THE LAW OF

MOTION PICTURES

INCLUDING THE LAW OF THE THEATRE

TREATING OF THE VARIOUS RIGHTS OF THE AUTHOR, ACTOR, PROFESSIONAL SCENARIO WRITER, DIRECTOR, PRODUCER, DISTRIBUTOR, EXHIBITOR AND THE PUBLIC, WITH CHAPTERS ON UNFAIR COMPETITION, AND COPYRIGHT PROTECTION IN THE UNITED STATES, GREAT BRITAIN AND HER COLONIAL POSSESSIONS

BY

LOUIS D. FROHLICH AND CHARLES SCHWARTZ

MEMBERS OF THE NEW YORK BAR

THE LAWBOOK EXCHANGE, LTD.

Clark, New Jersey

ISBN 978-1-58477-765-6

Lawbook Exchange edition 2007, 2016

The quality of this reprint is equivalent to the quality of the original work.

The Lawbook Exchange, Ltd.
33 Terminal Avenue
Clark, New Jersey 07066-1321

Please see our website for a selection of our other publications and fine facsimile reprints of classic works of legal history:
www.lawbookexchange.com

Library of Congress Cataloging-in-Publication Data

Frohlich, Louis D.
The law of motion pictures : including the law of the theatre treating of the various rights of the author, actor, professional scenario writer, director, producer, distributor, exhibitor and the public, with chapters on unfair competition, and copyright protection in the United States, Great Britain and her colonial possessions / by Louis D. Frohlich & Charles Schwartz.
p. cm.
Originally published: New York : Baker, Voorhis, 1918.
ISBN-13: 978-1-58477-765-6 (cloth : alk. paper)
ISBN-10: 1-58477-765-6 (cloth : alk. paper)
1. Copyright--Motion pictures. 2. Motion pictures--Distribution--Law and legislation 3. Copyright--Motion pictures--United States. 4. Motion pictures--Distribution--Law and legislation--United States. 5. Copyright--Motion pictures--Great Britain. 6. Motion pictures--Distribution--Law and legislation--Great Britain. I. Schwartz, Charles. II. Title.
K1474.F76 2007
343.09'9--dc22

2006035569

Printed in the United States of America on acid-free paper

THE LAW OF

MOTION PICTURES

INCLUDING THE LAW OF THE THEATRE

TREATING OF THE VARIOUS RIGHTS OF THE AUTHOR, ACTOR, PROFESSIONAL SCENARIO WRITER, DIRECTOR, PRODUCER, DISTRIBUTOR, EXHIBITOR AND THE PUBLIC, WITH CHAPTERS ON UNFAIR COMPETITION, AND COPYRIGHT PROTECTION IN THE UNITED STATES, GREAT BRITAIN AND HER COLONIAL POSSESSIONS

BY

LOUIS D. FROHLICH AND CHARLES SCHWARTZ

MEMBERS OF THE NEW YORK BAR

NEW YORK

BAKER, VOORHIS AND COMPANY

1918

THIS BOOK IS AFFECTIONATELY

DEDICATED TO

NATHAN BURKAN

TO WHOM WE OWE OUR ENTRANCE

INTO THE FIELD OF MOTION

PICTURE AND THEATRICAL

LAW

PREFACE

So rapid has been the growth of the motion picture industry that within a quarter of a century after its birth, it has taken its place among the five foremost business enterprises of this country.

Litigation between the different parties associated with the business has been frequent and has resulted in a large body of case law on the questions peculiar to the industry.

Notwithstanding the growth of this branch of the amusement life of the nation and of the importance of the law peculiar to it, no attempt has been made, so far as we know, to collect the decisions and to point out the general principles of law which have been developed by the courts with reference thereto.

To give such a statement of the motion picture law has been our object.

We have collected every available decision of the State and Federal Courts, as well as of the Courts of England and Canada relating to motion pictures. We have also collected all the more important decisions with reference to the theatre and literary property in general, as many of the principles established in those branches of the law apply to motion pictures.

If this work will assist the Bench and the Bar in clarifying the numerous legal questions constantly presented in litigation of this nature, we shall feel amply repaid for our efforts.

Thanks are due to William Leonard Berk, Esq., for assistance on the proofs.

LOUIS D. FROHLICH,
CHARLES SCHWARTZ.

165 BROADWAY, New York.
December 1, 1917.

TABLE OF CONTENTS

CHAPTER I

THE AUTHOR

Rights in his Literary Works

PAGE

SEC. 1. Where the motion picture is based upon a dramatic composition 1
2. Where the motion picture is based upon a novel or historical work 11
3. Where the motion picture is based upon a short story, sketch, poem, lecture, sermon or other kindred work 15
4. Where the motion picture is based upon an original scenario, that is one not based upon any other work 19
5. Where the motion picture is based upon a news item 23
6. Where the motion picture is based upon a work in the public domain 24
7. Where the motion picture is produced in serial form 25
8. Where the relationship is that of employer and employe 26
9. Where the motion picture material has been written by more than one person 35
10. Nature of the contract of co-authorship 45
11. Where music has been written specially to accompany the exhibition of the motion picture 51
12. Where the motion picture producer has not followed the text of the work upon which the motion picture is based 53
13. Criticism of the work 63

CHAPTER II

THE AUTHOR (CONTINUED)

Miscellaneous Questions

PAGE

SEC. 14. On the question whether the contract existing between the parties is a personal one 67
15. Where the contract contains a negative covenant 71
16. Where the work is to be to the satisfaction of the producer 73
17. Where the contract provides for the writing of a libelous, immoral or seditious work 73
18. Where the license granted is a sole and exclusive one 73
19. Where the contract contains limitations as to methods of exploitation 74
20. Where the work is to be produced at a definite time 75
21. Where the payment to the author is based upon a percentage of the gross receipts or net profits 77
22. Where the amount to be paid to the author is guaranteed 79
23. Where the payment to the author is a stipulated amount per performance or per period 80
24. Where the amount of damages in the event of a breach is stipulated 83
25. Where the contract provides for a forfeiture upon failure to pay the royalties due 84
26. Where the manuscript is lost or converted after submission to the producer 87
27. Where the work is secured by means of a prize contest .. 88
28. On the question whether an outright purchaser is required to reproduce the work 89
29. On the question whether the producer is entitled to a refund of advance payment 90
30. On the question whether the contract may be rescinded where the author made a poor bargain or where fraud is involved 90

PAGE

SEC. 31. On the question whether the contract may be rescinded where the producer made a poor bargain or where fraud is involved 91
32. On the question whether a contract to write will be specifically enforced 92
33. On the question whether the licensor may maintain an action against third parties 92
34. On the question whether courts grant injunctions pendente lite more readily in actions of this nature 92

CHAPTER III

THE PRODUCER

The Actor

SEC. 35. In general 95
36. Injunction for breach of contract where services are special, unique and extraordinary 95
37. Injunctions pendente lite 108
38. Services to be "satisfactory" 112
39. Length of engagement 117
40. Two weeks' custom and other customs 119
41. Contracts for work on Sunday 125
42. Services "actually performed" 131
43. Substantial performance 133
44. Anticipatory breach 135
45. Exposure to obscenity, ridicule, degradation, etc 136
46. Renewal of contract—modification 142
47. How many causes of action for breach 145
48. Actor's remedy for breach 146
49. Profits as a basis for damages 149
50. Producer's offer of re-employment after breach 154
51. Grounds for discharge 156
52. Actor's breach of the contract—damages 166
53. Changing motion picture 169

PAGE
SEC. 54. Contracts with infants 173
55. Inability of producer when studio closed by the authorities 176
56. Questions of travel 177
57. Booking agencies 178
58. Workmen's Compensation Acts 180
59. Garnishment 184
60. Serial stories 185
61. Escrow agents 186
62. Where joint venture 187
63. Royalties in addition to salary 190
64. Law governing validity of contract 190
65. Contract labor and exclusion laws 191
66. Performance in unlicensed theatre 192
67. Contracts for transportation—damages 193
68. Power of company's officer to contract—agency 195
69. Costumes 197
70. Enticement of actor 198
71. Libel of actor 202

CHAPTER IV

THE PRODUCER (CONTINUED)

His Other Employes

SEC. 72. Scenario writer 205
73. Director and other employes 209

CHAPTER V.

THE DISTRIBUTOR AND THE EXHIBITOR

SEC. 74. Distributor—in general 214
75. Exhibitor—in general 225
76. Advertising matter, programs, bill-posters 228

PAGE

SEC. 77. What are fixtures 232
78. Replevin of film and machine 235
79. Theatre leases 237
80. Theatre a nuisance 251
81. Franchise and booking agreements 256
82. Benefit performances—private exhibitions 258
83. Interstate commerce 260
84. Bankruptcy 261
85. Libel 264

CHAPTER VI

THE PUBLIC

Right of Privacy

SEC. 86. In general 267
87. When liable under statute 274
88. When not liable under statute 278
89. When use of name or picture is libelous 282
90. Weekly news motion pictures 284

CHAPTER VII

THE PUBLIC (CONTINUED)

Theatre Proprietor's Duty

SEC. 91. Right to exclude patrons 291
92. Liability for injuries sustained by patrons—In general.. 299
93. Falling over balcony 303
94. Seats and floors 305
95. Tripping in darkened theatre—aisles—steps—exits. 306
96. Articles dropping 311
97. Wild animals 313
98. Crowds 318

PAGE
SEC. 99. Hurt by performer.......... 319
100. Miscellaneous accidents.......... 322
101. Acts of strangers.......... 325
102. Assault.......... 326
103. Who is liable.......... 331
104. Property lost in theatre.......... 335

CHAPTER VIII

THE PUBLIC (CONTINUED)

License

SEC. 105. What is "Motion picture" "Theatrical performance" "Theatre".......... 337
106. Necessity for license.......... 345
107. Power to license discretionary—Revocation.......... 349
108. Extent of discretionary power.......... 351
109. Right to license on condition.......... 358

CHAPTER IX

THE PUBLIC (CONTINUED)

Regulation

SEC. 110. Buildings—Distances.......... 362
111. Standees—Aisles—Closing.......... 365
112. Operator and booth.......... 367
113. Firemen—Fire-escapes—Exits.......... 368
114. Admission of children.......... 370
115. Regulation amounting to prohibition.......... 371
116. Prohibition—Immorality.......... 372
117. Who is liable for penalty.......... 379
118. Ticket "Scalping".......... 381
119. Censorship.......... 383
120. Sunday performance.......... 391

CHAPTER X

UNFAIR COMPETITION

Titles—Marks and Devices

PAGE
SEC. 121. Using same or similar titles........................ 402
122. Use of title after copyright in work expires........... 438
123. Infringement of titles—Titles held to infringe........ 440
124. Infringement of titles—Titles held not to infringe..... 445
125. Acquiescence and abandonment..................... 449
126. Relief... 453
127. Marks and devices................................. 460
128. Transferability.................................... 463
129. Parties... 467
130. Actions at law..................................... 468
131. Trade-mark in title of cartoon...................... 469

CHAPTER XI

UNFAIR COMPETITION (CONTINUED)

Miscellaneous Matters

SEC. 132. Right to use or assign one's own name.............. 477
133. Limitations on use—price fixing..................... 481
134. Restraint of trade.................................. 487

CHAPTER XII

COPYRIGHT

In General

SEC. 135. Common-law rights.............................. 491
136. What is secured by copyright...................... 499
137. How copyright is secured.......................... 500

PAGE

Sec. 138. Publication 503
139. Notice of copyright 510
140. Licensee's failure to insert notice 519
141. False notice of copyright 520
142. Title—Changing title 521
143. Who may secure copyright 524
144. Belligerent aliens 527
145. In what name copyright may be taken out 532
146. Subjects of copyright—in general 534
147. Immoral and seditious works 535
148. Gags, stage business, contrivances, cartoons, advertisements 536
149. Burlesques, parodies, inferior copies 541
150. Copyrighting revised edition of work 543
151. Works in public domain 544
152. Component parts 544
153. Term of copyright 546
154. Renewal of copyright 547
155. Assignment of copyright 550
156. Difference between assignment and license 557

CHAPTER XIII

COPYRIGHT (CONTINUED)

Infringement

Sec. 157. Tests—What is protected 559
158. Primary test 561
159. Common sources 568
160. Substantial similarity by coincidence 574
161. Who may maintain action—Misjoinder of parties—Joinder of causes of action 577
162. Where action may be brought 585
163. Who is liable—Intent 586

PAGE
SEC. 164. What must be alleged and proved 593
165. Bill of particulars 599

CHAPTER XIV

COPYRIGHT (CONTINUED)

Remedies

SEC. 166. Actions in equity—In general 602
167. Preliminary injunction 602
168. Final hearing 608
169. Injunction as to part 619
170. Writ of seizure 621
171. Accounting 623
172. Actions at law 626
173. Actions purporting to be brought under the Copyright Act 628
174. Willful infringements 634
175. Statute of limitations 636
176. Construction of forfeiture and penalty clauses 636
177. Appeal 638

CHAPTER XV

COPYRIGHT (CONTINUED)

Miscellaneous Matters

SEC. 178. Return of copies deposited 639
179. Prohibition of importation of piratical copies 640
180. Ad interim protection 641
181. Bankruptcy—Title in trustee 643
182. Selling secondhand copies 646
183. Taxability 648
184. Music in theatres 649

PAGE
SEC. 185. Co-authorship 653
186. Employer and employe 653
187. Restraint of trade—Price fixing—Monopoly 653

CHAPTER XVI

COPYRIGHT (CONTINUED)

British, Colonial and International Copyright

SEC. 188. Copyright in United Kingdom and Protectorates 654
189. Copyright in Newfoundland 658
190. Copyright in Commonwealth of Australia 658
191. Copyright in Dominion of New Zealand 659
192. Copyright in Union of South Africa 660
193. Copyright in Dominion of Canada 660
194. International Copyright 672

APPENDIX

United States Copyright Act of 1909 as amended by the Acts of 1912, 1913 and 1914 677
Tabulated List of Presidential Proclamations conferring copyright protection upon foreign citizens or subjects 710
Rules of the Supreme Court of the United States for practice and procedure under section twenty-five of the United States Copyright Act of 1909 714
Presidential Proclamation of April 9th, 1910 719
Copyright Convention between the United States and Hungary 722
Copyright Convention between the United States and other American Republics 725
Order in Council of Great Britain of February 3, 1915 732
Presidential Proclamation of January 1, 1915 735
Statement of Register of Copyrights with respect to copyright of labels and prints 739

PAGE

Rules and Regulations for the registration of claims to copyright, as revised and issued in November, 1917 740
British Copyright Act of 1911 762
Previous British Copyright Acts not repealed by the British Copyright Act of 1911 801
Canadian Copyright Act 812
Rules of the Canadian Department of Agriculture under the Copyright Act 833
Convention creating the International Copyright Union, known as the Berne Convention of 1908 and commonly referred to as the Berlin Convention (text in English) 836
(text in French) 858

TABLE OF CASES CITED

PAGE

Aaron *v.* Ward.............. 291
Aborn *v.* Janis.....106, 174, 175
Abramovitz *v.* Tenzer...300, 312
Actiengesellschaft *v.* Arnberg 450
Adams *v.* Burke............ 481
Adams *v.* Grossmith........ 88
Adams *v.* Fellers........224, 236
Adams *v.* Fitzpatrick....... 143
Adams *v.* Folger.........460, 585
Adler, Matter of Samuel.... 183
Adler *v.* Miles............. 241
Agawam Co. *v.* Jordan..... 630
A. G. *v.* Shoreditch Corporation...................... 362
A. G. *v.* Vitagraph Co., Ltd.. 260
Ahlstrand *v.* Bishop........ 315
Akin *v.* Meeker............ 592
Albera *v.* Sciaretti......126, 127
Albert *v.* Interstate Amusement Co...178, 191, 196, 256, 258, 261
Albright *v.* Teas........553, 632
Alden *v.* Arnsky-Wilson..... 445
Alexander *v.* Potts......... 162
Alexander *v.* Manners Sutton 88
Allen *v.* Flood............. 202
Allen *v.* Walker.........452, 465
Allen Billposting Co. *v.* King 229
Almind *v.* Sea Beach Ry. Co. 281, 288

PAGE

American Acad. of Music *v.* Birt................... 124
American Clay Mfg. Co. *v.* American Clay Mfg. Co. 441, 463
American Hungarian Pub. Co. *v.* Miles Bros......... 151
American Law Book Co. *v.* Chamberlayne......27, 54, 55
American League *v.* Chase 96
American Malting Co. *v.* Keitel...............54, 603
American Music Stores *v.* Kussell................ 113
American Press Ass'n *v.* Daily Story Pub. Co.......... 520
American Tobacco Co. *v.* Werckmeister.........505, 623
American Trotting Reg. *v.* Gocher................. 603
American Waltham Watch *v.* U. S. Watch Co....... 463
Amoskeag Mfg. Co. *v.* Spear 452, 459, 460
Anderson *v.* Long.......... 198
Andre *v.* Mertens.......307, 308
Andrews *v.* Chandler....... 233
Andrews *v.* Kilgour........ 315
Andrus *v.* Berkshire Co..... 610

PAGE
Angers *v.* Leprohon........ 55
Angle *v.* Chicago & St. Paul Ry. Co................ 202
Anti-Vice Motion Picture Co., Inc., *v.* Bell......... 373
Appleton *v.* Welch......... 336
Appollinaris *v.* Scherer...... 468
Apthorpe *v.* Neville........ 73
Archbold *v.* Sweet........55, 65
Archer *v.* Willingrice...343, 348
Arden *v.* Lubin............ 84
Arena A. C. *v.* McPartland.. 103
Arkansas Smelting Co. *v.* Belden................ 645
Armstrong *v.* Majestic Motion Picture Co.......... 196
Armstrong *v.* Savannah Soap Works.................. 468
Armstrong *v.* Stair......... 329
Arnold *v.* State............ 321
Aronson *v.* Fleckenstein 44, 406. 417, 429, 438, 443, 492, 497, 531, 570, 581
Aronson *v.* Orlov.......... 628
Ashley *v.* Dixon........... 202
Aspinwall Mfg. Co. *v.* Gill.. 38
Associated Press *v.* International News Service...... 23
Astor *v.* W. 82 St. Realty Co. 437
Atchison-Ely *v.* Thomas.... 189
Atkinson *v.* Doherty....269, 272
Atlantic Milling Co. *v.* Robinson.................... 466
Atlas Mfg. Co. *v.* Street & Smith..404, 418, 419, 424, 434, 439, 447, 522, 534

PAGE
Atwill *v.* Ferrett........594, 596
Auckland & Brunetti *v.* Collins................... 179
Aughtrey *v.* Wiles......322, 323
Aunt Gemima Mills Co. *v.* Rignay Co.............. 458
Authors & Newspapers Ass'n *v.* O'Gorman Co.......... 486
Avery *v.* Langford......... 102

Babicz *v.* Riverview Sharpshooters................ 331
Bachman *v.* Belasco........ 572
Baglin *v.* Cusenier Co....... 450
Bainbridge *v.* City of Minneapolis........355, 357, 379
Baker *v.* City of Cincinnati.. 359
Baker *v.* Selden............ 560
Baker *v.* Taylor........... 514
Baldwin *v.* Baird.......... 632
Baldwin *v.* Burrows........ 47
Ball *v.* Broadway Bazaar 417, 433
Bancroft *v.* Scribner........ 645
Banker *v.* Caldwell......... 492
Banks Law Pub. Co. *v.* Lawyers Co-operative........ 552
Banks *v.* Manchester....511, 593
Barber *v.* Penley...252, 253, 344
Barclay *v.* Barclay.......... 37
Barnes *v.* Miner........... 537
Barnes *v.* Stern Bros....... 336
Barnett *v.* Q. & C. Co..6, 74, 85
Barnswell *v.* National Amusement Co............... 297
Baron *v.* Placide........... 139

PAGE

Barrett *v.* Lake Ontario Beach Imp. Co. 302, 323
Bartlette *v.* Crittenden. 506
Bartsch *v.* Herndon. 51, 69
Bass Furnace Co. *v.* Glasscock. 162, 163
Bassett *v.* French. 147
Batchelder *v.* Standard Plunger El. Co. 163
Batty *v.* Melillo. 178
Bauer *v.* O'Connel. 482
Baumeister *v.* Markham. . . . 137
Baxter *v.* Billings. 48, 49
Baylies *v.* Bulloch. 592
Baylies *v.* Curry. 298
Beck *v.* Carter. 302
Beckman *v.* Garrett. 156
Beer *v.* Canary. 229
Belford *v.* Scribner. .19, 532, 590, 598, 610
Belknapp *v.* Ball. 63
Bell, ex parte. 344
Bell *v.* Locke. 446
Bell *v.* Mahn. 340
Bellamy *v.* Wells. . .252, 254, 344
Bellis *v.* Beale. 344, 349
Bellis *v.* Burghall. 343
Beltinck *v.* Tacoma Theatre Co. 230
Bender *v.* King. 232, 234
Benn *v.* Le Clerq. 411
Bennett *v.* Carr. 637
Benson *v.* McMahon. 383
Bentley *v.* Tibbals. 544, 616
Benton *v.* Pratt. 202
Benton *v.* Van Dyke. 603

PAGE

Benyaker *v.* Scherz. 79, 190
Bergere *v.* Parker. 129, 196
Bernstein *v.* Meech. 79, 149
Besozzi *v.* Harris. 313
Betterton's Case. 252
Bettini *v.* Gye. 157, 166
Bien *v.* Abbey. 228
Bierce *v.* Stocking. 630
Billiken Co. *v.* Baker & B. Co. 455
Bilordeaux *v.* Bencke Lith. Co. 126
Binns *v.* Vitagraph Co. . .274, 280, 286, 288, 290
Binns *v.* Woodruff. 596, 619
Biograph Co. *v.* International Film Traders. . . .224, 225, 236
Bird *v.* Everhard. 336
Bird *v.* Thanhauser. 591
Birel *v.* Welsh. 592
Bishop *v.* Viviana & Co. . .20, 537
Black *v.* Allen 524, 550, 596, 608
Black *v.* Ehrich. . . .403, 405, 438
Black *v.* Imperial Book Co. 557, 661, 671
Blackledge *v.* Weir. . . .38, 42, 43
Blackwell *v.* Dibrell. 450
Blakely *v.* Sousa. .46, 48, 67, 479, 480
Blakely *v.* White Star Line. . 332
Blank *v.* Mfg. Co. 609
Bleistein *v.* Donaldson. .27, 32, 506, 539, 541, 574
Bliss *v.* Negus. 630
Blitz *v.* Toovey. 139
Block *v.* City of Chicago 337, 356, 372

PAGE

Bloom v. Nixon........19, 537
Bloomer v. McQuewan...... 481
Blount v. Societe........... 111
Blume v. Spear.....511, 516, 522
Bobbs-Merrill v. Equitable.. 573
Bobbs-Merrill Co. v. Snellenberg.................. 486
Bobbs-Merrill v. Strauss 486, 496, 560
Bobbs-Merrill Co. v. Universal Film Mfg. Co........ 78
Boisseau v. Scola Am. Co. 337, 344
Bole v. Pittsburgh A. C..... 318
Bolles v. Outing Co......513, 516
Bong v. Campbell Art Co... 527
Boosey v. Empire.......... 607
Booth v. Jarrett........... 480
Booth v. Lloyd............ 63
Booth v. Richards......... 67
Borman v. City of Milwaukee 317
Borthwick v. The Evening Post...............404, 448
Bosselman v. Richardson 594, 595, 598
Bossner, In re..........397, 398
Boston Glass Mfg. v. Binney 202
Boston Traveler Co. v. Purdy.................. 637
Boswell v. Barnum......292, 294
Boucicault v. Chatterton.... 568
Boucicault v. Delafield...... 526
Boucicault v. Fox...29, 492, 506
Boucicault v. Hart..492, 497, 506, 511, 568, 593, 594
Boucicault v. Wood.....492, 496

PAGE

Bourlier Bros. v. Macauley.. 200
Bowden v. Amalgamated Pictorials............274, 281
Boyd v. Dagenais.......... 272
Boyl v. Midland Lyceum Bureau................. 117
Bracken v. Rosenthal....... 539
Bradbury, Agnew v. Day.... 538
Bradbury v. Beeton........ 448
Bradbury v. Dickens....... 467
Bradner v. Mullen......... 336
Brady v. Daly.....563, 568, 638
Brady v. Reliance....12, 14, 552
Branch v. Klatt.......306, 308
Brand v. Godwin.......113, 159
Brandreth v. Lance........ 266
Brandt v. Goodwin.....157, 159
Brearley v. Morley.....341, 342
Brennan v. Fox Film Corp. 206, 210
Brewer v. Wynne......357, 372
Bridgeford v. Meagher..... 114
Briscoe v. Litt.........120, 140
British-American Tobacco Co. v. Brit. Am. C. S. Co.................424, 463
Broadhurst v. Nichols..405, 410, 445
Broder v. Zeno Mauvais Co. 536, 616
Broemel v. Meyer......... 449
Brooks v. Taylor.......... 314
Brown v. Baldwin & Gleason 141, 163
Brown v. Batchellor....320, 332
Brown v. Nugent.......... 349

PAGE

Brown v. Retsoff Mfg. Co... 114
Brown v. So. Kennebec..... 306
Brown v. Stubbs........... 350
Brown v. United States..... 528
Brown v. Weir............ 194
Browning v. Van Rensselaer 65
Bruce v. McManus........ 380
Bruce v. Reed............ 209
Bryant v. Logan........... 249
Buchanan v. Curry........ 530
Buenzle v. Newport........ 292
Buffalo Br. v. Breitinger.... 387
Bullen v. The Swan Electric 88
Bullen v. Ward............ 391
Bullinger v. Mackey....... 597
Bunnell v. Stern.......... 336
Bureau of National Literature v. Sells............ 648
Burnell v. Chown.......... 571
Burnett v. Snyder......... 47
Burns v. Burns............ 452
Burns v. Herman.......... 324
Burrow v. Marceau.....466, 480
Burrow-Giles Lithog. Co. v. Sarony...496, 513, 516, 596
Burton v. Schepf.......... 292
Burton v. Stratton......... 466
Bustanoby v. Revardel..... 166
Butcher v. Hyde........... 308
Butterick Publ. Co. v. Typographical Union......... 282
Buttman v. Dennett....... 336
Buxton v. James........... 662
Byrne v. Statist Co......26, 28
Bytovetzski v. Edward L. Wilson Co.............. 279

PAGE

Calcraft v. West........... 344
Caldwell v. Cline.......... 99
California Academy v. San Francisco............... 249
California Fig Syrup Co. v. Imp. Co............... 468
Caliga v. Interocean Newspaper Co...496, 523, 598, 637
Callaghan v. Myers...514, 532, 550, 598, 614, 625, 626
Camp v. Baldwin-Mellville Co.................... 121
Camp v. Wood........302, 304
Campbell v. Honakers...... 263
Campbell v. Portland Sugar Co.................... 302
Campbell v. Spottiswood.... 63
Canada Publ. Co. v. Beatty 440
Canary v. Russell.......99, 101
Candilis & Son v. Harold Victor & Co............... 530
Canterbury & Paragon, Ltd., v. Lloyd................ 107
Carlisle v. United States.... 531
Carlton Illustrators v. Coleman................56, 591
Carpenter Steel Co. v. Norcross................... 162
Carr v. Hood............. 64
Carte v. Duff............. 537
Carte v. Evans..27, 32, 523, 550
Carter v. Bailey..37, 41, 47, 493, 494, 504, 586
Carter v. Ferguson......98, 100
Cartwright v. Wharton..... 560
Caswell v. Hazard......410, 423

PAGE
Celluloid Mfg. Co. v. Cellonite 466
Central Brass v. Stuber..... 42
Central City Sav. Bank v. Walker................ 47
Central Lith. v. Moore..... 228
Central Trust Co. v. United States, etc.............. 617
Cescinsky v. Routledge..... 45
Chamberlayne v. Am. Law Book Co............... 27
Chancellor Oxford Univ. v. Wilmore Andrews....... 442
Chantrey, Chantrey & Co. v. Dey................. 32
Chaplin v. Essanay........ 171
Chapman v. Ferry......... 636
Chapman v. Waterman..... 477
Chappell v. Fields...20, 93, 527, 536, 562, 603
Chappell v. Harrison....... 124
Chappell v. Purday........ 661
Charley v. Potthoff..79, 134, 160, 247
Chatauqua School v. Nat'l School................. 598
Chatterton v. Cave........ 561
Cherry v. Des Moines Leader 203
Chicago Mus. Co. v. Butler.. 593
Chils v. Grouland......... 626
Christy v. Murphy......... 480
Church v. Hilliard..341, 392, 649
Church & Dwight v. Russ... 461
City of Boston v. Schaffer 347, 359
City of Buffalo v. Chadeayne 358
City of Buffalo v. Hill...... 355

PAGE
City of Chicago v. Powers.. 382
City of Chicago v. Shaynin 365, 372
City of Chicago v. Stratton.. 365
City of Chicago v. Weber 251, 344, 368
City of Clinton v. Wilton 396, 398
City of Duluth v. Marsh 352, 359, 365
City of Hartford v. Parsons.. 368
City of Indianapolis v. Dawson.................327, 328
City of Indianapolis v. Miller 251, 344, 367
City of Mobile v. Kiernan 260, 347, 361
City of New Orleans v. Hop Lee................... 369
City of New York v. Alhambra................ 396
City of New York v. Williams 399
City of St. Louis v. Nash.... 364
City of Topeka v. Crawford.. 398
Clark v. Bishop........339, 340
Clark v. Freeman.......... 270
Clark Paper & Mfg. Co. v. Stenacker.............. 96
Clark v. North American Co. 283
Clark v. West............ 77
Clarke v. Searle............ 349
Clary-Squire v. Press Publ. Co.................... 283
Clay v. People............ 210
Clemens v. Belford..57, 60, 62, 506, 533

PAGE
Clemens v. Estes 486
Clemens v. Press Pub. Co. . 53, 63
Clifford v. Brandon 330
Clifford's Olympia Co. v. Waters 121
Clinical Obstetrics, In re ... 557
Clinton Metallic Paint v. N. Y. Metallic Paint . . 421, 455
Clum v. Brewer 38, 42
Cluney v. Lee Wai 254
Clyne v. Helmes 303
Cobb v. Knapp 197
Cocks v. Purday 665
Coffeen v. Brunton 461
Coghlan v. Stetson 133
Cohen v. Mutual Life . . . 528, 530
Cole v. Rome Sav. Bank . . 320, 333
Coleman v. Wathen 497
Coles v. Sims 102
Colgate v. White 278, 607
Colles v. Mangham 179
Collier v. Imp. Films Co. . 435, 522
Collier v. Jones 442
Colliery Engineer Co. v. United Corresp. Schools Co 27, 32, 34, 208
Collins v. Public Ledger Co 61
Collister v. Hayman . . 291, 293, 294
Columbia Mill Co. v. Alcorn 410
Columbian Lyceum Bureau v. Sherman 134
Colyer v. Fox Publ. Co. . 281, 284, 287
Comerma v. Comerma 633

PAGE
Commercial Advertising Ass'n v. Hoques 446
Commonwealth v. Alexander 259, 260, 398
Commonwealth v. Cincinnati 255
Commonwealth v. Donnelly 340, 342
Commonwealth v. George ... 299
Commonwealth v. Keeler ... 345
Commonwealth v. Kneeland 210
Commonwealth v. McGann 345, 346, 349
Commonwealth v. Powell ... 329
Commonwealth v. Ray 383
Commonwealth v. Spiers 338, 342
Commonwealth v. Twitchell 346
Commonwealth v. Weidner . . 392
Comstock v. Lopokowa . . 93, 96, 111
Coney Island v. M'Intyre-Paxton Co 245
Connor v. The Princess Theatre 316
Conrad v. Clauve 321, 332
Conreid Metrop. Opera Co. v. Brin 83, 167
Cooper v. Stone 64, 65
Cooper v. Stephens 554
Cooper v. Whittingham 56
Corbett v. Purdy . . 403, 429, 522
Corelli v. Gray 576
Corelli v. Wall 270, 277
Corliss v. Walker 272, 278
Corsi v. Maretzek 157, 167

PAGE

Cort *v.* Lazzard.........99, 100
Cortesy *v.* Territory...... 391
Cosby *v.* Robinson......... 355
Cotton *v.* Sounes.......... 123
Cousineau *v.* Muskegon.... 325
Cox *v.* Coulson............ 320
Cox *v.* Cox..............33, 55
Cox *v.* Sports Publishing Co. 448
Cramer *v.* Klein........... 255
Crane *v.* Kansas City Baseball.................... 322
Crawford *v.* Mail and Express Pub. Co........104, 112, 208
Cream Co. *v.* Keller........ 477
Cremore *v.* Huber..298, 325, 327
Crepps *v.* Durden.......... 391
Croasdale *v.* Tantum....... 64
Cronin *v.* Bloewecke....... 255
Crookes *v.* Petter........56, 212
Crossman *v.* Griggs........ 465
Crotch *v.* Arnold...404, 449, 522
Crow *v.* State............. 397
Crowe *v.* Aiken....492, 584, 586
Crowley *v.* Rochester Fire Works................. 301
Crown Feature Film *v.* Betts 594, 622
Crown Feature Co. *v.* Levy 595, 596
Crutcher *v.* Big Four....... 269
Cuervo *v.* Henkell......... 450
Cumberland *v.* Copeland.... 552
Curran *v.* Birdsall......... 38
Currier *v.* Boston Music Hall................... 325
Currier *v.* Henderson....... 312

PAGE

Curtis & Dodd *v.* Struthers.. 144
Cutting *v.* Miner.......... 149

D'Altomonte *v.* N. Y. Herald 274
Da Prato Statuary Co. *v.* Giuliani Statuary Co..541, 545
Dailey *v.* Super. Court...... 266
Dale Reynolds *v.* Trade Papers Publ. Co........... 448
Dallas *v.* Murry........... 121
Dalton *v.* Hooper.......... 309
Daly *v.* Brady.........567, 568
Daly *v.* Palmer..20, 538, 562, 567, 569, 587
Daly *v.* Smith............. 96
Daly *v.* Stetson............ 80
Daly *v.* Wabash........... 61
Daly *v.* Walrath........496, 507
Daly *v.* Webster....20, 524, 540
Dam *v.* Kirk La Shelle..13, 17, 22, 546, 556, 558, 566, 614, 626, 627
Dana *v.* Fielder........... 125
Dann, In re............... 644
Danville Press *v.* Harrison.. 210
Daversa *v.* Davidson's Sons Co.................... 114
Davies *v.* Bowes..23, 24, 598, 616
Davis *v.* Dodge........140, 147
Davis *v.* Epoch Producing Co. 224, 228
Davis *v.* Foreman......... 100
Davys *v.* Douglas.......... 364
Day *v.* Klaw...........134, 178
Day *v.* Luna Park......251, 264
Day *v.* Simpson........339, 344

PAGE

Day *v.* Webster........455, 463
Day *v.* Woodworth........ 469
De Begnis *v.* Armistead.... 192
De Bekker *v.* Stokes.....57, 212
De Carlton *v.* Glaser....120, 125
De Francesco *v.* Barnum..107, 175
De Gellert *v.* Poole..121, 143, 164
De Gray *v.* Murray........ 316
De Jong *v.* Behrman....... 202
De Jong *v.* Brueker.....541, 593
De Koven *v.* Lake Shore & M. Co................. 110
De Loraz *v.* McDowell..155, 156
De Pol *v.* Sohlke........... 98
De Sando *v.* N. Y. Herald Co.................... 283
De Velin *v.* Swanson........ 311
De Vere *v.* Gilmore........ 122
De Witt *v.* Elmira Nobles Mfg. Co.........38, 39, 43, 46
De Zeichner *v.* Lamm....... 157
Dean *v.* Emerson.......... 479
Dearing *v.* Pearson. 148, 155, 156
Decatur *v.* Porter.......... 325
Decker *v.* Etchison.....513, 611
Delmour *v.* Forsythe....... 336
Delaney *v.* Root........... 40
Dennison *v.* Ashdown....... 28
Dennison Mfg. Co. *v.* Thomas Mfg. Co............... 461
Denny *v.* Wright & Cobb.... 181
Densmore *v.* Evergreen..... 365
Denver *v.* Hallett.......... 249
Deubert *v.* City of New York.................. 599
Development Co. *v.* King 140, 156

PAGE

Devlin *v.* Devlin........... 477
Deyo *v.* Kingston Consol. R. R. Co............... 301
Diamond *v.* Mendelsohn.... 114
Diamond Match Co. *v.* Roeber................... 102
Dibdin *v.* Swan............ 202
Dick *v.* Yates.....403, 404, 522
Dickey *v.* Linscott......... 157
Dickey *v.* Metro Pictures Corp...........421, 444, 457
Dickey *v.* Mutual Film Corp. 411, 418, 420, 422, 424, 444, 456
Dickinson *v.* Callahan...... 48
Dickson *v.* Waldron....301, 326
Dielman *v.* White.......27, 596
Dietze *v.* Riverview Park... 332
Dillon *v.* Pearson.......... 448
Dis Debar *v.* Hoeffle....... 136
Distington Hematite *v.* Possehl................528, 530
Dixey *v.* A. H. Woods Prod. Co.................... 131
Dixon *v.* Corinne.......... 623
Dixon Crucible Co. *v.* Guggenheim................ 479
D'Ole *v.* Kansas City Star 505, 609
Doan *v.* American Book Co. 486, 647, 648
Dockerell *v.* Dougall....... 270
Dockstader *v.* Reed.....108, 109
Dodd *v.* Smith............ 486
Doherty *v.* Allman......... 100
Donaldson *v.* Becket....... 495

PAGE

Donellan, In re. 398
Donnelly *v.* Ivers. 523
Douglas *v.* Merchants' Ins. Co. 143
Douglas *v.* Stokes. 272
Dow *v.* Henderson. 334
Dowling *v.* Livingstone. 63
Drake *v.* Hall. 42
Drayton *v.* Reid. 162
Dressler *v.* Keystone Film Co. 190, 221
Drew *v.* Peer. 328
Dreyfus *v.* City of Montgomery. 365, 372
Drummond *v.* Altemus. . .58, 212
Drummond *v.* Atty Gen'l. . . 140
Du Pont Powder Co. *v.* Masland. 213
Du Puy *v.* Post Telegram. . . 540
Du Tremble *v.* Poulin. 316
Duck *v.* Bates. 343
Duck *v.* Mayer. 593
Dudley *v.* Abraham. 311
Duff *v.* Russell. 99, 136
Dugan *v.* Anderson. 147
Duff *v.* Russell. 162
Dunham *v.* The Indianapolis R. R. Co. 39, 43
Duniway Publ. Co. *v.* The Northwest Printing & Publ. Co. 446
Dunlop *v.* United States. . . . 535
Dunn *v.* Agricultural Soc. . . 332
Dunning *v.* Jacobs. 304
Dunton *v.* Derby Desk Co. . . 144
Dutton *v.* Cupples. 457, 475

PAGE

Dwyer *v.* Hills Bros. 311
Dyckman *v.* Valiente. 40

E. C. T. Club *v.* State Racing Com. 355
Eaton *v.* Lake. 30
Economopoulos *v.* Bingham 338, 339, 348, 392
Eddy *v.* American Amusement Co. 145, 195
Edelstein *v.* Bell. . . .357, 376, 379
Edelstein *v.* Edelstein. . .461, 469
Eden *v.* People. 396
Eden Musee Co. *v.* Bingham 373, 393, 400
Edison *v.* Am. Mutoscope Co. 490
Edison *v.* Edison Polyform Co. 61, 269, 273
Edison *v.* Lubin. 338
Edison Storage Battery *v.* Edison. 460
Edling *v.* Kansas City Baseball. 322
Edwards *v.* Cissy Fitzgerald 97
Edwards *v.* Cotton. 558
Edward *v.* McClellan. .337, 338, 393
Edwards *v.* N. Y. & H. R. R. Co. 302, 304, 319, 333
Egan *v.* San Francisco. 249
Egbert *v.* Sun Co. 165
Eichel & Colligan *v.* Woods. . 573
Eiseman *v.* Schiffer. 465
Eisfeldt *v.* Campbell. 566
Elen *v.* London Music Hall 124, 204

PAGE

Elgin Nat. Watch Co. *v.* Illinois Watch Co......455, 463
Eliot *v.* Jones............. 275
Elkin & Co. *v.* Francis, Day & Hunter.............. 438
Ellis *v.* Marshall........... 539
Ellis *v.* No. American Theatres 361
Ellis *v.* Ogden............. 539
Ellis *v.* Thompson......... 79
Ellsler *v.* Brooks.......150, 153
Emerson *v.* Davies.....562, 570
Emerson *v.* Nash.......... 283
Empire City Am. Co. *v.* Wilton............538, 580, 593
Encyclopedia Britannica *v.* American Newspaper Ass'n 608
Engel *v.* Shubert.......143, 190
Epstein *v.* Gordon......327, 335
Ernst *v.* Grand Rapids Engr. Co.................... 162
Ervin *v.* Woodruff.......... 317
Estes *v.* Leslie..........439, 442
Estes *v.* Williams.......403, 439
Estes *v.* Worthington..439, 442, 591
Evans *v.* Morris........... 665
Everson *v.* Powers......145, 148
Evesson *v.* Ziegfeld........ 148
Ewen's Colonial Stamp Market, Ltd., *v.* Federal Stamp Co.................... 445
Ewing *v.* Chase........... 309
Ewing *v.* Osbaldiston....... 192
Excelsior *v.* Pacific......... 582
Exchange Telegraph Co. *v.* Howard............... 23

PAGE

Fagan *v.* Aborn........... 122
Fairbank Co. *v.* Windsor... 421
Fairbanks *v.* Luckel........ 452
Fairbanks *v.* Montreal St. Ry. Co................... 325
Fairfax *v.* Hunter.......... 528
Fake *v.* Addicks........... 316
Falk *v.* Donaldson......... 564
Falk *v.* Gast..505, 517, 623, 637
Farley *v.* Evening Chronicle Publ. Co................ 283
Farmer *v.* Calvert......... 594
Farmer *v.* Elstner.......564, 620
Farmers' Handy Wagon Co. *v.* Beaver...........460, 584
Farndale *v.* Bainbridge..... 348
Fay *v.* Bignell..........342, 649
Fay *v.* Harrington......264, 265
Fechter *v.* Montgomery..105, 207
Feinstein *v.* Jacobson....... 102
Fennar *v.* Atlantic Am. Co... 324
Fenning Film Service *v.* Wolverhampton.........225, 587
Fenstermaker *v.* Tribune Pub. Co.............270, 284
Fenton *v.* Clark........... 156
Ferguson, Ex parte........ 396
Ferris *v.* Frohman......509, 618
Fichtel *v.* Barthel.......... 608
Fichtenberg *v.* Atlanta...... 392
Filburn *v.* Peoples P. & A. Co.................... 317
Finney's Orchestra *v.* Finney's Famous Orchestra.. 465
Fire Department *v.* Hill..369, 380, 587

PAGE
Fire Department v. Stetson 369, 380
Fishel v. Lueckel...564, 591, 610
Fischer v. Automobile Supply Co.................... 600
Fischer v. Blanch.......... 459
Fisher v. Monroe.......121, 156
Fisher v. Star Co..474, 475, 631
Fitch v. Young..17, 498, 557, 558, 582
Fitzgerald v. George Newnes 162
Flagstaff Silver Co. v. Cullins 391
Flanagan v. Goldberg...311, 326
Fleron v. Lackaye......... 92
Fletcher v. New Orleans.... 636
Florence Co. v. J. C. Dowd.. 454
Folsom v. Marsh.......... 564
Forbes v. Howard......... 232
Ford v. Blaney Amusement Co..13, 16, 17, 22, 546, 556, 557, 594, 595
Ford v. Heaney........... 275
Forsythe v. McKinney..... 162
Foster-Milburn v. Chinn 273, 283
Foster's Agency, Lim., v. Romaine.................. 179
Fountain Sq. Theatre v. Evans..............130, 397
Fowler v. Holmes.......301, 327
Fox v. Buffalo Park..300, 302, 312, 332
Fox v. Dougherty.......... 322
Fox v. McClellan..351, 373, 394, 398
Francis v. Cockrell.....302, 303
Francis v. Flynn........... 273

PAGE
Francis v. Oliver........... 582
Francis Day & Hunter v. Feldman & Co.......506, 656
Frankenstein v. Thomas.... 499
Franklin Film Corporation, Matter of.............. 355
Fraser v. Barrei........... 586
Fraser v. Berkeley......... 65
Fraser v. Edwardes........ 591
Fraser v. Yack............ 526
Frazee v. Edeson.......... 104
Frazer v. Frazer........... 477
Fredericks v. Howie........ 344
Fredericks v. Payne........ 340
Freeman v. Trade-Reg..593, 595
Freligh v. Carroll.......... 538
French v. Day............ 588
French v. Gregory......... 590
French v. Jones........... 358
French v. Kreling......498, 632
French v. McGuire........ 492
French v. Quincy.......... 250
Frohman v. Fitch..2, 3, 8, 75, 418
Frohman v. Mason........ 149
Frohman v. Miller..404, 447, 459
Frohman v. Morris..407, 419, 429, 443, 456
Frohman v. Payton..417, 419, 429, 443, 456
Frohman Amusement Co. v. Blinkhorn.............. 225
Frowde v. Parish.......... 32
Fruit Cleaning Co. v. Fresno Home Packing Co....... 532
Fry v. Bennett............ 264

PAGE

Fuller *v.* Bemis..........20, 538
Fuller *v.* Brown........... 156
Fuller *v.* Downing......... 114
Fuller *v.* Huff............. 457
Fuller *v.* McDermott....... 280

Gabriel *v.* McCabe.......72, 172
Gaiety Theatre *v.* Cissy Loftus................. 100
Gaittin *v.* Searle........... 158
Gale *v.* Bingham.......... 396
Gale *v.* Leckie............. 76
Gallagher *v.* Rudd......... 367
Galliher *v.* Cadwell........ 608
Gallini *v.* Laborie.......... 192
Gannert *v.* Rupert......... 442
Garrett *v.* Messenger....... 349
Gast *v.* Falk.............. 610
Gates *v.* Fraser........... 38
Gath *v.* Interstate Amusement Co............138, 178
Gaumont *v.* Hatch......... 578
Gause *v.* Knapp........... 599
General Film Co. *v.* Kalem 223, 227
Genesee Recreation Co. *v.* Edgerton..351, 354, 355, 356, 373
George *v.* Smith........... 410
George *v.* Univ. of Minn.... 325
"George, the Count Joannes" *v.* Burt........ 65
Gerald *v.* Inter Ocean Pub. Co..................... 204
Gibson *v.* Carruthers Exchequer...............69, 70

PAGE

Gilbart *v.* Jefferson........ 132
Gilbert *v.* The Star........ 607
Gilbert *v.* Workman....... 57
Gill *v.* United States..27, 32, 550
Gillett *v.* Bate............. 644
Gilligham *v.* Ray.......223, 228
Gilman *v.* Lamson Co...... 113
Ginn *v.* Appollo........625, 648
Ginsberg *v.* Friedman...114, 163
Gilmore *v.* Anderson....... 590
Glaser *v.* St. Elmo..403, 429, 439, 447, 522, 571, 573
Glen & H. Mfg. Co. *v.* Hall 418, 467
Glenny *v.* Lacy........115, 208
Glenville *v.* Selig Polyscope Co.................... 589
Glinseretti *v.* Rickards..... 161
Glyn *v.* Miner............. 116
Glyn *v.* Western Feature Film Co........535, 542, 599
Glynn *v.* Lyceum Theatre Co.................303, 306
Goddard *v.* Morrissey...... 135
Goelet *v.* Frohman......... 239
Goldberg *v.* Popular Pictures Corporation. 153, 187, 216, 219
Golders Green Am. & Dev. Co. *v.* Relph............ 167
Goldmark *v.* Kreling..496, 569, 583
Goldstein *v.* Levy.......... 311
Gollansz *v.* Dent........... 77
Gonsolis *v.* Gearhart....... 163
Gooding *v.* Chutes......... 314
Goodrich *v.* Busse......... 365

PAGE
Goodyear Shoe Mfg. Co. *v.* Jackson................ 634
Gordon *v.* Barr..........99, 175
Gott *v.* Pulsifer..........64, 264
Gottsberger *v.* Aldine....... 504
Gould *v.* Banks............ 550
Gould *v.* Springer.......... 232
Gould *v.* State.........398, 400
Gould's Case.............. 181
Graddon *v.* Price.......... 157
Graham *v.* McKimm....... 65
Graham *v.* Payne.......... 316
Grannan *v.* Westchester Racing Ass'n............... 296
Grant *v.* Maddox.......105, 124
Grant Richards, In re....69, 647
Gran *v.* McVickar..135, 196, 237, 251
Graves *v.* Garrie........... 672
Gray *v.* Russell............ 564
Gray *v.* The Oxford, Lim. 164, 192
Gray *v.* Wulff............. 118
Greater N. Y. Film Rental Co. *v.* Biograph.......... 490
Green *v.* Botheroyd........ 344
Green *v.* Chapman......... 203
Green *v.* Luby..........503, 543
Green *v.* Minzensheimer.... 542
Green *v.* Savanah.......... 365
Greenburg *v.* Early........ 70
Greenburg *v.* West. Turf 292, 296
Greene *v.* Bishop.......... 621
Greene *v.* Seattle A. C...... 304
Greenhall Theat. Circ. *v.* Markowitz..........135, 146

PAGE
Greenough *v.* Allen Theatre 363
Gregory *v.* Brunswick...... 331
Gregory *v.* Tavernor..342, 343, 649
Gregory *v.* Tuffs..343, 344, 348
Griffin *v.* Brooklyn Ball Club 165
Griffith *v.* Tower Pub. Co. 51, 67, 68, 69, 646
Griggs *v.* Perrin........... 571
Grimston *v.* Cunningham. 96, 105
Grinnell *v.* Kiralfy......... 160
Griswold *v.* Ringling........ 319
Grocers Journal Co. *v.* Midland Publishing Co...... 446
Gross *v.* Seligman.......... 539
Gross *v.* Van Dyke..590, 618, 619
Grossman *v.* Canada Cycle Co................506, 665
Grote *v.* C., etc., H. R....... 302
Gunter *v.* Astor........... 202
Gustin *v.* Record Pub. Co... 623

Haag *v.* Rogers.........121, 162
Haas *v.* Feist..519, 533, 592, 613, 614
Hackett *v.* Walter......... 91
Hagan and Dodd Co. *v.* Rigbers............... 469
Haggard *v.* Waverly....... 519
Hahn *v.* The Concordia Society.................. 101
Haines *v.* Thompson....... 120
Hainque *v.* Cyclops Iron Works................. 461
Halcroft *v.* West End Playhouse, Ltd............. 176

PAGE

Hall *v.* Aronson 120
Hall *v.* Green 342, 343, 649
Hall *v.* Pritchett 184
Hallen *v.* Thompson 126
Halley *v.* Alloway 233
Hallyburton *v.* Burke Co.... 321
Halpern *v.* Manhattan Ave. Theatre Corp 251
Halstead *v.* Grinnan 608
Hamilton Shoe Co. *v.* Wolf 409, 463
Hamlin *v.* Bender 255, 396
Hammerstein, Matter of 351, 380, 398, 588
Hammerstein *v.* Belasco 238
Hammerstein *v.* Mann..100, 108, 110, 175
Hammerstein *v.* United Booking Offices 257
Hammond *v.* Melton 315
Hammond Publishing Co. *v.* Smythe 486
Hanfstaengl *v.* Smith 543
Hanlin *v.* Walters 138
Hanneton *v.* Eno 65
Hanover Milling Co. *v.* Metcalf 458, 475
Hanson *v.* Jaccard 583
Hapelman *v.* Poole 183
Hardacre *v.* Armstrong..552, 592, 596, 613
Hardie *v.* Balmain. 176, 177
Harley *v.* Henderson. ...158, 160
Harms *v.* Stern 33, 208, 615
Harper *v.* Donohue..495, 496, 554, 577, 649

PAGE

Harper *v.* Holman 603
Harper *v.* Klaw 2, 3, 8, 9
Harper *v.* Lare 446
Harper *v.* Ranous..403, 404, 437, 522
Harper *v.* Shoppell 587, 589
Harrington, ex parte 352
Harrington *v.* Stillman 599
Harris *v.* Carstens Packing Co 315
Harris *v.* Crawley 323
Harris *v.* Commonwealth ... 537
Harrison *v.* Baltimore 369
Harrison *v.* Conlan 70
Harrison *v.* Maynard-Merrill, 486, 632, 647
Hart *v.* Aldridge 202
Hart *v.* City Theatres 244
Hart *v.* Cort..6, 73, 124, 125
Hart *v.* Fox 82, 493, 592
Hart *v.* Thompson 119
Hart *v.* Townsend 65
Hart *v.* Wall 203
Hart *v.* Washington Park... 325
Hart *v.* Woodbury Dermat. Institute 283
Harte *v.* De Witt 57, 58
Hartford Fire Ins. Co. *v.* Wilcox 50
Hartford Print Co. *v.* Hartford Directory 609, 626
Harvey *v.* Tivoli, Manchester Ltd 161
Haskell *v.* Osborn 110
Hathaway *v.* Sabin 197
Hatton *v.* Kean 28, 52

PAGE

Haven *v.* Russell.......... 73
Hawkes *v.* Whaley, Royce & Co.................... 671
Hayes *v.* Smith............ 316
Hays *v.* Eldor Am. Co....... 324
Hays *v.* Miller............ 314
Hayward *v.* Hayward...... 184
Hazzard *v.* Hoxie.......... 230
Heap *v.* Hartley........... 71
Hearne *v.* Stowell.......... 283
Hefel *v.* White Land Co..... 516
Hegeman *v.* Hegeman...... 479
Hegeman *v.* Springer....... 637
Hein *v.* Harris............ 576
Heine *v.* Appleton......... 27
Heineman *v.* Smart Set..... 26
Hendershott *v.* Modern Woodmen.............. 310
Henderson *v.* Tompkins..534, 535, 594
Hendricks *v.* Thomas Publishing Co............... 617
Hene *v.* Samstag.......... 538
Heneky *v.* Stark........... 85
Hennessy *v.* Herrmann..... 467
Henry *v.* Cherry........... 269
Henry *v.* Dick..........46, 484
Henry Bill Publ. Co. *v.* Smythe................ 647
Herbert *v.* Fields......39, 40, 52
Herbert *v.* Shanley...340, 341, 348, 392, 649
Herbert *v.* Universal Talking Machine Co............ 277
Herbert *v.* Weber.......... 52
Hereford (Bishop) *v.* Griffin 29

PAGE

Herne *v.* Liebler......41, 68, 75
Herrick *v.* Wixon.......... 322
Herring *v.* Gas Consumers Ass'n................. 45
Herzog *v.* Heyman........ 633
Heye *v.* Tilford............ 47
Hicks *v.* Maxton.......... 181
Hier *v.* Abrahams.......... 456
Higgins *v.* Franklin Co..... 325
Higgins *v.* Keufel.......... 518
Higgins *v.* Lacroix......358, 371
Hill *v.* Gibbs............. 44
Hill *v.* Haberkorn.......... 105
Hill *v.* Lockwood.......... 468
Hill *v.* Whalen.........542, 582
Hillis & Co. *v.* Hoover...... 623
Hillman *v.* Star Publ. Co.269, 275
Hills *v.* Austrich........... 516
Hills *v.* Hoover.........516, 623
Hilson *v.* Foster........... 411
Hinton *v.* Locke........... 125
Historical Publishing Co. *v.* Jones......582, 584, 602, 620
Ho King, In re............ 192
Hodges *v.* Mayor.......... 359
Hodkins *v.* McDonald...... 191
Hoffman *v.* Bond.......... 349
Hoffman *v.* Le Traunik..535, 603
Hole *v.* Bradbury....51, 67, 646
Hollenback *v.* Clemmer..... 307
Hollis *v.* Kansas City Assoc. 332, 334
Holmes *v.* Hurst..13, 18, 496, 507, 546, 556, 560, 561
Holmes *v.* United Theatres.. 311
Home Fire Ins. Co. *v.* Barber 144

PAGE

Home of Inebriates v. San Francisco 249
Hopkins Amuse. Co. v. Frohman 417, 441
Horner v. Guardian Mut. Life Ins. Co. 143
Horney v. Nixon. . . 292, 293, 294
Hostetter v. Brueggeman. . . . 461
Houck v. Ingles 393
Howard v. Carlton 455
Howard v. Daly. 147, 148
Howard v. Henriques. 418
Howard v. Lovett. 443, 477
Howard v. Woodward 102
Howe v. Robinson 120
Howell v. Miller 591
Howley Dresser Co., In re. 646
Hoxey v. Chaney. 466, 479
Hoyt v. Bates 553
Hoyt v. Fuller 99
Hubbard v. Mathews. 530
Hubbard v. Miller 102
Hubbard v. Taunton 249
Hubbard v. Thompson 607
Hubbell v. Royal Pastime Amusement Co. 651
Hubges v. Belasco 565
Hudson Bldg. Co. v. Compagnie Gen. Transatlantique 143
Hubinger v. Eddy 461
Huebsch v. Crist. . 594, 598, 613, 618
Hughes v. Stratham 479
Hull, Re G. W. 395, 397

PAGE

Hull v. 86th St. Amusement Co. 298
Humiston v. Universal Film Mfg. Co. 285
Humphrey v. Sea Gull Specialty Co. 82
Humphries v. Armstrong. . . . 605
Humphries v. Thompson. . . 56, 57
Huneeke v. W. Brighton Am. Co. 306, 323
Hunt v. Bennett 209
Huntington v. Claflin 143
Hurst v. Picture Theatres, Ltd 297
Hyde v. Toronto Theatre. . . . 328
Hydecker v. Williams 116

Ickes v. State 210
Ide v. Brown 104, 175
Iliodor Picture Corp. v. Michailoff 431
Illinois Central v. Byrne. . . . 195
Imperial Curtain Co. v. Strauss 229
Imperial Film Exchange, In re 262
Inchbald v. Robinson 253
Indian Rubber Co. v. Rubber Comb. Co. 450
International Cheese Co. v. Phœnix Cheese Co. 450
Interstate Amusement Co. v. Albert. 178, 191, 196, 256, 258, 261
Interstate Am. Co. v. Martin 322, 328
Investor Publishing Co. of Mass. v. Dobinson 443

PAGE

Iolanthe Case.............. 61
Isaacs v. Daly..........408, 447
Ivan Film Productions v. Bell................356, 377

Jackel v. Nixon & Zimmerman.................. 259
Jacko v. State............. 537
Jackson, Matter of......... 489
Jackson v. Baker........... 317
Jackson v. Moore.......... 44
Jackson v. Walkie......511, 519
Jacob v. Schiff............. 271
Jacobson, Ex parte......... 392
Jacobson v. De Mille....... 573
Jacoway v. Young......... 465
Jaeger's Co. v. Le Boutillier.. 473
Janney v. Pan-Coast Ventilator Mfg. Co.........413, 449
Jaques v. Natl. Exhibit Co... 254
Jeffries v. N. Y. Evening Journal.....280, 281, 284, 287
Jeffrys v. Boosey...492, 560, 662
Jenkins v. Jackson......... 255
Jerome v. Queens City Cycle 156
Jeup v. State Fire Marshal.. 369
Jewelers' Mercantile Agency v. Jewelers......496, 505, 506
Jewel Theatre Co. v. Winship 362
Jewish Col. Ass'n v. Solomon 468
Johnson v. Donaldson..560, 573, 574
Johnson v. Humphrey Pop-Corn Co................ 340
Johnson Co. v. Hunt........ 97

PAGE

Johnson v. Sparrow.. 298
Johnson v. Wilcox.......... 310
Johnson v. Wilkinson.. ... 292
Johnston Harvester Co. v. Meinhardt.............. 202
Johnston v. Orr-Ewing..... 461
Jollie v. Jaques............ 403
Jones v. American Law Book Co.................... 62
Jones v. Sandford.......... 250
Jones v. Van Zandt........ 593
Joseph v. Bidwell.......... 298
Joseph v. Elliott........... 396
Journal Pub. Co. v. Drake.. 637
Joyner v. Moore........... 298
Julian v. Hoosier Drill Co.... 450
Jung Brewing Co. v. Commonwealth............. 255
Jurgens v. Woodberry...... 466

Kaiser v. Cinberg.......... 245
Kaiser Wilhelm Second..... 529
Kalem v. Harper..2, 338, 418, 431, 587, 610
Kalisthenic Ex. Co. v. Emmons...........379, 389, 390
Karno v. Pathe Freres...537, 589
Karst v. Prang Educational Co.................... 86
Kathreiner v. Pastor-Kneipp 456
Kay-Tee Film Exchange, In re..................227, 263
Keane v. Wheeler.......... 144
Keene v. Wheatley......... 582
Keener v. Moslander....... 244
Keith v. Kellerman..101, 168, 187

PAGE

Keith & Proctor *v.* Bingham 393, 400
Kelly *v.* Byles.............. 448
Kelly *v.* Caldwell.......123, 140
Kelly *v.* London Pavilion... 130
Kendall *v.* West........113, 208
Kennedy *v.* Press Pub. Co... 65
Kennedy *v.* Rolfe.......... 81
Kenyon *v.* Weissberg....111, 116
Kerker *v.* Lederer..78, 86, 93, 110
Kessler *v.* Chappelle....... 97
Kessler *v.* Deutsch......301, 327
Ketelbey *v.* Maggett....... 88
Keyes *v.* Allerdyce......... 181
Keyzor *v.* Newman........ 209
Kidd *v.* Johnson.......465, 479
Kiernan *v.* Man. Tel. Co.... 505
King *v.* Broadhurst........ 179
King *v.* McAuliffe......357, 379
King *v.* Ringling.......... 312
King *v.* Will J. Bloch Amusement Co............132, 195
King *v.* Woodfall.......... 283
Kingman *v.* Brockton...... 249
Kipling *v.* Fenno.......... 55
Kipling *v.* Putnam..455, 486, 544, 648
Kiralfy *v.* Macauley........ 151
Kirchner *v.* Gruban........ 100
Klaw *v.* General Film Co. 416, 419, 420, 421, 424, 429, 433, 444, 454
Klaw *v.* New York Press Co.................... 265
Klein *v.* Beach..2, 7, 8, 39, 42, 43
Kliger *v.* Rosenfeld......... 624

PAGE

Klinger *v.* Ryan........360, 394
Knottnerus *v.* North Park... 332
Koelble *v.* Woods.......259, 401
Kohn, Matter of (Wagener, Sisson)................ 365
Koppel *v.* Downing........ 497
Kramer *v.* Wein........... 114
Kreider *v.* State........... 398
Krier *v.* Mayor............ 371
Kries *v.* Dick............. 350
Kunz *v.* Bosselman.....270, 277
Kurlan *v.* Gutman......... 99
Kurtzmann *v.* Kurtzmann.. 481
Kyle *v.* Jefferys........... 552

La Crandall *v.* Ledbitter 130, 392
La Republique Française *v.* Saratoga Spring Co...... 463
La Societa *v.* San Francisco.. 249
Lacy *v.* Houck............ 99
Lacy *v.* Osbaldiston....124, 162
Lacy *v.* Toole.......22, 71, 557
Ladd *v.* Oxnard...505, 607, 618
Laird *v.* Pittsburg......... 249
Lalance & Grosjean Mfg. Co. *v.* Nat'l Enameling & Stamping Co.......39, 42, 43
Lamb *v.* Grand Rapids Furniture.................. 541
Landa *v.* Greenburg........ 61
Landeker *v.* Wolff..71, 552, 557
Landreth *v.* Landreth....... 477
Larrowe-Loisette *v.* O'Laughlin.................... 505
Lasky *v.* Celebrated Players Film Co............223, 228

	Page
Lasky v. Fox	201
Lasky Feature Co. v. Suratt	175
Latham v. Roach	306
Latour v. Bland	492
Laurelle v. Bush	345
Lauri v. Renad	44
Lavin v. Birch	592
Lawrence v. Aflalo	27
Lawrence v. Bushnell	544
Lawrence v. Dana	27, 511, 550, 609
Lawrence v. Dance	534
Lawrence v. Dixey	96, 101, 103
Lawrence Mfg. v. Tennessee Mfg	461
Leather Cloth Co. v. Am. Leather Cl. Co	479
Leavitt v. Kennicott	124
Leavitt v. Windsor Land & Investment Co	188, 245
Le Page Co. v. Russian Cement Co.	453, 466, 469
Lederer v. Ferris	586
Lederer v. Rankin	586
Lederer v. Saake	593, 598
Lee v. Gibbings	55
Lee v. State	345
Leeson v. General Council	360
Lempke v. State	398
Lennox v. Curzon	240
Leoncini v. Post	499
Lerner v. Tetrazzini	103
Leslie v. Robie	121
Lester v. Palmer	630
Lethridge v. Wilson	351, 352
Levin v. Goodwin	255
Levinsky v. Cooper	324
Levis v. Hitchkock	280
Levison v. Oes	79, 150, 190, 220
Levy v. Rutley	36, 37
Levy v. Yates	192, 344
Lewis v. Arnold	293, 328, 330
Leyland v. Stewart	552
Lichtenstein v. Fisher	143
Liddell v. Copp-Clark Co	599
Liedertafel Case, Jude's	580
Liedertafel Series, Re The	557
Life Photo Film v. Bell	357, 375
Liggett & Myers Tobacco v. Finzer	461
Lillard v. Sun Printing Co	637
Lindenmuller v. People	127
Lingenfelter, Ex parte	397
Linthicum v. Truitt	323
Linton v. U. F. Co	163
Lipshutz v. Proctor	116
Liquor Tax Cases	346
Little v. City of Madison	317
Little v. Gould	27, 550, 582
Littlefield v. Perry	582
Livingston, In re	175
Livingston v. Klaw	145
Loftus v. Roberts	117
London v. Biograph	573
London & Provincial El. Theatres, Ltd., ex parte	351
London Assurance Co. v. Dreunen	47
London Co. Council v. Bermondsey Bioscope Co.	361
London Music Hall v. Austin	96, 118, 124

PAGE
London Music Hall *v.* Poluski 107, 108
London Theatre of Varieties *v.* Evans.............6, 107
London University Press *v.* University Tutórial Press 29
Long *v.* Bowring.......... 102
Lorenz *v.* Bartuschek...142, 191
Lorette *v.* Collins.......... 177
Lorillard *v.* Clyde.......... 70
Lover *v.* Davidson......... 534
Lovering *v.* Miller......120, 123
Lowell *v.* Spaulding........ 303
Lowenfeld *v.* Curtis........ 60
Lubin *v.* Swaab....224, 235, 236
Lucas *v.* Cooke.........71, 557
Lucas *v.* Moncrieff......... 69
Ludwigh *v.* Payśon.....460, 585
Lumley *v.* Gye........... 202
Lumiansky *v.* Tessier....... 241
Lumley *v.* Wagner.......96, 99
Lumsden *v.* Thompson Scenic Ry.................. 323
Lusk *v.* Peck......300, 302, 312
Luxemburg *v.* Keith....... 292
Lyons, Sons & Co. *v.* Gulliver 252
Lyric Theatre *v.* State...... 399
Lytton *v.* Devey.......... 493

McAllister *v.* Simon........ 336
McBride & Co., In re D. H. 645
McCain *v.* Majestic Bldg... 333
McCaull *v.* Braham......... 96
McCrea *v.* Marsh.......... 292
McCullough *v.* Pence...... 86
McDermott *v.* Bd. of Trade.. 505

PAGE
McDonald *v* Hearst.197, 637, 591
McDonnell, In re.......... 644
McGee *v.* Kennedy........ 362
McGiffen *v.* Baird.......... 592
MacGowan *v.* Duff......... 328
MacGregar *v.* Gilmore...... 122
McIndoo *v.* Musson Book Co. 412, 448, 585
McIntosh *v.* Miner......... 123
McKeage *v.* Hanover Fire Ins. Co.............. 233
McKenzie *v.* McClellan. .350, 351
McLaughlin *v.* Hammerstein 119, 158, 160
McLaughlin *v.* Raphael. . . 521
McLean *v.* Fleming...405, 423, 430, 452, 456
McLellan *v.* Goodwin....168, 188
McLeod *v.* State.......... 398
Macleod *v.* Wakely... ... 65
Macmillan Co. *v.* Dent...493, 579
McMillan *v.* King......... 608
McNeill *v.* Williams...... . 603
McQuire *v.* Western News . 203
McVittie *v.* Turner.... ... 368
Macalay *v.* Press Pub.. Co. 158, 163
Mack *v.* Petter............ 445
Mackay *v.* Mackay...... . 551
Mackaye *v.* Mallory. 168
MacKenzie *v.* Soden Mineral Springs............270, 273
Macklin *v.* Richardson.. . . 497
Mahonoy City *v.* Hersker... 347
Mail & Express *v.* Life Pub. Co..............17, 545, 627

PAGE

Maitland *v.* Company...... 592
Majestic Theatre *v.* City of Cedar Rapids........... 399
Mallory *v.* Mackaye..32, 46, 51, 62, 67, 168, 187
Manchester Palace *v.* Manchester Corporation...... 360
Manger Bros. *v.* Shipman.. 313
Mann *v.* Maurel........... 76
Manners *v.* Triangle....427, 444
Mansell *v.* Valley Printing Co.................275, 492
Manufacturing Co. *v.* Wilson 461
Mapleson *v.* Bentham.96, 107, 124
Mapleson *v.* Del Puente..102, 109
Mapleson *v.* La Blache...... 101
Mapleson *v.* Sears......... 124
Maratta *v.* Heer Dry Goods Co..................... 164
Marble *v.* Ross............ 314
Marconi Wireless *v.* Simon.. 109
"Mark Twain" Case....... 212
Markham *v.* Southern Conservatory of Music....... 343
Marks *v.* Benjamin...341, 343, 344, 348
Marks *v.* Jaffa............ 270
Marks Realty Co. *v.* "Churchills"............ 232
Marks Realty Co. *v.* Hotel Hermitage.............. 232
Marks Realty Co. *v.* Rectors. 232
Marmet *v.* State........... 345
Marquet *v.* La Duke....... 317
Marrone *v.* Washington Jockey Club.........292, 294

PAGE

Marsh *v.* Conquest..550, 587, 588
Marshall *v.* Bull........... 554
Marshal *v.* Broadhurst..... 70
Marston *v.* Swett.......... 592
Martin *v.* Hunt........... 70
Martinetti *v.* Maguire...... 535
Marvin *v.* Brooks.......... 87
Marx *v.* Miller............ 140
Marx *v.* Ontario H. & A. Co. 324
Mary *v.* Hubert........... 670
Masson's Appeal........... 610
Mastad *v.* Swedish Brethren 327, 332
Matsell *v.* Flanagan........ 443
Mathers *v.* Green.......... 38
Matter of Allen........... 341
Matter of Armstrong *v.* Murphy.............350, 358
Matter of City of New York (Re Hammerstein)....... 338
Matter of Ormsby *v.* Bell 354, 357
Matter of Simons *v.* McGuire 350
Mattice *v.* Wilcox.......... 65
Maurel *v.* Smith..........36, 52
Mawman *v.* Tegg.......... 621
Mawson *v.* Leavitt......... 152
Maxwell *v.* Goodwin..560, 564, 591, 626, 627
Maxwell Steel Vault Co. *v.* Nat'l Casket Co......... 599
May *v.* Burdett........... 317
May *v.* Chaffee............ 41
Mayer *v.* Nethersole.....169, 187
Mayor of N. Y. City *v.* Eden Musee..............339, 341

PAGE
Meachem v. Jamestown R. R. Co....143, 191
Mecabe v. Jones.... 209
Meccano v. Wagner.... 541
Meeker v. Smith.... 325
Mehlos v. City of Milwaukee. 346
Meibus v. Dodge.... 316
Meisner v. Detroit.... 292
Melsheimer v. Sullivan.... 316
Menchen v. Denville.... 581
Menendez v. Holt..450, 452, 456
Merivale v. Carson.... 264
Merle v. Soc. Research..266, 272, 280, 282
Merrell v. Tice....593, 598
Merriam Co. v. Famous S. & C. Co....438, 439
Merriam Co. v. Halloway Pub. Co.... 438
Merriam Co. v. Ogilvie..438, 439, 442
Merriam Co. v. Strauss.... 438
Merriam Co. v. Saulfield.430, 438
Merriam Co. v. Texas Siftings Co.... 438
Merriam Co. v. United Dictionary Co....517, 593
Message Photoplay Co. v. Bell.... 354
Messenger v. Press Publ. Co.. 281
Messenger v. State.... 280
Messer v. Fadettes....466, 478
Metropolis Theatre Co. v. City of Chicago....352, 359
Metropolitan Opera Co. v. Hammerstein....246, 261, 489

PAGE
Metropolitan Ex. Co. v. Ward 109
Metts v. Charleston Theatre 331
Metzler v. Wood.... 440
Meyer v. Grand Rapids Chair Co.... 311
Meyer v. Redmund.... 197
Meyers v. Walton.... 179
Michelstree v. Stair.... 310
Mifflin v. Dutton..13, 18, 511, 546, 556
Mifflin v. White..13, 18, 511, 546, 556
Miles Medical Co. v. Park & Sons.... 202
Millar v. Taylor....496, 618
Miller v. Lawrence....143, 248
Millington v. Fox.... 461
Mills v. Standard Music Roll Co....545, 619
Mines v. Scribner.... 490
Ming v. Pratt.... 150
Miracle Co. v. Danziger..413, 443, 454
Mirsky v. Adler.... 333
Mitchell v. Hawley.... 481
Molloy v. Starin.... 315
Monahan v. Taylor....587, 588
Montague v. Flockton...123, 143
Montgomery v. Ladjing.... 336
Montgomery v. Waterbury.... 592
Moore v. Coyne.... 86
Moore v. Edwards.... 21
Moore v. Owen.... 398
Moore v. Rugg.... 596
Morang v. Le Sueur..58, 89, 207

PAGE

Morang *v.* Publishers' Syndicate 671
Morasse *v.* Brochu 283
Morgan *v.* Roberts 50
Morgan *v.* Rogers 466
Morgan *v.* Walton 455
Morgan Envelope Co. *v.* Albany Paper Co. 587
Morosco *v.* Fendall 574
Morris *v.* Briggs 144
Morris *v.* Colman 72, 96
Morris *v.* Kelly 497
Morrison *v.* Belcher 63, 203
Morrison *v.* Hurtig & Seaman 136, 162
Morrison *v.* Pettibone 623
Morrison *v.* Smith 283
Moshier *v.* Kitchell 50
Moss *v.* Donahue 529
Moss Motion Picture Corp. *v.* Ivan Film Prod., Inc. 426, 447
Moss *v.* Tompkins 150, 247
Motion Picture Patents Co. *v.* Universal Film 485
Motorboat Pub. Co. *v.* Motor Boating Co. 446
Mott Iron Works *v.* Clow ... 541
Moul *v.* The Coronet Theatre, Ltd. 588
Muckenfass, Ex parte...392, 397
Muller *v.* McKesson 315
Muller *v.* Rittersville Hotel .. 235
Munden *v.* Harris 273, 278
Munro *v.* Tousey..405, 406, 433, 447

PAGE

Murray *v.* Gast Lithographic Co. 269, 270
Murray *v.* Walter 203
Murrell *v.* Smith 318
Muser *v.* Robertson 599
Mutual Film Corp. *v.* City of Chicago 387
Mutual Film Corp. *v.* Hodges 387
Mutual Film Corp. *v.* Industrial Commission Ohio. 288, 384
Myers *v.* Callaghan 519

Nahser *v.* City of Chicago 255, 365, 371
Nash *v.* Krieling 141, 213
National Car Brake Co. *v.* Terre Haute Co. 457
Nat'l Cloak & Suit *v.* Kaufman 532, 541
Nat'l Cloak & Suit Co. *v.* Standard Mail Order Co... 541
Naulty *v.* Bulletin Co. 64
Neet, Ex parte 397
Neher *v.* Viviani 242
Neilson *v.* Horniman 578
Nelson *v.* A. H. Woods Prod. Co. 127
Nelson Theatre Co. *v.* Nelson 242, 247
Nephler *v.* Woodward 309
Nethersole *v.* Bell 567
Neuendorff *v.* Duryea 395
Neufeld *v.* Chapman 82
New Castle *v.* Genkinger 381
New Fiction Co. *v.* Star Co. 26, 531, 545, 553, 577, 578, 580

PAGE

New Theatre v. Hartlove... 308
New Tivoli v. Happy Fanny Fields.................. 106
New York v. Eden Musee... 398
New York City v. Pine...... 610
New York v. Williams...... 396
New York, Matter of....... 396
New York Academy of Music v. Hackett.......79, 150, 242,
New York Bank Note Co. v. Hamilton Engraving Co. 624, 625
New York Herald v. Ottawa 475
New York Herald v. Star Co.................... 475
New York Life Ins. Co. v. Allison.............233, 234
N. Y. Motion Picture Co. v. Universal Film.......... 489
N. Y. Phonograph Co. v. Davega................ 67
N. Y. Star Co. v. Sun Printing & Pub. Ass'n......... 598
N. Y. Times v. Star Co..502, 597, 598
Newcomer v. Blaney....... 120
Newhall v. Appleton....... 125
Newman v. Gatti.......105, 141
Newman v. Zachary........ 202
Nichols v. Amalgamated Press.................. 82.
Nillson v. De Haven.....82, 592
Nillson v. Lawrence..37, 39, 42, 44
Nisbet v. Golf Agency...... 32
Nixon v. Doran..93, 569, 570, 603

PAGE

Nixon & Zimmerman v. Lee Lash Co................ 230
N. K. Fairbanks Co. v. Windsor.................455, 456
Noack v. Wosslick......... 299
Noebius v. De Jong & Co.... 453
Norton v. Hudner.......... 311
Nottage v. Jackson........ 596

Oakes v. Tonsmierre....... 480
Oakland v. Bingham....301, 327
O'Brien v. Jones........... 592
O'Callaghan v. Dellwood Park Co................ 323
O'Connor v. Armour Packing Co.................... 139
Oellers v. Horn............ 343
Oertel v. Jacoby........... 506
Oertel v. Wood............ 492
Ogilvie v. Merriam Co...438, 442
Old Colony Trust Co. v. Dubuque Co............... 608
Oldknow v. City of Atlanta.. 367
Oliver v. Lansing.......232, 235
Oliver v. Rumford......67, 646
Oliver v. State............. 397
Ollendorf v. Black......... 662
Olympic A. C. v. Bingham... 400
Oneida Community v. Oneida 455, 459
O'Neill v. General Film Co. 25, 492, 493, 498, 573, 574,
Oriental Society, In re...... 262
O'Rourke, Matter of....... 371
Orr v. Johnson............ 457
Orton v. Brown........... 359

PAGE

Osborne *v.* Schenck.......40, 41
Osgood *v.* Allen....403, 446, 455
Osgood *v.* Aloe Instrument Co.............513, 593, 595
Outcault *v.* Bonheur.....91, 592
Outcault *v.* Lamar..405, 417, 443, 474
Owen *v.* Partridge......... 279
Owens *v.* Assoc. Realties 301, 308
Oxford *v.* Leathe.......... 334

Pagano *v.* Beseler.......... 539
Paige *v.* Banks.........548, 618
Palace Theatre *v.* Clency..99, 104
Palestine *v.* Minor......... 255
Palmer *v.* De Witt..21, 492, 493, 494, 496, 497, 504, 583, 586
Palmer *v.* Nat'l Sporting Club.................. 270
Palmer *v.* Snow........... 391
Pankhurst *v.* Kinsman...... 47
Pappas *v.* Miles........... 151
Paris *v.* Commonwealth.... 255
Park *v.* Morgan........... 359
Park & Pollard Co. *v.* Kellerstrass.................. 620
Parker *v.* Cushman........ 315
Parker *v.* Hyde & Behman Amuse. Co............. 113
Parkinson *v.* Laselle........ 511
Parry *v.* American Opera Co. 145
Parsons *v.* Manser......... 315
Partlow *v.* Haggerty........ 314
Parton *v.* Prang...492, 506, 554, 596

PAGE

Pastor *v.* Solomon......... 167
Patrick *v.* Wood........... 345
Patterson *v.* Ogilvie Publ. Co..523, 554, 594, 618, 619, 638, 644, 645
Pattison *v.* Hammerstein.... 335
Pattison *v.* Livingston Am. Co.................... 308
Paulton *v.* Keith........197, 345
Pavesich *v.* New England 273, 283
Pearce *v.* Spaulding........ 292
Pearson, Ltd., *v.* J. P. O'Connor.................... 448
Peck *v.* Tribune Co.....269, 283
Peerless Feature *v.* Fields 98, 110
Penrose *v.* Nixon.......... 254
People ex rel. Edison *v.* Assessors................. 648
People ex rel. Rota *v.* Baker 354, 375
People ex rel. Bonfiglio *v.* Bingham............... 350
People ex rel. Park Circle Am. Co. *v.* Board of Police 350
People *v.* Brown........... 393
People *v.* Busse............ 371
People *v.* Campbell......341, 342
People *v.* Coleman......... 359
People ex rel. Lodes *v.* Dept. of Health............... 354
People *v.* Dixon........... 399
People *v.* Doris........357, 373
People *v.* Dunford.......... 395
People *v.* Ewer............ 176

PAGE

People v. Finn.........393, 395
People ex rel. Jacques v. Flaherty............... 370
People ex rel. Burnham v. Flynn..............291, 296
People ex rel. Valensi v. Flynn 393
People ex rel. Moses v. Gaynor................358, 364
People ex rel. Schwab v. Grant..............350, 354
People v. Hammerstein..... 398
People v. Hart............ 294
People v. Haym............ 398
People v. Hemleb.......393, 394
People v. Jensen........... 370
People ex rel. Bender v. Joyce................. 394
People v. Keller........341, 348
People v. Kennedy......... 340
People v. King.....292, 298, 341
People v. Kingston......... 400
People v. Klaw............ 489
People ex rel. United States Aluminum Co. v. Knight.. 648
People ex rel. Kieley v. Lent 359, 360, 367, 395
People ex rel. Valensi v. Lynch................. 393
People v. Marks........... 382
People v. Martin.......341, 348
People ex rel. McNulty v. Maxwell............... 350
People ex rel. Armstrong v. Murphy................ 375
People ex rel. Keller v. Oak Park.................. 365

PAGE

People v. O'Gorman . . 396
People ex rel. Lange v. Palmitter.........365, 383
People ex rel. Klinger v. Rand 394
People ex rel. Johnson v Roberts.............. 648
People v. Royal 341, 342
People v. Samwick 370
People ex rel. Jacques v. Sheriff................ 381
People v. Steele........... 382
People v. Stevens.......... 176
People v. Trippi........... 370
People v. Wacke........... 341
People ex rel. Ritter v. Wallace.................. 346
People ex rel. Schau v. Williams................. 350
People ex rel. Cumiskey v. Wurster........349, 352, 354
Peple v. Comstock..... .68, 75
Pepper v. Labrot.......... 466
Perley v. Shubert.......... 258
Perris v. Hexamer......... 560
Perry v. Bates............ 117
Peters v. Borst...27, 34, 36, 208
Pettes v. American Clock Co. 463
Pevely v. Poole........114, 208
Phila. Ball Club v. Lajoie 96, 109
Philip v. Pennell........... 493
Philipp Co. v. New York Staats-Zeitung.......... 266
Phillips v. Alhambra Palace 161
Phillips v. Inez............ 391
Phillips v. Wisconsin State.. 325

PAGE

Phœnix Ins. Co. *v.* Continental Ins. Co. 102
Photo Drama Motion Pict. Co. *v.* Social Uplift Film Corp. . 2, 5, 9, 11, 12, 48, 110, 496, 553
Pierce *v.* Werckmeister. . 505, 511, 513, 593
Pierpont *v.* Fowle. 548
Pieschel *v.* Miner. 313
Piexotto *v.* Board of Education. 355
Pike *v.* Nicholas. 570
Pitts *v.* Hall. 37, 46
Placide *v.* Burton. 166
Planche *v.* Braham. 562
Planché *v.* Colburn. 77, 90
Pointer *v.* Mountain R. C. C. 323
Polk *v.* Daly. 147
Pollock *v.* Shubert. 131
Pollard *v.* Photographic Co. 272, 596
Popplewell *v.* Pierce. 314
Porter *v.* Freudenberg. 530
Posen *v.* Schwarz. 425
Posner Co. *v.* Jackson. 202
Pott *v.* Altemus. 604
Potter *v.* McPherson. . 406, 441, 506
Potter *v.* Watt. 366, 380
Poussard *v.* Spiers. 157
Powell *v.* Head. 37, 39
Powers *v.* O'Neill. 336
Pratt *v.* Montegriffo. 105, 106
Pratt *v.* Paris Gaslight & Coke Co. 630

PAGE

Press Association *v.* Northern, etc., Agency. 23
Press Publ. Co. *v.* Falk. 596
Press Publ. Co. *v.* Monroe 27, 493, 494, 498, 499, 556, 627
Prince Albert *v.* Strange. . 492, 506
Probosco *v.* Bonyon. 466
Pulte *v.* Derby. 19, 632
Purcell *v.* Daly. 292
Pusey *v.* Miller. 38, 42, 43, 44

Quaglieni *v.* Mathews. . 342, 343, 649
Quarg, Ex parte. 381
Quarles *v.* State. 398
Queen *v.* Commissioners of Inland Revenue. 361
Queen *v.* County Council. . . . 360
Queensberry *v.* Shebbeare. . . 492
Quong Wo, Ex parte. 365

Rafalo *v.* Edelstein. . 137, 139, 141, 142, 162
Raleigh *v.* Kinematograph Trading Company. 445
Ramonas *v.* Grand Rapids Ry. Co. 322, 323
Read *v.* Conquest. 496, 560
Reade *v.* Bentley. . 51, 67, 68, 646
Reade *v.* Sweetzer. 65
Record & Guide Co. *v.* Bromley. 515, 518
Rectanus Co. *v.* United Drug Co. 462
Redmond *v.* Nat'l Horse Show. 300

PAGE

Reed v. Carusi.........574, 597
Reed v. Holliday........591, 608
Rees v. Peltzer.........496, 505
Rees v. Robbins........... 573
Reeves v. Fourteenth St. Theatre................ 311
Reg. v. Barnes............. 398
Reg. v. Strugnell........344, 348
Reg. v. Tucker............ 341
Reichart v. Sapte.......... 574
Reid v. Wilson......349, 393, 400
Reinhardt v. Smith........ 623
Renard v. Carl Rosa Opera Co..................... 204
R. v. Ashton, Ex parte Walker................. 349
R. v. Baldoli.............. 635
Rex v. Carlile............. 254
Rex v. Charron............ 393
Rex v. Daoust............. 61
Rex v. Paton.............. 371
Rex v. Hazza.............. 365
R. v. Hannay.......349, 363, 369
Rex v. Jones............... 292
R. v. London County Council 358, 360
Rex v. Moore.............. 254
Rex v. Ouimet............. 398
R. v. Rosenthal............ 348
R. v. Sheerness County Council..................... 360
Rex v. Willetts............ 635
R. v. Wolfe............... 344
R. v. Yorkshire County Council..................... 360
Reymer & Bros. v. Huyler's.. 461

PAGE

Rhodes v. Sperry & Hutchinson.................... 271
Rice v. Miner..........176, 177
Richards v. Wreschner...... 529
Richardson v. Bosselman.... 623
Richardson v. D. M. Osborn & Co.................. 608
Richmond R. Co. v. Moore.. 332
Ricordi v. Hammerstein.... 605
Ricordi v. Mason.......... 562
Ridge v. English Illustrated Magazine............... 56
Ridgway Co. v. Amalgamated Press...............409, 448
Riddle v. McFadden....... 278
Rigney v. Dutton.......... 521
Rigney v. Raphael......... 521
Ritchie v. Sayres.......... 608
Ritter v. Wallace........354, 355
Roberson v. Rochester Folding Box Co......268, 273, 277, 280, 290
Roberts v. Myers........30, 581
Robertson v. Berry..61, 404, 441
Roberts v. Sheldon......... 468
Robey v. Arnold........... 145
Robey v. Stratton.......... 145
Robinson v. Davison.156, 157, 161
Robinson v. Illustrated London News.............. 552
Robinson v. Textile Publ. Co. 278
Robl v. Palace Theatre...571, 576
Rock v. Lazarus........... 532
Rodgers v. Nowill.......... 469
Rodwell v. Redge.......... 193
Rogers v. Evarts........... 202

PAGE

Rogers v. Rogers........... 313
Rogers v. International Silver Co.................... 468
Rolfs v. Pooley Furn. Co.... 156
Romeike v. Romeike....... 481
Root v. Railway........582, 609
Roquemore, Ex parte....... 397
Rosbach v. Sackett & Wilhelms Co............... 163
Rose Ball v. The Tribune.... 283
Rose v. McLean Publishing Co..................412, 440
Roseneau v. Empire Circuit. 257
Roserie v. Kiralfy.......... 139
Rosenwasser v. Amusement Enterprises............. 247
Ross v. Raphael........... 521
Roumfort Co. v. Delaney.... 369
Rosenberg v. Arrowsmith... 397
Rothenberg v. Packard..... 144
Routledge v. Low..661, 662, 665
Roy Watch Co. v. Carman Roy Watch Co........... 459
Royal Albert Hall v. London Council..............344, 347
Royal Aquarium Soc. v. Parkinson.................. 360
Royal Baking Powder v. Raymond...............450, 453
Royle v. Dillingham.......56, 59
Roys v. Johnson........... 193
Rudge-Whitworth, Ltd., v. Houck Mfg. Co.......... 110
Ruggles v. Eddy........... 582
Rupp & Wittgenfeld v. Elliot 587
Rushbrook v. Grimsby Palace Theatre............. 183
Russell v. Briant........... 588
Russell v. Notcutt......... 204
Russell v. Smith........339, 340
Russia Cement v. LePage... 466
Russo v. Orpheum Theatre 327, 331

Saake v. Lederer...531, 583, 593, 598
Saltus v. Bedford.......... 592
Salvation Army v. Salvation Army................. 455
Sampson & Murdock v. Seaver-Radford Co...111, 609, 620
Sanborn v. Dakin.......... 610
Sands v. N. Y. Life Ins. Co.. 528
Sargent v. McLeod.......48, 50
Sarony v. Ehrich........... 637
Sarpy v. Holland...348, 587, 649
Savage v. Hoffman...20, 496, 536
Savage v. Kerker.......... 420
Savage v. Neely........... 85
Savery v. Ingersoll......150, 151
Sawyer v. Kellogg.......452, 468
Saxe v. Shubert.........114, 208
Saxlehner v. Eisner.449, 450, 456, 468
Saxlehner v. Siegel-Cooper Co.................421, 456
Sayre v. Moore............ 561
Scarano v. Lemlein......... 164
Schimkevitz v. Bingham.... 400
Schleuter v. Billingheimer... 255

PAGE

Schmidt Case 182
Schnizer *v.* Philips. 300, 312
Schlesinger *v.* Bedford 622
Schlotz *v.* Amasis 560
Schoelkopf, Matter of 237
Schofield *v.* Wood 304
Schonberg *v.* Cheney 81
Schreiber *v.* Sharpless . . . 591, 637
Schulz *v.* Raimes 530
Schumacher *v.* Schwencke 27, 32, 550, 590, 627
Schuyler *v.* Curtis 270
Schwab *v.* Anderson Steamboat Co. 323
Schwab *v.* Muller 126
Schwartz *v.* India Rubber. . . 180
Schwarz *v.* Wylie 574
Schweitzer *v.* Hamburg, etc., Gesellschaft 182
Scott *v.* McNaughton 193
Scott *v.* University of Michigan 325
Scribner *v.* Allen Co. 532
Scribner *v.* Clark 532
Scribner *v.* Kelly 316
Scribner *v.* Strauss 46, 486
Scriven *v.* North 459
Sea Gull Specialty Co. *v.* Humphrey 82
Sebeck *v.* Plattdentsche Volkfest 332
Security Trust Co. *v.* Temple Co. 233, 234, 235
Selchow *v.* Baker 409
Selig Polyscope Co. *v.* Mutual Film Corporation 432, 444
Selig Polyscope Co. *v.* Unicorn Film Service Corp. 421, 422, 425, 441, 451, 454
Selinas *v.* Vermont State. . . . 325
Selwyn *v.* Waller 189
Serrena *v.* Jefferson . . 19, 538, 572
Sharpless *v.* Lawrence 421
Shaver *v.* Heller & Herz 463
Shaw's Jewelry Shop *v.* N. Y. Herald 253
Shaw *v.* Collins 449
Shaw *v.* McCreary 313
Sheehan *v.* Railroad Co. 38
Sheets *v.* Sunbry 311
Shelley *v.* Bethel . . 260, 344, 347, 348
Shelby *v.* Emerson 381
Shepheard *v.* Whitaker 283
Shepherd *v.* Bingham 400
Shepherd *v.* Conquest 31, 37
Sherman *v.* Marinelli 538
Sherwood *v.* Crane 117
Shook *v.* Daly 492
Shook *v.* Rankin 25, 492
Shook *v.* Woods 429, 459
Shubert *v.* Angeles 100
Shubert *v.* Coyne 103
Shubert *v.* Laughlin 245
Shubert *v.* Nixon 292, 294
Shubert *v.* Sondheim 243
Shubert *v.* Woodward . . . 111, 246
Shutt *v.* Lewis 343
Sigmon *v.* Goldstone 164
Silver *v.* Holt 632
Singer Mfg. Co. *v.* June Mfg. Co. 439

PAGE

Singer Mfg. Co. *v.* Long.... 457
Simmons *v.* Mansfield...... 461
Sims *v.* Marryat........... 557
Simms *v.* Stanton.......... 571
Simplex Automobile *v.* Kahnweiler.................. 438
Sizer *v.* Ray.............. 592
Skinner *v.* Oakes.......479, 480
Slingsby *v.* Bradford Truck Co.................... 615
Sloan *v.* Williams.......... 67
Smiles *v.* Belford.......... 671
Smith *v.* Benick........... 332
Smith *v.* City of Raton...248, 350
Smith *v.* Clinton........... 65
Smith *v.* Cumberland Soc.... 332
Smith *v.* Daily News, Ltd.. 591
Smith *v.* Dodd............ 647
Smith *v.* Dunn............ 47
Smith *v.* Herring-Hall-Marvin Safe Co............. 178
Smith *v.* Robson.......... 113
Smith *v.* Utley............ 209
Smith *v.* Wilcox........... 127
Snow *v.* Laird............. 637
Snow *v.* Mast............. 516
Snow *v.* McCracken........ 314
Snowden *v.* Noah.......... 446
Soane *v.* Knight........... 64
Social Register Ass'n *v.* Howard.................... 408
Social Register Assoc'n *v.* Murphy................ 446
Society *v.* Neusbach........ 341
Sociological Research *v.* Waldo..............356, 372

PAGE

Solman *v.* Arcaro.......103, 175
Solomon *v.* United States... 27
Sosman *v.* Coulon.......233, 234
Southern *v.* How.......... 469
Southern Ry. *v.* Myers...194, 195
Southey *v.* Sherwood....... 492
Spahn *v.* Winter Garden..... 118
Spain *v.* Manhattan Street Co. 113
Spaulding *v.* Rosa..48, 156, 157, 159, 161
Speake *v.* Powell........... 263
Speckman *v.* Kreig......... 315
Spicer *v.* Waters........... 499
Spiegel *v.* Zuckerman....... 411
Spires *v.* Los Angeles....... 249
Spooner *v.* Daniels.......64, 209
Spooner *v.* State........... 398
Spring *v.* Edgar........... 313
Springer *v.* Falk........... 637
Springfield *v.* Thame....... 23
S. F. Co. *v.* Siegel-Cooper 98
St. Cyr *v.* Sothern & Marlowe 81
St. James Hall Co. *v.* London County Council......... 244
St. Joseph *v.* Elliot......... 398
St. Louis *v.* Fischer......... 365
Stair *v.* Kane............. 325
Stamp *v.* 86th St. Am. Co.... 317
Standard Am. Pub. Co. *v.* Methodist Concern...... 68
Standard Fashion Co. *v.* Siegel-Cooper Co........ 96
Standard Sanitary Co. *v.* United States........... 489
Standard Scale & Foundry Co. *v.* McDonald........ 630

PAGE
Standing v. Brady......142, 162
Standidge v. Lynde........ 162
Star Co. v. Press. Pub. Co... 103
Star Co. v. Wheeler Syndicate.................... 470
State v. Burnes............ 399
State v. Chamberlain....... 393
State ex rel. Ebert v. Loden 350, 367
State v. French Opera Ass'n 380
State v. Herald............ 398
State v. Lynch............ 248
State v. Mason............ 210
State v. Morris........340, 393
State v. O'Hara........352, 359
State v. Penny.........393, 396
State v. Prather........... 397
State v. Rosenfield......... 346
State v. Ryan............. 398
State v. Scaffer........191, 345
State v. Schonhauser,...352, 359
State v. State Journal Co... 506
State Board of Agriculture v. Meyers................ 144
Stearns v. U. S............ 637
Stecher v. Dunston......505, 517
Stein v. Bell...........356, 375
Steppacher v. Karr......... 459
Sterling v. Bock........... 133
Stern v. Laemmle......6, 71, 72
Stern v. Remick........504, 517
Sternberg v. O'Brien....... 98
Stevens v. Benning..51, 67, 69, 646
Stevens v. Cady..496, 554, 610, 645

PAGE
Stevens v. Chicago Feature Co..................... 114
Stevens v. Gladding..534, 554, 590, 610, 626, 636, 645
Stevens v. McKibbin....... 47
Stevens v. Morenous....... 396
Stevens v. Wildy.......... 45
Stevens v. William......... 463
Stevenson v. Fox..25, 569, 573, 574, 620
Stevenson v. Glasgow....... 303
Stevenson v. Harris........ 573
Stewart v. Cobalt Curling... 303
Stewart v. Reuters Telegram 63
Stewart v. Thayer......129, 398
Stickel v. Riverview Sharpshooters............333, 334
Stiff v. Cassell............. 72
Stimpson v. Minsker Realty Co.................... 250
Stockdale v. Onwhyn....... 535
Stokes v. Allen & White.... 446
Stone v. Dugan............ 541
Stone v. Long............. 88
Stone v. Oconomowoc...... 250
Storer v. Downey.......... 365
Stott v. Gamble.......226, 351
Stott, Ex parte............ 226
Stover v. Lathrop.......... 499
Stowe v. Thomas.......560, 564
Strackosch v. Strackosch 118, 156
Strafford v. Stetson........ 123
Straus v. Victor........... 483
Strauss v. Am. Pub. Ass'n... 489
Strauss v. Francis.......... 64

PAGE
Strauss v. Hammerstein..127, 231
Strauss v. Notaseme Co..... 452
Strauss v. Pen Printing Co. 514, 617
Stringer v. Frohman....... 447
Strobridge Litho. Co. v. Crane 97
Stuart v. Smith........197, 590
Sturgis v. Coleman......... 366
Sturgis v. Grau............ 366
Sturgis v. Hayman......... 365
Sturtevant Co. v. Fireproof Film Co............... 196
Suburban Press v. Phila. Co. 61, 441
Suesskind v. Bingham...... 400
Sugar v. Monroe........... 250
Sutherland v. Wyer.....147, 148
Swan v. Tappan........... 64
Sweet v. Benning.......28, 550
Sweet v. Evans........... 28
Swezey, In re............. 479
Swords v. Edgar........... 302
Syers v. Conquest..342, 348, 649

Tabart v. Tepper.......... 64
Taft v. Smith, Gray & Co... 499
Taft v. Stevens............ 521
Tams v. Witmark...72, 583, 596
Taendsticksfabriks A. Vulcan v. Meyers...........455, 460
Tannenbaum v. Rehm...... 369
Tarling v. Fredericks....340, 346
Tasker v. Shepherd........ 70
Tate v. Fullbrook........21, 537
Taylor v. Caldwell.......48, 241
Taylor v. Cohn............ 292

PAGE
Taylor, v. Gilman.......591, 637
Taylor v. Hearst........... 283
Taylor v. Nast............ 443
Taylor v. Sawyer Spindle Co.................... 608
Taylor v. Waters.......... 292
Teichner v. Pope Mfg. Co... 114
Terry v. Brighton Aquarium 341, 398
Terry v. Moss's Empires, Ltd. 119
Texas State v. Britton...306, 332
Theatre De Luxe v. Gledhill 351, 361, 371
The King v. Dimock....... 352
The Mikado Case.......52, 508
The Sarah................ 140
Thedford Medicine Co. v. Curry.................. 469
Thill v. Hoyt............. 160
Thomas v. Abrahamson..... 420
Thomas v. Bayson......... 316
Thomas v. Beaver Dam Mfg. Co.................... 157
Thomas v. Bradbury.....63, 203
Thomas v. Gatti........... 263
Thomas v. Lennon......... 497
Thomas v. Springer.168, 187, 335
Thomas v. Williams........ 298
Thombleson v. Black....... 554
Thompson v. Hubbard..511, 513
Thompson v. Lowell.....321, 332
Thompson v. Shackell...... 64
Thompson v. Tillford....... 275
Thorne v. French.........77, 80
Thornton v. Agricultural Society.................. 332

PAGE

Thring *v.* Lucas..........176, 226
Tivoli, Manchester, *v.* Colley 96
Tobacco Co. *v.* Hynes...... 461
Todd Protectograph Co. *v.* Hirschberg.............. 213
Todd *v.* Keene.........150, 153
Tonson *v.* Collins.......... 492
Tomalin *v.* Pearson........ 180
Tompkins *v.* Hallock..493, 494, 504, 586
Town of Davis *v.* Davis..... 255
Trade Auxiliary Co. *v.* Middlesborough T. P. Ass'n... 37
Trailing *v.* Messenger...... 348
Tree *v.* Bowkett..36, 45, 71, 224, 228, 557
Trengrouse *v.* "Sol" Syndicate.................. 562
Triangle Film Corp. *v.* Artcraft................. 202
Tribune Co. of Chicago *v.* Associated Press..23, 540, 616
Triggs *v.* Sun Printing & Publishers Ass'n......... 65
Trow Directory *v.* Boyd.... 590
Troy City Directory *v.* Curtin............593, 594, 636
Trustees *v.* Lewis......249, 350
Tuck & Sons *v.* Priester..... 672
Tully *v.* Triangle..531, 580, 605
Turgeon *v.* Connecticut Co. 301, 306, 332
Turner *v.* Robinson........ 506
Tuttle *v.* La Dow.......... 67
Twiggar *v.* Rosenberg...... 399
Tyler *v.* Tyler............ 40

PAGE

United Drug Co. *v.* Rectanus Co............453, 455
United Oil Co. *v.* Grey...... 164
United States *v.* Edgar...... 192
United States *v.* Gay....... 192
United States *v.* Greathouse 531
United States *v.* Motion Picture Patents Co......261, 488
United States *v.* Taylor..... 280
United States *v.* Thompson.. 192
United States *v.* White...... 636
United Vaudeville Co. *v.* Zeller................. 396
Universal Film Mfg. Co. *v.* Bell...........355, 356, 373
Universal Film Mfg. Co. *v.* Copperman..485, 497, 507, 555, 617, 622
Universal Talking Machine *v.* English............. 97
Unwin *v.* Clarke........... 203

Vail *v.* Jersey Co.......... 143
Valenti *v.* N. Y. Theatre Co. 245
Valentine *v.* Richardt...... 610
Valentine Co. *v.* Sloan...308, 309
Van Antwerp *v.* Linton..... 306
Van Cleef *v.* Chicago....... 319
Vanderbilt *v.* Mitchell...... 273
Van Doren *v.* Balty........ 40
Van Norden *v.* Server Com................... 355
Vassar College *v.* Loose Wiles 272, 278
Vent *v.* Osgood........... 175
Vernon *v.* Shubert......567, 572

PAGE

Vernon Abstr. Co. v. Waggoner Title Co.......... 505
Victoria Pier Syndicate v. Reeve.................. 367
Village of Des Plaines v. Poyer..............252, 254
Violette v. Rice............ 140
Virginia Hot Springs v. Hegeman................... 452
Vitagraph v. Swaab.....224, 236
Vitascope Co. v. U. S. Phonograph Co............... 648
Vogel v. St. Louis Museum 196, 210
Von Thadorovich v. Franz Joseph Beneficial Ass'n... 273
Vredenburg v. Behan....... 315

Wade v. Hefner........... 162
Wade v. Rob't Arthur Theatres Co.............117, 144
Wade v. Waldon........... 204
Wagner v. Conried......... 506
Wagner v. Wilson.......... 586
Wagstaff v. Edison Bell..... 253
Wahle-Phillips Co. v. Fitzgerald................. 233
Wahle-Phillips v. Fifty-Ninth St. & Madison Ave. Co.................... 234
Waite v. Aborn............ 189
Waite v. O'Neil........... 610
Wakeman v. Wheeler....79, 150
Waldo v. Seelig........366, 380
Wales v. Baily............ 125
Walker, In re............. 363

PAGE

Walker v. Brewster........ 253
Walker v. Crown.......... 202
Walker v. Fuhrman........ 358
Walker v. Globe Newspaper Co.................... 496
Walker v. Tribune........63, 64
Wall v. Bailey............. 120
Wall v. Gordon............ 506
Wall v. Taylor.........348, 587
Wallenstein v. Herbert...... 52
Wallick v. Society......... 345
Walsh v. Hyde & Behman... 331
Walter Baker Co. v. Delapenha................. 411
Walter v. Emmott..404, 448, 455
Walter v. Howe........... 28
Walter v. Steinkopff....... 23
Walton v. Godwin......... 160
Walton v. Mather......... 118
Wamser v. Browning-King.. 336
Wandt v. Hearst's Chicago-American............... 340, 283
Ward v. Beeton........... 72
Ward Lock & Co. v. Long 28, 33, 76
Warheit v. The Day Pub. Co. 71
Warne v. Routledge........ 7
Warner v. Brighton Aquarium 340
Warner v. Roehr.......... 469
Warner v. The Rector and Trustees................ 139
Wash. Luna Park v. Goodrich..................... 323
Waterman v. McKenzie..... 582
Waterman v. Shipman..69, 74, 406, 633, 646

PAGE

Waters v. Leech........... 369
Watkins v. Thurman....... 114
Watson v. Cowdrey........ 499
Watson v. Russell.......122, 165
Watts v. Fraser........... 209
Watts v. Unione........528, 529
Watts v. Van Ness......... 391
Waycross v. Sossman....234, 235
Weatherby & Sons v. Intern'l Horse Agency........... 591
Weaver v. Klaw.......115, 208
Weber v. Freed.........379, 389
Weber v. Mapes........... 85
Weber-Stair v. Fisher....329, 331
Webb v. New Haven Theatre 234
Webb v. Powers........594, 621
Webber v. Chicago........ 340
Webster v. Daly........... 568
Weil v. Nevin............. 209
Weiner v. Scherer......305, 318
Weiss v. Skinner.......293, 329
Weistblatt v. Bingham..337, 339, 348, 392
Welcome v. Thompson..... 409
Weld v. Fruhling.......... 529
Weldon v. Dicks...403, 521, 532
Wells v. Haff.............. 157
Wells v. Minn. Baseball..... 299
Wells Am. Co. v. Means..... 331
Welty v. Jacobs........... 247
Wendell v. Baxter......... 302
Wendell v. Conduit Mach. Co. 281
Wentworth v. Riggs........ 336
Wentworth v. Whitney..... 158
Werckmeister v. Am. Lithographic Co.....486, 505, 513

PAGE

Werckmeister v. Springer Lith. Co................ 532
Werner v. Encyclopedia.... 610
West Publ. Co. v. Lawyers' Co-op.................. 590
West Publishing Co. v. Thompson......496, 543, 609
Westermann v. Despatch 612, 638
Westwater v. Rector....... 146
Wheaton v. Peters..495, 496, 506, 511
Wheeler v. Cobbey......636, 638
Wheeler v. Wheeler........ 40
Wheeler v. Woods......... 144
Wheeler Syndicate v. Star Co. 474
Whistler v. Ruskin......... 64
White v. Constable & Co.... 78
White v. Geroch........... 493
White v. Henderson........ 125
White v. Osborn........... 40
White v. Shapiro.......... 541
White v. White............ 281
White Dental Co. v. Sibley.. 574
White-Smith v. Apollo...550, 560
White-Smith v. Goff....... 548
Whittaker v. Howe........ 102
Whitten, Matter of.....350, 368
Whitwell, Ex parte.....252, 344
Whitwood v. Hardman....92, 99
Wichita Falls Co. v. Adams 333, 334
Widmer v. Thompson......6, 74
Wigan v. Strange.......... 21
Wilder v. Kent........554, 645
Willard v. Tayloe.......... 109

PAGE
Williams v. Butler.......... 157
Williams v. Davenport..... 203
Williams v. Feldman....... 11
Williams v. Mineral C. P. A. 312, 325
Williams v. Moray......... 314
Williams v. Wright.....348, 391
Willis v. Lowery........... 163
Willis v. Tibbals........... 73
Winter German Opera, Ltd., In re.................... 263
Wirth v. Calhoun 129, 398
Witkop & Holmes Co. v. Boyce................. 107
Witmark v. Peters......... 103
Witmark v. Standard Music Roll Co................ 545
Wm. Rogers Co. v. Rogers... 98
Wolf Cigar Stores v. Kramer 140
Wolfe v. Howes..48, 50, 133, 156, 165
Wood v. Butterworth...... 61
Wood v. Cunard Steamship Co..................... 499
Wood v. Leadbitter........ 292
Wood v. Miller............ 143
Wood v. Sandow.......... 203
Woodbridge v. Marks...... 314
Woodman v. Lydiard-Peterson Co 611
Woodruff v. Painter........ 336
Woods v. Broder... 251
Woods Prod. Co. v. Chicago 261, 396
Woodside v. Tonopah...... 111
Woolcott v. Shubert 295

PAGE
Wooster v. Crane..67, 531, 578, 582, 614, 618
Worden v. New Bedford.... 249
World Film Corporation v. Foy and N. Y. Motion Picture Corporation........ 110
Worthen v. Love.......... 316
Worthington v. Batty...... 579
Wright v. Eisle............ 505
Wright v. McCampbell..... 50
Wright v. Tullis.........24, 616
Wyatt v. Burnard......... 26
Wyatt v. Hall's Port Studio.. 278
Wyatt v. McCreery.275, 278, 281
Wyatt v. Phipps........... 125
Wyatt v. Rosherville Gardens.................. 313
Wyatt v. Wanamaker...278, 281
W. W. V. Co. v. Black...... 292

Yale & Towne Mfg. Co. v. Adler.................. 475
Yeamans v. Tannehill...... 76
Yerrington v. Greene.....50, 69
Yorkville v. Bingham...... 361
Young v. Am. Opera Co..157, 159
Younger v. Judah.......299, 328
Yuengling v. Schile.....526, 527

Zamco v. Hammerstein 161
Zenatello v. Hammerstein 128, 162
Zerralin v. Ditson.......... 248
Ziegfeld v. Norworth.....97, 112
Ziegfeld Follies, Inc., v. Gus Hill................445, 454
Zuccaro, Ex parte...... 397, 398

THE LAW OF MOTION PICTURES

CHAPTER I

THE AUTHOR

Rights in his Literary Works

SEC. 1. Where the motion picture is based upon a dramatic composition.
2. Where the motion picture is based upon a novel or historical work.
3. Where the motion picture is based upon a short story, sketch, poem, lecture, sermon or other kindred work.
4. Where the motion picture is based upon an original scenario, that is one not based upon any other work.
5. Where the motion picture is based upon a news item.
6. Where the motion picture is based upon a work in the public domain.
7. Where the motion picture is produced in serial form.
8. Where the relationship is that of employer and employe.
9. Where the motion picture material has been written by more than one person.
10. Nature of the contract of co-authorship.
11. Where music has been written specially to accompany the exhibition of the motion picture.
12. Where the motion picture producer has not followed the text of the work upon which the motion picture is based.
13. Criticism of the work.

Section 1.—Where the motion picture is based upon a dramatic composition.

We shall consider first the various rights and liabilities that are created when the author or proprietor of a play grants producing rights with respect to the same.

Where the author or proprietor of a play grants to a play producer the exclusive license for the dramatic production of that play by living actors upon the stage he may not thereafter grant to another the right to produce that play in motion picture form. This seems to be the accepted rule even where, at the time of the granting of the play rights, neither of the parties contemplated the production of the play by means of motion pictures.[1]

The reason for this rule is founded on the principle that the prior exclusive grant conveys a valuable property right. Inasmuch as a motion picture reproduction of such play is a dramatic work,[2] the exhibition of such motion picture constitutes an invasion of the exclusive dramatic rights originally granted to the producer of the play upon the stage with living actors.[3]

Were this not so, the anomalous situation would arise

[1] *Frohman* v. *Fitch* (1914), 164 A. D. (N. Y.) 231; 149 N. Y. Supp. 633, in which Clyde Fitch granted to Frohman in 1900 the exclusive producing rights to "Captain Jinks of the Horse Marines." Nothing was then contemplated or mentioned by the parties as to motion pictures. Thereafter, on the death of Fitch, his father granted to the American Play Company, the motion picture rights. It was held that Frohman was entitled to an injunction restraining the moving picture production. See also: *Klein* v. *Beach* (1916), 232 Fed. (D. C.) 240, opinion by Mayer, J.; aff'd 239 Fed. (C. C. A.) 108, opinion by Hand, J.; *Harper Bros.* v. *Klaw* (1916), 232 Fed. (D. C.) 609.

[2] *Kalem* v. *Harper* (1911), 222 U. S. 55; 32 Sup. Ct. 20.

[3] *Frohman* v. *Fitch* (1914), 164 A. D. (N. Y.) 231; 149 N. Y. Supp. 633; *Photo Drama Motion Pict. Co.* v. *Social Uplift Film Corp.* (1915), 220 Fed. (C. C. A.) 448; *Klein* v. *Beach* (1916), 232 Fed. (D. C.) 240; aff'd 239 Fed. (C. C. A.) 108; *Harper Bros.* v. *Klaw* (1916), 232 Fed. (D. C.) 609.

wherein the author could grant the exclusive dramatic rights to produce the play upon the stage and simultaneously with its production on the stage, could grant a license to reproduce the play in motion pictures to third parties, the exhibition of which would seriously interfere with, or even destroy, the production upon the stage with living actors.

This situation was imminent in the recent case of *Harper Brothers & ano.* v. *Marc Klaw & ano.*[4] In that

[4] *Harper Bros.* v. *Klaw* (1916), 232 Fed. (D. C.) 609, Hough, J.: "If by the agreement of 1899 the defendant had been granted the exclusive right of dramatizing 'Ben Hur' or producing any play or plays that might be made out of 'Ben Hur,' there would be no doubt at all as to their right to make a 'movie play' as well as the kind of play that has heretofore been produced. . . . But the grant made by that agreement was far more limited. The right conferred was to produce one version only, and that in a particular manner, and in places limited in cities of a certain size. The contract prohibits any change in the manner of performance or text, and contains provisions as to royalties and their computation confessedly incapable of application to any method of producing photo-plays in commercial use or known to witnesses or counsel. It is unnecessary to expand this thought, the whole arrangement made between the parties in 1899 is not only inconsistent with but repugnant to the thought of making 'movies' out of 'Ben Hur.'

"This differentiates the case at bar from *Frohman* v. *Fitch* (1914), 164 A. D. (N. Y.) 231, with which I fully concur, but these defendants never got so ample a grant as did Mr. Frohman.

"It follows, since the copyright covers a photo-play and Klaw & Erlanger got no license to make or produce one, they would infringe if their threat were carried out—therefore they must be enjoined.

"Plaintiffs assert and almost assume that since defendants cannot make a 'movie' out of 'Ben Hur' and such right must

case Klaw & Erlanger had acquired from Harper Bros. the exclusive right to produce a dramatization of the novel "Ben Hur." Klaw & Erlanger claimed that under the contract they had the right to reproduce the dramatization in the form of motion pictures. Harper Brothers contended that they had granted Klaw & Erlanger a license solely to produce the play upon the stage with

exist somewhere, it is in them,—as being an unconveyed portion of the copyright estate wherefrom was carved defendants' limited license.

"In strictness of law, I think this is true, *but it does not always follow that because one owns a certain thing he may use it to the detriment of another especially if the owner is under contractual obligations to such other.*

"The 'movie' rights to 'Ben Hur' undoubtedly existed in 1899, but in nubibus or (what is frequently the same thing) in contemplation of law only. As a matter of fact they are an accretion or unearned increment conferred of late years upon the copyright owners by the ingenuity of many inventors and mechanicians.

"*It is my opinion there is implied a negative covenant on the part of the plaintiffs (the grantors of defendants' restricted license) not to use the ungranted portion of the copyright estate to the detriment, if not destruction of the licensee's estate.*

"Admittedly if Harper Bros. (or Klaw & Erlanger for the matter of that) permitted photo-plays of Ben Hur to infest the country, the market for the spoken play would be greatly impaired if not destroyed.

"This being the fact, the law is analogous to that which implies from a covenant to make a certain use of property, a covenant negative against doing anything else with it (High on Injunction, 4th Ed., Section 1151a, and cases cited).

"The result is that plaintiffs may take the injunction prayed for against the defendants, and the defendants may have the same relief against plaintiffs. *The meaning of such double injunction is that as long as the contract of 1899 exists, neither party thereto can produce a photo-play of Ben Hur except by bargain with the other.*"

living actors, and sought to restrain them. The latter counterclaimed that even assuming they had nothing but the right of stage production, nevertheless they were entitled to enjoin the plaintiff from making a motion picture version of the play during the term of the license.

While the court found that the defendants Klaw & Erlanger had been merely granted a license to produce the play upon the stage with living actors and restrained them from making a motion picture version thereof, yet it granted judgment on the counterclaim, enjoining and restraining the plaintiffs, Harper Brothers, from making a motion picture reproduction of the play during the life of the license.

However, the original grant to produce the play upon the stage with living actors, does not divest the author of his right to produce the play in motion pictures. His right to produce the play in motion pictures is merely suspended during the term of the license granted by him to the producer of the play upon the stage.

When the agreement granting the exclusive license is silent on the question as to whether the play is to be produced with living persons upon the stage or fails to mention any other specific method of production,—in other words, where the author grants "all dramatization rights," the licensee secures not only the exclusive right to produce the play upon the stage with living actors, but he secures as well the exclusive right to make motion picture reproductions of such play.[5]

[5] *Photo Drama Motion Picture Co.* v. *Social Uplift Film Corporation* (1915), 220 Fed. (C. C. A.) 448, Lacombe, J.: "One Kaufman wrote a novel entitled 'The House of Bondage.' He assigned

The licensee secures the sole right to produce or reproduce the play and with it the accompanying right to restrain invasions of his license,[6] only when his grant is exclusive. Where no mention is made in the agreement of the exclusiveness of the grant, the court will assume that the grant is not exclusive, and the author may grant the same rights, for the same period, to third parties.[7]

his right to copyright the same to Moffatt-Yard & Co. Moffatt-Yard & Co. duly secured copyright. That gave them exclusive rights to publish and sell the novel; also to make dramatizations of it, whether in the usual form for acting on the stage of a theatre or in the more recent form of a motion picture play. Moffatt-Yard & Co. assigned *all dramatization rights* to Kaufman. *He then had exclusive right to make dramatizations of either kind.*"

See generally in this connection: *London Theatre of Varieties* v. *Evans* (Eng.) (1914), 30 T. L. R. 258. An actor agreed that he would not give or permit the giving of any colorable imitation, representation or version of his performance within a specified area. *Held* that it was a question of fact whether a motion picture reproduction of the act was in fact a colorable imitation, representation or version of the same; that the determination of the question of fact might depend on whether the performance was substantially one appealing to the eye which could be reproduced or to the ear which could not be reproduced. The court also stated that a reproduction of an operatic performance would not as a rule be a representation of the opera, the singing of which was the primary feature, while in the case of a music hall sketch it could be such a representation as to amount to a representation thereof.

[6] *Widmer* v. *Thompson* (1878), 56 How. Pr. (N. Y.) 91; *Barnett* v. *Q. & C. Co.* (1915), 226 Fed. (C. C. A.) 935; *Stern* v. *Laemmle* (1911), 74 Misc. (N. Y.) 262; 133 N. Y. Supp. 1082.

[7] *Hart* v. *Cort* (1913), 144 N. Y. Supp. 627; 83 Misc. (N. Y.) 44: A contract was made granting a license to the defendant to perform "LaTosca." The contract contained terms of limitation respecting time and place but no

Where, instead of a license for a limited period, there is an absolute sale, by the author or proprietor of the right to produce the play upon the stage, the right of the author or proprietor to reproduce the same play in motion pictures is forever suspended. Hence, in such a case, neither licensor nor licensee would have the right to make a motion picture reproduction of the play, nor grant such a right to third parties, except by mutual consent,—unless the play comes into the public domain.

In each instance where the question arises as to whether the grant is one of all the dramatic rights or merely of the motion picture rights or the right to produce the play upon the stage with living actors, it is a question of law for the court as to whether or not, from the context of the contract, the parties intended to convey an unlimited or limited grant.

It has been held in *Klein* v. *Beach* that the phrase "presentation on the stage" construed in connection with other provisions respecting production of a play by stock companies, stage scenery, &c., had reference only to the production of the spoken play in theatres, and that as

statement that the license was exclusive. It was held that unless the term "exclusive" or "sole" or other words expressing an intention to grant an exclusive license were used, there was no exclusive grant.

Warne v. *Routledge* (Eng.) (1874), 43 L. J. Ch. 604; L. R. 18 Eq. 497; 30 L. T. 857; 22 W. R. 750: An authoress contracted with one publisher for the publication of her work. Before the sale of all the copies of the edition issued by the first publisher she entered into a new contract with another publisher for a second edition of the same work. *Held*, that since she had granted no *exclusive* right to the first publisher she was at liberty to contract with other parties.

at the time the contract was made, the production of motion picture plays was a well-known business, it was not intended that the contract should carry the exclusive right to dramatize for that purpose, but that such right remained in the author.[8]

In *Harper & Bro.* v. *Klaw*, the preamble of the contract recited that the defendants were to obtain "the exclusive right of producing such dramatic version on the stage" and the body of the contract contained a provision that Klaw & Erlanger were granted the sole right of "producing on the stage" or "performing" the "dramatic version" thereof. It was there held that that portion of

[8] *Klein* v. *Beach* (1917), 239 Fed. (C. C. A.) 108, Hand, J.: "The actual words of grant are these: '*the sole and exclusive right to dramatize the said book for presentation on the stage.*' The plaintiff insists in view of *Kalem Co.* v. *Harper*, 222 U. S. 55, 32 Sup. Ct. 20, and *Frohman* v. *Fitch*, 164 App. Div. 232; 149 N. Y. Supp. 633, that dramatic rights include motion picture rights. If used alone that is doubtless true, especially if the contract antedate the commercial use of motion pictures. Yet Judge Hough in *Harper* v. *Klaw*, 232 Fed. (D. C.) 609, held on a contract dated in 1899 that the words '*the exclusive right of producing such dramatic version on the stage*,' did not give to the grantee any motion picture rights, although it is true, he also held that such a grant raised by implication a negative covenant against destroying the effect of such a grant by motion pictures. That decision would avail the plaintiff here, if the date of this contract had been so early; it will hardly serve at the end of November, 1911, long after motion pictures had become common and the distinction between them and the stage proper had for all purposes become well fixed.. There is no basis for an implied negative covenant, because the situation has not changed since the contract was made so as to create an unexpected situation if the terms be strictly interpreted."

the preamble and body of the contract, taken in conjunction with the fact that at that time (1899) the motion picture art was in its infancy, did not pass the motion-picture rights to the licensee.[9]

In *Photo Drama Picture Co.* v. *Social Uplift Film Co.*, complainants claimed that by securing all dramatization rights, complainants' assignor possessed the exclusive motion picture rights. This construction of the grant was admitted by the answer,[10] and was acquiesced in by the court.[11]

The situation may arise where the author or proprietor of a play before the play has been produced upon the stage, grants an exclusive license to reproduce the play in motion pictures, and subsequently thereto attempts to produce the play himself or grants to a third party the right to produce the play upon the boards. This may be the case with plays, which after being reproduced in motion pictures, become well known to the public.

Query: Has the motion picture producer the right to enjoin any stage production of such play upon the theory followed by the courts in *Frohman* v. *Fitch?*

While the question has not yet arisen before the courts, there seems to be good reason for believing that the rule laid down in the Frohman case will be followed.

[9] *Harper & Bros.* v. *Klaw & Erlanger* (1916), 232 Fed. (D. C.) 609. See excerpt of Judge Hough's opinion on pages 3 and 4.

[10] *Photo Drama Picture Co.* v. *Social Uplift Film Co.*, United States Circuit Court of Appeals for the Second Circuit, Record No. 102, January, 1915, also known under the designation Record No. 5150, U. S. Circuit Court of Appeals—Southern District of New York.

[11] *Photo Drama Picture Co.* v. *Social Uplift Film Co.* (1915), 220 Fed. (C. C. A.) 448.

The decision in that case is based upon the theory of unfair competition. Where all the elements of unfair competition exist, it would be only reasonable to assume that it makes no difference which is first granted and produced—the motion picture or the play. Since they are both in the same class, the production of each being a dramatic performance, the courts must protect him who was first given the grant and who first produced the work. Because I own a play and sell you the motion picture rights, I have no right thereafter to exploit my play to the detriment of your rights.

To avoid that situation, the author or proprietor of the play may provide in his contract with the motion picture producer that he *expressly reserves* to himself or his assigns, during the period of the motion picture grant, the right to perform the play with living actors upon the stage.

Then again, we may be confronted with a case wherein the proprietor of a successful and well-known play, after its performance on the stage for several years, finally grants an exclusive license for its reproduction in motion pictures. May he then, during the term of such grant, continue to perform his play with living actors upon the stage?

Here, a contrary situation is disclosed. The proprietor of the play was the first *user* of the property—the proprietor of the motion picture rights, the second user. The latter knows of the prior user. He makes his bargain with that in mind. If he wishes to have the exploitation of the play upon the stage suspended during the period of his license, he should not only bargain for the motion picture rights, but also obtain a covenant from the licensor, in which the latter agrees to refrain from continuing the stage performances during the period of his license.

Section 2.—Where the motion picture is based upon a novel or historical work.

With the coming in of the so-called "feature films" film producers soon found that their chief source of material for such films, to wit: dramatic compositions, was rapidly becoming exhausted. They naturally turned for new material to novels and historical works; and these have now become a prolific source of motion picture feature film material.

The question at once arises as to who may grant the motion picture rights to such works. A motion picture reproduction of a novel being a dramatization, the motion picture rights are vested in the owner of the dramatic rights.[12]

As between the author and the publisher it is always a question of contract in each case whether the author has retained or parted with his dramatic rights. A mere license to publish does not give any performing rights to the publisher.[13]

Under the Copyright Law the owner of the copyright

[12] *Photo Drama Motion Picture Co.* v. *Social Uplift Corp.* (1915), 220 Fed. (C. C. A.) 448, which holds that the grantee of the exclusive dramatization rights to a novel acquires two distinct rights: the right to make a play production of the novel with living actors upon the stage, and the right to reproduce the novel in motion pictures.

[13] *Williams et al.* v. *Feldman*, (Eng.) (1913), Times, Oct. 18.

in a novel has the exclusive right to dramatize the work.[14]

Hence, where the publisher of a novel copyrights the work of an author, a third party purchasing the motion picture rights to such novel, without notice of the rights of the author, buys them free from any claims which the author may have as against the publisher. If the record in the copyright office shows that the publisher is the owner of record of such copyright, the purchaser is not bound to inquire what relationship exists with respect to the work between the publisher and the author.[15]

As a matter of fact the publisher may be holding the copyright as trustee for the author; his rights may be limited to the extent only of reproducing the novel in copies for sale. But if the copyright record does not disclose any such relationship a purchaser for value without notice buys free and clear.

If the author wishes to retain his rights it is advisable

[14] Copyright Act of 1909, Section 1, subdivision (b). *Photo Drama Motion Picture Co.* v. *Social Uplift Corp.* (1915), 220 Fed. (C. C. A.) 448.

[15] *Brady* v. *Reliance Co.* (1916), 232 Fed. (D. C.) 259, Mayer, J.: "Where a publisher copyrights a work of an author there must of necessity exist some arrangement between them, and that, perchance the author may have reserved something undisclosed which the person dealing with the owner of the copyright should have suspected, although an examination of the record title provided for by law shows good title. This, to my mind, would place a duty upon a person dealing with the owner of a copyrighted work which the law never contemplated, and which from the standpoint of commercial requirements would be unjust, and seriously hamper legitimate dealings." See also: *Photo Drama Motion Picture Co., Inc.,* v. *Social Uplift Film Co.* (1915), 220 Fed. (C. C. A.) 448.

for him to file an instrument in the copyright office setting forth the fact that the copyright is held by his publisher as a trustee merely, subject to specified limitations. Anything which would put the prospective purchaser of the motion picture rights upon inquiry would probably be sufficient.

The author, by failing to have some notation made in the copyright office of his rights against the publisher, does not, however, lose his remedies against the *publisher* for the breach of the trust. The registration of the copyright in the name of the assignee (publisher) does not confer the dramatic rights upon the assignee where they had been retained by the author. Under such an arrangement the assignor (author) becomes the proprietor of the dramatic rights secured by the copyright in the name of the publisher.[16]

There arises the query, where motion pictures are produced by assignees both of the author who originally retained the right, and of the third party who purchased the rights from the publisher, as to who may enjoin, if at all, the exhibition of the motion picture of the other. It would seem to follow, from a reading of Judge Mayer's

[16] *Ford* v. *Blaney Amusement Co.* (1906), 148 Fed. (C. C.) 642: The work was published in a magazine which was copyrighted by the magazine proprietor. It was held that by selling his right to copyright but reserving to himself the dramatization rights, the work was copyrighted by the copyrighting of the magazine and that the dramatization rights remained in the author. See also: *Mifflin* v. *White* (1903), 190 U. S. 260; 23 Sup. Ct. 769; *Mifflin* v. *Dutton* (1903), 190 U. S. 265; 23 Sup. Ct. 771; *Holmes* v. *Hurst* (1899), 174 U. S. 82; 19 Sup. Ct. 606; *Dam* v. *Kirk La Shelle* (1910), 175 Fed. (C. C. A.) 902.

decision in *Brady* v. *Reliance Co.*, that the publisher's assignee has the exclusive right to the production of the picture, and that the right of the author's assignee is suspended during the term of the grant from the publisher to his assignee.

If there is an outright sale to the third party by the publisher of the motion picture rights, the author loses such rights forever.

Many of our most popular novels are based upon historical events. There is no question that these events are within the public domain. Let us take the case of a historical novel written to-day and based upon some familiar historical subject, the development of the theme adhering closely to the sequence of the events as they actually occurred. Let us assume that this novel is duly copyrighted, and that the author or proprietor of the novel grants away the motion picture rights. Will the licensee acquire such rights in the arrangement and development of his theme as will preclude another from producing a similar picture?

We do not think so. The arrangement and development of a well-known historical theme cannot strictly be said to be original, and while the novel as a whole may be the subject of copyright, yet those portions of it which treat of things within the public domain cannot acquire the protection of copyright.

Anyone may make an independent dramatization from the common source but must not make use of or resort to the licensee's dramatization or the novel from which the dramatization was made.

For the same reason a motion picture based directly

upon a well-known historical episode, instead of upon a novel and duly copyrighted can acquire no exclusive right, and the proprietor may not enjoin the reproduction of another picture portraying the same historical event or sequence of events.

This rule is, of course, subject to the limitation that in the original novel or motion picture the events spoken of are purely historical. When these events are so interspersed with imaginative fiction as to constitute a complete story in themselves, the treatment may then be said to be original and a reproduction of the work with the imaginative fiction contained therein, constitutes an infringement.

Historical events are themes in the public domain. What is accorded protection in the case of themes in the public domain is the *original development* and *treatment* of those themes. It is scarcely possible for two people to develop one theme in the identical manner; for that reason it is unlikely that we will have an exact duplication on films of even a popular and well-known theme unless there is an intent to infringe.[17]

Section 3.—Where the motion picture is based upon a short story, sketch, poem, lecture, sermon or other kindred work.

The rights of the author of a short story, sketch, poem, lecture, sermon or other kindred work are identical with those of a novelist.[18] The rights and liabilities which arise upon the sale of such work by the author or proprietor

[17] See cases of infringement under Sections 157 to 161.

[18] Copyright Act of 1909, Section 1, subdivisions (a), (b), (d).

to a motion picture producer are the same as those which arise between a novelist and motion picture producer.[19]

It is customary for the publisher of a periodical or newspaper to copyright the entire work in his own name. If he has been authorized by the author or proprietor of the work to secure copyright, but the rights granted to him are solely that of publication of the work, the magazine or newspaper proprietor holds the copyright as trustee for the author or proprietor of the work.[20]

[19] Section 2.

[20] *Ford* v. *Blaney* (1906), 148 Fed. (C. C.) 642: "I think, under this provision (referring to Section 4952 of the U. S. Revised Statutes) it is not necessary that the author himself should have taken out the copyright of a book, in order to preserve the right of dramatizing it, but that the author can sell the copyright of the book to a person, who, as proprietor, can take out the copyright, while the author, at the same time, retains the right of dramatization. If a copyright of a book has been obtained by anybody entitled by law to obtain it, I think that the author of the book or his assigns, a term which as used in Section 4952, means in my opinion an assignee of the right of dramatization, has the exclusive right to dramatize the work, if he reserved the right to dramatize upon the sale of the book, which is alleged in the complaint in this case. The object of the statute seems to have been to provide that the author's right of dramatization of a book shall not be protected unless the book be copyrighted; but *I do not see anything in the statute which requires that the author shall take out the copyright of the book.*"

In Drone on Copyright, at page 260: "A person who is not the author or owner of a work may take out the copyright in his own name, and hold it in trust for the rightful owner. Thus, when an article has first been published in a cyclopædia, magazine, or any other publication, the legal title to the copyright, if taken out in the name of the publisher, will vest in him. But it may be the property of the author, and held in trust for him. And the same is true when

Here, as in the case of a novel,[21] care must be exercised by the author or proprietor of the work, if he has retained any rights therein, to have something placed upon the copyright record to show what rights have been granted to the publisher and what rights have been retained.

Where the author or proprietor of the work wishes to reserve the dramatic rights, the usual arrangement is for him to make a contract with the publisher granting the exclusive publication rights to the publisher and authorizing him to copyright the work. The publisher on his part agrees to assign the copyright when secured by him to the author or proprietor of the work. This enables the publisher to copyright the entire periodical or newspaper and at the same time obtain the benefit of a *first* publication. The publisher then assigns his copyright to the author or proprietor of the work, who now becomes possessed of all the rights incidental to copyright, including, of course, the right to dramatize.

In this way there is no dedication, the magazine publisher is the first one to publish the work, and the author or proprietor of the work now has the dramatization rights which include the motion picture rights.[22]

the copyright of a book which belongs to the author is entered in the name of the publisher. In such case, a court of equity, if called upon, may decree a transfer of the copyright to be made by the owner." See also: *Dam* v. *Kirk La Shelle* (1910), 175 Fed. (C. C. A.) 902, and *Mail and Express* v. *Life Publ. Co.* (1912), 192 Fed. (C. C. A.) 899.

[21] Section 2.

[22] *Ford* v. *Blaney* (1906), 148 Fed. (C. C.) 642; *Dam* v. *Kirk La Shelle* (1910), 175 Fed. (C. C. A.) 902; *Fitch* v. *Young* (1911), 230 Fed. (D. C.) 743; aff'd 239 Fed. (C. C. A.) 1021.

If the author or proprietor of the work wishes to secure the copyright in his own name he may do so by placing the proper notice of copyright immediately after the title of his work and by depositing, promptly after publication, two copies of the periodical or newspaper in which his work is contained together with an application for copyright registration, and the required fee, in the office of the Register of Copyrights.[23]

Finally, it must be borne in mind that if the publisher is not given the right to copyright the work contained in his periodical or newspaper, though he has been given the right to publish such work, the work will not be protected by a copyright secured upon the entire publication by the proprietor of the periodical or newspaper, and the work will fall into the public domain.

In that event any motion picture producer may use the work without securing the consent of the publisher, or the author or proprietor of the work.[24]

[23] Copyright Act of 1909, Sections 9, 10 and 12; Rules and Regulations for Registration of Claims to Copyright, Section 33.

[24] *Mifflin* v. *White—Mifflin* v. *Dutton* (1903), 190 U. S. 260–265; 23 Sup. Ct. 769–771. The publication of a story in a magazine, the ownership of such story remaining in the author, and the publisher not being the agent of the author in securing copyright, constituted a dedication of the work. The magazine proprietor in copyrighting the magazine, secures copyright only in those parts of the magazine which belong to him or for the owners of which he is acting as agent. The fact that the work was published in serial form and subsequently combined in one complete work and such complete work entered in the copyright office did not validate the copyright. See also: *Holmes* v. *Hurst* (1899), 174 U. S. 82; 19 Sup. Ct. 606.

On the question whether there is

Section 4.—Where the motion picture is based upon an original scenario, that is one not based upon any other work.

Whether or not a scenario of a motion picture play may be the subject of copyright as an unpublished dramatic composition, is an open question. The Register of Copyrights has taken the position that Section eleven of the Copyright Act requires the deposit of "one *complete* copy of such work if it be a dramatic composition," and that a scenario is not a completed work and hence does not fulfill the requirements of that section.

In this respect we believe that he is wrong. To our mind a scenario is a completed work in that it is an exact reproduction, in words, of action upon the screen. It embodies within itself the orderly arrangement and development of a theme that enables actors to reproduce the same before the camera. In that respect it is similar to a play, which is primarily a vehicle to enable actors to portray the same upon the stage. Both the scenario and the play have as their primary object the attainment of this end. And the fact that in the play we have dialogue should not alter the situation. The scenario frequently has what the play lacks—minute directions as to acting. And while it is doubtless true that mere stage directions and stage business are not entitled to protection under the Copyright Law,[25] yet where the composition tells a

a presumption that the magazine proprietor acts as agent for the owner of the work in securing copyright. See: *Pulte* v. *Derby* (1852), 5 McLean, 328; *Belford* v. *Scribner* (1892), 144 U. S. 488; 12 Sup. Ct. 734.

[25] *Serrena* v. *Jefferson* (1888), 33 Fed. (C. C.) 347; *Bloom* v. *Nixon* (1903), 125 Fed. (C. C.)

story not in narrative form, but by words giving directions as to acting and display of emotions, it is as truly a dramatic composition as a work narrating a story in the form of dialogue.[26]

977; *Chappell* v. *Fields* (1914), 210 Fed. (C. C. A.) 864; *Savage* v. *Hoffman* (1908), 159 Fed. (C. C.) 584; *Fuller* v. *Bemis* (1892), 50 Fed. (C. C.) 926; *Bishop* v. *Viviana & Co.* (Eng.) (1909), Times, Jan. 5. For additional cases see Section 148.

[26] *Daly* v. *Palmer* (1868), 6 Blatchf. 256: A scenario is a dramatic composition under the description given in this case. "A dramatic composition is such a work in which the narrative is not related but is represented by dialogue and action. Where a dramatic composition is represented in dialogue and action by persons who represent it as real, by performing or going through with the various parts or characters assigned to them severally, the composition is acted, performed, or represented; and if the representation is in public, it is a public representation. To act in the sense of the statute is to represent as real, by countenance, voice or gesture that which is not real. A character in a play who goes through a series of events on the stage without speaking if such be his part in the play, is none the less an actor in it than one who, in addition to motion and gestures, uses his voice. A pantomime is a species of theatrical entertainment in which the whole action is represented by gesticulation without the use of words. A written work, consisting wholly of directions set in order for conveying the ideas of the author on a stage or public place, by means of characters who represent the narrative wholly by action is as much a dramatic composition designed or suited for public representation as if language or dialogue were used in it to convey some of the ideas."

The Circuit Court of Appeals in *Daly* v. *Webster* (1892), 56 Fed. (C. C. A.) at p. 486, approved of the excerpt of the opinion of Judge Blatchford quoted above.

Fuller v. *Bemis* (1892), 50 Fed. (C. C.) 926: "*It is essential to such a composition that it should tell some story. The plot may be*

A play may have greater literary value, yet the scenario usually possesses, for its own peculiar purposes, a greater practical value. The author of a scenario should not be compelled to publish his work in book form in order to secure copyright therein. The scenario is not written for the purpose of being reproduced in copies for sale.

If our position is correct, the rights of the author or proprietor of a scenario are coincident with those of the author or proprietor of a dramatic composition. He has the exclusive right to make other forms of dramatizations of the scenario, he may develop the scenario into the form of a short story or a novel.[27] He may reproduce the scenario in copies for sale. An outright sale of the manuscript of an uncopyrighted scenario or of the copyright of a copyrighted scenario conveys to the purchaser all the rights which the author had.[28]

simple. It may be but the narrative or representation of a single transaction; but it must repeat or mimic some action, speech, emotion, passion, or character, real or imaginary. And when it does, it is the ideas thus expressed which become subject of copyright."

Tate v. *Fullbrook* (Eng.) (1908), 77 L. J. K. B. 577; 1 K. B. 821; 98 L. T. 706; 24 T. L. R. 347. An idea or plot together with the manual and physical actions was held to be "a dramatic piece" within the meaning of Section 2 of the English Copyright Act of 1842.

Moore v. *Edwards* (Eng.) (1903), Times, March 3: *Held* that a "scenario" of a play when written down was the subject of protection, as a dramatic composition.

Wigan v. *Strange* (Eng.) (1865), L. R. 1 C. P. 175: A ballet was held to be a play.

[27] See Section 1.

[28] *Palmer* v. *DeWitt* (1872), 47 N. Y. 532: "This property in a manuscript is not distinguishable from any other personal property. It is governed by the same rules of transfer and succession and is protected by the same process, and has the benefit of all the

Hence in the usual transaction between a scenario writer and a film producer where the scenario is purchased for a lump sum of money, the author of the scenario divests himself of all rights in and to the same and the film producer acquires the sole right not only to make a motion picture reproduction of the scenario, but also to make any and all of the above mentioned versions of the same. Here, as in the case of a novel or drama, the author may limit the grant by express reservations in the contract of sale.

Where there is no contract of sale, but a sale, that is, where the manuscript and money are simultaneously exchanged, the producer acquires all rights in the scenario.[29]

remedies accorded to other property." It follows "the person of the owner, and is governed by the law of his domicile."

[29] *Dam* v. *Kirk La Shelle* (1910), 175 Fed. (C. C. A.) 901: "Now, as a matter of law, it seems possible to draw only one conclusion from the facts surrounding the acquisition of the story by the Ess Ess Publishing Company, and that is that it became the purchaser, and consequently, the proprietor of the work, with all the rights accompanying ownership. The author offered the story. The publisher accepted and paid for it, and the author transferred it without any reservations whatever.

"While it is probable that an author in assigning the right to publish and vend his work may retain and reserve the rights of translation or dramatization (*Ford* v. *Blaney Amusement Co.* (1906), 148 Fed. (C. C.) 642, a sale or assignment without reservations would seem necessarily to carry all the rights incidental to ownership. *And a transaction in which an author delivers his manuscript and accepts a sum of money 'in full payment for story' cannot be regarded as a sale with reservations.* The courts cannot read words of limitation into a transfer which the parties do not choose to use."

See also: *Lacy* v. *Toole* (Eng.) (1867), 15 L. T. N. S. 512, wherein it was held that a letter written by the owner of a copyright in a

It frequently happens that in vending his wares the scenario writer sends copies of the same work to a number of motion picture producers. Several of the producers purchase the scenario, each not knowing that some other producer has purchased the same work. The first purchaser in point of time will be the owner of the scenario, for at the time that the other producers accept the offer of the scenario writer, there is nothing that they can purchase, the author having been divested of his title to the scenario by the prior purchase of the work.

Section 5.—Where the motion picture is based upon a news item.

It is well settled that the facts and ideas contained in items in the daily newspapers, and held out to be statements of fact, may be appropriated and used in any manner by any one of the public.[30] The phrase above

dramatic piece to another in which he said: "to let you have my drama" assigned *all* the rights in the drama.

[30] *Tribune Co.* v. *Associated Press* (1900), 116 Fed. (C. C.) 126, and cases cited therein. In *Davies* v. *Bowes* (1913), 209 Fed. (D. C.) 53; aff'd 219 Fed. (C. C. A.) 178, the court said: "All that was ever copyrighted regarding this tale was the form of telling, the sequence and choice of words and arrangement of sentences coined by the plaintiff. . . ." See also: *Associated Press* v. *International News Service* (1917), 240 Fed. (D. C.) 983; aff'd June, 1917, opinion by Hough, J.; *Walter* v. *Steinkopff* (Eng.) (1892), 3 Ch. 489; *Springfield* v. *Thame* (Eng.) (1903), 89 L. T. 242; *Press Association* v. *Northern, etc., Agency* (Eng.) (1910), Times, Dec. 8.

See in this connection: *Exchange Telegraph Co.* v. *Howard* (Eng.) (1906), Times, Mar. 22. A news agency has a property right in unpublished news, and may prevent a rival agency from stealing the same.

used "held out" is used advisedly. Even where the news item is a creation of the mind of the reporter, and hence, an original work, yet if the work is published as news and not as fiction, the author or proprietor of the work will not be permitted to show that the work was one solely of his creation.[31]

Where, however, the work published in the newspaper is fiction and is presented to the public as such, the same rights accrue to the author or proprietor as in the case of a work published in a magazine.[32]

Section 6.—Where the motion picture is based upon a work in the public domain.

Whenever possible, motion picture producers of course make use of such works as are in the public domain. Care must be taken that in making use of such works, no use is made of other works based upon those in the public domain. It frequently occurs that in making adaptations of such public literary property, the ingenuity and originality of the adaptor has combined to create a new work.

Where the work is a novel or short story the adaptor may make a dramatization thereof; he may novelize a dramatic composition; he may rearrange the work and in so doing use originality; he may condense such work. Those portions of such new work which are due to the

[31] *Davies* v. *Bowes* (1913), 209 Fed. (D. C.) 53; aff'd 219 Fed. (C. C. A.) 178.

Wright v. *Tullis* (Eng.), 1 C. B. 873. Where a publisher pretended that a copyrighted work was a translation from a well-known foreign writer, *held* that such pretense vitiated the copyright.

[32] Section 3.

originality, ingenuity and literary effort of the adaptor will be fully protected.

The same applies to translations made of foreign works in the public domain. The translator is entitled to protect his translation as against everyone. No one may use his translation, although anyone may make his own independent translation of the original work and make whatever use of his own translation and the original work he sees fit.[33]

Section 7.—Where the motion picture is produced in serial form.

A recent development of the motion picture industry is the production of films in which the story is told in serial form, one or two reels being shown at a time. Simultaneously with the exhibition of the film the story of the picture is published in newspapers in installments.

The right to publish the story in the newspapers does not necessarily belong to the film producer. It belongs to the owner of the publication rights in the drama, novel,

[33] *Stevenson* v. *Fox* (1915), 226 Fed. (D. C.) 990; *Shook* v. *Rankin* (1875), Fed. Cas. (C. C.) No. 12804; *O'Neill* v. *General Film Co.* (1915), 152 N. Y. Supp. 599; modified and aff'd in 171 A. D. (N. Y.) 854; 157 N. Y. Supp. 1028; but not modified on question of infringement. The defendant was leasing out a photo play entitled "Count of Monte Cristo." "It is claimed that such motion picture play was prepared from and is an appropriation of the plaintiff's Fechter version and infringes upon plaintiff's common law property right therein. Defendant claims that the motion picture play was produced by resort to original sources, alleged to be open to all . . . and that in so far as there is any similarity between the motion picture play and the Fechter version, it is

story or scenario from which the film was reproduced.[34] The printing of the work whether in whole at one time or in parts at different times as in a serial story, constitutes merely a reproduction of the work in copies for sale within the meaning of the Copyright Act. It frequently happens that the film producer has merely the right to reproduce the work in the form of a motion picture, the publication rights having been retained by the author or having been granted to some third party.

The expression "serial rights" has acquired a secondary meaning in the publishing and motion picture business. Where one sells the "serial rights" the courts will construe the sale as a grant of "all publishing rights, including magazine and newspaper publishing rights, and excepting only book, dramatic and moving picture scenario rights." By book rights the court undoubtedly means the right to novelize.[35]

Section 8.—Where the relationship is that of employer and employe.

It frequently becomes necessary to decide whether the

lawful and proper in that the similar incidents and characters are found in the novel and earlier versions [that is the works in the public domain]." The court then finds that the defendant has infringed the plaintiff's work.

See also: *Byrne* v. *Statist Co.* (Eng.) (1914), 1 K. B. 622, and *Wyatt* v. *Burnard* (Eng.), 3 V. and B. 77.

See also Section 159.

[34] *New Fiction Pub. Co.* v. *Star Co.* (1915), 220 Fed. (D. C.) 994.

[35] *New Fiction Pub. Co.* v. *Star Co.* (1915), 220 Fed. (D. C.) 994.

See also: *Heineman* v. *Smart Set* (Eng.) (1909), Times, July 15. Defines "serial rights," "magazine rights" and "newspaper syndicate rights."

relationship existing between an author and a motion picture producer is that of independent contractors or that of master and servant.

If the relationship is one of independent contractors then the author retains all those rights in his work which have not been expressly or by necessary implication, from the circumstances of the case, granted to the motion picture producer.

If the relationship is one of master and servant there is a presumption in law that the parties bargained—one to give up the results of his mental labor in exchange for a stipend paid by the other; and unless the servant expressly reserves unto himself some rights in the work, the master will be deemed the sole proprietor thereof and entitled to all the benefits flowing out of such ownership.[36] In such case no formal assignment of all rights in the work is necessary.[37]

[36] *Colliery Engineer Co.* v. *United Corresp. Schools Co.* (1899), 94 Fed. (C. C.) 152; *Carte* v. *Evans* (1886), 27 Fed. (C. C.) 861; *Schumacher* v. *Schwencke* (1885), 25 Fed. (C. C.) 466; *Little* v. *Gould* (1852), Fed. Cas. No. 8395; 2 Blatchf. 362; *Lawrence* v. *Dana* (1869), Fed. Cas. No. 8136; *Solomon* v. *United States* (1890), 137 U. S. 342; 11 Sup. Ct. 88; *Gill* v. *United States* (1896), 160 U. S. 426; 16 Sup. Ct. 322; *Bleistein* v. *Donaldson Lith. Co.* (1903), 188 U. S. 239; 23 Sup. Ct. 298; *Dielman* v. *White* (1900), 102 Fed. (C. C.) 892; *Press Pub. Co.* v. *Monroe* (1896), 73 Fed. (C. C. A.) 196; *Chamberlayne* v. *Am. Law Book Co.* (1908), 163 Fed. (C. C.) 858; *Am. Law Book Co.* v. *Chamberlayne* (1908), 165 Fed. (C. C. A.) 313; *Peters* v. *Borst* (1889), 9 N. Y. Supp. 789; reversed in 142 N. Y. 62; 36 N. E. 814; *Heine* v. *Appleton* (1857), Fed. Cas. No. 6324 (C. C.)

[37] *Lawrence* v. *Aflalo* (Eng.) (1902), 20 T. L. R. 42; 1 Ch. 264; 85 L. T. 605. Where the publisher employed and paid one to write an article as part of a work which

Although the rule of law is clear, great difficulty has confronted the courts in arriving at the true relation

the publisher was producing at his own risk and expense, the natural inference of fact—no agreement in writing or express words being necessary to the assignment of copyright—was in the absence of evidence to the contrary that the publisher acquired copyright in such articles.

Sweet v. *Benning* (Eng.) (1855), 16 C. B. 459; 24 L. J. C. P. 175; 1 Jur. (N. S.) 543; 3 W. B. 519. Where the owner of a periodical contracted with one to write an article on the terms that the copyright should be the property of such proprietor, such terms were not required to be expressed but might be implied in fact.

Hatton v. *Kean* (Eng.) (1859), 7 C. B. (N. S.) 268; 29 L. J. C. P. 20; 6 Jur. (N. S.) 226; 1 L. T. 10; 8 W. R. Where a manager of a theatre, having designed to bring out an old play, with new scenery, dresses and musical accompaniments, hired A to compose the requisite music, who did so, and A was paid for his work, the sole right to the representation or performance of such musical compositions, as part of the whole, became thereby vested in the former, *without assignment or the consent in writing of A*, the terms of the contract between them being, that the compositions should become part of the entire dramatic piece, and that the manager should have the sole liberty of representing and performing the compositions with the dramatic piece. See also: *Byrne* v. *Statist Co.* (Eng.) (1914), 1 K. B. 622; *Walter* v. *Howe* (Eng.) (1881), 50 L. J. Ch. 621; 29 W. R. 776; 44 L. T. 727; *Sweet* v. *Evans* (Eng.) (1893), 1 Ch. 218; 62 L. J. Ch. 404.

Dennison v. *Ashdown* (Eng.) (1897), 13 T. L. R. 226. *Held* that an assignment of the copyright would be presumed from the conduct of the parties in dealing with each other for a long time, even though no actual assignment could be proved.

Ward Lock & Co. v. *Long* (Eng.) (1906), L. R. 2 Ch. 550; 75 Law Journal, Ch. 732; 95 Law Times, 345; 22 T. L. R. 798. An agreement whereby the author, in consideration of a sum of money, undertook to compose a book for the publisher, was a sufficient assignment of the copy-

existing between the parties. That has been specially the case where the person was engaged to perform services other than that of writing and he has merely as an incident to his employment composed literary works.

In one instance where the contract provided that the plaintiff should write a play to be produced at defendant's theatre and plaintiff and his wife were to act therein, and the profits to be divided equally between the parties, it was held that the parties were independent contractors and as there had been no express grant to the defendant the play belonged absolutely to the plaintiff.[38]

right, and was, as such, enforcible by the publisher.

See also Section 62 of the Copyright Act of 1909.

But see in this connection *Hereford (Bishop)* v. *Griffin* (Eng.) (1848), 16 Sim. 190; 17 L. J. Ch. 210; 12 Jur. 255. Where one was employed to write an article for an encyclopædia, the owner of that encyclopædia might not publish the article in any other form without the author's consent, unless the article was written under the express agreement that copyright in it should vest in the owner of the encyclopædia for all purposes.

And see: *London University Press* v. *University Tutorial Press* (Eng.) (1916), 2 Ch. 601; 115 L. T. 301; 32 T. L. R. 698. Where examiners getting up a set of examination papers were held not to be "employes," and entitled to copyright therein.

[38] *Boucicault* v. *Fox* (1862), 5 Blatchf. 87. Plaintiff who was an actor and author contracted with defendant to write a play to be produced at defendant's theatre and in which plaintiff was to act. He acted in it for a week, then withdrew, although the play was continued for some weeks more. Plaintiff took out copyright of the play in his own name. A few days later he attempted to enjoin defendant from continuing to produce the play. The court said: "That agreement was that he should write this play and, perhaps some other plays, and that he should contribute his and his wife's services at the Winter Garden

In another case where the contract provided that one who was engaged at a specified compensation should,

Theatre, as long as the plays would run there, and receive half the profits, as a compensation. This cannot be construed into a contract conferring upon Stuart, or anyone else, the legal or equitable title to this drama. The title to literary property is in the author whose intellect has given birth to the thoughts and wrought them into a composition, unless he has transferred that title, by contract, to another. In the present case no such contract is proved. The most that could possibly be said, in regard to the right of Stewart, or his trustee, in the play, is, that the arrangement entitled them to have it performed at the Winter Garden as long as it would run. There is not the slightest foundation upon which they, or either of them, can rest a claim to the literary property in the manuscript. That property was in the plaintiff, subject, at most, to a license or privilege in favor of Stewart & Fields, to have the piece performed at the Winter Garden. Whether the plaintiff was guilty of a breach of that part of his agreement which bound him to bestow his own and his wife's services, we need not inquire here. Such a breach if proved, would not vest the proprietors of the theatre with the title to 'The Octoroon.' *A man's intellectual productions are peculiarly his own, and although they may have been brought forth by the author while in the general employment of another, yet he will not be deemed to have parted with his right and transferred it to his employer, unless a valid agreement to that effect is adduced.*"

In *Roberts* v. *Myers* (1860), 20 Fed. Cas. No. 11,906 (C. C.), it was held that where an author had contracted with the proprietor of a theatre to write a play to be performed at the latter's theatre, the author was the owner of the copyright.

"By this agreement Stewart (proprietor) acquired no right or interest in the play to be written, except the privilege of having it performed at his theatre. All other rights were retained by the author."

In *Eaton* v. *Lake* (Eng.) (1888), 59 L. T. 100; 57 L. J. (Q. B.) 227, a music conductor, while in the employ of defendant for a term of years, had composed special music for the Christmas holidays,

among other things, compile and prepare instruction and question papers, it was held that the literary works of

which was performed. The defendant gave plaintff a week's notice to quit, and then took with him the score of the music and subsequently gave performances of the same. *Held*, liable, as the music was the independent composition of the plaintiff and belonged to him.

See also: *Shepherd* v. *Conquest* (Eng.) (1856), 17 C. B. 427; 25 L. J. C. P. 127; 2 Jur. N. S. 236; 4 W. R. 283.

In this case an author was engaged by the owner of a theatre to write a dramatic composition and he received therefor a specified weekly salary and travelling expenses. The action was brought by the proprietor of the theatre for damages for infringement of the play.

"The question is whether the plaintiffs by the transaction between them and Courtney (the writer) became entitled to the sole right of representation of this piece in London, so as to be able to maintain the action. We do not think it necessary in the present case to express any opinion whether under any circumstances, the copyright in a literary work or the right of representation can become vested ab initio in an employer other than the person who has actually composed or adapted the literary work. It is enough to say in the present case that no such effect can be produced where the employer merely suggests the subject and has no share in the design or execution of the work, the whole of which, so far as any character of originality belongs to it, flows from the mind of the person employed. It appears to us an abuse of terms to say, that in such a case, the employer is the author of a work to which his mind has not contributed an idea, and it is upon the author in the first instance that the right is conferred by the statute which creates it. We cannot bring our minds to any other conclusion than that Courtney, the person who actually made the adaptation, though at the suggestion of the plaintiffs, acquired for himself, as the author of the adaptation, and, so far as that adaptation gives any new character to the work, the statutory right of representing it; and that inasmuch as the plaintiffs have no assignment in writing of that

the writer belonged absolutely to the employer, the contract of employment being silent in whom the literary property was to vest.[39]

Where an author is engaged by a motion picture producer at a weekly, monthly, or yearly salary and the author agrees to furnish literary work as required by the producer, the relationship of master and servant is created, and the literary property belongs absolutely to the producer unless by express contract the parties thereto have agreed to the contrary.[40] Even where the author receives in addition to the fixed compensation a share of the profits the rule is the same.[41] The same is true as well

right, they cannot sue for an infringement of it."

[39] *Colliery Engineer Co.* v. *United Correspondence Schools Co.* (1899), 94 Fed. (C. C.) 152. "It seems equally clear that under his contract, which made it Ewald's duty while a salaried employe of complainant, inter alia, to compile, prepare and revise the instruction and question papers, the literary product of such work became the property of the complainant, which it was entitled to copyright, and which, when copyrighted Ewald would have no more right than any stranger to copy or reproduce." See also: *Schumacher* v. *Schwencke* (1885), 25 Fed. (C. C.) 466; *Frowde* v. *Parish* (Can.) (1896), 27 Ont. 526; *Nisbet* v. *Golf Agency* (Eng.) (1907), 23 T. L. R. 370; *Chantrey, Chantrey & Co.* v. *Dey* (Eng.) (1912), 28 T. L. R. 499.

[40] *Bleistein* v. *Donaldson Lith. Co.* (1903), 188 U. S. 239; 23 Sup. Ct. 298. Holmes, J.: "There was evidence warranting the inference that the designs belonged to the plaintiffs, they having been produced by persons employed and paid by the plaintiffs in their establishment to make those very things. *Gill* v. *United States* (1896), 160 U. S. 426; 16 Sup. Ct. 322; *Colliery Engineer Co.* v. *United Corresp. Schools Co.* (1899), 94 Fed. (C. C.) 152; *Carte* v. *Evans* (1886), 27 Fed. (C. C.) 861."

[41] *Mallory* v. *Mackaye* (1898), 86 Fed. (C. C.) 122.

when the author's compensation is based not upon time, but upon the quantity of the work produced, as, for instance, where he is paid a specified amount per page.[42]

Where the relationship is one of master and servant, and the author has not expressly reserved any rights, all the literary products belong to the producer as soon as they come into existence. If the writer should surreptitiously sell the work to some third party the producer is not deprived of such work, but may, on the contrary make use of the same and treat it as his own property in every respect.[43]

[42] *Cox* v. *Cox* (Eng.) (1853), 1 Eq. Rep. 94; 11 Hare, 118.

[43] *T. B. Harms* v. *Stern* (1915), 222 Fed. (D. C.) 581; aff'd 231 Fed. (C. C. A.) 645. Defendants agreed with one Romberg, a composer, by which he vested in them the exclusive publishing rights to his music for a term of years, and they agreed to do certain things for him. Subsequently he repudiated his contract, and plaintiffs claiming title to a song "Oh, Those Days," composed by Romberg subsequent to his agreement with defendants, sought to enjoin defendants from publishing it.

Judge Learned Hand held that the contract between Romberg and defendants, while not enforcible in equity, was valid at law, and that since defendants could under that contract obtain copyright of the song, even though the song was not in existence at the time of the making of the contract, the agreement operated as an executory contract to assign the copyright; that plaintiffs having taken with notice of the agreement were not entitled to injunction.

Ward Lock & Co. v. *Long* (Eng.) (1906), 75 L. J. Ch. 732; 2 Ch. 550; 95 L. T. 345; 22 T. L. R. 798. It was here held that an author could assign the copyright of a book not yet in existence and such an assignment might be in the form of an agreement to assign.

But a distinction must be carefully drawn between works created as an express part of the employment or as an incident to it and compositions made from information and knowledge acquired in the course of employment. In the former case the work belongs to the master, as has already been stated; but in the latter, it has been held that such literary property belongs to the author.[44] After leaving the employ of the producer he may develop the ideas which he has conceived during his employment. He may even go to the same original sources of information, and may make use in developing his work of whatever peculiar experience he may have acquired because of his former employment.[45]

[44] *Peters* v. *Borst* (1889), 9 N. Y. Supp. 789; reversed in 142 N. Y. 62; 36 N. E. 814, upon another ground.

The fact that one while in the employ of another composes a work from information and knowledge acquired in the course of his employment does not entitle the employer to the literary property unless there is an express agreement to that effect.

In *Colliery Engineer Co.* v. *United Corresp. Schools Co.* (1899), 94 Fed. (C. C.) 152, it was said: "Besides, it is thought that, although Ewald was not at liberty to reproduce such of his work as had been copyrighted by the employers for whom it was prepared, even by availing of his recollection of the contents of the copyrighted pamphlets, he was not debarred, after his contract terminated, from making a new compilation, nor from using the same original sources of information, nor from availing of such information as to the needs of students and the best methods of getting in mental touch with them as he may have acquired while superintending complainant's school."

[45] *Colliery Engineer Co.* v. *United Corresp. Schools* (1899), 94 Fed. (C. C.) 152. See part of opinion quoted on this page under footnote 44.

Section 9.—Where the motion picture material has been written by more than one person.

Motion picture producers have frequently found themselves involved in disputes because they have purchased from an author the motion picture rights to a play, or other work believing, in good faith, that the author was the sole owner of such rights, when in fact two or three men had collaborated in its writing. Those, who have not granted rights, come in and claim their share of the profits or proceeds, or seek an injunction upon the ground that the right granted by their co-author will destroy their interest in the common work.

The motion picture producer is bound to pay all the royalties to the party with whom he has contracted. If he ignores the rights of the other collaborators, they threaten to enjoin the picture or sue for damages. If he recognizes their rights the person with whom he has contracted threatens to bring an action for breach of contract. Hence, to properly safeguard his own interest, he must first inquire whether or not those claiming to be collaborators of the party with whom he contracted are such in fact.

The question as to what constitutes co-authorship has been constantly before the courts of this country and England. The test as laid down by Copinger contains all the elements which stamp a work as the product of co-authorship. "If there be a joint co-operation in carrying out the same design, it is not essential that the execution of the design shall be equally divided. Having agreed to a general design and structure, they may divide their parts and work separately. The pith of the joint authorship consists of the co-operation in a common design, and whether this co-operation takes place subsequently to the formation of the design by the one, and is varied in conformity with the suggestions or views of the other, it has equally the effect of creating a joint authorship as if the original design had been their joint conception."[46]

[46] Copinger's Law of Copyright (4th Edition), pages 109, 110.

A leading English case decided in 1871, *Levy* v. *Rutly*, L. R. 6 C. P. 523, gives a number of tests which may be applied with practical results in determining this question at page 529:

"If two persons undertake jointly to write a play, agreeing on the general outline and design and sharing the labor of working it out, each would be contributing to the whole production and they might be said to be joint authors of it, but to constitute a joint authorship there must be a common design." And again at page 530:

"But I take it that if two persons agree to write a piece, there being an original joint design and the co-operation of the two in carrying out that joint design, there can be no difficulty in saying they are joint authors of the work though one may do a larger share than the other."

This case has been cited with approval and followed in the state and federal courts of this country.

The latest decision defining what constitutes co-authorship is *Maurel* v. *Smith* (1915), 220 Fed. (D. C.) 195.

It was held that the plaintiff who wrote the scenario, the defendant Harry B. Smith who composed the libretto and the defendant Robert B. Smith who composed the lyrics of an operetta were co-authors.

Tree v. *Bowkett* (Eng.) (1896), 77 L. T. 77. It was held in this case that the adaptor of a play who introduced into his version material alteration was an "author of a dramatic piece" within the dramatic Copyright Act of 1833.

For cases where a co-worker was held not to be a co-author see: *Peters* v. *Borst* (1889), 9 N. Y. Supp. 789; reversed in 142 N. Y. 62; 36 N. E. 814, upon another ground.

Where a professor for thirty

In case of collaboration, where there is no express agreement to the contrary, the authors become tenants in common of the work.[47]

A tenant in common of literary property may grant a license to reproduce the common work in motion pictures without securing the consent of his co-tenant.[48] He can-

years had been engaged in compiling a work and had called in a student to help him tabulate the same, the literary product was held in that case to belong wholly to the professor in the absence of an agreement between them, although the student had placed considerable labor upon the work. *Shepherd* v. *Conquest* (Eng.) (1856), 17 C. B. 427; 25 L. J. C. P. 127; 4 W. R. 283; 2 Jur. (N. S.) 236; *Levy* v. *Rutley* (Eng.) (1871), 40 L. J. C. P. 244; L. R. C. C. P. 523; 24 L. T. 621; 19 W. R. 976.

[47] On this proposition see: *Carter* v. *Bailey* (1874), 64 Me. 458; *Trade Auxiliary Co.* v. *Middlesborough T. P. Ass'n* (Eng.) (1888), 58 L. J. Ch. 293; 40 Ch. D. 425; 60 L. T. 681; 37 W. R. 337. Three proprietors of three periodicals employed one to make certain compilations for them.

Held that each proprietor of each periodical had an equal interest in the copyright. See also: *Powell* v. *Head* (Eng.) (1879), 12 Ch. D. 686, where it was held that registered owners of a copyright took as tenants in common.

Barclay v. *Barclay* (1915), 155 N. Y. Supp. 221; aff'd 162 A. D. (N. Y.) 557; 156 N. Y. Supp. 1114. See this case for a valuable discussion of rights of tenants in common of copyrights, trademarks, etc., where they are made use of in a going business.

On the question whether the collaborators are co-partners or joint venturers, *Pitts* v. *Hall* (1854), 3 Blatchf. 201; also discussion and cases cited in Section 10.

[48] *Nillson* v. *Lawrence* (1912), 148 (N. Y.) A. D. 678; 133 N. Y. Supp. 293: "It is settled that with regard to property of this nature (a play), one tenant in common has as good a right to use it, or to license third persons to use it as has the other tenant in common, and neither can come into a court of equity and assert a superior right unless it has been

not, however, grant an exclusive right, as each has as good a right as the other to make use of the common prop-

created by some contract modifying the rights which belong to the tenants in common as such. [*De Witt* v. *Elmira Nobles Mfg. Co.* (1876), 66 N. Y. 459; *Clum* v. *Brewer* (1855), 2 Curt. 506.]"

It was held in this case, as well, that the complaint was bad because it did not allege that the defendant had *not* received a license from any co-owner. That allegation is essential when there is more than one owner.

Clum v. *Brewer* (1855), 2 Curtis C. C. 506. "One tenant in common has as good right to use and to license third parties to use the thing patented, as the other tenant in common has. Neither can come into a court of equity and assert a superior equity, unless it has been created by some contract modifying the rights which belong to them, as tenants in common."

Pusey v. *Miller* (1894), 61 Fed. (C. C.) 401. In this case where a patent was owned by several parties the court held:

"Where a patent belongs to several persons in common, each co-owner can assign his share, and sue for an infringement, and can also work the patent himself, give licenses to work it, and sue for royalties payable to him for its use, and is entitled to retain for his own benefit, whatever profit he may derive from the working, although he may be liable to account for what he receives in respect of the licenses. 1 Lindley Partn. 62; *Sheehan* v. *Railroad Co.* (Eng.), 16 Ch. Div. 59; *Mathers* v. *Green* (Eng.), L. R. 1 Ch. App. 29; *Clum* v. *Brewer* (1855), 2 Curt. 506; Fed. Cas. No. 2909; *Curran* v. *Burdsall* (1883), 20 Fed. (D. C.) 837; *Aspinwall Manufacturing Co.* v. *Gill* (1887), 32 Fed. (C. C.) 697; *De Witt* v. *Manufacturing Co.* (1876), 66 N. Y. 462; *Gates* v. *Fraser*, 9 Ill. App. 628; Hall, Pat. Est. 75."

Blackledge v. *Weir* (1901), 108 Fed. (C. C. A.) 71. This case gives a careful review of the American and English cases on the subject and reaches the same conclusion as the above cases.

Wood, C. J., said: "On principle, therefore, there can be no accountability on the part of a part owner of an invention to other owners for profits made by the exercise of his individual right, whether it be in the manu-

erty.[49] Unless, therefore, all the co-owners join in the grant of the motion picture rights, no exclusive rights can be secured. As a practical matter it is, for that reason, advisable to secure a grant from all claiming an interest in the motion picture rights in the work.

facture and sale or by granting to others licenses, or by assigning interests in the patent. . . . The separate rights of the other owners remain unaffected. They are equally free to use the invention in all legitimate ways for their individual profit. . . . *Lalance & Grosjean Mfg. Co.* v. *Nat'l Enameling & Stamping Co.* (1901), 108 Fed. (C. C.) 77, follows *Blackledge* v. *Weir.*

Herbert v. *Fields* (1915), 152 N. Y. Supp. 487. Plaintiff sought to enjoin the production in motion pictures of a play entitled "Old Dutch." The libretto had been written by Smith, the lyrics by Hobart and the music by Herbert. The defendants Smith and Fields licensed a motion picture reproduction of the libretto, Herbert's consent not having been secured. *Held* that consent of Herbert was unnecessary.

See also: *De Witt* v. *Elmira Nobles Mfg. Co.* (1876), 66 N. Y. 459; *Klein* v. *Beach* (1916), 232 Fed. (D. C.) 240; aff'd 239 Fed. (C. C. A.) 108; *Dunham* v. *The Indianapolis R. R. Co.* (1876), 7 Bissell, 223.

But see: *Powell* v. *Head* (Eng.) (1879), 48 L. J. Ch. 731; 12 Ch. D. 686; 41 L. T. 70. The part owner of a dramatic entertainment was here held to be unable to grant a license for its representation without the consent of all the other owners. Accordingly where the registered owner of an undivided part of the copyright of an opera alone granted a license for its representation, in an action by the other owners to recover a penalty under 3 & 4 Will. 4, c. 15, s. 2: *Held*, that having regard to that act and the act 5 & 6 Vict. c. 45, the license was illegally granted, and that the defendant was liable to pay to the plaintiffs one-half of the penalty fixed by the statute for each representation.

[49] *Nillson* v. *Lawrence* (1912), 148 (N. Y.) A. D. 678; 133 N. Y. Supp. 293; *Herbert* v. *Fields* (1915), 152 N. Y. Supp. 487.

This is subject to the further limitation that such grant does not injure or destroy the interest of the co-owner or co-owners in the common property.[50] Where the motion picture reproduction is of the same high standing and quality as the work itself, it will not ordinarily be regarded as injurious to or destructive of the original work, nor will the granting of such rights amount to an impairment of the co-tenant's interest in the common property.[51]

Where, however, a co-owner permits the making of an insignificant reproduction, with a poor cast, of a high-class drama or novel, equity will, in such cases, intervene

[50] *Osborn* v. *Schenck* (1880), 83 N. Y. 200. In discussing the question whether an owner in common of a chattel has a remedy against the other co-owner upon a destruction by such other co-owner of the common property, Finch, J., said: "If that possession develops into a destruction of the property or the interest of the co-tenant, or into such a hostile appropriation of it as excludes the possibility of beneficial enjoyment by him or ends in a sale of the whole property which ignores and denies any other right, then a conversion is established and trover may be maintained against the wrong-doer." The court then quotes in support of this proposition: *White* v. *Osborn* (1839), 21 Wend. (N. Y.) 72; *Tyler* v. *Taylor* (1850), 8 Barb. (N. Y.) 585; *Van Doren* v. *Balty* (1877), 11 Hun (N. Y.), 239; *Delaney* v. *Root*, 99 Mass. 547; *Wheeler* v. *Wheeler* (1851), 33 Me. 347; *Dyckman* v. *Valiente* (1870), 42 N. Y. 549.

[51] *Herbert* v. *Fields* (1915), 152 N. Y. Supp. 487. "Plaintiff urges that the production of the moving pictures to large crowds at low prices of admission 'destroys' the work. While the question whether the moving picture production detracts from or adds to its value as a musical comedy may be debatable, it seems perfectly clear that any analogy sought to be derived from the total physical destruction of an article owned in common is utterly inapplicable."

on behalf of the co-tenants and enjoin the reproduction of the common work.[52]

One of two or more co-authors may sell or assign his own share or right in the common work.[53]

With respect to the co-authors themselves, the law has not been definitely settled whether one must account to the other for his share of the profits. The rule seems to be that each may retain whatever moneys he may have secured from the exploitation of the motion picture rights of the work without accounting for any part thereof to his co-authors,[54] unless by contract the co-authors have agreed to the contrary.

[52] *Herne* v. *Liebler* (1902), 73 (N. Y.) A. D. 194; *Osborne* v. *Schenck* (1880), 83 N. Y. 200.

[53] *May* v. *Chaffee* (1871), 2 Dillon C. C. 385.

[54] *Carter* v. *Bailey* (1874), 64 Me. 458. "In the absence of any contract modifying their relations, copyright proprietors are simply owners in common . . . each owning a distinct but undivided part which or any part of which alone he can sell, as in the case of personal chattels."

"The statute confers upon all the owners full power, without exacting any obligation in return to print, publish and sell. . . . Each can exercise his own right alone without using, or receiving any aid or benefit whatever from the title or property of the other. But if none be allowed to enjoy his legal interest without the consent of all, then one, by withholding his consent, might practically destroy the value of the whole use. And a use only upon condition of an accounting for profits, would compel a disuse, or a risk of skill, capital and time with no right to call for a sharing of possible losses. When one owner by exercising a right expressly conferred upon him, in nowise uses or molests the right, title, possession or estate of his co-owners, or hinders them from a full enjoyment or sale and transfer of their whole property, we fail to perceive any principle of equity which would require him to account therefor. If owners

This is of great importance to the motion picture producer who has secured a license from only one of the co-authors. In such case, assuming that the co-authors have some agreement between themselves respecting the division of moneys secured from the exploitation of the work, the remedy of one co-author is against the other; and while he may compel the other to account, he may not compel the licensee to account to him. In other words, the motion picture producer is accountable only

of such property would have the result otherwise, they must bring it about by contract." If he takes "more than his share of the rents and income, without the consent of his co-owners," and refuses "in a reasonable time after demand, to pay such cotenants their share thereof . . . he will be liable to an action of special assumpsit."

Drake v. *Hall* (1914), 220 Fed. (C. C. A.) 905. Letters patent were issued to both parties to the suit as joint patentees. "Under such grant the rule is elementary that each of these patentees was vested with an undivided half interest therein, creating the relation between them of cotenants for all benefits of the grant, so that each became entitled to use thereof *without* accountability to the other cotenant. No relation of copartnership is involved in such ownership. . . ." To the same effect, *Central Brass* v. *Stuber* (1915), 220 Fed. (C. C. A.) 909; *Pusey* v. *Miller* (1894), 61 Fed. (C. C.) 401; *Clum* v. *Brewer* (1855), 2 Curtis C. C. 506; *Nillson* v. *Lawrence* (1912), 148 (N. Y.) A. D. 678; 133 N. Y. Supp. 293; *Blackledge* v. *Weir* (1901), 108 Fed. (C. C. A.) 71; *Lalance & Grosjean Mfg. Co.* v. *Nat'l Enameling & Stamping Co.* (1901), 108 Fed. (C. C.) 77. But see *Klein* v. *Beach* (1916), 232 Fed. (D. C.) 240; aff'd (1917) 239 Fed. (C. C. A.) 108. "Here both Beach and Klein became the owners of Klein's drama and each could then do with it what he pleased, with the duty of accounting over. . . . But in all these instances one would be obliged to account to the author."

to his licensor.[55] Nor is the licensee of one of the co-authors a proper party to an action brought by one co-author against the other.[56] It has also been held that

[55] *Pusey* v. *Miller* (1894), 61 Fed. (C. C.) 401. "In *Dunham* v. *Railroad Co.*, 2 Ban. & A. 327, 7 Biss. 223, Fed. Cas. No. 4151, it was said by Judge Drummond that, where a party owning less than the whole of the thing patented makes a grant or license under the patent, it would seem the better rule to hold, if there is any liability at all, that he shall be answerable to the others, rather than the other patentees shall look to the grantee or licensee. In *Curran* v. *Burdsall*, *supra* (20 Fed. 837), the court held that, if one of several joint patentees assigns to a third party, the estoppel upon the assignor must work a license to the assignee to use the patent, and the joint owners of the patent must look to the one who assigns, for an accounting. The rule deducible from the authorities would seem to be that the license of one or more of several owners in common of a patent confers a right as against all, and that the remedy of the other tenants in common, if they have any, is by a suit for an account for whatever may have been received by them. In other words, the licensee of a patent held by two or more co-owners is liable to his licensor only, and not to the other co-owners, for license fees or royalties, unless it is otherwise stipulated in the license."

Klein v. *Beach* (1916), 232 Fed. (D. C.) 240; aff'd 239 Fed. (C. C. A.) 108; *Lalance & Grosjean Mfg. Co.* v. *Nat'l Enameling and Stamping Co.* (1901), 108 Fed. (C. C.) 77; *Blackledge* v. *Weir* (1901), 108 Fed. (C. C. A.) 71; *De Witt* v. *Elmira Nobles Mfg. Co.* (1876), 66 N. Y. 459.

[56] *Dunham* v. *The Indianapolis R. R. Co.* (1876), 7 Bissell, 223. "What is the position of patentees with reference to their right to use the thing patented? The patentees are tenants in common of the right. One of them has no superiority of right over the other. One of them can manufacture and use the article pattented without the consent of the others; that is, each has the same right, although one may own a greater share of the thing patented than the other. The

where one co-author sues the licensee of the other co-author, the bill of complaint is demurrable.[57]

In any action brought by a co-author against a motion picture producer for an injunction or damages or both, other than an action brought by a co-author against his licensee for breach of the contract between them, he must join as parties thereto all his co-authors.[58] Where one

grant was in this case to the three to use and vend the improved car-brake shoes, and while it is clear that one of the patentees cannot grant what does not belong to him, and if he gives a license or makes a contract for the use of the thing patented, he can only grant that which he has himself, and not the rights of the other patentees, still he can clothe his grantee or his licensee with the same right that he has himself, namely, the right to sell or use the thing patented. And it seems to me the better rule is to hold, if there is a liability at all, that where a party owning less than the whole of a thing patented, makes a grant or a license, he shall be answerable to the others, rather than that the other patentees shall look to the grantee or licensee." *Pusey* v. *Miller* (1894), 61 Fed. (C. C.) 401.

[57] *Pusey* v. *Miller* (1894), 61 Fed. (C. C.) 401.

[58] *Nillson* v. *Lawrence* (1912), 148 (N. Y.) A. D. 678; 133 N. Y. Supp. 293. "We are also of the opinion that plaintiff's co-owner or co-owners should be made parties to the action. It is plain upon the face of the complaint that a complete determination of the controversy cannot be had in their absence."

Jackson v. *Moore* (1904), 94 (N. Y.) A. D. 504; 87 N. Y. Supp. 1101. "As a general rule tenants-in-common of personal property must join in bringing actions whether arising *ex contractu* or *ex delicto*. [*Hill* v. *Gibbs*, 5 Hil. (N. Y.) 56.]" *Aronson* v. *Fleckenstein* (1886), 28 Fed. (C. C.) 75.

Lauri v. *Renad* (Eng.) (1892), 61 L. J. Ch. 580; (1892), 3 Ch. 402; 67 L. T. 275; 40 W. R. 679. It was here held that any one or more of tenants in common in a copyright might maintain an action against a stranger for an infringement of the entire copy-

co-author has granted a license and the licensee has breached his contract, the licensor may maintain his action against his licensee without joining the licensor's co-authors.

One co-author may maintain an action against his co-authors for infringements of the common property.[59]

Section 10.—Nature of the contract of co-authorship.

Contracts between co-authors, and contracts between the manager or publisher and the co-authors for the crea-

right. See also: *Stevens* v. *Wildy* (Eng.) (1850), 19 L. J. Ch. 190.

In *Tree* v. *Bowkett* (Eng.) (1896), 77 L. T. 77, the question is discussed whether a licensee must be made a party to an action brought against an infringer by the co-authors.

[59] *Herring* v. *Gas Consumers' Assoc.* (1878), 3 McCrary C. C. 206. The question here presented was whether a joint author of a patent could infringe upon the patent owned jointly without being liable to his co-owner for the wrong done. The court held that he could not. The court says: "Can a part owner infringe the common patent and escape all liability? If he can it is obvious that, however small his aliquot part, he can make the enjoyment of the patent valueless to his joint owner. He has, by virtue of the joint ownership, a right to use the patent, but he has no right, more than a stranger, to infringe the same. If there is an infringement the right of recovery is in the party wronged. All the joint owners should ordinarily be parties plaintiff, but if the wrongdoer is one who is guilty to the damage of the other joint owner, the other should not be left remediless. As to such infringement they are strangers. . . . Were this not so, the door would be open to the gravest frauds by one joint owner against all other joint owners. See also: *Pitts* v. *Hall* (1854), 3 Blatchf. 201, at page 208.

Cescinsky v. *Routledge* (Eng.) (1916), 85 L. J. K. B. 1504; 115 L. T. 191.

tion and production of literary works are contracts for personal services.[60] The creation of a literary work resembles that of a patentable invention;[61] and since the co-owners of the copyright as of the patent are tenants in common, there is no partnership in the work, nor is there a joint venture.[62]

Of course, that relation may be modified by special contract,[63] but any such contract would have to create

[60] *Mallory* v. *Mackay* (1899), 92 Fed. (C. C. A.) 749; *Blakely* v. *Sousa* (1900), 197 Pa. St. 305; 47 Atl. 286. See also Section 14.

[61] *Henry* v. *Dick* (1911), 224 U. S. at page 45; 32 Sup. Ct. 364; *Scribner* v. *Strauss* (1904), 130 Fed. (C. C.) 389.

[62] *De Witt* v. *Elmira Nobles Co.* (1876), 5 Hun, 459; aff'd 66 N. Y. 459. "These parties are not partners in the ownership of this patent. Beyond doubt they are tenants in common each owning the undivided half."

Pitts v. *Hall* (1854), 3 Blatch. 201. "In the case of joint patentees, where no agreement of partnership exists, the relation of co-partners certainly does not result from their connection as joint patentees; and when one joint owner of a patent transfers his undivided interest to a stranger, the assignee does not become the partner of his co-proprietor. In both cases the parties interested in the patent are simply joint owners or tenants in common of the rights and property secured by the patent."

Robinson on Patents, Section 795.

"And it may be established as an accepted doctrine that whatever may be their relation to the monopoly such joint owners are *not co-partners* nor collective owners of the invention. . . ."

And we find this rule enunciated in Lindley on Partnership (6th Ed.) at p. 36:

"Mutual rights of co-owners of a copyright have not been much discussed; but it has been decided that a license to represent a dramatic entertainment granted by one only of several co-owners of the copyright in it does not bind the other."

[63] *Pitts* v. *Hall* (1854), 3 Blatch.

the mutually reciprocal obligations that are concomitant with partnership.[64] Where the parties have by special contract created a co-partnership, any cause which operates to dissolve the partnership remits them once more to their rights as co-tenants in the common work.[65]

Since death works a dissolution of partnerships, the death of one co-author would dissolve any relation of partnership or joint venture created between them by special contract.

Suppose that, in the absence of any special contract between them, one co-author dies before the completion of the work. What becomes of his rights to the work? To answer this one must examine the nature of their contract. When two men agree between themselves to write a play or book, the law spells out an implied cove-

201; *Pankhurst* v. *Kinsman* (1849), 1 Blatch. 488; *Carter* v. *Bailey* (1874), 64 Me. 463.

[64] *Heye* v. *Tilford* (1896), 2 A. D. (N. Y.) 346; 37 N. Y. Supp. 751; aff'd 154 N. Y. 757; 49 N. E. 1098; *Central City Sav. Bank* v. *Walker* (1876), 66 N. Y. 424; *Burnett* v. *Snyder* (1879), 76 N. Y. 344; *London Assurance Co.* v. *Drennen* (1886), 116 U. S. 461; 6 Sup. Ct. 442. "To constitute a partnership there must be a reciprocal agreement of the parties not only to unite their stock, but to share in the risks of profit or loss by the disposition to be made of it. . . ." *Baldwin* v. *Burrows* (1872), 47 N. Y. 199 at 206. And see *Smith* v. *Dunn* (1904), 44 (N. Y.) Misc. 288; 89 N. Y. Supp. 881; and *Stevens* v. *McKibbin* (1895), 68 Fed. (C. C. A.) 406, the latter case giving a most detailed and logical discussion of the essential elements of partnership.

[65] *Pankhurst* v. *Kinsman* (1849), 1 Blatch. 488. "The assignment (of the interest in the partnership) worked a dissolution and left the parties interested in the patent simply to their rights under it."

nant that they will remain alive to complete the work.[66] The contract is one which involves elements of confidence and skill, and each party is entitled to the active and continued collaboration of the other up to the completion of the work.[67] When death robs him of that essential, the contract is broken; it is at an end.[68] It cannot possibly survive, for obviously it cannot be carried out according to its terms. The surviving author is not bound to continue the work with a substitute appointed by the personal representative of the decedent, for no two people possess the same peculiar and valuable qualities.[69]

[66] *Blakely* v. *Sousa* (1900), 197 Pa. St. 305, at p. 318; 47 Atl. 286. "In all contracts of this character there is written by the law the condition that they are subject to the continuance of the lives of the parties contracting. . . ." See also: *Taylor* v. *Caldwell* (Eng.) (1863), 3 Best. & S. 826; *Spaulding* v. *Rosa* (1877), 71 N. Y. 40; *Baxter* v. *Billings* (1897), 83 Fed. (C. C. A.) 790.

[67] *Spalding* v. *Rosa* (1877), 71 N. Y. 40; *Blakely* v. *Sousa* (1900), 197 Pa. St. 305; 47 Atl. 286; *Sargent* v. *McLeod* (1913), 209 N. Y. 360; 103 N. E. 164; *Baxter* v. *Billings* (1897), 83 Fed. (C. C. A.) 790; *Wolfe* v. *Howes* (1859), 20 N. Y. 197.

[68] *Blakely* v. *Sousa* (1900), 197 Pa. St. 305; 47 Atl. 286. "Whatever Sousa may have done after Blakely's death he did for himself. The term of his employment *ended with the death of his employer*. . . ." See cases cited and excerpts in Section 14, page 67, footnote 6.

[69] *Blakely* v. *Sousa* (1900), 197 Pa. St. 305; 47 Atl. 286. "It would hardly be contended for a moment that if Sousa had died and Blakely had survived, Blakely could have been held to accept in lieu of Sousa's services the services of his legal representatives or of anyone selected by them."

Dickinson v. *Callahan* (1852), 19 Pa. St. 227, at 234. "It would seem absurd to say that the administrator of a physician *or author*, or a musician could be compelled to perform their professional engagements no mat-

On the other hand, he is not bound to throw away the product of their joint labor, nor divest himself of the knowledge and skill acquired thereby. He may continue the work to its completion and license third parties to exploit the same.

In like manner the manager or publisher who contracts with two or more co-authors is entitled to the joint product of their labors. He is not bound to accept the work of one, but may insist on genuine collaboration; and where one co-author dies before the completion of the work, the contract is at an end.[70]

ter how the contract might be expressed. The idea is ludicrous."

[70] *Baxter* v. *Billings* (1897), 83 Fed. (C. C. A.) 790. This was a case where a client retained two attorneys to prosecute some litigation; the attorneys were partners. Before the work had progressed at all, one of the attorneys, Yonley, died. Baxter, the survivor, was then asked to complete the work and he did so, bringing it to a successful issue. He brought an action for his services, basing the action on his original contract. Demurrer was sustained, the Circuit Court holding that: "An agreement with a lawyer to commence and prosecute a suit is of the same character as a contract *with an author to write a book. If the author dies*, or abandons his work when it is half written, no substitute or successor can complete the book, and recover its price, because the literary ability of the original author for the use of which the publisher contracted, has not been, and could not be applied to it. . . . That was a contract for the services of both Baxter and Yonley. Under that agreement their authority to commence and prosecute the suit was a joint authority, and their duty was a joint duty. A joint authority conferred on two persons can only be exercised by the act of both. An obligation to furnish and apply to the conduct of a lawsuit the learning, ability and experience of *two particular attorneys* is not performed by fur-

The manager may, however, contract anew with the surviving co-author, and a license so given to him is valid.[71]

What remedy may be open to the estate of the deceased co-author where he dies before the completion of the work is doubtful.[72] It is well settled that each co-author may exploit the work to the fullest extent, and his right to do so should not be curtailed because of the other's death—

nishing the services *of one of them. . . .*"

Sargent v. *McLeod* (1913), 209 N. Y. 360; 103 N. E. 164. In a similar case involving the death of an attorney the Court of Appeals said: "It is true that the cessation in performance was caused by his death, but it left undone that which he had agreed to do precisely as though it resulted from a physical or mental incapacitation at that time, or a capricious or unjustifiable abandonment of the case. . . . Not only was the performance which bound McLeod to pay the stipulated compensation incomplete at the death of the intestate, *but the death abrogated the contract.*" See also: *Morgan* v. *Roberts* (1865), 38 Ill. 65; *Moshier* v. *Kitchell* (1877), 87 Ill. 18; *Wright* v. *McCampbell* (1890), 75 Texas, 644; 13 S. W. 293; *Hartford Fire Ins. Co.* v. *Wilcox* (1870), 57 Ill. 180.

[71] *Yerrington* v. *Greene* (1863), 7 R. I. 594. "And if he would serve the administrators in winding up the estate it must be *under a new contract with them,* and under renewed powers granted by them. . . ."

[72] *Wolfe* v. *Howes* (1859), 20 N. Y. 197. The concurring opinion of Ch. J. Johnson observed " that it was material that the defendants had received actual benefits from the services of the plaintiff's testator and that quite a different question would be presented by a case where the services actually rendered should prove valueless, as, e. g., *if one should be retained to compose an original literary work and having faithfully employed himself in preparation should die without having completed any work of value to the employer.*"

if anything they should become greater, since the survivor must of necessity do more labor to complete the work.

Any rights which would enure to the estate of the deceased co-author must be determined by reservations which have been inserted in the contract of the co-authors. If there are no such reservations, his rights are problematical.

The contract of co-authorship is not assignable, nor is the contract with the publisher or manager. And being non-assignable, it will not pass to a trustee in bankruptcy.[73] It is entire and indivisible, and calls for complete performance before any rights under it are enforcible.[74]

Section 11.—Where music has been composed specially to accompany the exhibition of the motion picture.

There has been a strong tendency of late to provide

[73] *Griffith* v. *Tower Pub. Co.* (Eng.) (1897), 75 L. T. R. (N. S.) 330; 1 Ch. 21; *Hole* v. *Bradbury* (Eng.) (1879), 41 L. T. R. 153; 12 Ch. D. 886; *Stevens* v. *Benning* (Eng.) (1854), 24 L. T. R. (O. S.) 154; 1 K. and J. 169; *Reade* v. *Bentley* (Eng.) (1857), 30 L. T. R. (O. S.) 268; 3 K. and J. 271; and *Bartsch* v. *Herndon*, Circuit Ct. of Cook County, State of Illinois, March 16, 1917, which held that a license to produce a play did not pass to the trustee where the licensee became insolvent, the right to it being purely personal. In this case the licensee was a corporation.

[74] *Mallory* v. *Mackaye* (1889), 92 Fed. (C. C. A.) 749, at 751. "Such contracts are entire, not separable, and are governed by the rule, applicable to all entire contracts, that a breach by the one party as to any material part completely discharges and releases the other party from his obligations. It is hardly necessary to cite authorities on the proposition that such a contract is entire."

music, specially composed, to accompany the exhibition of motion pictures. This has raised some very interesting questions as to the rights of the various parties associated with that kind of a motion picture.

In the "Mikado Case" [75] it was held that where one wrote the libretto of an opera and another the music, the essence of the dramatic composition was in the libretto, stage-business, dialogue and vocal music rather than in the orchestral accompaniment. And since, in that case, Gilbert & Sullivan had abandoned their copyright to the exclusive dramatic representation of the opera by consenting to the multiplication and sale of the libretto and vocal score in England, they could not enjoin the presentation of the opera here, the orchestration not being theirs.

Following the line of reasoning in that case, it would seem that special music composed for a motion picture, is not in itself a dramatic composition. It is incidental to the picture, just as the music of an opera is incidental to the play itself. It is an integral and inseparable part of the motion picture,[76] and must stand or fall with it.

[75] The *Mikado Case* (1885), 25 Fed. (C. C.) 183. See also in this connection: *Herbert* v. *Fields*, 152 N. Y. Supp. 487.

[76] *Hatton* v. *Kean* (Eng.) (1859), 7 C. B. N. S. 268; 28 L. J. C. P. 20; 6 Jur. N. S. 226; 1 L. T. 10; 8 W. R. 7. Incidental music written for "Much Ado About Nothing" for defendant Kean who had designed and created the entire production, belonged to him, and the plaintiff had no separate property right therein and could not restrain the defendant from using it.

Wallenstein v. *Herbert* (Eng.) (1867), 15 L. T. N. S. 364; 16 L. T. N. S. 453; *Herbert* v. *Weber*, N. Y. Law Journal, Oct. 30, 1907, Judge Seabury; *Maurel* v. *Smith* (1915), 220 Fed. (D. C.) 195.

If there is no special contract between the composer of the music and the writer of the scenario both would naturally be co-authors in the completed work and their rights and liabilities would become fixed as such.[77]

Section 12.—Where the motion picture producer has not followed the text of the work upon which the motion picture is based.

In dealing with plays, novels, short stories and the like the motion picture producer is often confronted with the problem of how far he may go in making changes in the work when reproducing the same in motion pictures.

The literary product of an author or playwright is a thing jealously watched by him, and one in which the common law gives him certain well-defined rights, even where he has parted title with the work.[78] These rights

[77] See Sections 9 and 10.

[78] *Clemens* v. *Press Publishing Co.* (1910), 67 Misc. (N. Y.) 183; 122 N. Y. Supp. 206. "Even the matter of fact attitude of the law does not require us to consider the sale of the rights to a literary production in the same way that we would consider the sale of a barrel of pork. Contracts are to be so construed as to give effect to the intention of the parties. The man who sells a barrel of pork to another may pocket the purchase price and retain no further interest in what becomes of the pork. While an author may write to earn his living and may sell his literary productions, yet the purchaser, in the absence of a contract which permits him so to do, cannot make as free a use of them as he could of the pork which he purchased. . . . If the intent of the parties was that the defendant should purchase the right to the literary property and publish it, *the author is entitled not only to be paid for his work but to have it published in the manner in which he wrote it. The purchaser cannot garble it or put it out under another name than the author's, nor*

may not be violated even by one who purchases the product of the author; and it often becomes a serious question to determine just how far a producer may go in making changes in the work without invading the rights of the author or playwright.

It is necessary to bear in mind that there are two distinctive classes who may be guilty of such an invasion of rights. One may be an outright purchaser of a work, or, again, he may be nothing more than a mere licensee.

In the first case, that of an outright purchaser of the work, there was for a long time a conflict in the decisions as to how the author might be protected in his rights. The law was plain that while a purchaser of a work might go a great deal further than a mere licensee in making changes in it, nevertheless, he would not be permitted to mutilate the work or so alter it as to injure the reputation or standing of the author. But equity was reluctant to interfere; and after numerous decisions in England, it was finally determined and now seems to be the law both in England and this country, that a mutilation or radical change in a play by one who has purchased it outright amounts in essence to a *libel.*[79] And since a libel is both

can he omit altogether the name of the author unless his contract with the latter permits him so to do.

"The position of an author is somewhat akin to that of an actor. The fact that he is permitted to have his work published under his name or to perform before the public, necessarily affects his reputation and standing and thus impairs or increases his future earning capacity."

[79] *American Law Book Co.* v. *Chamberlayne* (1908), 165 Fed. (C. C. A.) 313; *American Malting Co.* v. *Keitel* (1913), 209 Fed. (C. C. A.) 351. This case reviews at length the history of this class of litigation.

a crime and a tort and equity will not restrain the commission of crimes, the author is relegated to the law side of the court for damages.[80] But where, in addition to

[80] *American Law Book Co.* v. *Chamberlayne* (1908), 165 Fed. (C. C. A.) 313. The action was brought in equity. The court held that the plaintiff having parted with his title to the manuscript should have brought an action for libel.

"If he has sustained damage because his article has been published in a mutilated or altered form or with some misrepresentation as to its authorship, he may, if he can prove his allegations, recover in an action for libel." The court then reversed the judgment secured after trial of the action.

Kipling v. *Fenno* (1900), 106 Fed. (C. C.) 692. In this case the work having been dedicated to the public it was held that the author could not regulate by injunction the manner in which his reprinted stories should be grouped and entitled.

Cox v. *Cox* (Eng.) (1853), 11 Hare, 118. Where there was an outright sale of a manuscript by the author, the purchaser was at liberty to alter and deal with it as he thought proper, unless there was a special contract reserving to the author any rights.

Archbold v. *Sweet* (Eng.) (1832), 1 M. & Rob. 62; 5 Car. & P. 219. The publisher of plaintiff's work was the owner of the copyright therein.

Held that plaintiff could maintain an action at law for any injury sustained by him by reason of the publication of an inaccurate edition of his work falsely purporting to have been executed by him.

Lee v. *Gibbings* (Eng.) (1892), 67 L. T. 263. The publisher in bringing out a second edition of a work omitted portions of it. The author sought to enjoin the publication of the book upon the ground that such publication caused an injury to his reputation.

Held that plaintiff's remedy was at law for libel.

Angers v. *Leprohon* (Can.), 22 Que. S. C. 170. It was here held that where a work was in the public domain, the publication of the same under a title different from that used by the author did not furnish ground for an in-

the libel, there is the element of "passing off" or fraud and deception of the public, equity will interfere.

In the case of a mere licensee, the rule is different. There we have the case of one injuring a work of which he is not the owner, or damaging the reputation of its author who is not a stranger to him, but, on the contrary, between whom and himself there is some privity. In such a case equity will intervene, and injunction will issue to restrain the irreparable damage that may be done.[81]

junction particularly where both the original publication and the later publication appeared under a pseudonym and it was not proven that the public knew the author under the assumed name.

Humphries v. *Thompson* (Eng.) (1908), Times, Apr. 29, 30, May 1. Even though the publisher owns the copyright in the book, he cannot so publish the work as to injure the reputation of the author. If he does so, he may be sued for libel.

Crookes v. *Petter* (Eng.) (1860), 6 Jur. (N. S.) 1131; 3 L. T. 225. The name of the editor of a newspaper was to appear on the title page and did appear there for some time. The editor sought to enjoin the removal of his name from such title page. It was agreed not to change the title.

Held that since his name was not part of the title he could not enjoin its removal, but that he could maintain an action at law for any damages he may have sustained.

See also: *Carlton Illustrators* v. *Coleman* (Eng.) (1911), 80 L. J. K. B. 510; 1 K. B. 771 (1911); 104 L. T. 413; and *Cooper* v. *Whittingham* (Eng.) (1880), 49 L. J. Ch. 752; 15 Ch. D. 501, followed.

Ridge v. *English Illustrated Magazine* (Eng.) (1913), Times, June 13. The publication of an inferior work under the name of an author of literary reputation when such work was not in fact written by him constitutes an actionable libel and plaintiff is not required to prove malice or actual damage.

[81] *Royle* v. *Dillingham* (1907), 53 Misc. (N. Y.) 383; 104 N. Y. Supp. 783. There the court said: "Probably under the common-

Equity will not restrain one from doing that which he pleases with his own property; and if in the conduct of it, he injures another, the latter must sue in damages for the tort. But where one attempts as in the case of a mere licensee, to injure property in which another has the title, equity will enjoin such acts.

The fact that a work is produced in serial form gives the producer no greater rights with respect to changes or mutilation than where the entire work is brought out at one time.[82]

The author has the strict right to preserve the identity of his creation.[83] So it would seem that if a producer of

law and certainly under his contract, the plaintiff is within his rights in invoking equitable jurisdiction. Whether we have gone quite so far as other countries whose literary history is longer in the protection of literary property, may be open to doubt; but there is as there should be, a growing tendency to bestow on authors that full measure of protection which their unique property requires. Whether the work is great or trivial, original or adapted, the principle should be the same so long as the work is the author's own. The court will not apply canons of literary taste, but leave that to the public. The tendency of our authorities is shown by such cases as *Clemmens* v. *Belford*, 14 Fed. 728; *Harte* v. *De Witt*, 1 Cent. Law Journal, 360.

Gilbert v. *Workman et al.* (Eng.) (1910), Times, Jan. 19th. Injunction was granted ex parte restraining introduction of a song in an operetta, which was not a part thereof.

[82] *Humphries* v. *Thompson* (Eng.) (1908), Times, Apr. 29, 30, May 1.

[83] *De Bekker* v. *Stokes Co.* (1916), 168 A. D. (N. Y.) 452; 157 N. Y. Supp. 576. The plaintiff sold to defendant the exclusive right to publish the work, prepared by plaintiff, and entitled "Stokes Encyclopedia of Music." The defendant, after selling the book in the regular way, authorized the defendant the University Company to publish the book

pictures took two or more separate scenarios written by two or more people, or even by the same person, and

together with eight other volumes under the title "Encyclopedia of Music." Defendants were enjoined.

Drummond v. *Altemus* (1894), 60 Fed. (C. C.) 338. Where there were published a few of a series of lectures given by plaintiff which lectures had been dedicated to the public, the lectures having been incorrectly copied and the book purported to contain the entire series of lectures, it was held that an injunction would issue to enjoin such publication.

Hart v. *De Witt*, 1 Cent. Law J. 360. "I think that the plaintiff has such an interest in his name and reputation as an author as entitles him to invoke the aid of equity in restraining the defendant from falsely representing that a literary production published and sold by the defendant, is the work of the plaintiff."

In this case the defendant published a book several chapters of which had been written by the plaintiff and other parts by another. The authorship of the entire book was ascribed to plaintiff, although at the end of the book there was an explanatory notice. The court granted a temporary injunction.

Excerpt from Editorial of the N. Y. Law Journal of March 21, 1916, in discussing *Morang* v. *Le Sueur* (Can.) (1911), 45 Can. Sup. Ct. 95.

The learned Chief Justice speaks of the absence of English authorities, but in a note to the story in Case and Comment it is stated that "in England apparently the same rule has been laid down in an unreported case," citing The Writer (Boston, vol. 26, No. 10, p. 150). Substantially in accord with these decisions was one of the German Imperial Court, the substance of which was stated in the Harvard Law Review for May, 1913, as follows:

"A Lady who owned a private residence in Berlin, of which she occupied the upper floor, while the lower floor was let to a tenant, desired to have the vestibule of the house decorated by a fresco painting and engaged a well known artist to do the work. The painting when finished represented an island with some nude figures of sirens. To these nudes the lady who had ordered the painting took exception, and

combined them all into one picture, he would be distinctly violating the right of separate identity, and would be liable in damages and injunction.

Where in the case of the granting of a license, the licensee agrees that no changes or alterations shall be made, or no artist shall be engaged without securing the consent of the licensor, a violation of such agreement will be enjoined.[84]

she had another artist overpaint the figures so that they appeared as draped. The first artist contended that this change violated rights which as an artist he had in the integrity of his work, and although the owner covered the altered portion of the fresco by a curtain, he was not satisfied, but brought an action demanding the restoration of the painting to its original condition, or failing in that demand, its entire withdrawal from where it might be visible to strangers. The lower court granted the latter prayers, and the plaintiff appealed. *Held*, that the overpainted drapery must be removed. (79 Entscheidungen des Reichsgerichts, 397, German Imperial Court, 1912). . . . ."

The court said that the principle of the decision must be deduced from the relative rights of the owners, of the public, of the artist to his reputation, and perhaps from a right of personality, which, even if not recognized as a distinct generic right, may yet be enforced with regard to particular interests.

Although the German law is codified, there is no explicit provision applicable to the particular controversy involved. It is significant that rights of control of a manuscript or a painting have been upheld both in code and common-law jurisdictions. A result similar to that reached in these cases ought to be worked out everywhere upon some theory, no matter what the general form or particular provisions of the local law may be. The remarks of Chief Justice Fitspatrick in the Supreme Court of Canada (supra) upon the unique and complex character of literary property may be taken as a guide in effectuating justice in any controversy of this nature.

[84] *Royle* v. *Dillingham* (1907),

An author may enjoin the exhibition of a motion picture which is purported to have been based upon his work when not so in fact.[85] And it would seem that this right

53 Misc. (N. Y.) 383; 104 N. Y. Supp. 783. It was here held that a producer of a play who agreed that no additions or alterations would be made without the consent of the author would be enjoined from making any unauthorized change or modifications in the text or structure of the work.

Lowenfeld v. *Curtis* (1896), 72 Fed. (C. C.) 105. Plaintiff made an agreement with defendant giving defendant a license to produce a play entitled "Gentleman Joe." The contract provided:

1. That no alterations or additions were to be made without the written consent of the plaintiff.

2. That the names of the artists who were to be engaged were to be submitted for the approval of the plaintiff.

Upon motion for an injunction it was held with respect to (1), "Additions to the play . . . are wholly unwarranted, except upon the written consent of the complainant. Defendant was entitled to produce the play only in strict conformity to the manuscript and score." The court also intimated that any alterations of the play would have violated the terms of the contract; with respect to (2) that failure to submit names of performers to plaintiff was a breach which entitled plaintiff to an injunction.

[85] *Clemens* v. *Beford* (1883), 14 Fed. (C. C.) 728. "An author of acquired reputation and perhaps, a person who has not obtained any standing before the public as a writer, may restrain another from the publication of literary matter purporting to have been written by him, but which, in fact, was never so written. In other words no person has the right to hold another out to the world as the author of literary matter which he never wrote; and the same would undoubtedly apply in favor of a person known to the public under a nom de plume, because no one has the right either expressly or by implication falsely or untruly to charge another with the composition or authorship of a literary

may be exercised by the executor of a deceased author.[86] An author's name has a property value. Its use amounts to the taking of another's property. Where the work is in the public domain, anyone using such work has the right to use the name of the author in connection therewith.[87]

Where he has applied a nom de plume to his work the nom de plume or the true name of the author may be

production which he did not write."

Robertson v. *Berry* (1878), 50 Md. 591. In the application of his name to a work the author has a property right which a court of equity will protect against such a use or imitation as may cause damage to the author's property.

Landa v. *Greenberg* (Eng.) (1908), 24 T. L. R. 441. One who contributes to the plaintiff's publication under a nom de plume may after dismissal restrain the use of such nom de plume, as she has an exclusive property right thereto.

Collins v. *Public Ledger Co.*, Court of Common Pleas, In Equity, Philadelphia, Pa., June Term, 1917, No. 2272; July 17, 1917, Barratt, P. J. Plaintiff had conducted a column in defendant's newspaper under the signature of "Girard." After leaving its employ, defendant continued to edit the column under the same name. Defendant was enjoined from so doing. *Suburban Press* v. *Phila. Suburban Publ. Co.* (1910), 227 Pa. St. 148; 75 Atl. 1037.

[86] *Wood* v. *Butterworth* (Eng.) (1901), Times, Dec. 23. An executor of a deceased author was granted an injunction ex parte enjoining one from falsely imputing the authorship of a work to plaintiff's testator.

[87] *Edison* v. *Polyform Mfg. Co.* (1907), 67 Atl. 392; *Iolanthe Case* (1883), 15 Fed. (C. C.) 439; *Daly* v. *Wabash* (1899), 40 A. D. (N. Y.) 220; 57 N. Y. Supp. 1125.

See in this connection: *Rex* v. *Daoust* (Can.), 28 D. L. R. 293; 26 Can. Cr. Cas. 69; 49 Que. S. C. 65. *Held* a criminal offense to suppress the name of a playwright, even though he was a foreigner, where his country was a party to the Berne convention.

used at the option of the motion picture producer in connection with the use of the work.[88] Where the motion picture producer is the owner of the work or where the literary product is in the public domain, it would seem that he is not bound to use the name of the author in connection with the exploitation of the work; that is, he is not required to use the name of the author, but, on the other hand he may not use any other name.[89]

[88] *Clemens* v. *Belford* (1883), 14 Fed. (C. C.) 728. "It does not seem to me that an author or writer has or can acquire any better or higher right in a nom de plume or assumed name than he has in his Christian or baptismal name. When a person enters the field of authorship he can secure to himself the exclusive right to his writings by a copyright under the laws of the United States. If he publishes anything of which he is the author or compiler, either under his own proper name or an assumed name, without protecting it by copyright, it becomes public property, and any person who chooses to do so has the right to republish it and to state the name of the author in such form in the book, either upon the title page or otherwise, as to show who was the writer or author thereof.

[89] *Jones* v. *American Law Book Co.* (1908), 125 A. D. (N. Y.) 519; 109 N. Y. Supp. 706. Plaintiff agreed to write legal articles for defendant for one year at a specified rate of payment per page. Contract provided that work was to belong absolutely to defendant, that defendant could make any and all charges it desired. It was held that in view of the contract made, plaintiff could *not insist* upon having his name printed as author of the work.

Mallory v. *Mackaye* (1898), 86 Fed. (C. C.) 122; modified in 92 Fed. (C. C. A.) 749, on another point. Plaintiff engaged defendant for a specified period and agreed to pay him a stipulated salary as well as a share of the profits. Defendant agreed that title in defendant's productions should belong to plaintiff. It was held that a patent for a revolving stage secured by defendant and a play written by him belonged to plaintiff; that omitting the

Section 13.—Criticism of the work.

"When an author places his book before the public he invites criticism; and, however hostile that criticism may be, and however much damage it may cause him . . . the critic is not liable in an action for libel, provided he makes no misstatement of any material facts contained in the writing, and does not attack the character of the author." [90]

The critic may use ridicule.[91] He may even underrate

name of the author from advertisements did not justify defendant in himself using the play.

Booth v. *Lloyd* (Eng.) (1910), 26 T. L. R. 549. Plaintiff was owner of the copyright of a musical composition. He granted the right to a third person to "print, publish and sell." *Held* that the licensee was not bound to print and publish the musical composition in his name.

But see *Clemens* v. *Press Publishing Co.* (1910), 67 Misc. (N. Y.) 183; 122 N. Y. Supp. 206.

[90] *Dowling* v. *Livingstone* (1896), 108 Mich. 321; 66 N. W. 225. Plaintiff published a book entitled "The Wage Worker's Remedy." The defendants in their newspaper severely criticised the composition as well as the theories of the author but made no personal attack on him. See also: *Campbell* v. *Spottiswood* (Eng.), 3 F. & F. 421; *Morrison* v. *Belcher* (Eng.), 3 F. & F. 614; *Belknapp* v. *Ball* (1890), 83 Mich. 589; 47 N. W. 674; *Walker* v. *Tribune* (1887), 29 Fed. (C. C.) 827.

Stewart v. *Reuters Telegram* (Eng.), 1911, Times, Feb. 1. Statements made concerning a publication which were untrue were held to be not *libellous per se when made in good faith.*

Thomas v. *Bradbury* (Eng.) (1905), Times, July 5-6-7; aff'd 95 L. T. 23. Plaintiff sued alleging that defendant, publishers of *Punch*, had criticised his work so harshly as to evince malice. He received a verdict of £300.

[91] *Dowling* v. *Livingstone* (1896), 108 Mich. 321; 66 N. W. 225. "One writer in exposing the follies and errors of another may make use of ridicule, however poignant, and if loss occurs it is

the author's talents.[92] But where the critic distorts the work [93] or uses the criticism as a means of attacking the character or private life of the author,[94] he is guilty of

damnum absque injuria. Carr v. *Hood*, 1 Campb. 354; *Strauss* v. *Francis*, 4 Fost. & F. 1114." To the same effect: *Soane* v. *Knight*, Moody & M. 74; *Thompson* v. *Shackell*, Moody & M. 187; *Swan* v. *Tappan*, 5 Cush. 105; *Gott* v. *Pulsifer*, 122 Mass. 235.

Walker v. *Tribune* (1887), 29 Fed. (C. C.) 827. An attorney who had written a pamphlet was referred to as a "crank." *Held* not libelous per se.

[92] *Naulty* v. *Bulletin Co.* (1903), 206 Pa. St. 128; 55 Atl. 862. A statement respecting a writer on historical subjects that he was not qualified as an expert in historical matters and that in sending certain letters and in acting as an officer of a historical society he was guilty of fraud and deception, was held not to be libelous as it did not impugn the good faith of plaintiff, but merely took issue as to the correctness of the facts set forth in the letters sent out by plaintiff.

[93] *Carr* v. *Hood* (Eng.), 1 Campb. 355. Where the critic introduced fiction in order to distort and make ridiculous the work, he was held liable for libel. See also: *Tabart* v. *Tepper* (Eng.), 1 Campb. 351; *Whistler* v. *Ruskin* (Eng.) (1878), Times, Nov. 26, 27.

[94] *Cooper* v. *Stone* (1840), 24 Wend. (N. Y.) 434. Criticism of the work of an author is permissible, but the critic may not attack the moral character of the author in his review; where he does so it becomes a question of good faith, and when the critic raises the question of privilege, it is for the jury to pass on.

"I do not speak of criticism upon the works of an author in the abstract; for this I admit no action can lie. Certainly not, unless the criticism be grossly false and work a special damage to the proprietor of the book at which the strictures are levelled."

Croasdale v. *Tantum* (1880), 6 Houst. (Del.) 60. A reference to an editor of a newspaper as a "miserable specimen of humanity" was held to be libelous in connection with a statement that defendant was obliged to write the article to apprise the public of an attempt to destroy the character of defendant.

Spooner v. *Daniels* (1854), Fed.

libel. That is true even where he attempts to justify his act upon the ground that it was a mere jest.[95] An oral imputation of insanity, however, was not held slanderous per se.[96]

Cas. No. 13,244a (C. C.). Where an author was referred to as a fraud, humbug and swindler, the words were held to be libelous.

Reade v. *Sweetzer* (1869), 6 Abb. Pr. (N. S.) (N.Y.) 9 (note). "The critic may say what he pleases of the literary merits or demerits of the published products of an author; but that with respect to his personal rights relating to his reputation the critic has no more privilege than any other person in assuming the business of criticism."

The court then holds that accusing an author of writing matter of a demoralizing effect is libelous. See also: *Kennedy* v. *Press Publ. Co.* (1886), 41 Hun (N. Y.), 422; *Hart* v. *Townsend* (1884), 67 How. Pr. (N. Y.) 88; *Archbold* v. *Sweet* (Eng.) (1832), 5 Car. & P. 219; *Macleod* v. *Wakely* (Eng.) (1831), 3 Car. & P. 311; *Graham* v. *McKimm* (Can.), 19 Ont. 475; *Browning* v. *Van Rensselaer* (1899), 97 Fed. 531 (C. C.); *Fraser* v. *Berkeley* (Eng.) (1833), 7 C. & P. 621.

95 *Triggs* v. *Sun Printing & Publishing Assn.* (1904), 179 N. Y. 144; 71 N. E. 739. "A publication, which in effect represents an author as a presumptuous literary freak and ridicules his private life, is not within the bounds of fair and honest literary criticism, is libelous per se, and cannot be justified upon the ground that it was a mere jest, when it is perfectly manifest from the language employed that it is an attack upon his reputation or business." The court cites *Cooper* v. *Stone*, 24 Wend. (N. Y.) 434; *Mattice* v. *Wilcox*, 71 Hun (N. Y.), 485; 24 N. Y. Supp. 1060; aff'd 147 N. Y. 624; 42 N. E. 270; *Hanneton* v. *Eno*, 81 N. Y. 116.

96 *"George, the Count Joannes"* v. *Burt* (1863), 88 Mass. 236. An oral imputation of insanity is not libelous per se.

See in this connection: *Smith* v. *Clinton* (Eng.) (1908), Times, Oct. 19–29. The printer is liable for libelous matter printed by him, and he cannot hold the proprietor of the work to account to him, even though it was expressly contracted that he be indemnified.

CHAPTER II

THE AUTHOR (CONTINUED)

Miscellaneous Questions

SEC. 14. On the question whether the contract existing between the parties is a personal one.
15. Where the contract contains a negative covenant.
16. Where the work is to be to the satisfaction of the producer.
17. Where the contract provides for the writing of a libelous, immoral or seditious work.
18. Where the license granted is a sole and exclusive one.
19. Where the contract contains limitations as to methods of exploitation.
20. Where the work is to be produced at a definite time.
21. Where the payment to the author is based upon a percentage of the gross receipts or net profits.
22. Where the amount to be paid to the author is guaranteed.
23. Where the payment to the author is a stipulated amount per performance or per period.
24. Where the amount of damages in the event of a breach is stipulated.
25. Where the contract provides for a forfeiture upon failure to pay the royalties due.
26. Where the manuscript is lost or converted after submission to the producer.
27. Where the work is secured by means of a prize contest.
28. On the question whether an outright purchaser is required to reproduce the work.
29. On the question whether the producer is entitled to a refund of advance payment.

30. On the question whether the contract may be rescinded where the author made a poor bargain or where fraud is involved.
31. On the question whether the contract may be rescinded where the producer made a poor bargain or where fraud is involved.
32. On the question whether a contract to write will be specifically enforced.
33. On the question whether the licensor may maintain an action against third parties.
34. On the question whether courts grant injunctions pendente lite more readily in actions of this nature.

Section 14.—On the question whether the contract existing between the parties is a personal one.

It has been generally settled that contracts between authors or proprietors of literary works with producers are personal and are not assignable by either party without the consent of the other.[1] Thus, where a license is

[1] "Contracts in which the personal acts and qualities of one of the contracting parties form a material ingredient are, in general not assignable." 2 Chitty on Contracts, 11th Am. Ed., p. 1363. To the same effect: *Mallory* v. *Mackay* (1899), 92 Fed. (C. C. A.) 749; *Blakely* v. *Sousa* (1900), 197 Pa. St. 305; 47 Atl. 286; *Sloan* v. *Williams* (1891), 138 Ill. 43; 27 N. E. 531; *Wooster* v. *Crane* (1907), 66 Atl. 1093; *Oliver* v. *Rumford* (1883), 109 U. S. 75; 3 Sup. Ct. 161; *Tuttle* v. *La Dow* (1889), 54 Hun (N. Y.), 149; 7 N. Y. Supp. 277; *N. Y. Phonograph Co.* v. *Davega* (1908), 127 A. D. (N. Y.) 222; 111 N. Y. Supp. 363; *Booth* v. *Richards* (Eng.) (1910), Times, July 14; *Hole* v. *Bradbury* (Eng.) (1879), 12 Ch. D. 886; 41 L. T. R. 153; *Stevens* v. *Benning* (Eng.) (1854), 1 K. & J. 169; 24 L. T. R. (O. S.) 154; *Reade* v. *Bentley* (Eng.) (1857), 3 K. & J. 271; 30 L. T. R. (O. S.) 268; *Griffith* v. *Tower Publ. Co.* (Eng.) (1897), 1 Ch. 21; 75 L. T. R. (N. S.) 330.

See in this connection: *Stand-*

given to produce a play, a subletting of the play to some third party has been held to be a breach of the contract.[2]

In the production of a play, which means the visualizing of the thoughts of the author employed in the manuscript, the greatest skill and ability are necessary. The success of the play is dependent to a large extent upon its proper casting, the selection of artists possessing the peculiar and particular talents necessary to properly interpret the parts and to portray the characters as conceived by the author, the planning of appropriate backgrounds, sceneries, costumes, paraphernalia and other accessories, the ability to secure bookings in desirable territory and in the best theatres. An element of confidence largely enters because the author is dependent for his compensation upon the royalties he receives from the manager for the performances. The manager has the exclusive handling of the funds and the making up of the daily and weekly receipts and a dishonest manager can easily defraud the author by means of false returns as well as a refusal to pay the royalties.

If the producer becomes a bankrupt either through vol-

ard Am. Publ. Co. v. *Methodist Concern* (1898), 33 A. D. (N. Y.) 409; 54 N. Y. Supp. 55.

[2] *Herne* v. *Liebler* (1902), 73 A. D. (N. Y.) 194; 76 N. Y. Supp. 762. Where the license was granted to defendants and the defendants agreed to produce the play, the subletting of the play to stock companies was held to be a breach of the contract. To the same effect: *Reade* v. *Bentley* (Eng.) (1857), 4 K. & J. 656; *Griffith* v. *Tower* (Eng.) (1897), 1 Ch. 21.

But when the contract granted a license to "*produce or have produced*" a production in "stock" it was held not a breach of the contract. *Peple* v. *Comstock*, N. Y. Law Journal, April 27, 1909.

untary or involuntary proceedings, the right to produce the play does not pass to the trustee in bankruptcy, but on the contrary, reverts to the licensor.[3] Upon bankruptcy the author is relieved of his obligation to complete the work.[4] Where the firm of the producer is changed subsequent to the making of the contract the license terminates.[5] Being a contract for personal services the death of either party terminates the contract.[6]

[3] *Waterman* v. *Shipman* (1893), 55 Fed. (C. C. A.) 982. A license granting the sole right to manufacture a patented article was personal and did not pass to a receiver appointed in proceedings supplementary to execution. *Bartsch* v. *Herndon*, Circuit Court of Cook County, Illinois, March 16, 1917.

Lucas v. *Moncrieff* (Eng.) (1905), 21 T. L. R. 683. Plaintiff wrote a book which was to be published by defendant, it being agreed that the profits were to be shared equally. After publication of several editions of the book, defendant became bankrupt. *Held:* that the agreement as to sharing profits did not vest the copyright in the book in the defendant; and that the contract was a personal one and that therefore defendant's trustee had no right to reprint and publish the book. *Griffith* v. *Tower Publ. Co.* (Eng.) (1897), 75 L. T. R. (N. S). 330.

See in this connection: *In re Grant Richards* (Eng.) (1907), Times, March 19; L. R. 2 K. B. 33; 76 L. J. K. B. 643; 96 L. T. 712. Where the publisher had secured the copyright and subsequently became bankrupt, the author's only remedy was to file his claim for royalties against the estate.

[4] *Gibson* v. *Carruthers Exchequer* (Eng.) (1841), 8 M. & W. 321.

[5] *Stevens* v. *Benning* (Eng.) (1854), 6 DeG. M. & G. 223; 3 Eq. Rep. 457; 24 L. J. Ch. 153; 1 Jur. (N. S.) 74; 3 W. R. 149. Where an author made a contract with a publisher, and the firm of the publisher was subsequently changed, *held* that the contract was of a personal nature and not assignable by either party without the other's consent.

[6] *Yerrington* v. *Greene* (1863),

A distinction must be carefully drawn between a license and an absolute assignment of a right. When there is

7 R. I. 593. Chief Justice Ames speaking of this class of contracts says: "The most obvious cases are the death of the party to a contract of marriage before the time fixed by it for the marriage; *the death of an author or artist before the time contracted for the finishing and delivery of the book, picture, statue or other work of art. . . .*"

Harrison v. *Conlan* (1865), 92 Mass. 85. Speaking of the rule that a contract ordinarily survives death, the court said: "But there is an exception to this rule when the contract of the deceased requires from its nature, or for other reason to be performed by him or to him personally; as, if he engages *to compose a book* or to make a painting or engraving, or engages to pay another during a specified time for attending on his person and for no other service, . . . his death ends such contracts. . . ."

Martin v. *Hunt* (1861), 83 Mass. 418. "There is a well-known class of cases where the rule is different, and the death of one of the parties discharges the contract or excuses its further performance. Such is the case where the engagement is of a strictly personal character, requiring personal skill or capacity; *as a contract to write books for a publisher* or a contract by a physician to cure a particular disease and the like." See also: *Tasker* v. *Shepherd* (Eng.), 6 Hurlst. & W. 575.

Williams on Executors, 4th American Edition, p. 1467.

Lorillard v. *Clyde* (1894), 142 N. Y. 456; 37 N. E. 489; *Greenburg* v. *Early* (1893), 4 Misc. (N. Y.) 99; 23 N. Y. Supp. 1009, which hold that contracts for personal services are abrogated by the death of the employer or the employe.

Marshal v. *Broadhurst* (Eng.) (1831), 1 Tyr. 349; 1 C. & J. 403; 9 L. J. (O. S.) Ex. 105. A contract by an author to write a book is purely personal and if he dies before its completion his estate is not liable.

Gibson v. *Carruthers* (Eng.) (1841), 8 M. & W. 343; 11 L. J. Ex. 138. Where the author becomes bankrupt while under contract to write a book, his trustee has no power to compel the completion of the work.

an assignment, the right of the producer to re-assign is unrestricted.[7]

Section 15.—Where the contract contains a negative covenant.

A negative covenant in a contract for the writing of literary works is enforceable in equity,[8] in the same

[7] *Heap* v. *Hartley* (Eng.) (1889), 42 Ch. D. 461. See this case for a detailed and careful discussion of the differences in rights conferred upon a licensee and those conferred upon an assignee.

The case holds that the fundamental difference lies in the fact that in the case of a licensee (even an exclusive licensee) no right in the property itself is given but a *personal* license to do an act which otherwise would be unlawful, while an assignment constitutes a grant conveying among other things the right to re-assign. See also: *Landeker* v. *Wolff* (Eng.) (1907), 52 Sol. J. 45; *Tree* v. *Bowkett* (Eng.) (1896), 74 L. T. 77; *Lucas* v. *Cooke* (Eng.) (1880), 13 Ch. D. 872; *Lacy* v. *Toole* (Eng.) (1867), 15 L. T. 512.

[8] *Stern* v. *Laemmle* (1911), 74 Misc. (N. Y.) 262; 133 N. Y. Supp. 1082. One Solman contracted with plaintiffs whereby they acquired the exclusive right to every song composed by him during a specified period. Solman composed a song and defendants copyrighted and published it. It was held that plaintiffs could enjoin defendants and secure accounting of defendants' profits upon the ground that under the contract with Solman the song belonged to plaintiffs; that plaintiffs could bring an action in the state court to protect their common-law rights and that defendants obtained nothing by their application for copyright registration.

Wahrheit v. *The Day Pub. Co.*, N. Y. Law Journal, Jan. 6, 1917. This was a motion for a temporary injunction. One Trufanoff was the author of a certain manuscript. He made a contract with plaintiff for the publication of the same in its newspaper, for which plaintiff paid him. Thereafter Trufanoff made some slight changes in the manuscript and contracted for the publication of the same in defendant's newspaper. The motion was granted,

manner as one contained in the contract of an actor. The same rules with respect to the unique and extraordinary character of the services contracted to be rendered, mutuality of obligations and remedies apply.[9] The third party producing the work will be enjoined and will be compelled to account for his profits derived from the exploitation of the work.[10]

enjoining the defendant newspaper from publishing such manuscript and Trufanoff from making any other disposition of the same.

Morris v. *Colman* (Eng.) (1812), 18 Vesey, 437. Lord Eldon held that a contract by a dramatist with the proprietors of a theatre not to write plays for any other theatre was enforcible.

Stiff v. *Cassell* (Eng.), 2 Jurist N. S. 348. Defendant Smith made an agreement with plaintiff to write tales for the plaintiff's journal, and a negative covenant to write for no one else. Smith then attempted to write for Cassell. *Held* that such a contract was enforcible.

Ward v. *Beeton* (Eng.) (1874), L. R. 19 Eq. 207; 23 W. R. 533. Plaintiff purchased the copyright of a book from defendant. Defendant agreed to give his whole time to plaintiff's service and not to engage in any other business. Defendant was restrained from advertising a rival work.

See in this connection: *Gabriel* v. *McCabe* (1896), 74 Fed. (C. C.) 743. Discusses the right of the licensee to publish the work in an abridged form, and holds that he had made no unfair use of his license.

[9] See Sections 36 and 37. *Tams* v. *Witmark* (1900), 30 Misc. (N. Y.) 293; 63 N. Y. Supp. 721; aff'd 48 A. D. (N. Y.) 632; 63 N. Y. Supp. 1117. It was held that it was sufficient in an action for infringement of property rights in a work where the plaintiff derived title from some third party to allege in the complaint that plaintiff duly acquired and became the exclusive owner of the work. The courts will not treat such an allegation as a conclusion of law.

[10] *Stern* v. *Laemmle* (1911), 74 Misc. (N. Y.) 262; 133 N. Y. Supp. 1082.

Section 16.—Where the work is to be to the satisfaction of the producer.

Where the author agrees to write a work which shall be satisfactory to the producer, the same rules of law apply which have been enunciated by the courts in the case of "satisfaction" contracts between actors and producers:[11]

Section 17.—Where the contract provides for the writing of a libelous, immoral or seditious work.

Neither the producer nor the author may maintain an action upon any contract which provides for the writing and reproduction of a work which is to contain a criminal libel, immoral or seditious matter.[12]

Section 18.—Where the license granted is a sole and exclusive one.

Unless it is expressly agreed that the license granted shall be a sole and exclusive one, the licensor may grant licenses to produce the same play for the same period and within the same territory to any number of persons.[13]

[11] See Section 38.

Haven v. *Russell* (1895), 34 N. Y. Supp. 292. Plaintiff agreed to write a play for defendants "if it proved satisfactory to them." *Held* that as the contract involved fancy, taste and judgment, actual satisfaction must be proved as a condition precedent to recovery.

[12] *Apthorpe* v. *Neville* (Eng.) (1907), Times, May 31.

[13] *Hart* v. *Cort* (1913), 83 Misc. (N. Y.) 44; 144 N. Y. Supp. 627.

Willis v. *Tibbals* (1871), 1 Jones & Spencer (N. Y.), 220. A license given to a publisher to print and vend a book upon a royalty basis is not a sole and exclusive license unless the contract expressly so provides.

But where the license is exclusive, the licensee may enjoin any and all third parties claiming through his licensor,[14] as well as the licensor himself,[15] from producing the work in the territory for which the sole license has been granted to him.

Section 19.—Where the contract contains limitations as to methods of exploitation.

If the contract provides that the motion picture shall be produced in a special manner only, as, where the producer agrees that the film shall not be shown without the playing of certain music written specially for use with the exhibition of the film, or that the film shall be shown in none but first-class theatres, the licensor can

[14] *Widmer* v. *Thompson* (1878), 56 How. Pr. (N. Y.) 91. Where defendant by agreement transferred to plaintiff the sole right to produce the play in America, the contract providing that unless the play was performed at least fifty times within one year from the date of the agreement and forty times yearly thereafter the rights of the plaintiff would cease, at the option of the defendant, and providing further that upon the payment of a specified sum within a year there was to be an absolute conveyance to plaintiff, it was held:

(1) Plaintiff succeeded to all of defendant's rights in such play in America.

(2) Plaintiff could enjoin defendant or any party claim through him from producing the play.

Barnett v. *Q. & C. Co.* (1915), 226 Fed. (C. C. A.) 935. An "exclusive license under a patent is a unique property right, against the destruction of which a court of equity will give protection by injunctive relief."

[15] *Waterman* v. *Shipman* (1893), 55 Fed. (C. C. A.) 982. An exclusive licensee of a patent may maintain an action under the patent laws where the patentee is guilty of infringement and the licensee may join all other parties who have combined with his patentee to infringe his rights.

restrain any violation of such covenants.[16] But in such case the licensor does not reserve to himself the right to have a film of his work produced without the special music or in other than first-class theatres.[17]

Section 20.—Where the work is to be produced at a definite time.

Where an author agrees to furnish the producer with a play or scenario on or before a specified date, his failure to do so renders him liable for whatever damages have been sustained by the producer, and the producer is

[16] *Herne* v. *Liebler* (1902), 73 A. D. (N. Y.) 194; 76 N. Y. Supp. 762. An injunction will be granted to enjoin the production of a play in stock by stock companies where the contract provides that the play shall be produced in none but first-class theatres.

See in this connection: *Peple* v. *Comstock*, N. Y. Law Journal, April 27, 1909. Bischoff, J.: "So far as a breach is alleged in the original complaint, the allegation proceeds upon a construction of the contract which would limit the defendant's rights in the play to a production by himself as manager, the plaintiff's assertion being that a breach occurred through the defendant's permitting the use of the play by 'stock' companies managed by other persons. Upon this question I am of the opinion that the contract does not bear the construction for which the plaintiff contends. Express permission was given the defendant 'to produce or have produced' this dramatic composition, and the words 'have produced' obviously extend to a production at the hands of others for the defendant's benefit."

[17] *Frohman* v. *Fitch* (1914), 164 A. D. (N. Y.) 231; 149 N. Y. Supp. 633. Where the licensor grants an exclusive right to produce a play in first-class theatres and in a first-class manner, he does not reserve to himself the right to produce such play in second-class theatres and in a second-class manner.

entitled to a return of all moneys advanced to the author under the contract.[18]

The producer, however, may waive his right to have the finished work delivered upon the specified day, and after such waiver he may not maintain an action for breach of contract before the expiration of a reasonable time after the giving of notice to the author to deliver the manuscript.[19]

Where an author is engaged to write a play or scenario and before the completion of the work the producer abandons the project of making a motion picture from such play or scenario, the author may maintain an action

[18] *Yeamans* v. *Tannehill* (1891), 15 N. Y. Supp. 958. Under a contract by which defendant agreed to write a play for plaintiffs, it was shown that the play was not completed in time, and plaintiffs brought their action to recover back the moneys advanced under the contract. Verdict in their favor sustained.

Ward Lock & Co. v. *Long* (Eng.) (1906), 75 L. J. Ch. 732; 95 L. T. 345; 22 T. L. R. 798; 2 Ch. 550. Here the author furnished a story of 70,000 words, instead of one of 80,000 words as agreed. *Held* a breach of the contract.

Gale v. *Leckie* (Eng.) (1817), 2 Stark, 107; 19 R. R. 692. Here the author refused to supply a manuscript after a part of the work had been printed. It was held that the publisher might maintain an action against him.

[19] *Mann* v. *Maurel* (1911), 126 N. Y. Supp. 731. Defendant agreed to furnish plaintiff with a complete manuscript in a specified month. Contract further provided that any extension granted to defendant to deliver the play should extend the time for its production for a proportionate period. Parties negotiated respecting the play after the time fixed for delivery of the manuscript. It was held that plaintiff could not maintain an action for breach before the expiration of a reasonable time after the giving of notice to defendant to deliver the finished manuscript.

for the reasonable value of his services without delivering or tendering the manuscript.[20]

If the contract provides for the writing of a number of plays, and the contract is not severable, and before the completion of the entire number of plays, the producer commits some breach of the contract, the author may maintain an action for breach of the entire contract.[21]

Section 21.—Where the payment to the author is based upon a percentage of the gross receipts or net profits.

We may have the situation where a work is sold for reproduction in motion pictures upon condition that the

[20] *Planché* v. *Colburn* (Eng.) (1831), 1 M. & Scott, 51; 8 Bing. 14; 5 Cas. & P. 58. Where an author was engaged to write a treatise for a periodical the publication of which was abandoned before the completion of such treatise.

Held that the author was entitled to compensation on the basis of quantum meruit, without delivering or tendering the treatise.

Gollancz v. *Dent* (Eng.) (1903), 88 L. T. 358.

Thorne v. *French* (1893), 4 Misc. (N. Y.) 436; 24 N. Y. Supp. 694; aff'd 143 N. Y. 679; 39 N. E. 494.

[21] *Clark* v. *West* (1910), 137 A. D. (N. Y.) 23; 122 N. Y. Supp. 380. Where the contract provides that B shall write a book, take out copyright in his own name and then assign the copyright to A for all of which A agrees to pay B, it is a breach of the contract for A to take out copyright in his name in the book.

Where B agrees to write five books for A and A agrees to pay B specified compensation upon publication of such books, B having written and delivered to A one book refuses to write or deliver balance because of some breach of the contract by A. *Held* that B may sue for breach of entire contract, contract not being severable, and secure damages for such breach.

author receive in lieu of all compensation a percentage of the gross receipts or net profits. If there is no time limit within which the film is to be made and exhibited, the author is entitled to have the work reproduced and exhibited within a reasonable time. Should the producer fail to do so, the author may either rescind the contract of sale or sue for damages for breach of the contract and recover the reasonable value of the work for motion pictures. If the agreement provides for the exhibition of the motion picture within a specified time the same principles apply.[22]

Difficulty, however, is encountered in fixing the value of a literary work for motion pictures. It is almost always problematical whether a work will be successful when reproduced in motion pictures. The play itself, the staging thereof, the acting of the performers who participate in its creation, the character of the advertising, the

[22] *Bobbs-Merrill Co.* v. *Universal Film Mfg. Co.* (1916), 160 N. Y. Supp. 37. Plaintiff licensed defendant to make photoplays from three books, defendant agreeing to pay a specified percentage of the gross receipts and paying an advance upon such royalties of a specified sum. Defendant further agreed to produce the motion pictures within nine months after the signing of the contract. Defendant failed to produce the films within the specified period and plaintiff notified defendant that because of such failure the contract was terminated and all rights granted to defendant reverted to it. Court granted injunction restraining defendant from asserting any rights under the contract.

White v. *Constable & Co.* (Eng.) (1901), Times, March 23. A failure to publish a book upon the date fixed by the contract renders the publisher liable for damages resulting from such delay. But see *Kerker* v. *Lederer* (1900), 30 Misc. (N. Y.) 651; 64 N. Y. Supp. 506.

methods of release are some of the elements that must be taken into account. Courts are reluctant to permit juries to fix the value of such rights, unless definite and concrete evidence of the value of such rights with respect to the work in question is adduced.[23]

If, however, the work has been reproduced in motion pictures and the producer fails or refuses to continue its exploitation, evidence showing how the motion picture was received, how the newspapers treated its production, criticism of the press, the gross rentals on account of exhibitions of the film, are all proper elements upon which the jury can base an estimate of the value of the motion picture rights of the work.[24]

Section 22.—Where the amount to be paid to the author is guaranteed.

The agreement may guarantee a specified amount as the author's share within a certain period. If the film is not reproduced and exploited during the period, or if the

[23] *Levison* v. *Oes* (1917), 98 Misc. (N. Y.) 260; *Wakeman* v. *Wheeler* (1886), 101 N. Y. 205; 4 N. E. 264; *Bernstein* v. *Meech* (1891), 130 N. Y. 354; 29 N. E. 255; *Benyaker* v. *Scherz* (1905), 103 A. D. (N. Y.) 192; 92 N. Y. Supp. 1089; *New York Academy of Music* v. *Hackett* (1858), 2 Hilt. (N. Y.) 217.

[24] *Ellis* v. *Thompson* (1896), 1 A. D. (N. Y.) 606; 37 N. Y. Supp. 468. Defendant agreed to produce a play in a first class theatre. The play was a failure. On the trial of an action for breach of the contract, the court held that plaintiff could show how the play was acted, what the audience said and did, how the newspapers treated its production, and the criticism of the press, and whether the actors were called before the curtain, and how many times, and whether there was applause. *Charley* v. *Potthoff* (1903), 95 N. W. 124.

author's share of the receipts or profits during such period is less than the guaranteed amount, then the author may recover an amount which, when added to the sum that he has received, will equal such guarantee.

Section 23.—Where the payment to the author is a stipulated amount per performance or per period.

Contracts have frequently been made for production of plays upon the stage whereby the producer has agreed to pay to the author a stipulated amount for each performance. It has been held that where the producer has agreed to exploit the play for a specified period, the author may recover for the entire period at the stipulated amount per performance, whether the play had been produced during such period or not. The same applies where the payment is made upon the basis of a specified amount per week or other period.[25] If the producer does not

[25] *Thorne* v. *French* (1893), 4 Misc. (N. Y.) 436; 24 N. Y. Supp. 694. Plaintiffs owned the opera "The Maid of Plymouth," and agreed to give defendant the performing rights during a specified time. The latter was to produce it after February 13, 1892. After that date defendant did not produce the opera but permitted Richard Mansfield to play in repertoire at his theatre. Plaintiff sought to enjoin him from using his theatre for that purpose. (1) The injunction was denied but plaintiff was permitted to recover $2,000 damages.

(2) *Held* also that as defendants had announced their intention not to go on with the contract, plaintiff was absolved from the necessity of tendering performance.

Daly v. *Stetson* (1890), 118 N. Y. 269; 23 N. E. 369. Plaintiff had contracted to sell to defendant the exclusive right to give performances of "Pique" and "Divorce" for thirty consecutive weeks for $200 a week.

obligate himself to produce the play for a definite period, he is only liable to pay for actual performances.[26]

He produced these plays for five weeks, then ceased doing so. Plaintiff sued for the balance due for 25 weeks amounting to $5,000. *Held* that plaintiff was entitled to recover as it was a breach of the contract.

[26] *Kennedy* v. *Rolfe* (1916), 174 A. D. (N. Y.) 10; 160 N. Y. Supp. 93. Plaintiff contracted with defendant to write a sketch for him which the latter was to produce in vaudeville. The contract provided that plaintiff was *"to be paid a royalty of $25 a week per each playing week for a period of 70 weeks."*

Held that this did not amount to a guarantee of 70 weeks, and a verdict in plaintiff's favor was reversed and complaint was dismissed.

Schonberg v. *Cheney* (1875), 3 Hun (N. Y.), 677. Defendant owned a theatre. He contracted with plaintiff to produce a play to be written by the latter, and to pay him $20 for each performance. Since the contract, however, only specified one date, May 7th, as the date of performance, and there was no other provision or extension it was held that plaintiff could not recover more than $20.

See in this connection: *St. 'Cyr* v. *Sothern & Marlowe* (1910), 140 A. D. (N. Y.) 888; 125 N. Y. Supp. 10. A contract was made between the parties to the action for the production by the defendants of a play owned by plaintiff. The contract provided that the defendants pay to plaintiff the sum of one thousand dollars as advance royalties, the said sum to be *forfeited* to plaintiff if the play was not produced within one year from the date of the contract. The contract also contained a clause that the defendants would give thirty public performances during the first year for which performances the plaintiff was to receive a minimum of $50 per performance. The contract was for a term of five years. Plaintiff contended that under the contract she was entitled to a minimum of $1,500 a year, thirty performances at fifty dollars each for a period of five years. Contract construed. *Held* that the guaranty clause was to be construed together with the forfeiture clause and

The author is entitled to his royalties for performances of his work whether such performances were given by the producer with whom he contracted or by the producer's licensee.[27] A producer will not be permitted to set up, as a defense, in an action for royalties, the invalidity of the author's copyright.[28]

upon defendant's failure to produce the play, they forfeited the $1,000 paid to plaintiff but were not liable for any other sum.

[27] *Neufeld* v. *Chapman* (Eng.) (1901), Times, Oct. 31. Plaintiff assigned copyright in his book to defendants who agreed to pay him a percentage on the published price of all copies sold beyond a specified number. *Held* that plaintiff was entitled to royalties upon all copies of magazines sold which contained his work in serial form, the published price to be estimated by taking a part of the published price of the magazine in proportion to the space taken up therein by the selection from plaintiff's book.

But see: *Nichols* v. *Amalgamated Press* (Eng.) (1908), C. A. May 12. Where the publisher was the sole owner of the copyright under a contract which contained no limitations, he could not be compelled to pay royalties for the publication of the work by a third party, even though made with the publishers' approval.

[28] *Nilsson* v. *De Haven* (1900), 47 A. D. (N. Y.) 537; 62 N. Y. Supp. 506; aff'd 168 N. Y. 656; 61 N. E. 1131.

Hart v. *Fox* (1917), N. Y. Law Journal, August 24th. "He secured a license from the plaintiff and cannot be heard to impeach his title."

See in this connection: *Sea Gull Specialty Co.* v. *Humphrey*, *Humphrey* v. *Sea Gull Specialty Co.* (1917), 242 Fed. (C. C. A.) 272; affirming the judgment upon the opinion of the court below.

The following opinion was filed in the court below:

In this case defendant was using certain patented box-making machines under a license from plaintiff and owed royalties. Another concern, using an infringing machine, invaded its territory and

Section 24.—Where the amount of damages in the event of a breach is stipulated.

If the parties fix a stipulated amount as damages in the event of the failure of one to deliver the finished manuscript or the other to reproduce and exhibit the work on or before a specified date, the courts will permit a recovery of the amount fixed by the parties as their damages.[29]

succeeded in taking away defendant's largest customer by underbidding its prices. Defendant retained the machines, but declined to pay royalties, on the ground plaintiff was obligated to prevent competition, and the loss on sales amounted to more than the royalties due. I sustained a demurrer to the jurisdiction of the court, and while the matter was pending in the Supreme Court on appeal the parties compromised and settled all of their differences, except the question of the amount of royalties due. The judgment dismissing the bill was reversed.

The bill prayed for an injunction, for cancellation of the license and the return of the machines, and for an accounting. Those questions are now out of the case, but the question as to the royalties is before me. Had the defendants' territory been invaded by a licensee of plaintiff, or by one allowed to infringe by connivance of, or agreement with, plaintiff, a different question might be presented. The license did not guarantee defendant against loss by the competition of infringers. The subsequent correspondence did not amend the contract, or create an estoppel to claim royalties already earned. The greatest right defendant could have exercised under the circumstances was to abandon the contract after notice to plaintiff and its failure to vigorously prosecute the infringers, but that course was not adopted.

There will be a decree in favor of plaintiff for $3,786.18 and for costs.

[29] *Conreid Metropolitan Opera v. Brin* (1910), 66 Misc. (N. Y.) 282; 123 N. Y. Supp. 6.

Section 25.—Where the contract provides for a forfeiture upon failure to pay the royalties due.

The producer may fail or refuse to pay the royalties due an author on account of the exhibition of the film. If the contract provides for the forfeiture of all rights by the producer upon his failure to pay the royalties when they become due the author by giving the producer the notice required by the contract between them, revokes all the rights granted to the producer and may enjoin him from making further use of the film should he attempt to do so.[30] He may also maintain an action at

[30] *Arden* v. *Lubin*, N. Y. Law Journal, Mch. 2, 1916. Cohalan, J.: "Action for an injunction and an accounting. The plaintiff, an actor and dramatist, entered into an agreement with the defendant Lubin whereby the latter agreed to present certain plays by means of motion pictures in consideration whereof Lubin agreed to pay the plaintiff a certain fixed sum as an actor, and further agreed to pay him a royalty of twenty per cent of the gross sales or rentals and extra charges of whatsoever name and nature to be derived by the defendant Lubin from the exploitation and distribution of the motion pictures in America. One play under this agreement was produced. It is admitted in the answer that the plaintiff complied with all the terms and conditions of the contract on his part to be performed. The plaintiff however alleges that the defendants violated the agreement by (1) failing to present all the plays, (2) failing to send stipulated statements, (3) failing to make payments of royalties at times fixed in the agreement, and (4) failing to render true statements and pay full amounts of the royalties as provided for in the agreement. The contract provided that statements and payments should be made commencing on the first day of August, 1914, and continuing quarterly thereafter. It appears that no statement was rendered on that date and no quarterly statements were rendered either on the first day of November, 1914,

law for the royalties which have become due. Where the contract does not contain a forfeiture clause, or where the payment is not made a condition of the grant, the failure to pay royalties does not terminate the producer's

nor on the first day of February, 1915, nor the first day of May, 1915. In fact, the first statement and check were received after the 26th day of July, 1915. I am satisfied that the failure to send these statements and pay the royalties thereunder within the time fixed by the agreement was a breach sufficient to warrant the termination of the agreement [*Heneky* v. *Stark*, 128 N. Y. Supp. 761; *Weber* v. *Mapes*, 98 A. D. (N. Y.) 165]. Furthermore, the plaintiff contends that he is entitled to twenty per cent of the gross income derived by the defendants from the pictures without any deduction. The defendant Lubin asserts that he is only accountable for twenty per cent of the gross profit and rentals which actually came into his hands. The contract, however, provides that the plaintiff was to receive twenty per cent of the gross sales and therein the words 'profits' or 'expenses' are not mentioned. In a word, the defendants claim that they should be permitted to deduct from the gross sales derived from the picture the expenses paid in exploiting the same. I am of the opinion that the contract shows that it was the defendant's duty to exploit the picture and that the charges therefor were not to be borne by plaintiff. Judgment for the plaintiff."

On the question of waiver of right of forfeiture, see: *Barnett* v. *Q. & C. Co.* (1915), 226 Fed. (C. C. A.) 935. "A reserved right of forfeiture for breach of an obligation may be waived before breach by an act or declaration inducing the licensee to continue in the performance of its obligations and upon which it was reasonably justified in relying as showing an intent to suspend the exercise of the right."

Savage v. *Neely* (1896), 8 A. D. (N. Y.) 316; 40 N. Y. Supp. 946. See on question of defendant's examination before trial, where action is brought by an author against a publisher for an accounting of sales where author is entitled to a specified royalty upon copies sold.

rights.[31] The author still has his remedy at law for the royalties which have become due.[32] It may also be noted

[31] *Kerker* v. *Lederer* (1900), 30 Misc. (N. Y.) 651; 64 N. Y. Supp. 506. The action was brought by the composers of "The Belle of New York," to restrain the defendants from producing the musical comedy and to compel defendants to account for royalties alleged to be due them. Defendants failed to give the notice required by the contract in order to secure a renewal of the performing rights for the theatrical season during which they were producing the play. *Held* that by accepting royalties, plaintiffs waived this provision of the contract. It was held further that upon their failure to pay the royalties, defendant's rights were not terminated as the contract contained no forfeiture clause and finally that it was doubtful whether plaintiffs had a cause of action in equity, the court intimating that the proper form of action was one at law for royalties due.

Karst v. *Prang Educational Co.* (1909), 132 A. D. (N. Y.) 197; 116 N. Y. Supp. 1049. Where the copyright in a work was in the defendant, a publisher, and the defendant refuses to pay the stipulated royalties, the author's remedy is an action at law and not one in equity.

[32] *Moore* v. *Coyne* (1906), 113 A. D. (N. Y.) 52; 98 N. Y. Supp. 892. When a state court of equity will refuse to entertain jurisdiction of an action for breach of a contract to pay royalties.

"The contract simply provides for the payment of royalties upon a patented article if manufactured or sold, and if the same have been manufactured or sold under the contract, then this gives the plaintiff the right, *not to an accounting*, but to the royalties stipulated to be paid, for which an action at law may be maintained. . . ."

Gollancz v. *Dent & Co.* (Eng.) (1903), 88 L. T. 358. Where an author is engaged to edit a work upon a royalty basis the remedy for the breach of the contract in refusing to permit him to edit the book is an action-at-law for damages.

McCullough v. *Pence* (1895), 85 Hun (N. Y.), 271; 32 N. Y. Supp. 986. "It is not of every action in which it is necessary to

here that where the contract provides that the license shall be contingent upon the giving of a specified number of performances during specified periods, a failure to give such required number of performances will terminate the license.

To sum up, if the contract specifies a definite date for the reproduction of the work, or no time is mentioned, and the work must be reproduced within a reasonable time, a breach of such provision of the contract gives the author the right to rescind. If, however, the only breach of the contract is the failure to pay the compensation therein provided, and payment is not made a condition of the grant, a breach gives the author nothing more than a right of action at law for his compensation.

Section 26.—Where manuscript is lost or converted after submission to the producer.

There is a good consideration to the producer when a manuscript is submitted to him, namely, the opportunity of reading the manuscript. For that reason he is not

take an account that equity has jurisdiction. There must be something more than the mere right to an account. It would seem that there must be some trust or fiduciary relation between the parties in order to justify a resort to a court of equity or a decree for an accounting. Even the existence of a bare agency is not sufficient. *Marvin* v. *Brooks*, 94 N. Y. 71. In the case at bar there was not the semblance of any trust. The action is brought to enforce a mere contract obligation to pay royalties, and the only final judgment would be a money judgment. The defendant in an action at law, could have a reference to take the accounts, if necessary, and, if a discovery was needed, an examination before trial was open."

a gratuitous bailee and will be liable to the author for its value if the same is lost through his or his employes' negligence.[33] But where the manuscript is submitted solely for criticism and advice, there is a gratuitous bailment and no liability attaches in the absence of gross negligence.[34] In the case of a conversion of the manuscript, the author is entitled to recover its value, and he may enjoin the possessor from publishing the same and compel him to deliver it up.[35]

Section 27.—Where the work is secured by means of a prize contest.

Where a producer offers a prize for any story or scenario submitted to him which he will accept and reproduce, the producer's rights are limited to the reproduction and exploitation of the work in motion pictures, unless the offer specifically provides that the prize will be given upon condition that all rights in the accepted work shall vest in him.[36]

[33] *Stone* v. *Long* (Eng.) (1903), the Author, Nov. issue.

[34] *Adams* v. *Grossmith* (Eng.) (1911), Times, March 9. An author who submits his play to an actor for criticism and advice has no claim for the loss of the manuscript unless the actor has been guilty of gross negligence. The actor is a gratuitous bailee.

Bullen v. *The Swan Electric* (Eng.) (1906), Times, Feb. 8, 22 T. L. R. 275. No liability attached to a printer who stored without charge plates belonging to his customer and the plates were lost. *Held* that the printer was a "gratuitous bailee" and that the fact of the loss did not raise any presumption on his part of negligence.

[35] *Alexander* v. *Manners Sutton* (Eng.) (1911), Times, March 28.

[36] *Ketelbey* v. *Maggett* (Eng.) (1911), Times, Feb. 8. Where a musical composition was submitted in a prize contest and the condition of the contest was that the publisher would publish and sell the accepted work it was

Section 28.—On the question whether an outright purchaser is required to reproduce the work.

A producer purchasing outright motion picture material is not required to reproduce the same unless he has contracted to do so.[37]

held that there was no implied condition that the winner would assign the copyright in the work to the publisher.

[37] In *Morang & Co.* v. *Le Sueur* (Can.) (1911), 45 Can. Sup. Ct. 95. An author sold his manuscript outright to a publisher. There was no undertaking on the part of the publisher, contained in the agreement, to publish the work. Upon the failure of the publisher to print and sell the work the author brought an action, after tendering back the amount he received in payment, to recover the manuscript. It was held by a divided court that in the case of a sale of a manuscript by an author to a publisher, there was implied an agreement on the part of the publisher to publish and upon his failure so to do, the author upon tendering the purchase money, was entitled to secure back his manuscript.

In a strong dissenting opinion Judge Duff takes issue with the decision of the majority court and what we believe is the more logical position. He says:

". . . It seems to me that it was necessary for the adequate protection of the publisher and of its enterprise that it should, on payment of the stipulated price, acquire the author's entire interest and property in the manuscript which he was employed to produce, with all rights which such proprietorship carries, including that of withholding the book from publication (quoting case) otherwise the publisher might find that it had brought about the production of a work which it could not make use of, but which might be used by the author very much to its detriment.

There can be no doubt that the parties, contemplating no event except publication, intended that for the $500, to be paid to the author, the defendant company should acquire all his rights in the book he was employed to write—his common-law literary property in it before

Section 29.—On the question whether the producer is entitled to a refund of advance payment.

If a license is granted for a specified period and an advance payment is made on account of royalties payable to the author under such license, the producer may not maintain an action against the author upon the termination of the contract period for any part of the advance which has not been earned unless the contract expressly provides for such refund.

Section 30.—On the question whether the contract may be rescinded where the author made a poor bargain or where fraud is involved.

The fact that the author in granting a license or making

publication, and his right to statutory copyright upon publication. Both parties expected that the plaintiff would succeed in producing a work of such character and merit that the defendant would publish it. Both took some risk at this point—the defendant took the risk of investing its $500 in an unsuitable book—the plaintiff the risk of failing to secure the opportunity of enhancing his literary reputation which the publication of his work might be expected to afford. I appreciate the observation of Tendal, C. J., in *Planche* v. *Colburn* that an author is actuated by the desire for literary reputation as well as for pecuniary profit. For his literary fame he depends on publication. But it is quite consistent with the contract now under discussion, reviewed in the light of all the circumstances surrounding it, that the author refrained from stipulating for publication, or in the alternative for the return of his manuscript and the right to have it published otherwise, because he relied upon his ability to produce a book of which the defendant's own business interests would ensure the publication, and he was prepared to take the risk of the defendant suppressing it."

See also: Copinger "Law of Copyright," 4th Edition, p. 793.

an outright sale had made a poor bargain, does not entitle him to rescind the contract, unless fraud has been practiced upon him.[38] And in the case of fraud he must tender back the benefits received by him before revoking the license or rescinding the sale.[39]

Section 31.—On the question whether the contract may be rescinded where the producer made a poor bargain or fraud is involved.

The same rules apply to a motion picture producer. He may not rescind the contract because he had paid too much for the rights; nor may he set up as a defense in an action to recover royalties that he has been induced to enter into the contract through fraud and misrepresentation without alleging that he has surrendered the license and the benefits received by him under the license.[40]

[38] *Hackett* v. *Walter* (1913), 80 Misc. (N. Y.) 340; 142 N. Y. Supp. 209. Here it was held that the court was not authorized to rescind a sale because the author used poor judgment in securing a small amount for his work.

[39] *Hackett* v. *Walter* (1913), 80 Misc. (N. Y.) 340; 142 N. Y. Supp. 209. Defendant Walter purchased a play from plaintiff, rewrote it, and thereafter the play was produced successfully. It was held that plaintiff could not have the sale set aside because of fraud, where he retained the benefits received by him under the contract of sale.

[40] *Outcault* v. *Bonheur* (1907), 120 A. D. 168; 104 N. Y. Supp. 1099. A defense to an action to recover royalties for the use of a play which alleges that the licensee was induced to enter into the contract by fraud and misrepresentation of the licensor who was not the author or owner, does not state a defense in the absence of allegations showing that the defendant rescinded the contract and offered such restoration as would place the licensor in the

Section 32.—On the question whether a contract to write will be specifically enforced.

Equity will not compel an author to specifically perform a contract providing for the writing of a book or play.[41]

Section 33.—On the question whether the licensor may maintain an action against third parties.

We have already discussed the right of a producer possessing a sole and exclusive license to enjoin his licensor as well as all other persons claiming through such licensor from violating his license.[42] It has also been held that the licensor, although he has for a period granted away his rights, may maintain actions against third parties for any infringement of his work, as such an infringement affects his remainder interest in his property.[43]

Section 34.—On the question whether courts grant injunctions pendente lite more readily in actions of this nature.

In conclusion, attention may be called to the fact that

position in which he stood before the granting of the license. If he elects to disaffirm, he must return the benefits received.

A counterclaim for royalties already paid, is demurrable when it does not allege that the license was surrendered and the benefits received by the licensee restored to plaintiff.

[41] *Whitwood* v. *Hardman* (Eng.) (1891), 2 Ch. 416.

[42] See Section 18.

[43] *Fleron* v. *Lackaye* (1891), 14 N. Y. Supp. 292. The owner of a dramatization who licenses a third party to produce such dramatization may in his own name maintain an action against one who pirates the dramatization. "An injury to it (the play) reaches his proprietary right, notwithstanding the temporary license given" to a third party "to perform the play for a limited period."

injunctions pendente lite are granted more readily in actions brought by or against authors or persons claiming through such authors on account of breaches of contracts with respect to their literary products than in other actions, because the delay involved in waiting for a final decree will frequently amount to a denial of justice.[44]

[44] *Chappell* v. *Fields* (1914), 210 Fed. (C. C. A.) 864; *Comstock* v. *Lopokowa* (1911), 190 Fed. (C. C.) 599; *Nixon* v. *Doran* (1909), 168 Fed. (C. C.) 575.

But see: *Kerker* v. *Lederer* (1900), 30 Misc. (N. Y.) 651; 64 N. Y. Supp. 506, where it was held that because of a sharp conflict of facts no temporary injunction would be granted.

CHAPTER III

THE PRODUCER

The Actor

SEC. 35. In general.
36. Injunction for breach of contract where services are special, unique and extraordinary.
37. Injunctions pendente lite.
38. Services to be "satisfactory."
39. Length of engagement.
40. Two weeks' notice and other customs.
41. Contracts for work on Sunday.
42. Services "actually performed."
43. Substantial performance.
44. Anticipatory breach.
45. Exposure to obscenity, ridicule, degradation, etc.
46. Renewal of contract—modification.
47. How many causes of action for breach.
48. Actor's remedy for breach.
49. Profits as a basis for damages.
50. Producer's offer of re-employment after breach.
51. Grounds for discharge.
52. Actor's breach of the contract—damages.
53. Changing motion picture.
54. Contracts with infants.
55. Inability of producer where studio closed by the authorities.
56. Questions of travel.
57. Booking agencies.
58. Workmen's Compensation Acts.
59. Garnishment.
60. Serial stories.

61. Escrow agents.
62. Where joint venture.
63. Royalties in addition to salary.
64. Law governing validity of contract.
65. Contract labor and exclusion laws.
66. Performance in unlicensed theatre.
67. Contracts for transportation—damages.
68. Power of company's officer to contract—agency.
69. Costumes.
70. Enticement of actor.
71. Libel of actor.

Section 35.—In general.

We have seen that the application of old legal principles to the evanescent forces of a new industry is not always easy of accomplishment.

Thus far we have viewed this shifting adjustment from the standpoint of the outsider—from him who occasionally rubs shoulders with those in the business.

We shall now discuss the outcome of the relationships of the various parties directly connected with the motion picture—the film producer, the actor, the scenario writer, the director and so on.

Section 36.—Injunction for breach of contract where services are special, unique and extraordinary.

When an actor of special ability breaches his contract with the motion picture producer, it becomes very important to know how the producer may seek redress, and avoid the irreparable damages that would follow such a breach of the contract.

The rule is that where the services of the actor are special, unique and extraordinary and the damage to the producer would be irreparable, the latter may restrain him from appearing elsewhere, provided his contract contains a negative covenant not to appear elsewhere.[1]

While this is in effect tantamount to decreeing specific performance of a contract for personal services, equity makes the exception to the general rule where the services of the artist are of such an unusual nature.

A contract for the exclusive services of an actor or dramatist is valid and not in restraint of trade.[2]

[1] *Lumley* v. *Wagner* (Eng.), (1852), 1 DeG. M. & G. 604; *Lawrence* v. *Dixey* (1907), 119 A. D. (N. Y.) 295; 104 N. Y. Supp. 516; *Standard Fashion Co.* v. *Siegel-Cooper Co.* (1898), 157 N. Y. 60; 51 N. E. 408; *Phila. Ball Club* v. *Lajoie* (1902), 202 Pa. St. 210; 51 Atl. 973; *Grimston* v. *Cunningham* (Eng.) (1894), 1 Q. B. D. 125; *Comstock* v. *Lopokowa* (1911), 190 Fed. (C. C.) 599.

McCaull v. *Braham* (1883), 16 Fed. (C. C.) 37. This case contains a summary of the English and early American decisions respecting the issuance of injunctions in actions of this character.

Daly v. *Smith* (1874), 49 How. Pr. (N. Y.) 150. This is a leading case in this country on the right to injunction in the case of unique and extraordinary services.

[2] *Morris* v. *Colman* (Eng.) (1812), 18 Ves. 437; *Tivoli, Manchester* v. *Colley* (Eng.) (1904), 20 T. L. R. 437; *Mapleson* v. *Bentham* (Eng.) (1871), 20 W. R. 176; *London Music Hall* v. *Austin* (Eng.) (1908), Times, Dec. 16; *Clark Paper & Mfg. Co.* v. *Stenacker* (1917), 100 Misc. (N. Y.) 173.

See in this connection: *American League* v. *Chase* (1914), 86 Misc. (N. Y.) 441; 149 N. Y. Supp. 6. Bissell, J. "A court of equity insisting that 'he who comes into equity must come with clean hands,' will not lend its aid to promote an unconscionable transaction of the character which the plaintiff is endeavoring to maintain, and strengthen by its application for this injunction. The court will not assist in enforcing an agreement which is a part of a general plan having for

In determining whether the services are special, unique and extraordinary the court will take into consideration the salary stipulated under the contract, the production, the probability of damage, and the indispensability of the actor. Indeed this last named quality is the acid test.[3]

its object the maintenance of a monopoly, interference with the personal liberty of a citizen, and the control of his full right to labor wherever and for whom he pleases; and will not extend its aid to further the purposes and practices of an unlawful combination, by restraining the defendant from working for anyone but the plaintiff."

[3] *Edwards* v. *Cissy Fitzgerald* (1895), N. Y. Law Journal, January 16. Passing on the question of replacement, the court said: "She has a charm peculiar to herself. By her grace, beauty, and artistic methods she has become a special attraction. The plaintiff would undoubtedly find it difficult to procure a substitute who would be likely to produce a similar impression upon the public."

Ziegfeld v. *Norworth* (1909), 134 A. D. (N. Y.) 951; 118 N. Y. Supp. 1151. On a question of injunction it was shown that the defendant was the real star around whom the whole production of plaintiff's play centred, and that she had been heavily featured in announcements and advertisements so as to give her real prominence.

Universal Talking Machine v. *English* (1901), 34 Misc. (N. Y.) 342; 69 N. Y. Supp. 813. "The important fact is that notwithstanding defendant's defection, plaintiff is still able to produce master records, which defendant swears and plaintiff does not deny are quite as good, if not a little better than those which defendant made. It does not appear, therefore, that the same services that defendant agreed to render cannot readily be obtained from another, and the application for an injunction upon this ground cannot prevail."

See also: *Johnson Co.* v. *Hunt* (1892), 66 Hun, 504; aff'd 142 N. Y. 621; 37 N. E. 564 (manager and advertising solicitor); *Strobridge Litho. Co.* v. *Crane* (1890), 58 Hun, 611; 12 N. Y. Supp. 898 (lithographer and designer); *Kessler* v. *Chappelle* (1902), 73 A. D.

If the actor may be substantially replaced the courts will not interfere by injunction; but if such is not the case, and the manager or producer is threatened with irreparable loss, equity will step in to give relief by injunction.

The fact that an actor is special, unique and extraordinary on the stage would seem to indicate necessarily that he is so for motion pictures. But the courts will not always enjoin in the case of motion pictures, unless there is some definite proof of damage. If an actor threatens to leave after the opening of the play the profits derived prior to its closing down may furnish some basis for measuring damages. On the other hand, a motion picture producer may have a great actor under contract to produce a single picture, and upon his failure to appear at the studio, the damage will run into future profits, with no basis upon which they may be computed.[4]

Of course, injunction will not be granted unless there

(N. Y.) 447; 77 N. Y. Supp. 285 (wine agent); *W. R. Mfg. Co.* v. *Rogers* (1890); 58 Conn. 356; 20 Atl. 467 (general manager); *Sternberg* v. *O'Brien* (1891), 48 N. J. Eq. 370; 22 Atl. 348 (installment collector); *De Pol* v. *Sohlke* (1867), 7 Robt. (N. Y.) 280 (actor); *S. F. Co.* v. *Siegel-Cooper* (1898), 157 N. Y. 60; 51 N. E. 408 (sale of patterns); *Carter* v. *Ferguson* (1890), 58 Hun, 569; 12 N. Y. Supp. 580 (actor).

[4] *Peerless Feature* v. *Fields* (1915), N. Y. Law Journal, Sept. 28. "The case is not like that of a theatrical manager who finds a prominent artist deserting him and thereby preventing the daily or nightly performance of a going play. The loss which this plaintiff will sustain is failure to get a photoplay with Lew Fields in it, and consequent inability to sell or hire out the films. It seems to me that such damages are altogether speculative and do not warrant the issue of a preliminary injunction if there be any means by which plaintiff's actual and provable loss can be secured to it."

is a negative covenant in the contract by which the actor binds himself not to take other employment during the term of the contract;[5] or in the absence of such negative covenant there may be an affirmative covenant to render "exclusive" services, or facts showing that it was the intention of the parties that the actor perform at no other place during the life of the contract,[6] or if the contract is so worded that it would be a physical impossibility for the actor to perform elsewhere.[7] Under these circumstances the negative covenant would be implied.

The courts do not favor the granting of injunctions in cases of this kind unless from the proof the right thereto appears to be reasonably free from doubt.[8]

First and foremost it must appear that the services of

[5] *Lacy* v. *Houck* (1899), 9 Ohio Dec. (Repr.) 347; *Caldwell* v. *Cline* (1830), 8 Mart. (N. S.) 684 (La.); *Lumley* v. *Wagner* (Eng.) (1852), 1 DeG. M. & G. 604.

[6] *Hoyt* v. *Fuller* (1892), 19 N. Y. Supp. 962. No negative covenant, yet injunction was issued as defendant's services were unique and extraordinary and she was engaged during the "run" of plaintiff's play. See also: *Cort* v. *Lassard* (1889), 18 Ore. 221; 22 Pac. 1054; *Kurlan* v. *Gutman* (1915), 90 Misc. (N. Y.) 14; 152 N. Y. Supp. 897; *Palace Theatre* v. *Clency* (Eng.) (1909), 26 T. L. R. 28; *Whitwood* v. *Hardman* (Eng.) (1891), 2 Ch. 416.

[7] *Duff* v. *Russell* (1891), 14 N. Y. Supp. 134; aff'd on opinion of court below in 133 N. Y. 678; 31 N. E. 622. Although the contract contains no negative covenant, an injunction will be granted where the intention of the parties can clearly be inferred from the contract to have been that the defendant was to render services exclusively for the plaintiff. The defendant agreed to give seven performances each week exclusive of Sunday.

[8] *Canary* v. *Russell* (1894), 9 Misc. (N. Y.) 558; 30 N. Y. Supp. 122; *Gordon* v. *Barr* (1917), N. Y. Law Journal, Jan. 20th, Hendrick, J.

the actor sought to be enjoined are special, unique and extraordinary. This does not mean that the parties themselves may stipulate that the services are such, but the services must appear to be special, unique and extraordinary from the facts.[9] Just what would bring an actor's services under these classifications cannot be stated with any degree of definitiveness. The salary paid him is one method of judging. Yet here again the decisions do not harmonize; for in one case an acrobat who received sixty dollars per week was enjoined,[10] while in another case an opera singer earning two hundred and fifty dollars per week was held not to come within the rule.[11] The better rule would be to say that the salary paid, in conjunction with the other circumstances of the case, is a fair guide to the nature of the services, and is some index to the relative degree of importance of the actor.

Injunction will be granted only for the term of the contract—that is to say, the actor will be enjoined from appearing elsewhere for as long a time as his contract with the plaintiff has to run.[12] And an actress will not

[9] *Carter* v. *Ferguson* (1890), 58 Hun (N. Y.), 569; 12 N. Y. Supp. 580; *Hammerstein* v. *Mann* (1910), 137 A. D. (N. Y.) 580; 122 N. Y. Supp. 276.

[10] *Cort* v. *Lazzard* (1889), 18 Ore. 221; 22 Pac. 1054.

[11] *Hammerstein* v. *Mann* (1910), 137 A. D. (N. Y.) 580; 122 N. Y. Supp. 276.

When services were held not to be exclusive. See also: *Kirchner* v. *Gruban* (Eng.) (1909), 1 Ch. 413; *Doherty* v. *Allman* (Eng.) (1878), 3 App. Cas. 709; *Gaiety Theatre* v. *Cissy Loftus* (Eng.) (1893), Times, Aug. 11th; *Davis* v. *Foreman* (Eng.) (1894), 3 Ch. 654.

[12] *Shubert* v. *Angeles* (1903), 80 A. D. (N. Y.) 625; 80 N. Y. Supp. 146. Modifying decision of lower court by limiting injunction to date when contract of employment would expire.

be enjoined from performing at another theatre during the summer months, where the employment contemplated under the original contract was only for a number of "seasons."[13] And where an actress enters into two contracts with the same management, one for winter performances and the other for summer performances, one contract may be enforced by injunction, and the other may not.[14]

In order to entitle him to injunction the damage to the plaintiff must be irreparable.[15] It has been held that where the parties have agreed in the contract that in the event of a breach the actress would become liable to a fixed penalty by way of liquidated damages, injunction would not lie, as the damages had been determined and agreed upon in advance.[16]

[13] *Canary* v. *Russell* (1894), 9 Misc. (N. Y.) 558; 30 N. Y. Supp. 122; *Lawrence* v. *Dixey* (1907), 119 A. D. (N. Y.) 296; 104 N. Y. Supp. 516.

[14] *Keith* v. *Kellerman* (1909), 169 Fed. (C. C.) 196.

[15] *Mapleson* v. *La Blache*, Superior Court, Spec. Term, Oct., 1883 (N. Y.). It was held that an injunction pendente lite to prevent defendant from signing would not be granted where the complaint did not aver that plaintiff would suffer irreparable injury or that a competent substitute could not be secured.

[16] *Hahn* v. *The Concordia Society* (1875), 42 Md. 460. The actor contracted to give performances and agreed that for his breach he would be liable in the sum of $200. After he broke the contract, plaintiff attempted to enjoin him from appearing elsewhere. *Held* that since the parties had already contracted for a specified sum as liquidated damages for any violation of the contract, they had themselves settled the question and amount of damages resulting:

"Having thus by their own contract, made presumably with full knowledge of the means and ability of the defendant, and

But this is not the true rule. The intent must clearly appear to substitute the liquidated damages for performance. Unless that intent is clearly expressed the employer will be entitled to an injunction nevertheless.[17]

The element of mutuality in the contract is indispensable to its enforcement by injunction. There must be reciprocal rights and obligations, otherwise a court of equity will not enforce the contract.

It frequently happens that while the contract purports to bind the actor to appear for a definite period, it fails to obligate the manager to furnish the actor with employ-

having fixed by their own estimate the extent of injury they would suffer from a nonobservance of this condition, and having indicated as clearly as if so stated in terms, that the only form in which they could seek redress and recover the stipulated penalty or forfeiture, was a court of law, the complainants are precluded from now resorting to a Court of Equity for relief by way of injunction, on the ground that a violation of this part of the contract would result in irreparable damage and injury to them."

To the same effect: *Mapleson* v. *Del Puente* (1883), 13 Abb. N. C. (N. Y.) 144.

[17] *Diamond Match Co.* v. *Roeber* (1887), 106 N. Y. 473; 13 N. E. 419; *Feinstein* v. *Jacobson* (1914), 161 A. D. (N. Y.) 121; 146 N. Y. Supp. 525; *Phœnix Ins. Co.* v. *Continental Ins. Co.* (1882), 87 N. Y. 400; *Howard* v. *Woodward* (Eng.) (1864), 10 Jur. N. S. 1123; *Coles* v. *Sims* (Eng.) (1853), 5 DeG. McN. & G. 1; *Avery* v. *Langford* (Eng.) (1854), Kay's Ch. 663; *Whittaker* v. *Howe* (Eng.) (1841), 3 Beav. 383; *Hubbard* v. *Miller* (1873), 27 Mich. 15.

Long v. *Bowring* (Eng.) (1864), 33 Beav. 585. It was said in this case which was an action in equity for the specific performance of a covenant, there being also a clause for liquidated damages, "all that is settled by this clause is that if they bring an action for damages the amount to be recovered is £1,000, neither more nor less."

ment during that period. This is a defect fatal to the contract.[18] So that a contract made for the services of a

[18] *Witmark* v. *Peters* (1914), 164 A. D. (N. Y.) 366; 149 N. Y. Supp. 642. In this case defendant Peters, a composer, had contracted with plaintiff to write music exclusively for it and for no other publishing house for a term of five years. While injunction was sought on the ground, strictly speaking, of the violation of a property right rather than a personal covenant, the question decided applied with equal force to both. The Appellate Division reversing a judgment in favor of the plaintiff, held that since the plaintiff had not *bound itself to publish* the defendant Peters' music within the contract period, the granting of an injunction would place that defendant at the mercy of the plaintiff, and would, in effect, prevent him from earning a livelihood.

Solman v. *Arcaro* (1911), 144 A. D. (N. Y.) 590; 129 N. Y. Supp. 689. A negative covenant in a musician's contract will not be enforced where the plaintiffs do not obligate themselves to furnish employment for any specified period.

Shubert v. *Coyne* (1908), 115 N. Y. Supp. 968. Plaintiff sought a temporary injunction to restrain an actor from appearing elsewhere, under a negative covenant. In the contract plaintiff had agreed to pay defendant $300 a week for "each and every week that he shall *actually* . . . perform." *Held*, that such a contract was of no value to defendant and lacked mutuality. Motion was denied.

Arena A. C. v. *McPartland* (1899), 41 A. D. (N. Y.) 352; 58 N. Y. Supp. 477. Where a club contracted with two boxers for an exhibition on March 29, 1897, "or upon such day or days and hour to which such exhibition, for any cause, may be mutually postponed" and they failed to appear, the court refused injunction, since under the contract plaintiff, by failing to agree *mutually* with defendants, might indefinitely deprive them of an opportunity to make a living.

See also: *Star Co.* v. *Press Pub. Co.* (1914), 162 A. D. (N. Y.) 486; 147 N. Y. Supp. 579; *Lerner* v. *Tetrazzini* (1911), 71 Misc. (N. Y.) 182; 129 N. Y. Supp. 889; aff'd 144 A. D. (N. Y.) 928; 129 N. Y. Supp. 1132; *Lawrence* v. *Dixey* (1907), 119 A. D. (N. Y.) 295;

motion picture "star" should always contain a provision for a guarantee of a certain number of pictures to be posed in or of a fixed minimum compensation to be paid to the actor within the contract period.

It is easy to see why this is necessary. Where an injunction is granted restraining the actor from appearing elsewhere and the plaintiff, under his contract, is under no obligation to furnish the actor with employment or to pay him a minimum wage, the actor is unable to earn his living.

Where, therefore, the injunction is granted, the employer must be under a duty to employ and pay the actor.[19] While equity will go far to enforce a personal covenant of an actor, it will not, in order to do so, condemn him to starvation.

It is essential, to the granting of the injunction, that the plaintiff shall have fully performed his part of the contract. So that where a grand-opera tenor was to receive a certain amount of publicity, and the manager failed to live up to that covenant, it was held that this was such a breach of the contract as justified the singer

104 N. Y. Supp. 516; *Ide* v. *Brown* (1904), 178 N. Y. 26; 70 N. E. 101; *Crawford* v. *Mail and Express Pub. Co.* (1900), 163 N. Y. 404; 57 N. E. 616; *Frazee* v. *Edeson*, Lehman, J., N. Y. Law Journal, April 29, 1915.

[19] *Palace Theatre, Ltd.*, v. *Clensy* (Eng.) (1909), 26 T. L. R. 28. While injunction was granted restraining the defendant from appearing at a rival music hall, the court announced that, this was done for the reason that it was possible to obtain an early trial, and that courts were reluctant in such cases to grant restraining orders where the practical result might mean the inability of the defendant to earn his livelihood. See also cases cited under footnote 18.

in not performing, and the manager was not entitled to injunctive relief.[20] And in another case the manager was refused injunction because he failed to show performance of a contract under which he was to give the defendant employment during the "acting weeks" of a term of years.[21]

A most unusual and interesting case in this connection is *Fechter* v. *Montgomery*.[22] There an actor was engaged for a stated term to commence some weeks ahead. In the meantime the manager had on the boards a play which was proving very profitable, and he was loath to discontinue it. When the time for performance of the contract arrived, he continued his old play, refused to give the defendant a part in any play, but paid him the salary stipulated in the contract. The defendant becoming tired of this inactivity, sought and obtained employment at a rival theatre. In an action to restrain him, plaintiff was defeated, the court holding that by failing to allow the actor to appear in a play as contemplated by

[20] *Pratt* v. *Montegriffo* (1890), 10 N. Y. Supp. 903.

[21] *Hill* v. *Haberkorn* (1889), 3 Silv. Sup. (N. Y.) 87; 6 N. Y. Supp. 474. Where defendant agreed to perform for plaintiff at such times and places as plaintiff might direct "to commence on or about Jan. 4, 1881, and continue during the acting weeks of six years," plaintiff accepted "the above contract on the terms and conditions therein stipulated" and bound himself to pay defendant a percentage of the profits. *Held* that plaintiff was bound to produce plays enough to give defendant employment in "the acting weeks" of every year.

[22] *Fechter* v. *Montgomery* (Eng.) (1863), 33 Beav. 22. See also: *Newman* v. *Gatti* (Eng.) (1907), 24 T. L. R. 18; *Grimston* v. *Cuningham* (Eng.) (1894), Q. B. D. 125; *Grant* v. *Maddox* (Eng.) (1846), 15 M. & W. 737.

the contract, plaintiff had breached the contract—that one of the objects of the contract was to enable the defendant to appear before a London audience and to display his talents and abilities.

This case is of prime importance, because it upholds the doctrine that the actor is not paid in terms of money alone, but that he is paid as well in opportunity to appear before the public, in publicity and in the fame and reputation that are concomitant with such opportunity—that a contract of employment with an actor is sui generis.[23]

It would seem to follow from the foregoing, that if a motion picture producer were to engage a prominent actor for a fixed term, pay him his salary, but make no picture, that would be a breach of the contract sufficient to justify a rescission by the actor.

Nor will an injunction be granted to the second manager with whom an actress contracted where to do so would subject her to a suit by the first manager.[24]

The courts will not, however, enjoin an infant where the services are unique and extraordinary.[25] And in a case where the plaintiff, a teacher of stage dancing, con-

[23] *Pratt* v. *Montegriffo* (1890), 10 N. Y. Supp. 903.

[24] *New Tivoli* v. *Happy Fanny Fields* (Eng.) (1906), Strong on "Dramatic and Musical Law," 3d Ed., p. 40. Defendant contracted in January, 1906, with the Robert Arthur Company to appear at the Adelphi. In July, 1906, she contracted with plaintiff to appear for three seasons at the Tivoli. The Tivoli was refused an injunction on the ground that to grant it would expose defendant to an action by the Robert Arthur Co. who had contracted first with her, and who had a prior claim on her services.

[25] *Aborn* v. *Janis* (1907), 62 Misc. (N. Y.) 95; 113 N. Y. Supp. 309.

tracted, not only with the infant, but with her mother as well, that during the apprenticeship the infant was not to perform at any place without his consent, injunction was denied.[26]

Managers frequently insert a "barring clause" in their contracts which provides that the actor is not to appear within a certain radius for a specified time before the commencement or after the termination of the contract. Such contracts are upheld, providing the restrictive covenants are not too broad.[27] But where the clause is unreasonably wide,[28] or no clear breach by the defendant is made out [29] or no likelihood of irreparable damage is shown,[30] the remedy will be denied. It is interesting to

[26] *De Francesco* v. *Barnum* (Eng.) (1889), 60 L. J. Ch. 63.

[27] *Witkop & Holmes Co.* v. *Boyce* (1908), 61 Misc. (N. Y.) 126; 112 N. Y. Supp. 874; aff'd 131 A. D. (N. Y.) 922; 115 N. Y. Supp. 1150; *London Music Hall* v. *Poluski* (Eng.), Strong on "Dramatic and Musical Law," 3d Ed., p. 42.

[28] *Canterbury & Paragon, Ltd.*, v. *Lloyd* (Eng.) (1898), Strong on "Dramatic and Musical Law," 3d Ed., p. 42.

[29] *London Theatre of Varieties, Ltd.*, v. *Evans C. A.* (Eng.) (1914), 31 T. L. R. 75. Defendant agreed to render his services exclusively for plaintiff and further agreed not to permit any representation or version of his performance to be given within a certain radius. Plaintiff contended that defendant had permitted the presentation of a motion picture version of one of his sketches to be given within the prescribed areas and sought to restrain him from permitting such performances.

Held that on the evidence defendant had not taken part in the alleged reproduction, hence no injunction would lie.

[30] *Mapleson* v. *Bentham* (Eng.) (1871), 20 W. R. 176. Where defendant, a tenor, had contracted to sing for plaintiff during the season commencing 1870, and agreed that after the expiration of his contract he would not sing within 20 miles of London during the year 1871. *Held* that in-

note that in measuring the distance defined in the "barring clause" the courts have construed the same to be from point to point.[31]

Section 37.—Injunctions pendente lite.

The parties frequently contract that in the event of a breach by the actor, an injunction may issue restraining him. That is a useless provision, and will be disregarded by a court of equity.[32] Parties may not by contract

junction to restrain his singing at Brighton in 1871, would not lie, as no irreparable injury or damage was shown.

[31] *London Music Hall* v. *Poluski* (Eng.), Strong on "Dramatic and Musical Law," 3d Ed., p. 42. Defendants there had agreed in a "barring clause" not to perform within a radius of a mile and a half of plaintiff's theatre. They contended that by "Phillip's Table of Distances," the place of performance was outside of the radius limited.

Held that the proper construction was between point and point or "as the crow flies."

[32] *Dockstader* v. *Reed* (1907), 121 A. D. (N. Y.) 846; 106 N. Y. Supp. 795. The contract provided that the services to be rendered by defendant were "special, unique and extraordinary." The defendant agreed that in the event of a breach by him, an injunction might be issued against him restraining him from rendering services for any other person. *Held* that the court was not bound by the statement of defendant that his services were unique nor that it should issue an injunction in case the defendant attempted to work for some person other than plaintiff. It is for the court to say, whether in the exercise of its sound discretion an injunction shall issue.

"Parties to an agreement cannot contract that courts will exercise their functions against or in favor of themselves. Whether or not a court will so exercise its powers is for the court itself to determine."

Hammerstein v. *Mann* (1910), 137 A. D. (N. Y.) 580; 122 N. Y. Supp. 276. *Held* that a clause in the contract giving the plaintiff

between themselves, usurp the functions of a court of equity, and stipulate that the court may or may not exercise its functions. The granting of a temporary injunction is always a matter of discretion [33] and that discretionary power may be exercised, not by the parties themselves, but by the court alone.[34]

the right to obtain an injunction was not binding on the court, as the parties could not by private agreement usurp the functions of a court of equity which may alone, in its discretion, grant or refuse injunctions.

[33] *Willard* v. *Tayloe* (1869), 8 Wall. 564. "When a contract is of this character it is the usual practice of courts of equity to enforce its specific execution upon the application of the party who has complied with its stipulations on his part, or has seasonably and in good faith offered, and continues ready to comply with them. But it is not the invariable practice. This form of relief is not a matter of absolute right to either party; it is a matter resting in the discretion of the court, to be exercised upon a consideration of all the circumstances of each particular case. The jurisdiction, said Lord Erskine, 'is not compulsory upon the court, but the subject of discretion. The question is not what the court must do, but what it may do under the circumstances, either exercising the jurisdiction by granting the specific performance or abstaining from it.'"

Marconi Wireless v. *Simon* (1915), N. Y. Law Journal, Nov. 22. Judge Hough states: "An injunction, and especially one pendente lite, is always of grace and not of right."

Mapleson v. *Del Puente* (1883), 13 Abb. N. C. (N. Y.) 144. "The granting of an injunction pendente lite is always in the discretion of the court, and should be ordered with caution and even with some reluctance, and only when the rights of the plaintiff on the law and the facts are clear, and the necessity for that form of equitable relief is manifest in order to prevent a failure of justice." See also: *Metropolitan Ex. Co.* v. *Ward* (1890), 9 N. Y. Supp. 779; *Phila. Ball Club* v. *Lajoie* (1902), 202 Pa. St. 210; 51 Atl. 973.

[34] *Dockstader* v. *Reed* (1907),

All disputed and doubtful questions of fact must be resolved in favor of the defendant upon a hearing for temporary injunction.[35] And the ex parte statements contained in the letters of third parties whose affidavits are not submitted on the motion are not competent and cannot be considered.[36]

Where the granting of a preliminary injunction might result in injury equal to or greater than its denial, the court, as a rule, will not enjoin.[37] So, too, in a case where the equities of the complainant's bill are fully and specifically denied by defendant's answer under oath, for in

121 A. D. (N. Y.) 846; 106 N. Y. Supp. 795; *Hammerstein* v. *Mann* (1910), 137 A. D. (N. Y.) 580; 122 N. Y. Supp. 276.

[35] *Photo Drama* v. *Social Uplift* (1914), 213 Fed. (D. C.) 374; aff'd 220 Fed. 448; *Kerker* v. *Lederer* (1900), 30 Misc. (N. Y.) 651; 64 N. Y. Supp. 506.

World Film Corp'n v. *Foy and N. Y. Motion Picture Corp'n* (1915), N. Y. Law Journal, June 30. "Plaintiff concedes that there was no contract in writing. There was not even a copy of a proposed contract to the provisions of which parties might be held by oral agreement. At most there was a draft of a proposed contract, which from its very terms was tentative and necessarily open to review and discussion. In any view there is nothing to show that by oral or written agreement plaintiff assumed any obligation or responsibility, and there being an absolute lack of mutuality, it cannot obtain provisional remedy by injunction. In addition there is a clear-cut question of fact involved, and the court at Special Term, will not determine that question on affidavits in advance of the trial. Application for injunction denied, with costs."

[36] *Haskell* v. *Osborn* (1898), 33 A. D. (N. Y.) 128; 53 N. Y. Supp. 361.

[37] *Peerless Feature* v. *Fields* (1915), N. Y. Law Journal, Sept. 28; *Rudge-Whitworth, Ltd.*, v. *Houck Mfg. Co.* (1914), 221 Fed. (D. C.) 678; *De Koven* v. *Lake Shore & M. Co.* (1914), 216 Fed. (D. C.) 955.

such case the answer is deemed to overcome the equities of the bill.[38]

Injunctions pendente lite are more readily granted in cases of this character, as the delay in waiting for final hearing will frequently be tantamount to a denial of justice.[39]

In a recent case,[40] the defendant, an actor, had contracted for his services. He agreed that his services "would be to the entire satisfaction of the employer." The employer also had the right to terminate the services. Judge Manton decided that the contract was so unjust and inequitable that while the employer might sue at law, he could not restrain the actor for his breach. In particular, the court said:

[38] *Woodside* v. *Tonopah* (1911), 184 Fed. (C. C.) 358. See also: *Sampson & Murdock* v. *Seaver-Radford Co.* (1904), 129 Fed. (C. C.) 761; *Shubert* v. *Woodward* (1909), 167 Fed. (C. C. A.) 47; *Blount* v. *Societe* (1892), 53 Fed. (C. C. A.) 98.

[39] *Comstock* v. *Lopokowa* (1911), 190 Fed. (C. C.) 599. Plaintiffs, managers, sued to enjoin defendants under a negative covenant. *Held* that the defendants being Russian dancers of a very high order and unusual attainments and personal characteristics, they could be restrained.

Also held that while the contract provided that they were to appear only in first class theatres (not vaudeville) the mere fact that in one theatre a vaudeville act was introduced was not a breach of the contract.

"In actions by managers against theatrical artists, relief to be of any avail must generally be given in the first instance because such artists are usually of doubtful financial responsibility and the season for which they engage is over before the cause can be reached for final hearing." See also: *Chappell* v. *Fields* (1914), 210 Fed. (C. C. A.) 864.

[40] *Kenyon* v. *Weissberg* (1917), 240 Fed. (D. C.) 536.

"I am of the opinion that the plaintiff is not entitled to the relief he seeks, to wit, a preliminary injunction. It confers a right upon plaintiff to bind Weissberg for a period of five years, but it gives no corresponding right to compel the plaintiff on his part to perform. The plaintiff may discharge Weissberg at any time when the manager determines that his services are not to his satisfaction. Nowhere is it expressed what would constitute satisfaction." [41]

Section 38.—Services to be "satisfactory."

Contracts are often made whereby the actor agrees to render services satisfactory to the manager, or the scenario writer agrees to write in a manner satisfactory to the company, or some other work in connection with a motion picture production is to be done in a like manner. Services so rendered may be terminated or dispensed with by the employer at any time at his own whim or caprice. He is the only one to say whether the services are satisfactory to him or not, and the court and jury may not substitute their judgment for his own.[42]

[41] *See on question of procedure where injunctive order is disobeyed, Ziegfeld* v. *Norworth* (1910), 140 A. D. (N. Y.) 414; 125 N. Y. Supp. 504; (1911), 148 A. D. (N. Y.) 185; 133 N. Y. Supp. 208.

[42] *Crawford* v. *Mail & Express Pub. Co.* (1900), 163 N. Y. 404; 57 N. E. 616. "He was not called upon to do the work of an ordinary reporter. . . . The evident design was that the articles should be interesting and attractive, involving art, taste, fancy and judgment. There is no provision in the contract in any manner limiting the publishers in the exercise of their judgment as to what is satisfactory, but if his services are unsatisfactory for any reason they are given the right to terminate the employment upon a week's notice, at any time they so elect." See

And although an attempt has been made in recent decisions to limit the employer to a bona fide exercise of his right and not to permit its use as a pretext merely,[43] it is difficult to see how this may consistently be done. There are no limitations upon the word "satisfactory"; and whether the employer's dissatisfaction arises because of the employe's work, or because of the burden of expense entailed upon him in paying his salary, or for any other one of a thousand reasons, is immaterial. We can see no distinction.

The courts which make a distinction seem to take for granted that "unsatisfactory" is equivalent to "incompetency" and that the employer may only become dissatisfied with the quality of the employe's work.

"Unsatisfactory" and "incompetent" are not necessarily correlative terms, and indeed have been squarely distinguished.[44] Why may not the employer become dissatisfied with the *fact* that the employe is in his employ? As these contracts are usually drawn, it seems reasonable to suppose that the employer has that privilege, and while the doctrine is harsh and seemingly one-sided, the parties should be held to their contract; and the decisions in the great majority of cases hold them to it.[45]

also Editorial in New York Law Journal, Jan. 24, 1917.

[43] *Am. Music Stores* v. *Kussell* (1916), 232 Fed. (C. C. A.) 306; *Gilman* v. *Lamson Co.* (1916), 234 Fed. (C. C. A.) 507; *Parker* v. *Hyde & Behman Amuse. Co.* (1907), 53 Misc. (N. Y.) 549; 103 N. Y. Supp. 731; *Smith* v. *Robson* (1896), 148 N. Y. 252; 42 N. E. 677. See in this connection: *Spain* v. *Manhattan Street Co.* (1917), 177 A. D. (N. Y.) 610.

[44] *Brand* v. *Godwin* (1890), 8 N. Y. Supp. 339; (1890), 9 N. Y. Supp. 743.

[45] *Kendall* v. *West* (1902), 196 Ill. 221; 63 N. E. 678. Appellant

The courts have been at pains to point out this distinction; that a contract calling for ordinary services containing a clause for "satisfaction" may only be broken in the event of good faith.[46] But that, regardless of good faith, the employer may discharge the employe for "unsatisfactory" service where the work involves taste, fancy, personal satisfaction or judgment.[47] But as

agreed to "render satisfactory services" and appellee agreed to pay for "satisfactory services." *Held* that the appellant did not undertake to render services which should satisfy a court or jury, but undertook to satisfy the taste, fancy, interest and judgment of appellee. It was the appellee who was to be satisfied, and if dissatisfied he had the right to discharge the appellant at any time for any reason, of which he was the sole judge.

Peverly v. *Poole* (1887), 19 Abb. N. Cas. (N. Y.) 271, note. The contract contained a clause providing that the defendants could discharge the plaintiff if his services should not "in the estimation of the" defendants "be satisfactorily rendered." *Held* defendants could discharge plaintiff without giving any reason therefor and it could *not* be left to a jury to say whether the services were satisfactorily rendered.

The footnote to this case summarizes all the early decisions in New York State on this question.

[46] *Kramer* v. *Wein* (1915), 92 Misc. (N. Y.) 159; 155 N. Y. Supp. 193; *Fuller* v. *Downing* (1907), 120 A. D. (N. Y.) 36; 104 N. Y. Supp. 991; *Brown* v. *Retsoff Mfg. Co.* (1908), 127 A. D. (N. Y.) 368; 111 N. Y. Supp. 594; *Ginsberg* v. *Friedman* (1911), 146 A. D. (N. Y.) 779; 131 N. Y. Supp. 517; *Diamond* v. *Mendelsohn* (1913), 156 A. D. (N. Y.) 636; 141 N. Y. Supp. 775; *Daversa* v. *Davidson's Sons Co.* (1915), 89 Misc. (N. Y.) 418; 151 N. Y. Supp. 872; *Teichner* v. *Pope Mfg. Co.* (1900), 125 Mich. 91; 83 N. W. 1031; *Stevens* v. *Chicago Feather Co.* (1913), 178 Ill. App. 455; *Watkins* v. *Thurman* (1906), 98 S. W. (Tex.) 904; *Bridgeford* v. *Meagher* (1911), 144 Ky. 479; 139 S. W. 750.

[47] *Saxe* v. *Shubert* (1908), 57 Misc. (N. Y.) 620; 108 N. Y. Supp. 683. Plaintiff, an actor, contracted with defendant for

almost any contract concerning itself with the conception, acting, directing or other preparation of a motion picture involves an element of artistic selection, it is safe to say that almost every contract which can come up for construction along these lines will fall within the latter rule.

So that if one undertook to write a scenario for a motion picture company to be "satisfactory" to it, or to its "satisfaction," the company could not be compelled to accept the same.[48]

his services which were to be "satisfactorily rendered" to the defendant. Said Judge Gerard:

"Where a contract contains a clause that the services are to be satisfactory to the employer, he has the right to discharge if the services are not satisfactory to him, if the employment is of the class involving taste, fancy, interest, personal satisfaction or judgment; and if the employer discharges the employe the question whether or not the services of the employe are satisfactory is to be determined solely by the employer and not by the court or jury. But where the employment is not of that class, and where the master has the power to discharge the employe if satisfied in good faith that he is incompetent, there the good faith is a question of fact, which must be submitted to the jury."

Defendant was sustained and plaintiff non-suited.

Weaver v. *Klaw* (1891), 16 N. Y. Supp. 931. Where a person is engaged and agrees to render services to the satisfaction of the employer, "if his or her work is not satisfactory to the employer, and particularly when it is a matter of taste, fancy or judgment, he may at any time discharge him, without subjecting himself to further claim." McCarthy, J. It is error to leave the question as to the competency of the employe in such case, to the jury.

[48] *Glenny* v. *Lacy* (1888), 1 N. Y. Supp. 513. Plaintiff agreed to complete a play "to the satisfaction" of the defendant. *Held* that defendant was not compelled to take and pay for the play unless he was satisfied with it.

The dissatisfaction can only be exercised by the person named in the contract.- And where under a contract a plaintiff could be discharged for specified reasons, and the defendant was to be "the sole arbiter and judge," it was held that discharge by an *employe* of defendant for one of the specified reasons did not relieve the defendant from liability.[49]

But there is a distinction between "satisfactory" services and services "satisfactorily" performed. In the latter case the employer obviously is not to be the judge of whether the services have been so performed, but the jury alone may pass upon it.[50] Where the employer may "deem" the services not satisfactory, this gives him the absolute right to discharge.[51]

The employer incurs one penalty, however, by having a "satisfaction" clause. In the event that the employe breaches the contract, an injunction to decree specific performance will not issue, and he cannot be restrained from appearing elsewhere, no matter how unique or extraordinary his services. This has lately been decided by Judge Manton in a motion picture case where the contract in question contained a clause to the effect that the actor's services "would be to the entire satisfaction of the employer." There were other clauses in the contract, which taken together, indicated such want of mutuality and reciprocal obligations that the court was constrained to hold specific performance impossible.[52]

[49] *Lipshutz* v. *Proctor* (1905), 95 N. Y. Supp. 566.

[50] *Hydecker* v. *Williams* (1892), 18 N. Y. Supp. 586.

[51] *Glyn* v. *Miner* (1894), 6 Misc. (N. Y.) 637; 27 N. Y. Supp. 341.

[52] *Kenyon* v. *Weissberg* (1917), 240 Fed. (D. C.) 536.

This decision is of prime importance, as it is the only theatrical or motion picture case reported where a contract containing a "satisfaction" clause was held incapable of being specifically enforced in a court of equity. The theory upon which it is decided is thoroughly sound and equitable, and we believe that it will stand as the law.

Section 39.—Length of engagement.

It is not easy to determine in every instance for how long a period the actor was engaged. The elements that enter into the calculations on this subject are the length of the season, the run of the play and the special language of the contract, which in each instance must be construed on its own merits.

While, as a general proposition, the language of a contract is to be construed by the court alone, ambiguities frequently occur which permit of the introduction of evidence to explain or amplify them.

The contract is often oral, with perhaps a letter or two, to confirm it. Such letters or writings are properly admissible in evidence.[53] In such event it becomes a question of fact, and by that token, a question for the jury to determine for how long a period the actor was engaged.[54]

[53] *Boyl* v. *Midland Lyceum Bureau* (1912), 138 N. W. (Iowa) 384; *Perry* v. *Bates* (1906), 115 A. D. (N. Y.) 337; 100 N. Y. Supp. 881.

[54] *Sherwood* v. *Crane* (1895), 12 Misc. (N. Y.) 83; 33 N. Y. Supp. 17. See also: *Loftus* v. *Roberts* (Eng.) (1902), 18 T. L. R. 532; *Wade* v. *Robert Arthur Theatre Co.* (Eng.) (1907), 24 T. L. R. 77.

A contract employing an actor for the "season" is not one for an indefinite hiring,[55] although in such a case there must be some evidence showing how far the season extends. But where the language of the contract as to the "season" is qualified, the court will, as a rule, infer an intention to terminate sooner, and will not penalize a defendant who has been compelled to close the play before the end of the season.[56]

A contract for a "long engagement" is uncertain and indefinite.[57]

Nor will the courts enforce a contract which is made subject to another contract which is to be substituted in its place at some future time, unless a waiver of such substitution is proved.[58] And it is for the jury to say

[55] *Spahn* v. *Winter Garden* (1912), 138 N. Y. Supp. 446.

[56] *Strakosch* v. *Strakosch* (1890), 11 N. Y. Supp. 251.

[57] *Gray* v. *Wulff* (1896), 68 Ill. App. 376. A leader of an orchestra sued to recover salary, and the defense was incompetence and justifiable discharge. Plaintiff introduced a letter in which he had written defendant "if you can make salary $15 weekly payable weekly, and can guarantee me a long engagement," to which he received a wire to come on.

Held that the term "*long engagement*" was uncertain and indefinite, and that defendant had the right to discharge him upon giving him the usual and customary notice.

London Music Hall v. *Austin* (Eng.) (1908), Times, Dec. 26th. Construing the expression "completion of the engagement."

[58] *Walton* v. *Mather* (1896), 16 Misc. (N. Y.) 546; 38 N. Y. Supp. 782; aff'g 15 Misc. (N. Y.) 453. Where a memorandum is signed which reads "subject to the conditions and regulations of a contract which is to be substituted for this memorandum" there is no binding contract until a subsequent contract is drawn unless the parties waive such subsequent contract and

whether or not a contract which had been changed by one of the parties was, as so modified, accepted by the other party.[59]

The term "season" has not acquired in the motion picture industry a secondary meaning, nor is there in the industry a well-defined period of time during which actors are generally engaged in posing, as there is in the theatrical profession.

Section 40.—Two weeks' notice and other customs.

There is frequently inserted in theatrical contracts a clause or phrase by which either side is to be relieved of the contract upon two weeks' notice. Evidence is always admissible to show the meaning of that phrase as well as the custom in the profession.[60] The custom is that

agree that the memorandum shall be regarded as the contract. Such waiver may be express or implied in fact from the conduct of the parties.

Terry v. *Moss's Empires, Ltd.* (Eng.) (1915), 32 T. L. R. 92. Where a contract between a music-hall artist and manager provided that the artist could transfer the dates of her performance and other dates were to be given her in lieu of the dates transferred, it was held that neither party had the absolute right to fix the dates but that both were bound to act reasonably in the matter.

[59] *McLaughlin* v. *Hammerstein* (1904), 99 A. D. (N. Y.) 225; 90 N. Y. Supp. 943. After the contract was signed by defendant, plaintiff upon signing the same crossed out one of its provisions. Plaintiff called the attention of the theatrical agency through which he had secured the engagement to the erasure and asked them to inform defendant of the same. Not hearing from the agency plaintiff entered upon the performance of the contract assuming that the erasure was satisfactory. *Held* a question for the jury whether defendant consented to the change.

[60] *Hart* v. *Thompson* (1899), 39 A. D. (N. Y.) 668; 57 N. Y.

where the actor is engaged for an indefinite period, either party may terminate the contract upon two weeks' notice.[61]

Supp. 334. This cause came up before the Appellate Division a second time after a trial before a jury [see 10 A. D. (N. Y.) 183 for opinion of Appellate Division upon appeal taken after first trial.] In affirming the judgment dismissing the complaint the court said: "The evidence shows that there was a custom at the time in the theatrical profession where no definite contract of employment has been made, to give on the one part, and accept on the other, a notice of two weeks to terminate an employment, and that in pursuance of such custom, that notice was given to the plaintiff.

Haines v. *Thompson* (1893), 2 Misc. (N. Y.) 385; 21 N. Y. Supp. 991. Where an actress was employed under an oral contract "for thirty-five or forty weeks, perhaps a year," it was held that no obligation was thereby created to continue the employment for a year, and hence the contract was not within the Statute of Frauds, and was not required to be in writing.

Plaintiff was employed upon "two weeks' notice either side." *Held* that evidence of the meaning of that phrase was admissible.

"The attempted proof of the meaning of the phrase 'two weeks' notice either side' was not to show that there was a custom in the theatrical profession whereby either of the parties could upon two weeks' notice to the other terminate any contract; but that, if defendant's version of the contract be true, a seemingly obscure part of it was understood by both contracting parties in a particular sense."

See also: *Newcomer* v. *Blaney* (1900), 33 Misc. (N. Y.) 95; 67 N. Y. Supp. 170; *Howe* v. *Robinson* (1895), 13 Misc. (N. Y.) 256; 34 N. Y. Supp. 85.

[61] *DeCarlton* v. *Glaser* (1916), 173 A. D. (N. Y.) 966; *Briscoe* v. *Litt* (1896), 19 Misc. (N. Y.) 5; 42 N. Y. Supp. 908; *Hall* v. *Aronson* (1891), N. Y. Law Journal, March 16; *Wall* v. *Barley* (1872), 49 N. Y. 464.

Lovering v. *Miller* (1907), 218 Pa. St. 212; 67 Atl. 209. By the contract appellants engaged plaintiff for a "regular season."

But where the contract is for a definite term, as for a season or year, and nothing is said therein as to the two weeks' notice, evidence of such custom is inadmissible.[62]

The notice terminating the contract need not be in writing, although actual notice of some kind is required,[63] and such notice posted on the "Call Board" of the theatre has been held sufficient.[64]

The object of the notice is to liquidate the damages, and in some measure protect the actor against sudden loss of employment.[65] The actor is entitled to two weeks' salary after such notice is given him,[66] and

"The number of weeks comprised in a regular season was, however, left undefined in the writing, and evidence was, therefore, properly admitted to show the common understanding in the theatrical business what that term included, and the writing with this evidence necessarily went to the jury to find the exact terms of the contract." See also: *Haag* v. *Rogers* (1911), 9 Ga. App. 650; 72 S. E. 46.

[62] *Camp* v. *Baldwin-Mellville Co.* (1909), 123 La. 258; 48 So. 927. An actor was engaged by telegrams "for next season." Subsequently he was given two weeks' notice and discharged. *Held* that evidence that either party had the right to terminate the contract in the customary two weeks' notice in the face of the telegrams was inadmissible. See also: *Dearing* v. *Pearson* (1894), 8 Misc. (N. Y.) 269; 28 N. Y. Supp. 715, on refusal of the court to charge on the two weeks' custom.

[63] *De Gellert* v. *Poole* (1888), 2 N. Y. Supp. 651.

[64] *Clifford's Olympia Co.* v. *Waters* (1898), 84 Ill. App. 664.

[65] *Dallas* v. *Murry* (1902), 37 Misc. (N. Y.) 599; 75 N. Y. Supp. 1040.

[66] *Leslie* v. *Robie* (1903), 84 N. Y. Supp. 289. Where the contract provides that it may be terminated by giving two weeks' notice, it makes no difference when the notice is given so long as plaintiff receives salary for two weeks after the giving of such notice.

Fisher v. *Monroe* (1893), 2

actual discharge has been held equivalent to notice in writing.[67]

In *Fagan* v. *Aborn*,[68] the plaintiff and his wife, vaudeville performers, contracted for four weeks' performances, with a three weeks' cancellation clause. Services were to begin December 4th, 1905. On October 31st, 1905, defendant wrote to plaintiffs cancelling the engagement. It was held that the notification by letter was a cancellation under the contract to take effect three weeks after its date, and the complaint was dismissed.

In view of the fact that the motion picture business is so closely allied to the theatrical profession, the question may arise as to whether or not such custom may be said to prevail in the motion picture business. We do not believe that such a custom obtains in the motion picture industry. A custom develops by slow growth and is the result of long usage. It concerns itself peculiarly with its own business, and after a time becomes so firmly fixed and is so well known to the parties engaged in that particular business, that all contracts made by such parties are made with a view to and with reference to such custom.

The growth of the motion picture industry is altogether

Misc. (N. Y.) 326; 21 N. Y. Supp. 995. Where an actress was discharged peremptorily where she had been hired on two weeks' notice she was entitled to recover two weeks' salary.

"Sedgwick on Damages lays down the doctrine that notice in such cases was provided in order to allow for liquidated damages."

[67] *MacGregar* v. *Gilmore* (1898), 25 Misc. (N. Y.) 312; 54 N. Y. Supp. 589; *Watson* v. *Russell* (1896), 149 N. Y. 388; 44 N. E. 161; *De Vere* v. *Gilmore* (1898), 25 Misc. (N. Y.) 306; 54 N. Y. Supp. 587.

[68] *Fagan* v. *Aborn* (1906), 50 Misc. (N. Y.) 666; 99 N. Y. Supp. 479.

too recent to admit of the development of any custom similar to the one above mentioned. Nor can it be argued that by analogy or association with the theatrical profession the custom in the latter has become the custom in the former. There are sufficient elements of dissimilarity between the two professions to refute that argument.

In addition to that custom, there are several other customs which have grown up in the theatrical profession. There is a custom that a "season" or a "regular season" begins in October and ends in May.[69] It has also been contended that when a theatre is booked for one company it may not at matinees book another;[70] that the "star" actor has the privilege of selecting parts which are consonant with his abilities[71] and that he is to receive prominent

[69] *Strafford* v. *Stetson* (1910), 41 Pa. Sup. Ct. 560. The question as to the length of "the theatrical season of 1902 and 1903" was properly submitted to the jury.

Lovering v. *Miller* (1907), 218 Pa. St. 212; 67 Atl. 209. In this case evidence was admissible to show a custom or general usage in the theatrical profession as to the number of weeks constituting a "regular season."

McIntosh v. *Miner* (1899), 37 A. D. (N. Y.) 483; 55 N. Y. Supp. 1074. Defendants engaged plaintiff as a star for three seasons, the first season to commence "sometime in the month of November, and the two ensuing seasons sometime in the month of September, *and shall continue as long as the same may be mutually agreed upon.*" No competent evidence of custom as to the length of the usual theatrical season having been introduced and no subsequent agreement as to the length of the seasons having been made, *Held* that the court could not enforce the contract nor ascertain damages.

Montague v. *Flockton* (Eng.) (1873), L. R. 16 Eq. 189. Custom that the manager may fix the length of the season.

[70] *Cotton* v. *Sounes*. Strong on "Dramatic and Musical Law," 3d Ed., p. 25.

[71] *Kelly* v. *Caldwell* (1832), 4 La. 38.

billing;[72] that a contract for "year" means for a season, and that no salaries are paid while the theatre is shut;[73] that the lease of a theatre building may be cancelled on a month's notice.[74] The courts have also permitted evidence to be offered tending to show a custom as to the manner of paying a manager his salary when the theatre is closed;[75] that no salaries are payable during rehearsals, that only half salaries are payable during Christmas holiday week, and that all salaries are payable at the end of the week.[76] There is no custom, however, that a grant of a license to produce a play is necessarily a "sole and exclusive" one.[77]

[72] *Elen* v. *London Music Hall* (Eng.) (1906), Times, May 31, June 1.

[73] *Grant* v. *Maddox* (Eng.) (1846), 15 M. & W. 737. Defendant refused to pay the artist for the time the theatre was closed. Evidence of a custom was admitted showing that while the theatres are shut no salaries are to be paid—that a contract for one or more *years* really meant for one or more *seasons*. See however: *Mapleson* v. *Bentham* (1871) (Eng.), 20 W. R. 176; *London Music Hall* v. *Austin* (Eng.) (1908), Times, Dec. 16.

[74] *American Acad. of Music* v. *Birt*, 26 W. N. C. (Pa.) 351.

[75] *Leavitt* v. *Kennicott* (1895), 157 Ill. 235; 41 N. E. 737.

[76] *Mapleson* v. *Sears* (Eng.) (1911), 105 L. T. 639.

[77] *Hart* v. *Cort* (1913), 83 Misc. (N. Y.) 44; 144 N. Y. Supp. 627; aff'd 165 A. D. (N. Y.) 583; 151 N. Y. Supp. 4. The burden was on the defendant to establish that a well-known custom existed and that the parties contracted with the intention and expectation that it should apply to their contract. Here the custom claimed was that a grant of a license to produce a play was a "sole and exclusive" one.

For other cases where the courts held that no custom existed see: *Chappell* v. *Harrison* (Eng.) (1910), 103 L. T. 594. No custom that piano makers will loan their pianos to theatres gratis.

Lacy v. *Osbaldiston* (Eng.) (1837), 8 C. & P. 80. No custom that the manager may reserve a private box.

For either party to avail himself of such custom in the suit, he must plead it in full, and allege that the same was well known to the parties at the time the contract was entered into; that it was a well-recognized and established custom and usage in the profession, and that both parties contracted with reference thereto.[78]

At the trial expert evidence of members of the profession is sufficient to prove the customs.[79]

Section 41.—Contracts for work on Sunday.

While Sunday, under the common law, was not regarded as a dies non, we find early statutes in England

Wyatt v. *Phipps* (Eng.) (1896), 40 Sol. Jo. 781. No custom that a tour on the road is for any number of weeks.

[78] *De Carlton* v. *Glaser* (1916), 173 A. D. (N. Y.) 966; *Hart* v. *Cort* (1913), 83 Misc. (N. Y.) 44; 144 N. Y. Supp. 627; aff'd 165 A. D. (N. Y.) 583; 151 N. Y. Supp. 4; *White* v. *Henderson* (Eng.) (1885), 2 T. L. R. 119.

Newhall v.. *Appleton* (1889), 114 N. Y. 140; 21 N. E. 105. "Every legal contract is to be interpreted in accordance with the intention of the parties making it, and, usage when it is reasonable, uniform, well-settled, not in opposition to fixed rules of law, not in contradiction of the express terms of the contract, is deemed to form a part of the contract, and to enter into the intention of the parties, when it is so far established and so far known to the parties, that it must be supposed that their contract was made with reference to it. (*Wales* v. *Baily*, 49 N. Y. 464.) And evidence is always admissible to explain the meaning which usage has given to words or terms as used in any particular trade or business, as a means of enabling the court to declare what the language of the contract did actually express to the parties. [Wharton on Evidence, Section 962; *Dana* v. *Fielder*, 12 N. Y. 40; *Hinton* v. *Locke*, 5 Hil. (N. Y.) 437.]"

[79] See cases cited in footnote 78 above.

prohibiting performances on that day. The question arises—is a theatrical contract for a Sunday performance valid and enforcible?

The weight of authority seems to indicate that such a contract is void. In New York, for instance, the older line of cases established the invalidity of such contracts without much discussion, irrespective of whether the performance contemplated on Sunday was permitted by the public authorities or not,[80] although later the courts seemed to lay more emphasis on the fact that such performances were within the prohibition of the Sunday statutes.[81] Finally, in the case of *Strauss* v. *Hammer-*

[80] *Bilordeaux* v. *Bencke Lith. Co.* (1889), 16 Daly (N. Y.), 78; 9 N. Y. Supp. 507; *Hallen* v. *Thompson* (1905), 48 Misc. (N. Y.) 642; 96 N. Y. Supp. 142.

[81] *Schwab* v. *Muller* (1916), N. Y. Law Journal, Feb. 18. "The contract between the parties provided that the defendant engaged five cabaret singers and musicians under the management and control of the plaintiff for a period of ten weeks to perform at his place of business in this city. That the employment of said cabaret singers and musicians should be between the hours of three P. M. and six P. M. each and every afternoon and from seven P. M. to the time of closing of the cafe and restaurant; that there should be at least three performers (musicians and singers) every week day and on Saturdays, Sundays and holidays there should be at least five performers (musicians and singers). In my opinion the contract provided for labor on Sundays that was not a necessity or charity. It is therefore in violation of Section 2143 of the Penal Law. It hardly can be said that such work is needful in the operation of a restaurant or cafe for the good order, health or comfort of the community. The case of *Albera* v. *Sciaretti*, 131 N. Y. Supp. 889, is not exactly in point as in that case the employe was required to render his services upon the Sabbath day at such theatres and in such characters in which he might be cast accord-

stein,[82] the Appellate Division of New York made the nice distinction that the parties would not be presumed

ing to the direction of the employer; but the principle decided in that case is in my opinion applicable to this in that the contract of employment provides for Sunday performances of a character prohibited by the laws of the state and hence is void and unenforceable. The demurrer is sustained and defendant's motion for judgment thereon granted."

Albera v. *Sciaretti* (1911), 72 Misc. (N. Y.) 496; 131 N. Y. Supp. 889. The contract provided: "It is agreed and understood by both parties that in the number of performances to be given each week, Sunday performances shall also be included in the week without extra compensation to the party of the second part." *Held* entire contract was void because:

Contract was not severable, hence entire contract was void and unenforceable as such performances are prohibited by statute and as contract was silent as to place of performance, court would presume that contract was performed within state where it was made. See also: *Smith* v. *Wilcox* (1862), 24 N. Y. 353; *Lindenmuller* v. *People* (1860), 33 Barb. (N. Y.) 538.

[82] *Strauss* v. *Hammerstein* (1912), 152 A. D. (N. Y.) 128; 136 N. Y. Supp. 613.

See also: *Nelson* v. *A. H. Woods Prod. Co.* (1913), N. Y. Law Journal, January 9. ". . . Finally the defendant claims that the contract is void on its face and no recovery can be had thereon for the reason that it provides for Sunday performances by the plaintiff, contrary to the Penal Law. The provision of the agreement referred to is as follows: 'It is understood and agreed that in the event that the party of the first part shall decide to give Sunday concerts or performances, such concerts or performances, shall be considered part of the regular weekly series, and the party of the second part shall render services thereat without extra compensation.' Though a contract for theatrical performances to be rendered in this state on Sunday is illegal and recovery cannot be had under it (*Albera* v. *Sciaretti*, 72 Misc. 496), I am of the opinion that this is not such a contract. There is here no absolute provision for

to have intended a violation of the statutes, and that if Sunday performances were contemplated, they would be such as were permitted by the authorities. The same rule was declared in Pennsylvania.[83]

This is the better rule. There has been an increasing demand on the part of the public for Sunday theatrical and motion picture entertainments, and the law-making bodies have given voice to this demand by the enactment of special statutes permitting the giving of certain kinds of performances on Sunday.

How then may it be said that a contract which calls for a performance of the kind especially permitted by statute

performances on Sunday. Such performances were to be entirely at the option of the defendant. The law will not presume that the defendant would exercise his option in breach of the law. If he should attempt to exercise his option he could not enforce it. This provision can be declared void without destroying the contract, for this provision is clearly severable. The contract is capable of being legally performed, and this court will not say that it is void because of the bare possibility of an attempt to require an illegal performance."

[83] *Zenatello* v. *Hammerstein* (1911), 231 Pa. 56; 79 Atl. 922. Plaintiff there bound himself "to sing in his capacity of tenor and shall sing in Italian in New York and in the United States of America the operas of his repertory and those which shall be indicated to him."

The court held that while the contract provided for Zenatello singing on week days and *Sundays*, the presumption was that the defendant would not require him to sing on Sunday in New York, but in places where such singing was permitted. The law would not presume that the parties would do an unlawful thing.

The validity of a contract as to matters affecting its performance is to be determined by the laws of the place of performance and not the place of execution.

on Sunday, is void? To hold that it is so seems illogical and absurd.

Motion pictures are permitted to be shown in New York City.[84] Under the circumstances, a contract between the releasing company and the exhibitor for the rental of a Sunday film would be a valid contract. Otherwise the ordinance above mentioned is without any effect. What would be the purpose of keeping it and similar statutes upon the books? If a thing may legally be done it may legally be contracted for.[85]

It is only when the contract prima facie calls for the doing of an act which would be in direct contravention to a Sunday statute, that it can be said to be an invalid contract.

These distinctions, however, are not made in other jurisdictions,[86] although the courts have gone so far as to

[84] Chapter 3, Article 1, Section 10, of the Code of Ordinances of the City of New York: "*Sunday observance:* No person shall exhibit on the first day of the week, commonly called Sunday, to the public, in any building . . . the performance of any tragedy, comedy, opera, ballet, farce . . . or rope dancers; but nothing herein contained shall be deemed to prohibit at any such place or places on the first day of the week, commonly called Sunday, sacred or other educational, vocal or instrumental concerts, lectures, addresses, recitations and singing, provided that such above mentioned entertainments shall be so given as not to disturb the public peace or amount to a serious interruption of the repose and religious liberty of the community. . . ."

[85] *Bergere* v. *Parker* (1914), 170 S. W. (Tex.) 808. A contract made through a booking agent for services upon Sunday *only where such services might be lawfully rendered* on that day, is a valid contract. See also: *Wirth* v. *Calhoun* (1902), 64 Nebr. 316; 85 N. W. 785.

[86] *Stewart* v. *Thayer* (1897), 168

attempt to split up or sever the contract; but where they have been unable to do so, and have been constrained to hold the contract entire and indivisible, they have declared it invalid.[87]

The Federal courts also hold such contracts invalid, where they are made in contravention of a state statute.[88]

But such contracts must be liberally construed with a view to their enforcibility. And where a contract was made between the manager of a music hall, and a performer, whereby the latter agreed to work "every evening" in the week, it was held that Sunday being a dies non in theatrical matters, the contract did not contemplate Sunday performances.[89]

A contract providing for the posing of the actor on

Mass. 519; 47 N. E. 420. Plaintiff sued to recover for actual work performed in playing with a band of musicians at defendant's resort. Some of the work was performed on Sunday. *Held* that the statute against Sunday violations precluded a recovery, as the entire contract was void.

[87] *The Fountain Sq. Theatre* v. *Evans* (1896), 4 Ohio Dec. 151. Plaintiff brought suit for breach of a contract to perform at its theatre. Defendant set up as a demurrer that the dates of performance stipulated in the contract included a Sunday. The court held that as the contract was entire, this went to the essence of it, and the same was void.

[88] *La Crandall* v. *Ledbitter* (1908), 159 Fed. (C. C. A.) 702. A contract providing for performances of artists on Sunday in theatres where admission fees are charged is unenforceable in the state of Texas in so far as it includes performances on Sunday under Article 199 of the Texas Penal Code.

[89] *Kelly* v. *London Pavilion* (Eng.) (1897), 77 L. T. 215. Accordingly where the artist sang at a social club on Sunday evening without pay, this was held not to be a performance which would breach the contract.

Sunday is void in its entirety. Where a contract provides for the entire services of the actor, the producer may not regard a refusal of the actor to pose on Sunday as a breach of the contract.

Section 42.—Services " actually performed."

Where the actor is hired for a definite term, the producer is bound to furnish him with employment. To insert in the contract that the actor will receive pay only "when services are rendered" or "when he shall actually perform" does not relieve the manager of responsibility for the entire contract period.[90] This is the later doctrine, and seems to have overruled the earlier cases which permitted the manager to provide an actor with work whenever he felt inclined that way.[91] Although in these deci-

[90] *Dixey* v. *A. H. Wood Prod. Co.* (1915), 168 A. D. (N. Y.) 337; 154 N. Y. Supp. 49; aff'g 88 Misc. (N. Y.) 506; 151 N. Y. Supp. 224. Here the plaintiff was engaged for a definite period, and agreed not to work for any other firm, person, or corporation during the term of the contract. He was to be paid the sum of $600 a week during each and every week when his services were actually rendered. The defendant was given work for one week only. He sued for the remainder of the contract period. The court held that the phrase "when services are rendered" intended to mean no more than the due performance of the contract of employment by the plaintiff. If the plaintiff was ready and willing to perform the defendant was bound to pay him for the entire contract period.

[91] *Pollock* v. *Shubert* (1911), 146 A. D. (N. Y.) 628; 131 N. Y. Supp. 386. On appeal from order denying motion for judgment on the pleadings. Order reversed and motion granted. Contract provided that plaintiff was to be paid "for each and every week that plaintiff publicly appeared and performed." Engagement was for a theatrical

sions the courts lay stress upon the language used in the contract, it is apparent that the policy of the court wherever possible, is to hold the defendant under such a contract bound to furnish the employment and to pay therefor.[92]

This kind of a contract is similar to the contract which provides "no play, no pay," and was intended by the managers to give them the privilege of paying for actual performances only. The English courts construed that expression to mean that the actor would not be entitled to compensation where he "could not" play or where he "would not" play, but that the manager was at all events bound to pay when the actor was ready, able and willing to perform.[93]

season. *Held* that defendant was under no obligation to pay plaintiff unless he publicly appeared and performed even though his failure to so appear was defendant's refusal to furnish plaintiff with work.

[92] *King* v. *Will J. Block Amusement Co.* (1908), 115 N. Y. Supp. 243; aff'd in 132 A. D. (N. Y.) 925; 116 N. Y. Supp. 1139. Defendant engaged plaintiff as an actress for thirty weeks and for a greater period if the production was a success; plaintiff was to select a play which would be satisfactory to defendant. Plaintiff selected a play and defendant accepted it. Plaintiff was ready and willing to perform but defendant failed and refused to furnish employment to the plaintiff. *Held* that plaintiff was entitled to recover as damages, compensation agreed to be paid for thirty weeks less any moneys earned by plaintiff during contract period. *Held* further that term "*actually performed*" as used in agreement did not excuse defendant where by its own wrongful act it prevented plaintiff from actually performing.

[93] *Gilbars* v. *Jefferson* (Eng.) (1902), Strong on "Dramatic and Musical Law," 3d Ed., p. 29. "No play, no pay," meant either "you won't play," or "you can't

Where performance is a condition precedent to payment, fulfillment must be shown in order to secure a recovery; but when performance is prevented or rendered impossible by the sickness or death of the actor, a recovery may be had on a quantum meruit.[94]

Section 43.—Substantial performance.

The actor who has been engaged for a stated period, and has rendered his services during its entire length, is entitled to recover for the full period. His right is not affected by reason of the fact that for a short interval within that period the producer had no work for him and the actor was perforce obliged to remain idle.[95]

play," and did not give the theatre manager the right to arbitrarily rescind the contract.

[94] *Wolfe* v. *Howes* (1859), 20 N. Y. 197. See in this connection Sections 10 and 14.

[95] *Sterling* v. *Bock* (1887), 37 Minn. 29; 32 N. W. 865. The action was brought against the defendants to recover for services rendered by the plaintiff as an actress under a written contract. *Held* that the evidence sustained the finding that the plaintiff performed the services contracted for, although she did not act in any play during the week in question, not having been called upon to do so. The contract was for the services of an actress for a period of about six months at a stipulated price per week, and it was immaterial that during a particular week her active service was not required.

Coghlan v. *Stetson* (1884), 19 Fed. (C. C.) 727. Plaintiff was engaged to appear at the Fifth Avenue Theatre and to appear as leading man at $100 a performance for seven performances each week. After playing for five weeks, he was not assigned to any part for three weeks. Subsequently he appeared in Boston under the defendant's auspices, and then brought this action to recover $2,100 for the aforesaid three weeks during which he was idle.

The actor is also entitled to recover for the time actually spent in travelling from one place of performance to another.[96]

And where one actor in a troupe was substituted for another, it was held the services were such as to permit a recovery.[97]

But where two performers out of thirteen and twelve musicians out of thirty are missing, there is a failure of compliance with the terms of the agreement.[98]

Held that plaintiff waived no rights by appearing in Boston and that there must be a reasonable construction of the contract—that it mattered nothing whether he sued as damages or wages, since he asked for a specified sum of money, pleaded all the facts, and defendants suffered no surprise. Plaintiff was given judgment.

[96] *Day* v. *Klaw* (1908), 112 N. Y. Supp. 1072. The defendants agreed to employ plaintiff for twenty-five consecutive weeks and pay him a stipulated salary per week. Plaintiff spent two weeks during the twenty-five weeks in travelling to certain theatres to perform pursuant to defendant's instructions. Action brought to recover salary for two weeks, also certain railroad fare. Judgment for plaintiff affirmed.

[97] *Columbian Lyceum Bureau* v. *Sherman* (1909), 19 N. D. 58; 121 N. W. 765. Plaintiff agreed to furnish six entertainments to defendant, stipulating that it was not to be liable if artists failed to appear because of illness or other unavoidable cause, also that it might at its option substitute another artist. It was held that plaintiff could recover contract price where because of illness of the artist who had been originally booked it substituted another performer.

[98] *Charley* v. *Potthoff* (1903), 118 Wis. 258; 95 N. W. 124. The fact that defendant made some of the payments required to be made under the contract did not constitute a waiver of his right to counterclaim for damages for inferior performances. Defendant could permit plaintiff to proceed with defective perform-

Section 44.—Anticipatory breach.

Where an actor who has contracted for his services for a period is notified, before the commencement of such period, that he will not be required, he need not go through the idle ceremony of presenting himself for performance or tendering his services. This is especially of importance since the services may have been contracted to be given at a distant place.[99]

Once the contract is breached, and treated as such by the other party, it cannot be kept alive by either party.[100]

ances without waiving his right to damages since to have prevented the continuance of such performances would have done serious injury to him (defendant had made an advance sale of seats, etc.).

[99] *Goddard* v. *Morrissey* (1899), 172 Mass. 594; 53 N. E. 207. Plaintiff and his company were engaged to perform for defendant for one week. Before date of first performance plaintiff was notified that because of defendant's inability to secure hall, plaintiff and his company would not be required. Jury gave verdict for less than amount agreed to be paid plaintiff for week's work, although plaintiff did not earn any other moneys during that week. On appeal by defendant it is *held:*

(1) It was not necessary for plaintiff and company to present themselves ready to work on the day originally agreed upon where he was notified before that day that his services would not be required.

(2) The contention that jury should have found for full amount or for nominal amount was invalid. Defendant was not harmed by such finding.

[100] *Greenwall Theat. Circ.* v. *Markowitz* (1904), 97 Tex. 479; 79 S. W. 1069. The manager of a theatre, after he is informed of his employer's intention to breach the contract, cannot, where he himself has treated the contract as breached, keep it alive, but must sue on the breach. See also: *Grau* v. *McVickar* (1874), 8 Biss. 7; Fed. Cas. No. 5708.

Section 45.—Exposure to obscenity, ridicule, degradation, etc.

Where the actor has contracted to play in any part which may be assigned to him, he is bound by the contract, and must obey the instructions of the director in so far as they are reasonable and consistent with his skill and reputation as an actor. And in such a contract an actress will not be permitted to maintain the defense that she has been ordered to don an immodest costume.[101]

[101] *Duff* v. *Russell* (1892), 14 N. Y. Supp. 134; aff'd on opinion below in 133 N. Y. 678; 31 N. E. 622.

Dis Debar v. *Hœffle*, N. Y. Law Journal, vol. 4, 1475. Plaintiff sued for damages in that defendant had published her picture representing her in the garb of Cupid. Plaintiff was an actress, and had contracted to appear in a play, and assume any part assigned to her. Judge McAdam held that having contracted to appear thus, it was her duty to dress in any part and in any costume assigned to her, and she could not complain. That it was one of the incidents of an actress's life to dress in costumes that were not always the height of modesty, and that she had no more cause for complaint than an artist's model would have because she might be required to pose in an immodest costume.

Morrison v. *Hurtig & Seaman* (1910), 198 N. Y. 352; 91 N. E. 842. Plaintiffs (husband and wife) were engaged to act for defendants. The plaintiffs agreed to furnish "at their own cost and expense, all *necessary* costumes, wigs, shoes, boots, tights, stockings and gloves in and about their performances," to "pay strict regard to make-up in the dressing of characters," and to "abide by and conform to all rules and regulations now made or hereafter to be made." Defendants requested Mrs. Morrison to change the costume which she was then using and in place thereof wear a "military costume." That was a costume in "tights" without skirts. *Held* that it was error to exclude conversations had at the time Mrs. Morrison was requested to change costumes, for the contract contemplated future discussions be-

She is bound absolutely by her contract, and the only way in which an actress can avoid the predicament of having to wear a costume repugnant to her sense of modesty, is by contracting with the manager. Unless she so contracts she is subject to discharge for which she cannot recover.[102]

tween the parties upon the subject of costumes and that such conversation would aid the jury in deciding whether the regulation of defendants was a reasonable one.

See also in this connection: Baumeister v. *Markham* (1897), 101 Ky. 122; 39 S. W. 844; 41 S. W. 816. An actress while on her way to the theatre to perform was injured through negligence of defendants. The lower court refused to charge the jury as follows, which was an alleged error of the court: "The court instructs the jury that if they believe from the evidence that a part of the business of the plaintiff was to go upon the stage and exhibit her legs in such manner as is indecent in fact and immoral in its tendencies, then, in that event, the loss of opportunity to earn money in such employment can form no basis for recovering damages." The appellate court sustained the lower court's refusal to so charge and said in support of its position: "It may be, as testified by appellant, such performance requires the artist to 'show her limbs in silk stockings,' but while it is tolerated by law and patronized openly and freely by the public, the court cannot arbitrarily outlaw those who earn a livelihood in that way."

[102] *Rafalo* v. *Edelstein et al.* (1913), 80 Misc. (N. Y.) 153; 140 N. Y. Supp. 1076. A part was assigned to one of the plaintiffs (the wife) which she refused to play upon the ground that such part was "artistically unfit" for her. Defendants were entitled to assign such part to the wife. Defendants asked her to reconsider her refusal. The following day the wife telephoned that she was willing to play the part but plaintiff refused to further employ her. *Held* that the request on the part of defendants to reconsider her refusal did not necessarily constitute a waiver of the breach of the contract, the

Nor may she object to portraying a lewd or immodest character, unless she has reserved that privilege to herself by contract. The theatre is an institution founded for "the imitation of virtue and the exposure of vice and folly." Of necessity somebody must play the villain, the adventuress, the harlot, just as one plays the hero and the innocent heroine. And the producer has the right to call upon any member of his troupe to play the disagreeable, as well as the desirable parts, subject to certain limitations which will be hereafter discussed.

The producer may not demand that the actor travel an unreasonable distance to perform,[103] or endanger his life and limb,[104] unless he has specifically contracted so

court holding that such question should have been submitted to the jury.

[103] *Gath* v. *Interstate Amusement Co.* (1912), 170 Ill. App. 614. Plaintiffs were engaged to perform a vaudeville act for five weeks in Montgomery, Ala., Little Rock, Ark., Fort Worth, Dallas and Houston, Texas, and "adjacent" towns. Defendants, seeking a pretext to break the contract, wired plaintiffs to appear in Beaumont which is 300 miles away. *Held* that the word "adjacent" did not convey any such meaning and that this was an unreasonable interpretation of the contract.

[104] *Hanlin* v. *Walters* (1893), 3 Col. App. 519; 34 Pac. 686. Defendant, manager of a theatre in Pueblo, was also an innkeeper and boarding-house keeper. He engaged plaintiff to work in his theatre and boarded and lodged her at his house. Becoming terrified at the actions of defendant's wife, plaintiff was compelled to leave.

Defendant kept her trunk and valise and plaintiff was forced to replevy them.

Held that defendant having been the cause of plaintiff's departure, the fault was with him, and he would not be permitted to say that her indebtedness to him of her board was not paid. The replevy was sustained.

to do and has accepted his employment with that understanding.[105]

The producer may not demand that the actor or actress do an act which is obscene or lewd, for that is clearly against public policy and is ground for rescission of the contract. But it would be for the jury to say what constituted such conduct.[106]

Nor may the producer insist that the actor play a part inferior to that for which he was hired.

Where the plaintiff was employed as a "premier second-danseuse," it was held that she was justified in refusing to dance in parlor dress with figurantes of the theatre.[107] So, too, where a dancer was engaged as a "premiere danseuse etoile" and had been asked to dance an inferior part by the stage management.[108] And a bass or baritone in a church choir could not be compelled to sing an inferior part.[109] In one case, where a "star" actress was

O'Connor v. *Armour Packing Co.* (1908), 158 Fed. (C. C. A.) 241. Generally on the question of exposing the servant to disease.

[105] *Blitz* v. *Toovey* (1890), 9 N. Y. Supp. 439. The plaintiffs (husband and wife) were engaged to perform at defendant's place of amusement, the husband to do the "fire act" and the wife, among other things, to walk on broken glass. The action was brought for wrongful discharge, defendant claiming that the wife failed to walk and dance on glass in the manner provided in the contract. *Held* that the wife substantially performed the contract by walking and jumping on the glass though she did not dance on it.

[106] *Rafalo* v. *Edelstein* (1913), 80 Misc. (N. Y.) 153; 140 N. Y. Supp. 1076; *Morrison* v. *Hurtig* (1910), 198 N. Y. 352; 91 N. E. 842.

[107] *Baron* v. *Placide* (1852), 7 La. Ann. 229.

[108] *Roserie* v. *Kiralfy*, 12 Phila. (Pa.) 209.

[109] *Warner* v. *The Rector and*

asked to play in a part assigned to her by the theatre manager, it was held that the evidence showed a custom or usage in the theatrical profession by which the "star" had the privilege of selection of such parts as she might shine into good advantage.[110]

In the case of *Violette* v. *Rice*,[111] the plaintiff, an actress, contracted "to render services at any theatres." It was held that evidence tending to show that the word "services" referred to particular kinds of services only, was

Trustees, etc. (1882), 1 City Court (N. Y.), 419. Plaintiff was employed to sing a bass or baritone part in a choir of the defendant's church. The defendant directed plaintiff to take a subordinate part which he refused. *Held* plaintiff could recover for breach of the contract.

Briscoe v. *Litt* (1896), 19 Misc. (N. Y.) 5; 42 N. Y. Supp. 908. "The employe is only required to engage in service of a character and grade equal to that from which he was discharged, and nothing inferior in rank or degree."

110 *Kelly* v. *Caldwell* (1832), 4 La. 38.

For miscellaneous non-theatrical cases see: Wolf Cigar Stores v. *Kramer* (1908), 109 S. W. (Tex.) 990; *Development Co.* v. *King* (1908), 161 Fed. (C. C. A.) 91; *Davis* v. *Dodge* (1908), 126 A. D. (N. Y.) 469; 110 N. Y. Supp. 787; *Marx* v. *Miller* (1901), 134 Ala. 347; 32 So. 765; *The Sarah*, 1 Stuart Adm. Rep. (Quebec) 87; *Drummond* v. *Atty. Gen'l* (Eng.), 2 H. L. Cas. 837.

111 *Violette* v. *Rice* (1899), 173 Mass. 82; 53 N. E. 144. An employment contract provided that plaintiff was "to render services at any theatres" and "to conform to and abide by all the rules and regulations adopted" by defendant "for the government of said companies." On the back of the contract were the rules of the company, one of them reading: "No person shall . . . refuse a part allotted to him or her by the manager" on certain penalties including the right of discharge. *Held* that evidence that the word "service" referred to particular services was *inadmissible*.

inadmissible, as varying the terms of the written contract. This rule seems to be in harmony with the language of the dissenting opinion of Mr. Justice Bijur in *Rafalo* v. *Edelstein*.[112] But in another case, involving the discharge of a traveling salesman, parol evidence was held admissible to ascertain the duties of the plaintiff.[113] And in another case it was held that it was for the jury to say what the duties of a stage manager were.[114]

On the other hand, an actress who is engaged for an inferior part or in the capacity of an understudy, may not demand that the producer permit her to perform when the principal becomes ill.[115]

[112] *Rafalo* v. *Edelstein* (1913), 80 Misc. (N. Y.) 153; 140 N. Y. Supp. 1076.

[113] *Brown* v. *Baldwin & Gleason* (1891), 13 N. Y. Supp. 893. Plaintiff alleged a wrongful discharge. He was hired as a traveling salesman, and at the trial defendants offered testimony to show that it was a custom in the trade for a salesman to take out a line of samples. Said Judge Pryer: "Doubtless the learned trial judge rejected the evidence on the ground that a written contract cannot be added to or in any way altered by oral testimony. By the contract the respondent was 'to serve as traveling salesman;' but what were his duties as such is not defined, nor does the law determine them. Parol evidence of trade usage ascertaining those duties was therefore in no sense contradictory of or inconsistent with the terms of the written instrument, but tended only to show the full meaning and effect of the words 'traveling salesman.'"

[114] *Nash* v. *Krieling* (1899), 56 Pac. 260; aff'd 123 Cal. xviii.

[115] *Newman* v. *Gatti* (1907), 24 (Eng.) T. L. R. 18. Plaintiff, an actress, was engaged for the run of a play to act as understudy to the principal character. Plaintiff received a weekly salary. She agreed not to appear at any other place of amusement during the term of the contract without defendant's consent. During the run of the play the principal actress left the show. Plaintiff

On the refusal of the actor to play the part assigned to him, the producer must give actual notice of discharge,[116] but if he fails to do so and continues him in his employ, it becomes a question of fact for the jury whether there was condonation.[117]

Section 46.—Renewal of the contract—modification.

Where nothing is said by the parties, and the actor under contract with the producer, continues in the employment, the law will imply a renewal of the original contract for an equal length of time up to one year, and upon the same terms.[118]

brought action for breach of contract for failure of defendant to permit her to act in the principal part. *Held* that under the contract no right was conferred upon plaintiff to play the part; that the contract merely imposed the obligation on the part of plaintiff to play if called upon so to do by defendant.

[116] *Standing* v. *Brady* (1913), 157 A. D. (N. Y.) 657; 142 N. Y. Supp. 656. Where the contract provided that plaintiff was to play such parts as were assigned to him and further that defendant could annul the contract during rehearsals. *Held* that verdict for plaintiff should be reinstated when although there was evidence that plaintiff refused to play part assigned to him, yet defendant failed to give notice of discharge to him.

[117] *Rafalo* v. *Edelstein* (1913), 80 Misc. (N. Y.) 153; 140 N. Y. Supp. 1076.

[118] *Lorenz* v. *Bartuschek*, City Court of the City of New York, unreported, judgment roll filed May 18, 1916. Plaintiff was a ballet-mistress employed by defendant in Berlin. Defendant contracted with Mr. Dillingham to produce his ice-ballet at the New York Hipprodrome, and plaintiff was sent over with the ballet in July, 1915, and after a rehearsal period of six weeks entered upon her duties. In November, 1915, defendant and Dillingham renewed their contract and extended the same for four months, with renewal op-

Where the original contract was for a graduated scale of compensation for several years, the contract will be

tions which Dillingham exercised down to July. The plaintiff continued to perform her duties, but after January 16, 1916, defendant refused to pay her, claiming that she was no longer in his employ, but in the employ of Dillingham, as no express contract of renewal had been made with her by the defendant.

Plaintiff went to the jury and received a verdict for $1,000, the full amount sued for, which was sustained by the Appellate Term without opinion.

(1) Plaintiff contended that where the original term of employment had expired and she was permitted to continue her duties, the contract was renewed by operation of law upon the same terms. [Labatt on Master & Servant, 2d Ed., Section 230; *Adams* v. *Fitzpatrick*, 125 N. Y. 124; *Wood* v. *Miller*, 78 N. Y. Misc. 377; *Douglas* v. *Merchants' Ins. Co.*, 118 N. Y. 484; *Huntington* v. *Claflin*, 38 N. Y. 182; *Vail* v. *Jersey Co.*, 32 Barb. (N. Y.) 564; *Lichtenstein* v. *Fisher*, 87 Hun (N. Y.), 397.] And the compensation was presumed to be the same. (Labatt, Section 232.) Besides which there was evidence to indicate that the contract had been extended by parol. (*Hudson Bldg. Co.* v. *Compagnie Gen. Transatlantique*, 169 N. Y. App. Div. 600; *Horner* v. *Guardian Mut. Life Ins. Co.*, 67 N. Y. 478.)

(2) The contract also provided that "In case of all *disputes* arising under this contract both parties shall submit to the jurisdiction of the Amstgericht, Berlin Mitte or Landericht I in Berlin. . . ." Plaintiff's contention was that this clause did not oust the American courts of jurisdiction. (*Meachem* v. *Jamestown R. R. Co.*, 211 N. Y. 346; *Engel* v. *Shubert*, 166 N. Y. App. Div. 394.)

(3) Evidence of the contract between defendant and Dillingham by the original instrument was properly admissible. (*Miller* v. *Lawrence*, 13 N. Y. Misc. 130.)

Montague v. *Flockton* (Eng.) (1873), L. R. 16 Eq. 189. A contract which renews a contract for services for another season is binding for the same length as the first contract.

De Gellert v. *Poole* (1888), 2 N. Y. Supp. 651.

For miscellaneous cases see:

deemed renewed for one year upon the same scale of compensation provided for in the last year of the original contract.[119]

It often happens that after an actor finishes an engagement for a long term he is asked to continue it for a short period, either to complete the run of a play or to finish a picture. In such case a breach by the management will entitle the actor to sue upon the additional period as if the same were a part of the period embraced in the original contract.[120]

Whether the written contract could be modified by a verbal agreement, is a question for the jury.[121]

Morris v. *Briggs* (1915), 179 S. W. (Mo.) 783; *Curtis & Dodd* v. *Struthers* (1915), 154 N. W. (Ia.) 872; *Dunton* v. *Derby Desk Co.* (1904), 186 Mass. 35; 71 N. E. 91; *State Board of Agriculture* v. *Meyers* (1904), 20 Col. App. 139; 77 Pac. 372; *Home Fire Ins. Co.* v. *Barber* (1903), 67 Nebr. 644; 93 N. W. 1024.

[119] *Wade* v. *Rob't Arthur Theatres Co.* (Eng.) (1907), 24 T. L. R. 77. Defendants engaged plaintiff to act in the principal part of a pantomime at a salary of £130 per week for the first year, £140 for the second year and £150 for the third year, with the option of retaining the services of plaintiff for the next pantomime season upon the same terms and conditions as set forth in the agreement. *Held* that the salary for the ensuing season if the option was exercised would be that payable for the third year and that the contract was not void for uncertainty.

[120] *Wheeler* v. *Woods* (1909), 120 N. Y. Supp. 80. Where plaintiff, an actor, had fully performed under a written contract and had been asked to perform for another two weeks in Chicago, and the show was disbanded during the second week, it was held that he could recover—not upon a quantum meruit,—but upon the extra two weeks' engagement. See also: *Keane* v. *Liebler* (1907), 107 N. Y. Supp. 102.

[121] *Rothenberg* v. *Packard* (1910), 97 Miss. 428; 52 So. 458. Plaintiff, manager of a produc-

And a contract made by the actor with the director general of a traveling show, may be renewed by that same director general so as to bind the company.[122]

Section 47.—How many causes of action for breach.

As a general rule the actor has but one cause of action for damages for a breach of the contract by wrongful discharge.[123]

But it is necessary to distinguish between a partial breach and a total breach. Where the contract is severable and of such a nature that it may be breached in part and performed in part, judgment recovered in an action for the partial breach is not a bar to a subsequent action for the total breach.[124]

tion, contracted with defendant to give performances at defendant's theatre, defendant agreeing to pay plaintiff 70% of gross receipts. Just before the opening of first performance plaintiff's actors and actresses refused to proceed with their acting unless they were paid salaries due them for previous performances. An agreement was made between plaintiff's traveling agent and defendant whereby defendant agreed to pay artists the 70% to be applied on account of salaries due them, which defendant did. Plaintiff sued for 70% of the gross receipts. *Held* that it was a question for the jury whether defendant, in view of the emergency, could make a verbal agreement with plaintiff's agent notwithstanding his original written contract with plaintiff.

Robey v. *Arnold* (Eng.) (1898), 14 T. L. R. 220. The meaning of the word "re-engagement" is for the jury. See also: *Arnold* v. *Stratton* (Eng.) (1898), 14 T. L. R. 537.

[122] *Eddy* v. *American Amusement Co.* (1913), 132 Pac. (Cal.) 83.

[123] *Everson* v. *Powers* (1882), 89 N. Y. 527; *Parry* v. *American Opera Co.* (1887), 19 Abb. N. Cas. (N. Y.) 269.

[124] *Livingston* v. *Klaw et ano.* (1910), 137 A. D. (N. Y.) 639; 122 N. Y. Supp. 264. Plaintiff

Where the employer has given notice of his intention to breach the contract, the employe who then treats the contract as breached, cannot keep it alive, but must sue on the breach.[125]

But there arises no cause of action, on a wrongful discharge, which is based upon the theory that such discharge was malicious and oppressive. The law will not give redress for such injury, but the action must be purely one for breach of contract and nothing more.[126]

Section 48.—Actor's remedy for breach.

Where the actor is ready, able and willing to continue in his employment and the producer does not permit him

was employed for a term of twenty consecutive weeks, services to commence December 2, 1907, at a weekly salary. Defendants failed to provide employment for weeks commencing January 6, 1908, and January 20, 1908. They did provide him with employment for weeks covering January 13, 1908, and January 27, 1908, respectively. Plaintiff sued for salaries due for weeks of January 6 and 20, and recovered judgment. Plaintiff now sues for total breach. Judgment secured because of partial breach is set up as bar to the action. *Held* that where there had been a partial breach, a recovery for such breach did not bar an action for a total breach subsequently occurring.

[125] *Greenwall Theat. Circ.* v. *Markowitz* (1904), 97 Tex. 479; 79 S. W. 1069.

[126] *Westwater et ano.* v. *Rector et al.* (1903), 140 Cal. 339; 73 Pac. 1055. Complaint alleged that the dismissal of the plaintiff, a vocal artist, was malicious and oppressive, and in consequence thereof plaintiff had been humiliated, suffered great mental agony, and had been sick in mind and body. *Held* that complaint was demurrable upon the ground that damage to health, reputation or feelings arising out of dismissal was too remote and uncertain.

to do so, or refuses to pay him for his services, there is a breach of the contract by the producer, and a cause of action arises in favor of the actor.

The latter may then sue for the entire amount due him for the unexpired term of the contract; and upon the trial the jury may give him a verdict up to such amount. Nor is the jury limited by the amount due at the time of the trial.[127]

After the occurrence of the breach it is not necessary for the actor to tender his services or be prepared at all times ready to perform for the producer.[128]

As against the plaintiff's recovery the defendant may set up the fact that plaintiff has earned other money elsewhere since the discharge, and the jury must be instructed to deduct such earnings from the damages claimed;[129] and they may also speculate on the amount of earnings of the plaintiff which he may secure before the expiration period of the contract. Indeed, the plaintiff is in duty bound to mitigate the damages, and to use all reasonable diligence in seeking other employment,[130] although where his

[127] *Howard* v. *Daly* (1875), 61 N. Y. 362; *Sutherland* v. *Wyer* (1877), 67 Me. 64; *Dugan* v. *Anderson* (1872), 36 Md. 567. See also concurring opinion of Gaynor, J., in *Davis* v. *Dodge* (1908), 126 A. D. (N. Y.) 469; 110 N. Y. Supp. 787.

See also: Editorial in the New York Law Journal of September 14, 1917.

[128] *Howard* v. *Daly* (1875), 61 N. Y. 362.

[129] *Bassett* v. *French* (1895), 10 Misc. (N. Y.) 672; 31 N. Y. Supp. 667. Defendant was permitted, after default in pleading, to come in upon assessment of damages and to show that during the contract period plaintiffs received other earnings which were to be allowed in mitigation of damages. See also: *Sutherland* v. *Wyer* (1877), 67 Me. 64.

[130] *Polk* v. *Daly* (1873), 4 Daly (N. Y.), 411. Plaintiff was dis-

absence does not prevent the defendant from reducing the damage he may recover for the full amount.[131]

However, if the defendant wishes to avail himself of this defense, he must plead it as a partial defense in mitigation of damages, and the burden of establishing it is upon him.[132]

Where the contract period has expired before the time of trial, the actor is entitled to recover full compensation up to the time of the expiration of the contract period, less other earnings.[133]

Where the earnings elsewhere are greater than the compensation agreed to be paid under the contract sued on, the defendant is entitled by way of mitigation of damages, only to a proportionate share of the earnings calculated upon the work done under each contract.[134]

charged before expiration of his contract. He tendered his services and upon defendant's refusal to furnish him with employment left for the south where he remained during the balance of the contract period. It was proved by defendant that plaintiff made no effort to find other employment, but on the contrary "went a fishing." *Held* that plaintiff was obligated to use "ordinary but active diligence" in securing new employment to mitigate damages. See also: *Howard* v. *Daly* (1875), 61 N. Y. 362; *Sutherland* v. *Wyer* (1877), 67 Me. 64.

[131] *Dearing* v. *Pearson* (1894), 8 Misc. (N. Y.) 269; 28 N. Y. Supp. 715.

[132] *Howard* v. *Daly* (1875), 61 N. Y. 362.

[133] *Everson* v. *Powers* (1882), 89 N. Y. 527.

[134] *Evesson* v. *Ziegfeld* (1903), 22 Pa. Super. 79. Under the contract plaintiff was to receive $100 per week; performances contemplated to be seven or eight per week. After discharge plaintiff secured other employment at $175 per week, number of performances to be given per week being fourteen. *Held* that defendant was only entitled to

Section 49.—Profits as a basis for damages.

The breach of a contract to play at a theatre often involves the difficulty of laying a basis on which damages may be predicated. Generally speaking, the prospective profits of a performance are vague and speculative, and not susceptible of such computation as to admit of proof.[135]

8/14 of $175 per week in mitigation of damages. *Held further* that plaintiff might show expenditures for costumes, etc., during period of employment by defendant not as an item of damage but for the purpose of showing performance on her part. *Held further* that a receipt in full for money actually earned did not release defendant from any and all claims for breach of contract as the money paid to plaintiff upon signing the release was actually due her, hence no consideration for absolute release.

Frohman v. *Mason* (1915), 89 Misc. (N. Y.) 380; 151 N. Y. Supp. 938. Defendant, counterclaiming, sought to recover for a breach of contract of employment. He had been employed by plaintiff at a salary of $700 a week and 7% of the profits over $7,000 weekly, but after the failure of the production, he contracted with another manager at $700 a week and a bonus of $1,700. His income for the season was greater than it would have been had he continued to play for the plaintiff, although in fact he was employed for 18 weeks instead of 20 weeks. *Held* that he was not actually damaged and could not recover.

[135] *Bernstein* v. *Meech et al.* (1891), 130 N. Y. 354; 29 N. E. 255. A contract was made whereby plaintiff was to give a specified number of performances at defendant's hall and receive 50% of the gross receipts from such performances. Defendant refused to permit plaintiff to perform. *Held* that although the value of the contract to plaintiff was in the profits, such profits were not susceptible of proof and could not be recovered.

Cutting v. *Miner* (1898), 30 A. D. (N. Y.) 457; 52 N. Y. Supp. 288. Plaintiff agreed to play her company at defendant's theatre and to receive a certain percentage of the receipts. The jury awarded her a substantial verdict but the Appellate Division reversed the judgment:

"There was no evidence in the case to warrant this finding. It was necessarily pure guess work. . . . If the performance had been permitted to proceed, and the play had been a success as evidenced by equally large audiences on subsequent occasions, there would have been some reasonable basis for the finding as to the prospective profits for the rest of the week. But here there was no basis at all. There was simply a first-night audience attracted by the production of a new play."

See also: *New York Academy of Music* v. *Hackett* (1858), 2 Hilt. (N. Y.) 217; *Wakeman* v. *Wheeler* (1886), 101 N. Y. 205; 4 N. E. 264; *Ellsler* v. *Brooks* (1886), 54 Super. Ct. (N. Y.) 73; *Levison* v. *Oes* (1917), 98 Misc. (N. Y.), 260; *Todd* v. *Keene* (1896), 167 Mass. 157; 45 N. E. 81.

Moss v. *Tompkins* (1893), 69 Hun (N. Y.), 288; 23 N. Y. Supp. 623; aff'd in 144 N. Y. 659; 39 N. E. 858. A contract was made between the parties whereby plaintiff, the lessee of a theatre, agreed to furnish defendant, the manager of a theatrical production, theatre and equipment for a specified period, the gross receipts to be shared between the parties. Before the date fixed for the giving of the first performance, defendant notified plaintiff that he would not produce the play at the plaintiff's theatre. Plaintiff was not permitted to show previous receipts of his theatre or the popularity and success of the production in the places where it had already been produced and that such receipts would have been greater during the contract period than those actually taken in by plaintiff.

The court makes this significant statement:

"The defendant's dramatic company was not shown to include artists of such exceptional and well-known talent as to guarantee, apart from the play, audiences of reasonably certain numbers. Nor was any special attraction of the latter kind contemplated by the contract."

But see in this connection: *Savery* v. *Ingersoll* (1887), 46 Hun (N. Y.), 176.

On the construction of the payment clause see: Ming v. *Pratt* (1899), 22 Mont. 262; 56 Pac. 279. Plaintiff owned an opera house; defendant was the proprietor of an opera company. The parties contracted for a per-

The plaintiff, however, will be permitted to recover the actual losses sustained by him.[136]

formance, and the court in passing upon the meaning of the payment clause said:

"The contract expressly provides that defendant shall have not less than $850 and 85 per cent of all monies received from the sale of seats. The language is clear, unambiguous and free from any uncertainty; its obvious meaning is that defendant was to receive $850, *and also* 85% of the gross receipts."

[136] *American Hungarian Pub. Co.* v. *Miles Bros.* (1910), 68 Misc. (N. Y.) 334; 123 N. Y. Supp. 879. Defendant agreed to furnish a motion picture display and suitable apparatus for the exhibition of motion pictures, advertisements and election returns. In an action for breach of the contract for failure to furnish such paraphernalia it was held that plaintiff could recover as damage the cost of preparing and advertising the display and that of preparing a special edition of a newspaper to have been distributed to the crowd during the exhibition.

Pappas v. *Miles* (1907), 104 N. Y. Supp. 369. Action for breach of contract because of defendant's failure to furnish apparatus for the giving of a motion picture exhibition. Plaintiff purchased films to be exhibited on the stated occasion. *Held* that plaintiff's measure of damage was the difference between the amount paid for the films by plaintiff and their market value.

Kiralfy v. *Macauley*, 9 Ohio Dec. (Rep.) 833; 17 Weekly Law Bulletin, 331. The manager was held to be entitled to recover all expenses which he had actually incurred in preparation for the production of the play.

Savery v. *Ingersoll* (1887), 46 Hun (N. Y.), 176. Defendant agreed to deliver lecture at plaintiff's hall for which he was to receive a specified sum of money but failed to appear. *Held* that the following excerpt of the trial judge's charge was proper:

"The plaintiff is entitled to recover his actual loss, his actual expenses, such expense of time and money as he had put himself to, as he had made in good faith and were reasonably made in view of the execution of the contract."

An examination of the above cited cases establishes the necessity for a liquidated damage clause in a contract between the manager of a company and the owner of a theatre. Such a clause is absolutely essential in the event of a breach, as it removes all uncertainty, and leaves only the question of the breach to be litigated.

In a case wherein defendant agreed to furnish his theatre in Denver for one week and plaintiff agreed to provide his theatrical company and play in the theatre for that week, the profits to be divided, and each party to pay, on a breach by it, the sum of five hundred dollars as liquidated damages, it was held that this sum was not a penalty and could be recovered.[137]

A frequent application of this principle is found in contracts made for the production of motion pictures. The owner of a play frequently contracts with a motion picture company to film the play; he may also agree to play the star part in it. In consideration he agrees to take a percentage of the profits.

In an action brought by the owner of the play for damages for breach of the contract, where the company fails to make a production, it would be impossible for him to prove his damage, for there is nothing which would serve as a basis on which the probable profits of the picture could be estimated. Hence, the wisdom in this instance, of a liquidated damage clause.

But where a defendant has agreed to compensate the plaintiff in profits, and the contract has been partially performed, and some performances have been given, this

[137] *Mawson* v. *Leavitt* (1896), 16 Misc. (N. Y.) 289; 37 N. Y. Supp. 1138.

establishes a basis on which future profits may be computed.[138] That alone is the guide for fixing the damagès. Neither the evidence of experts on what profits might have been made, or evidence on what plaintiff earned with a third party at some time prior thereto, is admissible.[139]

In a recent decision [140] plaintiff had contracted with the defendant company to manufacture a picture and turn the same over to it. Upon doing so he was to receive a lump sum equal to the cost of producing the pic-

[138] *Ellsler* v. *Brooks* (1886), 54 Super. Ct. (N. Y.) 73. Plaintiff was to receive under her contract in lieu of all compensation a portion of the profits of the undertaking. *Held* that the testimony of experts, theatrical managers, as to what profits would have been made was incompetent.

Held further that evidence of what plaintiff made under similar forms of agreement with some third party three or four years before was incompetent.

Held further that the proper manner to compute profits was to take the period during which the agreement was in operation and take the profits made during such period as the basis of computation.

[139] *Todd* v. *Keene* (1896), 167 Mass. 157; 45 N. E. 81. Defendant refused to permit plaintiff to perform, plaintiff was to receive a percentage of the receipts. It was held that testimony of plaintiff giving receipts of similar performances given by him, also showing his reputation, repute and popularity, also showing that during the previous year he had played in the same theatre to a large audience and that the town was the seat of an institution of learning and that his performance would appeal to a large number of students, was inadmissible on the question of damages and that plaintiff was entitled to nominal damages only.

[140] *Goldberg* v. *Popular Pictures Corporation* (1917), N. Y. Law Journal, Jan. 20, Greenbaum, J. The appeal taken in the action and reported in (1917), 178 A. D. (N. Y.) 86, was not from the order made in pursuance of the motion above reported.

ture and subsequently a share of the gross receipts realized from the exhibition of the picture. Defendant refused to take and pay for the picture, and plaintiff brought action. Judge Greenbaum held that the complaint should have set up a case for damages for the breach of a contract. Said he:

"Upon the defendant's failure or refusal to accept the negative and films the plaintiffs had the right to retain them and to hold the defendant liable for damages for the breach of contract if its refusal to accept was unjustifiable. These damages would be measured by the actual cost to the plaintiffs of producing the negatives and films, and of the proportionate amount of the gross receipts derived by the defendant from the picture, as provided in the contract. *It is obvious, however, that it would be impossible in this case to establish what the gross receipts would be where the defendants have failed to accept the films.*"

Section 50.—Producer's offer of re-employment after breach.

Since it is the duty of the actor, where he has been discharged, to mitigate the damages by seeking other employment, it is his duty to accept employment offered by the producer who has discharged him, providing the offer is made in good faith, is for the balance of the contract period, for the same kind of services as under the contract, and providing the actor is still out of employment.

Where the actor was discharged, the producer in his offer to re-employ, is required to tender all moneys due and accruing under the contract between the time of the discharge and the time of the offer. That is the test of good faith.

Where the actor was compelled to leave because of the brutality, abuse or other improper treatment of the producer or those in his employ, he may ignore such offer of re-employment, as he is not required to subject himself again to such treatment.

The services to be rendered under the re-employment and the duration of the same must be substantially the same as under the original contract.[141]

Where the actor has obtained employment elsewhere, he is not bound to abandon it in order to accept such offer of re-employment.[142]

[141] *DeLoraz* v. *McDowell* (1893), 68 Hun, 170; 22 N. Y. Supp. 606; aff'd 142 N. Y. 664; 37 N. E. 570. Plaintiff was employed for a definite period. Before entering upon the performance of her duties she was discharged. Later defendant made an offer to engage her for an *indefinite* period which plaintiff refused. *Held* that although defendant might have set up the offer to engage as a partial defense in mitigation of damages yet he might not set up such offer and refusal as a complete defense to the action. Defendant cannot substitute a contract of indefinite hiring for one of a definite period.

[142] *Dearing* v. *Pearson* (1894), 8 Misc. (N. Y.) 269; 28 N. Y. Supp. 715. "After the termination of the contract by defendant's breach it could not be reinstated and plaintiff deprived of her cause of action except by mutual consent. Defendant had a locus pœnitentiæ, but only to the extent of enabling him to reduce plaintiff's damages by providing her with employment of the same kind, which plaintiff would have been bound to accept unless in the meantime she had entered upon another's employment or her refusal was justifiable upon substantial grounds, under pain of suffering a diminution of her recovery to the extent of the earnings she would have re-

An offer of re-employment may be pleaded by defendant, but it is not a total defense to the plaintiff's cause of action. It may simply be set up in reduction of and in mitigation of damages.[143]

Section 51.—Grounds for discharge.

An actor, like any other employe, may be discharged for a violation of any express or implied covenant of his contract of employment.

A prolific source of discord between actor and producer is the failure of the actor to appear at rehearsals; and where this failure to attend is willful or intentional, the actor may properly be discharged.[144]

ceived from the employment offered her."

[143] *DeLoraz* v. *McDowell* (1893), 68 Hun (N. Y.), 170; 22 N. Y. Supp. 606; aff'd 142 N. Y. 664; 37 N. E. 570; *Dearing* v. *Pearson* (1894), 8 Misc. (N. Y.) 269; 28 N. Y. Supp. 715.

[144] *Fisher* v. *Monroe* (1891), 12 N. Y. Supp. 273. Where plaintiff had been engaged as an actress for a season of 30 weeks, and she failed to appear at a rehearsal. *Held* that her failure to appear was not explained and that it was, under the circumstances, ground for discharge, and a verdict in her favor should be set aside. *Reversing Fisher* v. *Monroe* (1890), 11 N. Y. Supp. 207, where, however, the court also said: "And if the failure to attend (rehearsal) was willful or intentional, the plaintiff was properly discharged, and cannot recover."

Spalding v. *Rosa* (1877), 71 N. Y. 40; *Strackosh* v. *Strackosh* (1890), 11 N. Y. Supp. 251. Compare *Robinson* v. *Davison* (Eng.) (1871), L. R. 6 Exch. 269, where illness was held to be an excuse. See also: *Wolfe* v. *Howes* (1859), 20 N. Y. 197; *Fuller* v. *Brown* (1846), 11 Metc. (Mass.) 440; *Jerome* v. *Queens City Cycle* (1900), 163 N. Y. 351; 57 N. E. 485; *Fenton* v. *Clark* (1839), 11 Vt. 557; *Rolfs* v. *Pooley Furn. Co.* (1912), 176 Ill. App. 93; *Beckman* v. *Garrett* (1902), 66 Ohio St. 136; 64 N. E. 62; *Development Co.* v.

But illness of the actor may excuse him, if the illness is not protracted and does not seriously affect the reproduction of the picture.[145]

Where the illness is, however, serious enough to prevent the actor from rehearsing or performing, the right of discharge arises, as a contract of employment is purely personal in its nature, and illness or other incapacity to perform terminates all rights under it.[146]

King (1908), 161 Fed. (C. C. A.) 91.

[145] *Robinson* v. *Davison* (Eng.) (1871), L. R. 6 Exch. 269. Where the contract of a performer requires the appearance of the artist on a particular day, failure to appear because of illness does not necessarily constitute a breach of the contract.

See also: *Spaulding* v. *Rosa* (1877), 71 N. Y. 40; *Brandt* v. *Goodwin* (1889), 3 N. Y. Supp. 807; *Dickey* v. *Linscott* (1841), 20 Me. 453; *DeZeichner* v. *Lamm* (1914), 187 Ill. App. 25; *Wells* v. *Haff* (1915), 165 A. D. (N. Y.) 705; 151 N. Y. Supp. 497; *Young* v. *Am. Opera Co.* (1887), N. Y. Daily Reg., May 27; *Williams* v. *Butler* (1914), 105 N. E. (Ind.) 387; *Thomas* v. *Beaver Dam Mfg. Co.* (1914), 157 Wis. 427; 147 N. W. 364; *Bettini* v. *Gye* (Eng.) (1876), 1 Q. B. 183.

See also: *Corsi* v. *Maretzek* (1855), 4 E. D. Smith (N. Y), 1. The owner of a theatre may make reasonable rules and regulations by which the artists are to be governed. The contract in the instant case provided that absence of the artist would cause a forfeiture of the contract unless such absence was caused by illness and provided further that such illness had to be proved by the doctor appointed by the director. The fact that the artist was a homeopathist did not excuse the artist from complying with the rule of the owner.

Graddon v. *Price* (Eng.) (1827), 2 C. & P. 610; 12 E. C. L. 286. The actress was given one day's notice to appear in the part in which she had previously played. *Held* that it was a question for the jury whether the absence of actress because of illness justified the imposition of a fine.

[146] *Poussard* v. *Spiers* (Eng.) (1876), 1 Q. B. D. 410. Where the contract provides for employ-

Illness of the star actor, preventing the continuance of the making of the film does not release the producer from his obligations toward the other members of the company.[147]

Incompetency is just ground for discharge.[148] But

ment for an extended appearance and the absence of the artist may result in serious injury, failure to appear although caused by illness gives the manager a right to rescind the contract. See also: *Harley* v. *Henderson* (Eng.) (1884), Times, Feb. 18, 19.

Macalay v. *Press Pub. Co.* (1915), 170 A. D. (N. Y.) 640; 155 N. Y. Supp. 1044. Plaintiff, a professional cartoonist, was discharged before the expiration of the term of his contract because of continued tardiness in coming to work. It was held that defendant was entitled to fix a reasonable time at which plaintiff should report for duty, and if the employe did not report at such time either through illness or any other cause, the defendant could at his option terminate the employment.

[147] *Wentworth* v. *Whitney* (1903), 25 Pa. Super. 100. Contract provided for weekly payment with deductions only "for any nights or days on which the party of the second part (plaintiff) may not be able to perform or sing, through illness or other unavoidable cause, or at such times that the company may not be giving performances." *Held* that failure to give performance because of absence of necessary artist where plaintiff was ready to go on, was no excuse for refusal to pay plaintiff her compensation for the performance even though defendant was not at fault.

Gaittin v. *Searle* (1881), 1 N. Y. City Court, 349. Defendant discharged plaintiff because of illness of star of production and her inability to perform. *Held* that such illness did not relieve defendant from his obligation to plaintiff.

[148] *McLaughlin* v. *Hammerstein* (1904), 99 A. D. (N. Y.) 225; 90 N. Y. Supp. 943. It was error for the trial judge to refuse to charge (at defendant's request): "If the plaintiff gave an *incompetent* performance the defendant was at liberty to terminate the agreement without

what is "incompetency" is often a debatable question. In one case "incompetency" was held not to be equivalent to "unsatisfactory" and really to mean the actual physical disability of the artist to appear,[149] and not the professional quality of the voice.[150] The rule as to competency is well stated in *Brandt* v. *Godwin*,[151] holding in effect that the actor impliedly warrants that he has the requisite ability and skill to perform.

any notice whatever, and was not compelled to permit him to perform for the entire period of the contract."

[149] *Brand* v. *Godwin* (1890), 8 N. Y. Supp. 339; (1890), 9 N. Y. Supp. 743. An opera singer was engaged, a portion of the contract reading: "In the event either of incompetency or of such continued illness or decrease of physical or vocal faculties as to prevent one from doing service for a period of more than two weeks, the company may in its discretion cancel or annul the contract with the party in question, without being subjected to any claim for damages. The vocal and musical directors shall be the sole judges of the fact and extent of the incompetency, in applying this rule."

The court held that "incompetency" was not equivalent to "unsatisfactory," and that some proof of actual incompetency should have been offered.

[150] *Young* v. *American Opera Co.* (1887), Daily Reg. (N. Y.), May 27. The contract there provided that in the event of *incompetency* for two weeks, the plaintiff could be discharged. The word incompetency was held to mean physical disability due to illness and not professional quality of the voice.

[151] *Brandt* v. *Godwin* (1889), 3 N. Y. Supp. 807. "It is the rule that where a person engages to perform a service requiring the possession of special skill and qualities, there is an implied warranty on his part that he is possessed of the requisites to perform the duties undertaken, and if found wanting, the right to discharge exists." To the same effect: *Spaulding* v. *Rosa* (1877), 71 N. Y. 40.

Discharge for incompetency must be made in good faith [152] and can only be made after the actor has been given a reasonable opportunity to perform or rehearse his rôle [153] and on sufficient evidence of his incompetency.[154] But where the artist has commenced rehearsal and the producer feels that he is incompetent, he is under no obligation to permit him to continue, but may discharge him at once.[155]

[152] *Grinnell* v. *Kiralfy* (1890), 55 Hun (N. Y.), 422; 8 N. Y. Supp. 623. A contract in which plaintiff was engaged as a soubrette and in which the manager reserved the right to discharge her for incompetency or other reasons if he became dissatisfied with her, held to be qualified by the use of the words "in good faith" and that plaintiff had bound himself by those words not to act arbitrarily or capriciously.

[153] *Walton* v. *Godwin* (1890), 58 Hun (N. Y.), 87; 11 N. Y. Supp. 391. The contract provided that "the vocal and musical directors shall be the sole judges of the fact and extent of the incompetency" of the plaintiff. *Held* that discharge was not justified where after signing of the contract plaintiff was never called upon to rehearse or perform.

[154] *Harley* v. *Henderson* (Eng.) (1884), Times, Feb. 19. Plaintiff was engaged to play at the Comedy Theatre in London. Four months afterward the defendant informed him that the author, the chorus mistress and the conductor complained that he was "frightfully out of tune" and plaintiff was accordingly discharged.

Held that the evidence was not sufficient to show that plaintiff was incompetent to perform his rôle, and judgment was rendered in his favor.

Charley v. *Potthoff* (1903), 118 Wis. 258; 95 N. W. 124. It was for the jury to say whether plaintiff gave the kind of performances contemplated by the contract.

[155] *Thill* v. *Hoyt* (1899), 37 A. D. (N. Y.) 521; 56 N. Y. Supp. 78. An actress was engaged to play a part, defendant agreeing to give her "a trial." She brought this action for breach of a contract of employment for a season and the court nonsuited her. See also: *Mc-*

The death of one or more members of a troupe will cancel a contract for their appearance, where the member who has died is one of the chief performers in the troupe.[156]

Laughlin v. *Hammerstein* (1904), 99 A. D. (N. Y.) 225; 90 N. Y. Supp. 943.

Zamco v. *Hammerstein* (Eng.) (1913), 29 T. L. R. 217. Defendant engaged plaintiff as an opera singer. After rehearsal defendant became dissatisfied with him and refused to let him appear. *Held* that it was open to proof whether or not defendant was justified in terminating the contract.

[156] *Spalding* v. *Rosa* (1877), 71 N. Y. 40. Allen, J.: "Contracts of this character, for personal services, whether of the contracting party or of a third person, requiring skill, and which can only be performed by the particular individual named, are not, in their nature, of absolute obligation, under all circumstances. Both parties must be supposed to contemplate the continuance of the ability of the person whose skilled services are the subject of the contract, as one of the conditions of the contract. Contracts for personal services are subject to this implied condition, that the person shall be able at the appointed time to perform them; and if he dies, or without fault on the part of the covenantor becomes disabled, the obligation to perform becomes extinguished."

This case further holds that where a theatrical troupe is engaged, it is of the essence of the contract that the chief artist shall perform.

Glinseretti v. *Rickards* (Eng.) (1907), Times, Jan. 26th, presents the interesting question whether a troupe of acrobats can insist on performance of a contract when some of the acrobats have died or left the troupe since the making of the contract. However, this point was not directly passed upon. See also: *Harvey* v. *Tivoli, Manchester, Ltd.* (Eng.) (1907), 23 T. L. R. 592; *Robinson* v. *Davison* (Eng.) (1871), L. R. 6 Exch. 269.

See in this connection: *Phillips* v. *Alhambra Palace* (Eng.) (1901), 1 K. B. 59. The death of one proprietor was held not to abrogate the contract with the performer, and the contract was held, as to such proprietors, not personal.

The immorality or lewd conduct of the artist is sufficient ground for discharge,[157] as well as violent and abusive language [158] and insolence [159] and insubordination; [160] so that where the conduct of a manager threatens the best interests of the theatre, he may be discharged.[161] Indeed, unfaithfulness generally is sufficient ground.[162] And where the actor claims an interest in the business when he has none in fact he may be dismissed.[163]

[157] *Drayton* v. *Reid* (1874), 5 Daly (N. Y.), 442. Where the plaintiff was guilty of lewd and indecent conduct, cursed and swore and had illicit intercourse with one of the performers, a married man, her discharge was justifiable.

[158] *Wade* v. *Hefner* (1915), 84 S. E. (Ga. App.) 598; *Ernst* v. *Grand Rapids Engr. Co.* (1912), 138 N. W. (Mich.) 1050; *Bass Furnace Co.* v. *Glasscock* (1886), 82 Ala. 452; 2 So. 315.

[159] *Forsythe* v. *McKinney* (1890), 8 N. Y. Supp. 561.

[160] *Zenatello* v. *Hammerstein* (1911), 231 Pa. 56; 79 Atl. 922. The defendant averred that plaintiff, an opera singer, was asked to sing the tenor rôle in "The Prophet" and that he declined to do so without reason.

Held that this was clearly a question for the jury. See also: *Haag* v. *Rogers* (1911), 9 Ga. App. 650; 72 S. E. 46, where the employe was engaged in a fight in the employer's place of business.

See also: *Standing* v. *Brady* (1913), 157 A. D. (N. Y.) 657; 142 N. Y. Supp. 656; *Rafalo* v. *Edelstein* (1913), 140 N. Y. Supp. 1076; 80 Misc. (N. Y.) 153; *Duff* v. *Russell* (1892), 133 N. Y. 678; 31 N. E. 622; aff'g 14 N. Y. Supp. 134; *Standidge* v. *Lynde* (1905), 120 Ill. App. 418; *Morrison* v. *Hurtig* (1910), 198 N. Y. 352; 91 N. E. 842.

[161] *Lacy* v. *Obaldiston* (Eng.) (1837), 8 C. & P. 80; 34 E. C. L. 300.

[162] *Alexender* v. *Potts* (1909), 151 Ill. App. 587; *Carpenter Steel Co.* v. *Norcross* (1913), 204 Fed. (C. C. A.) 537.

[163] *Fitzgerald* v. *George Newnes, Ltd.* (Eng.) (1902), Times, April 22. An editor who claimed an interest in a periodical because the magazine had been founded at his suggestion, was dismissed without notice. *Held* justified.

The producer may discharge the actor for drunkenness; one act of drunkenness is sufficient; [164] and where he is sued for a breach the producer may set up drunkenness as a rightful discharge.[165]

But where, after intoxication, the actor is retained in his employment, this would probably be a condonation, and he could not subsequently be discharged therefor,[166] unless he persisted in his derelictions.[167]

[164] *Bass Furnace Co.* v. *Glasscock* (1886), 82 Ala. 452; 2 So. 315. Where an employe while in the service of his employer becomes drunk and manifests such drunkenness by boisterous and disorderly conduct, the employer may discharge him as it "is such misconduct as to constitute a violation of the stipulation, implied in every contract of service, that the employe will conduct himself with such decency and politeness of deportment as not to work an injury to the business of the employer." "This he can do by a single act of drunkenness." To the same effect: *Gonsolis* v. *Gearhart* (1862), 31 Mo. 585.

[165] *Brown* v. *Baldwin-Gleason* (1891), 13 N. Y. Supp. 893. "Accordingly it was open to the defendant on the pleadings (under a general denial) to show that the plaintiff's dismissal was *rightful*, because of intoxication." See *Willis* v. *Lowery* (1912), 57 So. (Miss.) 418. And in particular *Linton* v. *U. F. Co.* (1891), 124 N. Y. 533; 27 N. E. 406, which holds that a defendant may not offer proof of justification for discharge under a general denial, but that the same must be pleaded as a defense, since a complaint which alleges a contract and a discharge prior to its expiration makes out a prima facie case. "The law will not presume that a servant has been derelict in his duty." The burden of proving this is upon the defendant.

[166] *Batchelder* v. *Standard Plunger El. Co.* (1910), 227 Pa. 201; 75 Atl. 1090.

[167] *Macaulay* v. *Press Pub. Co.* (1915), 170 A. D. (N. Y.) 640; 155 N. Y. Supp. 1044; *Ginsberg* v. *Friedman* (1911), 146 A. D. (N. Y.) 779; 131 N. Y. Supp. 517; *Rosbach* v. *Sackett & Wilhelms Co.* (1909), 134 A. D. (N. Y.)

It has been held that a musician may be discharged by his manager where the musical union to which they both belong will not permit the former to play.[168] And an actor who is violating the law by not obtaining a required license, may also be discharged.[169]

While actual notice is indispensable,[170] no precise words of discharge are required; any speech by which he is informed that his services are no longer desired suffices.[171]

The death of the actor at once terminates the contract.[172]

130; 118 N. Y. Supp. 846; *United Oil Co.* v. *Grey* (1907), 102 S. W. (Tex.) 934.

[168] *Scarano* v. *Lemlein* (1910), 66 Misc. (N. Y.) 174; 121 N. Y. Supp. 351. "Where both plaintiff and defendant were members of a musical union and entered into a contract of employment, there is a presumption that the contract is to be read in the light of the union's by-laws, in so far as such by-laws attempt to regulate the terms of employment of its members, and defendant could properly discharge the plaintiff when, under the by-laws of the union, the plaintiff was precluded from performing the work."

[169] *Gray* v. *The Oxford, Lim.* (Eng.) (1906), 22 T. L. R. 684. Defendant owned a music hall; plaintiff produced a sketch "The Fighting Parson" in it under a contract for six weeks. After five weeks defendant decided that this was a stage-play and could not be performed unless he had a theatre license. He cancelled the contract.

Held that this sketch was a stage-play and could not legally be produced in a music hall and that defendant was entitled to cancel his contract.

[170] *DeGellert* v. *Poole* (1888), 2 N. Y. Supp. 651.

[171] *Sigmon* v. *Goldstone* (1906), 116 A. D. (N. Y.) 490; 101 N. Y. Supp. 984.

As to the burden of proof see: Maratta v. *Heer Dry Goods Co.* (1915), 190 Mo. App. 420; 177 S. W. 718.

[172] For detailed discussion of this proposition, see Sections 10 and 14.

But where the actor was to receive part of his compensation during the term of the contract, and the balance at the end, his heirs may sue on a quantum meruit for the period during which he performed.[173]

Where the parties agree beforehand as to the manner and terms of discharge, it would seem that they would be bound thereby,[174] and that the damages recoverable would be such as were fixed by the contract.[175]

[173] *Wolfe* v. *Howes* (1859), 20 N. Y. 197. Where contract of employment provided that plaintiff's testate was to receive partial compensation during period of employment and balance upon termination of contract period it was held that plaintiff was entitled to recover for his testate's services upon a quantum meruit basis, where plaintiff's testate was incapable of carrying out the agreement because of illness.

[174] *Griffin* v. *Brooklyn Ball Club* (1902), 68 A. D. (N. Y.) 566; 73 N. Y. Supp. 864. "The contract between the parties contained a clause providing that the defendant might 'at any time after the beginning and prior to the completion of the period of this contract give the party of the second part (plaintiff) ten days' written notice of its option and intention to end and determine all its liabilities and obligations under this contract, in which event, upon the expiration of said ten days, all liabilities and obligations undertaken by said party of the first part or its assigns' should at once 'cease and determine.'

"It is urged that because defendant under this clause might have discharged plaintiff upon ten days' notice, it cannot be held liable upon its breach for damages for more than that period. (*Watson* v. *Russell*, 149 N. Y. 388.)

"We are unwilling to adopt this view. We are not interested in what defendant might have done under this contract, but in what it did do."

Watson v. *Russell* (1896), 49 N. Y. 388; 44 N. E. 161.

[175] *Egbert* v. *Sun Co.* (1903), 126 Fed. (C. C.) 568.

Section 52.—Actor's breach of the contract—damages.

While a producer who engages an actor and "features" him in an important rôle, may suffer considerable pecuniary loss because of the latter's breach of the contract, it is not an easy matter to collect damages therefor. Of course, the producer has a cause of action against the actor,[176] but that helps him very little, since it is next to impossible to find a true basis for damage.

The way in which this is usually overcome is to insert in the contract a clause for liquidated damages to be paid by the actor in the event of his breach. Where such damages are reasonable in amount, the court will uphold them.[177] The safest clause to insert is one providing that

[176] *Placide* v. *Burton* (1859), 17 Super. Ct. (N. Y.) 512. A manager may maintain an action against an actor who failed to appear upon the date agreed upon, for the damages sustained by him by reason of the breach.

Bettini v. *Gye* (Eng.) (1876), 1 Q. B. D. 183. Plaintiff was engaged especially as a tenor to appear in London. He failed to arrive in time to attend rehearsals, because of illness, and when he offered to perform defendant refused to permit him, claiming a breach.

Held that defendant could not rescind, but that he could have sued plaintiff at law for the damages sustained; that his covenant to appear on a specified opening date did not go to the *root of the matter*—in other words, it was not of the essence of the contract.

[177] *Bustanoby* v. *Revardel* (1911), 71 Misc. (N. Y.) 207; 130 N. Y. Supp. 894. Plaintiff was the owner of a restaurant. It agreed with defendants to employ them at $115 a week as musicians for two years, and the contract provided that in case defendants breached the same they should be liable for $1,000 as liquidated damages.

Held that in view of the fact that in case of a breach the damages to plaintiff would necessarily be uncertain, this was a reasonable provision.

the actor will pay as liquidated damages an amount equal to what he would have received, had he performed.[178]

It matters very little whether the words "penalty" or "liquidated damages" are used. The courts will not be bound by the language of the contract.[179]

The contract, however, was void for want of mutuality since the plaintiff did not agree to hire defendants for two years, and since it had the privilege of discharging them at any time.

Conried Metrop. Opera Co. v. *Brin* (1910), 66 Misc. (N. Y.) 282; 123 N. Y. Supp. 6. Where in a contract for services of a musical artist it is provided that upon a breach he shall pay as liquidated damages a specified sum, the court will award judgment for such sum to the injured party where it is impossible to ascertain the exact loss or damage which the injured party may sustain by reason of the breach.

[178] *Corsi* v. *Maretzek* (1855), 4 E. D. Smith (N. Y.), 1. *Held* that a provision in a contract between a singer and director of opera whereby the singer forfeited one month's salary upon his failure to appear at any entertainment for which he might be announced unless it was due to illness of the artist, such illness to be certified by the doctor appointed by the director, was valid.

Golders Green Am. & Dev. Co. v. *Relph* (Eng.) (1915), 31 T. L. R. 343. Defendant, an artist, agreed to perform twice an evening at plaintiff's music hall. For his default he agreed as liquidated damages to pay the amount he would have received for each performance. The contract was subsequently modified, and defendant defaulting, the court held him liable in damages as computed by the modification.

[179] *Pastor* v. *Solomon* (1899), 26 Misc. (N. Y.) 125; 55 N. Y. Supp. 956; aff'g 25 Misc. (N. Y.) 322. In a contract between a theatre manager and actors it was provided that upon a breach by the actors that they would become liable to a penalty of $500. *Held*, that was reasonable, and not disproportionate, and plaintiff recovered. *Held further* that the fact that the word "penalty" was used did not make it such. The courts would

It sometimes happens that the producer and actor agree to divide the profits, and that one of the parties subsequently refuses to carry out his agreement in that respect. The courts, construing a contract of this nature, usually hold it to be one of employer and employe, and not one of joint venture.[180]

Where the actress was required to pay her manager a specified percentage of the profits above twenty thousand dollars it was held that the word "profits" was intended to mean "net receipts" and that the actress

not be bound by the word, but rather by the intent of the parties, and by the facts.

[180] *Mallory* v. *Mackaye* (1899), 92 Fed. (C. C. A.) 749; *Mackaye* v. *Mallory* (cross bill). Mallory, a theatrical manager, made a contract with Mackaye whereby defendant agreed to give his exclusive services to Mallory for a period of ten years as actor, author, director and inventor, the literary property and invention of Mackaye to belong absolutely to Mallory. Mallory agreed to pay Mackaye a specified sum per annum and in addition thereto a portion of the profits. *Held* that the relationship between the parties was one of employer and employe and not one of joint ventures.

After the expiration of the second year Mackaye abandoned the contracts. *Held* that the contract was entire and not severable and that a breach as to a material part by one party discharged the other. *Held further* that where after an abandonment of the contract by one party, the other served notice of termination as provided by the contract, the giving of such subsequent notice of termination did not constitute a waiver of the breach.

To the same effect: *Thomas* v. *Springer* (1909), 134 A. D. (N. Y.) 640; 119 N. Y. Supp. 460; *Keith* v. *Kellerman* (1909), 169 Fed. (C. C.) 196; *McLellan* v. *Goodwin* (1899), 43 A. D. (N. Y.) 148; 59 N. Y. Supp. 290. For a discussion of and excerpts from the above cases, see Section 62.

could not charge the cost of production against the profits.[181]

Section 53.—Changing the motion picture.

In making a motion picture, scenes are taken according to a set plan, the scenario. The scenes are not taken consecutively, in their logical sequence, but in such sequence as will complete the picture most rapidly and involve the least expense.

Many scenes are taken over a number of times in order to insure perfection both from a photographic and acting viewpoint.

After all the scenes outlined in the plan are taken, the different portions of the film are assembled and viewed, and those scenes which are inferior in acting or in photography, those which are duplications and those which retard the action are "cut." The remaining scenes constitute the finished film.

The questions which naturally present themselves are: may the motion picture producer after the film is set up in its final form, change the order of the scenes; may he edit scenes, may he interpolate new scenes which were taken separately from the scenes of the film; may he take scenes of one picture for which the actor specially posed and make use of such scenes in an entirely different film; and may he take scenes which have been discarded because of inferior acting or poor photography or because they were "repeats" and make such use of them as he sees fit.

[181] *Mayer* v. *Nethersole* (1902), 71 A. D. (N. Y.) 383; 75 N. Y. Supp. 987.

None of the above questions has as yet come before the courts, but it is reasonable to assume that the courts will apply to such questions those rules of law which have developed in the common law for the protection of creators of literary work.

The analogy is very close between the owner of a novel or play to whom the author or playwright has sold his work outright or by whom the author or playwright was engaged to create such work, and that of an actor who has posed in a motion picture.

In the former case the effort of the artist has resulted in a work which portrays *by means of language* dramatic action. In the latter, the effort of the artist has resulted in a work which portrays *by means of pictures* dramatic action. In both instances the legal title in the product is in the owner of the finished work, who alone may exercise dominion over it. In both cases the artist has an interest remaining in the property *because his reputation and standing* are dependent upon the proper use of the property. Moreover, in both cases the owner of the work may use the name of the artist in the exploitation of the work.

We have already discussed the rights of an author or playwright who has parted with title to his work by outright sale, and those of an author or playwright who has never had title in the results of his labor because of the relationship of employer and employe.[182]

Let us apply those rules to the questions before us.

The finished film coming from the cutting room is similar to the work of the author or playwright delivered in final form to the purchaser thereof.

[182] See Section 12.

The motion picture producer may change the order of the scenes, may edit scenes and may add such scenes which have been discarded because they were "repeats" or because they were regarded in the cutting process as retarding the action; but only in so far as such changes in the picture are not radical in their nature or do not constitute a mutilation of the film. By radical is meant such a change as will occur for instance where a feature film is cut down to a two-reel film or vice-versa, where by adding a large number of discarded scenes a one or two reel film is stretched into a feature picture. With respect to mutilation it is a question of fact in each instance.

The remedy both in the case of a radical change and in that of mutilation is an action for libel.[183] Title in the work being in the motion picture producer the actor may not go into equity to enjoin the exhibition of such changed film,[184] unless in addition to the libel, there is the element of "passing off" or fraud and deception of the public.

[183] See Section 12.

[184] *Chaplin* v. *Essanay* (1916), N. Y. Law Journal, May 23d, Hotchkiss, J.; aff'd 174 A. D. (N. Y.) 866. Plaintiff posed for defendant in a two-reel film which was entitled "Burlesque on Carmen." The defendant, after the termination of plaintiff's employment, inserted a number of discarded scenes taken in the course of the making of the film and also added several scenes made without the participation of the plaintiff, and after he had completed his work therein. The film was then released as a four-reel feature film. The plaintiff contended that under his contract the defendant could not change the film in any manner, after its completion by him, without first securing his consent. He also contended that the stretching of the film by inserting discarded scenes and scenes taken without his participation, all of which retarded the action and destroyed his prominence in the film, seriously

In the same manner that an author or playwright has a right to have the identity of his work retained, so an actor is entitled to have the identity of the picture in which he posed retained. The motion picture producer may not separate particular scenes from the film and make use of them elsewhere, nor has he the right to in-

injured his reputation and standing as a motion picture "star."

In denying a motion for an injunction pendente lite, the court said:

"Notwithstanding the earnest argument of counsel for the plaintiff, I think this motion should be denied principally for the following reasons:

"(1) Plaintiff's right under paragraph third of the contract of December, 1914 (assuming such contract to have remained in force unaltered), to enjoin the production because he has not approved of the play is doubtful.

"(2) The play itself is undoubtedly the property of the Essanay Film Manufacturing Company, by which company plaintiff was employed, and the circumstances of plaintiff's services in connection with the creation of the play distinguish the case from those cases which have applied the principle of another's exclusive right of literary property.

"(3) The facts do not justify a claim that the association of plaintiff's name with the play as produced amounts to a fraud upon the public. A fair construction of the advertisements of the play is not that plaintiff is the author or producer, but that he is the star or principal actor.

"(4) It is not claimed that so far as he is pictured in the play his part is garbled or distorted. Whatever of him is shown is a truthful representation. Whether plaintiff's contract rights reserve to him, rather than to his employers, the sole privilege of determining what of his pictures shall be incorporated into the play as produced is at least doubtful.

"(5) Whether plaintiff will suffer any damage from the production is problematical, while an injunction is certain to work considerable loss to defendants."

See also in this connection: *Gabriel* v. *McCabe* (1896), 74 Fed. (C. C.) 743.

corporate new scenes taken from some other film or photographed separately from those taken specially for the film in question. The actor has the same remedies for any such breach that an author or playwright has.

Finally, any use made by the motion picture producer of those scenes which have been discarded because of their inferiority either in their photography or acting, constitutes a libel.

Coming now to the exhibition of the film, the positives and the negatives are the absolute property of the motion picture producer. He may release them at any time he sees fit, and through whatever exchanges are agreeable to him. The films may be shown in any theatres wherein the positives are delivered. In other words, the actor has no control over the exploitation of the film unless he has contracted otherwise.

Nor has the actor any control of the advertising issued in connection with the exploitation of the film, except as by contract between the parties.

Section 54.—Contracts with infants.

Infants are engaged to pose in motion pictures, not only in minor parts, but in important as well as occasionally in stellar rôles.

Contracts of hire are voidable at the option of the infant. Upon avoiding the contract the infant may generally recover for services rendered, although the producer would be entitled to set off any damage he may have sustained by reason of the infant's avoidance.

The motion picture producer may not enforce a negative covenant to restrain the infant from working for anyone else during the contract period.[185] The courts will not enforce such a negative covenant even where the guardian or parents and the infant are both parties to the agreement.[186]

[185] *Aborn* v. *Janis* (1907), 62 Misc. (N. Y.) 95; 113 N. Y. Supp. 309.

[186] *Aborn* v. *Janis* (1907), 62 Misc. (N. Y.) 95; 113 N. Y. Supp. 309. The defendant Elsie Janis, an infant, had contracted through her general guardian with the plaintiff for her services as an actress. She subsequently rendered services for one Percy Williams and plaintiff sought to restrain her under a negative covenant. The court, denying the motion, said: "An adult, who was bound to render peculiar and valuable services to another, and has agreed to render them for no one else during the term of the contract, will, it is to be assumed, continue to observe his contract, if restrained from rendering his services to another person; that is, the injunction in its cogent effect upon adult intelligence would result in performance of the contract, and it is for this reason that the courts have adopted the remedy by injunction in cases of contract for personal services as a means to the desired end—specific performance of the agreement made by the party thus enjoined. But if prior to the attainment of the age of twenty-one years, a person may not ordinarily make a contract because of that absence of mature intelligence which the law presumes to arise from nonage, *how may it be said that the infant's intelligence will be affected by an injunction, as though the wisdom of an adult were present?* To determine that such a contract should be specifically enforced by resort to an injunction prohibiting the breach of the negative covenant would be to say, in effect, that the infant, a person lacking sufficient judgment to contract, must yet exercise sufficient judgment as to his or her personal interest to elect between performing a contract not necessarily wisely made, and indeed, presumably unwisely made, or take the harsh alternative of starvation for a refusal to perform at all or for an omission to perform in a satisfactory manner; and all this while the

And while it has been said that a contract of the infant beneficial in its character may be enforced,[187] nevertheless neither in this country nor in England will the contract for personal services of the infant be deemed such a contract.[188]

infant, because of immaturity, is deemed to be under the protection of the court as its ward."

Vent v. *Osgood* (1837), 36 Mass. 572; *Ide* v. *Brown* (1904), 178 N. Y. 26; 70 N. E. 101.

See also: *Gordon* v. *Barr* (1917), N. Y. Law Journal, Jan 20. Hendrick, J.: "In this motion to restrain defendants from 'rendering services as artists or theatrical performers,' the complaint alleges that defendants have broken their contract and threaten to continue 'to do the various things and matters in contravention of the said agreement.' Defendants state in an affidavit that they were only twenty years of age when they signed the contract, but infancy is not alleged as a defense. Plaintiff is a 'manager' and acts as an intermediary between theatrical performers and their employers. Defendants are twin sisters and perform dancing acts and sing at music halls and cabarets. They claim that their services are neither 'unique, extraordinary or peculiar' and, therefore, if they have broken the contract, plaintiff has an adequate remedy at law, and cite *Hammerstein* v. *Mann*, 122 Supp. 278; *Lasky Feature Co.* v. *Suratt & Fox Film Corp'n*, 154 Supp. 974. They also argue that as plaintiff was not a theatrical manager, but simply had an interest in their compensation, he has an ample legal remedy. To this point they cite *Solman* v. *Arcaro*, 129 N. Y. Supp. 689. I do not think that the remedy of injunction can be invoked unless plaintiff makes a case reasonably clear and in my opinion plaintiff's case lacks the usual requisites. The motion is denied."

[187] *In re Livingston* (1866), 34 N. Y. 555.

[188] *Aborn* v. *Janis* (1907), 62 Misc. (N. Y.) 95; 113 N. Y. Supp. 309; *De Francesco* v. *Barnum* (Eng.) (1889), 60 L. J. Ch. 63.

In New York it is a misdemeanor to employ minors under specified ages for singing or danc-

Section 55.—Inability of producer—when studio closed by authorities.

The inability of a manager to open his theatre does not relieve him from liability under his contract of employment.[189] In like manner a producer is not freed from liability because he cannot make use of his studio.

But the manager frequently inserts a clause, intended to modify his liability in that respect, and if the clause is properly worded, he may succeed in doing so.[190] But

ing—see *People* v. *Ewer* (1894), 141 N. Y. 129; 36 N. E. 4; *People* v. *Stevens* (1893), 70 Hun (N. Y.), 243.

[189] *Rice* v. *Miner* (1915), 89 Misc. (N. Y.) 395; 151 N. Y. Supp. 983. "The defendant attempts to excuse his failure to furnish employment for the week of December 8th, 1913, on the ground that no license had been obtained for the theatre in which the performances were to be given, and it is claimed that this was an 'interference or restraint of a legal authority. . . .' That clause plainly contemplates active interference by public officials, and does not mean restraint by law, or include a case where defendant failed to obtain or cause to be procured a theatre license."

Hardie v. *Balmain* (Eng.) (1902), 18 T. L. R. 539.

[190] *Halcroft* v. *West End Playhouse, Ltd.* (Eng.) (1916), S. C. 182. Where defendant, owners of a theatre in the course of construction, had contracted with a performer to appear therein after its completion, and the building of the theatre was not completed, it was held that defendant was not liable, as the contract contained a clause that it was "subject to the said theatre being in the occupancy and possession of the management."

Thring v. *Lucas* (Eng.) (1903), Strong on "Dramatic and Musical Law," 3d Ed., p. 30. Where the theatre was closed by the authorities in order that certain repairs should be made. *Held* that the owner was not liable under a contract which contained a clause that "Engagement to be void if the performance is objected to by the public

just as often the language may be too broad or inartificial and the result will be that the actor may recover damages.[191]

But the language of such a contract is strictly construed, and the manager who assigns his interest in the show to another may not evade liability, for that is not a closing of the theatre.[192]

Section 56.—Questions of travel.

In filming a play it is frequently necessary to take scenes at places other than at the studio of the motion picture producer. An actor who agrees to participate in the making of a picture knows that he may be required to travel while engaged in the making of the picture. He is

authorities, or stopped by any cause over which the management have no control."

[191] *Hardie* v. *Balmain* (Eng.) (1902), 18 T. L. R. 539. Plaintiff, manager of a company, contracted with defendant, manager of a theatre, to appear for six nights, profits to be divided; if the theatre was closed through fire, death in the Royal Family, "or any cause whatsoever," contract to be terminated.

The theatre was closed on what was to be the opening night, not having been completed. *Held* that the manager of the theatre was liable under the contract.

"Any cause whatsoever" meant any cause external to that outside the control of the parties to the contract. See also: *Rice* v. *Miner* (1915), 89 Misc. (N. Y.) 395; 151 N. Y. Supp. 983.

[192] *Lorette* v. *Collins* (Eng.) (1906), Strong on "Dramatic and Musical Law," 3d Ed., p. 27. In the contract for plaintiff's appearance for a week at the Hippodrome, it was provided that in the event of the hall closing for any cause the contract was to terminate. The manager *assigned* his interest to another. *Held* this was not a closing, and plaintiff recovered.

engaged to pose in the picture and hence agrees to present himself at the places where the picture can be taken. Unless, therefore, he expressly provides otherwise in his contract of employment he must attend at the places where the picture is to be taken and the cost of transportation, as well as of his board and lodging, must be borne by him.[193]

Section 57.—Booking agencies.

In several of the states, laws have been passed requiring all agencies that procure employment for actors to obtain licenses and otherwise comply with certain requirements. These agencies are not permitted to charge more than a fixed rate and for a stated period during which the actor receives a salary.[194]

Attempts are often made to evade the statute, by inserting a provision in the booking contract that the person procuring the engagement is a "manager" and that the increased rate of compensation is paid in consideration of certain services rendered or to be rendered—more or

[193] *Batty* v. *Melillo* (Eng.) (1850), 10 C. B. 282; *Smith* v. *Herring-Hall-Marvin Safe Co.* (1909), 115 N. Y. Supp. 204. See in this connection: *Day* v. *Klaw* (1908), 112 N. Y. Supp. 1072.

On the question of the distance he may be required to travel see: Gath v. *Interstate Amusement Co.* (1912), 170 Ill. App. 614.

[194] Chapter 700 of the Laws of 1910 (New York), as amended by Chapter 587 of the Laws of 1916.

Interstate Amusement Co. v. *Albert* (1913), 161 S. W. (Tenn.) 488. A booking agency which had made a contract in one state for the performance of certain acts in another state, was held not to have complied with the provisions of the latter state with respect to license and tax, and so could not recover.

less fictitious. The courts have prevented recovery upon such contracts.[195]

The booking agent is entitled to his compensation when the introduction is effected and the actor is eventually accepted.[196]

Where the contract of employment was postponed by the actor through *force majeure* the actor is not obligated to pay until he actually enters upon his engagement.[197]

[195] *Meyers* v. *Walton* (1912), 76 Misc. 510; 135 N. Y. Supp. 574. *Held* that the plaintiff who sued for services which he claimed he rendered as "manager" under a contract calling for a compensation of 5% of any salary received by defendants for performing in a vaudeville sketch, was evading the Theatrical Agency License law (Chap. 700, Laws 1910, amended 1916), and a judgment in his favor was reversed.

[196] *Colles* v. *Mangham* (Eng.) (1909), Times, Dec. 21. One who is in the business of placing dramatic compositions for production is entitled to compensation when in his business capacity he introduces an author to a manager who eventually accepts his play.

See also: *King* v. *Broadhurst* (1914), 164 A. D. (N. Y.) 689; 150 N. Y. Supp. 376. An actor who made a contract with a playwright whereby he agreed to procure a producer of a play provided he was given the leading rôle may recover for the reasonable value of his services for securing such a manager where he waived his right to play the leading rôle upon the representation of the playwright that he would "do what is right" and other similar expressions.

[197] *Foster's Agency, Lim.*, v. *Romaine* (Eng.) (1916), 32 T. L. R. 545. Plaintiff sued for breach of a contract whereby he was to be compensated by defendant for procuring an engagement in Australia. Because of the dangers incidental to submarine warfare defendant *postponed* her engagement. *Held* there could be no recovery, as defendant had not breached the contract.

Auckland & Brunetti v. *Collins* (Eng.) (1898), 14 T. L. R. 348. A booking agent's agreement for

Section 58.—Workmen Compensation Acts.

Most of the states as well as the federal government have enacted compensation acts.

Actors who are engaged to pose in motion pictures as well as directors, camera men and the other employes of the studio probably come within the protection of the statute in a number of states. In each instance it is always a question of the construction of the statute involved.[198]

The interesting question arises whether an actor employed in a state where a workmen's compensation act is in force with respect to members of the theatrical profession can enforce his rights under the act against his employer when the injury occurs without the state while he is en tour.

The question is ordinarily one of construction of the statute. In Massachusetts the court following the English rule [199] has held that the statute has no extraterritorial

commission was held enforcible where theatre had been torn down and re-built.

[198] See Bulletin No. 203 (January, 1917), of the United States Department of Labor; Bureau of Labor Statistics, entitled "Workmen's Compensation Laws of the United States and Foreign Countries" for the text of all the statutes in force at the present time.

See also: Bulletin No. 2 (Jan., 1913, p. 5), of the Massachusetts Industrial Accident Board on the question whether vaudeville actors come within the provisions of the Massachusetts statute.

See also for recent New York Statute, Laws of 1916, Chap. 622, Group 40. Entitling to compensation those engaged in "printing, engraving, photo-engraving, stereotyping, electrotyping, lithographing, embossing, *manufacture of moving picture machines and films. . . .*"

[199] *Tomalin* v. *Pearson* (Eng.) (1909), 2 K. B. 61; *Schwartz* v. *India Rubber* (Eng.) (1912), 2 K.

effect. It held that the employe, a citizen and resident of that state, could not claim the benefits under the statute although the employer was a Massachusetts corporation and the contract of hire was made in that state, the accident having occurred in the state of New York.[200]

The court held that his right to recover damages was determined by the law of the state where the accident took place.

The same rule has been enunciated in Michigan.[201] In New Jersey, however, the contrary conclusion was reached.[202] The court held that although the statute was not binding without the limits of the state, yet the statute could require a contract to be made by two parties to a hiring and that such contract should have an extraterritorial effect. The court found that there was an implied contract between the parties to compensate for injuries arising out of the employment, and that such contract could be enforced irrespective of the place where the injury was sustained.

In Ohio the same result was arrived at as in New

B. 299; *Hicks* v. *Maxton* (Eng.), 124 L. T. Rep. 135.

[200] *Gould's Case* (1913), 215 Mass. 480; 102 N. E. 693. "The subject of personal injuries received by a workman in the course of his employment is within the control of the sovereign power where the injury occurs. 'It must certainly be the right of each state to determine by its laws under what circumstances an injury to the person will afford a cause of action.'"

[201] *Keyes* v. *Allerdyce*, Michigan Industrial Accident Board, April, 1913.

[202] *Deeny* v. *Wright & Cobb*, 36 N. J. L. J. 121, referred to in Bradbury on "Workmen's Compensation."

Jersey, not, however, upon the theory of an implied contract, but by a construction of the statute which provided for compensation for injuries or death "wherever occurring." [203]

In New York an action was brought by a seaman for injuries received through negligence of his employer.[204] It appeared that the plaintiff was employed by defendant on one of its ships for a voyage from Hamburg, Germany, to New York and return. While in New York harbor the injury complained of occurred. The defendant relied upon a workmen's compensation law of Germany as a bar to the action. The court held "a foreign law, to which both employer and employe engaged in interstate and foreign commerce and transportation, have subscribed, and upon the basis of which the contract of employment was made and entered into, where the cars or ships of the employer enter our state, and in or upon which, while within our borders an accident occurs to the employe through his employer's negligence, particularly where the contract provides for a fixed compensation in case of specified injury to take the place of a right of action at law, and which is lawful both in the place where made and that in which the cause of action arose, should obtain recognition and enforcement here."

The Workmen's Compensation Commission of New

[203] *Schmidt Case,* Ohio State Liability Board of Awards, July 10, 1912 (Claim No. 6).

[204] *Schweitzer* v. *Hamburg, etc., Gesellschaft* (1912), 78 Misc. (N. Y.) 448; 138 N. Y. Supp. 944. See also same case on appeal from order to compel service of a reply to the defense set up in the answer, 149 A. D. (N. Y.) 900; 134 N. Y. Supp. 812.

York has ruled that the operation of a theatre did not fall within the class of "hazardous" occupations.[205]

Under the English Compensation Act a workman employed by a lion tamer was killed, and it was held that the accident "arose out of his employment." [206] And whether or not a deceased was a stage manager entrusted with important duties or whether his duties were manual was the question involved in another case.[207]

[205] *Matter of Samuel Adler*, Workmen's Compensation Commission of New York, Claim No. 52,437. It was held that the operation of a theatre did not fall within the class of "hazardous" occupations and a widow was denied compensation for the death of her husband, a property-man, who was killed by falling through a trap-door.

[206] *Hapelman* v. *Poole* (Eng.) (1908), Strong on "Dramatic and Musical Law," 3d Ed., p. 56. The Workmen's Compensation Act of 1906 is here construed. A workman was employed by a lion tamer to clean out the lion cages, etc. While in charge of the cages, a lion broke loose, and in trying to get the lion back in the cage, the lion turned on him and killed him.

Held that the accident arose "out of and in the course of his employment" and decedent's personal representatives were entitled to compensation.

[207] *Rushbrook* v. *Grimsby Palace Theatre* (Eng.) (1908), 25 T. L. R. 258. The question was whether a "stage manager to take charge of the electric plant and to bill" was a "workman" within the meaning of the Employers' Liability Act of 1880. *Held* that he was. "Stage-managers in some theatres, no doubt, involved important duties, but that term must be considered in connection with the actual duties the deceased man was called upon to perform, and from the evidence in this case it seemed clear that the deceased was really nothing more than a foreman scene-shifter or carpenter earning 25s. a week; he was mostly if not entirely engaged in manual labor."

Section 59.—Garnishment.

The salary of the actor is subject to garnishment in such states where garnishee statutes have been enacted, the manner and procedure of the garnishment, of course, following the particular state statute.

The New York statute is typical of the statutes of other states. The proceeding is regulated by Section 1391 of the Code of Civil Procedure, which provides that the Marshal or Sheriff may serve a garnishee execution upon the employer, who is then required to deduct from the actor's salary, if the same be more than twelve dollars weekly, a sum equal to ten per cent thereof, and pay it over to the levying officer; in default of so doing, he may be sued by the judgment creditor for an amount up to the amount of the judgment.

It has been held in England that an actor's salary may not be attached or garnisheed until it is actually due, and only while it is unpaid.[208]

A distinction is drawn between the remedy of garnishment and that of proceedings supplementary to execution. Where the salary has not been wholly earned and become wholly due, the judgment creditor may only proceed by garnishee proceedings.[209]

[208] *Hall* v. *Pritchett* (Eng.) (1877), 3 Q. B. D. 215.

[209] *Hayward* v. *Hayward* (1917), 178 A. D. (N. Y.) 92. "It is quite true that a fund representing a salary earned, whether in the possession of the employer, or of the employe, or of a third person, is not exempt from levy, under execution, and that such fund may be seized wherever found. But this is no such case. When the execution was issued there was no fund belonging to the defendant representing salary earned in the hands of the Palace Operating Corporation (employer). The salary was not

Section 60.—Serial stories.

In the production of the serial picture an interesting question arises. For this kind of a picture the actor employed is usually one of considerable fame and popularity, and consequently is able to dictate, to a great extent, the terms of his contract. He usually demands that each installment of the serial picture shall be approved by him and so marked before its release, and the contract provides therefor.

Suppose the artist arbitrarily and in bad faith refuses to approve of an installment of the picture? The producer has invested his money, and is seemingly at the mercy of the artist who, perhaps already contracting with another producer, finds it to his interest to impede and delay the release of the installment. In such case, the producer is at liberty to disregard that covenant in the contract, and proceed with the release of the installment without obtaining the actor's approval.

On the other hand, where the actor is actuated by proper motives and there is no element of fraud or bad faith involved, the producer is at his mercy, and may not release the film without the approval of the actor, no matter how whimsical and arbitrary the latter may be.

In some respects, a contract containing a clause of this kind is very similar to a contract where the services to

only not due at that time but was only partially earned. There is only one way provided by statute for reaching an accruing salary, and that is the means provided in Section 1391 of the Code. Upon the return of the execution unsatisfied, an order may be obtained garnishing a percentage of salary due or to become due."

be performed are to be "satisfactory" to the employer. Complete satisfaction with all the work is in each instance made a condition precedent.[210]

Section 61.—Escrow agents.

A number of artists who are sought after a great deal by producers, have devised a rather unique method of insuring payment of the salaries agreed to be paid to them under their contract.

A bank or trust company is made escrow agent. The motion picture producer deposits with the escrow agent a sum equal to the total amount agreed to be paid the artist, and the bank or trust company is directed to make payments to the artist at stated periods.

The artist is thus assured his salary if he lives up to the terms of his agreement, regardless of changes in the financial condition of the producer. The contract usually provides as well that in the event of bankruptcy, the unpaid balance shall become due and payable at once to the artist.

On the other hand, the producer is protected by a provision to the effect that in the event the artist breaches his contract, he may give notice to the escrow agent who is then required to withhold payments to the artist until arbitrators provided for under the contract render their decision.

The escrow agent is made a party to the agreement. Its duty ends if it complies with the terms of the agreement. If it arbitrarily assumes to act on its own initiative and disregards the express terms of the contract, it be-

[210] See Section 38.

comes liable to the injured party for whatever damages he has sustained thereby.

Section 62.—When joint venture.

The fact that an actor and a manager agree to share the receipts of a play does not necessarily stamp the transaction as a joint venture. An agreement to share in the losses is the true test of a joint venture.[211]

[211] *Thomas* v. *Springer* (1909), 134 A. D. (N. Y.) 640; 119 N. Y. Supp. 460. An agreement between a manager of a theatrical company and a theatre owner whereby the latter is to receive a percentage of the gross receipts, the proprietor of the theatre to furnish the scenery, equipment and regular employes of the theatre, does not create a partnership. The parties are independent contractors. Unless there be an agreement to share profits and losses there is no copartnership.

Keith v. *Kellerman* (1909), 169 Fed. (C. C.) 196. The agreement between the parties provided that defendant was to render her specialty as actress, in consideration of fifty per cent of the profits. It was held that the contract was not one of copartnership but one of employment; the test being "whether the parties are jointly interested as principals and may bind each other by their acts or engagements within the scope of the enterprise."

Mallory v. *Mackaye* (1899), 92 Fed. (C. C. A.) 749. Plantiff, a theatrical manager, contracted with defendant, an actor, whereby defendant agreed to render his exclusive services to plaintiff as an actor, author, director and inventor, all of his creations to become the property of the plaintiff in consideration for all of which plaintiff bound himself to pay defendant a specified sum per annum and in addition thereto a portion of the profits. The relationship existing between them was held to be that of employer and employe and not that of joint ventures.

See also: *Mayer* v. *Nethersole* (1902), 71 A. D. (N. Y.) 383; 75 N. Y. Supp. 987; *Goldberg* v.

Where the relationship is that of employer and employe the remedy for a breach is an action at law in damages.[212]

But where the contract provided that defendant furnish the building and pay certain of its expenses, and the plaintiff was to give his time and skill in carrying on a theatre therein and act as manager thereof, the defendant to receive a fixed sum as rent, and in addition thereto one-half of the net profits, losses to be borne equally by the parties, this was held to create a partnership, and it made no difference that the parties referred to themselves throughout as lessor and lessee.[213]

Popular Pictures Corp. (1917), N. Y. Law Journal, Jan. 20. The appeal taken in the action and reported in (1917), 178 A. D. (N. Y.) 86, was not from the order made in pursuance of the motion above reported.

[212] *McLellan* v. *Goodwin* (1899), 43 A. D. (N. Y.) 148; 59 N. Y. Supp. 290. Plaintiff, a theatrical manager, agreed to conduct a tour of the defendant, an actor. Defendant was to receive 50% of the receipts and was to pay his company of players and for costumes out of such moneys. Plaintiff agreed to pay other expenses out of his share of the receipts. Plaintiff did not conduct a tour for defendant and defendant earned moneys by employment elsewhere. The action was brought for an accounting of moneys earned by defendant. *Held* plaintiff was not in any event entitled to share in earnings of defendant as such earnings were not received by defendant from a tour conducted by plaintiff; that plaintiff's remedy, if at all, was one at law for damages for breach of contract.

[213] *Leavitt* v. *Windsor Land & Investment Co.* (1893), 54 Fed. (C. C. A.) 439.

See also: *Cole* v. *Rome Savings Bank* (1916), 96 Misc. (N. Y.) 188; 161 N. Y. Supp. 15. Defendant Rome Savings Bank made an agreement with one Edwards whereby R. gave the use of a theatre which it owned for one year upon the following conditions:

E. agreed to deduct from the gross receipts a specified sum to

Where a joint venture or copartnership is created for the exploitation of literary works, the loss of prestige in the business of one of the partners is a valid cause, it would seem, for a dissolution.[214]

The joint venturers are bound to use the utmost of good faith toward each other.[215]

be applied to his own uses and from the balance pay for insurance, taxes, cost of theatre license, advertising, labor employed and other incidental expenses necessary to the operation of the theatre and pay to R. a specified sum per year and at the end of the year pay to R. one-half of the surplus profits. If upon the termination of the lease the net receipts proved insufficient to make the above payments then the entire net receipts were to be paid to R., less a specified sum per month to be retained by E.

Held not to create a co-partnership. See also: *Atchison-Ely* v. *Thomas* (1905), 104 A. D. (N. Y.) 368; 93 N. Y. Supp. 693.

[214] *Waite* v. *Aborn* (1901), 60 A. D. (N. Y.) 521; 69 N. Y. Supp. 967. Plaintiff and defendant entered into a copartnership for a specified period to conduct the business of "making productions of operas, extravaganzas and for general amusement purposes." Plaintiff was to have charge of the business of the enterprise and defendant of the artistic branch. *Held* that a complaint asking for a dissolution of the partnership because the carrying on of the business had become impracticable on account of the bad reputation acquired by defendant in the theatrical world and that its continuance could not be effected save with loss, stated a cause of action.

[215] *Selwyn & Co.* v. *Waller et ano.* (1914), 212 N. Y. 507; 106 N. E. 321. Under an agreement for the production of a play and the sharing of profits and losses including the payment of royalties to the authors, one of the parties to the enterprise was held bound to disclose to his associate the fact that he had previously acquired from the authors a one-fourth interest in such royalties. Parties about to engage in a joint venture whether as partners inter sese or not owe to each

Section 63.—Royalties in addition to salary.

Contracts of employment occasionally provide for compensation of the actor who poses for motion picture companies by salary and royalties based upon the earnings of the picture.[216]

If the contract is silent as to the period during which such royalties are to be paid, the actor is nevertheless entitled to them even where his contract of employment has expired by limitation; and his right to such royalties continues as long as the picture is exploited.

He may not, however, compel the producer to exhibit the film in which he has posed. A failure to exploit the picture merely relegates the actor to his remedy at law for damages for the breach, with the difficulty of establishing some basis upon which damages may be awarded.[217]

Section 64.—Law governing validity of contract.

Where a contract is made in a foreign jurisdiction, but is to be wholly performed within the United States, the interpretation and validity of the contract will generally be subject to review by the American courts. And the courts will not be ousted of jurisdiction by the contract of the parties between themselves.[218]

other the utmost good faith and the most scrupulous honesty.

[216] *Dressler* v. *Keystone Film Co.* (1915), N. Y. Law Journal, Aug. 5th.

[217] *Benyakar* v. *Scherz* (1905), 103 A. D. (N. Y.) 192. See also: *Levison* v. *Oes* (1917), 98 Misc. (N. Y.) 260, containing a valuable discussion of the method by which future profits may be estimated as to motion pictures.

For additional cases, see Section 49.

[218] *Engel* v. *Shubert* (1915), 166 App. Div. (N. Y.) 394; 151 N. Y.

In general, the contract must be valid in the place of its performance.

Where a booking agency conducting a business from its headquarters in Chicago, had contracted to provide troupes for theatres in Tennessee, it was held that since it had not complied with the laws of that state, it could not recover, as performance was held to be within that state.[219]

Section 65.—Contract labor and exclusion laws.

Under the Federal statutes a contract made with an alien to perform labor or services within the United States or its territories previous to the immigration or importation of such person into the United States is void, and any person, firm or corporation which assists or encourages such immigration or importation is guilty of a crime and is subject to heavy penalties.[220]

Supp. 593. The contract between the parties provided that: "In case of a dispute, both contracting parties agree to submit to the jurisdiction of the Vienna courts."

Held that such provision was not exclusive, and that the courts would not look with favor upon attempts to oust them of jurisdiction.

"It is entirely plain that such agreements should be strictly construed and should not be extended by implication."

Meachem v. *Jamestown R. R. Co.* (1914), 211 N. Y. 346; 105 N. E. 653; *Lorenz* v. *Bartuschek*, City Court of N. Y., No. 116. Judgment Roll filed May 18, 1916.

[219] *Albert* v. *Interstate Amusement Co.* (1913), 161 S. W. (Tenn.) 488.

On the question whether a phrase of limitation relates to all the preceding terms or modifies the term immediately preceding such phrase see: Hodkins v. *McDonald* (1907), 123 Mo. App. 566; 100 S. W. 508; *State* v. *Scaffer* (1905), 95 Minn. 311; 104 N. W. 139.

[220] Compiled Statutes of the

These statutes, however, have been strictly construed and it has been held that only manual unskilled laborers are intended to come within the prohibition,[221] and the making of contracts with actors, directors or skilled mechanics would not be a violation of the statute.[222]

Nor would a Chinese actor be excluded, since he has been held to be no "laborer" under the exclusion laws.[223]

Section 66.—Performance in unlicensed theatre.

An actor who performs in an unlicensed theatre is estopped from recovering for his services, and the owner of such theatre is likewise powerless to enforce a contract to which he is a party.[224]

United States (pub. 1913), Sections 4245, 4246, 4248, 4250, 4251.

[221] *United States* v. *Gay* (1899), 95 Fed. (C. C. A.) 226.

[222] *United States* v. *Thompson* (1889), 41 Fed. (C. C.) 28; *United States* v. *Edgar* (1891), 45 Fed. (C. C.) 44; aff'd 48 Fed. (C. C. A.) 91.

[223] *Re Ho King* (1883), 14 Fed. (C. C.) 724. The relator, Ho King, was a Chinese actor. Landing at Portland, he was detained under the Exclusion Law. A writ of habeas corpus issued, and it was held that an actor or theatrical performer was not a "laborer" under that Act, and that he could come and go at pleasure.

[224] *Levy* v. *Yates* (Eng.) (1838), 8 Ad. & El. 129; 35 E. C. L. 352. Where the owner of a theatre has not obtained a license as required by law, a contract made between himself and a theatrical company through a booking agency cannot be enforced.

De Begnis v. *Armistead* (Eng.) (1833), 25 E. C. L. 47; 10 Bing. 107. The contract of a theatre owner was held unenforceable because of his failure to comply with the law.

As to what constitutes an illegal contract for performance at a theatre. See also: *Ewing* v. *Osbaldiston* (Eng.) (1837), 2 My. & Cr. 53; *Gallini* v. *Laborie* (Eng.) (1793), 5 Term Rep. 242; *Gray* v. *The Oxford* (Eng.) (1905), 21

But the actor who so performs must have actual notice of the fact that his performance is unlicensed. The distinction is made between ignorance of the law and ignorance of a fact; and the want of notice on the actor's part in this case would be ignorance of a fact only, and would not bar a recovery.[225]

From the foregoing it may be concluded that a distributor, who has contracted for film rental with an exhibitor who has failed to secure the proper license from the authorities, may recover damages for the breach, providing he is unaware of the exhibitor's derelictions. In dealing with the exhibitor he is not bound to make any special inquiries, as he may be permitted to assume that the theatre is licensed. That presumption exists in law.[226]

Section 67.—Contracts for transportation—damages.

When a common carrier undertakes the transportation

T. L. R. 664; aff'd 22 T. L. R. 684; *Scott* v. *McNaughton* (Eng.) (1908), Times, Nov. 25th.

[225] *Roys* v. *Johnson et al.* (1856), 7 Gray (Mass.), 162. The actor rendered his services and brought this action to secure compensation therefor. Defendants set up the fact that the plaintiff acted in an unlicensed theatrical exhibition and not entitled to compensation as the giving of an unlicensed theatrical performance was unlawful. *Held* that so long as plaintiff did not know that the performance was unlicensed he was entitled to recover, and defendants would not be permitted to sustain such defense, having themselves been guilty of the unlawful act.

[226] *Rodwell* v. *Redge* (Eng.), 1 C. & P. 220; 11 E. C. L. 374. The action was brought against an actor for breach of contract for failure to appear. *Held* that there was a presumption that the theatre was licensed from the fact that performances had been going on uninterruptedly.

of an actor and his scenery, the carrier is not prima facie charged with any unusual degree of responsibility. To hold the company liable for neglect or delay, it must be established that a contract existed by which the company was fully apprised of all the facts in order that it may be said that the loss of profits of the actor was within its contemplation. Such a contract is not proven merely by showing that the actor bought a ticket; more than that is required.[227]

But where such a contract is proven, it becomes important to determine whether the actor may prove and recover damages including the profits he might have made had he been able to perform. In New York the rule seems to be that such damages are not incidental to and proximate to the injury, and may not be proven.[228]

[227] *Southern Ry.* v. *Myers* (1898), 87 Fed. (C. C. A.) 149. An actor was injured by the overturning of a sleeping-car. "In the absence of a definite contract for carriage to a given point by a given time, with such reasons for its making as would naturally lead the agent of the carrier to contemplate the profits the passenger expected to realize, it is clear that the damage claimed for the failure to realize such profits is too uncertain and remote, and that, until competent proof tending to show such contract was offered and admitted, it was error to admit any testimony in reference to the speculative profits which the passenger might have made if he had been safely carried through on schedule time."

[228] *Brown* v. *Weir* (1904), 95 A. D. (N. Y.) 78; 88 N. Y. Supp. 479. Plaintiff, an actress, delivered a trunk containing all of her theatrical costumes to the Adams Express Co. for transmission. The trunk was not delivered for a period of ten days because of dispute as to charges, the company having demanded an improper amount. *Held* that plaintiff could not recover as damages, loss of earnings during the period,

But in Illinois the courts have held otherwise; [229] and the rule in that jurisdiction seems to be in accord with the dicta of the Federal court in *Southern Railway* v. *Myers*.

Section 68.—Power of company's officer to contract—agency.

A contract of employment with an actress has been held valid when signed by the president and general manager of the company.[230] So too, where the director-general of a traveling show extends a contract for an additional season.[231]

first, because she failed to make reasonable exertions to make the injury as light as possible, and secondly because damage for breach of contract was only that which was incidental to and was directly, caused by the breach, and might reasonably be presumed to have entered into the contemplation of the parties.

[229] *Illinois Central* v. *Byrne* (1903), 205 Ill. 9; 68 N. E. 720. Suit to recover damages for failure to haul car loaded with scenery and theatrical property. It was claimed that by reason of such failure appellee missed an engagement which had been advertised and for which tickets had been sold.

Held that it was proper for the jury to consider the nature of the plaintiff's business and his profits for a reasonable period next preceding the time when the contract was violated.

[230] *King* v. *Will. J. Block Am. Co.* (1908), 115 N. Y. Supp. 243; aff'd 132 A. D. (N. Y.) 925; 116 N. Y. Supp. 1139. It is within the implied powers of the president and general manager of the defendant to bind the defendant in the employment of an actress.

[231] *Eddy* v. *American Amusement Co.* (1913), 132 Pac. (Cal.) 83. A person, having charge generally of the defendant's traveling show having the title of director general and having the authority, when authorized in writing by the general manager of the defendant to employ and discharge artists and who employed plaintiff for one season may bind the defendant in ex-

But it has been held that the president of a theatrical company could not appoint a general business manager without the consent of the directors, and that the business manager did not have the inherent power to engage performers for a year.[232]

A booking-agent may contract within his apparent authority, and secret instructions are not binding upon third parties with whom he contracts.[233]

And a contract signed by a manager will make him personally liable if there is nothing in the body of the contract to indicate that the contract is made with his principal.[234]

tending the employment agreement for an additional season.

See in this connection: *Armstrong* v. *Majestic Motion Picture Co.* (1914), 87 Misc. (N. Y.) 141; 149 N. Y. Supp. 1039.

[232] *Vogel* v. *St. Louis Museum* (1880), 8 Mo. App. 587.

[233] *Interstate Amusement Co.* v. *Albert* (1913), 161 S. W. (Tenn.) 488. *Held* that plaintiff, who operated a booking-agency in Chicago was the agent of the defendants, who operated a theatre in Tennessee.

Bergere v. *Parker* (1914), 170 S. W. (Texas) 808. *Held* that where a person was held out as defendant's booking agent, private instructions to such agent were not binding upon parties who without knowledge of such instructions contracted with defendant through the agent and that his acts were within his apparent authority.

[234] *Grau* v. *McVicker* (1874), 8 Biss. 7; 10 Fed. Cas. No. 5,708. The lessee of a theatre was described as "M. G., representing Messrs. C. A. C. & Co., manager of the A. O. B. Co.," and the contract stated that he, Grau, was to have the privilege of giving a certain number of performances. One of the clauses provided: "The said Maurice Grau, in consideration of the above, agrees to pay to the said McVicker." *Held* that M. G. was liable as principal and that the words added to his name were merely words of description.

B. F. Sturtevant Co. v. *Fireproof*

Where the plaintiff had contracted as "The Redpath Lyceum Bureau" but brought suit in the name of Geo. H. Hathaway, the real party in interest, it was held that he could properly do so.[235]

Section 69.—Costumes.

While stock costumes for the company are usually rented, in more elaborate productions of plays and motion

Film Co. (1915), 216 N. Y. 199; 110 N. E. 440. "When an offer, proposal or contract is expressed in clear and explicit terms, matter printed in small type at the top or bottom of the office stationery of the writer where it is not easily seen, which is not in the body of the instrument or referred to therein, is not necessarily to be considered a part of such offer, proposal or contract."

Cobb v. *Knapp* (1877), 71 N. Y. 348. "There is no hardship in the rule of liability against agents. They always have it in their own power to relieve themselves, and when they do not, it must be presumed that they intend to be liable."

Meyer v. *Redmund* (1912), 205 N. Y. 478; 98 N. E. 906. Defendants were auctioneers, acting and presumably known to be acting as agents. Yet the court held that: "Even where he discloses the name of his principal, if he (the agent) signs a written contract in his own name merely, which contract does not show upon its face that he was acting as the agent of another, or in an official capacity in behalf of the Government, he will be personally bound thereby."

[235] *Hathaway* v. *Sabin* (1889), 61 Vt. 608; 18 Atl. 188.

See also: *Stuart* v. *Smith* (1895), 68 Fed. (C. C.) 189. Where an officer of a corporation was held not liable for the acts of the corporation when done without his consent; and *McDonald* v. *Hearst* (1899), 95 Fed. (C. C.) 656.

On the question whether the proprietor of a theatre is liable for the act of his manager in refusing to permit an officer to enter the theatre to serve legal process upon an actor see: *Paulton* v. *Keith* (1901), 23 R. I. 164; 49 Atl. 635.

pictures, these costumes must be made up specially. It is the custom to have plates prepared by the designer of the costumes, and these plates are furnished to the costumer.

In a case where the costumer, an English resident, had himself prepared and designed the plates for costumes to be used in the defendant's production, it was held that he had fully performed, and judgment in his favor was sustained.[236]

Section 70.—Enticement of actor.

Because of the great competition existing between producers to secure the services in the making of motion pictures of actors and actresses of established reputation, one motion picture producer frequently will attempt to secure the services of an actor who has contracted to perform with his competitor. It is important for him to know how far he may go in inducing the artist to leave his competitor's employ without committing an actionable wrong.

His competitor may have expended large sums of money and assumed obligations in reliance upon his contract with the actor.

It has been generally held in this country that where the breach is induced solely by argument and persuasion and no false representation is made, the producer whose contract has been breached, has no remedy against his

[236] *Anderson* v. *Long* (1914), 56 Pa. Sup. Ct. 183. Plaintiff was a designer of theatrical costumes and defendant a playwright. The former was commissioned to draw plates for designs of costumes. *Held* that he had fully performed and was entitled to recover.

competitor. He is left to his remedy against the actor for damages for the breach of the contract.

If the actor, however, has been induced to breach his contract by false representations, by fraud or by force or coercion, the competitor has committed a wrong for which he is accountable to the producer. The motive of the person enticing the servant away is immaterial.

The law is stated in a recent case as follows:

"The gist of the wrong lies in overpowering or circumventing the freedom of will and the intent of the one obligated to perform as distinguished from procuring him by fair means to elect not to perform."

The wronged party may in any case where the contract has been breached by false representations, fraud, force or coercion, maintain an action at law against the wrongdoer for his damages.

Where the services of the artist are unique and extraordinary and the producer's damages irreparable the courts have gone one step further and permitted him to go into equity to enjoin, not only the actor, but the wrongdoer as well and prevent such wrongdoer from availing himself of the services of the actor.

It seems that there are only three cases reported in this country where one, contracting with an actor, has brought an action against a third party for enticement.

One action was brought at law. The defendant induced an actor who had contracted to perform at plaintiff's theatre to breach the contract and to perform at defendant's theatre upon the days he had agreed to act at plaintiff's theatre. The court held that the motives of defendant in inducing the actor to breach his contract were immaterial so long as the means used by him in inducing the breach were legal, and plaintiff had no cause of action against defendant.[237]

The other two actions were brought in equity. In *Jesse L. Lasky Feature Play Co.* v. *Fox* the complaint alleged that plaintiffs had made a contract with an actress of unique and extraordinary ability whereby she had agreed to pose for plaintiffs in the making of motion pictures for a specified period; that defendant by making false representations had induced her to breach the contract; that the false representations consisted of statements to her that the contract between plaintiffs and her was void, that plaintiffs had no intention of furnishing her with employment as provided for in the contract, that plaintiffs had violated the agreement in failing to make the necessary preparations for posing and that she was under no obligation to perform the agreement. The contract contained a negative covenant. The defendant, who was a business rival of plaintiffs, had caused the actress to pose for a motion picture subsequent to the making of the above mentioned agreement and prior to its termination; and the relief asked for was, among other things, for an injunction restraining defendant from exhibiting the photo-play for which the actress had posed.

[237] *Bourlier Bros.* v. *Macauley* (1891), 91 Ky. 135; 15 S. W. 60. ". . . For, to enforce a doctrine making the hirer responsible for breach by the person hired of a previous contract with another involves legal recognition of personal dominion, bordering on pure servitude, which is neither in harmony with our form of government nor well for those who labor for subsistence. . . ."

The defendant's demurrer to the bill of complaint was overruled.[238]

The latest decision is that of *Triangle Film Corporation* v. *Artcraft Pictures Corporation* wherein plaintiff sought to enjoin the defendant from employing one Hart as one of its motion picture actors.

Hart had entered into a contract with the plaintiff in which he agreed to render to it his exclusive services as a motion picture actor for a number of years. The contract provided that one Ince was to supervise all the productions made with the participation of Hart. It appeared that Ince had left plaintiff's employ and at the time of the commencement of this action was associated with the defendant. Hart refused to remain in plaintiff's employ after the withdrawal of Ince and had accepted employment from the defendant.

The theory of the action was that the defendant had combined with Ince to induce Hart to leave plaintiff's employ by means of false representations, and to enter into its own employ.

Judge Manton denied the application for an injunction pendente lite upon the ground that Hart was not obligated to perform under his contract since the condition of his employment was that Ince should act as director-general

[238] *Jesse L. Lasky Feature Play* v. *Fox* (1916), 93 Misc. (N. Y.) 364; 157 N. Y. Supp. 106. "In this jurisdiction interference by a stranger with a contract of service by any class of employes gives rise only to such remedies as exist under like circumstances in the case of other contracts the parties to which have assumed mutual obligations. For inducing the termination or other breach of such a contract a third party is liable only when he has been guilty of unlawful means."

of all pictures to be made with his participation; and that since no action could be maintained against Hart, none could be maintained against the defendant.[239]

Section 71.—Libel of actor.

Members of the theatrical profession will be permitted to maintain actions for libel where the criticisms of their performances are instigated through malice, or where the critic in his zeal has made statements which are untrue.

Where statements were made concerning a public singer that he falsely claimed to be the owner of certain songs, and that he procured the giving of applause, the court held the defendant guilty of a libel.[240]

[239] *Triangle Film Corp.* v. *Artcraft* (1917), D. C. U. S., S. D., N. Y., July 31st. "If Hart could not be held for breach of contract, how can this defendant be held for inducing Hart to break his contract?"

For the first English case on this subject where the services of an actor were involved, see: Lumley v. *Gye* (Eng.) (1853), 2 E. & B. 216. See also: *Allen* v. *Flood* (Eng.), 67 L. J. Q. B. 112.

And for more recent miscellaneous cases in enticement, see: *Rogers* v. *Evarts* (1891), 17 N. Y. Supp. 264; *Johnston Harvester Co.* v. *Meinhardt* (1880), 9 Abb. Cases, 393; *DeJong* v. *Behrman* (1911), 148 A. D. (N. Y.) 37; 131 N. Y. Supp. 1083; *Posner Co.* v. *Jackson* (1915), 166 A. D. (N. Y.) 920; 152 N. Y. Supp. 1105; *Angle* v. *Chicago & St. Paul Ry. Co.* (1893), 151 U. S. 1; 14 Sup. Ct. 240; *Dr. Miles Medical Co.* v. *Park & Sons* (1911), 220 U. S. 373; 31 Sup. Ct. 376.

For some of the earlier enticement cases not involving the services of an actor see: *Benton* v. *Pratt* (1829), 2 Wend. (N. Y.) 386; *Walker* v. *Crown* (1871), 107 Mass. 555; *Ashley* v. *Dixon* (1872), 48 N. Y. 430; *Boston Glass Mfg.* v. *Binney* (1827), 4 Pick. (Mass.) 425; *Newman* v. *Zachary* (Eng.) (1646), Aleyn, 3; *Hart* v. *Aldridge* (Eng.) (1774), Cowp. 54; *Gunter* v. *Astor* (Eng.) (1819), 4 J. B. Moore, 12.

[240] *Dibdin* v. *Swan* (Eng.)

In another case where the performances of a troupe of public performers were referred to as being coarse, farcical, wholly without merit and ridiculous, it was held that unless malice was established there could be no recovery.[241] A reference to the manners of an actor as "ungentlemanly and discourteous" was however held actionable.[242]

As the reputation of an actor is dependent to a great extent upon the nature of the publicity given to him, improper forms of advertisement or type will sustain a cause of action for libel. Thus where a high class actor's name was billed in very small type whereas he was accustomed to having it starred, the courts permitted a

(1793), 1 Esp. 28. "The editor of a newspaper may fairly and candidly comment on any place or species of public entertainment; but it must be done fairly and without malice or view to injure or prejudice the proprietor in the eyes of the public. If so done, however severe the censure, the justice of it screens the editor from legal animadversion; but if it can be proved that the comment is malevolent, or exceeding the bounds of fair opinion then such is a libel and therefore actionable."

To the same effect: *Hart* v. *Wall* (Eng.) (1877), 25 W. R. 373. See also: *Green* v. *Chapman* (Eng.) (1837), 4 Bing. N. C. 92; *Morrison* v. *Belcher* (Eng.), 3 F. & F. 614.

[241] *Cherry et al.* v. *Des Moines Leader* (1901), 114 Iowa, 298; 86 N. W. 323.

McQuire v. *Western News* (Eng.) (1903), 88 L. T. 757. Referring to certain songs delivered during the performance of a play and to certain dancing therein as "*vulgar*" was not held to be libelous. See also: *Thomas* v. *Bradbury* (Eng.) (1906), 95 L. T. 23; *Unwin* v. *Clarke* (Eng.) (1908), Times, March 31; *Murray* v. *Walter* (Eng.) (1908), Times, May 6, 7, 8, 9.

See also: *Wood* v. *Sandow* (Eng.) (1914), Times, June 26, 30. The publication of an actor's picture in connection with an advertisement is not ipso facto libelous.

[242] *Williams* v. *Davenport*

recovery; [243] and where the singer's name was placed third on the list of concert singers printed on the handbills and advertising, the court held that that was calculated to injure the plaintiff's reputation and constituted a libel.[244]

On the other hand, to accuse an actress of being in the company of a man late at night and being mixed up in a quarrel was held not libelous in the absence of special damage.[245]

(1890), 42 Minn. 393; 44 N. W. 311.

[243] *Elen* v. *London Music Hall* (Eng.) (1906), Times, May 31, June 1.

[244] *Russell* v. *Notcutt* (Eng.) (1896), 12 T. L. R. 195. See also: *Renard* v. *Carl Rosa Opera Co.* (Eng.) (1906), Times, Feb. 15; *Wade* v. *Waldon* (Eng.) (1909), S. C. 571.

[245] *Gerald* v. *Inter Ocean Pub. Co.* (1899), 90 Ill. App. 205.

CHAPTER IV

THE PRODUCER (CONTINUED)

His Other Employes

SEC. 72. Scenario writer.
73. Director and other employes.

Section 72.—Scenario writer.

The professional scenario writer is a new figure; he is unique to the motion picture industry, and it is rather difficult to define with any reasonable degree of accuracy the peculiar rights and liabilities involved between himself, his employers and third persons.

We have discussed in a previous chapter the scenario writer who is employed to write original motion pictures, and the author who writes original scenarios and sends them in for sale, confining ourselves principally to the rights retained or transferred in the scenario.[1] But it is becoming customary for the film producers to employ scenario writers whose principal function it is to adapt novels, plays and other works which have come into their control for representation in motion pictures.

Such a scenario writer has no independent rights in the scenario, as such, nor does he secure copyright in the motion picture reproduced from that scenario. He is

[1] See Section 4.

acting as an intermediary only, and while he creates something, that which he creates belongs to his employer and not to him.

The above is subject to one exception, however, for should the film producer multiply the scenario in copies for sale, and should he, in the process mutilate it to any appreciable extent, the scenario writer would undoubtedly have the right to seek redress, as this would be an invasion of his common-law rights, which he has not lost.[2] Also, where he has so contracted, he may enforce the display of his name upon the picture and billing matter.[3]

It must be remembered, however, that his common-law rights are limited to the scenario alone.

It frequently happens that a scenario writer goes out of his way to plagiarize from another work or picture, to libel another, to invade a private right or to write that which is obscene or indecent. In such case the rule of respondeat superior applies.

Many scenario writers have adopted the system of doing independent work for one or several companies. They are usually given a novel or play and told to turn it into a scenario. Where the contract provides that no compensation is to be paid for the scenario until the picture is actually produced, the scenario writer may not recover until there is an actual reproduction, nor may he compel such a reproduction.

In Canada, it was held in *Morang* v. *LeSueur* that an author who sold his manuscript to the publisher without

[2] See Section 12.

[3] *Brennan* v. *Fox Film Corp.* (1916), N. Y. Law Journal, August 25th, Mullan, J. See excerpt from opinion under Section 73.

any reservation as to publication, could tender back the advance royalties, where the publisher failed to publish the work, and compel a re-assignment of the same. In that case, however, the author, under the contract, was to receive his remuneration in royalties based *only* upon the actual retail sale of the work, and this was an element that carried great weight with the court in arriving at its conclusion.

The bench was divided, three to two, and Judge Anglin in an elaborate dissenting opinion expressed the sounder doctrine that, unless the contract especially so provided, the publisher was under no obligation to risk his money in producing the work; and while it is true that an author sells his work with an eye to the enhancement of his reputation and fame which publication would bring about, he ought to expressly contract for the publication of it, if he thinks enough of himself and his work.[4]

It would follow that where a scenario writer sells his scenario to the motion picture producer, the latter is

[4] *Morang & Co.* v. *Le Sueur* (1911), 45 Canadian Sup. Ct. 95. See excerpt from dissenting opinion quoted in Section 28.

See in this connection: *Fechter* v. *Montgomery* (Eng.) (1863), 33 Beav. 22, where an actor was engaged for a specified period, the performances of the artist to commence several weeks after the making of the contract. When the time for the performance of the contract arrived, the manager refused to give the defendant a part in any play, but paid him the stipulated salary. The defendant becoming tired of his inactivity obtained employment at a rival theatre. In an action for an injunction plaintiff was defeated, the court holding that one of the objects of the contract was to enable the defendant to appear in public; that the actor was paid not in terms of money alone but in opportunity to appear in public, and to acquire reputation and fame.

under no obligation to make a production of the picture, unless the contract especially covenants him to do so.

If the acceptance of the work is contingent upon the satisfaction of the producer, the latter may reject the scenario for any cause he sees fit.[5]

Where the scenario writer leaves the employ of his company, he may subsequently make use of any and all ideas which he may have acquired in the course of his employment. He may even go to the same sources for information and ideas which he had made use of while so employed, and he may later develop them in any way that he sees fit—provided that such sources are not the property of his former employers.[6]

But where the scenario writer has reduced to writing while in such employment, any ideas whatsoever, whether the material has been developed in the form of scenario or not, such writings, whether complete or in unfinished narrative form, are the absolute property of his former employers.[7]

The writer is engaged specifically to write this kind of material, and it is well settled that as soon as the material

[5] *Glenny* v. *Lacy* (1888), 1 N. Y. Supp. 513; *Crawford* v. *Mail & Express Pub. Co.* (1900), 163 N. Y. 404; 57 N. E. 616; *Peverly* v. *Poole* (1887), 19 Abb. N. Cas. (N. Y.) 271; *Kendall* v. *West* (1902), 196 Ill. 221; 63 N. E. 683; *Saxe* v. *Shubert* (1908), 57 Misc. (N. Y.) 620; 108 N. Y. Supp. 683; *Weaver* v. *Klaw* (1891), 16 N. Y. Supp. 931.

For additional cases, see Sections 16 and 38.

[6] *Peters* v. *Borst* (1889), 9 N. Y. Supp. 789; reversed 142 N. Y. 62; 36 N. E. 814; upon another ground: *Colliery Engineer Co.* v. *United Corresp. Schools* (1899), 94 Fed. (C. C.) 152.

[7] *T. B. Harms* v. *Stern* (1915), 222 Fed. (D. C.) 581.

comes into existence, and takes concrete, tangible form, it becomes the property of the one who has paid him for such work. If he attempts to use the same thereafter, he is as much of an infringer as a stranger, and he may be restrained and punished.[8]

Section 73.—Director and other employes.

Directors, camera men and other employes of film companies are amenable to the general rules governing master and servant. Directors in particular have been recognized, like competent actors, as being artists possessing in greater or lesser degree the attributes of skill, taste and judgment, and as such their rights and duties must be defined in accordance with the rules heretofore set out for special, unique and extraordinary employes.

For example, a skillful director who has contracted for a definite period for his services, may not arbitrarily breach his contract; if he does so, he may be restrained.

He is, for many purposes, the agent of the company. Where he supervises or directs the production of a libelous picture he becomes personally liable as a joint tort feasor with his employer.[9] Even though the motion picture producer has no actual knowledge of the libel, his failure to control his agent would be equivalent to such disregard of the rights of others as to amount to intentional

[8] See Section 8.

[9] *Spooner* v. *Daniels* (1854), 22 Fed. Cas. (C. C.) No. 13,244a; *Watts* v. *Fraser* (Eng.) (1837), 7 C. & P. 369; *Hunt* v. *Bennett* (1859), 19 N. Y. 173; *Bruce* v. *Reed* (1883), 104 Pa. St. 408; *Weil* v. *Nevin*, 1 Pa. Sup. Ct. Cas. 65; *Keyzor* v. *Newman* (Eng.), 1 F. & F. 559; *Mecabe* v. *Jones* (1881), 10 Daly (N. Y.), 222; *Smith* v. *Utley* (1896), 92 Wis. 133; 65 N. W. 744.

wrong.[10] And such liability would seem to be criminal as well as civil.[11]

And where a director has placed an actor in a dangerous part wherein he sustains injury he is the alter ego of the employer in the same manner as the foreman or superintendent of a shop. The rule applies as well to acts of omission as to acts of commission.

He is ordinarily vested with the right to employ and discharge actors and other employes. But he has no inherent authority to engage an actor for a year and thereby bind the company.[12]

He is entitled to a reasonable amount of publicity where he has contracted therefor, and in that event may insist that the display advertising and billing matter have his name printed thereon.[13] Where his name is so advertised,

[10] *Danville Press* v. *Harrison* (1901), 99 Ill. App. 244.

[11] *State* v. *Mason* (1894), 26 Oregon, 273; 38 Pac. 130; *Ickes* v. *State* (1898), 8 Ohio Circ. Dec. 442; *Com.* v. *Kneeland* (1834), Thach. Crim. Cas. (Mass.) 346; aff'd 20 Pick. 206; *Clay* v. *People* (1877), 86 Ill. 147.

[12] *Vogel* v. *St. Louis Museum* (1880), 8 Mo. App. 587.

[13] *Brenan* v. *Fox Film Corp.* (1916), N. Y. Law Journal, Aug. 25. "The plaintiff who is the author of a photoplay known as 'The Daughter of the Gods' seeks to enjoin the exhibition of it by the defendant without an accompanying ascription to him of the authorship, and without giving prominent publicity, in the various ways customarily employed in the motion picture business to advertise photoplays, to the fact that the plaintiff 'is the originator, author and producing director of such photoplay.' The plaintiff was employed by the defendant in January, 1915, at a weekly salary to write for it scenarios and direct the production of motion picture or photoplays. The engagement was oral, for no definite period, and contained no provision to insure to the plaintiff the pub-

licity for himself, upon the importance of which he lays such stress in his complaint and in his moving papers upon this application, although he states that shortly before entering the employ of the defendant he severed his connection with persons conducting a similar business for the reason that they denied to him the publicity he felt he was entitled to. In July of this year the plaintiff voluntarily severed his connection with the defendant by resignation. Although I have no disposition to pass upon the merits of the dispute in advance of the trial, which presumably will bring out the true and full situation, I think it is at least doubtful whether any engagement that may possibly be spelt out by defendant's conduct and the custom of the business to advertise plaintiff's connection with the plays he wrote and produced while in the defendant's employ may hold good and continue after a severance of the relation of employe and employer. If the defendant were to be bound for all time to advertise the plaintiff in connection with the plays he wrote while in the pay of the defendant, it is more than strange that the plaintiff should not have made such advertisement an express condition of the employment, and procured the protection of a written instrument, particularly when, as he says, he left his former employer for the sole reason that he was not sufficiently advertised. Many grounds of opposition are urged by the defendant, among them, that even if it should be thought from a reading of the papers submitted upon this motion, that the plaintiff may have contractual rights for the breach of which he should be entitled to suitable redress, it would be impossible in such a case as this for a court of equity suitably and appropriately to exercise its powers. While the proper enforcement in equity of the plaintiff's rights, if it be ultimately decided that he has any, may present certain difficulties, I am not prepared to say that an appropriate scheme of relief could not be worked out; but it is not necessary for me to pass upon that question. I rest my decision upon the belief that the ultimate success of the plaintiff is too doubtful to warrant a mandatory injunction which may give to the plaintiff in advance of the trial a considerable measure of the relief he might be entitled

but he has not directed the picture, he may enjoin such use of his name.[14] Where he has directed a picture, and the producer or distributor places another name thereon, he may restrain the production.[15]

The director, being responsible to his employer for the proper filming of the picture, is given wide discretionary powers. He may alter the sequence of the taking of scenes; he may make changes in the scenario, eliminate scenes, change about the cast and in general, supervise and conduct the production to meet with his individual notion, taste and judgment.

The director cannot be delegated by the producer to do other work, and his refusal to perform work other than

to upon making out his case before the trial court. As the condition of the calendar is such that a trial may be had speedily, the risk of damage to the plaintiff is not in my judgment sufficient to require what would in effect be a determination in his favor prior to the taking of proofs. Motion denied."

[14] *The "Mark Twain" Case* (1883), 14 Fed. (C. C.) 728. "So, too, an author of acquired reputation, and perhaps a person who has not obtained any standing before the public as a writer, may restrain another from the publication of literary matter purporting to have been written by him, but which in fact was never so written. In other words, no person has the right to hold another out to the world as the author of literary matter which he never wrote."

Drummond v. *Altemus* (1894), 60 Fed. (C. C.) 338. Here defendant published what purported to be a series of lectures delivered by the plaintiff entitled: "The Evolution of Man; being the Lowell lectures delivered at Boston, Mass., April, 1893, by Professor Drummond." The court restrained him. See also Section 12.

[15] *DeBekker* v. *Stokes* (1915), 168 A. D. (N. Y.) 452; 153 N. Y. Supp. 1066; *Crooks* v. *Petter* (Eng.) (1860), 3 L. T. Rep. (N. S.) 225. See also Section 12.

such within the scope of his employment is not grounds for discharge.[16]

He, as well as all the other employes of the producer will be restrained from disclosing the trade secrets of their employer to a rival, in the same manner and under the same conditions as in other commercial pursuits.[17]

[16] *Nash* v. *Krieling* (1899), 56 Pac. 260; aff'd 123 Cal. xviii. For additional cases see: Section 45.

[17] *For the latest expression of the courts on this subject see: DuPont Powder Co.* v. *Masland* (1917), 244 U. S. 100; *Todd Protectograph Co.* v. *Hirschberg* (1917), 100 Misc. (N. Y.) 418.

CHAPTER V

THE DISTRIBUTOR AND THE EXHIBITOR

SEC. 74. Distributor—in general.
75. Exhibitor—in general.
76. Advertising matter, programs, bill-posters.
77. What are fixtures.
78. Replevin of film and machine.
79. Theatre leases.
80. Theatre a nuisance.
81. Franchise and booking agreements.
82. Benefit performances—private exhibitions.
83. Interstate commerce.
84. Bankruptcy.
85. Libel.

Section 74.—Distributor—in general.

It has become a practice in the motion picture industry to have separate organizations take care of the manufacture and distribution of the motion picture. A number of the concerns manufacturing the films turn over the finished product to a distributing agency. The distributing agency is usually the main organization, the manufacturing companies being subsidiaries of the releasing or distributing company. The distributing company maintains branches in the principal cities of the country, known in the trade as "exchanges" through which the motion pictures are rented out to the individual exhibitors.

One of two methods is usually followed by the distributor to compensate the manufacturer for the films. In the one case the negative of the film is sold outright to the distributor for a lump sum, usually amounting to the actual cost of production, and positive prints of the film are sold at a specified amount per foot; the other method is to have the producer lease the positive prints of the film to the releasing agency, the gross receipts being divided between the two upon a fixed percentage basis. The former method was the one first adopted in the industry, but the latter has become more popular in the past few years and will undoubtedly ultimately supplant the older method entirely.

That is true especially because of the growing custom of forming manufacturing organizations to make the pictures of a single star and giving him a part of the capital stock of the company. The star, being a stockholder, will turn the films over to a releasing company, only upon condition that a share of the receipts are returned to the company. In this manner a profit is derived from the exploitation of the film, from which the star receives a share on account of his stock holdings.

Litigation between the producer and the releasor is infrequent. Their interests are, as a rule, closely allied and, as the control of each one is in the same group of men, all disputes between them are usually settled intra mura. Occasionally, disputes arise which reach the courts, and the questions which come up are complicated and difficult of adjustment.

In the case of *Goldburg* v. *Popular Pictures Corporation* the producer, under his contract with the distributor, made for and tendered to it a negative of a film. Under the contract the producer was to receive a sum equal to the actual cost of the manufacture of the negative plus a percentage of the gross receipts when the film was released. The distributor failed to accept or pay for the film, and when suit was brought, the court was at a loss to understand whether the action was upon a lease, a sale, or a joint venture.

After a careful array of the facts, Judge Greenbaum decided that the complaint should be based upon a breach of contract. The measure of damages would be solely the actual cost of producing the picture. The percentage of the gross receipts was entirely too speculative, as the picture had not been exhibited by the defendant Popular Pictures Corporation, and plaintiff was directed to amend his complaint accordingly.[1]

[1] *Goldberg* v. *Popular Pictures Corp.* (1917), N. Y. Law Journal, April 20. Greenbaum, J.: "The subject-matter of the contracts upon which the defendants are sought to be held is the production by the plaintiffs of a feature motion picture to consist of not less than 4,500 feet, to be delivered on or before a fixed date to the defendants Popular Pictures Corporation, who will be referred to as 'the defendant.' The legal obligations flowing from the contracts are of a somewhat composite nature, embodying those that are peculiar to a sale, a lease and a joint venture. It lacks, however, all the essential features of any of these transactions. It is not a sale, because the title in the production is reserved in the plaintiffs, the defendant having merely the right to rent, exhibit or otherwise use the films produced by the plaintiffs. It is not altogether a lease, because it is indefinite as to the terms of duration, and it obligates the defendant the Popular Pictures Corporation to the performance of certain active duties or obligations in handling the production. The total amount of what may be termed the 'rentals' to be paid to the plain-

After the amendment of the complaint the defendants interposed answers in which they set up as a partial

tiffs is dependent in fact upon the gross receipts obtained by the defendant from the exhibition or use or lease of the pictures. By the terms of the agreement the compensation or rental to be paid is an advance payment in a single sum, equal to the actual cost to the plaintiffs of manufacturing the pictures, not exceeding, however, the sum of $14,000, plus 50 per cent. of the gross receipts obtained by the defendant in producing the pictures, after the defendant shall have first reimbursed itself from these receipts to the extent of the advance payment. Although the contract embodies some of the substantial features of a joint venture, nothing is stated therein which would indicate that the parties so regarded it, and upon the argument of this motion no suggestion was made by either party that it is a joint venture, and, besides, it lacks the element of 'profits.' The result of this conglomerate relationship is that the learned counsel for the respective parties variously attempt to apply the rules of law applicable to a sale to a lease. It is also claimed on the one side that the contract implies a fixed or absolute obligation in part and the right to uncertain damages in part. On the other hand, it is contended that the situation set forth in the complaint would permit the plaintiffs only to [recover] general or special damages, if provable, as for a breach of the entire contract. Eliminating the technical points urged upon the argument as to whether the complaint sets forth any cause of action, the conceded facts apparent from the complaint and answers are that the plaintiffs and the defendant Popular Pictures Corporation entered into a written agreement, annexed to the complaint; that the plaintiffs tendered a negative and films in alleged conformity with the provisions of the contract; that the defendant refused to accept them, and that the plaintiffs subsequently leased the production to third parties, upon which considerable sums of money have thus far been paid to the plaintiffs. By the contract the defendant agreed to pay as rental, in advance, a sum not exceeding $14,000, upon the receipt by it of 'the original

defense that plaintiff had received moneys from other exhibitors on account of the leasing of the film and that they should be allowed to offset as against the plaintiff's

negatives and a sample print thereof.' The plaintiffs undoubtedly would become entitled, upon an acceptance of the negative and films, to an absolute payment of a sum representing the actual cost expended by the plaintiffs in producing the picture. Upon the defendant's failure or refusal to accept the negative and films the plaintiffs had the right to retain them and to hold the defendant liable for damages for the breach of contract if its refusal to accept was unjustifiable. These damages would be measured by the actual cost to the plaintiffs of producing the negatives and films, and of the proportionate amount of the gross receipts derived by the defendant from the picture, as provided in the contract. It is obvious, however, that it would be impossible in this case to establish what the gross receipts would be where the defendants have failed to accept the films. Hence, under the peculiar circumstances of this case, the plaintiffs would have the right to retain the negatives and films and to lease or rent them to third parties upon the best terms obtainable, for the purpose of recouping themselves against the unknowable loss sustained by them by reason of the Popular Pictures Corporation's alleged refusal to produce the pictures which deprived them of their proportionate share of the gross receipts. It seems to me that upon the alleged breach of the contract on the part of the defendant, by its refusal to accept the negatives and films, a cause of action thereupon accrued for damages for breach of the entire contract. Unless the complaint is amended to set up a case for damages for the breach, no cause of action is established. As the complaint now reads, there is no allegation as to what the actual cost of the production was. The defendant London & Lancashire Indemnity Company of America will also be liable as indemnitor, limited to the amount of the actual cost of the production."

claim the amount so received. The plaintiff moved for judgment on that special defense, which was granted by the special term. On appeal the order of the special term was reversed and it was held that the defendants were entitled to set off such amounts received by the plaintiff.[2]

[2] *Goldberg* v. *Popular Pictures Corp.* (1917), 178 A. D. (N. Y.) 86. Headnote: The plaintiff agreed to manufacture and deliver to the defendant a moving picture film which the defendant was to have the sole right to exhibit in the United States and Canada and on the delivery of the film the defendant was to advance to the plaintiff the actual cost of manufacture, not to exceed $14,000. The defendant also agreed to pay to the plaintiff fifty per cent of its gross receipts from the exhibition of the film, but the plaintiff was not to be entitled to said percentage until the defendant had first reimbursed itself out of the receipts for the manufacturing cost advanced to the plaintiff on delivery of the film, so that the original cost of manufacture was ultimately to be borne solely by the plaintiff out of its share of the receipts of the defendant. To secure performance the defendant gave a bond of the defendant surety company, upon which this action is based, which recited and referred to the aforesaid agreement and provided that nothing therein contained shall modify the right of the defendant to repayment of the advances made to the plaintiff out of the moneys realized by the defendant on said production. The answer of the defendants alleged that acceptance of the film was refused because the plaintiff had delivered to another exhibitor substantially the same film under an agreement by which the plaintiff was to receive from the other exhibitor a percentage of its receipts from the production of the picture in the United States and Canada and that it had actually received certain sums of money from said exhibitor.

Held, that the obligation of the defendant surety company to pay arose, not only when there was an acceptance of the film manufactured by the plaintiff,

In *Levison* v. *Oes* [3] the contract between the parties provided for the sale and delivery of a single film entitled "In the Hands of Impostors" by the defendant to plaintiff. The defendant refused to deliver the film and this action was brought to recover for the breach.

As to the measure of plaintiff's damages the court held that "The ordinary rule of damage for the breach of such a contract is the difference between the market value of the film and the contract price. . . . I think it is fair to assume that there was no market price in this city for this particular film, and that the plaintiff is therefore entitled to recover as special damages both the expenses incurred by him in preparing to exhibit the film and loss of profits. . . . In this case, however, I do not think that he has properly proven them. In order to recover anticipated profits under actual contracts, the plaintiff must plead and prove that he has made such contracts and that the defendant when he agreed to sell the film, knew that the plaintiff had made or contemplated making such contracts which he could not fulfill unless the defendant delivered the film to him."

Further on in the opinion the court furnishes a basis for the measurement of damages as follows:—"Before the jury can however return a verdict based upon loss of future profits the plaintiff must present to the jury some

but also when the plaintiff in other respects did what it was required to do under the contract, and that hence the special defenses aforesaid are good and the plaintiff is not entitled to recover the full amount of $14,000, as the moneys received from the other exhibitor should be offset against the claim.

[3] *Levison* v. *Oes* (1917), 98 Misc. (N. Y.) 260.

evidence from which it can draw a reasonable inference as to the probable approximate amount of such loss."

In *Dressler* v. *Keystone Film Co.*,[4] the plaintiff, an actress, sued to restrain defendant from granting rights to third parties in a film which was the joint property of both, and for an accounting. The question arose whether the rights granted by the defendant with respect to the film were in the nature of an outright sale or a lease.

In holding that the relationship existing between the defendant and the third parties was that of lessor and lessee the court said:—"What the Keystone Film Company has done was to grant the exclusive right to use the picture for a limited term, upon the payment of a fixed sum. This certainly is a lease and not a sale. No absolute or general property in the picture was conveyed or assigned. The use of the picture for a term was all that was granted. The sum paid was not therefore consideration for a sale, but was rent for the use of property. That rent is payable in one sum, rather than in installments, does not change its character."

The producer is entitled to maintain as high a standard as he can attain to in the production of his picture, and the distributor or releasor may not arbitrarily injure that reputation or good will. For instance, where the contract provides that the picture is to be released for a first run only in first-class theatres, the distributor is not at liberty to lease the picture to cheaper or smaller houses.

Nor may he mutilate or change the picture, for in that

[4] *Dressler* v. *Keystone Co.* (1915), N. L. Law Journal, Aug. 5th; aff'd 172 A. D. (N. Y.) 954.

respect the rights of the producer are as sacred as the rights of the actor who played in it.

The distributor may not omit to release regularly as provided for in his contract, for the producer is entitled to have his pictures exhibited before the public at such stated intervals as he may deem compatible with his interest, and a distributor, by holding back the release of pictures, is in a position to seriously affect the standing and good name of the producer.

Where the producer has contracted for a certain size of type or display in the advertising of the picture, he may insist on receiving the same, and for a failure to receive it, may bring an action in damages. If the releasor distributes the picture with a name other than the producer upon the advertising matter, cause for injunction would be made out.

We have not discussed the situation of a producer who sells outright a number of positive films of motion pictures for use in various territories. "State right" sales are often made, and where a lump sum is paid, the transaction is closed, unless by special contract the producer reserves the right to have the picture exhibited in a certain manner, and to have the same advertised along certain lines. Where those reservations are not made by contract, the distributor may exhibit the picture and advertise the same in any manner which will be most profitable to him.

Where third parties come in, within the states for which the exclusive rights have been granted, and infringe upon such picture, the distributor who has obtained the rights for that territory, may enjoin such infringers.

And it would seem that he need not join, in such an action, the producer from whom he obtained the rights. If the producer attempts to license another for the same territory and for the same film, he will also be restrained.[5]

[5] *General Film Co.* v. *Kalem Co. & Kinetograph Co.* (1913), United States District Court, South. Dist. of N. Y., April 16. The action was brought to enjoin defendant Kalem from granting a license to represent a copyrighted drama and the defendant Kinetograph Company from exhibiting the same.

Ward, J.: "The effect of the contract between the complainant and the Kalem Company was to give the complainant the exclusive right to represent and grant to others the right to represent by moving pictures the copyrighted drama. There was nothing left in the Kalem Company to grant to anyone else during the continuance of the complainant's exclusive license. The complainant may properly ask for an injunction restraining a similar representation by anyone else *even though acting in good faith and without notice.* The motion is granted."

Jesse L. Lasky Co. v. *Celebrated Players Film Co.* (1914), 214 Fed. (D. C.) 861. Defendant contracted with plaintiff for Illinois and other state rights for "Brewster's Millions." The Chicago censor eliminated several scenes and while defendant was attempting to adjust this matter plaintiff contracted for the same state rights with another company.

Held that plaintiff was not entitled to enjoin the exhibition of the pictures and that it should be enjoined.

Gilligham v. *Ray* (1909), 157 Mich. 488; 122 N. W. 111. The complaint set forth that plaintiff had acquired from the Chicago Film Exchange the sole right to exhibit the "Gans-Nelson Fight" pictures. That defendants had obtained films from the same exchange and were about to exhibit them. Said the court:

"The Chicago Film Exchange, so far as the bill shows, owed no duty to complainant to protect him against the unlawful or fraudulent use of their film by others. If complainant had any cause of action whatever, it was against defendants. Having ob-

Where the producer has entered into a contract for the sale of "state rights" and before performance of the same, sells the right to the same territory to a third party, who purchases in good faith, it would seem that equity will not decree specific performance of the contract, but leave the injured party to his remedy at law.[6]

However, the purchaser of state rights has no right to duplicate the number of positive prints by "duping" or any other method.

Where state rights are granted upon condition that royalties be paid and the distributor breaches that condition, the producer may maintain replevin for his films.[7]

tained the exclusive right to exhibit this film in Muskegon, he had the same right of action against any person unlawfully or fraudulently invading that exclusive right that the Film Exchange Company itself would have had in the absence of the contract. It would hardly be contended that the corporation owning and controlling the use of this film could not protect its rights by suit to prevent the unauthorized use thereof. No good reason is perceived for denying the same right to the assignee of the corporation's exclusive rights within the contract limits of time and place."

Tree v. *Bowkett* (Eng.) (1896), 12 T. L. R. 181. Mr. Beerbohm Tree having licensed one Abud to produce "Trilby" in certain territory, it was held that Abud was the proper person to maintain an action for infringement of the play in that territory, and not Tree.

See also Section 18.

[6] *Davis* v. *Epoch Producing Co.* (1915), 91 Misc. (N. Y.) 631; 155 N. Y. Supp. 597.

[7] *Vitagraph* v. *Swaab* (1915), 248 Pa. 478; 94 Atl. 126; *Lubin* v. *Swaab* (1913), 240 Pa. 182; 87 Atl. 597; *Biograph Co.* v. *International Film Traders* (1912), 76 Misc. (N. Y.) 436; 134 N. Y. Supp. 1069; *Adams* v. *Fellers* (1910), 88 S. C. 212; 70 S. E. 722. For a discussion of and excerpts from the above cases, see Section 78.

See generally on the rights of a

Section 75.—Exhibitor—in general.

The relationship existing between the distributor and the exhibitor is that of licensor and licensee. The motion picture is rented to the exhibitor to be used by him at a stipulated place and for a stated time. Any use of the film at any place other than that agreed upon or at a time other than that specified, constitutes a violation of the license agreement, and subjects the exhibitor to an action for damages.[8] The courts will also construe it as an infringement of the copyright.[9] They have even gone to the extent of construing such an act as a conversion of the film.[10]

The exhibitor must use ordinary care in the handling

principal to recover moneys received by his agent from the leasing of films: Frohman Amusement Corp. v. *Blinkhorn* (1917), 178 A. D. (N. Y.) 431.

[8] *Fenning Film Service, Ltd.*, v. *Wolverhampton, etc., Cinemas, Ltd.* (Eng.) (1914), 3 K. B. 1171. Plaintiff agreed to lease a certain motion picture to defendants for a period of one week to be exhibited at certain specified theatres. Defendants agreed not to exhibit the film at any theatres other than those specified. The defendants exhibited the film at theatres other than those agreed upon and announced their intention by posters and handbills of exhibiting the film at another theatre.

Held that in addition to its right to damages for breach of its contract plaintiff was entitled to recover damages under the English Copyright Act of 1911, as performances of the film at places other than those agreed upon constituted an infringement of plaintiff's sole right to perform the work in public.

[9] *Fenning Film Service, Ltd.*, v. *Wolverhampton, etc., Cinemas, Ltd.*, (Eng.) (1914), 3 K. B. 1171.

[10] *Biograph Co.* v. *International Film Traders* (1912), 76 Misc. (N. Y.) 436; 134 N. Y. Supp. 1069. See summary of case under Section 78.

of films. The film being fragile in its nature, it is easily ruined. If the operator in projecting the film handles it roughly and renders it unfit for further use the exhibitor will be liable for the value of the print. The courts will always give due consideration to the fact that each exhibition leaves its imprint upon the film and that films are peculiarly susceptible to "wear and tear."

Where the film is destroyed by accident or fire which is not due to any fault on the part of the exhibitor or his employes, the distributor must bear the loss.

Where the film is libelous, and the exhibitor has notice thereof, he is a joint tort feasor.

If the exhibitor is prevented from showing the film because of the closing of his theatre by the public authorities he remains liable for the license fees.[11] But if the public authorities prohibit him from exhibiting the film because of its immoral, lewd, or lascivious character he is under no obligation to pay such license fees; as in the latter instance it would be contrary to public policy to compel one to carry out a contract which in its performance would contravene the law.[12]

There may be said to have arisen, with the coming in of the motion picture industry, a new warranty, that is,

[11] *Thring* v. *Lucas* (Eng.). Strong on "Dramatic and Musical Law," 3d Ed., p. 30. See also cases under Section 55.

[12] *Stott* v. *Gamble* (Eng.) (1916), 115 L. T. 309; 32 T. L. R. 579; 85 L. J. (K. B.) 1750; 2 K. B. 504. Where the licensing authority had refused to permit the theatre proprietors to exhibit a film, plaintiff, the distributor who had contracted with the proprietors, could not recover any damages as of a breach of contract. Also held in this connection that plaintiff was not an *aggrieved* party. *Stott, ex parte* (Eng.) (1916), 114 L. T. 234; 32 T. L. R. 84.

an implied warranty of "clarity of outline and fitness for exhibition." As has been already noted, the film is a very delicate substance, easily injured through use, and the clarity of outline, and the fitness generally for exhibition decrease in proportion to the number of times the film has been exhibited. There has gradually developed in the trade the implied warranty that a film released for exhibition shall be reasonably fit to be shown. If the film furnished to the exhibitor violates this warranty, he may upon discovering the same, either rescind the contract and sue for the return of the money paid by him as license fees, or he may stand upon the contract and sue for his damages.

A license to exhibit a motion picture film is purely personal, and may not be assigned by the licensee without the consent of the licensor. So that where an exhibitor has an agreement with the distributor or releasor for a certain number of releases for a specified period, and the exhibitor sells his business to another, he may not assign his contract with the producer, to the purchaser, nor is such a contract an asset or good will of the business. It does not, in the event of the exhibitor's bankruptcy, pass to his trustee.[13]

Where an exhibitor, who has been given an exclusive license to exploit a film, finds that his licensor is attempting to violate such sole grant, he may enjoin his licensor as well as the one with whom his licensor has contracted.[14]

[13] *In re Kay-Teė Film Exchange* (1911), 193 Fed. (D. C.) 140. See cases cited in Section 14.

[14] *General Film Co.* v. *Kalem Co.* (1913), United States District Court, South Dist. of N. Y., April 16; *Jesse L. Lasky Co.*

But where the defendant had, after the making of his contract with the plaintiff, sold some of his rights to an innocent third party, equity would not decree specific performance.[15]

Section 76.—Advertising matter, programs, bill-posters.

The methods of advertising productions of both plays and motion pictures have been gradually extended, until they have reached a stage where they embrace every known form of publicity medium. The usual and customary mode, however, is by the old-fashioned billboard, the poster and newspaper.

On the other hand, quite an industry has been built up for the advertising of merchants so as to reach the theatre audiences by means of programs, curtain displays and motion picture slides.

A contract with a lithographer for the making of posters has been held to be one for work and labor, in one state,[16] and one for goods sold and delivered in another state.[17]

v. *Celebrated Players Film Co.* (1914), 214 Fed. (D. C.) 861; *Gillingham* v. *Ray* (1909), 157 Mich. 488; 122 N. W. 111; *Tree* v. *Bowkett* (Eng.) (1896), 12 T. L. R. 181. See Section 74, footnote 5, for excerpts from above cases. See also Section 18.

[15] *Davis* v. *Epoch Producing Co.* (1915), 91 Misc. (N. Y.) 631; 155 N. Y. Supp. 597.

[16] *Central Lith.* v. *Moore* (1889), 75 Wis. 170; 43 N. W. 1124. A contract to manufacture lithographs and engravings as advertisements for a theatrical manager held to be not a sale, but a contract for work and labor.

And where, after the work was completed and set aside for the manager, and he did not come for it, and the goods were destroyed by fire, the plaintiff was permitted nevertheless to recover as for *work and labor*.

[17] *Bien* v. *Abbey* (1891), 13 N. Y. Supp. 286. In an action for goods sold and delivered,

Under a contract for display on a drop curtain it was held that plaintiff could recover for the weeks when performances in the theatre were given.[18]

Where the owner of the theatre had contracted with the plaintiff for a drop curtain, and the latter, on the strength of this, had erected the curtain and entered into advertising contracts with third parties, the owner of the theatre was compelled to permit the use of the curtain in the theatre during the term of the contract.[19]

made pursuant to a sample lithograph furnished to plaintiff by defendant, it was reversible error for the court to refuse to charge that "if the jury find that they [the lithographs] were not according to the sketches the plaintiffs cannot recover," the appellate court holding that under a general or specific denial the defendant might give evidence which showed or tended to show that the evidence relied upon by the plaintiff to establish a material fact was untrue.

David Allen Billposting v. *King* (Irish) (1915), Div. Ct., 2 I. R. 213. Defendant, proprietor of a theatre, held liable for breach of a contract for bill posting.

[18] *Imperial Curtain Co.* v. *Strauss* (1912), 76 Misc. (N. Y.) 533; 135 N. Y. Supp. 577. When in a contract for the display of defendant's advertisement on a theatre drop curtain, the defendant agreed to pay a specified sum per week during the period of the contract and "credit was to be given for each entire week" the advertisement was not shown: *Held* that plaintiff was obligated to display the advertisement during those weeks when performances were given and was entitled to recover for display of the advertisement after defendant had directed its discontinuance.

[19] *Beer* v. *Canary* (1896), 2 A. D. (N. Y.) 518; 38 N. Y. Supp. 23. Defendants agreed to permit plaintiff to erect a curtain in front of the proscenium of their theatre, the curtain to be covered by advertisements and the plaintiff to pay a monthly rental for the privilege. *Held* that plaintiff was entitled to an order directing defendant to use

But where the owner of the curtain is remiss in the payment of his rentals, the owner of the theatre may rescind the contract and remove the curtain.[20]

A change in the character of the productions given at the theatre from high-class to cheap and inferior drama and vaudeville, breaches the contract, and the curtain may be removed.[21]

In a contract for program advertising made for three theatres, it was held that the contract was not divisible, and a closing of one of the theatres breached the entire contract.[22] And in a contract of this kind made for the

the curtain, it appearing that plaintiff had been put to some expense in furnishing and setting up the curtain and had entered into contracts for the display of advertisements thereon, the order of special term denying the motion for an injunction pendente lite being reversed.

[20] *Beltinck* v. *Tacoma Theatre Co.* (1910), 61 Wash. 132; 111 Pac. 1045. Defendant permitted plaintiff to hang an advertising curtain in its theatre for which it was to receive $175 a month payable in advance. Plaintiff made partial payments. Defendant rescinded the contract, and the court held that while the contract was silent on that point, that time was nevertheless of the essence of the contract, and plaintiff was properly non-suited.

[21] *Nixon & Zimmerman* v. *Lee Lash Co.* (1911), 46 Pa. Sup. Ct. 89. Where the owner of a drop curtain contracts to put his curtain in a theatre, for a term of five years, and after a time the performances given at the house are changed from legitimate dramatic productions to cheap vaudeville, the contract is breached and the owner of the curtain may take it back and be relieved from future payments under the contract.

[22] *Hazzard* v. *Hoxsie* (1889), 53 Hun (N. Y.), 417; 6 N. Y. Supp. 295. The action was brought upon a contract:

"I hereby agree to pay Edward J. Hazzard the sum of $8.50 per week for publishing my advertisement in the Fifth Avenue, Union Square and Lyceum Thea-

length of a theatrical season, the jury was permitted to determine what period constituted such a season.[23] A failure to give the specified number of performances makes the owner of the theatre liable under the contract.[24]

Where the performance of the contract "depends upon

tre, to occupy one inch on program page for the theatre season. Season 1886, 1887.

"Anna P. Hoxsie."

Held that this was an entire contract, and where the Fifth Avenue Theatre closed first, the contract was terminated at that time and defendant was liable only up to that time.

[23] *Strafford* v. *Stetson* (1910), 41 Pa. Sup. Ct. 560. The contract was:

"Insert our advertisement in the Kieth's Chestnut Street Theatre programme for the (no other piano house ad. but Blasius & Sons) theatrical season of 1902 and 1903, to occupy space of opposite page 4, on page, for which we agree to pay ten dollars per week payable every four weeks." Properly submitted to the jury as to the length of the "theatrical season of 1902 and 1903."

[24] *Strauss* v. *Hammerstein* (1912), 152 A. D. (N. Y.) 128; 136 N. Y. Supp. 613. Defendant granted to plaintiff the exclusive license to circulate programs in defendant's theatre for a specified period; paragraph second provided that there would be given six performances a week for twenty consecutive weeks in each year, plaintiff agreeing to pay a specified sum per performance; the contract further provided that if the giving of grand opera should be discontinued, the plaintiff should at its option have all the program rights with respect to such other performances as might be given at the theatre. *Held* that the agreement contained in paragraph second was absolute and unqualified and that upon defendant's failure to give the specified number of performances for the period therein stated plaintiff could maintain action for the breach of the contract, subject, however, to this: that if plaintiff availed itself of its option and furnished program at performances other than that of grand opera, it could not then recover for a breach of paragraph second.

the happening of an event over which neither party has any control, an implied condition will be read into the agreement to the effect that the contract shall be abrogated upon the non-happening of such an event." [25]

Section 77.—What are fixtures?

In considering what tests to apply to the various parts of the theatre building to determine whether or not they are fixtures, regard must be had to the use for which they are intended, the manner in which they are attached to the realty, and what the condition of the theatre would be were they removed.

Chairs on the floors of the orchestra and balconies and in the boxes are fixtures attached to the realty and may not be removed,[26] although a distinction has been made

[25] *Marks Realty Co.* v. "*Churchills*" (1915), 90 Misc. (N. Y.) 370; 153 N. Y. Supp. 264. See also *Marks Realty Co.* v. *Hotel Hermitage* (1915), 170 A. D. (N. Y.) 484; 156 N. Y. Supp. 179; *Marks Realty Co.* v. *Rectors* (1915), 156 N. Y. Supp. 180.

[26] *Gould* v. *Springer* (1912), 206 N. Y. 641; 99 N. E. 149. Lessee of a theatre was notified by the Board of Health to remove torn and unclean carpets and unsafe and broken chairs from the orchestra floor. Plaintiffs made the repairs and brought action for the sum expended. *Held* that chairs on the floor of the orchestra were fixtures attached to the realty. The rights of the parties being fixed by the lease, the plaintiff was under no duty to make the repairs, and a verdict in plaintiffs' favor was affirmed.

Forbes v. *Howard* (1856), 4 R. I. 364. Where in a contract for the construction of a building the defendant agreed to furnish the fixtures of such a building it was held that seats were fixtures and should have been furnished by defendant.

To the same effect: Bender v. *King* (1901), 111 Fed. (C. C.) 60; *Oliver* v. *Lansing* (1899), 59 Neb. 219; 80 N. W. 829.

between such chairs as were, and such as were not fastened to the floor.[27] Intention of the parties is of paramount importance,[28] although such intention may be spelt out by the fact that a chattel mortgage was placed upon the articles in question.[29]

Lighting and Gas Appliances that are essential to the operation of the theatre are fixtures.[30] This is especially true where these appliances have been so built as to harmonize with the general decoration of the theatre, thereby showing an intent to make them a permanent part of the realty.[31]

[27] *Security Trust Co.* v. *Temple Co.* (1904), 67 N. J. Eq. 514; 58 Atl. 865.

[28] *Sosman* v. *Conlon* (1894), 57 Mo. App. 25. In an action to establish a mechanic's lien it was held that the test whether the materials furnished for the building of the theatre were fixtures, was whether such materials were furnished and received with the intention of forming an integral part of the theatre. *To the same effect: Halley* v. *Alloway* (1882), 78 Tenn. 523.

[29] *Andrews* v. *Chandler* (1888), 27 Ill. App. 103. *Held* that chairs contained in an opera house were not fixtures upon the ground it was the intention of the owners of the opera house and those furnishing the chairs that they should not be regarded as such, such intention being evidenced, among other things, by a chattel mortgage given thereon.

[30] *Security Trust Co.* v. *Temple Co.* (1904), 67 N. J. Eq. 514; 58 Atl. 865. *But see: McKeage* v. *Hanover Fire Ins. Co.* (1880), 81 N. Y. 38; *N. Y. Life Ins. Co.* v. *Allison* (1901), 107 Fed. (C. C. A.) 179.

[31] *Wahle-Phillips Co.* v. *Fitzgerald* (1914), 83 Misc. (N. Y.) 636; 146 N. Y. Supp. 562; aff'd 157 N. Y. Supp. 1150. Action to foreclose mechanic's lien upon a theatre building and office building. The question was whether certain lighting fixtures were part of the realty. Judge Cohalan held that the lighting fixtures in the office building were not of a permanent character. But that in the theatre

The Switchboard was also held to be a fixture as well as the wires and lighting plant.[32]

The Drop Curtain has been held to be an integral part of the realty and not capable of being removed.[33]

Scenery which is not of a permanent character and not fastened in particular to anything is not a fixture,[34] al-

building the lighting fixtures were *part of a scheme to harmonize* with the decorations and interior construction of that part of the building. To the same effect: *Wahle-Phillips Co.* v. *Fifty-Ninth Street and Madison Ave. Company* (1912), 153 A. D. (N. Y.) 17; 138 N. Y. Supp. 13; aff'd 214 N. Y. 684; 108 N. E. 1110.

[32] *Webb* v. *New Haven Theatre* (1913), 87 Conn. 129; 87 Atl. 274. *Held* that the lighting plant, switchboard, wires and the like were fixtures and not removable, even where the lessee had taken out the old ones and replaced them by a new plant, since the house was practically useless without such plant, and an intent to make it a permanent part of the freehold had to be presumed.

[33] *Bender* v. *King* (1901), 111 Fed. (C. C.) 60; *Waycross* v. *Sossman* (1894), 94 Ga. 100; 20 S. E. 252.

[34] *Bender* v. *King* (1901), 111 Fed. (C. C.) 60. *Held* that opera house chairs screwed to the ground, appliances to facilitate handling of scenery during performances and drop curtain were fixtures and went with the realty; that scenery which was in no way attached to the building and was shown to be capable of being used in other buildings was personalty. To the same effect: *Security Trust Co.* v. *Temple Co.* (1904), 67 N. J. Eq. 514; 58 Atl. 865; *New York Life Ins. Co.* v. *Allison* (1901), 107 Fed. (C. C. A.) 179.

But see: *Sosman* v. *Conlon* (1894), 57 Mo. App. 25. *Held* that while stage fittings and scenery were removable, they were nevertheless fixtures.

"The question is not whether they composed integral parts of a building, but whether they were furnished or received with the intention of forming integral parts of a *theatre building*. . . ."

though special scenery constituting part of the permanent stage equipment has been held to be a fixture.[35]

Ticket-booths are not fixtures; nor are portable dance floors put up in sections,[36] nor a carousel in an amusement park, even though an old one had been removed and a new one substituted by the lessee.[37]

Section 78.—Replevin of film and machine.

Where the plaintiff, the owner of motion picture films, had leased them to defendant under a license agreement which the latter had violated, the plaintiff was entitled to maintain replevin for the possession of the films.[38] The

[35] *Oliver* v. *Lansing* (1899), 59 Neb. 219; 80 N. W. 829. *Held* that "the stage appointments, such as scenery, etc.," as well as the opera chairs fastened to the floors, all of which had been built and designed specially for the building were fixtures and passed with the realty; that a piano, carpets and curtains were personalty.

Waycross v. *Sossman* (1894), 94 Ga. 100; 20 S. E. 252. *Held* that scenery and other articles constituting the stage and scenic outfit of an opera house as well as drop-curtain, wings, borders, set-houses, settees and balustrades, were fixtures. To the same effect: *Grewar* v. *Alloway*, 3 Tenn. Ch. 584.

[36] *Security Trust Co.* v. *Temple Co.* (1904), 67 N. J. Eq. 514; 58 Atl. 865. *Held* that the following were not fixtures of a theatre: stage-scenery, chairs not fastened to the realty, combination closet, clock, ticket-boxes, mirrors, tools, wrenches and oilfitter, large portable dance-floor in sections.

[37] *Muller* v. *Rittersville Hotel* (1913), 240 Pa. 79; 87 Atl. 424.

[38] *Lubin* v. *Swaab* (1913), 240 Pa. 182; 87 Atl. 597. This was an action in replevin to recover nine motion picture films leased under a licensed agreement. Plaintiff had been licensed by the Moving Picture Patents Co., owner of patents, to make and lease films to exchanges; defendant operated an exchange. The contract provided that on termination for a breach plaintiff

physical property of the films is in the licensor, which is sufficient for the purposes of the action.

Likewise, the owner of a motion picture machine may replevy the same, even though the same was taken out of the state and sold to a bona fide third party.[39]

In each case, the rule is that while a license in the use of the thing may be granted, title to the physical film

would after 20 days have the right to possession.

Defenses were mainly undue oppression and conspiracy to harm the defendant, and the premature issuance of the writs of replevin.

Judgment in favor of defendant was reversed on assignments of error that defendant, after notice of cancellation of the contract, had no right to license the exhibition of the films to third parties.

Vitagraph Co. v. *Swaab* (1915), 248 Pa. 478; 94 Atl. 126. This case, like *Lubin* v. *Swaab*, 240 Pa. 182, presents the question of the right to replevin motion picture films, the defenses also being conspiracy and bad faith.

Biograph Co. v. *International Film Traders* (1912), 76 Misc. (N. Y.) 436; 134 N. Y. Supp. 1069. Plaintiff was a licensed manufacturer of the Motion Picture Patents Co. It rented film to exhibitors licensed by the Motion Picture Patents Co., in accordance with its agreement with the Patents Co. The title in the film was in plaintiff. Defendant was not a licensed exhibitor and could not clearly show how it came into possession of the films. *Held* that plaintiff could replevin the films and that defendant in refusing to deliver up the same was guilty of conversion.

[39] *Adams* v. *Fellers* (1910), 88 S. C. 212; 70 S. E. 722. A motion picture machine was rented in Georgia by plaintiff to one Heatherly, under an oral agreement that the machine was not to be taken outside of the state; the rental agreement was not recorded, the state of Georgia not requiring such recording. The machine was removed to South Carolina and there sold to a bona fide purchaser, the defendant. *Held* plaintiff was entitled to a return of machine.

or machine still remains with the licensor; and on the breach of the agreement. between them, the licensor may rescind the contract and get back the physical possession of his property.

Section 79.—Theatre leases.

While there was an old English custom with reference to one month's termination of a lease of a theatre upon notice, the modern lease of a theatrical building, theatre or music hall does not differ from leases of real property in general. However, as productions increase in magnitude, and the relationship between the theatre and the various forms of amusement offered in it becomes more and more complex, covenants more or less peculiar to the theatrical profession are inserted into the lease, and come up for construction by the courts from time to time.

Where the lessee of a theatre was described as "M. G. representing Messrs. C. A. C. & Co. Manager of the A. O. B. Co." it was held that "M. G." was liable as a principal and the words added to his name were merely words of description.[40]

A theatre is often spoken of as a "first-class theatre" to distinguish it from theatres in which cheaper and inferior grades of plays are produced. Where, in the lease, the parties have covenanted that none but "first-class" productions are to be given in the theatre, a breach of such covenant by the giving of inferior productions, entitles the lessor to maintain hold-over proceedings.[41]

[40] *Grau* v. *McVickar* (1874), 8 Biss. 7; 10 Fed. Cas., No. 5,708.

[41] *Matter of Schoelkopf* (1907), 54 Misc. (N. Y.) 31; 105 N. Y. Supp. 477. Hold-over proceedings by lessor of theatre because

In *Hammerstein Opera Co.* v. *Belasco*,[42] the interesting question arose as to whether the exhibition of motion pictures violated a covenant in a lease. The lease provided that the premises were "to be used and occupied by the said tenant as a first-class theatre" and that the tenant would not use them or permit them to be used "for any business purpose deemed disreputable or extra hazardous on account of fire, etc." Belasco had used the theatre for high-class plays for which he charged from fifty cents to two dollars admission; he had, however, licensed the Universal Film Company to exhibit in the theatre a motion picture to which admission fees, ranging from twenty-five cents to one dollar, were charged. It was claimed that such motion pictures were not "first-class" plays, and that the premises were rendered "extra hazardous by fire."

The court sustained the plaintiff and granted the injunction.[43]

of breach of covenant to operate "for any other purpose than a theatre and opera house of strictly the first class, etc." Defendant gave exhibitions of a cheaper standard, and the court held that the lease was violated, and the landlord was entitled to an order.

[42] *Hammerstein* v. *Belasco* (1914), 161 A. D. (N. Y.) 199; 146 N. Y. Supp. 341.

[43] *Hammerstein* v. *Belasco* (1914), 161 A. D. (N. Y.) 199; 146 N. Y. Supp. 341. ". . . If the facts set out in the affidavits presented by the plaintiff are true, then the premises are not being used as a first-class theatre, and if such use is continued the value of the property will be greatly diminished. . . . Not only this but the fact is not disputed but that the use to which the theatre is now being put is extra hazardous on account of fire. In answer to this the defendants state they have complied with all the requirements of the municipal authorities, but

In a later decision, however, it was held that a covenant to exhibit pictures for admission ranging from twenty-five cents to two dollars was not violated by charging only twenty-five cents to fifty cents.[44]

if so the present use of the theatre would seem to be a violation of the clause with reference to an increased hazard on account of fire."

[44] *Goelet* v. *Frohman* (1916), N. Y. Law Journal, Feb. 23. "Application pendente lite for injunction. The plaintiff, the owner of the Knickerbocker Theatre, seeks to enjoin the defendant from presenting in said theatre a continuous motion picture performance at admission prices 25 and 50 cents. They assert that such action on the part of defendants is a violation of the covenants of the lease of the theatre. It appears that the defendants Hayman, Klaw & Erlanger and Charles Frohman, Inc., are lessees from the plaintiff, and under their lease, entered into an agreement with the defendant Aitken, granting the use of the theatre to the defendants under certain restrictions. The following provisions are contained therein: 'The parties of the first part let unto the party of the second part (Aitken) for the purpose of exhibitions of first-class motion pictures only for a period of one year, commencing Sept. 1, 1915, and terminating August 31, 1916, the Knickerbocker Theatre. . . . The second party defendant (Aitken) agrees that said premises are to be used only for the exhibition of first-class motion pictures, and not otherwise, prices of admission to be and maintained at the same standard as that of other first-class theatres on Broadway; evening prices to be 25 cents to $2.00. The second party (Aitken) agrees further to use said theatre as a theatre of the first class in the City of New York. . . . The party of the second part hires the said theatre subject to the lease of the parties of the first part with the owners of the said building. . . .' It is asserted that the defendant Aitken and the defendant Triangle Film Co. are violating this agreement by offering the theatre as a continuous moving picture house at the prices above stated, and presenting an addition to motion

Rent is suspended, when so covenanted, when the theatre is closed by the authorities, but the covenant must be express.[45] Where, however, the lessee has not made any such reservation, and the police or the local authorities, because of non-compliance with their regu-

picture songs, musical numbers and other acts; that the defendant, it is claimed, has further violated the agreement by transferring the said lease or rights thereunder to the Triangle Film Co. I am of the opinion that the acts complained of are not clearly such as to constitute a breach of the covenant contained in the lease for violation of which this relief is sought. The case is novel and far-reaching in its importance. It is a matter of serious question whether or not it can be decided on affidavits. Through the introduction of moving picture and photo plays into the theatrical field there has occurred therein an evolution in the production and presentation of plays; in fact, the entire trend of the business may have so evolved as to permit the defendants to carry on their business as now being conducted without violating the restrictive covenants of the lease. Even though irreparable injury be shown, in view of the short time which the lease has to run, unless the right of those seeking the injunction is clear and unmistakable this court may not intervene to prevent the use of the theatre in the manner that it is now conducted. The issues are important and the determination should be left to the trial court, and the injunction ad interim must be denied."

[45] *Lennox* v. *Curzon* (Eng.) (1906), 22 T. L. R. 611. Under a lease for a theatre which was in process of construction it was provided that when "closed by order of any superior authority, etc.," the rent was to be suspended. An adjoining railway building collapsed and the theatre structure becoming unsafe, the London County Council refused to issue a license.

Held, that the theatre was "closed by order of a superior authority" and that the rent was suspended.

lations, shut down the theatre, the rent reserved accrues nevertheless and the lessee is liable therefor.[46]

Where the theatre is destroyed by fire before the commencement of the term of the lease, the lessee is relieved from his obligation thereunder.[47]

In *Adler* v. *Miles*,[48] where the lease provided that the demised premises were "to be used and occupied for the purposes of a place of amusement for the exhibition of moving pictures and for no other purposes whatsoever" a city ordinance subsequently enacted making the giving of motion pictures in this theatre unlawful, was held sufficient to exonerate both the lessee and his surety from the obligation of paying rent.

[46] *Lumiansky* v. *Tessier* (1912), 213 Mass. 182; 99 N. E. 1051. The demised premises were leased for a vaudeville and moving picture theatre. Under the lease, the lessee was required to make all inside repairs. The state police notified the lessor that unless certain interior alterations were made the license would be revoked. The lessee, knowing of the requirements of the state police, but not complying with them although he was obligated so to do under his lease, cannot excuse himself from paying the rent stipulated under the lease when the license is revoked because of non-compliance with the state police requirements.

[47] *Taylor* v. *Caldwell* (Eng.) (1863), 3 Best. & S. 826.

[48] *Adler* v. *Miles* (1910), 69 Misc. (N. Y.) 601; 126 N. Y. Supp. 135. After the making of the lease a city ordinance was enacted prohibiting the use of premises such as the demised premises for the exhibition of moving pictures. In an action on the lease against the surety of such lease it was held that neither the original lessee nor his surety were obligated to pay rent after the passage of the ordinance, the court applying the rule expressed in the maxim "lex non cogit ad impossibilia."

A covenant against assignments is valid; but where there have been numerous assignees, and the lessor has accepted rent from all, this would amount to a waiver on the part of the lessor.[49]

In building and other contracts for the construction of theatres, it is well to define with every degree of exactness what the theatre building is to be, with special reference to the unique elements of the building, such as the proscenium, stage, seats and so on.[50] And for delay in such construction, the lessee may, in an action for the rent, counterclaim for damages sustained by him by reason of such delay,[51] or the lessee is entitled to maintain an action

[49] *Nelson Theatre Co.* v. *Nelson* (1913), 216 Mass. 30; 109 N. E. 926. Where defendant had leased a theatre to a tenant with the usual covenants against assignments unless consented to in writing, and where the tenant had subsequently assigned without such written consent, and there had been subsequent assignments without written consents, and the defendant had accepted rent from all these assignees: *Held,* that he would be enjoined from ousting the last tenant, as his acceptance of the rent amounted to a waiver of that clause in the lease. *Held also* that evidence of experts on the receipts of the theatre for the past year as a basis for computing the damages was admissible.

[50] *Neher* v. *Viviani* (1910), 15 N. M. 460; 110 Pac. 695, passes on the meaning of a building contract for a theatre, and holds in particular that the phrase "a modern thirty thousand dollar theatre building" includes in addition to the bare building, the usual necessary permanent equipment, such as plumbing, heating and lighting apparatus, seats, curtains and scenery adapted to and intended for use in that particular building, but *not* the piano, furniture, carpets, etc.

[51] *New York Academy of Music* v. *Hackett* (1858), 2 Hilt. (N. Y.) 217. Defendant leased plaintiff premises for two months, plaintiff to use diligence in completing the construction of building,

for liquidated damages under the contract, where the theatre was not constructed and the lessor has utterly failed to perform.[52]

lessee to be evicted on account of non-payment of rent. Plaintiff failed to use diligence in completing the building and defendant failed to pay rent. Action was for rent. *Held* that defendant might counterclaim for his damages by reason of plaintiff's breach in failing to diligently complete the building; that defendant was entitled to be allowed in abatement of the rent, expenses incurred by him in advertising the performances announced for the week following the eviction but was not entitled to set off damages by reason of loss of the services of one of the artists who contracted a severe cold on account of the unfinished condition of the building as the gains or profits, which the defendant might have made through the artist's performances, were too speculative and conjectural.

[52] *Shubert* v. *Sondheim* (1910), 138 A. D. (N. Y.) 800; 123 N. Y. Supp. 529; aff'd 203 N. Y. 636; 97 N. E. 1116. Where a written agreement to make a lease, rental to commence when a building on the property was completed, provided that the lessee was to deposit money in escrow as security for the rent, and the proposed lessee, having the necessary funds failed to do so solely because the lessor refused to designate a depository when requested so to do, the lessee may maintain an action for liquidated damages provided for by the agreement, if the proposed lessor put it out of his power to fulfill the contract by leasing the lands to third parties.

It was held that the provision for liquidated damages was enforceable as the plaintiff "might have sustained very large damages which could not be proved with sufficient definiteness to warrant a recovery thereof, if he relied throughout the period of the construction of the building on obtaining a lease of this theatre, and then did not receive it." It is not essential to the validity of a liquidated damage clause that it be reciprocal. Interest may be recovered on stipulated damages.

For penalties for defective struc-

Agreements between the theatre owner and adjoining property owners to break through walls for the purpose of making exits and vestibules must be made as provided for by the ordinances of the local authorities. Otherwise the contract may be held void and unenforcible, and a recovery thereon will be denied.[53] In a similar suit brought in equity where the theatre owner had not fully performed under his contract, relief was denied him.[54]

tural defects see: St. James Hall Co. v. *London Co. Council* (Eng.) (1901), 2 K. B. 250.

[53] *Hart* v. *City Theatres Co.* (1911), 71 Misc. (N. Y.) 427; 128 N. Y. Supp. 678; reversed 156 A. D. (N. Y.) 673; 141 N. Y. Supp. 386; judgment of Appellate Division reversed, and that of trial affirmed in 215 N. Y. 322; 109 N. E. 497. A contract between the owner of a theatre and the owner of an adjoining non-fireproof building to cut through the wall which separated the buildings, for an exit through the latter building, was held to violate the building code of the City of New York and the owner of the latter building was not permitted to maintain an action to recover the agreed compensation.

"Courts will not be astute to sustain contracts when the effect will be to weaken the efficacy of law and regulations designed for the protection of human life. Where a contract on its face, whether so intended by the parties or not, offends against statutes intended to promote public safety, the courts will not enforce it" (excerpt from opinion in 215 N. Y. 322; 109 N. E. 497).

[54] *Keener* v. *Moslander* (1911), 54 So. (Ala.) 881. Plaintiff owned a theatre and motion picture house in Mobile. Defendant conducted a candy business in the rear of the theatre—the parties contracted to give plaintiff a right of way through defendant's storeroom into the theatre, after which plaintiff constructed improvements and made an entrance and vestibule through the storeroom. Defendant then erected a board fence, cutting off the entrance and egress of patrons and this suit for injunction was brought. Relief denied upon the ground that plaintiff had failed to perform

Where a building was rented for the purpose of being conducted as a motion picture theatre, the landlord could not be held to have covenanted to have allowed the lessee an exit from the rear through property owned by the landlord where such property was not included in the lease.[55]

It is not always an easy matter to determine whether the contract between the parties is a lease or a license. In a late case the question was fully discussed,[56] but the agreement there construed was rather unusual. In *Leavitt* v. *Windsor Co.*,[57] it was held that where in addition

his part of the contract, and so could not obtain relief in equity.

[55] *Kaiser* v. *Cinberg* (1909), 130 A. D. (N. Y.) 254; 114 N. Y. Supp. 716.

As to the liability of the owner of a theatre for repairs made therein under direction of the lessee, see Valenti v. *N. Y. Theatre Co.* (1917), N. Y. Law Journal, April 6th.

[56] *Coney Island Co.* v. *M'Intyre-Paxton Co.* (1912), 200 Fed. (C. C. A.) 901. An agreement made for the use of an amusement park construed, and its tenure defined.

Whether the rights of a concessionaire amounted to a license revocable at will of owner, quære.

[57] *Leavitt* v. *Windsor Land & Investment Co.* (1893), 54 Fed. (C. C. A.) 439. Where contract provides that defendant furnish building and pay certain of its expenses and the plaintiff give his time and skill in carrying on a theatre therein and to act as manager of such theatre, the defendant to receive a fixed sum as rent and in addition thereto one-half of the net profits; the contract also providing that the losses be borne equally by the parties it was held that a partnership had been created though the parties had referred to themselves as lessee and lessor. See also Section 62.

On the question of the dissolution of such joint venture see: Shubert v. *Laughlin* (1907), 107 N. Y. Supp. 708. Plaintiff contributed his theatre lease and defendant his skill as a manager and booking-agent in a joint

to rent the lessor was to receive a stipulated portion of the profits, and pay certain charges and to share in the losses, the relation was that of partners or joint venturers, and not that of lessor and lessee.

The lessee may sell out his interest in the theatre to a third party; and in such a contract a covenant by him not to engage in business in a limited territory for a limited term has been held valid and binding. And where, in violation of such covenant, he subsequently attempts to manage a theatre within the prohibited area during the prescribed term, he will be enjoined.[58]

However, injunction is not a remedy usually favored by the courts with respect to leases and their breaches, for to do so "would be to compel supervision by the courts for a long term of years and the enforcement of negative covenants which would in effect be to decree specific performance." [59]

Where the owner of the theatre had contracted first with one company, then with another company, for the

venture. In an action brought by one of the partners an order appointing a receiver was reversed on the ground that plaintiff was not asking for a dissolution, and that the proper parties had not been brought in.

[58] *Metropolitan Opera* v. *Hammerstein* (1914), 162 A. D. (N. Y.) 691; 147 N. Y. Supp. 532. Defendant Oscar Hammerstein in 1914 sold his opera properties, good will and business to the Metropolitan Opera Co. He covenanted not to engage in grand opera in New York City for ten years. On injunction to restrain defendant from giving grand opera, *held*, that such a covenant was not in restraint of trade, and was reasonable.

[59] *Shubert* v. *Woodward* (1909), 167 Fed. (C. C. A.) 47.

lease of his theatre for the same term, injunction was likewise refused.[60]

In an action between the lessor and lessee of a theatre who had agreed to divide the profits of a play to be produced therein, evidence of the previous receipts of the theatre, of the popularity of the production in places where it had already been produced and the probable amount of the receipts was inadmissible.[61]

But in an action on the breach of a lease for a theatre, evidence of experts on the receipts of the theatre for the past year as a basis for computing the damages was held admissible.[62]

Where the issue involved is whether the performances given were in compliance with the contract, declarations of the patrons at the very moment they are leaving the theatre, of their reasons for so doing, are a part of the "res gestæ" and admissible.[63]

Where a defendant was sued for services rendered and the question was whether he or his landlord was liable

[60] *Welty* v. *Jacobs* (1898), 171 Ill. 624; 49 N. E. 723. Plaintiff, manager of "The Black Crook" entered into a contract with defendant for the use of the latter's theatre. Subsequently defendant entered into another contract with a rival "The Black Crook" company for the use of his theatre for the same period. Plaintiff sued for injunction to restrain such use of the theatre. *Held* untenable.

[61] *Moss* v. *Tompkins* (1893), 69 Hun (N. Y.), 288; 23 N. Y. Supp. 623; aff'd 144 N. Y. 659; 39 N. E. 858. In this connection, see Sections 21 and 49.

[62] *Nelson Theatre Co.* v. *Nelson* (1913), 216 Mass. 30; 109 N. E. 926. See also: *Rosenwasser* v. *Amusement Enterprises* (1914), 88 Misc. (N. Y.) 57; 150 N. Y. Supp. 561.

[63] *Charley* v. *Potthoff* (1903), 118 Wis. 258; 95 N. W. 124.

therefor, it was held that the lease between himself and the landlord was admissible in evidence.[64] Where the contract was evidenced by a letter, oral testimony showing a qualification of the letter was held inadmissible.[65]

The question has occasionally arisen whether a municipality has the right to establish and maintain a place of amusement.

In a recent Ohio case it was held that the powers to be exercised by a municipality did not include the maintenance of a motion picture theatre.[66]

[64] *Miller* v. *Lawrence* (1895), 13 Misc. (N. Y.) 130; 34 N. Y. Supp. 161.

[65] *Zerralin* v. *Ditson* (1875), 117 Mass. 553. Plaintiff sued for services rendered in conducting of "The World's Peace Jubilee." Defendant set up a special contract whereby the services were rendered upon the understanding, expressed in a letter, that the management would not be responsible in case the music festival resulted in a loss.

On the trial defendants offered the letter in evidence and plaintiff attempted to give oral testimony to show a qualification of the terms of the letter, which was rejected as varying the express terms of the letter.

Held on appeal that the oral evidence was properly rejected.

[66] *State* v. *Lynch* (May, 1913), 102 N. E. (Ohio) 670. "Whether a municipality acquires authority 'to exercise all the powers of local self-government' by adopting a charter, or adopts a charter as an indispensable mode of exercising the authority, the powers to be exercised, being governmental, do not authorize taxation to establish and maintain moving picture theatres."

The decision was by a divided court. A strong dissenting opinion was written by Judge Wanamaker.

See also: *Smith* v. *City of Raton* (1914), 140 Pac. 109 (N. M.) Under the powers granted to cities and towns by the statute to erect all needful buildings for their use, such municipalities are limited to the erection of such needful buildings as may be required for public uses or for

In California a decision was rendered a month after the opinion in the Ohio case was handed down, holding that a municipal corporation *might* have the power to erect and maintain a place of public amusement, although it could not contract with a private corporation for the erection of the buildings by the private corporation on land belonging to the municipality, where the property was to be managed by a board of trustees, a majority of which were not to be selected by the municipality.[67]

municipal uses and purposes as distinguished from private or quasi public use. Where the paramount purpose is to use such building for theatrical performances, "legislative authority is lacking in this state for the erection of such buildings by cities and towns." See also: *Trustees, etc.*, v. *Lewis* (1912), 63 Fla. 691.

See in this connection *Worden* v. *New Bedford* (1881), 131 Mass. 23, where it was held that if the building was, in good faith, erected for municipal purposes but later became vacant, the municipality had a right to permit its uses for a private enterprise. See also: *Bryant* v. *Logan* (1904), 56 W. Va. 141; 49 S. E. 21.

[67] *Egan* v. *San Francisco* (June, 1913), 165 Cal. 576; 133 Pac. 294.

The court cites in support of the proposition that a municipality may devote money for the pleasure and amusement of its inhabitants: *Hubbard* v. *Taunton* (1886), 140 Mass. 467; 5 N. E. 157; *Denver* v. *Hallett* (1905), 34 Col. 393; 83 Pac. 1066; *Kingman* v. *Brockton* (1891), 153 Mass. 255; 26 N. E. 998; *Spires* v. *Los Angeles* (1906), 150 Cal. 64; 87 Pac. 1026; *Laird* v. *Pittsburg* (1903), 205 Pa. St. 1; 54 Atl. 324.

The court cites the following cases in support of the proposition that the public use of public property cannot coexist with private management and control of such property. *California Academy* v. *San Francisco* (1895), 107 Cal. 334; 40 Pac. 426; *Home, etc., of the Inebriate* v. *San Francisco* (1898), 119 Cal. 534; 51 Pac. 950; *La Societa, etc.*, v. *San Francisco* (1900), 131 Cal. 169; 63 Pac. 174.

See also in this connection:

Lessees of theatres are customarily required to deposit a sum of money with their lessors as security for the due performance of all of the provisions of the lease.

The agreement sometimes provides that in case of any default by the lessee, the lessor may retain the moneys deposited with him as liquidated damages. The courts will not be bound by the language of the parties. If the result is to penalize the lessee the courts will permit him to recover back his deposit.

In *Stimpson* v. *Minsker Realty Co.*, the plaintiff as receiver brought an action to recover back $68,500, part of a deposit of $72,000, made by the lessee with the lessor under a lease for a theatre. In view of the fact that the amount sought to be retained was out of all proportion to the damages sustained by the defendant the court was constrained to treat the amount as a penalty, notwithstanding the express provision of the lease that the lessor was entitled to retain the entire amount as liquidated damages in the event of a breach.[68]

An action to recover back a deposit under a lease may be maintained only upon the expiration of the period of

French v. *Quincy* (1861), 3 Allen (Mass.), 9; *Stone* v. *Oconomowoc* (1888), 71 Wis. 155; 36 N. W. 829; *Jones* v. *Sanford* (1877), 66 Me. 585; *Sugar* v. *Monroe* (1902), 108 La. 677; 32 So. 961.

[68] *Stimpson* v. *Miasker Realty Co.* (1917), 177 A. D. (N. Y.) 536. "We also think that the $72,000 retained by the lessor is out of all proportion to the probable loss in case of a breach as viewed at the time the lease was made. In the event of a breach by the lessee, the lessor could assume absolute control of the premises and relet them for its own account. It is hardly credible that it would fail to relet them to advantage, situated as they were in the midst of numerous and theatre going population."

the lease, unless every contingency under which the defendant might have had a claim for damages against said fund has been exhausted.[69]

The lessee may maintain an action for breach of the contract before the date arrives for his entry upon the premises, where he is informed prior thereto by the lessor that he will not be permitted to enter upon such premises.[70]

The lessor, when suing for rent on a guaranty, is not required to prove that the defaulting tenant was in actual physical possession of the premises.[71]

Section 80.—Theatre a nuisance.

A theatre is not a nuisance per se.[72] But under certain

[69] *Halpern* v. *Manhattan Ave. Theatre Corp.* (1916), 173 A. D. (N. Y.) 610.

[70] *Grau* v. *McVickar* (1874), 8 Biss. 7, 10 Fed. Cas. No. 5,708. The performances were to commence Feb. 9th. It was held that a complete cause of action accrued prior to that date where the lessee notified the lessor that he would not comply with the terms of the agreement.

[71] *Woods* v. *Broder* (1908), 113 N. Y. Supp. 335.

For a case where a bar privilege was leased see: Day v. *Luna Park* (1912), 174 Ill. App. 477. A concession granted by the defendant, an amusement park, for a bar privilege, which contains a restrictive covenant against its assignment to third parties, is personal and does not, in the event of bankruptcy of the bar, pass to the trustee in bankruptcy.

[72] *City of Indianapolis* v. *Miller* (1907), 168 Ind. 285; 80 N. E. 626. "While theatres are subject to the police power of the state in some particulars, yet it can by no means be said that the business of conducting a playhouse is in its own nature a nuisance. 1 Hawk. P. C. 693; Joyce, Nuisances, Section 115; Wood, Nuisances, 3d Ed., Section 52."

City of Chicago v. *Weber* (1910), 246 Ill. 304; 92 N. E. 859. "A city may declare and abate nuisances, but a theatre is not a

conditions it may easily become one, as when large crowds gather in front and extend in line, boisterous patrons congregate, noises issue from the theatre, and the like.

The most frequent complaint is that great crowds are attracted to the theatre, and extend in long queues down the street, obstructing entrance upon and egress from adjacent property, and interfering with the free use thereof.

Where this is a common occurrence, it unquestionably constitutes a nuisance, and may be abated by appropriate remedy.[73] This is true not only of a theatre, but of other

nuisance per se, and a declaration by the city would not make it a nuisance unless it was such in fact. [*Village of Des Plaines* v. *Poyer* (1888), 123 Ill. 348; 14 N. E. 677.]"

To the same effect: 1 Hawkins P. C. (8th Ed.), 693; *Barber* v. *Penley* (Eng.) (1893), 2 Ch. 447; *Bellamy* v. *Wells* (Eng.) (1890), 63 L. T. N. S. 635; *Ex parte Whitwell* (1893), 98 Cal. 73; 32 Pac. 870.

Holt, C. J., in *Betterton's Case* (1695), Holt K. B. 538; 5 Mod. 142; 5 Kin. 625. "It hath been holden that a common playhouse may be a nuisance if it draw together such a number of coaches or people, etc., as to prove generally inconvenient to the places adjacent. And it seems that playhouses, having been originally instituted with a laudable design of recommending virtue to the imitation of the people, and exposing vice and folly, are not nuisances in their own nature, but may only become such by accident."

[73] *Lyons, Sons & Co.* v. *Gulliver* (Eng.) (1913), C. A. (1914), 1 Ch. 631; 30 T. L. R. 75. Defendant conducted a theatre. A large number of people assembled in and about the theatre before each performance. Long lines were formed extending for some distance from the theatre, five persons abreast. Plaintiff's premises were adjacent to those of defendant. *Held* that the collection of such crowds constituted an actionable nuisance, and that the failure of police to keep proper gaps for passage of public and

forms of public exhibition and advertising.[74] The crowd or line need not necessarily be noisy or unruly or bois-

regulate the crowds was no defense.

Dissenting opinion by Phillimore, L. J., that every trader had the right to make his shop as attractive as possible and was not responsible for crowds who collected before his shop; that defendant was not responsible for collection of crowd before the hour at which they were invited to attend; that it was the duty of the police to prevent obstruction of passageways; that formation of a line or queue did not constitute an actionable nuisance.

Barber v. *Penley* (Eng.) (1893), 62 L. J. Ch. Div. 623. Plaintiff kept a lodging house adjacent to defendant's theatre. She sought to enjoin defendant, claiming that access to her premises was shut off by the great crowds which collected in front of the theatre two hours before it opened.

The court held that if after the opening night of the show crowds continued to gather in front of defendant's theatre, that would constitute a nuisance; but as it appeared from the affidavits that the police had taken control and no nuisance existed at the time when the application for the injunction was made, no injunction was necessary and hence refused. Defendant, however, was required to pay plaintiff's costs of the action. To the same effect: *Wagstaff* v. *Edison Bell* (Eng.) (1893), 10 T. L. R. 80.

Inchbald v. *Robinson* (Eng.) (1869), L. R. 4 Ch. 388. A temporary injunction was refused because of insufficient evidence before the court, although it approved of the rule of law "that the collecting of crowds immediately before a residence, so as to block up the approaches to it, might be a nuisance, and that if the collection of those crowds was to be attributed to the act of a particular individual, that individual might be restrained from the commission of that act." The statement of the law by Lord Cairn as above quoted was approved on appeal by Lord Justice Selwyn.

Walker v. *Brewster* (Eng.) (1867), L. R. 5 Eq. 25. *Held* that the collection of large crowds in front of defendant's amusement resort constituted a nuisance and should be enjoined.

[74] *Shaw's Jewelry Shop* v. *N. Y.*

terous; its mere presence in sufficient numbers to interfere with the adjoining owner's rights constitutes the nuisance.

Where a place of amusement is so conducted that noises issue therefrom so as to disturb the peace and rest of the neighbors, it becomes a nuisance, whether such noises are caused by the patrons or by the performers.[75]

Herald (1915), 170 A. D. (N. Y.) 504; 156 N. Y. Supp. 651. The maintenance of an automatic baseball playograph which caused the collection of thousands of spectators and impeded traffic to the extent of requiring the presence of a large number of police officers and interfered with the ingress to and egress from plaintiff's store constituted a nuisance, for which plaintiff was entitled to damages, and if not abated at time of trial, to an injunction.

Jaques v. *Natl. Exhibit Co.* (1884), 15 Abb. N. C. (N. Y.) 250. It was held that a puppet show in a window for advertising purposes, which drew together crowds of persons, was a nuisance.

Bellamy v. *Wells* (Eng.) (1890), 63 L. T. N. S. 635. The assemblage of large groups of persons before defendant's club wherein boxing exhibitions were conducted was held to be a nuisance.

Rex v. *Carlile* (Eng.) (1819), 6 C. and P. 636. Defendant exhibited some effigies in his window, which caused the collection of large crowds in front of the window and obstructed passage along the street. *Held* a nuisance.

Rex v. *Moore* (Eng.) (1832), 3 B. & Ad. 184. The collection of a large number of persons on the road leading to defendant's shooting grounds was held to be a nuisance. The court said: "If a person collects together a crowd of people to the annoyance of his neighbors, that is a nuisance for which he is answerable."

[75] *Cluney* v. *Lee Wai* (1896), 10 Hawaii, 319. The playing of instruments at defendant's theatre from which such noises emanated as interfered with plaintiff's slumber was enjoined.

See also: *Penrose* v. *Nixon* (1891), 140 Pa. St. 45; 21 Atl. 364, where injunction was refused to restrain noises caused by the shifting of scenery.

Village of Des Plaines v. *Poyer*

The close proximity of the theatre to a church has also been held to constitute a nuisance.[76] So, too, where patrons were continually trespassing on the adjacent owner's property.[77]

(1888), 123 Ill. 348; 14 N. E. 677. Where the noise and commotion of a public resort reaches such a point as to interfere with the rights of the public, they will constitute a nuisance.

Commonwealth v. *Cincinnati, etc., Rd. Co.* (1908), 139 Ky. 429; 112 S. W. 613. An indictment charging that defendant permitted the congregation of large numbers of persons at its public resort on and near a public highway, who made loud noises, and otherwise misbehaved themselves to the discomfort and annoyance of the inhabitants residing in the vicinity, sufficiently alleged acts constituting a nuisance.

See also: *Cramer* v. *Klein* (1908), 127 A. D. (N. Y.) 146; 111 N. Y. Supp. 469; *Jung Brewing Co.* v. *Commonwealth* (1906), 123 Ky. 507; 96 S. W. 595; *Levin* v. *Goodwin* (1906), 191 Mass. 341; 77 N. E. 718; *Palestine* v. *Minor* (1905), 86 S. W. (Ky.) 695; *Town of Davis* v. *Davis* (1895), 40 W. Va. 464; 215 S. E. 906; *Schleuter* v. *Billingheimer*, 9 Ohio Dec. (Repr.) 513; *Paris* v. *Commonwealth*, 4 Ky. Law Rep. 597; *Jenkins* v. *Jackson* (Eng.) (1888), 40 Ch. D. 71.

[76] *Nahser* v. *City of Chicago* (1915), 271 Ill. 288; 111 N. E. 119. *Held* that a motion picture theatre within 200 feet of a church constituted a *nuisance.*

Hamlin v. *Bender* (1915), 92 Misc. (N. Y.) 16; 155 N. Y. Supp. 963; aff'd 173 A. D. (N. Y.) 996. Where large crowds congregate about the entrance of a moving picture theatre to such an extent as to cause at times congestion of travel in front of the building and where those attending a church in the immediate vicinity of the theatre are called upon to pass and repass it, an injunction may be granted restraining the operation of the theatre, on Sundays, as a nuisance.

[77] *Cronin* v. *Bloewecke* (1899), 58 N. J. Eq. 313; 63 Atl. 605. Defendants conducted baseball games at their park. A number of balls fell upon plaintiff's premises and persons trespassed thereon to recover the balls. Injunction

Section 81.—Franchise and booking agreements.

Many plays are booked through so-called "booking circuits." The circuit company makes agreements with the owners of theatres, whereby it agrees to furnish them with companies of players together with the plays customarily produced at such theatres, and the theatre proprietors agree to pay to the performing companies a specified compensation, which is usually a percentage of the gross receipts. The theatres are known as the circuit.

The circuit company thereupon enters into agreements with managers of performing companies, the agreements being known as "franchises," in which it agrees to secure bookings for the managers' productions.

The circuit company is the agent of the theatre owner for whom it arranges bookings.[78] This becomes important on the question of suit. Where the owner of the theatre has breached the terms of the contract and has refused

issued restraining defendants from permitting ball games to be conducted in such manner as to annoy and injure plaintiff, either because of the driving or dropping of balls upon the premises or by permitting the collection of idle or disorderly persons in the streets.

The rule of law is that Courts of Equity will restrain an existing or threatened nuisance at the suit of the people by their attorney general, or of a private individual who sustains special and peculiar injury therefrom distinct from that suffered by him in common with the public.

[78] *Interstate Amusement Co.* v. *Albert* (1913), 161 S. W. (Tenn.) 488. Plaintiff operated a booking agency in Chicago. Defendant operated a theatre in Tennessee. Plaintiff booked certain acts for defendant for which the latter became indebted to it in a sum of money.

Held that plaintiff was the agent of the defendant to book these acts for which it was to receive $10 a week and 5% of the amounts paid to the troupes.

to pay the manager of the company whose play has been booked for his theatre, he may be directly sued by the manager. There is privity of contract between the parties, and the manager may allege the making of the contract, through the medium of the circuit company, although in fact one contract was made between the manager and the circuit company, and another between the circuit company and the theatre owner.

A burlesque booking circuit which opened a theatre in proximity to the plaintiff's theatre and thereby forced it to shut down, was held not guilty of conspiracy, since it had done nothing illegal, and its motives were immaterial.[79]

A booking agent will not be compelled to specifically perform its contract and book through its offices acts for a theatre proprietor, as that would require the continuous supervision of the court, and a court of equity will not assume such a duty.[80]

[79] *Roseneau* v. *Empire Circuit* (1909), 131 A. D. (N. Y.) 429; 115 N. Y. Supp. 511. Action by plaintiff as Receiver of the Court Street Theatre for a conspiracy to bring about the ruin of that theatre by the defendant which controlled a burlesque booking circuit.

Held untenable as defendant had merely done lawfully the things which it had a right to do.

"If the means employed to do a certain act are legal and lawful, it is of no consequence that the motive which induced such act was malicious."

[80] *Hammerstein* v. *United Booking Offices* (1915), N. Y. Law Journal, Nov. 4. Defendant had entered into an agreement with a number of owners and managers of vaudeville theatres whereby defendant agreed to act as booking agent for the managers and the managers agreed to book through defendant exclusively. The managers agreed with each other that during the term of the agreement

Booking agents and circuit companies have been held not to be engaged in interstate commerce.[81]

A booking agency or circuit company contract must be construed in the light of reasonableness, so that in a contract in which territory was to be set aside before a day certain, it was held that time was not of the essence, and the defendant could later set aside such territory or route.[82]

Section 82.—Benefit performances—private exhibitions.

It is a common practice for clubs, lodges and societies to arrange with theatre owners for benefit performances, the proceeds of which are as a rule donated to some worthy

they would not become directly or indirectly interested in the operation of any vaudeville theatre other than their own in the City of New York except as provided in the agreement. Plaintiff became in effect a party to the above agreement by a subsequent agreement made between itself and other parties and the defendant. Plaintiff in violation of his agreement became interested in another theatre and defendant thereupon refused to book any acts for plaintiff's theatre. A motion was made to compel defendant to specifically perform, to wit: to book acts for plaintiff. The motion was denied, among other reasons, because the court would not assume the duty of requiring the doing of acts which would require its continuous supervision.

[81] *Interstate Amusement Co.* v. *Albert* (1913), 161 S. W. (Tenn.) 488.

[82] *Perley* v. *Shubert* (1907), 121 A. D. (N. Y.) 786; 106 N. Y. Supp. 593. Where the parties, theatrical managers, contracted for a certain territory for bookings, defendants to set aside a certain territory or route prior to May 1st of each year, it was held nevertheless that time was not of the essence of the contract, and that there was no evidence of a breach.

charity. As these performances are often held on Sunday, the question arises whether, in states where Sunday performances are prohibited, these classes of performances are exempt. In some of the states performances or exhibitions for charitable or benevolent purposes are expressly permitted to be given on Sunday.

In *Koelble* v. *Woods*,[83] an outdoor celebration, consisting of foot-races, bicycle and motorcycle races was stopped by the authorities. In proceedings brought to restrain the Police and Sheriff, the court held that the fact that proceeds were to be given to charity did not give the promoters the right to violate the law. But this was clearly an "outdoor" sport or exhibition, and there was no exemption in the New York statutes for that kind of entertainment.

A performance of that nature is not taken out of the statute because the expenses of the house are paid. The test is whether the proceeds derived from the sale of tickets are devoted to charity.[84]

Where a benefit performance had been scheduled to take place, and there was a breach by the theatre owner, the association giving the performance could not recover where it had suffered no damage.[85]

[83] *Koelble* v. *Woods* (1916), 159 N. Y. Supp. 704.

[84] *Commonwealth* v. *Alexander* (1904), 185 Mass. 551; 70 N. E. 1017.

[85] *Jackel* v. *Nixon & Zimmerman* (1907), 33 Pa. Sup. Ct. 30. Plaintiff, an association, contracted with defendant for a benefit performance at its theatre. Subsequently, and after plaintiff had sold many of the tickets, defendant rescinded the contract. *Held*, that since plaintiff had refunded all the moneys for the tickets so purchased of it, it could not recover.

"Proceeds" derived from a benefit or charitable performance have been defined as the balance remaining after deductions for the expenses necessarily incurred for the giving of such a performance.[86]

Unless specifically exempted by statute, a charitable organization must secure a theatrical license and pay the required tax before giving public exhibitions.[87]

It is not a public exhibition for a motion picture company to exhibit its reels to dealers by running them off for the purpose of renting or leasing the same.[88]

Section 83.—Interstate commerce.

In New York it has been squarely held that the theatrical business does not constitute "interstate commerce" within the meaning of the "Sherman anti-trust law." The fact that theatrical companies travelled from state to

[86] *Commonwealth* v. *Alexander* (1904), 185 Mass. 553; 70 N. E. 1017.

[87] *City of Mobile* v. *Kiernan* (1910), 54 So. (Ala.) 102.

Shelley v. *Bethell* (Eng.) (1883), 12 Q. B. D. 11. Defendant who had a private house fitted up as a private theatre turned it over to another who advertised performances therein for the benefit of a School for Dramatic Art. *Held* that defendant was guilty irrespective of the fact that the performance was for charity.

See also Section 106.

[88] *A. G.* v. *Vitagraph Co., Ltd.* (Eng.) (1915), 1 Ch. 206; 13 L. G. R. 148; 84 L. J. (Ch.) 142; 31 T. L. R. 70; 112 L. T. 245; 79 J. P. 150. The term "*Exhibition*" in Section 1 of the Cinematograph Act 1909, refers to the exhibition of cinematograph pictures in places of public entertainment, and does not include a case where dealers in the exercise of their trade of selling or renting films merely show their films by running them through their machines in the presence of one or more customers.

state giving grand opera made no difference in this respect.[89] But in Illinois the court has intimated that the sending of theatrical troupes from one state to another is interstate commerce.[90]

The business of a booking agent has been held not to constitute interstate commerce, even where it booked acts in various states throughout the Union.[91]

And the making of contracts in one state for the production of plays in another has been held not to violate a statute forbidding foreign corporations from doing business in the latter state without first complying with the statutory requirements.[92]

In *United States* v. *Motion Picture Patents Co.*, however, it was held that the shipment of motion picture films from one state to another constituted interstate commerce.[93]

Section 84.—Bankruptcy.

It has been held that a distributor of motion picture films is not a "trader" within the meaning of the Bank-

[89] *Metropolitan Opera* v. *Hammerstein* (1914), 162 A. D. (N. Y.) 691; 147 N. Y. Supp. 532.

[90] *Woods Production Co.* v. *Chicago, etc., R. R.* (1909), 147 Ill. App. 568.

[91] *Interstate Amusement Co.* v. *Albert* (1913), 161 S. W. (Tenn.) 488. Here plaintiff operated a booking agency in Chicago and defendant operated a theatre in Tennessee.

[92] *A. H. Woods Production Co.* v. *Chicago, Cincinnati, etc., R. R.*, 147 Ill. App. 568. See in this connection: *Interstate Amusement Co.* v. *Albert* (1913), 161 S. W. (Tenn.) 488.

[93] *United States* v. *Motion Picture Patents Co.* (1915), 225 Fed. (D. C.) 800. See Section 134, for discussion of this case.

ruptcy Act, and may not avail itself of the provisions of that Act.[94] These decisions follow the principle laid down in the case *In re Oriental Society*,[95] where it was held

[94] *In re Imperial Film Exchange* (1912), 198 Fed. (C. C. A.) 80. "It seems too clear for argument that a corporation which leases moving picture films is not engaged in trading as above defined."

The petition alleged:

"That the said Imperial Film Exchange, for the greater portion of six months preceding the date of the filing of this petition, has been engaged in the business of selling and leasing moving pictures, films, machines and accessories for the exhibition of moving pictures, and has its principal place of business at No. 44 West Twenty-Eighth Street, borough of Manhattan, City of New York."

The court said:

"Assuming that the business of selling moving picture films, machines, and accessories is within the act, the difficulty is that it is not alleged that the principal business of the corporation was such selling. It was not enough to allege that a part of the business of the corporation was within the statute. . . . Taking the petition as it stands, there is nothing to negative what appears to have been the fact that the principal business of the corporation was leasing picture films, although occasional sales were made."

[95] *In re Oriental Society* (1900), 104 Fed. (D. C.) 975. "A corporation engaged in giving theatrical performances is, of course, not engaged in manufacturing, printing or publishing. In my opinion, also, it is clearly not trading, or following mercantile pursuits, in the ordinary meaning of these words. A trader or merchant is one who either sells, or buys and sells, and a theatrical society does neither. It gives performances of one kind or another, to which the public are attracted by the skill of the performers. But the skill is not sold; it is merely exhibited for hire. The fact that the society must buy scenery and stage appliances and furniture, which it may afterwards sell again, is of no importance. This is a mere incident, and not the principal business of the bankrupt."

that a corporation engaged in giving theatrical performances could not avail itself of the benefits of the Bankruptcy Act.

It has, however, been held in a state court, that one conducting a motion picture business was engaged in a "trade" or "profession" and entitled to certain exemptions thereby on execution and levy.[96]

An actor is a wage-earner, and as such entitled to a special preference for salary due him from his bankrupt employer.[97]

A license agreement is personal and does not pass to the trustee in bankruptcy.[98]

[96] *Campbell* v. *Honakers* (1914), 166 S. W. (Tex.) 74. The question was whether the property used by appellant in conducting his motion picture business was exempt from levy and sale under execution, as "tools, apparatus and books belonging to any trade or profession." *Held* that an Edison machine and an Edison Perfecting Kinetoscope Manufacturing sale machine and metal machine outfit were exempt. But the chairs used in the theatre were *not* exempt. *Held further* that a person engaged in the motion picture industry was following a trade.

But see: *Speake* v. *Powell* (Eng.) (1873), L. R. 9 Ex. 25, where it was held that the occupation of an actor was not a "trade."

[97] *Winter German Opera, Ltd.* (Eng.) (1907), 23 T. L. R. 662. *Held* that under the Preferential Payments and Bankruptcy Act of 1888, the artists of the company were considered "servants" and that their salaries up to £50 would have preferences in the estate. See also: *Thomas* v. *Gatti* (Eng.) (1906), Times, Feb. 1 and 2.

[98] *In re Kay-Tee Film Exchange* (1911), 193 Fed. (D. C.) 140. The Lubin Co. had leased a number of films to the bankrupt more than four months prior to the adjudication. On petition for reclamation the referee held that the trustee had no title in such films and decreed that they be given up to the petitioners (at p. 149).

Section 85.—Libel.

To accuse a theatrical manager of fraud, insolvency and embezzlement was held a libel.[99] And to include statements in a newspaper that a theatrical production was immoral when not so in fact was also held to be libelous.[100] A statement that a theatrical manager had

"So far as this proceeding is concerned it is one to recover the identical property belonging to the petitioner and traced into the hands of the trustee in bankruptcy. The petitioner never intended to sell, and had no right to sell, and did not sell said moving pictures or reels to the bankrupt."

Day v. *Luna Park* (1912), 174 Ill. App. 477. A bar concession in an amusement park is personal and does not pass to the trustee in bankruptcy. For detailed discussion, see Section 14.

[99] *Fry* v. *Bennett* (1863), 28 N. Y. 324. A charge that a theatrical manager has designed to cheat and defraud the subscribers to an opera by a fraudulent discontinuance of performances, that he had become insolvent at Philadelphia and was about to become insolvent at New York, that he had misappropriated the moneys received from subscribers, and that gamblers patronized performances given by him was held to constitute a libel.

See also: *Gott* v. *Pulsifer* (1877), 122 Mass. 235. The plaintiff brought this action because of statements made in defendant's newspaper concerning a scientific curiosity belonging to plaintiff.

Gray, C. J., said: "This action is not for a libel upon the plaintiff, but for publishing a false and malicious statement concerning his property, and could not be supported without an allegation and proof of special damage. The special damage alleged was the loss of the sale of the plaintiff's statue to Palmer. Evidence of the value of the statue as a scientific curiosity was therefore rightly rejected as immaterial.

[100] *Merivale* v. *Carson* (Eng.) (1888), L. R. 20 Q. B. Div. 275; 58 L. T. N. S. 331.

Fay v. *Harrington* (1900), 176 Mass. 270; 57 N. E. 369. Plaintiffs, proprietors of a theatre, brought this action for libel

forced out one of his copartners and had, together with the other surviving partner, appropriated the entire profit of the brains and capital of their associate to themselves constituted an actionable libel.[101]

When the articles charged plaintiffs with discriminating unfairly against the Irish population, in their business of giving entertainments, they were held not actionable without proof of special damage.[102]

A motion picture company was held to libel the plaintiff, the owner of a shop, where a "White Slave" picture

against the publisher of a newspaper. *Held* that where the articles charged plaintiffs with giving indecent exhibitions, evidence showing that the costumes worn by the dancers at the performance which defendant asserted was indecent, were similar in style to those usually worn by young women dancing on the stage at public performances, was properly excluded.

[101] *Klaw* v. *New York Press Co.* (1910), 137 A. D. (N. Y.) 686; 122 N. Y. Supp. 437. Plaintiff contended that defendant published false statements concerning him because of the withdrawal by him of advertisements of his theatrical productions. The article contained a statement to the effect that plaintiff had forced out of his business one of his co-partners and that he and the other remaining partner had seized "the whole profits of the brains and capital of their associate for themselves" —*Held* libelous per se.

The court said: "Although this article does not directly relate to acts of the plaintiff in his business and profession of producing and booking plays, it does indirectly and would naturally, if believed, affect him in his business and profession which necessarily involves the making of contracts, for most people dislike to deal with men who would be alert to take advantage of them and are known to have been guilty of sharp practices."

[102] *Fay* v. *Harrington* (1900), 176 Mass. 270; 57 N. E. 369.

had been taken purporting to hold the shop out as a rendezvous for questionable characters.[103]

An interesting discussion as to the limits a newspaper may go in criticizing a production or its management is contained in *Philipp Co.* v. *New York Staats-Zeitung*.[104]

Where a man on trial for murder sought to enjoin the production of a play upon the ground that it prevented the conducting of an impartial trial and interfered with the administration of justice, the court refused to grant equitable relief, holding that his remedy, if any, was at law for libel.[105]

[103] *Merle* v. *Sociological Research Film Corp.* (1915), 166 A. D. (N. Y.) 376; 152 N. Y. Supp. 829.

[104] *Philipp Co.* v. *New York Staats-Zeitung* (1914), 165 A. D. (N. Y.) 377; 150 N. Y. Supp. 1044. "The press is accorded, for the public interests, a qualified privilege to discuss and criticize the management of and productions at a theatre to which the public are invited, and this privilege in the absence of actual malice extends even to ridicule and is without limitation; but since it is accorded for the benefit of the public only and the guidance of public opinion and taste, when the discussion or criticism exceeds the bounds of fair and honest criticism, and becomes an intemperate, aspersive attack upon the motive of the management of the theatre, or the character of the production thereat, an evil and malicious motive for the publication may be inferred; and if found to exist, the publication is not protected by the qualified privilege, but may, of course, be justified by absence of malice or by pleading and proving that it was true (cases cited)."

[105] *Dailey* v. *Super. Court* (1896), 112 Cal. 94; 44 Pac. 458. See also: *Brandreth* v. *Lance* (1839), 8 Paige (N. Y.), 26.

CHAPTER VI

THE PUBLIC

Right of Privacy

SEC. 86. In general.
87. When liable under statute.
88. When not liable under statute.
89. When use of name or picture is libelous.
90. Weekly news motion pictures.

Section 86.—In general.

When we come to review the rights of the public in their relation to the motion picture industry, we must take up as of paramount importance the "right of privacy." This is a very recent development of the law, and is evidentiary of the growing tendency of the courts and law-making bodies to protect the citizen in his personal rights as well as in his property rights.

The policy of the English common law has in the main been a policy of protection of property rights. For the protection of his personal rights the individual was relegated to the narrow limits of his remedy in tort or to the criminal branch of the law.

The person of the individual was considered a thing apart from his brain, his mind, his feelings and the entire incorporeal part of him. So that when the phrase "personal injury" was used, reference was had to a physical injury, suffered directly to the bodily person. And when the courts desired to protect a personal right, recourse was had to the pretense of protecting some fictitious property right.

For instance, in actions for breach of promise, where the injury is purely in the mental suffering, there was woven in, with the element of tort, one of contract. In libel, redress was offered on the theory that it tended to provoke a breach of the peace. Slander was based on the assumption of a pecuniary loss suffered.

In none of these cases was it pretended that the individual had such vested inherent rights in his person per se that law or equity would extend to them the full measure of protection afforded him in his property rights. Indeed, a review of the law of unfair competition discloses that even the right to protection in a man's name, for trade purposes, was not recognized until the nineteenth century; and a considerable period elapsed before legislators extended that right to include protection against other modes of invasion of purely personal rights.

With the advent and rapid advance of the arts of photography and lithography, the spread of advertising, the motion picture film and other innovations of a like nature, a new form of invasion of the individual's personal rights came into practice—the reproduction and general dissemination of his likeness.

In 1900 an action was brought in New York [1] in which

[1] *Roberson* v. *Rochester Folding Box Co.* (1902), 171 N. Y. 538; 64 N. E. 442. Chief Justice Parker who wrote the opinión said: "Nevertheless the courts reached the conclusion that plaintiff had a good cause of action against defendants in that defendants had

this question was squarely presented. There, one of the defendants engaged in the general milling business, had printed and sold, without the knowledge or consent of the plaintiff, about twenty-five thousand lithographic prints or likenesses of the plaintiff, which were distributed broadcast and exhibited in various places throughout the country. The likeness was a good one. Plaintiff, however, claimed that she had suffered great distress and anguish of mind and body, and sought injunction and damages.

The Court of Appeals reversed a decision in her favor upon the ground that in the absence of statute there was no principle of the common law which would sustain her cause of action.

It was held in England that the sale of picture post-

invaded what is called 'a right of privacy'—in other words the right to be let alone. Mention of such a right is not to be found in Blackstone, Kent or any of the other great commentators upon the law, nor so far as the learning of counsel or the courts in this case have been able to discover, does its existence seem to have been asserted prior to about the year 1890 when it was presented with attractiveness and no inconsiderable ability in the Harvard Law Review (Vol. IV, page 193), in an article entitled 'The Right of Privacy.'"

Henry v. *Cherry* (1909), 73 Atl. (R. I.) 97. Approves of *Roberson* v. *Rochester Folding Box Co.* and reiterates the doctrine that independently of statute there is no such thing as a right of privacy.

See also: *Murray* v. *Gast Lithographic etc. Co.* (1894), 8 Misc. (N. Y.) 36; 28 N. Y. Supp. 271; *Atkinson* v. *Doherty* (1899), 121 Mich. 372; 80 N. W. 285; *Peck* v. *Tribune Co.* (1907), 214 U. S. 185; 29 Sup. Ct. 554; *Edison* v. *Edison Polyform Co.* (1907), 73 N. J. Eq. 136; 67 Atl. 392; *Crutcher* v. *Big Four* (1908), 132 Mo. App. 311; 111 S. W. 891; *Hillman* v. *Star Publ. Co.* (1911), 64 Wash. 691; 117 Pac. 594.

cards bearing plaintiff's likeness was not actionable;[2] that a physician could not as an individual control the use of his name in connection with advertisements,[3] and that a pugilist could not enjoin the exhibition of a motion picture showing him defeated in a contest.[4]

Not only was the individual helpless, under the common law, but his parents, guardians and personal representatives were likewise without remedy.[5]

[2] *Corelli* v. *Wall* (Eng.) (1906), 22 Times L. R. 532. Unless the matter complained of was libelous plaintiff could not maintain injunction independently of statute, where defendant placed her pictures on post-cards with alleged scenes of her life.

See also: *Kunz* v. *Bosselman* (1909), 131 A. D. (N. Y.) 288; 115 N. Y. Supp. 650, where defendant was held liable for a similar offense under the Civil Rights Law.

[3] *Clark* v. *Freeman* (Eng.) (1848), 11 Beav. 112 and *Dockrell* v. *Dougall* (Eng.) (1898), 78 L. T. N. S. 840, 80 L. T. R. 556, involving the right of a physician to the use of his name where an advertisement had been issued; and *Mackenzie* v. *Soden Mineral Springs* (1891), 20 Abb. N. C. (N. Y.) 402; 18 N. Y. Supp. 240.

[4] *Palmer* v. *National Sporting Club* (Eng.) (1906), Ch. D., Nov. 16.

[5] *Murray* v. *Gast Lithographic etc. Co.* (1894), 8 Misc. (N. Y.) 36; 28 N. Y. Supp. 271. A father was held to have no cause of action against one for publishing the photograph of his daughter.

But where the picture or article is libelous and reflects on the other members of the family, a cause of action arises as to each. *Fenstermaker* v. *Tribune Pub. Co.* (1895), 12 Utah, 439; 43 Pac. 112.

Schuyler v. *Curtis* (1893), 24 N. Y. Supp. 509; rev. 147 N. Y. 434; 42 N. E. 22. The court below granted injunction at the suit of relatives of a decedent, restraining the defendant, a voluntary association, from making, setting up and exhibiting in public a *statue* of the deceased.

The Court of Appeals reversed, holding that there was no invasion of the right of privacy.

See: *Marks* v. *Jaffa* (1893), 6 Misc. (N. Y.) 290; 26 N. Y. Supp. 908.

As a result of the Roberson decision the Legislature of New York in 1903 passed a law designed to meet that situation, which law was incorporated in the Civil Rights Law [6] and came up for construction by the same court in 1908. It was there held to be constitutional, but the court at the same time declared the Act to be purely prospective in its nature, and that such law did not limit the right of one to use the portrait of another which had been acquired prior to the enactment of the statute.[7]

Later decisions have discussed the right to sue for a violation of this statute in law and in equity.[8] In a case wherein a picture was made purporting to show the evils

[6] Laws of New York, 1903, Chap. 132.

[7] *Rhodes* v. *Sperry & Hutchinson* (1908), 193 N. Y. 223; 85 N. E. 1097; aff'd 220 U. S. 502; 31 Sup. Ct. 490. "It is wholly prospective in its operation, and, therefore, wholly good . . . and does not apply to previously acquired pictures at all. Upon portraits the ownership of which was in others at the time when the act took effect its provisions are inoperative. Such pictures the owner is still at liberty to use for advertising or trade purposes without being held thereby to have been guilty of a crime or to have committed a tort. His property rights therein are unaffected by the statute."

[8] *Jacob* v. *Schiff* (1913), 149 N. Y. Supp. 273. Suit was brought to restrain the use of plaintiff's portrait. *Held* that the main remedy was injunction with damages as incidental relief.

"It may be said that the whole statute (Civil Rights) undoubtedly was passed with a view of affording to a plaintiff a right to a jury trial in all the relevant issues, *if he elects to pursue his remedy at law;* but the bringing of the suit in equity, with reliance upon recovery for damages as incidental thereto, is either a waiver of the right to a jury trial, or, perhaps, more strictly speaking, the abandonment of an intention to seek that mode of trial."

of the traffic in vice, plaintiff's factory was photographed exhibiting the firm name upon it. He brought suit on two causes of action, one for libel, and one for a violation of the statute. The court sustained a demurrer on the second cause of action, but held that the exhibition of plaintiff's factory in which a large number of girls were employed, in connection with a picture of that kind, might reflect seriously upon his good name, and overruled a demurrer as to the first cause of action.[9]

The English courts, while refusing to recognize any right to protection in the person, have occasionally protected the individual in his property rights, if the same were affected by an exhibition or dissemination of this kind, and they granted injunctions on the theory of a breach of a trust relationship.[10] This doctrine has been followed in some cases by our Federal courts and in some of the states.[11]

Some of the American jurisdictions have taken issue

[9] *Merle* v. *Sociological Research* (1915), 166 A. D. (N. Y.) 376; 152 N. Y. Supp. 829.

[10] *Pollard* v. *Photographic Co.* (Eng.) (1888), L. R. 40 Ch. Div. 345, in which a photographer was restrained from putting in his window a photograph of a patron.

See also: *Boyd* v. *Dagenais* (Can.) (1897), Rap. Jud. Quebec, 11 C. S. 66.

[11] *Corliss* v. *Walker* (1893), 57 Fed. (C. C.) 434; 64 Fed. (C. C.) 280.

In *Douglas* v. *Stokes* (1912), 149 Ky. 506; 149 S. W. 849, a photographer was employed by the parents to photograph the dead body of a deformed child. He thereafter copyrighted the same and published it. *Held*, that he was liable in damages on the theory that it constituted a breach of a trust relationship.

See also: *Atkinson* v. *Doherty* (1899), 121 Mich. 372; 80 N. W. 285.

See in this connection: *Vassar College* v. *Loose Wiles* (1912), 197 Fed. (D. C.) 982.

with the rule laid down by the Roberson case and have granted protection "on the score of it (the right to display one's likeness) being a property right of material profit." [12]

[12] *Munden* v. *Harris* (1911), 153 Mo. App. 652; 134 S. W. 1076. The court holds that the right of privacy exists independent of any statute; that one whose picture is being exhibited may restrain such use thereof or sue for damages in an action at law.

In taking issue with the doctrine laid down by the prevailing opinion in *Roberson* v. *Rochester Folding Box Co.* (1902), 171 N. Y. 538; 64 N. E. 442, the court said:

"We therefore conclude that one has an exclusive right to his picture, on the score of it being a property right of material profit. We also consider it to be a property right of value in that it is one of the modes of securing to a person the enjoyment of life and the exercise of liberty; and that novelty of the claim is no objection to relief. If this right is, in either respect invaded, he may have his remedy, either by restraint in equity, or damages in an action at law. If there are special damages, they may be stated and recovered; but such character of damages is not necessary to the action, since general damages may be recovered without showing a specific loss; and if the element of malice appears, as that term is known to the law, exemplary damages may be recovered."

Edison v. *Edison Polyform Co.* (1907), 73 N. J. Eq. 136; 67 Atl. 392. This case also holds that there is a property right in one's photograph, and that where defendant was advertising Mr. Edison's name and picture without his consent, he could restrain such acts.

See also: *Von Thadorovich* v. *Franz Joseph Beneficial Asso.* (1907), 154 Fed. (C. C.) 911; *Vanderbilt* v. *Mitchell* (1906), 71 N. J. Eq. 632; 63 Atl. 1107; *Foster-Milburn* v. *Chinn* (1909), 134 Ky. 424; 120 S. W. 364; *Mackenzie* v. *Soden Mineral Springs* (1891), 20 Abb. N. C. (N. Y.) 402; 18 N. Y. Supp. 240; *Francis* v. *Flynn* (1885), 118 U. S. 385; 6 Sup. Ct. 148.

Pavesich v. *New England* (1904), 122 Ga. 190; 50 S. E. 68. This case contains an excellent sum-

Section 87.—When liable under statute.

For a leading case illustrating the application of the Civil Rights Law to motion pictures *Binns* v. *Vitagraph Co.* is of great interest.[13] There the defendant released a film which purported to depict the story of a shipwreck. Plaintiff, although he had never posed for the picture nor authorized the use of his name therein, was widely advertised as the hero. Although it was claimed that the actual photograph of the hero in the story was not that of plaintiff, the court nevertheless restrained the use of the film as coming clearly within the statute.

A newspaper was held to violate the plaintiff's rights in publishing a photograph after a severance of business relations between them; [14] and in another case defendant was

mary of the law relating to the right of privacy.

[13] *Binns* v. *Vitagraph Co.* (1913), 210 N. Y. 51; 103 N. E. 1108. "A picture within the meaning of the statute is not necessarily a *photograph* of the living person, but includes any *representation* of such person. The picture represented by the defendant to be a true picture of the plaintiff and exhibited to the public as such, was intended to be, and it was, a *representation* of the plaintiff. The defendant is in no position to say that the picture does not represent the plaintiff or that it was an actual picture of a person made up to look like and impersonate the plaintiff."

In this connection see also: *D'Altomonte* v. *N. Y. Herald* (1913), 154 A. D. (N. Y.) 453; 139 N. Y. Supp. 200; modified 208 N. Y. 596; 102 N. E. 1101.

[14] *Bowden* v. *Amalgamated Pictorials, Lim.* (Eng.) (1911), 80 L. J. Ch. 291; 1 Ch. 386; 103 L. T. 829. Where plaintiff supplied photographs to a newspaper at agreed rates, and after he severed his connection with it, the newspaper continued to publish photographs of plaintiff, some copyrighted, and some uncopyrighted, *Held* that the termination of the contract amounted to a with-

not permitted to advertise his lengthy association in business with plaintiff.[15]

Where defendant, without consent, used the name of Dr. Charles W. Eliot for a series of books, calling the same "Dr. Eliot's Five-foot Shelf" and "Dr. Eliot's Set" it was held that he was violating the statute.[16]

The New York statute provides that the consent of the person whose name or picture is used must be obtained in writing, and an oral authorization is insufficient.[17]

drawal of all open offers and plaintiff could enjoin both the publication of the copyrighted and uncopyrighted photographs.

See also: *Mansell* v. *Valley Printing Co., Lim.* (Eng.) (1908), 77 L. J. Ch. 742; 2 Ch. 441.

See in this connection: *Hillman* v. *Star Pub. Co.* (1911), 64 Wash. 695; 117 Pac. 594.

[15] *Thompson* v. *Tillford* (1913), 152 A. D. (N. Y.) 928; 137 N. Y. Supp. 523.

[16] *Eliot* v. *Jones* (1910), 66 Misc. (N. Y.) 95; 120 N. Y. Supp. 989; aff'd 140 A. D. (N. Y.) 911; 125 N. Y. Supp. 1119.

[17] *Wyatt* v. *McCreery* (1908), 126 A. D. (N. Y.) 650; 111 N. Y. Supp. 86. Plaintiff, an actress, had orally authorized the defendant to sell and make any use it saw fit of her photograph. *Held*, that where plaintiff brought an action under the Civil Rights Law, a defense of that kind was demurrable. The authorization should have been in writing.

Ford v. *Heaney* (1910), N. Y. Law Journal, July 22, Bischoff, J. "Plaintiff moves for an injunction pendente lite restraining defendant from manufacturing the positive print from a certain negative motion picture of the plaintiff in their possession, and from exhibiting or producing the same in violation of the rights claimed by her under sections 50 and 51 of the Civil Rights Law. It is undisputed that the defendants intend to use the said picture for the purposes of trade, and it is admitted by them that they have not obtained the written consent of the plaintiff to such use, as provided for in said sections. The defendants, by certain mesne transactions, duly acquired said negative, originally owned by a certain Cameraphone Company, for whom the plaintiff posed and to whom she gave her consent to the exhibition of said picture for one year. The said agreement was entered into by the plaintiff with said company, under date of 9th of October, 1908, and granted the right to said company to exhibit the picture so taken for the year ending on the 2nd of November, 1909. The said agreement is in the form of a letter written on behalf of the said company to the plaintiff, but is not signed by her. There can be little doubt, however, that the acceptance of the latter and the subsequent posing by her pursuant to the terms thereof should be regarded as a written consent within the statute. The defendants admit in the brief filed in their behalf that the right given to said company was limited to one year, but state that they were unaware of the existence of such agreement at the time of their purchase, and therefore cannot be bound by its terms. They assert that they are bona fide purchasers for value, and that the rule which is applied upon the purchase of personal property, that the purchaser must have notice that he buys with only a qualified right of use, if such is the fact, should prevail and prevent the defendants being bound by some special and secret agreement made by the plaintiff with the Cameraphone Company. The difficulty with such a contention is that it does not meet the point made by the plaintiff that the said statutory consent has not been obtained. The defendants, in ordinary prudence, were charged with the duty of ascertaining, before they made the purchase, as to whether the latter would involve the right to use the picture for purposes of trade, notwithstanding the provisions of the Civil Rights Law. If, because of omission to make due inquiry in that respect, embarrassment exists, they have no one but themselves to blame. The further circumstances that the plaintiff was an actress, of more or less renown, and that therefore her picture would have value as being of some public interest, might well have put the defendants upon inquiry to ascertain whether the apparently valuable rights they intended to acquire were unquestioned. The cases cited by the defendant and wherein the persons giving the privileges as to their pictures or names attempted to curtail their use, although no limitation had been placed on the rights granted, it will be seen, can have

Dissemination of picture-postcards with a likeness of plaintiff is a violation.[18]

Defendant's good faith is entirely immaterial so far as the injunction is concerned.[19]

no application here. The statute does not prevent the person giving a written consent limiting or qualifying it in any way he may see fit, and that was precisely what was done in the present circumstances, as appears by said agreement. I think from what thus appears that the plaintiff is entitled to prevent the use of the said picture pendente lite, and to the relief demanded herein. Motion granted."

[18] *Kunz* v. *Bosselman* (1909), 131 A. D. (N. Y.) 288; 115 N. Y. Supp. 650. On demurrer it was held that a complaint which stated that the defendant was engaged in the business of selling portraits and post-cards and among other places in the City of New York he used, displayed, circulated and offered for sale for the purpose of trade the plaintiff's portrait and picture, stated a cause of action under the New York statute.

See also: *Corelli* v. *Wall* (Eng.) (1906), 22 T. L. R. 532.

[19] *Herbert* v. *Universal Talk. Mach. Co.* (1904), N. Y. Law Journal, March 9. "I am of the opinion that the plaintiff brings himself squarely within the provisions of Chapter 132 of the Laws of 1903, giving a person whose name is used for advertising purposes or for the purpose of trade without written consent first obtained, the right to maintain an equitable action to restrain the use of his name and recover damages for any injury sustained by reason of such use. . . . The statute is invoked to restrain the further sale of those wares through the aid or instrumentality of the added commercial value given them by the use of plaintiff's name for purposes of trade or advertising. *No question of defendant's good* faith is necessarily involved, it may well have been misled. But the plaintiff is entitled to the relief which the statute—passed to remedy a theretofore irremediable injustice (*Roberson* v. *Rochester, F. B. Co.* (1902), 171 N. Y. 545; 64 N. E. 442)—was intended to give. Injunction should issue."

Plaintiff is not barred from maintaining the action by reason of his infancy.[20]

Both the photographer who takes the picture and the author who uses it in the book are liable as joint tort feasors.[21]

Section 88.—When not liable under statute.

The right of privacy is purely a personal right, and does not survive the death of him whose right has been invaded, so as to give his personal representative a cause of action.[22] Nor may it be exercised by everybody in his lifetime.

A person who has become prominent in public affairs, and whose comings and goings are more than of ordinary interest to the public, such as a president or other high state official or a famous general, has in fact abandoned his right of privacy and may not invoke the statute.[23] A

[20] *Munden* v. *Harris* (1911), 153 Mo. App. 652; 134 S. W. 1076; *Wyatt* v. *McCreery* and *Wyatt* v. *Wanamaker* (1908), 126 A. D. (N. Y.) 650; 111 N. Y. Supp. 86.

[21] *Riddle* v. *McFadden* (1907), 116 A. D. (N. Y.) 353; 101 N. Y. Supp. 606.

Robinson v. *Textile Publ. Co.* (1916), N. Y. Law Journal, June 14. See for lengthy discussion of Sections 50 and 51 of the New York Civil Rights Law.

[22] *Wyatt* v. *Hall's Port. Studio* (1911), 71 Misc. (N. Y.) 199; 128 N. Y. Supp. 247. A cause of action for violation of the right of privacy under sections 50 and 51 of the Civil Rights Law of New York is personal in its character and does not survive the death of the person to whom the statute gives it.

[23] See in this connection: *Corliss* v. *Walker* (1894), 64 Fed. (C. C.) 280; *Munden* v. *Harris* (1911), 153 Mo. App. 652; 134 S. W. 1076; *Vassar College* v. *Loose Wiles* (1912), 197 Fed. (D. C.) 982; *Colgate* v. *White* (1909), 169 Fed. (C. C.) 887; 180 Fed. (C. C.) 882 (final hearing).

criminal, also, has no such right, and it was held that he could not restrain the exhibition of his picture in a Rogue's Gallery.[24]

Statutes which prohibit the use of the name or picture for advertising purposes are held to be penal and are strictly construed. A complaint therefore which alleged that a picture was printed in a magazine "in adornment thereof" failed to state a cause of action.[25] When the

[24] *Owen* v. *Partridge* (1903), 82 N. Y. Supp. 248.

[25] *Bytovetzski* v. *Edward L. Wilson Co.* (1917), N. Y. Law Journal, Jan. 24. "The action is brought to recover damages under section 51 of the Civil Rights Law, as amended by chapter 226, Laws of 1911, which provides as follows: 'Any person whose name, portrait or picture is used within this state for advertising purposes or for the purposes of trade, without the written consent first obtained, as above provided, may maintain an equitable action in the Supreme Court of this state against the person, firm or corporation so using his name, portrait or picture, to prevent and restrain the use thereof, and may also sue and recover damages for any injuries sustained by reason of such use, and if the defendant shall have knowingly used such person's name, portrait or picture in such manner as is forbidden or declared to be unlawful by the last section, the jury, in its discretion, may award exemplary damages. But nothing contained in this act shall be so construed as to prevent any person, firm or corporation practicing the profession of photography from exhibiting in or about his or its establishment specimens of the work of such establishment, unless the same is continued by such person, firm or corporation after written notice objecting thereto has been given by the person portrayed.' The complaint in substance alleges that defendant owned, published and circulated for commercial purposes in connection with its business a booklet or magazine, and in the July number exhibited on one of its pages, 'in adornment thereof,' the portrait or picture

statute gives the right of action to "citizens" alone, a failure to allege the citizenship of the plaintiff makes the complaint demurrable.[26]

of plaintiff without his consent. The publication of a person's portrait is not in itself illegal. *Roberson* v. *Rochester Folding Box Co.*, 171 N. Y. 538. To come within the statute the use of the portrait must be for advertising purposes or purposes of trade. In *Jeffries* v. *N. Y. Evening Journal Pub. Co.*, 124 N. Y. S. 780, it was held that the publication of a portrait in a newspaper in connection with the biography of the person was not within the statute; that a picture is not used for advertising purposes unless it is part of an advertisement, and that the purposes of trade refer to commerce or traffic and not to the dissemination of information. There is nothing in the complaint to show either expressly or by fair intendment that the picture was used as part of an advertisement or for purposes of trade, commerce or traffic. It is alleged to have been inserted on the top of the page 'in adornment thereof.' If inserted for adornment merely, or for any other purpose not specified in the statute, plaintiff cannot recover. It is stated in *Binns* v. *Vitagraph Co.*, 210 N. Y. 55, that "the statute is very general in its terms, but when a living person's name, portrait or picture is used it is not necessarily and at all times so used either for advertising purposes or for the purposes of trade. The statute is, in part at least, penal, and should be construed accordingly. So construed, and also construed in connection with the history of chapter 132, Laws of 1903, which was enacted at the first session of the Legislature after the decision in the Roberson case, it does not prohibit every use of the name, portrait or picture of a living person." That its use was for one of the purposes enumerated cannot be assumed; it must be alleged and proved."

See also: *Merle* v. *Sociological Research* (1915), 166 A. D. (N. Y.) 376; 152 N. Y. Supp. 829.

[26] *Fuller* v. *McDermott* (1904), 87 N. Y. Supp. 536.

See also: *Levis* v. *Hitchkock* (1882), 10 (D. C.) Fed. 4; *U. S.* v. *Taylor* (1880), 3 Fed. (C. C.) 563; *Messenger* v. *State* (1889), 25 Neb. 674; 41 N. W. 638.

The Civil Rights Law as enacted in New York was not intended to prevent the dissemination of news, and it was held that the defendant newspaper was not liable for the publication of plaintiff's name and picture in a single issue; to hold otherwise would be tantamount to muzzling the press.[27]

It seems that one may be estopped from invoking the aid of the statute, as where he has lent his name to a business in which his name or picture is being advertised, and has permitted the owner of the business to expend large sums of money to exploit such name or picture,[28] or sells the business and stock of a corporation bearing his name.[29]

[27] *Moser* v. *Press Pub. Co.* (1908), 59 Misc. (N. Y.) 78; 109 N. Y. Supp. 963; *Colyer* v. *Fox-Pub. Co.* (1914), 162 A. D. (N. Y.) 297; 146 N. Y. Supp. 999; *Jeffries* v. *N. Y. Evening Journal Pub. Co.* (1910), 67 Misc. (N. Y.) 570; 124 N. Y. Supp. 780.

[28] *Wendell* v. *Conduit Mach. Co.* (1911), 74 Misc. (N. Y.) 201; 123 N. Y. Supp. 758. Where one who is in another's employ voluntarily poses for a portrait to be used in his master's business and with knowledge that he was to make its present use thereof, he may not, after the latter has incurred expenses in its use to build up his business maintain an action under the Civil Rights Law upon the termination of the employment, to restrain the further use of his portrait for advertising purposes. *Wyatt* v. *McCreery* and *Wyatt* v. *Wanamaker* (1908), 126 A. D. (N.Y.) 650; 111 N.Y. Supp. 86, distinguished upon the ground of plaintiff's infancy, the infant not being estopped to invoke the protection accorded under the act.

See also: *Almind* v. *Sea Beach R. Co.* (1913), 157 A. D. (N. Y.) 230; 141 N. Y. Supp. 842. But see: *Bowden* v. *Amalgamated Pictorials L'mtd* (Eng.) (1911), 103 L. T. 829.

[29] *White* v. *White* (1914), 160 A. D. (N.Y.) 709; 145 N.Y. Supp. 743. While this case holds that one selling his right to a corporation sells therewith the right to

In no case will the court grant relief pendente lite where the plaintiff's right is involved in doubt.[30]

Section 89.—When use of name or picture is libelous.

It frequently happens that the use of the person's name or picture is not such as may be restrained under the Civil Rights Law, but that such use will amount to a libel. In that case equity will not restrain, but the plaintiff may recover damages at law.[31]

Defendant exhibited a "White Slave" film in which plaintiff's factory was depicted as being a rendezvous for vicious characters. It was held that this amounted to a libel, although it was not a violation of the Civil Rights Law.[32]

A publication of plaintiff's portrait in conjunction with

the use of his own name where the corporation had borne it, it seems to us that this rule is limited by the rule that where the skill and personal qualities of the vendor are peculiarly valuable as in the case of an artist, musician, actor or director, a transfer of the name is not permissible as it would tend to work a fraud upon the public. See *Blakely* v. *Sousa* (1900), 197 Pa. 305; 47 Atl. 286.

[30] *Butterick Publ. Co.* v. *Typographical Union* (1906), 50 Misc. (N. Y.); 100 N. Y. Supp. 292. "Where plaintiffs' right to the equitable relief sought is involved in doubt the court will not grant an injunction pendente lite containing the same relief that would ultimately be granted if the plaintiff succeeded upon the trial of the action."

[31] *Butterick Publ. Co.* v. *Typographical Union* (1906), 50 Misc. (N. Y.) 1; 100 N. Y. Supp. 292. A court of equity will not enjoin a libel even where the plaintiff by reason of his inability to prove special damage has no remedy at law. (See cases cited therein.)

See also: Section 12.

[32] *Merle* v. *Sociological Research* (1915), 166 A. D. (N. Y.) 376; 152 N. Y. Supp. 829.

a whiskey advertisement was held to be libelous, and defendant was bound to respond in damages even though it had made an innocent mistake.[33] And a newspaper was held liable for the publication of a picture of plaintiff over an article which was true of another but not of plaintiff.[34]

[33] *Peck* v. *Tribune Co.* (1908), 214 U. S. 185; 29 Sup. Ct. 554. Plaintiff's portrait was published in defendant's newspaper in connection with an advertisement of whiskey. Some name other than plaintiff's was printed at the foot of the picture. The court held that the publication of plaintiff's portrait in connection with such an advertisement with the statement made therein that plaintiff had drunk the whiskey was libelous. It was further held that it was immaterial whether the publication was caused through an innocent mistake.

The court cites in support of the proposition that it is immaterial whether the error is caused innocently. *King* v. *Woodfall* (Eng.) Lofft. 776, 781; *Hearne* v. *Stowell* (Eng.) 12 A. and E. 719, 726; *Shepheard* v. *Whitaker* (Eng.), L. R. 10 C. P. 502; *Clark* v. *North American Co.* (1902), 203 Pa. St. 346; 53 Atl. 237; *Morasse* v. *Brochu* (1890), 151 Mass. 567; 25 N. E. 74.

See generally: *De Sando* v. *New York Herald Co.* (1904), 88 A. D. (N. Y.) 492; 85 N. Y. Supp. 111; *Clary-Squire* v. *Press Publ. Co.* (1901), 58 A. D. (N. Y.) 362; 68 N. Y. Supp. 1028; *Farley* v. *Evening Chronicle Publ. Co.* (1905), 113 Mo. App. 216; *Emerson* v. *Nash* (1905), 124 Wisc. 369; 102 N. W. 921; *Wandt* v. *Hearst's Chicago American* (1906), 129 Wis. 429; 109 N. W. 70; *Foster Milburn Co.* v. *Chinn* (1909), 134 Ky. 424; 120 S. W. 364; *Morrison* v. *Smith* (1904), 177 N. Y. 366; 69 N. E. 725; *Hart* v. *Woodbury Dermat. Institute* (1906), 113 A. D. (N. Y.) 281; 98 N. Y. Supp. 1000; *Taylor* v. *Hearst* (1895), 107 Cal. 262; 40 Pac. 392; *Pavesich* v. *New England* (1904), 122 Ga. 190; 50 S. E. 68.

[34] *Farley* v. *Evening Chronicle Co.* (1905), 113 Mo. App. 216; 87 S. W. 565.

Rose Ball v. *The Tribune* (1905), 123 Ill. App. 235. Where defendant's newspaper printed an article and picture, the likeness

In one case it has been held that where the libel published related to the family as a whole, a cause of action arose to each member of the family.[35]

Section 90.—Weekly news motion pictures.

The issuance of motion pictures as "Weekly News" wherein are depicted the current events of the day, has become a regular feature of several of the larger producers. The scenes are taken from the actual happenings, and are reproduced without any embellishments or changes whatsoever.

The position taken by the motion picture producers is that their "Weekly News Service" has become one of the means of disseminating news, and is to all intents and purposes a newspaper with all the rights and privileges of the press.

They contend that since newspapers are not prohibited by the Civil Rights Statutes from printing and publishing the likenesses of persons [36] they as well have the

being that of plaintiff, but the article referring to one as "young composer secured morphine late in the night of her death," relating to another person, held a question for the jury.

[35] *Fenstermaker* v. *Tribune Pub. Co.* (1895), 12 Utah, 439; 43 Pac. 112.

[36] *Colyer* v. *Richard Fox Pub. Co.* (1914), 162 A. D. (N. Y.) 297; 146 N. Y. Supp. 999. The plaintiff, a professional high-diver, was photographed and her picture printed in defendant's magazine.

"When the statute was enacted originally in 1903 the custom of publishing in papers the portraits of individuals who were distinguished in their activities of life was very general. If the Legislature had intended to wipe out this custom, it could have said so easily in positive language."

Jeffries v. *N. Y. Evening Jour-*

right to reproduce such likenesses in their current event services.

This question was squarely presented to a court for the first time in the case of *Humiston* v. *Universal Film Mfg. Co.* where the learned justice held that the motion picture industry, as a whole, was a private enterprise and that there were no substantial points of resemblance between the motion picture weekly news service and the newspaper. For that reason the court held that the motion picture reproduction and exhibition of a portrait of a prominent woman lawyer, featuring her in a sensational news event, constituted an invasion of her personal rights under the statute.

In view of the importance of this decision the entire opinion is given below.[37] It must, however, be remembered that it is not a decision of a court of last resort.

nal (1910), 67 Misc. (N. Y.) 570; 124 N. Y. Supp. 780. Plaintiff, a famous pugilist, sought under Section 51 of the Civil Rights Law of N.Y. (formerly Chap. 132, Laws 1903) to enjoin the defendant from publishing a biography in which he was pictured.

The court there held: "In my opinion a picture is not used 'for advertising purposes within its meaning unless the picture is part of an advertisement, while 'trade' refers to 'commerce or traffic,' not to the dissemination of information. According to the plaintiff's construction the picture of a pugilist or president would bring the case within the statute where that of an obscure and quiet citizen would probably not; nor does he, indeed, object to his picture, except in connection with his biography. Motion for temporary injunction denied."

[37] *Humiston* v. *Universal Film Mfg. Co.* (1917), N. Y. Law Journal, Aug. 10th, Ordway J.:

Motion for injunction pendente lite to restrain defendants from using and displaying the plaintiff's name, photograph and portrait in their moving picture films, contrary to the provisions of sections

Whether or not it will be finally determined that the "weekly news service" is in its essence a newspaper, the

50 and 51 of the Civil Rights Law. The defendants have organized and are conducting a business called the "Universal Animated Weekly," in which they produce and distribute for use by their customers reels of films of motion pictures, which are photographs of actual current events which they deem of public interest. These reels are produced and distributed weekly and are exhibited all over the country in moving picture theatres as soon as possible after the occurrence of the events depicted. The defendants furnish with them to their customers posters which are used as bulletins for display outside of the place of exhibition to inform the public what will be shown within. The defendants admit that "this service is marketed and sold" by them, and is "a source of substantial profit" to the defendants.

In their reel of films used as above described and called "Universal Animated Weekly No. 77," the defendants have included photographs or pictures of the plaintiff accompanied with the following "legends:"

"Woman lawyer solves Ruth Cruger mystery. After world-wide search, Mrs. Grace Humiston's persistent efforts lead to discovery of high school girl's murder—New York City. Sub. The woman who succeeded where police failed—Mrs. Grace Humiston. In Cocchi's cellar—passed by millions—the crime was hidden for months. Thousands attracted to scene of crime."

They have also furnished posters or publicity matter accompanying said number of the "Weekly" films, to be used by their customers as above described, containing in large display type the same words as appear in the main legend above quoted. These reels of films and posters are being used by at least fifty customers of the defendants in moving picture theatres in New York City and other parts of the country.

The plaintiff has not given her written consent to this use of her name and picture, and now brings suit for an injunction against such use and for damages. In my opinion this case cannot be distinguished in principle from the case of *Binns* v. *Vitagraph Co.*, 210 N. Y. 51. The defendants

producer may in no event under a statute of this kind, take the name or photograph of a person without his con-

attempted to distinguish it on the ground that in the Binns case the films were not photographs of an actual event and of actual people, but were photographs of actors posed for the purpose and of scenery simulating the actual scenes of the wreck of the "Republic," that is, were really a photoplay, whereas in this case the films are photographs of actual people and events precisely as they acted and happened, and further argue that there is a legal distinction between photoplay as commonly known and used and their service, which they contend is a regular weekly news service for the dissemination of information to the public, and analogous to a regular newspaper or at least to a weekly newspaper or magazine.

In my opinion there is no foundation for any legal distinction between the two cases. The "information" which is being "disseminated" by defendants' films is of the same character as that "disseminated" by the Binns films. The fact that the defendants' films are photographs of actual current events and are called "Universal Animated Weekly" and are produced and distributed weekly and used as soon as possible after the occurrence of the events does not make them a newspaper, or bring them within the protection extended to newspapers by the cases of *Colyer* v. *Fox Publishing Co.*, 162 App. Div. 297, and *Jeffries* v. *N. Y. Evening Journal Publishing Co.*, 67 Misc. 570, on which defendants rely. I do not understand that in those cases the courts founded their decisions upon the constitutional protection of the freedom of the press, and defendants expressly disclaim that they are relying upon such constitutional provisions. As I understand those cases the courts merely held that the Legislature did not intend by chapter 132 of the Laws of 1903, now sections 50 and 51 of the Civil Rights Law, to extend the prohibitions of that statute to newspapers. But that is very far from holding that such a service as the defendants conduct is a newspaper or that the acts complained of are not prohibited by the statute. The Supreme Court of the United States has recently had occasion to consider the character of such a service in the case of *Mutual Film Corporation* v. *Industrial Commission of Ohio*, 236 U. S. 230, where the question was involved of the constitutionality of a censorship of a service which included (p. 232) "events of historical and current interest—the same events which are described in words and by photographs in newspapers, weekly periodicals, magazines and other publications, of which photographs are promptly secured a few days after the events which they depict happen, thus regularly furnishing and publishing news through the medium of motion pictures under the name of "Mutual Weekly," and said (p. 244): "It cannot be put out of view that the exhibition of moving pictures is a business pure and simple, originated and conducted for profit, like other spectacles, not to be regarded, nor intended to be regarded by the Ohio Constitution, we think, as part of the press of the country or as organs of public opinion."

The defendants argue that they are not using the plaintiff's name and picture "for advertising purposes or for the purposes of trade." I cannot agree with them. The films are used in the defendants' regular business, for purposes of profit, and the posters are used to advertise the films and to induce the public to patronize the theatres where the films are exhibited. In other words, the defendants are exploiting the plaintiff's name and picture in their business for profit, and even if they are incidentally disseminating information as to current news of the day, the plaintiff has the right to object and to an injunction against the continuance of such conduct. In *Binns* v. *Vitagraph Co.*, supra, the court said (p. 58):

"We hold that the name and picture of the plaintiff were used by the defendant as a matter of business and profit and contrary to the prohibition of the statute. It is urged that there is danger of serious trouble in the practical enforcement of any rule which may be adopted in construing and enforcing the statute so far as it relates to purposes of trade. If there is any basis for the suggestion of danger in enforcing a part of the statute under consideration it is the duty of the Legislature to repeal such part thereof," etc.

As the court said in *Almind* v. *Sea Beach Railway Co.*, 157 App. Div. 230, 232: "The right of privacy under the statute cannot be invaded for purposes purely informative or redemptive, whether the altruist be entirely a charitable envoy or a railway company. No cause is so exalted that it may allure by exposing the portrait of a person to the public gaze."

The defendants argue that if this motion is granted it will seriously interfere with, if not destroy, their business, which gives information as to current events and innocent amusement to thousands, and they set out at length the services they are rendering to the government and to the Red Cross in connection with the present war and the activities of good citizens in connection therewith. Even if this were true, the remedy is by an appeal to the Legislature, but the results they pretend to fear are not likely to follow. While I am not called on to decide the point, it is not probable that any court will enjoin the use of moving picture films of current events of real public importance, because they happen as a mere incident to include among many the picture of an individual. As the court said in the Binns case (p. 57): "It is not necessary in this opinion to discuss the question whether a person, firm or corporation would be liable under the statute for making and using a picture of a living person when it is included in a picture of an actual event in which such person was an actor, and such picture is a mere incident to the actual event portrayed. The use of the plaintiff's name and picture, as shown by the testimony in this case, was not a mere incident to a general picture representative of the author's understanding of what occurred at the wreck of the Republic."

There is a clear distinction between a merely incidental and fortuitous use of an individual's picture as an incident to some important public event, and the exploitation of that individual as the important and central part of an event which is not of real public importance, however great may be the public interest therein. In this case it is clear that Mrs. Humiston's name and picture are the main point of that part of defendants' film relating to the Cruger murder, and that the defendants are seeking by the use of her name and picture to make money out of her reputation and prominence. She is not the commander of an army, a visiting ambassador or even a

sent, weave fiction about it and represent the whole in motion pictures.[38]

public official, but a private citizen practicing her profession as a member of the bar, who is entitled to be protected in her right of privacy.

It is conceded that the plaintiff gave no written consent to the use of her name and picture, and although it is claimed that she orally consented she denies that fact, and it is immaterial on this motion. So also the fact, if it be a fact, that her name and picture have appeared frequently with her consent in the daily newspapers is not material on this motion. All these facts may perhaps be material on the question of her damages, but that is not before me now. As Judge Gray said in the case of *Roberson* v. *Rochester Folding Box Co.*, 171 N. Y. 538, at p. 566: "It would be, in my opinion, an extraordinary view which, while conceding the right of a person to be protected against the unauthorized circulation of an unpublished lecture, letter, drawing, or other ideal property, yet, would deny the same protection to a person whose portrait was unauthorizedly obtained and made use of for commercial purposes. The injury to the plaintiff is irreparable, because she cannot be wholly compensated in damages for the various consequences entained by defendant's acts. The only complete relief is an injunction restraining their continuance. Whether, as incidental to that equitable relief, she should be able to recover only nominal damages is not material, for the issuance of the injunction does not, in such a case, depend upon the amount of the damages in dollars and cents."

Motion for injunction during the pendency of this action granted on plaintiff giving an undertaking in the sum of $2,500.

[38] *Binns* v. *Vitagraph* (1913), 210 N. Y. 51; 103 N. E. 1108.

CHAPTER VII

THE PUBLIC (CONTINUED)

Theatre Proprietor's Duty

SEC. 91. Right to exclude patrons.
92. Liability for injuries sustained by patrons—In general.
93. Falling over balcony.
94. Seats and floors.
95. Tripping in darkened theatre—aisles—steps—exits.
96. Articles dropping.
97. Wild animals.
98. Crowds.
99. Hurt by performer.
100. Miscellaneous accidents.
101. Acts of strangers.
102. Assault.
103. Who is liable.
104. Property lost in theatre.

Section 91.—Right to exclude patrons.

The exclusion of certain people or classes of people from the motion picture theatre is another one of the public's rights which has assumed considerable importance, and which has been the subject of statutory enactment.

Under the common law a theatre proprietor could exclude whom he wished.[1] It was held in the leading case

[1] *Collister* v. *Hayman* (1905), 183 N. Y. 250; 76 N. E. 20; 1 L. R. A. (N. S.) 1188; *Aaron* v. *Ward* (1911), 203 N. Y. 351; 96 N. E. 736; *People ex rel. Burnham* v. *Flynn* (1907), 189

of *Purcell* v. *Daly* that the ticket of admission was merely a revocable license, and that the only penalty which the proprietor of the theatre would incur for its revocation would be the cost of the ticket and incidental loss suffered.[2] As the relationship is a purely contractual one, a refusal to

N. Y. 180; 82 N. E. 169; *People* v. *King* (1888), 110 N. Y. 418; 18 N. E. 245; *Luxemburg* v. *Keith* (1909), 64 Misc. (N. Y.) 69; 117 N. Y. Supp. 979; *Purcell* v. *Daly* (1886), 19 Abb. N. C. (N. Y.) 301; *Marrone* v. *Wash. Club* (1912), 227 U. S. 633; 33 Sup. Ct. 401; *Wood* v. *Leadbitter* (Eng.) (1845), 13 M. & W. 838; *Shubert* v. *Nixon* (1912), 83 N. J. L. 101; 83 Atl. 369; *McCrea* v. *Marsh* (1858), 12 Gray (Mass.), 211; *Burton* v. *Schepf* (1861), 1 Allen (Mass.), 133; *Johnson* v. *Wilkinson* (1885), 139 Mass. 3; 29 N. E. 62; *Greenburg* v. *West. Turf* (1903), 140 Cal. 357; 73 Pac. 1050; 148 Cal. 126; 82 Pac. 684; aff'd 204 U. S. 359; 27 Sup. Ct. 384; *Taylor* v. *Cohn* (1906), 47 Ore. 538; 84 Pac. 388; *Meisner* v. *Detroit* (1908), 154 Mich. 545; 118 N. W. 14; *Buenzle* v. *Newport Ass'n* (1908), 29 R. I. 23; 68 Atl. 721; *Horney* v. *Nixon* (1905), 213 Pa. 20; 61 Atl. 1088; *W. W. V. Co.* v. *Black* (1912), 113 Va. 728; 75 S. E. 82; *Taylor* v. *Waters* (Eng.), 7 Taunt. 374; *Younger* v. *Judah* (1892), 111 Mo. 303; 19 S. W. 1109; *Boswell* v. *Barnum* (1916), 185 S. W. (Tenn.) 692; *Rex* v. *Jones* (Eng.) 1 Leach C. C. 204; *Pearce* v. *Spaulding* (1882), 12 Mo. App. 141.

[2] *Purcell* v. *Daly* (1886), 19 Abb. N. C. (N. Y.) 301. "The proprietor of a theatre has a perfect right to say whom he will or will not admit to his theatre, and should any one apply at the box-office of a theatre and desire to purchase tickets of admission, and be refused, there can be no question that he would have no cause of action against the proprietor of the theatre for such refusal. And in the same way, if tickets are sold to a person the proprietor may still refuse admission, in which case the proprietor would be compelled to refund only the price paid for the tickets of admission, together with such other expense as the party might have been put to, but which expense must be directly connected with the issuing of the ticket of admission."

admit one who has purchased a ticket is a breach of the contract and nothing more.[3]

Not only may the proprietor refuse admission to a ticket holder, but he may refuse in the absence of a prohibitory statute, to sell a ticket to any particular person. Under the doctrine that the theatre is a purely private enterprise, the proprietor may contract with whomsoever he pleases.

He may also attach any condition to the sale of the ticket that he sees fit, and where the ticket is sold subject to a condition that it be not resold on the sidewalk by a speculator, and such condition is brought to the attention of one buying it at or before its purchase, the proprietor may exclude the purchaser from admission.[4]

[3] *Horney* v. *Nixon* (1905), 213 Pa. 20; 61 Atl. 1088; 1 L. R. A. (N. S.) 1184. "The proprietor of a theatre is a private individual, engaged in a strictly private business, which, though for entertainment of the public, is always limited to those whom he may agree to admit to it. There is no duty as in the case of a common carrier, to admit everyone who may apply and be willing to pay for a ticket, for the theatre proprietor has acquired no peculiar rights and privileges from the state, and is therefore under no implied obligation to serve the public. When he sells a ticket he creates contractual relations with the holder of it, and whatever duties on his part grow out of these relations, he is bound to perform or respond in damages for the breach of his contract, if it is of that only that complaint can be made."

Weis v. *Skinner* (1915), 178 S. W. (Tex.) 34.

On the question whether one who buys a seat may demand the return of his money if the house is full see: Lewis v. *Arnold* (Eng.) (1830), 4 C. & P. 354, which holds that he is entitled to a refund of his money.

[4] *Collister* v. *Hayman* (1905), 183 N. Y. 250; 76 N. E. 20; 1 L. R. A. (N. S.) 1188.

And he may revoke the license either before or after admission [5] and may even eject him.[6]

The mere fact that the theatre is licensed does not make it a public or quasi-public institution. The license conferred is not in the nature of a franchise as in the case of a common carrier,[7] for in the case of the latter the state delegates certain of its rights and powers to the holder of the license, whereas in the case of a theatre the license is in the nature of a special tax.[8]

To overcome the evils which grew out of the applica-

[5] *Boswell* v. *Barnum & Bailey* (1916), 185 S. W. (Tenn.) 692. "Amusement places are private enterprises, and the law does not confer upon the public the right to demand admission thereto. No legal duty is breached by refusing admission to anyone, or excluding anyone *after* admission. If such person had bought a ticket there is a breach of contract, but there is no tort."

[6] *Marrone* v. *Wash. Jockey Club* (1912), 227 U. S. 633; 33 Sup. Ct. 401; 43 L. R. A. (N. S.) 961. "The fact that the purchase of the ticket made a contract is not enough. A contract binds the person of the maker, but does not create an interest in the property that it may concern, unless it also operates as a conveyance. . . . But if it did not create such an interest, that is to say, *a right in rem*, valid against the landowner and third persons, the holder had no right to enforce specific performance by self-help. His only right was to sue upon the contract for the breach."

The court upholds the right of the proprietor to eject the ticket holder after the revocation of the license if he refuses to leave the premises. To the same effect: *People* v. *Hart* (1910), 56 Ill. App. 523; *Shubert* v. *Nixon* (1912), 83 N. J. L. 101; 83 Atl. 369.

[7] *Collister* v. *Hayman* (1905), 183 N. Y. 250; 76 N. E. 20. "A theatre may be licensed, like a circus; but the license is not a franchise, and does not place the proprietors under any duty to the public or under any obligation to keep the place open."

[8] *Horney* v. *Nixon* (1905), 213 Pa. 20; 61 Atl. 1088.

tion of the foregoing doctrine, the Federal Government[9] and the several states have enacted statutes making it unlawful generally to discriminate against members of the public because of their "race, creed and color." These statutes being in derogation of the common law, have been strictly construed, and unless the exclusion has been because of the race, creed or color of the individual excluded, he has no remedy against the proprietor.

This proposition is singularly illustrated in *Woolcott* v. *Shubert*[10] where the defendants sought to exclude from their theatres a critic of the "New York Times" on the ground that his criticisms of their productions had been highly displeasing to them. In New York there was a statute at the time when this action was brought which provided that "all persons within the jurisdiction of this State shall be entitled to the full and equal accommodations, advantages and privileges of any place of public accommodation, resort or amusement, subject only to the conditions and limitations established by law and applicable alike to all persons."[11] The statute further provided that no person shall directly or indirectly refuse to accord the same accommodations, advantages and privileges to any person on account of his "race, creed or color."

The Court of Appeals held that the management was limited in its undoubted right to exclude the plaintiff only by the Civil Rights Law "except for reasons applicable alike to all citizens of every race, creed or color."

[9] Civil Rights Act, 18 Stat. 335.

[10] *Woolcott* v. *Shubert* (1916), 217 N. Y. 212; 111 N. E. 829.

[11] Laws 1913, Chap. 265 (New York).

Since Woolcott was a critic writing for pay, and the discrimination against him was not based on race, creed or color, but was based on his criticisms of the defendants' plays, the court held that he could not enjoin the defendants.[12]

The reasoning in that case follows closely the principles laid down in the Civil Rights cases,[13] where the Federal Statute was held to be constitutional, and wherein it was decided that in the absence of any other statutes preventing them, proprietors could exclude from their theatres persons, if the exclusion was based on something other than race, creed or color.

On the other hand, the Civil Rights Statute of California provides that any orderly person presenting a ticket of admission acquired by purchase is entitled absolutely to admission. It was there held that such ticket holder on being excluded from a race course, was entitled to recover the penalty under the statute, although his exclusion had been based upon some ground other than race, creed or color.[14]

[12] See: *Grannan* v. *Westchester Rac. Ass'n* (1897), 153 N. Y. 449; 47 N. E. 896.

People ex rel. Burnham v. *Flynn* (1907), 189 N. Y. 180; 82 N. E. 169. An association of theatrical managers combining to exclude a critic from witnessing their performances on the ground that his criticisms were scurrilous and highly unfair was held not to violate the law with respect to conspiracy to prevent one from exercising his lawful trade, and it was held that they could lawfully exclude such critic from their theatres.

[13] Civil Rights Cases (1883), 109 U. S. 3.

[14] *Greenberg* v. *Western Turf Assoc'n* (1903), 140 Cal. 357; 73 Pac. 1050; 148 Cal. 126; 82 Pac. 684; aff'd 204 U. S. 359; 27 Sup. Ct. 384.

While it was the accepted rule in England since 1845 when *Wood* v. *Ledbitter* was decided, that a ticket was a revocable license and could be revoked either before or after entry into the theatre, the recent English case of *Hurst* v. *Picture Theatres* has modified this rule.[15] There plaintiff had purchased a ticket entitling him to an unreserved seat, entered the theatre, and occupied a seat therein. Shortly after the commencement of the performance he was requested to leave the auditorium, and upon his refusal to do so, force was threatened, and he walked out.

The prevailing opinion held that "the license was a license to enter the building and see the spectacle from its commencement until its termination. . . . The defendants had, I think, for value contracted that the plaintiff should see a certain spectacle from its commencement to its termination. They broke that contract, and it was a tort on their part to remove him." [16]

The English rule, as established by *Hurst* v. *Picture Theatres* is that a theatre ticket is a license coupled with a

[15] *Hurst* v. *Picture Theatres, Ltd.* (Eng.) (1915), 83 L. J. (K. B.) 1837; 111 L. T. 972; 30 T. L. R. 642; 58 Sol. Jo. 739.

[16] The *Hurst* v. *Picture Theatres Ltd.* decision was followed in *Barnswell* v. *National Amusement Co.* (Eng.), 23 D. L. R. 615; 31 W. L. R. 542. A patron once having entered and taken the proper seat was held entitled to retain his seat under the contractual relation existing between himself and the proprietor of the theatre, and might maintain an action on the contract as well as for assault if he was forcibly ejected. Dissenting opinion by McPhillips, J. A., to the effect that the proprietor of the theatre has "complete control over those who are permitted to attend" the entertainment, and may eject patron if he refuses to leave theatre.

grant—the grant to see the spectacle, and the license to go upon the premises to enjoy the grant; and for that reason it may not be revoked.

The American rule is, by the great weight of authority, that the purchase of the ticket confers but a license revocable at any time, and that this right is limited only in so far as it may be affected by the various Federal and state statutes.

To exclude a negro from a theatre is to violate the provisions of the statute.[17] And it was even held that where a negro was not excluded, but was asked to exchange the seat purchased by him for a seat in another part of the house, there was equally a violation of the statute.[18] It was, however, held in another state that where the accommodations afforded by the part set aside for the use of the negro were equal to that afforded to the other

[17] *Joyner* v. *Moore* (1913), 152 A. D. (N. Y.) 266; 136 N. Y. Supp. 578; *Cremore* v. *Huber* (1897), 18 A. D. (N. Y.) 231; 45 N. Y. Supp. 947; *Joseph* v. *Bidwell* (1876), 28 La. Ann. 382; *People* v. *King* (1888), 110 N. Y. 418; 18 N. E. 245; *Johnson* v. *Sparrow* (Can.), Q. J. R. 15 S. C. 104; Q. J. R. 8 Q. B. 379.

Thomas v. *Williams* (1905), 48 Misc. (N. Y.) 615; 95 N. Y. Supp. 592. A negress was denied admission to a theatre because of her color. *Held* that the proprietor was not liable when the defendant did not personally exclude or authorize the exclusion of plaintiff and when he on the contrary had made rules to the contrary and customarily permitted negroes to enter.

Hull v. *68th St. Amusement Co.* (1913), 144 N. Y. Supp. 318. Action was brought under Civil Rights Law because of refusal to sell seat for orchestra balcony to negro. *Held* there was no violation where all the seats were already sold at the time plaintiff sought to purchase the seat.

[18] *Baylies* v. *Curry* (1889), 128 Ill. 287; 21 N. E. 595.

portions of the theatre, there was no violation of the statute.[19]

Section 92.—Liability for injuries sustained by patrons—In general.

While the proprietor of the theatre is not regarded as an insurer of the safety of his patrons [20] he is required as a general rule to exercise reasonable care and prudence in maintaining his premises in a safe condition.[21] In many of the states the measure of this duty has been defined as analogous to that owed by the owner of a tenement house. The trend of the decisions, however, has of late years been away from this doctrine, and indications are not wanting that a *high* degree of care is imposed upon the proprietor, in keeping with the peculiar conditions that exist when great crowds gather for the purpose of recreation and amusement.

"Where, however, a person invites others to come upon his premises to view an exhibition conducted by him for hire, he warrants the reasonable safety of the place, and by reason of that warranty is not under a passive duty

[19] *Commonwealth* v. *George* (1915), 61 Pa. Super. Ct. 412.

See also: *Younger* v. *Judah* (1892), 111 Mo. 303; 19 S. W. 1109; 16 L. R. A. 558.

[20] See: *Wells* v. *Minn. Baseball* (1913), 122 Minn. 327; 142 N. W. 706, where the owner of a baseball park while required to use care and precaution to protect his patrons, was not, however, held to be an insurer and bound to anticipate the improbable.

[21] See: *Noack* v. *Wosslick* (1913), 182 Ill. App. 425, where a manager of a restaurant or summer garden was held bound to exercise reasonable care to keep the premises in a safe condition.

merely, but is under an active duty, to guard against all risks which might reasonably be anticipated." [22]

He is bound to inform himself of the condition of the premises [23] and to ascertain their special fitness for the accommodation of surging crowds and other unusual occurrences that the owner of other property need not generally anticipate. He is responsible for structural defects [24] as well as for the acts of omission and commission

[22] *Redmond* v. *Nat'l Horse Show Ass'n* (1912), 78 Misc. (N. Y). 383; 183 N. Y. Supp. 364. Plaintiff as a patron while viewing an exhibition was struck by a heavy gate which fell from the impact with a horse which had become unmanageable. *Held* negligence on the part of plaintiff, upon ground that defendant should have reasonably foreseen and guarded against such an accident.

[23] *Lusk* v. *Peck* (1909), 132 A. D. (N. Y.) 426; 116 N. Y. Supp. 1051; aff'd 199 N. Y. 546; 93 N. E. 377. "The owner of a place of entertainment is charged with an affirmative positive obligation to know that the premises are safe for public use. He may not be exonerated merely because he had no precise knowledge of the defective condition of the place to which he invited the public."

[24] *Schnizer* v. *Philips* (1905), 108 A. D. (N. Y.) 17; 95 N. Y. Supp. 478. "The law is well settled in this state that where a party in possession of premises throws the same open to the public for the purpose of gain, he impliedly warrants the premises reasonably safe for the purposes for which they were designed and where as in the case at bar, the plaintiff is injured by the fall of a structure which she is using at the invitation of the person in charge and in the manner which such person has a right to expect the same would be used, *the burden of explaining the accident and of showing freedom from negligence is upon the defendant.*

See also: *Abramovitz* v. *Tenzer* (1911), 144 A. D. (N. Y.) 170; 128 N. Y. Supp. 951; *Fox* v. *Buffalo Park* (1897), 21 A. D. (N. Y.) 321; 47 N. Y. Supp. 788; aff'd 163 N. Y. 559; 57 N. E. 1109.

on the part of agents and servants while engaged in the business of operating the theatre.[25] And that duty extends not alone to those who pay the price of admission to his premises, but also to all others upon the same by his invitation.[26]

This liability on the part of the owner of the building is not evaded by a lease of the structure, for even here the courts have gone so far as to read into the lease an

[25] *Oakland* v. *Bingham* (1892), 4 Ind. App. 545; 31 N. E. 383; *Dickson* v. *Waldron* (1893), 135 Ind. 507; 34 N. E. 506; 35 N. E. 1; *Fowler* v. *Holmes* (1889), 3 N. Y. Supp. 816.

Kessler v. *Deutsch* (1908), 44 Misc. (N. Y.) 209; 88 N. Y. Supp. 846. The master is responsible for an act of the servant done within the general scope of the employment while engaged in the master's business and to further it, whether the act be done *negligently, wantonly* or *willfully*. The burden, however, is on the plaintiff to establish that the servant acted within the scope of his authority.

See in this connection: *Deyo* v. *Kingston Consolidated R. R. Co.* (1904), 94 A. D. (N. Y.) 578; 88 N. Y. Supp. 487. Plaintiff was injured through negligence of employes of a fireworks manufacturer giving exhibition in defendant's amusement park. Defendant not held liable since exhibition was done entirely by manufacturer's employes and defendant had no control nor assumed to exercise any control over them. See also *Crowley* v. *Rochester Fire Works* (1906), 183 N. Y. 353; 76 N. E. 470.

See also Section 102.

[26] *Owens* v. *Assoc. Realties* (1911), 81 N. J. L. 586; 80 Atl. 325. Plaintiff, a minor, was permitted to enter defendant's park by defendant's employes, without paying an admission fee, in exchange for which plaintiff rendered certain services. *Held* that plaintiff was there at defendant's invitation and that defendant was thereby under an obligation to exercise care for his safety.

See also *Turgeon* v. *Connecticut Co.* (1911), 84 Conn. 538; 80 Atl. 714.

implied covenant by the lessor that the premises are fit and safe for the purposes for which they are intended to be used.[27]

[27] *Fox* v. *Buffalo Park* (1897), 21 A. D. (N. Y.) 321; 47 N. Y. Supp. 788; aff'd 163 N. Y. 559; 57 N. E. 1109. "While it is undoubtedly true in ordinary cases in the leasing of buildings that there is no implied warranty on the part of the lessor that the buildings are fit and safe for the purposes for which they are leased, the rule is different in regard to buildings and structures in which public exhibitions and entertainments are designed to be given and for admissions to which the lessors directly or indirectly receive compensation. In such cases the lessors or owners of the buildings or structures hold out to the public that the structures are reasonably safe for the purposes for which they are let or used, and impliedly undertake that due care has been exercised in the erection of the buildings. *Francis* v. *Cockrell* (Eng.) (1870), L. R. [5 Q. B.] 501; *Swords* v. *Edgar* (1874), 59 N. Y. 28; *Camp* v. *Wood* (1879), 76 N. Y. 92; *Beck* v. *Carter* (1877), 68 N. Y. 283; *Grote* v. *C. etc. H. R.* (Eng.) (1848), 2 Exch. 251; *Campbell* v. *Portland Sugar Co.* (1873), 62 Me. 552; *Wendell* v. *Baxter* (1859), 12 Gray (Mass.) 494."

Lusk v. *Peck* (1909), 132 A. D. (N. Y.) 426; 116 N. Y. Supp. 1051; aff'd 199 N. Y. 546; 93 N. E. 377. A lessor who rents baseball grounds containing a grand stand which was in a decaying condition at the time of the letting is liable for injuries sustained by a patron.

Where the premises are in a proper condition at the time he originally rents them but become defective during the term of the lease and where at the expiration of the lease he relets the premises to another party without repairing the premises, the lessor is liable to a patron during the period of the second lease for an injury sustained by reason of such defective condition.

Barrett v. *L. O. B. Impr. Co.* (1903), 174 N. Y. 310; 66 N. E. 968; 61 L. R. A. 829. Where the lessor let a structure for public use which was structurally defective or did not afford adequate protection to persons using it he was held liable.

See also: *Edwards* v. *New York* (1885), 98 N. Y. 245.

But in any event, whether by an implied covenant or an express covenant by the lessor, there must be notice, actual or constructive on his part, before liability can attach.[28]

Section 93.—Falling over balcony.

A frequent cause of accidents is the giving way of the railing of a balcony thereby precipitating a spectator into the auditorium below. It then becomes a question of fact to determine whether the rail was insecurely fastened. The proprietor's liability has been rigidly enforced in Canada, where even the employment by him of an expert architect did not prevent the plaintiff's recovery.[29]

In this country, recovery for such an accident is difficult, as it is not an easy matter to prove the faulty or insecure construction of the railing. In one case, the lessee was

[28] *Lowell* v. *Spaulding* (1849), 58 Mass. 277. A lessor of a theatre who covenants to make reasonable repairs on the leased premises is not liable to his lessee or patrons of the theatre for a breach of this covenant unless he had knowledge, actual or constructive, of the defects complained of.

See also: *Glynn* v. *Lyceum Theatre Co.* (1913), 87 Conn. 237; 87 Atl. 796. Contra: *Clyne* v. *Helmes* (1898), 61 N. J. L. 358; 39 Atl. 767.

[29] *Stewart* v. *Cobalt Curling* (Can.) (1909), 19 Ont. L. R. 667; 14 Ont. W. Rep. 179; aff'd 14 Ont. W. Rep. 1063. Plaintiff, in leaning against a railing of a balcony where he was seated, was precipitated to the floor below because of the giving way of the railing. *Held* that defendant was liable notwithstanding the fact that he had employed a competent architect who supervised the erection of the rink. The court quoted with approval *Francis* v. *Cockrell* (Eng.) (1870), L. R. 5 Q. B. 501.

See also: *Stevenson* v. *Glasgow Corp.* (Scotch) (1908), Sc. Ct. Sess. 1034.

held not liable because he had a right to assume that the rail was properly constructed.[30] In another case, the lessor was held blameless as the lessee had weakened the structure.[31] In a third case the proprietor was permitted to maintain a balcony at an angle of fifty-five degrees without a second guard rail in front of the aisles.[32] At best it is a question of fact for the jury.[33]

[30] *Greene* v. *Seattle A. C.* (1910), 60 Wash. 300; 111 Pac. 157. Defendant leased an armory for one night only for a sporting exhibition, mostly of foot races. Plaintiff was on the balcony. During the races the crowd surged forward and caused the railing to break, injuring plaintiff. It was not claimed that the balcony was overcrowded, but that the posts that held the railing were insecure.

Held that defendant was not bound to have the balcony inspected by experts, but had a right to assume that the building was structurally sound.

See: *Edwards* v. *N. Y. & H. R. R.* (1885), 98 N. Y. 245.

[31] *Bard* v. *New York* (1882), 10 Daly (N. Y.), 520. Where the lessee of a hall had changed the balcony and put in boxes and had so weakened the structure that it fell and injured plaintiff, the landlord was held not liable, the lessee being at fault alone.

[32] *Dunning* v. *Jacobs* (1895), 15 Misc. (N. Y.) 85; 36 N. Y. Supp. 453. Plaintiff, in changing his seat in the gallery of the theatre slipped, fell over several rows of seats, over the guard rail and was precipitated into the orchestra. *Held* that the accident was not caused by defendant's negligence, that it was not negligent for theatre manager not to provide a second guard rail or to maintain the gallery at an angle of 55 degrees.

See also: *Camp* v. *Wood* (1879), 76 N. Y. 92.

[33] *Schofield* v. *Wood* (1898), 170 Mass. 415; 49 N. E. 636. Plaintiffs, while seated in the gallery of defendant's hall, leaned on the rail, which gave way and caused their injury. There was some evidence to show that the rail was improperly constructed and insecurely fastened. *Held*, a question for the jury.

"A person erecting and using a hall for such exhibitions must

The American rule is extremely unfair to the public. It would be more in keeping with justice if the proprietor were held strictly to account for the giving way of the balcony rail, regardless of whether he knew anything about its construction, or had received notice of any defects.

There are some elements of responsibility resting upon the theatre proprietor which, because of the peculiar arrangement of the building and the methods of its use, impose a greater duty upon him than the American jurisdiction exacts.

It seems hard to understand why a common carrier, which is bound to accept everyone presenting himself as a passenger, is charged with the highest degree of care, while the proprietor of a theatre, more or less free to fill his house, may expose great numbers of the public to unusual dangers and be liable for ordinary care only.

If this rule were modified, it would do more to insure the safety of an audience than is accomplished by all the numerous statutes and ordinances that are passed every year. *Weiner* v. *Scherer* [34] comes nearer to expressing this doctrine than any of the other reported American cases.

Section 94.—Seats and floors.

While the duty of the theatre proprietor has been de-

use reasonable care in the construction, maintenance and management of it, having regard to the character of the exhibitions given and the customary conduct of spectators who witness them. . . ."

[34] *Weiner* v. *Scherer* (1909), 64 Misc. (N. Y.) 82; 117 N. Y. Supp. 1008. Here the rail gave way because of the surging of the crowd, causing several people to fall upon the plaintiff who was seated in the orchestra.

fined as ordinary care, even where the seats of a grand stand had collapsed it was held nevertheless that he was liable for defects in the structure of the building which resulted in the giving way of the flooring.[35]

The safer practice on the part of the proprietor is to make a thorough inspection of his building every day, paying particular attention to the seats. An inspection of this kind has been judicially defined as a full compliance with the proprietor's duty to his patrons.[36]

Section 95.—Tripping in darkened theatre—aisles—steps—exits.

The case of *Branch* v. *Klatt* [37] has laid down the best

[35] *Texas State* v. *Britton* (1902), 118 Fed. (C. C. A.) 713. Plaintiff was injured by the falling of seats in a grand stand. *Held* that the corporation operating the State Fair and advertising the side-show was liable in damages.

See also: *Van Antwerp* v. *Linton* (1895), 89 Hun (N. Y.), 417; 35 N. Y. Supp. 318; aff'd 157 N. Y. 716; 53 N. E. 1133; *Huneke* v. *West Brighton Am. Co.* (1903), 80 A. D. (N. Y.) 268; 80 N. Y. Supp. 261.

Brown v. *So. Kennebec* (1859), 47 Maine, 275. The proprietor was held liable to a patron for injuries caused because of negligence in the construction of a building resulting in the fall or giving way of the flooring.

See also: *Latham* v. *Roach* (1874), 72 Ill. 179.

[36] *Glynn* v. *Lyceum Theatre Co.* (1913), 87 Conn. 237; 87 Atl. 796. "The lessee did not insure the absolute safety of the theatre seats; it, by its invitation to its guests, assumed the duty toward them of exercising reasonable care to see that the seats were in a reasonably safe condition for its guests, *Turgeon* v. *Connecticut Co.* (1911), 84 Conn. 538, 541; 80 Atl. 714. It performed this duty by having its servant examine the seats each day and report their condition, and thereafter repairing the defective ones."

[37] *Branch* v. *Klatt* (1911), 165 Mich. 666; 131 N. W. 107; after retrial 173 Mich. 31; 138

rule of all the reported decisions with respect to the liability of the theatre proprietor when his theatre is darkened during a performance. It holds that the patron, in such case, has the right to rely on the premises being in safe condition, and that his duty is lighter than that of a pedestrian. That is an eminently sensible doctrine, and should be followed in all the states. Unfortunately, it is not. The courts generally adhere to the old rule of ordinary care and contributory negligence,[38] something which in the

N. W. 263. Plaintiff was hurt by descending the steps situated at the exit of a theatre after dark. The question was whether by using this exit plaintiff was guilty of contributory negligence.

"One would have the right to presume that the defendant had discharged his duty of having the premises in a reasonably safe condition, as to lights and construction; and the ordinary person would naturally suppose that it would be safe to pass along a passageway provided for his exit, with reasonable assurance of its being in safe condition. The very fact of the premises being maintained in a darkened condition might give him added assurance of its being reasonably safe. . . . The duty of a person in a theatre, where he has been invited, is lighter than that resting upon one passing along the public streets."

See also: *Andre* v. *Mertens et al.* (1916), 96 Atl. (N. J.) 893. "It is next argued that the plaintiff was negligent as a matter of law in attempting to leave the theatre before the show was finished. Not so. The defendants commonly exhibited the same pictures over and over again on the same evening, and it was quite usual for patrons to depart at any time."

[38] *Hollenback* v. *Clemmer* (1912), 66 Wash. 565; 119 Pac. 1114. Plaintiff had attended a moving-picture show and on leaving the theatre was directed by the usher to take a particular exit. There was a step down of seven inches at this exit. Not noticing this step she was precipitated to the ground and injured. *Held* that defendant was not liable; that plaintiff should have used her sense of sight and looked where she was stepping.

light of the facts that usually obtain, seems unnecessarily harsh and unjust.

It has been held that the theatre proprietor is under a

New Theatre v. *Hartlove* (1914), 123 Md. 78; 90 Atl. 990. The appellee was injured by reason of a fall while seeking a seat in a darkened theatre.

Ordinary care and diligence was held to be the measure of defendant's duty, and a verdict in favor of plaintiff was upheld in view of all the evidence.

Pattison v. *Livingston Am. Co.* (1913), 156 A. D. (N. Y.) 368; 141 N. Y. Supp. 588. Plaintiff entered the balcony while the theatre was dark. Her seats were in the fifth row from the front. Without waiting for any assistance, she groped her way along, and was injured.

Held, that she was guilty of contributory negligence as a matter of law.

Butcher v. *Hyde* (1897), 152 N. Y. 142; 46 N. E. 305. It was held error for the trial court to refuse to charge that if plaintiff fell from the fourth or fifth step the verdict must be for the defendants where there was no proof of any defect in the stairway of a theatre except in the condition of a strip of rubber on the sixth step.

Andre v. *Mertens et al.* (1916), 96 Atl. (N. J.) 893. Plaintiff in leaving defendant's motion picture theatre, descended a stairway leading from the balcony to the entrance floor. Because of the dark condition of the stairway, she lost her footing in a turn of the stairs and was precipitated to the platform below. In affirming a judgment in plaintiff's favor the court said:

"The proprietor of a theatre conducted for reward or profit, to which the general public are invited to attend performances must use ordinary care to make the premises as reasonably safe as is consistent with the practical operation of the theatre, and if he fails in this duty, he may be held liable for personal injuries occasioned thereby; and this rule applies to the proprietor of a moving picture show."

See also: *Owens* v. *Associated Realties* (1911), 81 N. J. Law, 586; 80 Atl. 325; *Branch* v. *Klatt* (1911), 165 Mich. 666; 131 N. W. 107; same case after retrial 173 Mich. 31; 138 N. W. 263; *Valentine Co.* v. *Sloan* (1912), 53 Ind. App. 69; 101 N. E. 102.

duty to make proper inspections of his premises, and it is for the jury to say whether such inspections were made a sufficient length of time before to have enabled him to repair the premises.[39]

The violation of a statute or ordinance by the proprietor renders him prima facie liable; and a failure to build inclines as required was held to be the proximate cause of the injury.[40]

[39] *Dalton* v. *Hooper* (1914), 168 S. W. (Tex.) 84. Plaintiff, while descending a stairway in a theatre, caught her foot on a projecting metal strip, and sustained injuries. *Held*, that while defendants were not insurers, yet they owed the duty of exercising reasonable care.

"It is their duty to make proper inspections to see that the place is in proper condition to avoid injury. In this case there was proof to show inspection, and whether the projecting metal strip that caused appellee to fall was known to be in that condition, or should have been known to appellants by reasonable care, a sufficient length of time before the accident to have been repaired by appellants, was a question for the jury's determination."

Valentine Co. v. *Sloan*, 53 Ind. App. 69, 101 N. E. 102. Plaintiff, while attempting to descend an aisle in the theatre, tripped and fell. The light provided was not sufficient for her to distinguish the uneven steps, and she was quite unfamiliar with their condition. *Held*, that there was no such thing here as assumption of risk.

"One who conducts a theatre for reward or profit, to which the general public are invited to attend performances, must use ordinary and reasonable care to make the premises as reasonably safe as is consistent with the practical operation of the same."

Nephler v. *Woodward* (1906), 200 Mo. 179; 98 S. W. 488. Plaintiff, a patron of defendants' theatre while passing down one of the aisles to her seat fell, her foot having caught in a hole in the carpet. *Held*, that jury could find that defendants failed to use the proper care required of them to protect their patrons, and judgment entered on verdict of jury was affirmed.

[40] *Ewing* v. *Chase* (1911), 37

In *Micheltree* v. *Stair* [41] the proprietor was sought to be held liable by reason of an injury suffered by an actress who used an iron stairway to reach her dressing-room. It was held that she assumed the risk. We cannot reconcile this decision with the cases in the same state which hold that a tenant who has no method of egress from or ingress to his apartment other than the stairway on which he is injured, is not, by reason of his using such stairway, guilty of contributory negligence. We do not believe that that decision will be followed.

On the other hand, a patron of a theatre has no right to leave by a rear exit which is not intended for general use, and where he does so, and is hurt, he cannot recover.[42]

App. Cas. (D. C.) 53. The defendant violated a statute in failing to build proper inclines leading to exits, in his theatre. The court held that one who failed to comply with a statute was guilty of negligence as a matter of law where the person injured was free from contributory negligence and the violation of the statute was the proximate cause of the injury.

[41] *Micheltree* v. *Stair* (1909), 135 A. D. (N. Y.) 210; 120 N. Y. Supp. 540. Plaintiff, an actress, slipped, while using stairway leading to her dressing room, because of the slippery condition of the iron treads on the stairs. *Held* that as she had used the stairway a number of times before, she must have known the condition of the stairway and assumed the risk. *Held further* that the appellants not being plaintiff's employers, were only bound to use reasonable care in keeping the building, including the stairway in repair, but under no obligation to furnish her with a reasonably safe place to work.

[42] *Hendershott* v. *Modern Woodmen* (1911), 66 Wash. 155; 119 Pac. 2. Plaintiff while leaving a hall by the back stairway was injured. *Held*, no liability, as there was no invitation to enter or leave by that way.

Johnson v. *Wilcox* (1890), 135 Pa. St. 217; 19 Atl. 939. Plaintiff had attended a dance-hall. Instead of leaving by the lighted

Nor is the owner liable because plaintiff had tripped over a mat in the foyer near the ticket office.[43]

Section 96.—Articles dropping.

When a patron is injured by the fall of a part of the ceiling or chandelier, the rule of res ipsa loquitur applies, and the burden is on the proprietor to show that he was free from negligence. In such a case proof that the premises were regularly and carefully inspected will not relieve him from liability.[44] To hold otherwise would be to place a premium upon carelessness on the part of theatre proprietors.

It has been held in *Flanagan* v. *Goldberg* [45] that a charge

entrance he stepped out upon a dark platform. *Held* that defendant was not liable for the injury resulting.

[43] *Holmes* v. *United Theatres* (1915), 152 N. W. (Mich.) 987.

See generally: *Norton* v. *Hudner* (1913), 213 Mass. 257; 100 N. E. 546; *De Velin* v. *Swanson* (1909), 72 Atl. (R. I.) 388; *Dwyer* v. *Hills Bros.* (1903), 79 A. D. (N. Y.) 45; 79 N. Y. Supp. 785; *Reeves* v. *Fourteenth St. Theatre* (1906), 110 A. D. (N. Y.) 735; 96 N. Y. Supp. 448; *Dudley* v. *Abraham* (1907), 122 A. D. (N. Y.) 480; 107 N. Y. Supp. 97; *Meyer* v. *Grand Rapids Chair Co.* (1914), 180 Mich. 604, 147 N. W. 488.

[44] *Goldstein* v. *Levy* (1911), 74 Misc. (N. Y.) 463; 132 N. Y. Supp. 373.

But see: *Sheets* v. *Sunbry* (1912), 237 Pa. St. 153; 85 Atl. 92. Plaintiff, while attending an amusement park, stopped under a tree. A limb or branch fell upon him, injuring him, and the testimony showed that it appeared to be decayed, although there was some dispute as to that. It appeared that two days prior thereto an inspection of the park had been made. *Held* that defendant was not liable and judgment in plaintiff's favor reversed.

[45] *Flanagan* v. *Goldberg* (1910), 137 A. D. (N. Y.) 92; 122 N. Y. Supp. 205. Plaintiff was injured by a board falling in a

to this effect was error, but the special facts in that case must be considered, as there was indication that the board had been placed by strangers. The better rule would be to give the patron the benefit of every liberal construction, for he enters at the invitation of the owner, and relies upon the latter's prudence and carefulness in the maintenance of the premises.[46]

Special circumstances might arise when the proprietor would not be held liable, as in case of a sudden panic [47] on where the article dropped had not been fastened to the premises and might have been so dropped by a stranger.[48]

motion picture theatre. The court held that it was error to charge that the burden was on defendant to show freedom from negligence rather than on plaintiff to show negligence.

[46] *Currier* v. *Henderson* (1895), 85 Hun (N. Y.), 300; 32 N. Y. Supp. 953. Defendant was held liable for injuries received by plaintiff by the fall of a batten from the flies in defendant's theatre.

Schnizer v. *Phillips* (1905), 108 A. D. (N. Y.) 17; 95 N. Y. Supp. 478; *Fox* v. *Buffalo Park* (1897), 21 A. D. (N. Y.) 321; 47 N. Y. Supp. 788; aff'd 136 N. Y. 559; 57 N. E. 1109; *Abromowitz* v. *Tenzer* (1911), 144 A. D. (N. Y.) 170; 128 N. Y. Supp. 951; *Lusk* v. *Peck* (1909), 132 A. D. (N. Y.) 426; 116 N. Y. Supp. 1051; aff'd 199 N. Y. 546; 93 N. E. 377.

[47] *King* v. *Ringling* (1910), 145 Mo. App. 285; 130 S. W. 482. Plaintiff was injured by falling of a board at defendant's circus, during a panic caused by a windstorm. *Held* defendant not liable as no evidence was brought out showing that defendant was guilty of a breach of any duty owing to plaintiff.

[48] *Williams* v. *Mineral C. P. A.* (1905), 128 Iowa, 32; 102 N. W. 783; 1 L. R. A. (N. S.) 427. While seated below a grand stand in a park where races were being held, a bottle was dropped upon plaintiff. *Held* that as reasonable care was the measure of duty, the charge was correct and the

Section 97.—Wild animals.

Under one line of cases the rule of liability on the part of an owner of wild animals was a very stringent one, so that where the animal escaped and injured another, the owner at once and in any event became liable.[49] The owner was legally presumed negligent [50] and was charged with knowledge of the propensities of such animals to do injury.[51] He was bound to "absolutely prevent" the

jury's verdict for the defendant would not be disturbed. There was no evidence to show how the bottle had been dropped or by whom.

Pieschel v. *Miner* (1900), 30 Misc. (N. Y.) 301; 63 N. Y. Supp. 508. "Plaintiff moves to set aside a dismissal. He showed that while in the orchestra of defendant's theatre, he was injured through the fall of an iron hook from above the stage. The defendant through a witness called by the plaintiff, showed that the hook fell while in use by the stage carpenter; there was no evidence of the character of any defect which existed prior to the accident, or that the tool was unsuited to the work. . . . The dismissal was therefore proper."

[49] 1 Hale, P. C., chap. 33, p. 430. The doctrine was laid down by Hale that when the animal escapes, the owner is at once liable irrespective of the degree of care exercised by him in keeping the animal confined.

See: *Besozzi* v. *Harris* (Eng.) (1858), 1 Fost. & F. 92; *Wyatt* v. *Rosherville Gardens* (Eng.) (1886), 2 Times L. R. 282; *Manger Bros.* v. *Shipman* (1890), 30 Neb. 352; 46 N. W. 527; *Shaw* v. *McCreary* (Can.), 19 Ont. Rep. 39.

[50] *Rogers* v. *Rogers* (1887), 4 N. Y. St. Rep. 373. Negligence of the owner is the legal presumption. While a man might by a wanton act, provoke an attack "every failure to use care is not negligence nor does the rule of contributory negligence in the sense in which that term is ordinarily applied, govern in such cases."

[51] *Spring* v. *Edgar* (1878), 99 U. S. 645. "Animals ferae naturae as a class are known to be mischievous; and the rule is well settled that whoever undertakes

injury [52] and the fact that plaintiff was a trespasser upon the premises whereon the animals were kept did not defeat a recovery.[53]

to keep such an animal in places of public resort is or may be liable for the injuries inflicted by it on a party who is not guilty of negligence and is otherwise without fault . . . in actions for injuries by such beasts it is not necessary to allege that the owner knew them to be mischievous, for he is presumed to have such knowledge, from which it follows that he is guilty of negligence in permitting the same to be at large."

See also: *Woodbridge* v. *Marks* (1896), 5 A. D. (N. Y.) 604; 40 N. Y. Supp. 728; *Brooks* v. *Taylor* (1887), 65 Mich. 208; 31 N. W. 837; *Popplewell* v. *Pierce* (Eng.) (1852), 10 Cush. 509; *Snow* v. *McCracken* (1895), 107 Mich. 49; 64 N. W. 866; *Partlow* v. *Haggerty* (1870), 35 Ind. 178; *Williams* v. *Moray* (1881), 74 Ind. 25.

[52] *Gooding* v. *Chutes* (1909), 102 Pac. (Cal.) 819; 23 L. R. A. (N. S.) 1071. Defendant was keeping animals for exhibition at a place called "The Chutes." Plaintiff was employed to look after them, and in particular a camel of vicious propensities.

"It is the duty of one who owns or keeps domestic animals known to be vicious to guard them in such a manner as will absolutely prevent the occurrence of an injury to others through such vicious acts of the animals as they are naturally inclined to commit. . . . This language is used in the authority cited with respect to the duty of an owner of wild animals, which are presumed to be ferocious."

Hays v. *Miller* (1907), 43 So. (Ala.) 818. The owner of a wolf was held liable for injuries inflicted by the animal.

"On the other hand the owner of wild animals ferae naturae is as a general rule liable for injuries done by them. It is not necessary to prove that the owner had knowledge of the vicious nature of a wild animal causing injury, as he is conclusively presumed to have such knowledge. Neither is it necessary to show that the owner was negligent in permitting the animal to be at

[53] *Marble* v. *Ross* (1878), 124 Mass. 44.

"It is the duty of those who keep them (wild beasts) to do it in such a manner as will absolutely prevent the occurrence of an injury to others through such vicious acts of the animals as they are naturally inclined to commit, and such liability exists without notice of the previous misconduct of such animals. In other words, such notice is conclusively presumed from the nature of the animal." [54]

But wild animals have become a very necessary feature of the motion picture business as well as of theatrical exhibitions and the rule of absolute liability has been recognized as harsh and unjustly severe. It has for that reason been modified to the extent that some negligence must be shown on the part of the owner before he may be held liable.[55]

large for he is bound to keep it secure at his peril."

See: *Parsons* v. *Manser* (1903), 119 Iowa, 88; 93 N. W. 86.

Andrew v. *Kilgour* (Can.), 19 Manitoba, 545; 13 West. L. Rep. 608. *Held* the owner absolutely liable for injuries caused by his pet racoon.

Vredenburg v. *Behan* (1881), 33 La. Ann. 627. Where plaintiff's intestate was set upon by a bear and mortally attacked, his estate could recover of the defendants, members of a club, which had kept the bear upon the adjoining premises.

See also: *Speckman* v. *Kreig* (1899), 79 Mo. App. 376.

Harris v. *Carstens Packing Co.* (1906), 86 Pac. (Wash.) 1125. Defendant, the owner of a vicious steer, held liable for one injured by the animal.

See also: *Muller* v. *McKesson* (1878), 73 N. Y. 195; *Hammond* v. *Melton* (1891), 42 Ill. App. 186; *Ahlstrand* v. *Bishop* (1899), 88 Ill. App. 424.

[54] *Parker* v. *Cushman* (1912), 195 Fed. (C. C. A.) 715. Plaintiff attended a wild-animal show, and a lion reached through the bars and injured her.

[55] *Molloy* v. *Starin* (1908), 191 N. Y. 21; 83 N. E. 588. The owner of a boat was transporting several trained bears. Plaintiff,

"Hence the gist of such an action as this is not the keeping of the dog with knowledge of his dangerous nature, but rather the negligent failure to properly *restrain* the animal, and to keep him so safely that he may not injure anyone who is lawfully at the place." [56]

Where the owner is free from all negligence and the animal escapes, the owner is not liable.[57] Nor is the owner

a boy of nine years, came upon the cages and was injured. *Held* that the defendant was not brought within the rule making it absolutely liable for beasts ferae naturae, unless negligence on his part could be shown, and that as no negligence was here shown, a verdict in favor of plaintiff was reversed.

[56] *Hayes* v. *Smith* (1900), 62 Ohio St. 161; 56 N. E. 879.

See also: *Thomas* v. *Bayson* (1901), 21 Ohio C. C. 778; *Fake* v. *Addicks* (1890), 45 Minn. 37; 47 N. W. 450; *Melsheimer* v. *Sullivan* (1891), 1 Colo. App. 22; 27 Pac. 17; *Meibus* v. *Dodge* (1875), 38 Wis. 300; *Worthen* v. *Love* (1888), 60 Vt. 285; 14 Atl. 461; *Graham* v. *Payne* (1889), 122 Ind. 403; 24 N. E. 216.

[57] *Connor* v. *The Princess Theatre* (Can.), 10 D. L. R. 143; 4 O. W. N. 502; 27 Ont. L. Rep. 466; 49 C. L. J. 118. Plaintiff was injured by a trained monkey which performed in the theatre of defendants. *Held* that defendants were not liable as they had not been guilty of any negligence, the monkey having been insecurely fastened by a stranger.

See also: *Du Tremble* v. *Poulin* (Can.), 42 Que. S. C. 121.

De Gray v. *Murray* (1903), 69 N. J. L. 458; 55 Atl. 237. Defendant was accustomed to keeping a vicious dog locked up for the night. The dog managed to chew away the woodwork around the lock of his house, and escaped, injuring plaintiff early the following morning. Defendant held not liable.

Scribner v. *Kelly* (1862), 38 Barb. (N. Y.) 14. Defendant owned an elephant. Plaintiff's horse became frightened thereat and caused the injury. *Held* that while the defendant's negligence was presumed, there was no proof here that he was anything but careful, and the complaint was dismissed.

liable when the plaintiff has himself been guilty of contributory negligence or has provoked the animal.[58] And the owner has been held harmless where the plaintiff was employed to look after the animal, for in that case the latter is presumed to have accepted the risk incidental to his employment.[59]

There seems to have been a reversion to the old doctrine in a recent New York decision where a proprietor was held liable although no actual negligence on his part was shown.

It is rather surprising to see the old doctrine of absolute liability invoked and enforced at the present time, but *Stamp* v. *Sixty-eighth Street Amusement Company*[60] seems to be based wholly on that theory. There a lion had escaped during a performance, and a panic ensued, causing the plaintiff's injuries. While the learned court rightly held that the panic and injury were a direct result of the animal's escape, it also held that the pro-

[58] *Ervin* v. *Woodruff* (1907), 119 A. D. (N. Y.) 603; 103 N. Y. Supp. 1051. One who places himself in danger of attack by a bear is guilty of contributory negligence.

See: *Marquet* v. *LaDuke* (1893), 96 Mich. 596; 55 N. W. 1006; *Jackson* v. *Baker* (1904), 24 App. D. C. 100.

[59] *Borman* v. *City of Milwaukee* (1896), 93 Wis. 522; 67 N. W. 924; 33 L. R. A. 652. Plaintiff was employed in a park where deer and elk were kept and while in an enclosure with the animals, was attacked by them and injured. He was held to have accepted the ordinary risks incident to the business, and defendant was not liable.

See: *Little* v. *City of Madison* (1877), 42 Wis. 643; S. C., 49 Wis. 605; 6 N. W. 249; *May* v. *Burdett* (Eng.) (1846), 9 Q. B. 101; 9 Adol. & E. (N. S.) 101; *Filburn* v. *Peoples P. & A. Co.* (Eng.) (1890), 25 Q. B. Div. 258.

[60] *Stamp* v. *68th St. Am. Co.* (1917), 159 N. Y. Supp. 683.

prietor of the theatre was liable irrespective of whether he was negligent or not.

To this doctrine we cannot subscribe. We do not think that the case will stand.

Section 98.—Crowds.

It has been held negligence on the part of the theatre proprietor to so overcrowd his balcony as to cause the giving way of the rail.[61] Narrow passageways, resulting in a jamming of the crowd, and injury to the plaintiff will also make him liable, as it has been held to be the proximate cause of the injury.[62] And a failure to guard the space under a platform which collapsed and killed a boy who had strayed underneath was sufficient to charge the defendant with liability.[63]

[61] *Weiner* v. *Scherer* (1909), 64 Misc. (N. Y.) 82; 117 N. Y. Supp. 1008. Plaintiff while seated in the orchestra was injured by the giving way of a rail on the balcony, causing several people to fall upon him.

"The defendant must be assumed to have known the capacity of the balcony, and he had no right to permit it to become so overcrowded as to cause undue pressure upon the rail. The pressing forward of the people to view the performance was also to be expected, and that this would naturally be done by the standees should have been anticipated; and the admission of a much greater number of people than the balcony in ordinary use was intended to contain . . . made it a question for submission to the jury."

[62] *Bole* v. *Pittsburgh A. C.* (1913), 205 Fed. (C. C. A.) 468. Plaintiff was injured while attending a baseball game. *Held* that the proximate cause of the accident was the act of defendant in maintaining a narrow passageway, and judgment in defendant's favor was reversed.

[63] *Murrell* v. *Smith* (1910), 152 Mo. App. 95; 133 S. W. 76. Plaintiff's intestate, a boy of

In one case fire broke out in the defendant's circus, and plaintiff was injured. Defendant's liability was rested upon his failure to supply fire extinguishers.[64]

From the foregoing cases the rule might be adduced that the proprietor of a theatre or other place of amusement is bound to anticipate the gathering of great crowds, and he is in duty bound to make some suitable provision for their safe entry and exit, their disposal, and for the common emergencies that may arise, such as fire and panic.[65]

Section 99.—Hurt by performer.

The proprietor of a theatre is under a duty to exercise reasonable care in safeguarding the audience from injury

eight years, met his death under a platform erected by and under the charge of the defendant's managers in the midst of fair grounds. The surging of the crowd caused the platform to collapse. *Held* that barriers should have been placed, as children might have been expected to go into this space. That reasonable diligence and caution was the measure of defendant's duty. (See: *Van Cleef* v. *Chicago*, 23 L. R. A. (N. S.) 642.)

[64] *Griswold* v. *Ringling* (1915), 165 A. D. (N. Y.) 737; 150 N. Y. Supp. 1022. It was held that the question of negligence was for the jury in a case where a spectator of a circus was injured in endeavoring to get out upon the breaking out of fire in the tent and the defendant failed to have chemical extinguishers therein.

[65] *Edwards* v. *N. Y. & H. R. R.* (1885), 98 N. Y. 245. Defendant had leased Gilmore's Gardens to one Kelley, who was to make all alterations. Kelley permitted a large crowd to enter upon a gallery, and as a result of the overcrowded condition and the stamping of the people, the gallery fell, injuring plaintiff.

By a divided court, four to three, the defendant was held not liable. Ch. J. Ruger writing a long dissenting opinion in which

likely to be suffered at the hands of performers.[66] It has been said in England that the proprietor impliedly warrants his play to be safe.[67] But this theory would seem to break down where the entertainment given is known

he maintained that inasmuch as the defendant knew the purposes for which the hall was let and the inadequacy of the gallery to accommodate a large crowd, he was guilty of negligence, and should have been held liable.

The dissenting opinion seems to have carried greater weight than the prevailing opinion in the later case of *Atchison Ely* v. *Thomas*, 104 A. D. (N. Y.) 368; 93 N. Y. Supp. 693.

[66] *Brown* v. *Batchellor* (1908), 69 Atl. (R. I.) 295. It was held that a bill of complaint alleging that defendants were negligent in failing to provide suitable protection upon the stage to prevent a performer on a bicycle from riding off the stage stated a good cause of action.

Cole v. *Rome Sav. Bank* (1916), 96 Misc. (N. Y.) 188; 161 N. Y. Supp. 15. Defendant Edwards had engaged a trapeze act. During the progress of the performance the mechanism broke and an iron hook flew out and struck plaintiff in the audience.

"I think upon the evidence in the case a fair question of fact was presented as to whether the Campbell Brothers used due care in the erection and securing of the casting net and as they were hired to give the exhibition from which the proprietor derived profit it was the business of the proprietor and not that of Campbell Brothers. The relation of respondeat superior therefore existed, and the proprietor was chargeable with their negligence."

[67] *Cox* v. *Coulson* (Eng.) (1916), 85 L. J. K. B. 1081; 2 Ch. 177; 114 L. T. 599; 60 S. J. 402; 32 T. L. R. 406; rev. 31 T. L. R. 390. Plaintiff was in the audience of a theatre. An actor on the stage, discharging a pistol, injured him. A verdict in plaintiff's favor was reversed, the Court of Appeal holding that while defendant impliedly covenanted that he would use reasonable care and diligence, he did not warrant that the members of his company would do likewise.

to be attended with some danger, although it might be said that the warranty would extend to the place where the performance is given. At any rate a question of fact would be presented as to whether the proprietor had taken all reasonable precautions to prevent injury to the patrons.[68]

It has been held that one attending a baseball game does so with full knowledge of the risk he takes in being

[68] *Arnold* v. *State* (1914), 163 A. D. (N. Y.) 253; 148 N. Y. Supp. 479. Where the State Fair Commission permitted a race of high power automobiles on its grounds and protected the part assigned to spectators from the track by a wooden fence of flimsy construction, it was held liable for death and injury of person by an automobile which broke through such fence.

Conrad v. *Clauve* (1883), 93 Ind. 476. Defendants were the owners and managers of an amusement park to which an admission fee was charged. A part of the ground was allotted to target shooting. Plaintiff was not informed upon entering the park that a part thereof was allotted to target shooting and hitched his horse within the proscribed area. Defendants were held liable for the value of the horse which was shot, upon the ground that there was a duty imposed upon defendants to inform plaintiff of the danger of hitching his horse within the ground set aside for target shooting.

Thompson v. *Lowell* (1898), 170 Mass. 577; 49 N. E. 913; 40 L. R. A. 345. Where a spectator at a grove was struck in the eye by a bullet fired by a performer therein, he was entitled to go to the jury on the question whether defendant had taken due precaution to guard against injury.

A railroad corporation which owned and maintained such a grove also held liable.

Hallyburton v. *Burke Co.* (1896), 119 N. C. 526; 26 S. E. 114. Where a horse, on a racetrack, bolted from his course and injured a spectator who was sitting on the railings, the proprietor of the track was held not liable.

struck by a foul ball.[69] But where the screen which is provided is inadequate plaintiff may recover.[70]

Nor is this a duty owed to a patron alone, but the proprietor, it has been held, owes a duty to a trespasser as well, if he knows of the latter's presence.[71]

The proprietor is liable to a patron for insulting and defamatory language addressed to the latter by a performer.[72]

Section 100.—Miscellaneous accidents.

One who operates a scenic railway is a carrier of passengers and is likewise bound to the highest degree of

[69] *Crane* v. *Kansas City Baseball* (1912), 168 Mo. App. 301; 153 S. W. 1076. Plaintiff had purchased a seat in the grand stand which was protected against danger of being struck by foul balls. He voluntarily chose to take a seat in an unprotected area. Defendant held not liable.

[70] *Edling* v. *Kansas City Baseball* (1914), 181 Mo. App. 327; 168 S. W. 908. Plaintiff was witnessing a ball game on defendant's amusement grounds. Plaintiff was sitting in a stand which was screened. A foul ball struck the screen, broke through and hit plaintiff. Defendant was held liable.

See also: *Fox* v. *Dougherty*, 2 W. N. C. (Pa.) 417; where it was held not to be contributory negligence to sit in the front row of the orchestra.

[71] *Herrick* v. *Wixon* (1899), 121 Mich. 384; 80 N. W. 117; 81 N. W. 333. The fact that plaintiff forced his way into a show tent, where he was injured by the explosion of a giant firecracker in the course of the performance, will not preclude a recovery based on the proprietor's negligence, since the duty of reasonable care is owed even to trespassers when their presence is known.

See in this connection: *Aughtrey* v. *Wiles* (1917), 91 S. E. (S. C.) 303; *Ramonas* v. *Grand Rapids Ry. Co.* (1917), 160 N. W. (Mich.) 382.

[72] *Interstate Am. Co.* v. *Martin* (1913), 8 Ala. App. 481.

care.[73] And one who operates a "merry-go-round" may not start it until every passenger in it has been seated.[74] A swing erected in an amusement park must not be maintained in a defective condition [75] and the owner of a park

[73] *Wash. Luna Park* v. *Goodrich* (1910), 110 Va. 692; 66 S. E. 977. A judgment in favor of plaintiff was affirmed. He had been a passenger in a "roller coaster" car, and while therein another car had collided with him, causing the injury.

O'Callaghan v. *Dellwood Park Co.* (1909), 242 Ill. 336; 89 N. E. 1005. One operating a scenic railway was held to be a carrier of passengers and bound to use the same degree of care as any other carrier of passengers.

Pointer v. *Mountain R. C. C.* (1917), 189 S. W. (Mo.) 805. The rule of res ipsa loquitur on scenic railways not held to apply.

Lumsden v. *Thompson Scenic Ry.* (1909), 130 A. D. (N. Y.) 209; 114 N. Y. Supp. 421. Action for negligence on scenic railway. Verdict for plaintiff reversed.

See: *Huneeke* v. *W. Brighton Amusement Co.* (1903), 80 A. D. (N. Y.) 268; 80 N. Y. Supp. 261; *Barrett* v. *Lake Ontario Beach Imp. Co.* (1903), 174 N. Y. 310; 66 N. E. 968.

On the question of liability to a trespasser see: Aughtrey v. *Wiles* (1917), 91 S. E. (S. C.) 303. Plaintiff non-suited after injury suffered on automobile race-track on the ground that he was a trespasser. *Ramonas* v. *Grand Rapids Ry. Co.* (1917), 160 N. W. (Mich.) 382.

[74] *Harris* v. *Crawley* (1912), 170 Mich. 381; 136 N. W. 356. The question in this case was whether defendant was negligent in starting his "merry-go-round" before plaintiff was seated.

See *Linthicum* v. *Truitt* (1911), 2 Boyce (Del.), 338; 80 Atl. 245, on the question whether it was negligence to attempt to board a "merry-go-round" while it was in motion.

[75] *Schwab* v. *Anderson Steamboat Co.* (1911), 66 Wash. 236; 119 Pac. 614. The owner of a park was held not liable for an injury to the plaintiff upon a swing erected just outside the limits of the park, although there is a short and logical dissenting opinion by Judge Chadwick which gives the better rule.

is likewise liable to one who is injured by a turnstile at the gate.[76]

While one who was riding on an amusement device was non-suited by reason of his failure to show a faulty construction of the device,[77] it was held that where the accident was caused by the act of the defendant's employe, a question of fact was presented for the jury.[78]

To leave one's position in a grand stand and go to an exposed part of the field has been held contributory negligence.[79] The proprietor of a swimming bath was held not liable because the attendants furnished by him failed to rescue plaintiff's intestate.[80]

[76] *Marx* v. *Ontario H. & A. Co.* (1914), 211 N. Y. 33; 105 N. E. 97. It was held that a sudden backward movement of a turnstile through which it was necessary for patrons of an amusement park to pass, by one of defendant's attendants, causing an injury to a ticket holder, rendered the defendant liable.

[77] *Fennar* v. *Atlantic Am. Co.* (1913), 84 N. J. L. 691; 87 Atl. 344. Plaintiff while riding on the "Human Niagara Falls" was injured. *Held* that in the absence of any evidence to show faulty construction or want of repair, the complaint was bad.

[78] *Hays* v. *Eldor Am. Co.* (1912), 51 Pa. Sup. Ct. 426. A bamboo slide in an amusement park was used by plaintiff, who alleged that by reason of the start or shove given him by the defendant's employe he was injured. *Held* a question for the jury.

[79] *Burns* v. *Herman* (1910), 48 Colo. 359; 113 Pac. 310. Where defendant provided a grand stand where the spectators were to sit and the plaintiff voluntarily left the place furnished by defendant and went to a place where he was in danger of being injured, it was held that plaintiff was guilty of contributory negligence.

[80] *Levinsky* v. *Cooper* (1911), 142 S. W. (Tex.) 959. Defendants conducted a natatorium, and plaintiff's intestate, while swimming therein was drowned. While it was held that the proprietor of the place was bound to exercise reasonable care in furnishing

It is a negligent act for a street railway company to run its car at full speed opposite a point where people are leaving a theatre in large numbers.[81]

Section 101.—Acts of strangers.

The proprietor is not liable for the acts of patrons or strangers unless they are such as could have reasonably been foretold.

"While the defendants were bound to exercise reasonable care to protect their invitees from peril, they were not insurers of their safety, and if the accident occurred through the willful act of a third party, the defendants could not be held liable therefor." [82]

Depredations by boys committed at intervals would be

attendants, he was not responsible if the attendants failed to rescue the intestate.

[81] *Fairbanks* v. *Montreal St. Ry. Co.* (Can.), 31 D. L. R. 728.

See generally on accidents: *Cousineau* v. *Muskegon* (1906), 145 Mich. 314; 108 N. W. 720; *Phillips* v. *Wisconsin State* (1884), 60 Wisconsin, 401; 19 N. W. 377; *Higgins* v. *Franklin Co.* (1906), 100 Maine, 565; 62 Atl. 708; *Currier* v. *Boston Music Hall* (1888), 135 Mass. 414; *Hart* v. *Wash. Park* (1895), 157 Ill. 9; 41 N. E. 620; *Scott* v. *University of Mich.* (1908), 152 Mich. 684; 116 N. W. 624; *Selinas* v. *Vermont State* (1888), 60 Vt. 249; 15 Atl. 117; *Stair* v. *Kane* (1907), 156 Fed. (C. C. A.) 100; *Decatur* v. *Porter* (1907), 137 Ill. App. 448; *George* v. *Univ. of Minn.* (1909), 107 Minn. 424; 120 N. W. 750.

[82] *Meeker* v. *Smith* (1903), 84 A. D. (N. Y.) 111; 81 N. Y. Supp. 1067. Plaintiff's intestate while visiting defendant's amusement park was killed by the falling of a jack, a part of an apparatus used in defendant's park. The accident occurred through the willful act of a stranger.

See also: *Williams* v. *Mineral C. P. A.* (1905), 128 Iowa, 32; 102 N. W. 783; *Cremore* v. *Huber* (1897), 18 A. D. (N. Y.) 231; 45 N. Y. Supp. 947.

something to put the proprietor on his guard, and he would be bound to guard against future acts of a like nature; but if no prior acts had occurred, he would not be liable for the injury sustained on this occasion.[83]

Section 102.—Assault.

The proprietor of a theatre owes his patron the duty of protecting him against assault, both of the theatre employes and strangers. "Common carriers, inn-keepers, merchants, managers of theatres and others who invite the public to become their patrons and guests, and thus submit personal safety and comfort to their keeping, owe a more special duty to those who may accept such invitation. Such patrons and guests have a right to ask that they shall be protected from injury while present on such invitation and particularly that they shall not suffer wrong from the agents and servants of those who invited them."[84] The proprietor is in duty bound to maintain

[83] *Flanagan* v. *Goldberg* (1910), 137 A. D. (N. Y.) 92; 122 N. Y. Supp. 205. Plaintiff attended a motion-picture show and during the performance a board fell upon her.

"If defendants negligently so placed the board that it fell and did the injury, they are liable. They would not be liable for an injury caused by a board thrown into the hall, unless the facts show that they had knowledge, actual or constructive, that the boys were committing depredations, or had done so, and thereupon negligently failed to protect those invited to the entertainment."

[84] *Dickson* v. *Waldron* (1893), 135 Ind. 507; 34 N. E. 506; 35 N. E. 1. The court held that in such case, where the duty of the servant was to preserve order in the theatre and to remove offensive patrons, the servant was of necessity the judge whether the conduct of the patron was such as to require his removal and that the master was liable where the

order and quiet during performances in the theatre and may request patrons to be quiet, but this should be done politely and without any undue humiliation.[85]

While the proprietor as a general rule is not responsible for the act of other patrons [86] he is nevertheless liable for such acts when committed through his agency or where he has had reason to anticipate such acts and could have taken measures to prevent them.[87] He is likewise an-

servant erred, and that this rule applied to a special policeman engaged by the theatre proprietor.

Oakland v. *Bingham* (1892), 4 Ind. App. 545; 31 N. E. 383. One conducting an amusement park was held liable for injuries sustained by a patron through an assault made by a gatekeeper.

Fowler v. *Holmes* (1889), 3 N. Y. Supp. 816. A person collecting tickets at entrance to defendant's theatre assaulted plaintiff who attempted to enter, having a ticket of admission. *Held* that the trial court properly submitted the question to the jury whether defendant's ticket taker was acting within the scope of his employment at the time he assaulted plaintiff.

See also: *Epstein* v. *Gordon* (1909), 114 N. Y. Supp. 438; *Kessler* v. *Deutsch* (1904), 44 Misc. (N. Y.) 209; 88 N. Y. Supp. 846.

[85] *Russo* v. *Orpheum Theatre* (1914), 66 So. (La.) 385.

[86] *Cremore* v. *Huber* (1897), 18 A. D. (N. Y.) 231; 45 N. Y. Supp. 947.

[87] *Mastad* v. *Swedish Brethren* (1901), 83 Minn. 40; 85 N. W. 913. A person managing and controlling a public place of amusement, to which he invites the public, on payment of an admission fee to attend, and at which place he sells to his customers and patrons intoxicating liquors, and who sells such liquors to one in attendance at such place, and thereby renders him drunk and disorderly, well knowing that when in that condition he is likely to commit assaults upon others without cause or provocation is bound to exercise reasonable care to protect his other customers and patrons from such assaults and insults, and for a failure to do so is liable in damages at the suit of one assaulted and injured.

See: *Indianapolis* v. *Dawson*

swerable for the insulting and abusive language of the performers.[88]

Colored people may not be ejected from the theatre [89] and for an assault committed by the servants of the proprietor, he is liable.

A patron who occupies a seat to which he is not entitled may be asked to give it up, and if he refuses the usher or other servant may use such reasonable degree of force as will accomplish the purpose.[90] But he must

(1903), 31 Ind. App. 605; 68 N. E. 909.

[88] *Interstate Am. Co.* v. *Martin* (1913), 8 Ala. App. 481; 62 So. 404. The defendant, the proprietor of a theatre, was held liable in damages to plaintiff, a patron of the theatre, for the act of a performer in addressing to plaintiff insulting and defamatory language.

The court said: "It is not to be doubted that one of those duties is to accord to the ticket holder civil treatment while he is exercising the privilege for which he has contracted. This duty is one that may be breached by the proprietor himself or by mistreatment at the hands of an employe while acting within the scope or range of his employment, and the mistreatment may consist in the use of uncivil and offensive language addressed to or spoken about the ticket holder."

[89] *Drew* v. *Peer* (1880), 93 Pa. 234. Defendant held liable for ejecting a colored man and his wife from his theatre.

Indianapolis v. *Dawson* (1903), 31 Ind. App. 605; 68 N. E. 909. Defendant, a street railway company, having knowledge of a conspiracy to attack all colored persons who attended at its amusement park, which it owned, transported a negro to its park. It was held liable for injuries sustained by plaintiff because of an assault at the park.

[90] *Hyde* v. *Toronto Theatre* (Can.), 17 O. W. R. 380. The usher may use reasonable force in ejecting from the theatre one whose ticket does not entitle him to that particular seat.

See also: *MacGowan* v. *Duff* (1887), 14 Daly (N. Y.), 315; *Younger* v. *Judah* (1892), 111 Mo. 303; *Lewis* v. *Arnold* (Eng.) (1830), 4 C. and P. 354.

be given a reasonable opportunity to explain,[91] and if it turns out that the proprietor has made the mistake, the patron may recover punitive as well as compensatory damages.[92]

Commonwealth v. *Powell* (1873), 10 Phila. (Pa.) 180. "A visitor at a theatre or other place of amusement is entitled to a seat. This right to some extent depends upon the character of his ticket. If for a reserved seat, he has a right to that particular seat. If not reserved, then to any one he may find unoccupied, and which had not previously been sold to another. I instructed the jury that if the prosecutor selected a seat in that portion of the building called for by his ticket, and that there was nothing upon the said seat to indicate that it was 'taken', and no notice had in fact been given prosecutor prior thereto that it had been sold to someone else, he had a right to occupy it, and the act of the defendant in ejecting him therefrom was an assault and battery. Subsequent reflection has satisfied me that it is not so much a question of notice, as of whether there had been an actual bona fide sale of that particular seat to a third party. If so, no neglect on the part of the proprietor of the museum in marking said seat as 'taken' could give the prosecutor a right to that which someone else had previously bought and paid for. . . ."

[91] *Armstrong* v. *Stair* (1914), 217 Mass. 534; 105 N. E. 442. Plaintiff purchased a balcony ticket. He gave it to the usher who left him standing, and plaintiff then occupied the last seat. Later, when asked for his check he tried to account for its absence, and a special officer was sent for. The latter took him into custody and brought him to a police station where he was forced to remain all night. *Held* that the defendants, including the managers of the theatre, were liable for assault, false imprisonment and malicious prosecution.

See in this connection: *Weiss* v. *Skinner* (1915), 178 S. W. (Tex.) 34. For wrongful ejection from the theatre because of the purchase of a ticket for another performance than that attended, the manager of the theatre was held not liable in contract, because he was not a party thereto, nor in tort, for he did not eject plaintiff.

[92] *Weber-Stair* v. *Fisher* (1909),

The patron also owes a duty to the proprietor to conduct himself in a peaceable and orderly manner, to retain the seat sold to him and to refrain from causing any riot or disturbance.[93] He cannot hold the proprietor liable where he has violated that duty.

119 S. W. (Ky.) 195. Plaintiff received evening tickets instead of tickets for a matinee by a mistake of the theatre employe. *Held* that he was entitled to punitive damages.

[93] *Lewis* v. *Arnold* (Eng.) (1830), 4 C. and P. 354. Action for assault and false imprisonment. Plaintiff had bought a ticket for the pit. There being standing room only, he attempted to climb into a box. From this he was ejected and escorted out of the theatre. An altercation arose, and plaintiff was arrested. Chief Justice Tindall said: "Even if this plaintiff had been informed that there was room in the pit of this theatre when there was not, which in this evidence is matter of doubt, he had still no right to go into this private box. His proper course, if there was not room, was to go out of the theatre and demand the return of his money. . . . Mr. Arnold has therefore a right to turn the plaintiff out of the private box, using no more force than was necessary."

In this case plaintiff was accompanied by two other people, and in the altercation that took place outside of the theatre one of these people struck a blow. *Held* that even if plaintiff was passive, all three were engaged in a common purpose, and he was therefore nonsuited.

Clifford v. *Brandon* (Eng.) (1810), 2 Camp. 358. Action for assault and false imprisonment. Plaintiff had entered Covent Garden during a disturbance in the audience due to the raise in prices of the seats. On going out, although not actively taking part in the rioting, he was arrested. Subsequently he was discharged and on this action, Chief Justice Mansfield said: "The jury will consider whether Mr. Clifford was an instigator of the riot, which one of his witnesses has represented as resembling a quarrel among a thousand drunken sailors. The law is that if any person encourages or promotes, or takes part in riots, whether by words, signs or gestures, or by wearing the badge or ensign

The rule as to punitive damages is that where the assault was wanton or vicious, such damages are recoverable. Proof of knowledge of viciousness of the servant has been held necessary in one state and not necessary in another.[94] It is always for the jury to pass on the question whether the manager himself instigated the assault,[95] and where the reason assigned for the ejectment was that the patron was drunk and disorderly, evidence showing that on prior occasions he was not drunk and disorderly is inadmissible.[96]

Section 103.—Who is liable.

The general rule is that the proprietors of parks, fairs and amusement grounds are liable for injuries sustained because of the negligence of their concessionaires,[97]

of the rioters, he is himself to be considered a rioter. . . ."

See: *Russo* v. *Orpheum Theatre* (1914), 66 So. (La.) 385; *Gregory* v. *Brunswick* (Eng.) (1843), 6 Man. & G. 205.

[94] *Walsh* v. *Hyde & Behman Amuse. Co.* (1906), 113 A. D. (N. Y.) 42; 98 N. Y. Supp. 960. Plaintiff, a ticket holder, was ejected from defendant's theatre and was badly beaten and bruised. Verdict granting specified amount for compensatory damages and an additional amount for punitive damages was modified to the extent of disallowing the sum awarded as punitive damages upon the ground that no proof had been adduced showing knowledge on defendant's part of viciousness of his servants.

But see: *Weber-Stair* v. *Fisher* (1909), 119 S. W. (Ky.) 195, where punitive damages were allowed.

[95] *Metts* v. *Charleston Theatre* (1916), 89 S. E. (S. C.) 389.

[96] *Wells Am. Co.* v. *Means* (1911), 56 So. (Ala.) 594.

[97] *Babicz* v. *Riverview Sharpshooters* (1911), 161 Ill. App. 356; aff'd 256 Ill. 24; 99 N. E. 860. A general admission was charged to each person entering the park. *Held* that proprietor of park was

although in one or two states it has been held otherwise.[98] The test of liability seems to be a participation in the

liable for injuries sustained while on concessionaire's apparatus.

Dietze v. *Riverview Park* (1913), 181 Ill. App. 357.

Smith v. *Cumberland Soc.* (1913), 163 N. C. 346; 79 S. E. 632. Plaintiff, while attending a fair, was requested to take hold of the rope of a balloon. On doing so, his foot was caught and he was carried up. Nonsuit was reversed, as there was sufficient evidence to have gone to the jury.

Turgeon v. *Connecticut Co.* (1911), 84 Conn. 538; 80 Atl. 714. This case holds that it makes no difference whether an admission fee is charged with respect to the liability of a proprietor of an amusement park where the patron is injured while on a device operated by a concessionaire. The court holds that the defendant is not relieved from his obligation because the device is run by an independent contractor and cites the following cases in support of its position: Note to *Hollis* v. *Kansas City etc. Assoc.* (1907), 14 L. R. A. (N. S.) 284; 205 Mo. 508; 103 S. W. 32; *Thornton* v. *Agricultural Society* (1902), 97 Me. 108; 53 Atl. 979; *Sebeck* v. *Plattdeutsche Volkbest* (1900), 64 N. J. L. 624; 46 Atl. 631; *Richmond etc. Ry. Co.* v. *Moore* (1897), 94 Va. 493; 27 S. E. 70; *Texas State Fair* v. *Brittain* (1902), 118 Fed. (C. C. A.) 713; *Conradt* v. *Clauve* (1883), 93 Ind. 476; *Thompson* v. *Lowell etc. Co.* (1898), 170 Mass. 577; 49 N. E. 913; *Blakeley* v. *White Star Line* (1908), 154 Mich. 635; 118 N. W. 482; *Dunn* v. *Agricultural Society* (1888), 46 Ohio St. 93; 18 N. E. 496; *Mastad* v. *Swedish Brethren* (1901), 83 Minn. 40; 85 N. W. 913; *Fox* v. *Buffalo Park* (1897), 21 A. D. (N. Y.) 321; 47 N. Y. Supp. 788; *Brown* v. *Batcheller* (1908), 29 R. I. 116; 69 Atl. 293; 2 Cooley on Torts (3d Ed.), p. 1259.

[98] *Knottnerus* v. *North Park* (1892), 93 Mich. 348; 53 N. W. 529. Plaintiff was injured while riding on a switch-back railway operated by owner at defendant's pleasure resort. The owner of the switch-back railway was a concessionaire of defendant. Defendant was held not liable.

Smith v. *Benick* (1898), 87 Md. 610; 41 Atl. 56. A balloonist was engaged by defendant to make ascensions in defendant's park. The balloonist furnished

profits derived from the payment of admission and other sources, and a reservation of some rights in the premises, even though leased away.[99] But where the proprietor parts with all control he is not liable.[100] Even where the

his own help. One of the poles used in connection with the ascensions fell and caused an injury to plaintiff. The balloonist was a competent person. *Held* that the balloonist was an independent contractor and that defendant having used care in engaging him, was not liable for injuries sustained by plaintiff through an act of the independent contractor. There was a dissenting opinion holding that defendant should have used sufficient care to have foreseen such an accident.

[99] *Stickel* v. *Riverview Sharpshooters* (1910), 159 Ill. App. 110. Where the proprietor of an amusement resort receives a share of the receipts of one of his concessionaires he is liable for injuries sustained by a patron on the structure or apparatus of the concessionaire.

Wichita Falls Co. v. *Adams* (1912), 146 S. W. (Tex.) 271. An amusement park pavilion was owned by a railroad. Plaintiff's son was injured therein. *Held* that the company was liable for while it had leased away some rights therein, it has also reserved some, and so was chargeable with negligence.

[100] *McCain* v. *Majestic Bldg.* (1908), 120 La. 306; 45 So. 258. The owner of a theatre held not liable for injury caused to one who fell on the sidewalk in front of it, as he was no longer in control, but had leased the theatre away.

Mirsky v. *Adler* (1910), 123 N. Y. Supp. 816. Where the defendant established that he had leased the theatre to some third party reserving solely the right to use it on Sundays and where the evidence also showed that even on Sundays the defendants had leased it to other persons; *Held* that defendant was not in control of the theatre and was not liable for injuries sustained by a patron while on the premises on a Sunday.

See: *Edwards* v. *N. Y. & H. R. R.* (1885), 98 N. Y. 245; *Cole* v. *Rome Sav. Bank* (1916), 96 Misc. (N. Y.) 188; 161 N. Y. Supp. 115.

lessee is holding over after the term of his lease, the proprietor is nevertheless liable.[101]

One who is not the proprietor, but is in charge of grounds where exhibitions are given, participates in the distribution of advertising matter, and derives a share of the proceeds taken in from the use of appliances upon which the plaintiff was injured, is liable.[102]

It occasionally happens that a member of the company playing in a theatre is injured by a stage-hand. The rule here is that although the theatre was leased for a percentage of the gross receipts, such stage-hand, hired and paid by the proprietor, while temporarily under the control of the company, is actually the servant of the proprietor, and the latter is liable for his tortious acts.[103]

[101] *Oxford* v. *Leathe* (1896), 165 Mass. 254; 43 N. E. 92. Defendant leased his building for four days for use in theatrical entertainments. He had charge of box office until specific sum was received by him and also furnished the lights. He was held liable for injuries sustained by plaintiff by reason of the falling of a platform at a time when the lessee was holding over, upon the same terms, after the expiration of the original term.

[102] *Hollis* v. *Kansas City* (1907), 205 Mo. 508; 103 S. W. 32. One having general charge of grounds where exhibitions are given, participates in distribution of advertising matter and derives share of proceeds taken in from use of appliance upon which plaintiff was injured is liable.

See also: *Stickel* v. *Riverview Sharpshooters* (1910), 159 Ill. App. 110; *Wichita Falls Co.* v. *Adam* (1912), 146 S. W. (Tex.) 271.

[103] *Dow* v. *Henderson* (1895), 85 Hun (N. Y.), 300; 32 N. Y. Supp. 953. Plaintiff, while acting as directress for the Julia Marlowe company, was injured by the negligent act of a stage-hand, who was under the general employ of the defendant. The fact that for a percentage of the receipts the defendant had agreed

On the other hand, the proprietor of the theatre is not liable for the torts of the company's own employes even though the company is playing under a like arrangement of a percentage of the gross receipts.[104]

The lessees of a theatre were held liable for an assault committed by an usher in their employ, on the theory that while they were not joint tort-feasors they were employers, and as long as the usher was acting within the scope of his duty, they were responsible for his acts.[105]

Section 104.—Property lost in theatre.

The theatre proprietor is no insurer of the property of his patrons, where the same has not been committed to his care especially. And where so committed he can only be held liable for his negligence.[106]

to furnish to the company the stage, scenery, and stage-hands, did not alter his liability. They were still his servants. *Held* liable.

[104] *Thomas* v. *Springer* (1909), 134 A. D. (N. Y.) 640; 119 N. Y. Supp. 460. Although the theatre proprietor retained possession and control of the house and sold the tickets of admission he was held not estopped from denying that the employes of the theatrical company were his servants.

[105] *Epstein* v. *Gordon* (1909), 114 N. Y. Supp. 438. The usher of a theatre took hold of plaintiff's coat, called him vile names, struck him, arrested him, and appeared against him in court, where plaintiff was discharged. There was no justification.

Held that the question presented for the jury was whether the usher was acting within the scope of his duty.

"It is true that there is no proof tending to show that the defendants, (the lessees) or either of them, in any way personally participated in the misconduct complained of, and neither of them can be held liable as joint tort-feasors; *but this fact does not relieve them from their liability as employers of the usher.*"

[106] *Pattison* v. *Hammerstein* (1896), 17 Misc. (N. Y.) 375; 39

N. Y. Supp. 1039. "The manager of a theatre, in the absence of a special agreement, is not, unlike an innkeeper and common carrier of goods, upon which classes the common law, from motives of public policy then prevailing imposed an extraordinary liability, an insurer of his patron's property though the property may consist of apparel such as is necessarily or usually worn by the patrons and laid aside by them while attending the play. His liability is, at most, that of every person except innkeepers and common carriers of goods."

It was also held that the burden was on the plaintiff to show negligence on the part of the defendant.

See generally on this proposition the following non-theatrical cases: *Barnes* v. *Stern Bros.* (1915), 89 Misc. (N. Y.) 385; 151 N. Y. Supp. 887; *Wentworth* v. *Riggs* (1914), 159 A. D. (N. Y.) 899; 143 N. Y. Supp. 955; *McAllister* v. *Simon* (1899), 27 Misc. (N. Y.) 214; 57 N. Y. Supp. 733; *Wamser* v. *Browning King* (1907), 187 N. Y. 87; 79 N. E. 861; *Bunnell* v. *Stern* (1890), 122 N. Y. 539; 25 N. E. 910; *Woodruff* v. *Painter* (1892), 150 Pa. 91; 24 Atl. 621; *Bradner* v. *Mullen* (1899), 27 Misc. (N. Y.) 479; 59 N. Y. Supp. 178; *Appleton* v. *Welch* (1897), 20 Misc. (N. Y.) 343; 45 N. Y. Supp. 751; *Buttman* v. *Dennett* (1894), 9 Misc. (N. Y.) 462; 30 N. Y. Supp. 247; *Bird* v. *Everhard* (1893), 4 Misc. (N. Y.) 104; 23 N. Y. Supp. 1008; *Delmour* v. *Forsythe* (1911), 128 N. Y. Supp. 649; *Montgomery* v. *Ladjing* (1899), 30 Misc. (N. Y.) 92; 61 N. Y. Supp. 840; *Powers* v. *O'Neill* (1895), 89 Hun (N. Y.), 129; 34 N. Y. Supp. 1007.

CHAPTER VIII

THE PUBLIC (CONTINUED)

License

SEC. 105. What is "Motion picture," "Theatrical performance," "Theatre."
106. Necessity for license.
107. Power to license discretionary—Revocation.
108. Extent of discretionary power.
109. Right to license on condition.

Section 105.—What is "Motion picture," "Theatrical performance," "Theatre."

Just what constitutes each particular form of theatrical entertainment cannot be stated with any degree of finality. Even as between the several kinds of pictures, such as motion-pictures and stereopticons, the statutes of some states have differentiated.[1] And it has been a mooted question whether a motion picture exhibition given in conjunction with some other business comes within the letter and spirit of statutes regulating motion pictures generally.[2]

[1] *Block* v. *City of Chicago* (1909), 239 Ill. 251; 87 N. E. 1011. An ordinance which referred only to motion-picture licenses, and not to stereopticon exhibitions was held constitutional.

[2] *Boisseau* v. *Scola Am. Co.* (Can.) (1913), 22 Can. Cr. Cas. 31; *Edward* v. *McClellan* (1909), 118 N. Y. Supp. 181; *Weistblatt* v. *Bingham* (1908), 58 Misc. (N. Y.) 328; 109 N. Y. Supp.

However, there is no longer any uncertainty as to the status of such an entertainment. In the early case of *Edison* v. *Lubin* [3] a motion picture was held to be for purposes of copyright merely a series of photographs. Places where they were exhibited were not required to be licensed. Later on, with their development and growing popularity, licensing restrictions became the rule in all the states. *Harper* v. *Kalem*,[4] which for the purpose of copyright stamped the exhibition as a dramatic entertainment, brought it within the then existing statutes regulating theatrical entertainments, and really made it unnecessary and superfluous to pass special restrictions.

A motion picture is to all intents and purposes a theatrical or dramatic exhibition,[5] and decisions which seek to draw a distinction between it and the spoken drama are compelled to resort to quibbling.[6] A statute which requires a license for a dramatic exhibition or entertainment requires a license, unless expressly excepted, for a motion picture.

545; *Economopoulos* v. *Bingham* (1907), 109 N. Y. Supp. 728; *Commonwealth* v. *Spiers* (1912), 51 Pa. Super. Ct. 59.

[3] *Edison* v. *Lubin* (1903), 122 Fed. (C. C. A.) 240.

[4] *Kalem* v. *Harper* (1911), 222 U. S. 55; 32 Sup. Ct. 20.

[5] *Matter of City of New York* (*re Hammerstein*) (1907), 57 Misc. (N. Y.) 52; 108 N. Y. Supp. 197. *Held* that Section 1481 of the Greater New York Charter forbids all performances of any character in a place of public amusement on Sunday. That the phrase "*any other entertainment of the stage*" is broad enough to include any public exhibition whatsoever given upon the stage.

[6] *Edwards* v. *McClellan* (1909), 118 N. Y. Supp. 181. It was held that a motion-picture exhibition was not a "public show" within the meaning of a Sunday statute.

The courts have been greatly divided on what constitutes a "theatrical performance," and have included in that category and demanded a license of an orchestral concert given on a raised dais,[7] a performance consisting of the singing of a song at a piano,[8] a pantomime,[9] motion pictures shown in an ice-cream saloon,[10] motion pictures

[7] *Mayor etc. of New York City* v. *Eden Musee* (1886), 102 N. Y. 593; 8 N. E. 40.

[8] *Russell* v. *Smith* (Eng.) (1848), 12 Q. B. 217; 17 L. J. Q. B. 225; 12 Jur. 723. The singing of a song at a piano although without scenery or costume was held to be a "dramatic piece."

It was also held that the hall in which the song was sung was a place of dramatic entertainment. Under this decision *semble* that any place where a dramatic piece is performed is a place of dramatic entertainment.

See also: *Clark* v. *Bishop* (Eng.) (1872), 25 L. T. 908.

[9] *Day* v. *Simpson* (Eng.) (1865), 18 C. B. N. S. 680. A play in which but two persons appear on the stage and the reflection of other persons is thrown upon a mirror in back of the stage in such a manner as to deceive the audience in believing them to actually appear is an "entertainment of the stage" and the owner of the house, who had procured no license for the same, was held guilty.

[10] *Weistblatt* v. *Bingham* (1908), 58 Misc. (N. Y.) 328; 109 N. Y. Supp. 545. Plaintiff operated an ice-cream saloon and to attract customers gave moving picture exhibitions. No admission fee was charged. *Held* that although no admission fee was charged it was a public performance, a "common show" within the contemplation of the statute and an illegal public performance unless the license issued to "common shows" was secured.

To the same effect see: *Economopoulos* v. *Bingham* (1907), 109 N. Y. Supp. 728.

"I do not think the charging of an admission fee or the failure to charge a fee changes the situation: but if it has any bearing, the affidavits show that the plaintiff collects admission by an extra charge on soda water and the like sold to people who are permitted to view the exhibition and listen to the music."

fitted up with a vaudeville stage,[11] a circus,[12] an opera,[13] horse-racing,[14] a medical museum,[15] a booth,[16] a bowling alley,[17] and an aquarium.[18]

See also: *Herbert* v. *Shanley*, 242 U. S. 591; 37 Sup. Ct. 232.

[11] *Commonwealth* v. *Donnelly* (1912), 51 Pa. Super. Ct. 61. Where the building is fitted up with a stage and other accessories for theatrical productions, and where moving picture exhibitions are alternated with performances of artists and vocal entertainment, the theatre is subject to the tax required of theatrical entertainments.

[12] *State* v. *Morris* (1910), 76 Atl. (Del.) 479. Under a statute providing that no person shall be engaged in exhibiting circuses and further that all buildings wherein "*theatrical*" performances were given shall be deemed a circus within the meaning of the statute it was held that the giving of motion picture exhibitions constituted a theatrical performance.

[13] *Bell* v. *Mahn* (1888), 121 Pa. St. 225; 15 Atl. 523. "The opera is essentially and in every point of view a dramatic composition and its representations a dramatic exhibition. . . . It may be conceded that music is in some sense an essential element in the opera; in this respect it is distinguished from the spoken drama, but the fundamental and really essential element of both is action."

[14] *Webber* v. *Chicago* (1892), 50 Ill. App. 110. "There is no more uncertainty as to horse racing in Garfield Park being an exhibition within an enclosure than as to selling whiskey in a bar room being such a business as requires a dram shop license."

[15] *People* v. *Kennedy* (1913), 141 N. W. (Mich.) 887.

[16] *Fredericks* v. *Payne* (Eng.) (1862), 1 H. and C. 584. A booth which has been erected temporarily is a "place" within the meaning of Section Eleven of the Theatres Act of 1843. [See *Tarling* v. *Fredericks* (Eng.) (1873), 21 W. R. 785 for that section.]

See also: *Russell* v. *Smith* (Eng.) (1848), 12 Q. B. 217; 17 L. J. Q. B. 225; 12 Jur. 723; *Clark* v. *Bishop* (Eng.) (1872), 25 L. T. 908.

[17] *Johnson* v. *Humphrey Pop-Corn Co.* (1902), 24 Ohio Cir. Ct. 135. "Places of accommodation and amusement" include a bowling-alley.

[18] *Warner* v. *Brighton Aquarium* (Eng.) (1875), L. R. 10 Exch.

On the other hand, a cabaret "was held not to be an exhibition.[19] In view of the decision of the United States Supreme Court in *Herbert* v. *Shanley* [20] holding that the public performances of songs in cabarets and hotels are given for "profit," the Martin case will probably not

291; *Terry* v. *Brighton Aquarium* (Eng.) (1875), L. R. 10 Q. B. 306.

On the question whether the proprietor of a skating rink where music is played is liable if he does not have a license, see: *Reg* v. *Tucker* (Eng.) (1877), L. R. 2 Q. B. D. 417.

See also: *People* v. *King* (1886), 42 Hun. (N. Y.), 186; aff'd 110 N. Y. 418; 18 N. E. 245.

See also *as to whether skating is dancing, and whether the public must actually participate. Marks* v. *Benjamin* (Eng.) (1839), 5 M. & W. 565.

[19] *People* v. *Martin* (1912), 137 N. Y. Supp. 677. A "cabaret," consisting of dancing and singing, accompanied by music from an orchestra, was held not to be a "public exhibition" within the contemplation of a statute making it a misdemeanor to conduct a public exhibition without a license, upon the ground that the entertainment constituted a gratuitous contribution by the management, no admission having been charged.

The court then cites the following cases in support of this proposition: *Mayor etc. of New York City* v. *Eden Musee* (1886), 102 N. Y. 593; 8 N. E. 40; *People* v. *Campbell* (1900), 51 A. D. (N. Y.) 565; 65 N. Y. Supp. 114; *People* v. *Royal* (1898), 23 A. D. (N. Y.) 258; 48 N. Y. Supp. 742; *Society* v. *Neusbach* (1883), 16 Wkly. Dig. (N. Y.) 349; *Matter of Allen* (1901), 34 Misc. (N. Y.) 698; 70 N. Y. Supp. 1017.

See *People* v. *Wacke* (1912), 77 Misc. (N. Y.) 196; 137 N. Y. Supp. 652 where motion pictures were shown in a hotel and *People* v. *Keller* (1916), 96 Misc. (N. Y.) 328; where a cabaret performance was given.

See also: *Brearley* v. *Morley* (Eng.) (1899), 2 Q. B. 121; where a public house was held not to require a license where the piano was played by guests.

[20] *Herbert* v. *Shanley* (1917), 242 U. S. 591; 37 Sup. Ct. 232; *Church* v. *Hilliard* (1917), 242 U. S. 591; 37 Sup. Ct. 232.

stand.[21] A motion picture theatre having no stage, was likewise held exempt from obtaining a license; [22] so too, a saloon having a piano in a balcony,[23] exhibitions given to aid the sale of a book,[24] a private subscription

[21] See in this connection: *Gregory* v. *Tavernor* (Eng.) (1833), 6 C. & P. 280; *Hall* v. *Green* (Eng.) (1853), 9 Exch. 247; *Quaglieni* v. *Matthews* (Eng.) (1865), 6 B. & S.. 474; *Syers* v. *Conquest* (Eng.) (1873), 37 J. P. 342; *Fay* v. *Bignell* (Eng.) (1883), Cab. & El. 112.

[22] *Commonwealth* v. *Spiers* (1912), 51 Pa. Super. Ct. 59. A moving picture theatre cannot be taxed as a theatrical or operatic entertainment where it appears that the place is not equipped with any stage or facilities for vaudeville, and the entertainment consists only of moving pictures and illustrated songs.

But where the moving picture exhibitions are alternated with performances by artists and the building is fitted up with a stage and other theatrical accessories the building comes under the Act providing for the licensing of theatres and payment of tax required. *Commonwealth* v. *Donelly* (1912), 51 Pa. Super. Ct. 61.

[23] *People* v. *Campbell* (1900), 51 A. D. (N. Y.) 565; 65 N. Y. Supp. 114. Defendant was the proprietor of a liquor saloon and had paid the tax which authorized him to sell liquor, but had no concert license. On a balcony was a piano which was played during the evening. *Held* that this did not constitute a theatrical performance.

Brearley v. *Morley* (Eng.) (1899), 2 Q. B. 121. A music license was not required by a licensed victualler who kept a piano in his smoking room for his customers to play upon.

[24] *People* v. *Royal* (1898), 23 A. D. (N. Y.) 258; 48 N. Y. Supp. 742. Defendant leased a store and had an assistant exhibit various gambling devices, all being done to induce the sale of his book on gambling. *Held* that as the sale of the book was perfectly lawful, he had a right to give such exhibitions.

"As long as he conducts such a business, using his exhibitions, illustrations and explanations to accomplish that end, we think he offends no law and does not violate this ordinance."

dance,[25] where music and dancing were a secondary feature,[26] an amateur dramatic performance [27] and public concerts given by a music school.[28] An exhibition of actors and motion pictures did not require a motion picture li-

[25] *Bellis* v. *Burghall* (Eng.) (1788), 2 Esp. 722. Where a dancing master invited people to his house for dances by subscription. *Held* that as the public were not admitted indiscriminately, no dance license was required.

See also: *Marks* v. *Benjamin* (Eng.) (1839), 5 M. & W. 565.

But see *Archer* v. *Willingrice* (Eng.) (1802), 4 Esp. 185. Where though the admission fee for the dancing was paid to one who taught the dances and not to the proprietor, he was required nevertheless to obtain a license.

See also: *Shutt* v. *Lewis* (Eng.) (1804), 5 Esp. 128; *Gregory* v. *Tuffs* (Eng.) (1833), 6 C. & P. 271; *Gregory* v. *Tavernor* (Eng.) (1833), 6 C. & P. 280.

[26] *Guaglieni* v. *Matthews* (Eng.), 34 L. J. M. C. 116. Where the music and dancing are not the chief business of the house but merely a secondary feature, a license will not be required.

But see *Hall* v. *Green* (Eng.) (1853), 9 Ex. 247.

[27] *Oellers* v. *Horn* (1897), 3 Pa. Sup. Ct. 537. Performances given by amateurs by an organization of university undergraduates, are not theatrical performances within the purview of the statute, and no license need be procured.

Duck v. *Bates* (Eng.) (1884), 13 Q. B. D. 843. A performance given by an amateur dramatic society in a hospital, admission to which was by free ticket issued to friends of the performers, was held not to be a public performance.

[28] *Markham* v. *Southern Conservatory of Music* (1902), 130 N. C. 276; 41 S. E. 531. A school for musical instruction owned a hall wherein as an incident of its instruction, it gave concerts. Distinguished specialists were contracted with to give performances to which the pupils and general public were admitted upon the payment of an admission fee. The concerts were run at a loss, the purpose of selling tickets of admission being solely to reduce in part the loss sustained by the institution. *Held* that the school was not liable for an opera house tax.

cense,[29] and a license given for musical concerts or dances did not cover or authorize the license to give stage plays.[30]

A theatre is an institution sui generis. It is not a nuisance,[31] nor a bawdy house,[32] nor a

[29] *Boisseau* v. *Scola Amuse. Co.* (Can.) (1913), 22 Can. Cr. Cas. 31; Statute 3 Geo. V. (Que.), ch. 36 (R. S. Q. 1301d) (1913), construed. *Held* that a theatre at which a number of actors appeared was not subject to the provincial tax placed upon moving picture halls although the exhibition of moving pictures constituted almost half of the performance.

[30] *Levy* v. *Yates* (Eng.) (1838), 8 A. & E. 129; 3 Nev. & P. (Q. B.) 249.

See generally the following English cases: *Fredericks* v. *Howie* (1862), 1 H. & C. 381; *Shelley* v. *Bethell* (1883), 12 Q. B. D. 11; *Marks* v. *Benjamin* (1839), 5 M. & W. 565; *R.* v. *Strugnell* (1865), L. R. 1 Q. B. 93; *Day* v. *Simpson* (1865), 18 C. B. (N. S.) 680; *Calcraft* v. *West* (1845), 2 Jo. & Lat. 123; *Gregory* v. *Tuffs* (1833), 6 C. & P. 271; *Bellis* v. *Beale* (1797), 2 Esp. 592; *Royal Albert Hall* v. *London Council* (1911), 27 T. L. R. 362.

[31] *City of Indianapolis* v. *Miller* (1907), 168 Ind. 285; 80 N. E. 626; *City of Chicago* v. *Weber* (1910), 248 Ill. 304; 92 N. E. 859; *Ex parte Whitwell* (1893), 98 Cal. 73; 32 Pac. 870; *Barber* v. *Penley* (Eng.) (1893), 2 Ch. 447; *Bellamy* v. *Wells* (Eng.) (1890), 63 L. T. N. S. 635; 1 Hawkins P. C. (8th Ed.) 693.

For detailed discussion of this subject see Section 80.

[32] *Ex Parte Bell* (1893), 32 Tex. Crim. App. 308. The City charter of Houston authorized the City to pass ordinances prohibiting and punishing keepers and inmates of bawdy houses and variety shows. In pursuance thereof the city passed an ordinance declaring that any variety theatre or show where there was music, dancing or singing and where intoxicating liquors were sold to the patrons, should be regarded as a bawdy house. Ordinance held invalid.

But see: *R.* v. *Wolfe* (Eng.) (1849), 13 J. P. 428; *Green* v. *Botheroyd* (Eng.) (1828), 3 C. & P. 471. Under the Disorderly Houses Act of 1751, (25 Geo. 2, ch. 36) s. 2, a music or dance

dwelling-house,[33] nor a place where valuable goods are stored.[34]

It has also been held that the term "theatre" in a statute with respect to the securing of licenses for the giving of theatrical performances, referred not to the building but the performance.[35]

Section 106.—Necessity for license.

It is well settled that statutes requiring the securing of a license as a condition to build or operate a theatre, motion picture exhibition or other form of public entertainment are constitutional.[36] And the statute may im-

hall which did not obtain a license was considered a disorderly house.

See also: *Patrick* v. *Wood* (Eng.) (1905), 4 Adam, 648.

[33] *Paulton* v. *Keith* (1901), 23 R. I. 164; 49 Atl. 635.

[34] *Lee* v. *State* (1876), 56 Ga. 478. "The word theatre does not, ex vi termini import that it is a place where valuable goods are stored." The court then held that an indictment which did not allege that valuable goods were contained therein was bad.

[35] *Commonwealth* v. *Keeler* (1850), 3 Pa. Dist. 158.

[36] *Commonwealth* v. *McGann* (1913), 213 Mass. 213; 100 N. E. 355. Upholds the statutes regulating the licensing of motion-picture theatres.

"The Liberty of the Press" does not apply to the oral presentation of a play in a theatre.

Laurelle v. *Bush* (1912), 17 Cal. App. 409; 119 Pac. 953. Upholds the legality of an ordinance regulating the licensing of motion-picture theatres.

Marmet v. *State* (1887), 45 Ohio St. 63; 12 N. E. 463. The state has the right to regulate private businesses and require their licensing.

State v. *Scaffer* (1905), 95 Minn. 311; 104 N. W. 139.

Wallick v. *Society* (1876), 67 N. Y. 23. Plaintiff sued to restrain the defendant from bringing an action against him to

pose penalties for the giving of performances without first obtaining such license.[37]

recover penalties and close his theatre because he, plaintiff, had not secured a license as required by law. Plaintiff contended that such law was unconstitutional.

Held that he could not maintain an action of this kind.

See also: *Liquor Tax cases* (1866), 5 Wall. 462.

On the right to regulate dance halls and the form such regulation may take see *Mehlos* v. *City of Milwaukee* (1914), 156 Wis. 591; 148 N. W. 882, and cases therein cited. *State* v. *Rosenfield* (1910), 111 Minn. 301; 126 N. W. 1068; *People ex rel. Ritter* v. *Wallace* (1914), 160 A. D. (N. Y.) 787; 145 N. Y. Supp. 1041.

Two licenses for the same act may be required. See: *Commonwealth* v. *McGann* (1913), 213 Mass. 213; 100 N. E. 355. It was held that a statute was valid which required one license issued by the Chief of Police for the safety of the public, and one license issued by the Mayor' to protect the morals of the public. The business may be permitted or licensed in part and prohibited in part.

[37] *Commonwealth* v. *Twitchell* (1849), 58 Mass. 74. Defendant was found guilty of a crime under the statute, for promoting and setting up a theatrical exhibition without first securing a license as required.

Tarling v. *Fredericks* (Eng.) (1873), 21 W. R. 785. Under Section 11 of the Theatres Act of 1843 it is provided: "And be it enacted that every person who for hire shall act or present or cause, permit or suffer to be acted or presented any part in any stage-play, in any place not being a patent theatre, or duly licensed as a theatre shall forfeit such sum as shall be awarded by the court in which, or the justices by whom, he shall be convicted, not exceeding ten pounds for every day on which he shall so offend."

Mr. Justice Blackburn said that this section was enacted for the purpose of preventing anyone from acting stage plays for hire anywhere where there was no license.

On the question whether a municipal corporation may be estopped from maintaining an action for a penalty for giving theatrical exhibitions without a license where it has retained moneys paid to it sub-

The question has occasionally arisen whether a particular organization was required to secure a license.

A charter granted to a group of men, under which the corporation was given the right to give public performances of stage plays in its building did not relieve the corporation of its obligation to obtain a license before giving such performances.[38]

In like manner it has been held that a charitable organization was obligated to obtain a license and pay the required tax unless specifically exempted by statute;[39] and generally it may be said that one vested with the licensing power may not except a special person or organization from either obtaining a license or paying the required tax, unless the statute specifically provides for such exemption.

The license itself need not be in writing.[40]

sequently as a license fee, see *Mahanoy City* v. *Hersker* (1911), 231 Pa. 319; 80 Atl. 539.

[38] *Royal Albert Hall* v. *London Co. Council* (Eng.) (1911), 104 L. T. 894; 75 J. P. 337; 9 L. G. R. 626; 27 T. L. R. 362. Although the corporation of Albert Hall has full powers under its charter to give public performances of stage plays in its buildings, such powers are not letters patent to give stage plays, and the corporation must obtain a theatre license.

[39] *City of Mobile* v. *Kiernan* (1911), 54 So. (Ala.) 102.

Shelley v. *Bethell* (Eng.) (1883), 12 Q. B. D. 11. A defendant who had a private house fitted up as a private theatre turned it over to another. The latter advertised performances therein for the benefit of a school for Dramatic Art. Admission was by ticket which cost £1 1s.

Held that inasmuch as the owner of the house had not procured a license he was guilty, irrespective of the fact that the performance was for charity, construing Section Two of the Theatres Act of 1843.

[40] *City of Boston* v. *Schaffer*

There is some conflict as to whether a license is required for an entertainment for which no direct admission fee is charged. In New York a cabaret was held exempted from procuring a license.[41] In England, however, the contrary seems to be the rule.[42] And *Herbert* v. *Shanley*,[43] decided by the United States Supreme Court, subsequent to the New York decision above mentioned, by holding that a performance given at a restaurant to which no direct admission fee was charged, was a public performance for profit, has made the English rule, the American doctrine in this respect.

(1830), 9 Pick. (Mass.) 415. A license exacted by the mayor and aldermen need not be in writing.

"No formal written license was given to the defendants, but that is not material; for there was a vote of the city that the license to the theatre should be renewed, on the proprietors giving bond and paying $1000 a year, and the defendants have proceeded as under a license."

[41] *People* v. *Martin* (1912), 137 N. Y. Supp. 677; *People* v. *Keller* (1916), 96 Misc. (N. Y.) 92; 161 N. Y. Supp. 132. But see: *Weistblatt* v. *Bingham* (1908), 58 Misc. (N. Y.) 328; 109 N. Y. Supp. 545; *Economopoulos* v. *Bingham* (1907), 109 N. Y. Supp. 728.

[42] *Farndale* v. *Bainbridge* (Eng.) (1898), 42 Sol. Jo. 192; *Sarpy* v. *Holland* (Eng.) (1908), 99 L. T. 317; *Wall* v. *Tayler* (Eng.) (1883), 52 L. J. Q. B. 558; *Gregory* v. *Tuffs* (Eng.) (1833), 6 C. & P. 271; *Archer* v. *Willingrice* (Eng.) (1802), 4 Esp. 186; *Trailing* v. *Messenger* (Eng.) (1867), 31 J. P. 423; *Williams* v. *Wright* (Eng.) (1897), 13 T. L. R. 551.

[43] *Herbert* v. *Shanley* (1917), 242 U. S. 591; 37 Sup. Ct. 232.

See generally as to defendant's scienter and the manner of use of the premises the following English cases: *Shelley* v. *Bethell* (Eng.) (1883), 12 Q. B. D. 11; *Marks* v. *Benjamin* (Eng.) (1839), 5 M. & W. 565; *Gregory* v. *Tuffs* (Eng.) (1833), 6 C. & P. 271; *Syers* v. *Conquest* (Eng.) (1873), 37 J. P. 342; *R.* v. *Rosenthal* (Eng.) (1865), 30 J. P. 101; *R.* v. *Strugnell* (Eng.) (1865), L. R. 1 Q. B.

Section 107.—Power to license discretionary—Revocation.

The power to license, by the great weight of authority, has been held to be purely discretionary in the official or body in whom it is vested, even though such power may be granted or revoked "at their pleasure." [44] The courts will not interfere in the exercise of that discretion, nor substitute their judgment in place of the licensing body, unless that discretion is abused.[45]

In a leading case the New York Appellate Division held that "The question which we have here presented therefore is whether the refusal of the commissioner to grant the license is a 'judicial act.' . . . But with that determination when reached the court has no right to interfere. In other words, the granting of licenses is referred to the judgment and discretion of the commissioner, and there is no authority in any particular instance for

93; *Clarke* v. *Searle* (Eng.) (1793), 1 Esp. 25; *Bellis* v. *Beale* (Eng.) (1797), 2 Esp. 592; *Ried* v. *Wilson* (Eng.) (1895), 1 Q. B. 315; *Hoffman* v. *Bond* (Eng.) (1875), 32 L. T. N. S. 775; *Brown* v. *Nugent* (Eng.) (1872), L. R. 7 Q. B. 588; *Garrett* v. *Messenger* (Eng.) (1867), L. R. 2 C. & P. 583; *Regina* v. *Hannay* (Eng.) (1891), 2 Q. B. 709.

[44] *Commonwealth* v. *McGann* (1913), 213 Mass. 213; 100 N. E. 355.

[45] *People ex rel. Cumiskey* v. *Wurster* (1897), 14 A. D. (N. Y.) 556; 43 N. Y. Supp. 1088. The power granted to a mayor to issue theatrical licenses is discretionary and when not abused, will not be interfered with by the courts.

See also cases cited in Section 108.

R. v. *Ashton, ex parte Walker* (1915) (Eng.), 113 L. T. 696; 79 J. P. 444. Discusses the proposition as to who is entitled to notice of appeal from the refusal to grant a music license.

substituting for the conclusion which he may reach that of the court . . . our conclusion being that the power vested in the police commissioner is purely discretionary and one not reviewable by the courts." [46]

The police powers of the state to grant licenses may be delegated to subordinate boards and commissions; [47] but the delegation must be express, so that school trustees may not overstep their authority by leasing school property for motion picture exhibitions. [48]

[46] *Matter of Armstrong* v. *Murphy* (1901), 65 A. D. (N. Y.) 126; 157 N. Y. Supp. 534.

See also: *Matter of Whitten* (1913), 152 A. D. (N. Y.) 506; 137 N. Y. Supp. 360; *Matter of Simons* v. *McGuire* (1912), 204 N. Y. 253; 97 N. E. 526; *People ex rel. Schau* v. *McWilliams* (1906), 185 N. Y. 92; 77 N. E. 785; *People ex rel. McNulty* v. *Maxwell* (1908), 123 A. D. (N. Y.) 591; 108 N. Y. Supp. 49; *People ex rel. Park Circle Amuse. Co.* v. *Board of Police* (1901), 36 Misc. (N. Y.) 89; 72 N. Y. Supp. 583; *People ex rel. Bonfiglio* v. *Bingham* (1910), 67 Misc. (N. Y.) 539; 124 N. Y. Supp. 751; *People ex rel. Schwab* v. *Grant* (1891), 126 N. Y. 473; 27 N. E. 964.

[47] *McKenzie* v. *McClellan* (1909), 62 Misc. (N. Y.), 342; 116 N. Y. Supp. 645. *State* v. *Loden* (1912), 117 Md. 373; 83 Atl. 564.

Brown v. *Stubbs* (1916), 97 Atl. (Md.) 227. An ordinance passed by the City of Baltimore requiring an applicant seeking to secure a license for the erection of a moving picture theatre, to first obtain a permit from the mayor and city council was held valid even though the ordinance did not prescribe any rules or regulations limiting the exercise of the discretion of the mayor and city council.

See also: *Kries* v. *Dick* (1914), 141 Pac. (Col.) 505. Where by statute a town clerk is the person designated to issue licenses for motion picture exhibitions, the town clerk alone is the proper party in mandamus proceedings. It is improper to join the mayor and members of the town board.

[48] *Trustees etc.* v. *Lewis* (1912), 63 Fla. 691; 57 So. 614.

See also *Smith* v. *City of Raton* (1893), 104 Pac. (N. M.) 109.

Just as they may grant, so may the licensing powers *revoke* the license where grounds for so doing, exist. And they may do this without holding any formal hearing or giving any notice to the licensee.[49] Indeed, in a recent case it was held that where the theatre was unsafe for use and the interior arrangement was not in compliance with the law, the mayor was under an express obligation to so revoke the license.[50]

Section 108.—Extent of discretion of licensing power.

The power of the licensing authorities to grant licenses is restricted in three respects—first, by its reasonableness, second, in respect of the use of the licensed premises, and third, by the interest of the public. Subject to these restrictions, there is no fetter upon the power of the licensing authorities.[51]

[49] *McKenzie* v. *McClellan* (1909), 62 Misc. (N. Y.) 342; 116 N. Y. Supp. 645. The mayor revoked the licenses issued to the plaintiffs without any notice or hearing. *Held* that such power was vested in him.

See also: *Matter of Hammerstein* (1907), 52 Misc. (N. Y.) 606; 102 N. Y. Supp. 950; *Fox Am. Co.* v. *McClellan* (1909), 62 Misc. (N. Y.) 100; 114 N. Y. Supp. 594; *Ex parte Stott* (Eng.) (1916), 1 K. B. 7; W. N. 362; 32 T. L. R. 84.

[50] *Genesee Recreation Co.* v. *Edgerton* (1916), 172 A. D. (N. Y.) 464; 158 N. Y. Supp. 421.

[51] *Theatre de Luxe* v. *Gledhill* (Eng.) (1915), 2 K. B. 49; W. N. 16; 84 L. J. (K. B.) 649; 112 L. T. 519; 79 J. P. 238; 31 T. L. R. 138; 13 L. G. R. 541.

Lethridge v. *Wilson* (Can.), 8 A. L. R. 178; 8 W. W. R. 424. Statute regulating erection and operation of theatres including licensing control and supervision of use and operations of moving picture machines and regulations of exhibition, sale and leasing of films construed. The Theatres Act, ch. 25, 1911–12.

Ex parte London & Provincial El. Theatres, Ltd. (Eng.) (1915), 31 T. L. R. 329. County Coun-

As an illustration of the first limitation upon its power, reference may be had to ordinances imposing a specified license fee. Unless the amount of the tax is excessive, the courts will not interfere.[52]

A statute imposing a license tax upon places of amusement graded according to the size of the city wherein the theatre was situated, was held valid; [53] so also, where the tax was upon a graded scale according to the price of admission charged.[54]

A mayor in whom was vested the power to license was permitted to look behind an application to ascertain whether its actual purpose was truly represented, and if not so, to refuse to issue a license.[55]

cils in considering applications for license under the Cinematographic Act of 1909 are not confined to matters relating to safety alone.

See also: *Ex parte Harrington* (Eng.) (1888), 4 T. L. R. 435; C. A.

[52] *City of Duluth* v. *Marsh* (1898), 71 Minn. 248; 73 N. W. 962. A license fee of $125 for six months was held not to be excessive.

See in this connection: *The King* v. *Dimock* (Can.), 30 D. L. R. 217; 26 Can. Cr. Cas. 311; 44 N. B. R. 124. Under an Act which imposes generally a license fee of $50 on "public places of amusement," motion pictures may not be required to pay $300 as a license fee.

See in this connection: *Lethbridge* v. *Wilson* (Can.), 8 A. L. R. 178; 8 W. W. R. 424. *Held* that in the absence of a special provision the licensing authority had no right to impose a license fee on theatres.

[53] *State* v. *O'Hara* (1884), 36 La. Ann. 93.

To the same effect: *State* v. *Schonhausen* (1885), 37 La. Ann. 42.

[54] *Metropolis Theatre Co.* v. *City of Chicago* (1912), 228 U. S. 61; 33 Sup. Ct. 441.

[55] *People ex rel. Cumiskey* v. *Wurster* (1897), 14 A. D. (N. Y.) 556; 43 N. Y. Supp. 1088. The

There are numerous instances illustrative of the third limitation. The question has usually come up in cases where the one vested with the authority to license, has either refused to issue or threatened to revoke the license of a theatre because of the exhibition therein of a motion picture which in his opinion, is obscene, immoral, seditious or apt to create race prejudice.

The courts have been increasingly prone to give the licensing power wide scope in the exercise of its discretion, until now the broad rule followed by the courts seems to be that unless the element of bad faith, capriciousness or misinformation is apparent, they will not interfere with the discretion exercised.

"These statutory provisions and ordinances, the validity of which is not and could not well be questioned, necessarily delegate to the commissioner authority to issue and to revoke licenses according to his judgment and discretion, to be exercised, of course, in good faith and impartially and conscientiously according to what he believes

mayor may refuse to grant a theatrical license to a club where it appears that only prize-fight exhibitions are contemplated.

"It would certainly be remarkable to deny to the mayor to look behind an application made for a license to ascertain whether its actual purpose was truly represented, and if not so, to refuse it. He undoubtedly would have that power. He exercised it in the relator's case. The mayor was justified in the conclusion that a license for a first-class theatre was not applicable to the purposes for which the Surf Athletic Club had prepared its building and to which it was to be devoted. And it may be assumed that his refusal to grant the license was founded upon the facts in that respect as they then existed, and were reasonably inferable from them."

to be in the interest of morality or decency or public safety or public welfare. It is not the judgment and discretion of those who are interested in exploiting a film commercially, as is the plaintiff, or of citizens generally, or even the courts, but that of the commissioner *only* [italics that of the court] that is called into action. The commissioner, however, must not abuse the discretion vested in him by acting capriciously or arbitrarily or on false information and without reasonable ground for apprehending that the public morality, or decency, or safety, or welfare will be endangered, but the extent of inquiry collaterally by the courts with respect to his action is whether there is reasonable ground upon which such apprehension may honestly rest in the exercise of a fair and legal discretion, and if not, the court may require him to act or enjoin him from acting: but if the question be doubtful, and there be room for an honest difference of opinion, then the matter must be left to the official to whom the Legislature has delegated authority, and his action in refusing to grant a license, or in revoking one granted, cannot be annulled or controlled collaterally as by mandamus or injunction." [56]

[56] *Message Photoplay Co.* v. *Bell* (1917), New York Appellate Division; N. Y. Law Journal, July 20th. Citing: *People ex rel. Schwab* v. *Grant* (1891), 126 N. Y. 473; 27 N. E. 964; *Matter of Ormsby* v. *Bell* (1916), 218 N. Y. 212; 112 N. E. 747; *People ex rel. Rota* v. *Baker* (1910), 136 A. D. (N. Y.) 7; 120 N. Y. Supp. 161; *Genesee Recreation Co.* v. *Edgerton* (1916), 172 A. D. (N. Y.) 464; 158 N. Y. Supp. 421; *People ex rel. Cumiskey* v. *Wurster* (1897), 14 A. D. (N. Y.) 556; 43 N. Y. Supp. 1088; *Ritter* v. *Wallace* (1914), 160 A. D. (N. Y.) 787; 145 N. Y. Supp. 1041; *People ex rel. Lodes* v. *Dep't of Health* (1907), 189 N. Y.

This is the language of the Appellate Division of New York (First Department) with reference to the film known

187; 82 N. E. 187; *Piexotto* v. *Board of Education* (1914), 212 N. Y. 463; 106 N. E. 307; *Matter of Franklin Film Corporation* (1917), 253 Pa. St. 422; 98 Atl. 623; *Van Norden* v. *Sewer Comm'r* (1904), 90 A. D. (N. Y.) 555; 84 N. Y. Supp. 445; *Bainbridge* v. *City of Minneapolis* (1915), 131 Minn. 195; 154 N. W. 964. "For decisions in which the same rule is stated but mandamus was issued see: *E. C. T. Club* v. *State Racing Comm'n* (1907), 190 N. Y. 31; 82 N. E. 723; *Cosby* v. *Robinson* (1910), 141 A. D. (N. Y.) 656; 126 N. Y. Supp. 546.

"There is no evidence that the threatened action of the defendant is in bad faith, and it must therefore be presumed that he is acting honestly in the exercise of fair and impartial discretion and judgment. *City of Buffalo* v. *Hill* (1903), 79 A. D. (N. Y.) 402; 79 N. Y. Supp. 449.

"The merits of the action should not be determined on conflicting affidavits, nor should a temporary injunction issue in such case against the official in whom the law has vested the duty of acting in the premises. *Matter of Whitten* (1913), 152 A. D. (N. Y.) 506; 137 N. Y. Supp. 360; *Genesee Recr.* v. *Edgerton* (1916), 172 A. D. (N. Y.) 464; 158 N. Y. Supp. 421; *Ritter* v. *Wallace* (1914), 160 A. D. (N. Y.) 787; 145 N. Y. Supp. 1041."

Universal Film Mfg. Co. v. *Bell* (1917), N. Y. Law Journal, June 5th, Greenbaum, J. "Indeed it is wholly immaterial what the court's opinion may be as to the wisdom of the commissioner's action as long as he acted in good faith. The court cannot act as a commissioner of licenses. That the commissioner did not act arbitrarily or capriciously, it is but fair to state that the affidavits submitted indicate that he based his opinion of the character of the production after he had thoroughly familiarized himself with its theme, the pictures and the words employed in its presentation and considered the effect it was likely to produce upon those who witness it. Among the answering affidavits a number of them are made by persons of high standing and by representatives of civic societies to the effect that the play is *contra bonos mores*. Whether their opin-

as "Birth Control," in which case the order of the justice at special term enjoining the commissioner of licenses from in anywise interfering with the exhibition of the picture was reversed.[57]

ions are correct or not it is not necessary for the court to pass upon, but they are merely referred to as bearing upon the question of whether or not the defendant has abused his discretion. Under the statute the commissioner is to consider whether the play is 'immoral, indecent or against the public welfare.' One of the definitions of the word 'decency' found in the Century Dictionary is 'propriety of action, speech, dress, etc.' What constitutes decency, or, in other words, what is propriety of action, must be determined by standards in vogue among highly civilized peoples and not those that may prevail among the Fiji or South Sea Islanders. Lewd men and women have no sense of decency, and what may be regarded as decent by one person may not be thus regarded by another. The discretion honestly exercised by the commissioner in the discharge of his duties may not be overthrown by the court excepting only where it may be shown that his actions were influenced by corrupt or dishonest considerations, the burden of proving which rests upon the moving party."

[57] *For other cases where the licensing power attempted to enjoin the exhibition of an obscene or immoral picture* see: *Universal Film Manufacturing Co.* v. *Bell* (1917), N. Y. Law Journal, Greenbaum, J. (The Hand that Rocks the Cradle); *Sociological Research* v. *Waldo* (1914), 83 Misc. 605; 145 N. Y. Supp. 492 (The Inside of the White Slave Traffic); *Genesee Recreation Co.* v. *Bingham* (1916), 172 A. D. (N. Y.) 464; 158 N. Y. Supp. 421 (no title given in decision); *Block* v. *City of Chicago* (1909), 239 Ill. 251; 87 N. E. 1011 (James Boys and Night Riders); *Stein* v. *Bell* (1917), N. Y. Law Journal, May 2nd (The Awakening of Spring); *Ivan Film Productions* v. *Bell* (1916), N. Y. Law Journal, December 5 (The Sex Lure).

For cases where a production on the stage with living actors was involved see: *People* v. *Doris*

A court has refused to interfere where the licensing authority threatened to revoke a license upon the ground that the proposed exhibition of a motion picture would tend to cause breaches of neutrality; [58] and in like manner where the motion picture was likely to create race prejudice.[59]

The courts also upheld a commissioner of licenses in his refusal to grant a license, where the owner of the adjacent property stored combustibles.[60]

(1897), 14 A. D. (N. Y.) 117; 43 N. Y. Supp. 571; appeal dismissed, 153 N. Y. 678; 48 N. E. 1106 (A pantomime entitled "Orange Blossoms"); *Brewer* v. *Wynne* (1913), 163 N. C. 319; 79 S. E. 629 (The Girl from Rector's); *King* v. *McAuliffe* (Can.), 8 Can. Cr. Cas. 21 (Ballet Dancing).

[58] *Life Photo Film* v. *Bell* (1915), 90 Misc. (N. Y.) 469; 154 N. Y. Supp. 763. Plaintiff was about to exhibit a motion-picture depicting scenes of the German War. Defendant, Commissioner of Licenses, threatened to revoke the license of the theatre producing the same, and plaintiff was granted injunction on the ground that it would be impossible for him to obtain any relief otherwise.

[59] *Edelstein* v. *Bell* (1915), 91 Misc. (N. Y.) 620; 155 N. Y. Supp. 590. The court would not interfere with a commissioner of licenses where he refused to grant a license permitting the exhibition of a photoplay entitled "The Frank Case" based on the incidents of the famous murder trial in Georgia.

Bambridge, Jr. v. *City of Minneapolis* (1915), 131 Minn. 195; 154 N. W. 964. Action was brought to enjoin mayor from revoking license of theatre wherein plaintiff had arranged to exhibit the film "The Birth of a Nation." *Held* that mayor was not abusing his discretion or exercising it capriciously.

[60] *Matter of Ormsby* v. *Bell* (1916), 218 N. Y. 212; 112 N. E. 747. Since the power of the commissioner to grant a license to a motion picture theatre is discretionary, it was held that it was not an abuse of his dis-

It was also held to be a proper exercise of discretion to refuse a license because of the proximity of the building wherein the motion pictures were contemplated to be given, to a church and school.[61]

And, in England, the courts refused to interfere where a municipality refused a license for a motion picture theatre, when the applicant for the license was a company of which the majority of the stockholders were alien enemies.[62]

Attention, however, may be here called to cases where it was held that where there had been full compliance with the requirements of a statute for the issuance of a license for a motion picture theatre, the applicant was prima facie entitled to such license.[63]

Section 109.—Right to license on condition.

Provisions contained in a licensing act requiring the payment of specified sums, as a condition precedent to the issuance of a license, have been held valid.[64]

cretion to refuse a license because the owner of the adjacent property stored combustibles and would lose his permit if the theatre were opened.

See also: *Matter of Armstrong* v. *Murphy* (1901), 65 A. D. (N. Y.) 123; 157 N. Y. Supp. 534; *City of Buffalo* v. *Chadeayne* (1889), 7 N. Y. Supp. 501; aff'd 134 N. Y. 163; 31 N. E. 443; *French* v. *Jones* (1906), 191 Mass. 522; 78 N. E. 118.

[61] *People ex rel. Moses* v. *Gaynor* (1912), 77 Misc. (N. Y.) 576; 137 N. Y. Supp. 196.

[62] *R.* v. *London County Council, ex parte* (Eng.) (1915), 2 K. B. 482; W. N. 154; 84 L. J. (K. B.) 1795; 113 L. T. 122; 31 T. L. R. 329; 70 J. P. 417.

[63] *Walker* v. *Fuhrman* (1914), 84 Misc. (N. Y.) 118; 146 N. Y. Supp. 519; *Kries* v. *Dick* (1914), 141 Pac. (Col.) 505.

[64] *Higgins* v. *Lacroix* (1912), 119 Minn. 145; 137 N. W. 417. A license fee of $200 as a prerequi-

Where the licensing power is vested by statute in a political subdivision of the state, it may insert and enforce a stipulation that the theatre shall be kept open only during specified hours.[65]

site to operate a motion-picture theatre in a village held not to be excessive.

"The village is presumably a growing community now having more than one thousand inhabitants. These shows are usually carried on every day in the week with several performances each day. Fifty-five cents per day does not appeal to us to be so high that it necessarily results in prohibiting moving picture shows from locating at Deer River."

Park v. *Morgan* (1912), 64 Fla. 414; 60 So. 347. An ordinance imposing a license tax upon theatrical shows was held valid.

Baker v. *City of Cincinnati* (1860), 11 Ohio St. 534. A provision in a licensing act which exacted the payment of $63.50 from the applicant for license held legal.

To the same effect: *City of Boston* v. *Schaffer* (1830), 26 Mass. 415; *Hodges* v. *Mayor* (1840), 21 Tenn. 61; *State* v. *O'Hara* (1884), 36 La. Ann. 93; *State* v. *Schonhauser* (1885), 37 La. Ann. 42; *City of Duluth* v. *Marsh* (1898), 71 Minn. 248; 73 N. W. 962; *Metropolis Theatre Co.* v. *City of Chicago* (1912), 228 U. S. 61; 33 Sup. Ct. 441.

People v. *Coleman* (1854), 4 Cal. 46. For an exhaustive summary of the right of the state to tax trades, professions and occupations.

See in this connection: *Orton* v. *Brown* (1858), 35 Miss. 426. Discussing a tax of $25 a day imposed upon a circus the court said:

"Hence the law taxes the exhibition as a matter of public policy, and thereby gives the right to make the exhibitions upon payment of the sum required. This, in effect, is a license to do an act, and not a tax upon property; and therefore when the sum required is paid, the right is conferred without further exaction."

In other words where the owner had paid his tax, he was not required to pay an additional county tax.

[65] *People ex rel Kieley* v. *Lent* (1915), 166 A. D. (N. Y.) 550;

The applicant for a license may also be required to pledge himself not to apply for a liquor license, as a condition to the granting of the theatre license.[66]

And generally, the licensing power may impose conditions for the grant of the license,[67] and reasonable limits may be placed upon the exercise of the rights granted thereunder.[68]

It may not, however, impose a condition that the theatre shall remain closed on Sunday, as that in the language of the courts "must be deemed 'tyrannical' and a usurpation of power and not 'discretionary' . . . for the mayor thus makes a Sunday law unto himself and seeks to impress it upon the community in hostility to the general law of the state and judges that of which the legislature is the sole judge." [69]

152 N. Y. Supp. 18. "A license may be conditionally granted. It may be given subject to certain reasonable hours of opening and other limits upon its exercise."

[66] *Queen* v. *County Council* (Eng.), 2 Q. B. D. 386. The County Council may require, as a condition to granting a theatre license, that the applicant pledge himself not to apply for a liquor license.

[67] *R.* v. *Yorkshire County Council* (Eng.) (1896), 2 Q. B. 386; *Manchester Palace* v. *Manchester Corporation* (Eng.) (1898), 62 J. P. 425; *R.* v. *Sheerness County Council* (Eng.) (1898), 62 J. P. 563, C. A.

And as to procedure where license is opposed see: *Royal Aquarium Soc.* v. *Parkinson* (1892), 1 Q. B. 431, C. A; *R.* v. *London Co. Council* (Eng.) (1892), 1 Q. B. 190; *R.* v. *London Co. Council* (Eng.) (1894), 71 L. T. 638; *Leeson* v. *General Council* (Eng.) (1889), 43 Ch. D. 366, C. A.

[68] *People ex rel. Kieley* v. *Lent* (1915), 166 A. D. (N. Y.) 550; 152 N. Y. Supp. 18.

[69] *Klinger* v. *Ryan* (1915), 91 Misc. (N. Y.) 71; 153 N. Y. Supp. 71; 153 N. Y. Supp. 937. Re-affirming the doctrine of *People ex rel. Kieley* v. *Lent*, that since a municipality could not enforce a Sunday closing ordi-

Where the theatre license is issued by one bureau and the liquor license by another, the theatrical licensing bureau is not thereby necessarily deprived of its control over the sale of liquor in the theatre. The liquor licensing bureau may be required to first secure the consent of the other bureau before issuing its license to the theatre.[70]

nance by fines or imprisonment unless *expressly authorized* by the Legislature, it could not accomplish the same purpose by the *conditions of a license.*

But see: *Ellis* v. *No. American Theatres* (Eng.) (1915), 2 K. B. 61; 112 L. T. 1018; W. N. 61; 79 J. P. 297; 13 L. G. R. 735; 84 L. J. (K. B.) 1077; 31 T. L. R. 201. A condition contained in a license, that the theatre be kept closed on Sunday was held valid, and might lawfully be imposed.

Also to same effect, *London Co. Council* v. *Bermondsey Bioscope Co.* (Eng.) (1915), 27 T. L. R. 141.

In this connection see: *City of Mobile* v. *Kiernan* (1911), 54 So. (Ala.) 102; *Yorkville* v. *Bingham* (1909), 64 Misc. (N. Y.) 636; 118 N. Y. Supp. 753.

See also: *Theatre De Luxe* v. *Gledhill* (Eng.) (1914), 31 T. L. R. 138; 112 L. T. 519. A theatre license was granted upon condition that no child under ten years of age should be allowed to attend under any circumstances after 9 P. M. *Held,* that the act was ultra vires upon the ground that there was no connection between the ground upon which the condition was imposed and the subject matter of the license. Dissenting opinion by Atkin, J., that county councils were properly entitled to take into account the public interest so far as children were affected.

[70] *Queen* v. *Commissioners of Inland Rev.* (Eng.), 57 L. J. M. C. 92. The question was as to whether the Empire Theatre could obtain an excise license from the commissioners of Inland Revenue. *Held* that since it was licensed as a music-hall, application would have to be made in the regular way to a justice as required by 5 & 6 Wm. IV, c. 39, s. 7 and that the Licensing Act of 1872 did not apply.

CHAPTER IX

THE PUBLIC (CONTINUED)

Regulation

SEC. 110. Buildings—Distances.
111. Standees—Aisles—Closing.
112. Operator and booth.
113. Firemen—Fire-escapes—Exits.
114. Admission of children.
115. Regulation amounting to prohibition.
116. Prohibition—Immorality.
117. Who is liable for penalty.
118. Ticket "Scalping."
119. Censorship.
120. Sunday performance.

Section 110.—Buildings—Distances.

It is a valid exercise of the police power to regulate the construction of the theatre building,[1] the nature and kind of materials to be used in certain parts therein and the like.[2] The authorities may also demand that changes be

[1] *McGee* v. *Kennedy* (1908), 114 S. W. (Ky.) 298; *People* v. *Busse* (1910), 248 Ill. 11; 93 N. E. 327.

Jewel Theatre Co. v. *Winship* (1914), 144 N. W. (Mich.) 835. A statute requiring that all motion picture theatres shall have their auditoriums on the level with the street was held constitutional.

[2] *A. G.* v. *Shoreditch Corporation* (Eng.) (1915), 2 Ch. 154; 79 J. P. 369; W. N. 184; 31 T. L. R. 400; 84 L. J. (Ch.) 772; 59 Sol. Jo. 439; 112 L. T. 628; 13 L. G. R. 1141. The authorities

made in the building to reduce fire hazards and other risks.[3] Where, however, the relator had equipped and used a building as a motion picture theatre, the mayor of the City of New York was held to be not authorized to withhold a license from him under the provisions of an ordinance which was passed subsequent to such equipment.[4]

It was held in England that a tent was not a "place"

permitted the owners of a public swimming bath to turn it into a motion picture theatre.

[3] *R.* v. *Hannay* (Eng.) (1891), 2 Q. B. 709.

[4] *In re Walker* (1914), 84 Misc. (N. Y.) 118; 146 N. Y. Supp. 519. Where the relator had equipped and used a building as a motion picture theatre prior to December 1st, 1912, the Mayor of the city was not authorized to withhold a license from him under the provisions of an ordinance which was passed in March, 1913.

"If the mayor may withhold a license then it is within his power to destroy valuable property rights of owners who, acting under competent authority have invested large sums in the construction of moving picture shows, by simply refusing to renew such licenses when such licenses expire. It is one thing to refuse a license to build and construct in the first instance, and quite a different thing to refuse to permit the continued use of such a theatre when once lawfully constructed under a lawful permit."

See however: *Greenough* v. *Allen Theatre etc.* (1911), 80 Atl. (R. I.) 260. Defendants had secured a permit to alter a stable into a theatre in accordance with plans theretofore filed by them. The plans filed by defendants conformed to the laws then in force. Subsequently a statute was enacted requiring that all theatres thereafter "erected" shall be built in accordance with such statute. *Held* that the statute being one for the health and safety of the public it should be freely construed and that the word "erected" was intended to include alterations made to buildings, erected prior to the passage of the statute, to transform them into theatres.

within the meaning of the Act of 1843,[5] but in this country a tent was classified as a "building" on the question of fire limits.[6]

In some jurisdictions it has been held that the municipality has not the power to construct a building for the giving of theatrical performances, such being purely private enterprises, while in other jurisdictions the contrary rule has been applied.[7]

The right to withhold licenses from theatres unless they are situated beyond a certain radius of a school or church is a valid exercise of the police power.[8]

[5] *Davys* v. *Douglas* (Eng.), 4 H. and N. 180. Section two of the Theatres Act of 1843:

"It shall not be lawful for any person to have or keep any house or other *place* of public resort in Great Britain, for the public performance of stage-plays, without authority by virtue of Letters Patent from Her Majesty, her heirs and successors or predecessors, or without license from the Lord Chamberlain of Her Majesty's household for the time being, or from the justices of the peace as hereinafter provided; and that every person who shall offend against this enactment shall be liable to forfeit such sum as shall be awarded by the Court in which, or the justices by whom he shall be convicted, not exceeding twenty pounds for every day on which such house or place shall have been so kept open by him for the purpose aforesaid without legal authority."

[6] *City of St. Louis* v. *Nash* (1916), 18 S. W. (Mo.) 1145. Defendant built a tent-like structure within the fire-limits of St. Louis in which he gave motion picture exhibitions.

Held that the structure was not a "tent" but was a "building" within the classification of an ordinance which prohibited the erection of a so-called fourth-class building within the fire-limits.

[7] See Section 79, p. 248, for a detailed discussion of this subject and for all the cases.

[8] *People ex rel. Moses* v. *Gaynor* (1912), 77 Misc. (N. Y.) 576;

Section 111.—Standees—Aisles—Closing.

As a precautionary measure against panics, statutes and ordinances have been passed prohibiting patrons from standing in the aisles of a theatre.[9] While in an early

137 N. Y. Supp. 196. Where the power to grant licenses for motion-picture shows is vested solely in the Mayor, it is not an abuse of his discretion to refuse a license to an applicant for a site next to a public school and opposite a church, where it is shown that parents have remonstrated, and clergy protested against the issuance of the license.

Nahser v. *City of Chicago* (1916), 271 Ill. 288; 111 N. E. 119. It was held that under its police power a municipal corporation could refuse to grant a license for a moving picture theatre which was situated within two hundred feet of a church.

See also: *Matter of Kohn* (Wagener, Sisson) (1917), N. Y. Law Journal, May 29; *Goodrich* v. *Busse* (1910), 247 Ill. 367; 93 N. E. 292; *Ex parte Quong Wo* (1911), 161 Cal. 220; 118 Pac. 214; *Storer* v. *Downey* (1913), 215 Mass. 273; 102 N. E. 321; *St. Louis* v. *Fischer* (1902), 167 Mo. 654; 67 S. W. 1100; *Green* v. *Savanah* (1849), 6 Ga. 1; *People ex rel Lange* v. *Palmitter* (1911), 71 Misc. (N. Y.) 158; 128 N. Y. Supp. 426; aff'd 144 A. D. (N. Y.), 894; 128 N. Y. Supp. 1140; aff'd 202 N. Y. 608; 96 N. E. 1126; *City of Duluth* v. *Marsh* (1898), 71 Minn. 248; 73 N. W. 962; *City of Chicago* v. *Stratton* (1896), 162 Ill. 495; 44 N. E. 853; *People ex rel. Keller* v. *Oak Park* (1915), 266 Ill. 365; 107 N. E. 636; *Densmore* v. *Evergreen* (1910), 61 Wash. 230; 112 Pac. 255; *City of Chicago* v. *Ripley* (1911), 249 Ill. 468; 94 N. E. 931; *City of Chicago* v. *Shaynin* (1913), 258 Ill. 69; 101 N. E. 224; *Dreyfus* v. *Montgomery* (1912), 4 Ala. App. 270; 58 So. 730.

[9] *Sturgis* v. *Hayman* (1903), 84 N. Y. Supp. 126. *Held* a violation of the statute to permit persons to stand in the side aisles, where such aisles were used to reach the side exit.

Rex v. *Hazza* (Can.) (1916), 28 D. L. R. 373; 25 Can. Cr. Cas. 306; 34 W. L. R. 97. Spectators at a motion-picture theatre may stand in the space between the box-office and the entrance of the theatre, known as the lobby, while waiting for admission; and

decision the space in the rear of the orchestra chairs was held to be not an "aisle," [10] a later decision in the same state held that such space was an "aisle." [11]

The fact that in the aisles in which patrons were permitted to stand, seats might have been lawfully installed, did not relieve the proprietor from liability; [12] and this was true where stools and chairs had been placed in the aisles, although fixed seats might have been installed.[13]

this will not be a violation of an ordinance which prohibits the standing of patrons in the aisles or exits.

[10] *Sturgis* v. *Grau* (1902), 39 Misc. (N. Y.) 330; 79 N. Y. Supp. 843. The space in the rear of the orchestra of the Metropolitan Opera House was occupied by a large number of standees. *Held* no violation of the statute, as this space was not an aisle or passageway, and was not used by the audience for ingress or egress.

[11] *Waldo* v. *Seelig* (1911), 70 Misc. (N. Y.) 254; 126 N. Y. Supp. 798; aff'd 146 A. D. (N. Y.) 879; 130 N. Y. Supp. 1133. Action was brought by the Fire Commissioner to recover a penalty from the proprietor of a theatre for obstructing the aisles in his theatre. *Held* that the space directly back of the seats of the main floor was an "aisle."

[12] *Potter* v. *Watt* (Eng.) (1914), 84 L. J. (K. B.) 394; 79 J. P. 212; 112 L. T. 508; 31 T. L. R. 84. The respondent was found guilty of permitting people to stand in the aisles of his theatre, in violation of the Cinematograph Act of 1909.

The fact that he had not installed the full number of seats in the theatre was no justification.

[13] *Sturgis* v. *Coleman* (1902), 38 Misc. (N. Y.) 303; 77 N. Y. Supp. 886. While the side-aisles of a theatre were much wider than the minimum prescribed by law, it was held, nevertheless, to be a violation to place stools and chairs therein, even though permanent seats might have been built up.

A theatre exit may open upon an alley.[14]

Regulations as to closing are reasonable and valid.[15]

Section 112.—Operator and booth.

It is a reasonable exercise of the police power to require all persons operating motion picture machines to submit to examinations before obtaining a license.[16]

"The danger to life and property incident to the use of moving picture machines when operated by incompetent persons is known to all. The films used in connection with the machine are highly explosive and dangerous in their character, and if not properly managed and cared for are liable to explode." [17]

[14] *City of Indianapolis* v. *Miller* (1907), 168 Ind. 285; 80 N. E. 626. Action for violation in maintaining an alley entrance to the theatre. *Held* that the ordinance was invalid in that it deprived the defendant of the use of a public highway.

[15] *People ex rel. Kieley* v. *Lent* (1915), 166 A. D. (N. Y.) 550; 152 N. Y. Supp. 18; aff'd 215 N. Y. 626; 109 N. E. 1088.

Gallagher v. *Rudd* (Eng.) (1898), 1 Q. B. 114. The time for closing under the Licensing Act of 1874 held to apply equally to theatres and to music-halls.

As to whether an ordinance requiring all female patrons attending theatres, motion picture exhibitions or other amusements to remove their hats was valid see: *Oldknow* v. *City of Atlanta* (1911), 71 S. E. (Ga.) 1015.

[16] *State ex rel. Ebert* v. *Loden* (1912), 117 Md. 373; 83 Atl. 564. A statute which required all persons to submit to examination before obtaining a license as motion-picture operator was held constitutional.

[17] *State ex rel. Ebert* v. *Loden* (1912), 117 Md. 373; 83 Atl. 564.

Victoria Pier Syndicate v. *Reeve* (Eng.) (1912), 28 T. L. R. 443. The word "inflammable" as used in the Cinemetographic Act of 1909 is not limited to films which are "inflammable" only while being used in the proecting machine.

The booth in which the machine is inclosed may also be required to be fireproofed.[18]

It has been held that an officer entering the theatre premises for the purpose of making an inspection to see whether inflammatory films were being used, may make other observations as well, and will not be considered a trespasser.[19]

Section 113.—Firemen—Fire-escapes—Exits.

The licensing powers have the undoubted right to have firemen inspect the theatres and remain throughout the performances.[20] But they may not compel the proprietor of the theatre to pay for such fireman, for that would be manifestly unfair. As one judge said, they could apportion a goodly number of firemen and policemen throughout the amusement places of the city, and thereby saddle such proprietors with the cost of maintaining almost the entire fire and police departments.[21]

[18] *Matter of Whitten* (1912), 152 A. D. (N. Y.) 506; 137 N. Y. Supp. 360. It was held not to be an abuse of discretion to deny a license because the motion picture booth was not fireproofed.

[19] *McVittie* v. *Turner* (Eng.) (1915), 60 S. J. 238; 113 L. T. 982; 13 L. G. R. 1181; 79 J. P. (Journal) 400.

[20] *City of Hartford* v. *Parsons* (1913), 87 Conn. 412; 87 Atl. 736; *City of Chicago* v. *Weber* (1910), 246 Ill. 304; 92 N. E. 859.

[21] *City of Hartford* v. *Parsons* (1913), 87 Conn. 412; 87 Atl. 736. *Held* that where statute required that a fireman or police officer should be stationed in each theatre during performances and was silent as to who shall pay such person, the obligation to pay rested upon the municipality and not upon the owner of the theatre. *Held* further also that such statute was reasonable and proper.

City of Chicago v. *Weber* (1910), 246 Ill. 304; 92 N. E. 859. *Held*

Safeguards against fire and attendant loss of life are of prime importance where theatres are concerned, and the regulating powers may require any precaution deemed necessary in that respect. For that reason, statutes and ordinances regulating fire inspection have been upheld as constitutional and reasonable,[22] as well as acts requiring exits, fire-escapes, fire-extinguishers and the like.[23] In addition, the penalties for infraction are severe and rigidly enforced.[24]

that while the city might pass an ordinance compelling the theatre to have a fireman in attendance, the proprietor of the theatre could not be compelled to pay for the fireman.

To the same effect see: *Waters* v. *Leech* (1840), 3 Ark. 110; but see contra: *Tannenbaum* v. *Rehm* (1907), 152 Ala. 494; 44 So. 532; *City of New Orleans* v. *Hop Lee* (1901), 104 La. 601; 29 So. 214; *Harrison* v. *Baltimore* (1843), 1 Gill. (Md.) 264, where the proprietors were compelled to pay.

[22] *Jeup* v. *State Fire Marshal* (1914), 182 Mich. 231; 148 N. W. 340. A statute regulating the operation and construction of theatres and moving picture exhibitions, providing for fire inspection and issuance of licenses was held constitutional as it did not conflict with provisions of the constitution prohibiting passage of local or special acts or invade the constitutional requirements for municipal charters and local self-government.

[23] *Roumfort Co.* v. *Delaney* (1911), 230 Pa. St. 374; 79 Atl. 653. An act requiring exits, fire escapes, fire extinguishers for buildings used as theatres and other places where the public assembled was held valid.

R. v. *Hannay* (Eng.) (1891), 2 Q. B. 709. The authorities may demand that changes be made in the building to reduce fire hazards.

[24] *For liability to penalties for infraction of the fire regulations* see: *Fire Department* v. *Hill* (1891), 14 N. Y. Supp. 158; *Fire Department* v. *Stetson* (1887), 14 Daly (N. Y.), 125. Where the lessees and managers were held liable even though the house had been leased away for a period.

Section 114.—Admission of children.

The licensing power may regulate how and when and under what conditions children may be admitted to a theatre. In many states and cities statutes and ordinances have been passed making the admission of a child without a guardian a criminal offense.[25] In such case, however, a "guardian" has been construed as not necessarily being a legal guardian, but as meaning even a neighbor or friend.[26]

The fact that the person admitting the minor is de-

[25] *People* v. *Trippi* (1912), 152 A. D. (N. Y.) 717; 137 N. Y. Supp. 599. The conviction of defendant for admitting minors under the age of sixteen to a moving picture show in violation of section 484 of the Penal Law of New York was sustained.

See also: *People* v. *Jensen* (1904), 99 A. D. (N. Y.) 355; 90 N. Y. Supp. 1062; aff'd 181 N. Y. 571; 74 N. E. 1122.

[26] *People ex rel. Jacques* v. *Flaherty* (1907), 122 A. D. (N. Y.) 878; 107 N. Y. Supp. 415; aff'd 191 N. Y. 525; 84 N. E. 1118. Under a statute providing that "a person who . . . admits to or allows to remain in any . . . theatre . . . owned, kept or managed by him in whole or in part," any minor under the age of sixteen unless accompanied by its parent or guardian was guilty of a misdemeanor, *Held* that the ticket taker was not included as one of the persons liable under the statute.

See also: *People* v. *Samwick* (1908), 127 A. D. (N. Y.) 209; 111 N. Y. Supp. 11, for a construction of the above mentioned statute. The court held that the owner of a motion picture theatre could not be convicted under the statute where there was no proof that the place was injurious to the health and morals of the minors. The court also held that the word "guardian" in the statute did not necessarily refer to a legal guardian but might refer to a neighbor or friend.

To the same effect as the principal case is *People ex rel. Jacques* v. *Sheriff* (1907), 122 A. D. (N. Y.) 878; 107 N. Y. Supp. 415; aff'd 191 N. Y. 525; 84 N. E. 1118.

ceived as to his age is no defense for a violation of the statute.[27]

The license may also provide that children under a specified age shall not be admitted after a certain hour of the night.[28]

Section 115.—Regulation amounting to prohibition.

In Illinois it has been definitely settled that the power to regulate does not include the power to *prohibit;* if it is sought to prohibit, a nuisance must be established.[29] And this rule has been followed in several of the other states of the union.[30]

[27] *Rex* v. *Paton* (Can.) (1911), 20 Ont. W. Rep. 533.

[28] *Theatre De Luxe* v. *Gledhill* (Eng.) (1915), 31 T. L. R. 138.

[29] *Nahser* v. *City of Chicago* (1916), 271 Ill. 288; 111 N. E. 119. Clause 41 of the ordinance gives the city the same power in that respect as the state possessed, which is similar to the Amendatory Act of 1901 of the Laws of New York where the Board of Aldermen of New York City was given power to pass ordinances of a restrictive character upon places of amusement within the City of New York.

In this case it is held that it would be a valid exercise of the police power to enact a law prohibiting a motion picture show within 200 feet of a church, since such a show in such proximity would constitute a nuisance. See also: *People* v. *Busse* (1909), 240 Ill. 338; 88 N. E. 831; (1910), 248 Ill. 11; 93 N. E. 327.

[30] *Krier* v. *Mayor etc.* (1914), 26 Col. App. 150; 141 Pac. 505. *Held* that a local ordinance regulating the running of motion-picture theatres was void as it *absolutely prohibited* the same in the discretion of the local authorities.

See also: *Matter of O'Rourke* (1894), 9 Misc. (N. Y.) 564; 30 N. Y. Supp. 375.

But see in this connection: *Higgins* v. *Lacroix* (1912), 119 Minn. 145; 137 N. W. 417. "To say the least, opinions are quite at variance as to the merits of moving picture shows as an in-

This rule, however, does not deprive the licensing power from prohibiting motion picture exhibitions or other forms of amusement in certain parts of a town or city.[31]

Section 116.—Prohibition—Immorality.

It is within the police power of the state to prohibit the exhibition of any picture that is licentious, obscene, corrupt, seditious or apt to cause riots and disturbances, and this power may be delegated to the municipality.[32]

fluence for good or evil in a community. It must therefore be classed among those pursuits which are liable to degenerate and menace the good order and morals of the people, and may therefore not only be licensed and regulated, but also prevented by a village council."

[31] *Dreyfus* v. *City of Montgomery* (1912), 58 So. (Ala.) 730. Ordinance prohibiting motion picture shows in certain parts of a city was held valid.

See also: Section 110, p. 364, for instances where licenses were refused because of proximity to a church or school.

[32] *Sociological Research* v. *Waldo* (1914), 83 Misc. (N. Y.) 605; 145 N. Y. Supp. 492. The police interfered with the exhibition of plaintiff's film, "The Inside of the White Slave Traffic," describing the working of prostitutes. This action was brought in equity to enjoin the police from interfering with the exhibition of the picture. *Held* that a court of equity would not interfere with the police in enforcing the criminal law. *Held* further that the exhibition of a picture of the kind in question was not entitled to protection by a court of equity.

City of Chicago v. *Shaynin* (1913), 258 Ill. 69; 101 N. E. 224. A municipal corporation may prohibit the giving of exhibitions which tend to corrupt public morals or pander to morbid tastes and arouse the sexual desires.

Block v. *City of Chicago* (1909), 239 Ill. 251; 87 N. E. 1011. Holds that the city of Chicago may regulate motion picture theatres so as to prohibit the exhibition of immoral or obscene pictures.

Brewer v. *Wynne* (1913), 163 N. C. 319; 79 S. E. 629. Action

It is no defense to allege that the picture teaches a moral lesson,[33] nor need there be any exposure of the person to make it obscene.[34]

for false arrest and imprisonment. The defendant Stell, chief of police, arrested plaintiff under a statute permitting the police to prevent or suppress an indecent or immoral show, without a warrant, where the exhibition was imminent. *Held* that such a statute was constitutional.

Universal Film Mfg. Co. v. *Bell* (1917), N. Y. Law Journal, June 5, Greenbaum, J. The photoplay involved was entitled "The Hand that Rocks the Cradle."

See excerpt from opinion on p. 355.

Message Photo Play Co. v. *Bell* (1917), New York Appellate Division, N. Y. Law Journal, July 20. The court on appeal refused to interfere with a license commissioner who threatened to revoke the license of a theatre where the exhibition of a photoplay entitled "Birth Control" was in contemplation.

See excerpt contained on pp. 353 and 354.

See in this connection: *Genesee Recreation Co.* v. *Edgerton* (1916), 158 N. Y. Supp. 421; *Fox* v. *McClellan* (1909), 62 Misc. (N. Y.) 100; 114 N. Y. Supp. 594; *Eden Musee Co.* v. *Bingham* (1908), 125 A. D. (N. Y.) 380; 110 N. Y. Supp. 210.

[33] *Genesee Recreation Co.* v. *Edgerton* (1916), 158 N. Y. Supp. 421. Even though a motion picture may teach a moral lesson, it does not necessarily follow that the exhibition may not offend against public decency.

Anti-Vice Motion Picture Co., Inc., v. *Bell* (1916), N. Y. Law Journal, September 22. "Application for an injunction pendente lite to restrain the defendant from interfering with the exhibition by the plaintiff of a motion picture photoplay entitled 'Is any Girl Safe?' The Commissioner of Licenses of the City of

[34] *People* v. *Doris* (1898), 14 A. D. (N. Y.) 117; 43 N. Y. Supp. 571; appeal dismissed 153 N. Y. 678; 48 N. E. 1106. A pantomime entitled "Orange Blossoms," showing the retiring of a couple upon their wedding night was held a public nuisance even though there was no indecent exposure of the person.

New York asserts the right to prohibit the exhibition of this play upon the ground that it is immoral and indecent and in violation of law; in other words, that it would tend to the corruption of the morals of the public under section 1140a of the Penal Law. The film or photoplay is now being produced at one of the city theatres and it depicts the methods by which certain types of men procure young girls for houses of prostitution. It further pictures scenes in a house of prostitution and purports to show how young girls are led to ruin. The papers in opposition convince me that if the play is not of a revolting character, it certainly has many objectionable features, all of which are sufficient to condemn it. One affidavit sets forth that the play is a crude presentation, wholly devoid of moral or educational value, and that it caters to the lower and sensual side of human nature. Communications from many reputable citizens interested in the welfare of the stage and of motion picture theatres condemn this effort to appeal to a morbid public taste. The statements of these people, many of them experienced in the work of setting proper standards for moving picture houses and the productions made therein, and in protecting the morals of society, particularly the young members thereof, are of the utmost importance on this application. The preponderance of proof adduced herein shows that the City of New York is not benefited by such a realistic depiction of the sordid side of human life. The declaration is made in behalf of the scenario that 'it is literally a picturized sermon.' Such a statement does not appeal to me. Moving pictures may point a way or teach a lesson, but no depicted film that leads the beholder through scenes of such depravity and degradation can influence or help society. I think that such a play offends public decency and tends to the injury not only of the young of the community, but of all persons who witness it. It tends to deprave and corrupt the morals of those whose minds are open to such influences. Even if there was nothing so openly displayed, as is here claimed on behalf of the defendant, there is danger in an appeal to the imagination, and when the suggestion is immoral, the more that is left to the imagination the more subtle and seductive is the influence. *People*

v. *Doris*, 14 App. Div. 119. Moreover, the act of the commissioner of licenses in acting in the manner complained of is reasonable and is a proper exercise of the powers vested in him. The courts of this state have repeatedly held that they will not interfere with the exercise of the discretion vested by law in a departmental official unless such official has abused his discretion by acting in an unreasonable and tyrannical manner. *People ex rel. Rota* v. *Baker*, 136 App. Div. 7; *People ex rel. Armstrong* v. *Murphy*, 65 App. Div. 123. The defendant shows that the photoplay is not a proper production to be presented in licensed theatres of this city, and the motion is denied."

For a "war picture" see *Life Photo Film* v. *Bell* (1915), 90 Misc. (N. Y.) 469; 154 N. Y. Supp. 763. "Plaintiff, a manufacturer and lessor of photoplays, made and placed upon the market a film entitled "The Ordeal." The film portrayed events which presumably occurred during the Franco-Prussian war. The defendant, the commissioner of licenses, threatened to revoke the license of any theatre which exhibited the film upon the ground that because of the unfavorable manner in which the German soldiers were portrayed upon the screen, the exhibition of the film might arouse racial strife. In granting an injunction enjoining the commissioner from in anywise interfering with the film the court said: "Being of the opinion that the play itself is not offensive to any person of ordinary sense and that it is a perfectly proper play in all respects to be put before the public, and it appearing that the judgment of the defendant in preventing its exhibition according to defendant's brief is based upon the judgment of an unofficial body and his deputy, Mr. Kaufman, and not upon his own, and that by defendant's own testimony the play is unobjectionable, and that the reason assigned by defendant himself is insufficient to justify him in refusing to allow its exhibition, and that unless defendant is restrained there will be no way by which the plaintiff, as matter of right, will be able to test the question. I feel in justice to the plaintiff that the defendant should be restrained and that the relief prayed for in the complaint be granted."

Stein v. *Bell* (1917), N. Y. Law Journal, May 2. "An injunction is sought to prevent official interference with the plaintiff's attempt to produce a play entitled 'The Awakening of Spring,' the defendant, the commissioner of licenses, having announced his purpose of revoking the license of the theatre chosen for the performances should the plaintiff persist with the production. While a point is made that the threatened revocation of the license would be excessive of the commissioner's powers, the statute and the ordinances apparently afford him discretionary authority so to proceed (Charter, sec. 641; Laws 1914, chap. 475; Code of Ordinances, June 20, 1916, chap. 14, art. 1, secs. 2 and 5; chap. 3, art. 1, secs. 1, 2 and 3; *Edelstein* v. *Bell*, 91 Misc. 620). That the disapproval of this play is not an abuse of discretion is, to my mind, hardly open to argument. As addressed to the senses of a general audience it offends public decency. If intended for parents as a warning to instruct their children in sexual matters there is no promise that the audience is to be limited to parents. Apparently the young are to be equally enlightened by the play without giving the parents a prior choice of some less turgid channel of education. True, the plaintiff is not without the support of several well-meaning and intelligent persons in his opinion that the dramatization of these sex questions will serve a good end, but it appears to me that the subject is thus approached only from the standpoint of an adult's ability to reject indecent suggestions while assimilating the moral to be drawn from patent uncleanliness. The inquiring mind of youth has not this balanced equipment and is quicker to seize upon what is novel than to indulge in the abstractions of a more or less obscured philosophy. A general audience of theatregoers will see what is to be seen and take the obvious impressions from what is to be heard. Some may find a moral in this play which is beneficial; the majority, particularly the younger element, would find in the portrayal only what is portrayed—a pruriency attributed as typical of youth—to which type, happily, many do not conform. The play has been acted for my advisement upon this application, and I have also read the text. My judgment upon the subject being invited, I express the view that such a play has no proper place upon the stage of a public theatre and does infinitely more harm than good. Motion for injunction denied."

Even where the picture is in itself harmless but the title and posters are suggestive, it has been held that the picture should be suppressed.[35]

[35] *Ivan Film Productions* v. *Bell* (1916), N. Y. Law Journal, December 5. "This is a motion for an injunction pendente lite restraining the commissioner of licenses from prohibiting or interfering in any manner with the plaintiffs in the exhibition, presentation or production of a certain film or motion picture photo-play entitled "The Sex Lure." The position taken by the defendant is correctly stated in the brief of the corporation counsel to be this: "The commissioner objects to theatres under his jurisdiction producing said play on account of the title and the method of advertising the same. The affidavits in opposition show clearly that the title of the play, 'The Sex Lure,' and the method of advertising are an offense against morality, decency and public welfare, and that the title of the photo-play and the method of advertising are purely for the purpose of holding out to the public that the photo-play is of an indecent character, thus creating an immoral curiosity as to the nature of the same." That there is nothing objectionable about the photo-play itself is distinctly stated in the commissioner's affidavit, in which he says: "I learned from the report made to me by the deputy commissioner that the film itself was such that a production of the same in the theatres of this city could be had without harmful results." The question presented, therefore, is whether the commissioner of licenses has power to revoke the license of a theatre simply upon the ground that the name of the play and the methods of advertising on billboards and elsewhere are objectionable. The power of the commissioner of licenses to suspend or revoke any license or permit issued by him is undoubted, but it is equally clear that the power cannot be exercised arbitrarily or upon grounds that are entirely foreign to the commissioner's jurisdiction. The commissioner's jurisdiction for his official action in this case must be found in section 41, chapter 3, article 2, of the Code of Ordinances of the City of New York, which reads as follows: "Sec. 41. Public Morals. The inspectors of the

department of licenses shall investigate the character of exhibitions in motion picture theatres and open air motion picture theatres, and shall report to the commissioner any offense against morality, decency or public welfare committed in said exhibitions." Plainly it is the "character of exhibitions" and offenses "committed in said exhibitions" which, under this section, constitute the subject matter of the commissioner's jurisdiction. The method of advertising a play may be disgusting, offensively sensational and even dishonest, either on billboards or in the newspapers or elsewhere, but this has nothing to do with the character of the exhibition itself and is obviously not an offense committed in the exhibition. Whether it is desirable and necessary to give the commissioner of licenses jurisdiction over methods of advertising and the selection of names for plays is not for the court to say. Plainly, however, no such authority has been vested in the commissioner, and he has no more legal right to revoke the license of a theatre on these grounds than he would have because the moral character of the author of a play or of the actors employed to produce it was bad. If it appeared that the title of the play was exhibited in the theatre as a part of the film or production, a different question might be presented, but there is no proof that such is the case. There is another feature of this case, however, that should be considered. That the name and the method of advertising invite the public to a prurient and disgusting performance is only too obvious. The performance itself, however, is said to be a clean one, as indeed it would have to be to obtain the sanction of the commissioner. So it is established that the plaintiff is inviting the public to the theatre upon false pretenses and seeking to capitalize whatever degenerate interest there may be created by the use of this name and the posters that go with it. Furthermore, the name and the posters taken together are indecent, nasty and offensive. Such practices result, too, in bringing odium unjustly upon the many respectable members of the important motion picture industry. The plaintiffs do not come into court with clean hands, and upon this ground the motion for an injunction is denied."

Pictures that tend to create race feeling and threaten disturbances of the peace may be prohibited,[36] as well as exhibitions of prizefighting.[37]

On the other hand, it has been held that ballet dancing does not constitute ground for suppression.[38]

Section 117.—Who is liable for penalty.

The courts have held proprietors of places of amusement to a strict accountability for violations of statutes governing the licensing and control of such places and have

[36] *Bainbridge, Jr.* v. *City of Minneapolis* (1915), 131 Minn. 195; 154 N. W. 964. On an attempt to enjoin the Mayor from revoking the license of a theatre wherein the film "The Birth of a Nation" was about to be produced.

Edelstein v. *Bell* (1915), 91 Misc. (N. Y.) 620; 155 N. Y. Supp. 590. The court refused to interfere with the exercise of discretion rested in the Commissioner of Licenses where he refused to grant a license permitting the exhibition of a photoplay entitled "The Frank Case" based on the incidents of the famous murder trial in Georgia.

[37] *Weber* v. *Freed* (1915), 239 U. S. 325. *Held* that Congress had power to prohibit the introduction, importation or transportation from abroad of any tangible object, and that prizefight films of the Willard-Johnson fight came under that prohibition.

Kalisthenic Ex. Co. v. *Emmons* (1915), 225 Fed. (D. C.) 902; aff'd 229 Fed. (C. C. A.) 124. Plaintiff, the owner of negative films of the Willard-Johnson prizefight, sought to make entry of them with the defendant, collector of the port of Portland, Me. The court held that under Section 10416 of the U. S. Compiled Statutes of 1913 this film could not be brought in.

[38] *The King* v. *McAuliffe* (Can.) (1904), 8 Can. Cr. Cas. 21. Ballet dancing is not in itself indecent and in order to convict the proprietor of a theatre of conducting an immoral show, affirmative evidence of indecency and obscenity must be produced.

not permitted them to relieve themselves of liability by showing that they were not guilty of the wrongful acts, or that they had no knowledge of the misdeeds.[39]

In a case where an ordinance prohibited the proprietor of a place of amusement from causing, consenting to, or "allowing" certain exhibitions, a proprietor was held liable, although he himself did nothing, was ignorant of the act or made ineffectual attempts to stop the wrongful act.[40]

And even where the premises had been let to some third party but defendant furnished the ushers and other employes he remained liable.[41]

But when the proprietor gives up all control of the premises and his lessee is in complete possession he is not liable.[42]

[39] *Bruce* v. *McManus* (1915) (Eng.), 3 K. B. 1; 113 L. T. 332; W. N. 170; 79 J. P. 294; 84 L. J. (K. B.) 1860; 31 T. L. R. 387; 13 L. G. R. 727. Even though a motion picture is managed or superintended by a subordinate, the owner himself is liable for a penalty under the statute.

See also: *Waldo* v. *Seelig* (1911), 70 Misc. (N. Y.) 254; 126 N. Y. Supp. 798; aff'd 146 A. D. (N. Y.) 879; 130 N. Y. Supp. 1133; *Potter* v. *Watt* (Eng.) (1914), 84 L. J. (K. B.) 394; 79 J. P. 212; 112 L. T. 508; 31 T. L. R. 84.

[40] *Matter of Hammerstein* (1907), 52 Misc. (N. Y.) 606; 102 N. Y. Supp. 950.

[41] *Fire Department* v. *Hill* (1891), 14 N. Y. Supp. 158. Defendant, lessee of theatre premises, had let to another the privilege of giving performances for four weeks. During these performances, persons were permitted to stand in the aisles in violation of the fire regulations, and suit was brought for a penalty. Defendant furnished the ushers and other employes.

Defendant held liable, even though the servants were under the direction of the manager of the performance, and he claimed ignorance of the infractions.

Following *Fire Dept.* v. *Stetson* (1887), 14 Daly (N. Y.), 125.

[42] *State* v. *French Opera Ass'n* (1902), 107 La. 284; 31 So. 630.

Under a penal statute making it a misdemeanor to permit a child under a specified age to enter a place of amusement unless accompanied by its guardian, a mere ticket taker was held not included within the class of persons embraced by the section.[43]

Section 118.—Ticket " Scalping."

Under Act of March 18, 1905, of California, known as Penal Code, Sec. 526, it was declared a misdemeanor to sell or offer to sell any tickets of admission to any theatre or other place of amusement at a price in excess of that charged originally by the management.

This statute was declared unconstitutional upon the ground that it prevented the free disposition of property by the owner thereof, which was guaranteed to him under the state constitution.[44]

The owner of a theatre is not liable for a tax imposed upon the theatre where the property has been leased to a third party and the lessee conducts the theatre.

New Castle v. *Geukinger* (1908), 37 Pa. Super. Ct. 21. Where the defendant did not exhibit an immoral show, but merely rented his opera house to another, who without his knowledge or consent, gave such performances, he is not liable, and a judgment of conviction against him under Sec. one, Act 1 of ordinances of the City of New Castle approved March 22, 1904, will not be upheld.

[43] *People ex rel. Jacques* v. *Sheriff* (1907), 122 A. D. (N. Y.) 878; 107 N. Y. Supp. 415; aff'd 191 N. Y. 525; 84 N. E. 1118.

Section 290 of the Penal Code of New York.

On the question whether the license of the lessees of a theatre covered also the performers see *Shelby* v. *Emerson* (1880), 4 Lea. (Tenn.) 312. "We think the license includes and protects the employes of the managers, who furnish the entertainments, and the minstrel troupe is but an essential agency in carrying on the business licensed."

[44] *Ex parte Quarg* (1906), 149 Cal. 79; 84 Pac. 766.

Illinois enacted a similar statute. This statute as well was declared unconstitutional as an abuse by the state of its police power. The court held: "There is nothing immoral in the sale of theatre tickets, at an advance over the price of the box office. Such sale is not injurious to the public welfare and does not affect the public health, morals, safety, comfort or good order. It does not injure the buyer or proprietor of the theatre. The buyer purchases voluntarily. He is under no compulsion. If the conducting of a theatre is a mere private business, there is no reason why the proprietor may not sell the tickets when and where, at what prices and on what terms he chooses." [45]

In New York the business of a ticket speculator was held to be a lawful occupation.[46] A city ordinance, however, making it a misdemeanor to sell tickets on the streets in front of any licensed theatre or place of amuse-

[45] *People* v. *Steele* (1907), 231 Ill. 340; 83 N. E. 236. The state under its police powers has a right to regulate a theatre but only to the extent that it may regulate any other private business. It may impose a license fee and pass such regulations as will safeguard the public health, safety, morals, comfort and general welfare of the public.

But the legislature may not enact laws to prevent speculation in theatre tickets, frequently called "scalping" as such legislation has no reference to the public health, safety, morals, comfort or general welfare of the public and such laws would deprive those engaged in such business of their liberty and property without due process of law.

City of Chicago v. *Powers* (1907), 231 Ill. 560; 83 N. E. 240. Where the courts of the state held a statute forbidding "ticket scalping" to be void, the city of Chicago could not pass an ordinance of like effect.

[46] *People* v. *Marks* (1909), 64 Misc. (N. Y.) 679; 120 N. Y. Supp. 1106.

ment was held constitutional as within the police powers of the municipality.[47]

Section 119.—Censorship.

We have seen that under its police power, the different states of the union have enacted laws regulating the erection and operation of buildings wherein motion picture exhibitions are contemplated to be given.[48] We have also noted that some states have indirectly controlled the exhibition of the motion picture itself by giving to those in whom they have vested the regulation of the operation of such buildings, discretionary powers in withholding, granting or revoking the *licenses* required to operate them.[49] Instances have been also given where the police have been upheld by the courts when they have suppressed films under penal statutes prohibiting the giving of obscene or immoral exhibitions, or because such exhibitions constituted a nuisance.[50]

Several of the states have gone one step further and have enacted statutes creating boards of censorship, the approval of which must be obtained before the motion picture may be exhibited within the state. Such laws

[47] *People ex rel. Lange* v. *Palmitter* (1911), 71 Misc. (N. Y.) 158; 128 N. Y. Supp. 426; aff'd 144 A. D. (N. Y.) 894; 128 N. Y. Supp. 1140; aff'd 202 N. Y. 608; 96 N. E. 1126.

See in this connection: *Benson* v. *McMahon* (1888), 127 U. S. 457; 8 Sup. Ct. 1240. One who causes to be printed tickets for an operatic performance and sells them as and for the tickets of the management when not so in fact is guilty of forgery at common law.

See also: *Commonwealth* v. *Ray* (1855), 69 Mass. 441.

[48] See Sections 110 to 117.

[49] See Sections 107 to 110.

[50] See Section 116.

have been held to be constitutional and a proper exercise of the police power of the state.

The first case to reach the United States Supreme Court and which declared motion picture censorship laws constitutional, was that of the *Mutual Film Corporation* v. *Industrial Commission of Ohio.*[51] The statute involved was one enacted by the legislature of Ohio, creating under the authority and superintendence of the Industrial Commission of the state a board of censors of motion picture films.

Section three of the statute made it the duty of the board to examine and censor those films which were to be publicly exhibited within the state. The films were required to be exhibited to the board before their delivery to the exhibitor.

Section four provided, "Only such films as are in the judgment and discretion of the board of censors of a moral, educational or amusing and harmless character shall be passed and approved by such board."

Section five granted authority to the board to work in conjunction with censor boards of other states as a congress, and permitted the action of such congress to be considered that of the state board.

Section seven imposed penalties for the exhibition of motion pictures without first complying with the statute.

Section eight provided for a review of the action of the board "as is provided in the case of persons dissatisfied with the orders of the industrial commission."

[51] *Mutual Film Corp.* v. *Industrial Com.* (Ohio) (1915), 236 U. S. 230; 35 Sup. Ct. 387. See also opinion of the lower court reported in 215 Fed. 138.

Three objections as to the constitutionality of the statute were raised by the appellant.

The first objection was that the statute imposed an unlawful burden upon interstate commerce. The court held that when the film was brought into the state for exhibition therein, and sent to "exchanges" to be delivered to the exhibitors, they became subject to the laws of the state. In the words of the courts, "There must be some time when the films are subject to the law of the State, and necessarily when they are in the hands of the exchanges ready to be rented to exhibitors or have passed to the latter, they are in consumption, and mingled as much as from their nature they can be with other property of the State."

The appellant's second contention was that motion picture exhibitions were in the same category with the press and that any censorship thereof was a violation of freedom of speech and publication guaranteed by the state constitution.

The court held that the motion picture industry was a private enterprise, not organized primarily for the purpose of expressing public opinion, but on the contrary its primary aim was to amuse and entertain. It further held that the manufacture and exhibition of pictures of an educational character, were merely one of the incidental branches but not by any means, the main branch of the industry.

To quote the court: "They (motion pictures), indeed, may be mediums of thought, but so are many things. So is the theatre, the circus, and all other shows and spectacles, and their performances may be thus brought by the like reasoning under the same immunity from repression or supervision as the public press." And again, "It cannot be put out of view that the exhibition of moving pictures is a business pure and simple, originated and conducted for profit, like other spectacles, not to be regarded or intended to be regarded by the Ohio constitution, we think, as part of the press of the country as organs of public opinion."

The final objection to the statute raised by the Mutual Film Corporation was that the statute delegated *legislative powers* to a board in that it furnished no standard of what was educational, moral, amusing or harmless, and thus left the decisions of the board to their "arbitrary judgment, whim and caprice," permitting the "personal equation" to enter into the consideration of the approval of the films. The court brushed aside this argument. It summed up its position upon this objection by saying, "But the statute by its provisions guards against such variant judgments, and its terms like other general terms, get precision from the sense and experience of men and become certain and useful guides in reasoning and conduct. The exact specification of the instances of their application would be as impossible as the attempt would be futile. Upon such sense and experience, the law properly relies (citing cases). If this were not so, the many administrative agencies created by the State and National governments would be denuded of their utility and government in some of its most important exercises become impossible."

The state of Kansas also passed a censorship act prohibiting the exhibition of any motion picture film unless it had first been submitted to and approved by the Superintendent of Public Instruction. The Supreme Court, following its decision in the Ohio case, held that the statute was constitutional, that the statute was a valid exercise of the police power of the state, that it did not interfere with interstate commerce, did not infringe upon the liberty of opinion and that there was no delegation of legislative power to administrative officers.[52]

The highest state court of Pennsylvania held that a statute requiring the submission of all films to be exhibited within the state to a board of censors was constitutional.[53]

The most recent case upholding the constitutionality of censorship statutes was that of the *Mutual Film Corporation* v. *City of Chicago, et al.*[54] An ordinance of the City of Chicago provided that no motion picture should be exhibited in any public place without first submitting the film to the censorship of the police. The court held the ordinance constitutional upon the authority of the two above mentioned cases decided by the United States Supreme Court.

Louisiana has a censorship law upon its statute books authorizing any city, town or village of the state to adopt any ordinance for the regulation by censorship of motion picture theatres and all other places wherein films are

[52] *Mutual Film* v. *Hodges* (Kansas) (1915), 236 U. S. 247; 35 Sup. Ct. 393.

[53] *Buffalo Br.* v. *Breitinger* (1915), 250 Pa. 225; 95 Atl. 433.

[54] *Mutual Film* v. *City of Chicago* (1915), 224 Fed. (C. C. A.) 101.

exhibited.[55] The statute has not yet come before the courts as to its constitutionality.

Attempts have been made to secure the passage of a bill through Congress establishing a Federal census board, but up to the present writing Congress has not seen fit to legislate upon that subject. Although Congress, under its control of interstate commerce, probably has the constitutional right to require all films shipped through the different states, to be submitted to a Federal board of censors, it is doubtful whether it will exercise its rights. It will probably leave the censoring of films to state boards, which can take into consideration the habits, prejudices and modes of thought peculiar to the state in which they act.

Congress has already enacted a law prohibiting the transportation from one state to another or the importation into this country of films representing prize fights and other pugilistic encounters for purposes of public exhibition.[56] And that statute has been held to be con-

[55] Acts of Louisiana, 1914, (Special Session of 1913), Act No. 180, July 9, 1914.

[56] Act of July 31, 1912, Chapter 263, Sections 1, 2, 3; 37 Stat. 240; (United States Compiled Statutes of 1916, Sections 10416, 10417, 10418, pp. 12856, 12857.)

Sec. 10416. "It shall be unlawful for any person to deposit or cause to be deposited in the United States mails for mailing or delivery or to deposit or cause to be deposited with any express company or other common carrier for carriage, or to send or carry from one State or Territory of the United States or the District of Columbia to any other State or Territory of the United States or the District of Columbia, or to bring or to cause to be brought into the United States from abroad, any film or other pictorial representation of any prize fight or encounter of pugilists, under whatever name, which is designed to be used or may be

stitutional, under the commerce clause of the constitution.[57]

Congress has also provided in the tariff act of 1909 for a censorship by the Secretary of the Treasury of all films imported into this country. The Secretary of the Treasury, however, has not as yet to the knowledge of the writers, attempted to exercise that right.[58] The Circuit

used for purposes of public exhibition."

Sec. 10417. "It shall be unlawful for any person to take or receive from the mails or any express company or other common carrier with intent to sell, distribute, circulate or exhibit any matter or thing herein forbidden to be deposited for mailing, delivery, or carriage in interstate commerce."

Sec. 10418. "Any person violating any of the provisions of this act shall for each offense, upon conviction thereof, be fined not more than one thousand dollars or sentenced to imprisonment at hard labor for not more than one year, or both, at the discretion of the court."

Kalisthenic Exhibition Co. v. *Emmons* (1915), 225 Fed. (D. C.) 902; aff'd 229 Fed. (C. C. A.) 124. The plaintiff sought to import a negative film of a prize fight exhibition. The court held that where the positive prints of the film were contemplated to be exhibited before "clubs, societies, associations, athletic clubs, and their guests" and no limitation was placed upon the number of their guests, such exhibitions of the film were public and came within the prohibition of the statute.

See opinion of the United States Circuit Court of Appeals.

[57] *Weber* v. *Freed* (1915), 239 U. S. 325; 36 Sup. Ct. 131. See also opinion of lower court in 224 Fed. 355.

[58] Tariff Act of October 3, 1913, Chapter 16, Section 1, Subsection 380 38 Stat. 114; (United States Compiled Statutes of 1916, Section 5291, p. 6389.)

". . . photographic film negatives imported in any form, for use in any way in connection with moving picture exhibits or for making or reproducing pictures for such exhibits exposed but not developed, two cents per linear or running foot; if exposed

Court of Appeals in *Kalisthenic Exhibition Co., Inc.,* v. *Emmons,* holds that the censorship provision of the statute may permit the barring of the entry of a film until the Secretary of the Treasury subjects it to his censorship.[59]

As in the case of authorities in whom are vested the right to issue and revoke licenses for the giving of motion picture exhibitions, the action of Boards of Censorship will not be interfered with by the courts, unless the element of bad faith, capriciousness or misinformation is apparent.[60]

and developed, three cents per linear or running foot; photographic film positives, imported in any form for use in any way in connection with moving-picture exhibits, including herein all moving, motion, motophotography or cinematography film pictures, prints, positives or duplicates of every kind and nature and of whatever substance made, one cent per linear or running foot. *Provided, however, that all photographic films imported under this section shall be subject to such censorship as may be imposed by the Secretary of the Treasury.*"

[59] *Kalisthenic Exhibition Co. Inc.* v. *Emmons* (1916), 229 Fed. (C. C. A.) 124. The following is the language of Putnam, C. J.: "The later act . . . by its closing provision apparently bars importations except subject to censorship and as no censorship has been imposed which reaches this case, the bar therefore continues, so far as we perceive."

[60] *In re Franklin Film Mfg. Co.* (1916), 253 Pa. 422; 98 Atl. 623. "Every order for an elimination made by the board of censors, necessarily comprehends a finding that the picture in question is 'sacrilegious, obscene, indecent or immoral' and, as such, tends to 'debase or corrupt morals' . . . yet it (the court below) did not find the censors were guilty of an arbitrary or oppressive abuse of discretion, and, in the absence of such a determination, the order complained of cannot stand."

". . . The evident intent was to grant a right of appeal to

Section 120.—Sunday performance.

Sunday was not a *dies non* under the common law, and all regulations respecting the observance of Sunday and the prohibition of particular lines of activity are purely of statutory creation.

However, Sunday statutes are very old.

The earliest general statute on the subject is contained in the Act of 1677 (29 Car. 2, Chap. 7), more generally known as the "Lord's Day Act." Under this statute it was declared "that no tradesman, artificer, workman, labourer or other person whatsoever shall do or exercise any worldly labour, business or work of their ordinary callings upon the Lord's Day or any part thereof, works of necessity and charity only excepted." The statute imposed a fine of five shillings for a violation thereof.

For many years thereafter the courts were occupied with construing the meaning of "works of necessity."[61] Under a later statute[62] it was made a crime to open a

the Common Pleas so that that tribunal could correct any arbitrary or oppressive orders which the Board of Censors might make, and nothing more; in other words, that the court might reverse the censors when the latter were guilty of an abuse of discretion . . ."

See for detailed discussion of subject, Sections 107 to 110.

[61] For a construction of what constitutes "*Works of Necessity*" see *Crepps* v. *Durden* (Eng.) (1777), Comp. Pt. 2, p. 640; *Phillips* v. *Inez* (Eng.) (1837), 42 R. R. 19; *Palmer* v. *Snow* (Eng.) (1900), 1 Q. B. 725; *Bullen* v. *Ward* (Eng.) (1905), 93 L. T. N. S. 439; *Williams* v. *Wright; Watts* v. *Van Ness* (1841), 1 Hill (N. Y.), 76; *Cortesy* v. *Territory* (1892), 6 N. M. 682; 30 Pac. 947; *Flagstaff Silver Co.* v. *Cullins* (1881), 104 U. S. 176.

[62] Sunday Observance Act of 1780 (21 Geo. III, c. 49) s. 1.

See in this connection: *Williams* v. *Wright* (Eng.) (1897), 41 S. J. 671; 13 T. L. R. 551.

room or house for public entertainment, amusement or debate on Sunday and to charge an admission fee therefor.

The charge of an admission fee has often been the determining factor in establishing whether or not there has been a violation of the statute, but the decisions on that point are not harmonious.[63] We should have no hesitancy in saying that since the intent of the legislature, as a rule, is to prohibit a performance from which *a profit* may be derived, the mere fact that admission fees are charged is not very material. There frequently are other and perhaps more subtle and indirect methods of deriving gain and profit, and *Herbert* v. *Shanley* [64] would now seem to be controlling on that point.

The New York Statutes are typical of many Sunday statutes throughout the country. Indeed, New York was one of the first states to adopt statutes which prohibited theatrical performances on Sunday, but it has not yet passed any statute expressly prohibiting the exhibition of motion pictures on Sunday. The result is a generally chaotic state of the law with respect to Sunday performances. The history of the construction of these statutes is instructive.

Chapter 42 of the Laws of 1788 of the state of New

[63] *Ex parte Jacobson* (1909), 55 Tex. Crim. 237; 115 S. W. 1193; *Weistblatt* v. *Bingham* (1908), 58 Misc. (N. Y.) 328; 109 N. Y. Supp. 545; *Economopoulos* v. *Bingham* (1907), 109 N. Y. Supp. 728; *La Crandall* v. *Ledbetter* (1908), 159 Fed. (C. C. A.) 702; *Muckenfuss* v. *State* (1909), 55 Tex. Crim. 229; 116 S. W. 51; *Fichtenberg* v. *Atlanta* (1906), 126 Ga. 62; 54 S. E. 933; *Com.* v. *Weidner* (1887), 4 Pa. Co. Ct. 437.

[64] *Herbert* v. *Shanley* (1917), 242 U. S. 591; 37 Sup. Ct. 232; *Church* v. *Hilliard* (1917), 242 U. S. 591; 37 Sup. Ct. 232.

York prohibited servile work, traveling and shooting, fishing, sporting, playing, horse racing, hunting or frequenting tippling houses or any unlawful exercise or pastimes on Sunday. This Chapter was carried into the Revised Laws of 1813 without change and into the Revised Statutes of 1830 with the addition of "gaming." It was later incorporated into Section 265 of the Penal Code.

In 1908 the statute came up for construction in a case where the owner of a theatre had been convicted for giving a motion-picture exhibition on Sunday. It was held that the phrase "*or other public sports, exercise or shows*" in that section of the Penal Code was to be construed in the light of the *ejusdem generis* rule and that the words above quoted referred merely to outdoor amusement or such as would in their nature desecrate or profane the Sabbath; that they had no application whatever to the exhibition of a motion-picture.[65] This interpretation of the statute was followed in later cases.[66]

[65] *People* v. *Hemleb* (1908), 127 A. D. (N. Y.) 356.

See also: *State* v. *Penny* (1910), 42 Mont. 118; 111 Pac. 727; *People ex rel. Valensi* v. *Flynn* (1908), 108 N. Y. Supp. 208; *Reid* v. *Wilson* (Eng.) (1895), 1 Q. B. 315; *People ex rel Valensi* v. *Lynch* (1908), 108 N. Y. Supp. 209; *Keith & Proctor* v. *Bingham* (1908), 125 A. D. (N. Y.) 791; 110 N. Y. Supp. 219; *Edwards* v. *McClellan* (1909), 118 N. Y. Supp. 181; *Eden Musée* v. *Bingham* (1908), 125 A. D. (N. Y.) 780; 110 N. Y. Supp. 210; *State* v. *Chamberlain* (1910), 112 Minn. 52; 127 N. W. 444; *Rex* v. *Charron* (Can.) (1909), 15 Can. Cr. Cas. (Quebec), 241; *Houck* v. *Ingles* (1914), 126 Minn. 257; 148 N. W. 100; *State* v. *Morris* (1916), 155 Pac. (Idaho), 296; *People* v. *Brown* (1912), 137 N. W. (Mich.), 535.

[66] *People* v. *Finn* (1908), 57

In 1916, the statute again came before the court for construction. It was held in effect that a motion-picture *was* one of the "*other public sports, exercises or shows*" and should be prohibited.[67] The highest court, not having had the question before it as yet, the conflicting decisions have left the law in New York in a very unsettled state.[68]

In construing Sunday statutes, the courts have taken into consideration the fact whether at the time the act was passed motion pictures had become well known and

Misc. (N. Y.) 659; *Fox Amusement Co.* v. *McClellan* (1909), 62 Misc. (N. Y.) 100; 114 N. Y. Supp. 594; 110 N. Y. Supp. 22; *Klinger* v. *Ryan* (1915), 91 Misc. (N. Y.) 71; 153 N. Y. Supp. 71; 153 N. Y. Supp. 937; *People ex rel. Klinger* v. *Rand* (1915), 91 Misc. (N. Y.) 276; 154 N. Y. Supp. 293.

[67] *People ex rel. Bender* v. *Joyce* (1916), 174 A. D. (N. Y.) 574; 161 N. Y. Supp. 771. Holds that Sec. 2145 of the Penal Law applies to motion-picture theatres, and relator, convicted of conducting such a theatre on Sunday, was remanded. This decision has aroused considerable discussion, as it is directly opposed to *People* v. *Hemleb* (1908), 127 A. D. (N. Y.) 356, wherein Judge Gaynor decided that the exhibition of motion pictures was not a violation of the statute.

[68] At the present writing the Appellate Divisions of the State of New York are diametrically opposed to each other in construing the foregoing section. We even doubt whether a decision of the Court of Appeals would clear the situation, for any section upon which the principle must rest, it must be remembered, was passed before the advent of motion-pictures. Direct and plain legislation on the subject is the real necessity, and the reason that there is none is that the people want Sunday motion-pictures and the religious organizations do not want them to have it. It is to be deplored that so important a feature of the motion-picture business and of the life of the people should be subject to the whim and caprice of individual judges rather than to special legislative enactment.

for that reason in the minds of the legislators at that time.[69]

The legislature alone is the sole judge of observances or profanities of the Sabbath and a Mayor or other municipal officer unless expressly authorized so to do, has no inherent authority to regulate the same.[70]

[69] *People* v. *Finn* (1908), 57 Misc. (N. Y.), 659; 110 N. Y. Supp. 22.

"This act was framed before the idea of moving pictures was conceived by the mind of man and must be interpreted with relation to the then intent of the Legislators."

Re G. W. Hull (1910), 18 Idaho, 475; 110 Pac. 256. The Supreme Court of Idaho speaking of a scenic railway said:

"The prohibition of public amusements on Sunday must therefore rest on the theory that it is necessary either for the protection of the public morals, the public health, or the public peace and safety. (Citing cases.) This amusement is not per se, unlawful or criminal, nor is it immoral or dangerous or detrimental to the public health. It is apparently a wholesome, innocent outdoor amusement. In order to prohibit such an amusement we ought to find the prohibition within the statute, either in positive terms or by clear implication. *No such means of amusement existed at the time of the passage of this act,* and if this is to be prohibited under the statute, it must be by reason of it being 'such a place of amusement' as some one of those specifically enumerated. We do not feel that we would be justified in extending the statute to cover this means of amusement, and thereby make its maintenance and operation a crime."

[70] *Neuendorff* v. *Duryea* (1877), 69 N. Y. 557. See also: *People* v. *Dunford* (1912), 207 N. Y. 17; 100 N. E. 433.

People ex rel. Kieley v. *Lent* (1915), 166 A. D. (N. Y.) 550; 152 N. Y. Supp. 18; aff'd 215 N. Y. 626; 109 N. E. 1088. The legislature alone has power to enforce ordinances by penalties, forfeitures and imprisonment, and unless it has expressly delegated this power to a municipality, the latter may not enforce a Sunday closing ordinance as to motion picture houses.

In many of the states exhibitions of motion pictures have been held exempt from the operation of statutes forbidding the keeping open of a theatre on Sunday,[71] the operation of "other places of amusement"[72] and of "amusements disturbing the peace."[73]

City of New York v. *Alhambra Theatre* (1910), 136 A. D. (N. Y.) 509; 121 N. Y. Supp. 3; aff'd 202 N. Y. 528; 95 N. E. 1125. The municipality had by express enactment (Greater N. Y. Charter) been given the power to pass ordinances regulating the observance of Sunday and the defendant had been held liable in a penalty for giving a theatrical performance on Sunday. See also: *People* v. *O'Gorman* (1908), 124 A. D. (N. Y.) 222; 108 N. Y. Supp. 737; *New York* v. *Williams* (1905), 48 Misc. (N. Y.) 77; 96 N. Y. Supp. 237; *Matter of New York* (1909), 131 A. D. (N. Y.) 767; 116 N. Y. Supp. 353; *St. Joseph* v. *Elliott* (1891), 47 Mo. App. 418; *Ex parte Ferguson* (1914), 80 Wash. 102; 141 Pac. 322.

[71] *State* v. *Penny* (1910), 111 Pac. (Mont.) 727. *Held* that a statute making it a misdemeanor to keep open a theatre on Sunday was not violated by the giving of a motion picture exhibition.

[72] *City of Clinton* v. *Wilson* (1913), 257 Ill. 580; 101 N. E. 192. The statute prohibited "any billiard room, ball or pin alley, baseball grounds *or other places of amusement* to operate on Sunday. *Held* that it did not apply to motion picture performances.

[73] *Stevens* v. *Morenous* (1912), 169 Ill. App. 282. Under a statute prohibiting amusements disturbing the peace and good order of society it was held that the proprietor of a theatre could not be restrained from giving Sunday performances when such performances were proper and moral.

See also: *Eden* v. *People* (1896), 161 Ill. 296; 43 N. E. 1108; Contra with respect to a motion picture exhibition: *United Vaudeville Co.* v. *Zeller* (1908), 58 Misc. (N. Y.) 16; 108 N. Y. Supp. 789; *Hamlin* v. *Bender* (1915), 92 Misc. (N. Y.) 16; 155 N. Y. Supp. 963; *Gale* v. *Bingham* (1907), 110 N. Y. Supp. 12.

See also: *A. H. Woods Prod. Co.*

On the other hand, they have been held to come within the provisions of statutes prohibiting "theatrical performances" [74] and the keeping open of "any place of public amusement." [75]

v. *Chicago R. R.* (1909), 147 Ill. App. 568. A theatrical performance on Sunday was held not to violate a statute prohibiting "any noise, rout or amusement on the first day of the week disturbing the peace of any private family."

[74] *Ex parte Lingenfelter* (1911), 64 Tex. Crim. 30; 142 S. W. 555. "Being of the opinion that a moving picture show of the character and kind presented in this state, comes within the definition of amusements of like character, kind and species as a theatre, and while not a theatre, yet it is of the same genus, relator is remanded. Our statutes refer to a "horse" and this term has been held to embrace a mare, a mule, a jack, a jenny, as they are all of the same species, and many illustrations might be cited as holding that all things of the same genus are embraced, even when not followed by general words, but we deem it useless."

Cases referred to by the court include: *Ex parte Roquemore* (1910), 60 Tex. Crim. 282; 131 S. W. 1101; *Ex parte Muckenfuss* (1908), 52 Tex. Crim. 467; 107 S. W. 1131; *Crow* v. *State* (1851), 6 Tex. 334; *In re Hull* (1910), 18 Idaho, 475; 110 Pac. 256; *State* v. *Prather* (1909), 79 Kansas, 513; 100 Pac. 57; *Ex Parte Neet* (1910), 157 Mo. 527; 57 S. W. 1025. To the same effect: *In re Bossner* (1910), 18 Idaho, 519; 110 Pac. 502.

Rosenberg v. *Arrowsmith* (1914), 89 Atl. (N. J.) 524. The statute in question prohibited "worldly employment or business, interludes and plays, fiddling, or other music for the sake of merriment on Sunday." Moving picture exhibitions were held to be included within that statute.

See in this connection: *Foun-*

[75] *Oliver* v. *State* (1911), 144 S. W. (Tex.) 604. *Held* that a motion picture exhibition was included under a statute prohibiting the keeping open of "any place of public amusement" on Sunday. See also: *Ex parte Zuccaro* (1913), 162 S. W. (Tex.) 844.

To manage a theatre on Sunday has been held to be "*labor*" within Sunday statutes.[76]

tain Sq. Theatre v. *Evans* (1896), 4 Ohio Dec. 151; *Matter of Hammerstein* (1907), 57 Misc. (N. Y.) 52; 108 N. Y. Supp. 197; *People* v. *Haym* (1860), 20 How. Pr. (N. Y.) 76; *State* v. *Herald* (1907), 47 Wash. 538; 92 Pac. 376; *In re Donellan* (1908), 49 Wash. 460; 95 Pac. 1085; *People* v. *Hammerstein* (1913), 155 A. D. (N. Y.) 204; 139 N. Y. Supp. 1075; *Kreider* v. *State* (1912), 103 Ark. 438; 147 S. W. 449; *Reg.* v. *Barnes* (Can.), 45 U. C. Q. B. 276; *N. Y.* v. *Eden Musée* (1886), 102 N. Y. 593; 8 N. E. 40; *Stewart* v. *Thayer* (1897), 168 Mass. 519; 47 N. E. 420.

[76] *City of Topeka* v. *Crawford* (1908), 78 Kan. 583; 96 Pac. 862. "If to keep open a store and receive and sell wares therein is the common *labor* of a merchant, it is fair to say that to keep open, manage and superintend a theatre and sell tickets therein is the *labor* of such manager." *Held* that managing a theatre on Sunday was *labor* and was a violation of the statute.

Quarles v. *State* (1891), 55 Ark. 10; 17 S. W. 269. To superintend and manage the giving of a theatrical performance on Sunday, and to sell tickets therefor is "*labor*" within the meaning of a statute that prohibits all labor on Sunday.

See also: *City of Topeka* v. *Crawford* (1908), 78 Kan. 583; 96 Pac. 862; *Wirth* v. *Calhoun* (1902), 64 Nebr. 316; 89 N. W. 785; *Comm.* v. *Alexander* (1904), 185 Mass. 551; 70 N. E. 1017; *Rex* v. *Ouimet* (Can.) (1908), 14 Can. Cr. Cas. (Quebec) 136; *Moore* v. *Owen* (1908), 58 Misc. (N. Y.) 332; 109 N. Y. Supp. 585; *Re Bossner* (1910), 18 Idaho, 519; 110 Pac. 502; *Ex parte Lingenfelter* (1911), 64 Tex. Crim. 30; 142 S. W. 555; *Ex parte Zuccaro* (1913), 72 Tex. Crim. Rep. 214; 162 S. W. 844; *St. Joseph* v. *Elliott* (1891), 47 Mo. App. 418; *State* v. *Ryan* (1908), 80 Conn. 582; 69 Atl. 536; *Fox* v. *McClellan* (1909), 62 Misc. (N. Y.) 100; 114 N. Y. Supp. 594; *Terry* v. *Brighton Aquarium* (Eng.) (1875), L. R. 10 Q. B. 306; *City of Clinton* v. *Wilson* (1913), 257 Ill. 580; 101 N. E. 192; *McLeod* v. *State* (1915), 180 S. W. (Tex.) 117; *Spooner* v. *State* (1916), 182 S. W. (Tex.) 1121; *Gould* v. *State* (1911), 134 S. W. (Tex.) 695; *Lempke* v. *State* (1915), 171

A statute which prohibits the operation of motion picture theatres on Sunday is constitutional.[77] It is in its essence a police regulation [78] and a defendant may be prosecuted simultaneously under it for both the civil and criminal penalties.[79]

Equity will not restrain a defendant from giving such performances, but will relegate the state to its criminal remedy.[80]

S. W. (Tex.) 217; *People* v. *Dixon* (1915), 154 N. W. (Mich.) 1.

[77] *State* v. *Barnes* (1911), 22 N. D. 18; 132 N. W. 215. A statute prohibiting the operation of a theatre, show, moving picture exhibition or theatrical performance on Sunday was held constitutional.

See cases cited in opinion of the above case for decisions in the different states of the union to the same effect.

[78] *Majestic Theatre* v. *City of Cedar Rapids* (1911), 153 Ia. 219; 133 N. W. 117. There was introduced in the city council for enactment a proposed ordinance prohibiting theatrical exhibitions on Sunday. Plaintiffs, proprietors of a theatre in the city sought to restrain the passage of such ordinance upon the ground that its passage and enforcement would be in violation of the constitution of the state forbidding discrimination between classes of persons, and further in violation of the fourteenth amendment of the Federal constitution. The demurrer to the bill was sustained upon the ground that the ordinance was in the nature of a police regulation, and if void for unreasonableness or not within the power delegated to the city, the courts would not enforce it.

[79] *City of N. Y.* v. *Williams* (1905), 48 Misc. (N. Y.) 77; 96 N. Y. Supp. 237.

[80] *Twiggar* v. *Rosenberg* (1916), 98 Misc. (N. Y.) 86; 163 N. Y. Supp. 771. The court will not restrain the defendant from conducting a motion-picture show on Sunday.

"It has long been held that courts may not resort to injunction to enforce the criminal law."

Lyric Theatre v. *State* (1911), 136 S. W. (Ark.) 174. Suit was instituted in the name of the state of Arkansas to enjoin defendant from giving public per-

Nor will it restrain the police officials from carrying out the provisions of the statute.[81]

To sustain a conviction under the statute the defendant must be in some way responsible for the performance. If as proprietor, it must have been given with his knowledge and consent,[82] and a manager is also responsible.[83]

formances of vaudeville and motion pictures in its theatre. These performances were given gratis, and were wholly proper and moral.

Held that chancery would not enjoin the doing of an act which was purely criminal.

Held further that a theatre was not per se a nuisance, although it might attract the lawless and the noisy so as to become a public nuisance.

See also: *Eden Musée* v. *Bingham* (1908), 125 A. D. (N. Y.) 780; 110 N. Y. Supp. 210; *Shepherd* v. *Bingham* (1908), 125 A. D. (N. Y.) 784; 110 N. Y. Supp. 217.

[81] *Eden Musée* v. *Bingham* (1908), 125 A. D. (N. Y.) 780; 110 N. Y. Supp. 210; *Shepherd* v. *Bingham* (1908), 125 A. D. (N. Y.) 784; 110 N. Y. Supp. 217; *Suesskind* v. *Bingham* (1908), 125 A. D. (N. Y.) 787; 110 N. Y. Supp. 213; *Keith & Proctor* v. *Bingham* (1908), 125 A. D. (N. Y.) 791; 110 N. Y. Supp. 219; *Schimkevitz* v. *Bingham* (1908), 125 A. D. (N. Y.) 792; 110 N. Y. Supp. 219; *Olympic A. C.* v. *Bingham* (1908), 125 A. D. (N. Y.) 793; 110 N. Y. Supp. 216.

[82] See *People* v. *Kingston* (1912), 139 N. Y. Supp. 649, for a very able discussion of Sunday performances of motion pictures and as to the sufficiency of the evidence to hold the defendant liable.

Reid v. *Wilson* (Eng.), 1 Q. B. D. 315. An attempt was made to convict the persons responsible for a series of educational lectures given on Sunday evenings, under the provisions of 21 Geo. III, ch. 49, but it was unsuccessful.

[83] *Gould* v. *State* (1912), 146 S. W. (Tex.) 172. While, in a criminal prosecution for keeping open a theatre on Sunday, the defendant showed that he was not the proprietor, he was held nevertheless liable as it was shown that he had been held out as the manager.

While the fact that the proceeds of the performance are devoted to some worthy charitable enterprise is in general no defense [84] it would amount to a defense in such states which except "works of charity or necessity." [85]

[84] *Koelble* v. *Woods*, 159 N. Y. Supp. 704. *Held* that the fact that the proceeds of the performance were given to a worthy charity did not take it out of the operation of the statute.

[85] For detailed discussion see Section 82.

CHAPTER X

UNFAIR COMPETITION

Titles—Marks and Devices

SEC. 121. Using same or similar titles.
122. Use of title after copyright in work expires.
123. Infringement of titles—Titles held to infringe.
124. Infringement of titles—Titles held not to infringe.
125. Acquiescence and abandonment.
126. Relief.
127. Marks and devices.
128. Transferability.
129. Parties.
130. Actions at law.
131. Trade-mark in title of cartoon.

Section 121.—Using same or similar titles.

In dealing with the title of a work, we shall disregard entirely the body of it. We shall assume that in all cases where the question of title arises, there is no resemblance in the body of the work as between the two plays or motion pictures. The remedy in all cases arising out of infringement of the text, plot, situation or characterization of the work is under the Copyright Act, or under the common law in the case of an uncopyrighted and unpublished work.

The title of a play or motion picture is the most valuable part of this species of literary property. It is the medium through which the production becomes identified with the public, and by which it is advertised, lauded and made valuable to the owner. It is also a most prolific source of infringement, and withal the least protected part of the work.

Copyright does not extend to the title. An author or dramatist acquires the benefit of the copyright law in every part of his work, except where he most needs it—in the title itself. To that, copyright will not extend, no matter how original or admirable the author's conception.[1]

[1] *Glaser* v. *St. Elmo* (1909), 175 Fed. (C. C.) 276. "The complainants claim, however, that, as they have a legal copyright of a play named 'St. Elmo,' the defendants have no right to apply the name 'St. Elmo' to the play produced by them. There is some doubt, under the authorities, whether a person who has a valid copyright in a book or play has an exclusive right to the title. Some cases hold that the title of a book or play is a part of the thing copyrighted and that no other person can adopt such title. *Weldon* v. *Dicks* (Eng.) (1878), L. R. 10 Ch. Div. 247; *Estes* v. *Williams* (1884), 21 Fed. (C. C.) 189. Other authorities hold that a copyright only extends to a literary production and that a mere title of a book is not a subject of copyright. *Harper* v. *Ranous* (1895), 67 Fed. (C. C.) 904; *Corbett* v. *Purdy* (1897), 80 Fed. (C. C.) 901; *Black* v. *Ehrich* (1891), 44 Fed. (C. C.) 793; *Dick* v. *Yates* (Eng.) (1881), L. R. 18 Ch. Div. 76; *Osgood* v. *Allen* (1872), (C. C.) Fed. Cas. No. 10603; Copinger's Law of Copyright (4th Ed.), p. 64; 9 Cyc., p. 928 and cases cited, and see *Jollie* v. *Jaques* (1850), (C. C.) Fed. Cas. No. 7,437."

"I think that the authorities, particularly the American cases, preponderate that the copyright of a book does not prevent other persons from taking the same title for another work, even in the case of an entirely unexpired copyright."

Corbett v. *Purdy* (1897), 80 Fed. (C. C.) 901. Lacombe, C. J.: "The right secured by the copy-

But the title may be protected by a court of equity under the general equity powers of the court, on the theory of unfair competition.[2] It can only be protected, however,

right act is the property in the literary composition and not in the name or title given to it. In no case, so far as this court is advised has protection been afforded by injunction under the copyright laws to the title alone, separate from the book or dramatic composition which it is used to designate."

Harper v. *Ranous* (1895), 67 Fed. (C. C.) 904. "The application, however, for an injunction against the mere use of the name 'Trilby' as the title of any dramatic composition which does not present such scenes, incidents, plot, or dialogue, or simulated or colorable imitation or adaptation thereof, is denied. It is the name in connection with the novel, not the name alone, which the copyright law protects."

Dick v. *Yates* (Eng.) (1881), 18 Ch. D. 76; 50 L. J. Ch. 809; 44 L. T. 660; *Walter* v. *Emmott* (Eng.) (1885), 54 L. J. Ch. 1059; *Borthwick* v. *Evening Post* (Eng.) (1888), 37 C. D. 460; *Crotch* v. *Arnold* (Eng.) (1909), 54 S. J. 49.

See also: *Atlas Mfg. Co.* v. *Street & Smith* (1913), 204 Fed. (C. C. A.) 398 at p. 403, which contains an exhaustive summary of the authorities on this point.

[2] *Robertson* v. *Berry* (1878), 50 Md. 591. "A *publisher* or *author* has either in the *title* of his work or in the application of his name to the work or in the particular marks which designate it, a species of property similar to that which a trader has in his trade-mark, and may like a trader claim the protection of a Court of Equity against such a use or imitation of the name, marks or designations, as is likely in the opinion of the Court to be a cause of damage to him in respect of that property."

Frohman v. *Miller* (1894), 8 Misc. (N. Y.) 379; 29 N. Y. Supp. 1109. "While there is no doubt as to the power of the court to enjoin the use of a title calculated to deceive the public into the belief that the defendants were performing the plaintiff's play etc. etc."

". . . Therefore, whether copyrighted or not, the author's

in conjunction with the work with which it has become associated.

The case of *Munro* v. *Tousey*,[3] has strongly emphasized the proposition that "a publication is the subject of property and there is no reason why, like every other kind of property, it should not be the subject of the law's protection. To put out a colorable imitation of it, by which the public may be easily misled into supposing that it is the literary article they had in mind to obtain and read, is an act of deception, which injures the publisher."

In 1909, the Appellate Division of New York in *Outcault* v. *Lamar*,[4] held that the plaintiff, who had invented

right to the title of his attraction is to be protected from unlawful invasion."

See also: *Broadhurst* v. *Nichol* (Australian) (1903), N. S. W. 3 S. R. 147; *McLean* v. *Fleming* (1877), 96 U. S. 245. See in this connection *Black* v. *Ehrich* (1891), 44 Fed. (C. C.) 793.

[3] *Munro* v. *Tousey* (1891), 129 N. Y. 38; 29 N. E. 9. "That the plaintiff would be entitled to the protection of the law against the use by others of the words 'Old Sleuth Library' as used to describe a series of publications, or against the use of the name 'Old Sleuth the Detective' for a work of fiction, may be conceded. That is plainly right, and in order to afford a protection more adequate than would be afforded by an action at law, the equity power of the courts might be successfully invoked to restrain a similar use by others of such names and to prevent a species of literary piracy. This power is exerted upon the same principle upon which the court acts in trademark cases, in restraining the unauthorized use of the label, or sign, constituting the trademark."

[4] *Outcault* v. *Lamar* (1909), 135 A. D. (N. Y.) 110; 119 N. Y. Supp. 930. "The theory of the complaint is that the cartoonist invented this title and these names, and that he and his associates were the first to use them in connection with a public play, and that a court of equity

a series of cartoons called "Buster Brown" and around which he had written a play of that name, could restrain the defendant from producing a play under a similar title, under the general equity powers of the court.

Earlier cases had paved the way for this decision by defining with precision the rights acquired in the substance or body of the work, and the rights acquired in the title.

Potter v. *McPherson* [5] clearly separates these two rights.

should protect them in that use upon the principles upon which trade names and trade marks are protected by the courts, notwithstanding the fact that they are used in connection with a copyright or a patent. *Munro* v. *Tousey*, 129 N. Y. 38; 29 N. E. 9; *Waterman* v. *Shipman*, 130 id. 301; 29 N. E. 111; *Potter* v. *McPherson*, 21 Hun, 559." The court then held that the lower court erred in dismissing the complaint and directed a new trial.

See also: *Aronson* v. *Fleckenstein* (1886), 28 Fed. (C. C.) 75. ". . . The name given the composition by its author and under which it has become known to the public, became, as it seems to me, a property right,—not strictly on the principle of a trade mark because the name and literary composition become blended and united, so that the name identifies the composition to the public—so that the name of this composition belongs to this complainant as identifying and describing his literary property, and as a part of the piece itself, and defendants have no right to profit by using this name to the injury of complainant."

[5] *Potter* v. *McPherson* (1880), 21 Hun (N. Y.), 559. "According to these principles, which are well sustained by the authorities, so much of the injunction ordered as restrains the defendants from publishing this book or any imitation of any book or pamphlet representing that sold by the plaintiffs was unauthorized and to that extent, it must certainly be vacated. The only portion of the injunction therefore, concerning which it can be claimed on the part of

There the work itself had been dedicated by its publication without securing copyright. The defendant published a similar work under a similar title. It was held that while the plaintiffs could not restrain defendants from making use of the substance of their work, they nevertheless could enjoin the defendants from appropriating their title; and that, to accomplish this, they could invoke the general equity powers of the court.

To be susceptible of exclusive appropriation by the owner, the title of a play or motion picture must not be descriptive. Much has been said on what constitutes descriptiveness—"words or names which simply indicate the quality or character of the goods to which they refer are as a rule words which others may employ for the same purpose with equal truth, and hence cannot be exclusively appropriated by any one as a trade-mark." [6]

the plaintiffs that it should be continued, is that relating to the title under which the plaintiff's book has been published, for as to that, the law does not deprive them of their rights of property by the mere publication and sale of the book itself. That is the distinguishing mark by which their publication becomes known in the market and as to that they have a right to maintain the exclusive use where it has been properly devised for the purpose of maintaining their trade, and preventing it from being appropriated to the business of other persons."

[6] *Frohman* v. *Morris* (1910), 68 Misc. (N. Y.) 461; 123 N. Y. Supp. 1090. "Words or marks merely indicating superior excellence, popularity or universality in use, such as 'best,' 'favorite', etc., cannot be exclusively appropriated as a trade-mark. . . . . The name of a drama or other theatrical production not published as a book cannot, of course, constitute a trade-mark, but *it is a trade-name*, and will be protected against unauthor-

It is extremely rare that the title of a play is descriptive, for the reason that this form of literary creation does not lend itself to description in the sense that commodities in trade do.

The theory of descriptiveness, as it has been developed in the law of unfair competition, is that no one will be permitted to appropriate to his own exclusive use a word or words which describe the physical properties of the

ized use or imitation amounting to unfair competition. In the light of these principles it is evident that no one can appropriate a trade-mark or title which describes the thing to which it is affixed. Thus, no one could appropriate the word 'play,' or 'dramatic composition,' 'comedy,' 'farce,' 'tragedy' or any similar word in connection with a stage-production, because it describes the thing itself."

Social Register Ass'n v. *Howard* (1894), 60 Fed. (C. C.) 270. "These words 'Social Register,' are clearly selected arbitrarily to designate the publication of the complainant, and cannot be properly called descriptive, in any sense. Hence, the words, when chosen, associated together, and applied to a list of persons selected at will by the compiler, as in the case at bar, become a trade-mark, and are entitled to protection as such. It is not necessary to cite authorities to sustain this statement."

But see: *Isaacs* v. *Daly* (1874), 7 Jones & Spencer (N. Y.) 511. Plaintiff copyrighted a play called "Charity." Shortly thereafter defendant became the owner of a play under the same title. The court denied injunction on the ground that the word "charity" is "a virtue that has been symbolised and portrayed in every stage and department of art for all ages."

The defendant had acted in good faith, and the court denied injunction.

We think that this decision is unsound, and is not expressive of the law as it exists to-day. No matter what the title is, or what it symbolizes or embodies, once it is attached to a play or motion picture and becomes known to the public, it acquires

article;[7] for if that were done, others selling the same commodity might be hindered from accurately describing their own property.[8]

Thus, every man may offer for sale "tan shoes" or "black shoes" or "women's shoes," but when one calls his shoes "The American Girl" he chooses an altogether arbitrary title which does not describe any physical property in the article and he may prevent others from using the same title.[9]

a *secondary meaning* in conjunction with such work, and is from that time on entitled to the protection of the courts.

[7] *Welcome* v. *Thompson* (Eng.) (1904), 1 Ch. 736. "When one is dealing with this question of whether a word is descriptive, I think one must always bear in mind that for a word really to be descriptive it must describe something which is material to the composition, i. e., the quality, form or purpose of the article to which the trade-mark is intended to apply."

[8] *Selchow* v. *Baker* (1883), 93 N. Y. 59. "The reason for not permitting names, descriptions of the article or its component parts, to be appropriated as trade-marks is that inasmuch as all persons have an equal right to produce and vend similar articles, they also have the right to properly describe them and to use any appropriate language in words for that purpose, and no person can appropriate to himself exclusively any word or expression, properly descriptive of the article, its qualities, ingredients or characteristics."

[9] *Ridgway Co.* v. *Amalgamated Press* (Eng.) (1911), 28 T. L. R. 149. Plaintiffs, American publishers of "Everybody's Magazine," issued monthly and sold at a shilling, brought action to restrain defendants from selling a periodical called "Everybody's Weekly" issued weekly and sold for a penny.

Held that these publications were not likely to compete with each other. Also that the court could not restrain the use of a common and popular expression like "Everybody's."

Hamilton Shoe Co. v. *Wolf*

Thus, any producer may apply the terms "play," "sketch," "drama," "act" to his film without fear of restraint by another who has used that same word as the title of his motion picture; but if he adopts a word such as "The Rosary" or "Life" or phrases such as "Home Comfort" or "A Fool There Was" and his literary work becomes known to the public under such title, equity will protect him in his exclusive use of such word or expression.

But in order to receive this protection, there must be such use of the title that it will have acquired a secondary meaning, and the public will have identified it with the particular play or motion picture. The first one to make use of the title is entitled to it as against all subsequent persons.[10] Priority of actual use in point of time is the test. "Priority of use rather than priority of invention confers the right." [11]

(1916), 240 U. S. 251; 36 Sup. Ct. 409.

[10] *Broadhurst* v. *Nichols* (Australia) (1903), N. S. W. 3; S. R. 147. Plaintiff's play "The Wrong Mr. Wright" had been produced in England, America and in parts of Australia. Defendants threatened to produce an entirely dissimiliar play under the title "The Wrong Mrs. Wright" in a place in Australia where the plaintiff's play had not yet been performed and as defendants claimed, where plaintiff's play was entirely unknown. *Held* that plaintiff was entitled to maintain his action for injunction upon the ground that the reputation acquired by the play elsewhere gave rise to plaintiff's cause of action.

See also: *Columbia Mill Co.* v. *Alcorn* (1893), 150 U. S. 460; 14 Sup. Ct. 151; *Caswell* v. *Hazard* (1890), 121 N. Y. 484; 24 N. E. 707.

[11] *George* v. *Smith* (1892), 52 Fed. (C. C.) 830. "It is the party who uses it first as a brand for his goods, and builds up a business under it, who is entitled to

The monopoly of the title is acquired by him who first appropriates and not by the man who was the first to suggest, design, invent or conceive the title. So that a mere deposit of the work and title in the office of the Register of Copyrights is not actual user.[12] And if one releases a motion picture prior to another motion picture having the same title, which has been previously copyrighted, but not released, equity will protect the former, for that one is entitled to the benefits accruing from prior user. The burden, however, is upon the plaintiff to show that he was the first to use the title.[13]

But it is interesting to note that the cases are not very clear as to what constitutes prior user.

A situation may arise where two motion pictures are being made simultaneously, and in good faith the same

protection, and not the one who first thought of using it on similar goods, but did not use it. *The law deals with acts, not intentions.*" (p. 832).

See also: *Walter Baker Co.* v. *Delapenha* (1908), 160 Fed. (C. C.) 746.

[12] *Dickey* v. *Mutual Film* (1916), 160 N. Y. Supp. 609.

See in this connection: *Benn* v. *Le Clerq* (1873), 3 Fed. Cas. 1308. *Held* that a person who deposited in the copyright office the title of a drama, not original with himself, did not secure to himself such title to the exclusion of others who have applied such title to a dramatic composition founded on the same story, before the date of such deposit.

[13] *Spiegel* v. *Zuckerman* (1910), 175 Fed. (C. C.) 978.

See also: *Hilson* v. *Foster* (1897), 80 Fed. (C. C.) 896. Not only the intrinsic merit of a work, but the amount of publicity and advertising given thereto and the popularity derived therefrom will be considered by the court on the question of unfair competition.

See also: *Selig Polyscope* v. *Unicorn* (1917), 163 N. Y. Supp. 62.

title is applied to each. The period intervening between the release of the two films may be very short.

It is doubtful whether the courts will enjoin the one released subsequent in point of time. The court will probably direct that each producer affix to the title some name or phrase which will enable the public to distinguish between the two, and thus avoid confusion or deception.

In a late Canadian case,[14] a closely analogous situation was presented to the court in the case of two books. One book was entitled *The New Canadian Bird Book* and the other *The Canadian Bird Book*. A period of about three months intervened between the publication of the books. The court held that the publication of the first book *The New Canadian Bird Book* was not such a prior user of the title as to entitle the plaintiff to an injunction.

But where the defendant has had knowledge of the plaintiff's title and then has applied the same to his own motion picture, it matters not that the priority of the

[14] *McIndoo* v. *Musson Book Co.* (Can.) (1915), 35 O. L. R. 42. Plaintiff published a book entitled "The New Canadian Bird Book" which he copyrighted. Defendant published a book entitled "The Canadian Bird Book." There was no claim that defendant used any of plaintiff's material. Action was brought *first* on copyright, *second* on theory of trade name. *Held*: *first* that unless the "title itself amounted to a literary, scientific or artistic work or composition" it could not be the subject of copyright; *second* that in order to succeed plaintiff was required to show that his book had become known to the public and sought for under the title adopted by him, and furthermore the fact that plaintiff published his work three or four months before defendant published his work did not establish such prior user as to entitle plaintiff to an injunction.

Rose v. *McLean Publishing Co.* (Can.) (1896–7), 27 O. R. 325; 24 A. R. 240 distinguished.

plaintiff's use was for a short time. An interval of a day, in that case, would be sufficient prior user to entitle the plaintiff to an injunction.

And even where the plaintiff has stopped the production of his work for a short time, another may not step in with a work under a similar title.[15]

We have thus far discussed the elements necessary to maintain an action to enjoin the use of the same or similar title, assuming that the title in each instance was applied to a motion picture.

As between a play and a motion picture it has been settled by the decisions of *Harper* v. *Kalem* and *Frohman* v. *Fitch*, that both are dramatic works, and that one may be in competition with the other.[16]

Several cases have arisen in this country wherein the proprietor of a dramatic composition has attempted to enjoin the production of a motion picture under the same title under which his play was performed before the public.

The first case in which this question arose was that of the *Miracle Co.* v. *Danziger*.[17] In that case the plaintiff

[15] *Janney* v. *Pan-Coast Ventilator Mfg. Co.* (1904), 128 Fed. (C. C.) 121. *Held* that the fact that plaintiff was not manufacturing the patented article and placing the same upon the market under its trade name at the time of the commencement of the suit was no defense to an action for unfair use of plaintiff's trade name.

[16] For full discussion of these two cases see Section 1.

[17] *Miracle Co.* v. *Danziger* (1913), N. Y. Law Journal, March 8. "The plaintiffs Max Reinhardt and Karl Vollmoeller are the owners and producers of a pantomime play, known as 'The Miracle.' This play was produced with great success in London. The plaintiff, the Miracle

which was the owner of the production rights of Maeterlinck's play called "The Miracle," sought to enjoin the

Co. Inc., acquired the exclusive cinematograph rights in this play or spectacle for the United States and Canada in April, 1912. The play has been reproduced on films for moving pictures and these films were produced at the Park Theatre in the City of New York on February 17th, 1913. It appears that prior to the time when the Miracle Co. acquired the exclusive rights to this play the defendants arranged with a German corporation for the production of a moving picture play under the same name of 'The Miracle.' Since May, 1912 they have been advertising this film for rental under the name of 'The Miracle' and actually produced the film before the plaintiffs. The Miracle Co. produced its play here, but after it had notice of plaintiff's claim to the exclusive right to produce such play. The play owned by the plaintiff and the play owned by the defendant are both founded upon an old legend of a miracle of St. Beatrice. The legend became famous when dramatized by Maeterlinck under the title of Sister Beatrice. It is not claimed on this application that the defendant's play is similar to the plaintiff's play except that they are both founded on the same legend, nor is it claimed that the plaintiffs have any copyright on that legend. The claim is simply that the defendants are engaged in an unfair competition in that by using the name of 'The Miracle' they are intentionally deceiving or tending to deceive the public into the belief that their play is the play produced in London under the same title and to which the plaintiffs have the exclusive rights. I have no doubt that the defendants in using the name 'The Miracle' for their play are trying to obtain the benefit of the reputation of the London production. While the title is not wholly fanciful and bears a direct relation to the subject matter of the play and is to some extent descriptive of that subject matter, yet the legend of the miracle of St. Beatrice is not so well known that it has even been known or even could be appropriately called 'The Miracle.' It seems to me that it is absolutely improbable that any person attempting to dramatize this legend would call

exhibition of a motion picture of the same title. A temporary injunction was granted.

it 'The Miracle' except with intent to obtain the benefit of the reputation of the earlier play called by this name. Even though the plaintiffs may not have an exclusive right to the name, they have to the enjoining of others from using that name in such manner as would intentionally deceive the public. In this case too, the intent to deceive the public into the belief that the defendant's play is really a reproduction of the play owned by the plaintiff rests not alone on the improbability of the same name having been chosen without any intent to appropriate the benefit of the reputation of the plaintiff's play, but as a fair inference from the undisputed facts. The defendants originally advertised their film as 'The Miracle—the one million dollar spectacular production played at the Olympia, London, for more than a year.' It is true that they discontinued all reference to the London production when plaintiffs notified them that they would restrain any attempt on their part to use the name 'The Miracle' as the title of any films of moving pictures, but the fact remains that when the defendant first used the name it was coupled with an open intent to deceive the public. Moreover, it is shown that even thereafter and on July 9 one of these defendants wrote to a motion picture exhibitor a letter describing the film which contained the significant words, 'We are being advised now by our attorney that may give us rights to use the music that was written for the original play.' These words can only refer to the Humperdinck music written for the original play in Europe, and shows to my mind clearly an attempt to appropriate the reputation of that play. We have therefore the following points clearly shown: First, that plaintiffs are the owners and assignees of the play which has achieved a great reputation in Europe under the name 'The Miracle;' Second, the defendants are offering a film of another play under the same title, founded on the same subject; Third, the defendant selected his title with knowledge that it had clearly been appropriated by the owners of the first play; Fourth, the title is not so descriptive of the subject

Then came the case of *Marc Klaw* v. *The General Film Co.*,[18] where the plaintiffs, the producers of a play entitled

matter of the play that it would naturally be used, except for a desire to obtain the benefit of the reputation of the original play; Fifth, this desire is clearly shown by the defendant's acts in offering their films to the public. Sixth, the natural result of the defendant's acts is to deceive the public. Under the circumstances it seems to me that the plaintiffs are clearly entitled to the injunctive relief demanded. Motion granted."

[18] *Klaw* v. *General Film Co.*, New York Law Journal, March 4, 1915; 154 N. Y. Supp. 988; aff'd 171 A. D. (N. Y.) 945; 156 N. Y. Supp. 1128. Platzek, J: "Some five years ago Robert Hilliard, one of the plaintiffs, a popular and gifted actor, first produced an elaborate dramatic production entitled "A Fool There Was," at the Liberty Theatre, in the City of New York. From that time the play has been presented and is now being produced throughout the United States and Canada with success, both from an artistic and financial standpoint. Large sums of money have been expended by the plaintiffs for actors, actresses, hiring of theatres, the equipment of the play and in extensive advertising for more than four years. After the dramatic representation "A Fool There Was" acquired a reputation, and its title became well known, the defendant appropriated the title "A Fool There Was" and produced it in connection with one of its photo dramas, with knowledge that the plaintiffs had been and were producing a dramatic representation under such title. It appears that the title "A Fool There Was" is an original title in connection with a play, and that no other play under such title was presented prior to the production of the drama by Robert Hilliard. The circumstance that defendant's play is dissimiliar to plaintiff's play or that it was produced as a photo play does not militate against their right to enjoin the appropriation of and use by the defendant of the title. "The question, 'What's in a name?' has been answered by the courts in many well considered cases, where the exclusive right to a name possessed or owned by a successful business enterprise has been maintained against imita-

"A Fool There Was" secured an injunction against the defendant which had produced a motion picture under the same title.

tors and wrongdoers who sought by an unauthorized use to deceive the public and profit by the wrong." *Frohman* v. *Payton*, 34 Misc. 275; *Hopkins Amus. Co.* v. *Frohman*, 202 Ill. 541; *Outcault* v. *Lamar*, 135 App. Div. 110; 38 Cyc. 837. In *Aronson* v. *Fleckenstein*, 28 Fed. Rep. 75, it is stated: "The name given the composition by its author, and under which it has become known to the public, became, as it seems to me, a property right—not strictly on the principle of a trade mark, but because the name and literary composition became blended and united, so that *the name identifies the composition to the public*—so that the name of this composition belongs to this complainant as identifying and describing his literary property and as a part of the piece itself, and *defendants have no right to profit by using this name to the injury of the complainant*, ... and defendants have no right to avail themselves of the merits and popularity of complainant's play to draw audiences to the performance of theirs, even if, as is claimed, their composition is a new and original dramatic arrangement. *It is a fraud upon the public, as well as upon the complainant, to attempt to do so.*" In *Ball* v. *Broadway Bazaar*, 194 N. Y. 435, Werner, J., writing for the court, says: "Although we agree with the learned Appellate Division in recognizing the technical distinction between trade marks and trade names, we think the same fundamental principles of law and equity are applicable to both. 'All such cases, whether of trade mark or trade name or other unfair use of another's reputation, are concerned with an injurious attack upon the good will of a rival business; customers are diverted from one trader to another, and orders intended for one find their way to the other' (Sebastian on the Law of Trade Marks, p. 17). Trade marks and trade names are in reality analogous to the good will of the business to which they appertain. The trade mark represents it in the market, and the trade name proclaims it to those who pass the shop. In either case such unfair conduct as is calculated to deceive the public into

The case of *Paul Dickey* v. *Mutual Film Corporation* followed.[19] Dickey, the author as well as the proprietor

believing that the business of the wrongdoer is the business of him whose name, sign or mark is simulated or appropriated, constitutes the gist of the offense." It was also held in this case that "trade names are protected by the application of the same principles of equity that relate to technical trade marks," *Howard* v. *Henriques*, 3 Sandf. S. C. 725; *Glen & H. Mfg. Co.* v. *Hall*, 61 N. Y. 226; Paul on Trade Marks, sec. 182. It is not disputed that plaintiffs' play was produced with success by leading actors and actresses in the principal cities of the United States, and was a valuable theatrical production. It is not disputed that the defendant presented a moving picture presentation under the title "A Fool There Was." It affirmatively appears that the defendant produced its photo play under said title in different cities of the Union no less than three thousand times without authority. In *Kalem Company* v. *Harper*, 222 U. S. 55, it is held that the owner of dramatic rights might forbid the dramatic representation by moving pictures and to the present time the only right to protect moving pictures arises from the words "dramatic" or "drama." *Photo Drama Co.* v. *Social Corp'n*, 213 Fed. Rep. 374–377; *Atlas Mfg. Co.* v. *Smith*, 204 Fed. Rep. 398; *Frohman* v. *Fitch*, 149 N. Y. Supp. 633. The plaintiffs have established and acquired an exclusive proprietary right as a trade name and trade mark in the words "A Fool There Was" as a title in connection with their play, and that they are entitled to a permanent injunction restraining the defendant from the continuance of the infringement and impairment of their right in and to such trade mark or trade name. Judgment for plaintiffs. An interlocutory decree may be entered herein making final the injunction to restrain defendant from the further use of the title "A Fool There Was" and for an accounting by the defendant, and for this purpose the appointment of a referee."

[19] *Dickey* v. *Mutual Film Corp.* (1916), 160 N. Y. Supp. 609. Clark, J: "This is an action for an injunction and an accounting. Plaintiff is a dramatic writer. Defendant is a moving picture

of a one-act play entitled "The Come-Back," sought to enjoin the defendant from exhibiting a film under the

producer. Plaintiff wrote a one-act play called "The Come-Back" which was produced on the stage first in March, 1911. It has been produced as recently as March, 1915. Defendant has since at least June, 1915, produced upon the screens a photoplay called "The Come-back." It is not claimed that the story of the play and the photoplay are similar; indeed, the sole similarity is in the title. I shall hold that although not now actually being produced, plaintiff's play is sufficiently of value to be the subject of loss from competition, and that the name "The Come-Back" is not descriptive but fanciful and therefore subject in a proper case to the protection of an equity court. In the first place I do not think that the prior copyright of two dramatic compositions under a similar name affects plaintiff's rights. The title not being subject to copyright, its use is protected under the equitable rule applicable to trade marks; that is, priority of actual use gives priority of right to use and to protection. *Columbia Mill Co.* v. *Alcorn*, 150 U. S. 460, 463. Defendant's chief defense is that the case is merely one of coincidence, and that not every case of coincidence is unfair competition, at least in the absence of fraudulent intent. I do not think that fraudulent intent is involved in this case. It is true that coincidence in title is not per se unfair competition, as witness numerous cases cited by defendant, beginning with the Apthorp case, *Astor* v. *West 62nd St. Realty Co.*, 167 App. Div. 273. These cases, as I read them, are decided on the ground that no competition exists. For instance, the Apthorp case held that there was no competition between a hotel and an apartment house. In the case of *Atlas* v. *Street & Smith*, 204 Fed. 388, it was held that there was no competition between novels and moving pictures of the same titles. It is clear that competition may exist between a play and a photoplay, and that an injunction may arise from the mere use of a similar title I think is held by the case of *Frohman* v. *Morris*, 68 Misc. 46, *Klaw & Erlanger* v. *General Film Co.*, 154 N. Y. Supp. 988 and *Frohman* v. *Payton*, 34 Misc.

same title. Here again, an injunction was granted. In another action the same plaintiff enjoined another motion

275. An injunction must therefore be granted in the present case. On the question of an accounting it appears that plaintiff had submitted his play in three-act form to various theatrical managers and moving picture producers subsequent to defendant's production and that it had been rejected. This is sufficient evidence of damages and loss of profits to allow an accounting. Defendant contends that where no fraud is found there can be no accounting or damages. The rule, as I read the cases, is rather that in case of innocent competition courts are reluctant to decree an accounting and damages. While not specifically finding fraud or intentional unfair competition here, I nevertheless feel that on the facts the case is one for an accounting and damages to be determined by a referee to be appointed for the purpose."

See also: *Thomas* v. *Abrahamson* (1916), N. Y. Law Journal, August 31. "Motion for injunction pendente lite restraining the use by the defendant of the title 'Her Husband's Wife' is granted. *Klaw* v. *General Film Co.*, 154 N. Y. Supp. 988; *Dickey* v. *Mutual Film Corp'n*, N. Y. Law Journal, August 11, 1916."

See also: *Henry W. Savage, Inc.*, v. *Kerker* (1914), N. Y. Law Journal, April 25th. "The fact that the title of 'Magda, the Modern Madame X,' which was assumed by the defendant for his films, is being used to deceive the public, is clearly shown by the method adopted in some of his advertising, where the words 'Madame X' are made unduly prominent, being printed in much larger type than any other words and separated from the descriptive adjective and given an entire line in heavy block type; nor is this avoided by the note in small type on one of defendant's advertisements that 'this production is not taken from a play with a title somewhat similar,' for other advertisements issued by those to whom defendant has sold the films refer to them as 'The original and only production of this wonderful play, Madame X.' For the protection of the public from deception and to prevent unfair competition the

picture distributor from exhibiting a film produced under the same name.[20]

plaintiff is entitled to have the injunction continued during the pendency of the action."

[20] *Dickey* v. *Metro Pictures Corporation* (1917), N. Y. Law Journal, April 28. Platzek, J: "There can be no doubt that plaintiff is entitled to the injunction prayed for, *Klaw* v. *General Film Co.*, 154 N. Y. Supp. 988; aff'd 171 App. Div. 945; but I think the further relief demanded must be largely curtailed.

The case rests on the theory of unfair competition. It can, therefore, only be sustained by showing that the defendant knew of plaintiff's prior use of the title in question while itself making use of the same title. This is shown as to defendant's use of the title, which is admitted by the answer, at times subsequent to the date when notice of plaintiff's claim was proved to have been given. Its use prior to that time appears to have been only a coincidence. It was innocent and accidental.

Plaintiff did not undertake to show when the letter written by his attorney on Saturday, April 22, 1916, was received by the defendant. The testimony of the defendant's witness on the point is not as clear as it might be but in one place he testifies that it was not received until Monday, the 24th, the day when, in the ordinary course of business, the defendant released its films throughout the country. In the absence of any evidence on the point on the part of the plaintiff I shall find that it was received on April 24th, and the accounting which may include damages and profits, (*Sharpless* v. *Lawrence*, 213 Fed. Rep. 426; 38 Cyc. 908, 913), must be limited to damages sustained and profits derived from sales, leases or other dispositions of the films made after that date. *Saxlehner* v. *Siegel-Cooper Co.*, 179 U. S. 42; *N. K. Fairbank Co.* v. *Windsor*, 124 Fed. Rep. 200; *Clinton Metallic Paint Co.* v. *N. Y. Metallic Paint Co.*, 23 Misc. 66, 73; *Wolf Bros. Co.* v. *Hamilton Shoe Co.*, 240 U. S. 251.

In so far as the title was innocently used without knowledge of plaintiff's right the case differs from *Selig* v. *Unicorn Film Corpn.*, 163 N. Y. Supp. 62. There the appropriation was knowingly and deliberately made. The case

In the case of *Selig Polyscope et al.* v. *Unicorn Film Service Corporation* the plaintiffs were the owners of a dramatic composition as well as a motion picture reproduction thereof entitled "The Rosary." Plaintiffs, Rowland and Clifford, were originally the owners of all rights in and to the play. The Selig Polyscope Co. was the assignee of the motion picture rights therein, and it produced a motion picture of the play, using the same title to identify its motion picture. The defendant put out upon the market a motion picture under the same title. Here, as well, the court, after a trial upon the merits, granted injunction,[21] although a temporary injunction had been refused.[22]

is also said by counsel to differ from *Dickey* v. *Mutual Film Corpn.*, 160 N. Y. Supp. 609, in the fact that the advertisements in that case were expressly found to convey the impression that the defendant's picture was a reproduction of plaintiff's play. The findings I have made, relating to the defendant's improper appropriation, use and advertisement of plaintiff's title will be understood to relate to the conduct of the defendant after notice of plaintiff's rights.

The requests for findings have been passed upon. Settle a decision on notice which shall embody all findings made by me and which shall further provide for the injunction and accounting proposed by plaintiff except that the profits and damages to be accounted for and assessed shall be limited as above indicated and that this relief shall be granted only against the defendant served, and which shall provide for final judgment on the coming in and confirmation of the referee's report; and shall further provide that all questions as to costs and allowances be reserved until final judgment."

[21] *Selig Polyscope Co.* v. *Unicorn Film Service Corp.* (1917), 163 N. Y. Supp. 62. Opinion after final hearing. "The plaintiffs have brought this action for an injunction to restrain the defendant's use of the words "The Rosary" as the title of a photo-

play and for damages for the alleged unauthorized use of that title. There can be no doubt that the plaintiffs Rowland and Clifford first adopted this title in connection with a dramatic composition. Their play by that name which was copyrighted in the year 1910 was successfully produced in the following year and during four seasons afterwards. In June, 1915, this play under the same title was produced as a motion picture by the plaintiff Selig Polyscope Company, which concern had acquired from Rowland and Clifford the right so to reproduce the original play.

It appears from the evidence that this representation both on the stage and as a motion picture had met with marked acceptance by the public and that the good will acquired by the plaintiffs in the production under this chosen title "The Rosary" became of substantial value.

While the title of a copyrighted play is not protected by the copyright, the use of that title is none the less to be secured to the owner of the copyrighted matter as a trade mark, if the title so first employed by him has acquired a trade significance as an arbitrary designation. *Outcault* v. *Lamar*, 135 App. Div. 100, 117; *Caswell* v. *Hazard*, 121 N. Y. 484, 494; *McLean* v. *Fleming*, 96 U. S. 245, 254.

As was said in the case last cited: "Phrases or even words in common use may be adopted for the purpose, if, at the time of their adoption, they were not employed by another to designate the same or similar articles of production or sale."

Here the phrase "The Rosary," while well known in its reference to a form of religious observance, is in no sense descriptive of a drama, as such. It is an arbitrary title when so employed, and, as appears, the authors and producers of the plaintiffs' play adopted this title to identify rather than describe the composition itself. Indeed, the phrase is not aimed to be, nor is it, serviceable as a description of the subjects portrayed in the play, whether as acted or as exhibited upon the screen.

I have no doubt therefore that this phrase was open to adoption by the plaintiffs and that, having acquired a secondary meaning in identification of the plaintiffs' dramatic composition, it became associated with the good will of the business established in the production of the play, and was a trade mark. *Outcault* v. *Lamar*, 135 App. Div. 110; *Klaw & Erlanger* v. *General Film Company*, 154 N. Y. Supp. 988. As such, its character continued when applied to a representation in the form of a motion picture. *Dickey* v. *Mutual Film Corporation*, 160 N. Y. Supp. 609. In June, 1916, the defendant corporation, which was engaged in the business of buying motion picture films and of distributing them for exhibition released to its customers a film acquired by it and renamed "The Rosary." It appears that this was an old film, representing a dramatic portrayal, and had been exhibited under some other name. When choosing the title "The Rosary" and advertising the motion picture under it, the defendant knew of the plaintiffs' widely advertised and successful production; its President, Mr. Schlank, was thoroughly familiar with the play, as he testifies, and I am satisfied from the evidence that the choice of this title for an old film was not merely accidental. *British-American Tobacco Co.* v. *British-American Cigar Store Co.*, 211 Fed. R. 933, 935. Justification for this use of the plaintiffs' trade-mark cannot be found in the fact that the catalogues in evidence disclose the designation of other motion picture films by the use of the word "Rosary." So far as these catalogues have any value as proof, they indicate no more than that other persons in three instances have so named their films at dates long after the plaintiffs Rowland and Clifford acquired their trade mark by original adoption. Whether the films referred to were actually exhibited under conditions which the plaintiffs might or might not have found to be injurious to their rights, is a matter of speculation, but the defendant's case is not aided by pointing to a possible invasion of these rights by others, nor is it of importance that a well-known song and novel had been published under the title 'The Rosary' before the date when the plaintiffs Rowland and Clifford so named their play. There is no similarity of enterprise in a dramatic composition when compared with a song or novel, such as to suggest or to present conflicting rights to a trade mark. *Atlas Co.* v. *Street & Smith*, 204 Fed. Rep. 398.

"There should be judgment for the plaintiffs for an injunction and for damages to be ascertained on a reference. Proposed decision and judgment as heretofore submitted by plaintiffs should be noticed for settlement."

See also: *Posen* v. *Schwarz* (1917), N. Y. Law Journal, Jan. 3d, Hendrick, J.: "Plaintiff's affidavit states that the film 'The Battles of a Nation' was copyrighted as a photoplay in the office of the Register of Copyrights on Oct. 8, 1915, and received entry No. L. 6579. This copyright included the photoplay itself, the title thereof and the synopsis thereof. He also states that the pictures were made at large expense by special correspondents of plaintiff, 'who visited the scenes of battle and who took the pictures especially for this film.' It is also stated that defendant is using plaintiff's advertising matter in a manner to convey the impression that he is leasing the film produced by plaintiff. Defendant admits that he is renting a film entitled 'The Battles of a Nation' and claims that said title is a common one without commercial value; that the picture consists of a patchwork of battle scenes, old and new and that he 'believes that the 'Battles of a Nation' is not a copyright. I think a proper case has been made for an injunction pendente lite."

[22] *Selig Polyscope Co.* v. *Unicorn Film Service Corp.* (1916), N. Y. Law Journal, Sept. 16, Cohalan, J.: "Plaintiffs seek by an injunction pendente lite to restrain the defendant from using as the title of a moving picture film the term 'The Rosary.' It is asserted the plaintiffs Rowland and Clifford acquired the sole right to use this title on March 22, 1910, when a play called 'The Rosary' was produced. The rights of this dramatic production were secured by the Selig Company on June 15, 1914, for moving picture purposes. The plaintiffs' photoplay is of seven parts, and is known as a long photoplay. The defendants are presenting also a two-part picture play called 'The Rosary.' There is no similarity in the subject matter of the respective productions. The themes and the import thereof are wholly dissimilar. It is conceded that if the defendant attempted to deceive the public and to represent its photo drama as the photo drama of the plaintiffs that an action would lie and an injunction would be the proper remedy. But such a claim is not borne out by the moving papers. No effort

The New York Supreme Court in another case involving two motion pictures entitled respectively "The Girl Who did Not Care" and "The Girl Who Doesn't Know" held that there was no conflict between such titles.[23]

to deceive has been made and no means calculated to perpetrate a fraud upon the public have been employed. The plaintiffs cannot claim that the term 'The Rosary' is a fanciful device to which they are absolutely entitled. They neither acquired proprietorship therein by origin or purchase. The words are descriptive and they have been variously and commonly used in this country, and in fact in every Christian country for years, and undoubtedly other plays so named, particularly of a religious nature, have been and are now being produced. I am satisfied that not only has there been no attempt made on the part of the defendant to imitate the plaintiffs' drama or to mislead the public, but that no ownership in the title can be predicated herein. Motion denied."

[23] *B. S. Moss Motion Picture Corp.* v. *Ivan Film Prod. Inc.* (1917), N. Y. Law Journal, Jan. 23, Cohalan J.: "Plaintiff moves for an injunction pendente lite. It seeks to restrain the defendant from using in the production of a photoplay the name "The Girl Who Did Not Care." The plaintiff is the owner of a photoplay which is entitled "The Girl Who Doesn't Know." It is claimed that the name of the defendant's play conflicts with that of the plaintiff. The defendant asserts that the name of its play was selected by the deputy commissioner of licenses out of a list of six names submitted to him. As a matter of unfair competition, I am of opinion that the papers do not show clearly the plaintiff's right to injunctive relief. Moreover, it is not shown that it has actually sustained any damage. There is no proof that confusion has arisen through the respective titles of the play or that any advantage has accrued to the defendant or any disadvantage to the plaintiff. The titles do not conflict with each other; the method of advertising the defendant's play is distinctive from that of the

The most recent case is that of *Manners* v. *Triangle* wherein the Federal court enjoined the use of a title of a dramatic composition in connection with a motion picture upon the theory of unfair competition.[24]

plaintiff, and in that respect apparently no attempt has been made to deceive the public. The plaintiff cannot claim that the term "The Girl Who Did Not Care" is a fanciful device to which it is absolutely entitled. The words are descriptive, and as no attempt has been made on the part of the defendant to imitate the plaintiff's drama or to mislead the public, no complete ownership in the title may be predicated herein. Motion denied."

[24] *Manners* v. *Triangle* (1917), U. S. District Court, Southern District of New York, N. Y. Law Journal, June 21. Manton, D. J.: "The plaintiff is a well known playwright and seeks, in this action, to restrain, by injunction, the defendants from using the title "Happiness" as the title of a play or photoplay. He claims that in violation of his sole right in the title "Happiness" as a trade name or trade mark, the defendants should not only be restrained in its use, but should compensate him for the damages he has sustained. The action has been removed from the state court.

The defendants move to dismiss the complaint on the ground that it does not state facts warranting equitable relief.

Much is claimed by plaintiff as to delays on the part of the defendants in defending the action and, it is argued, that this practice is indulged in so as to avoid a trial of the action before the summer recess of this court, to the advantage of the defendants, in that the defendants may profit by the use of the title "Happiness" in the interim. It is claimed that the life of a motion picture of the type produced by the defendants is but a few months, and that since this cause cannot be tried until the October session of the court, unless an injunction be granted now, an injunction resulting from the trial of the action would be of little avail.

The plaintiff is the author of "Peg o' My Heart," "The Harp of Life" and "Out There." His

In the case of *Selig Polyscope Co.* v. *Mutual Film Corporation*, the plaintiff exhibited a motion picture entitled

wife, under the stage name of "Miss Laurette Taylor," is well known to the theatre-going public and has had a successful career. The play "Happiness," written by the plaintiff, has been copyrighted. In March, 1914, it was presented at the Cort Theatre in New York City, and after some performances taken off. The moving affidavits indicate that the play is to be used in the future under this title.

The plaintiff's attention was called, in April last, to the announcement of the production of the photoplay at the Rialto Theatre in this city, under the title "Happiness." Notice was served upon the theatre and the producers of the play, defendants herein, of the claim of ownership by the plaintiff of the title "Happiness" as the title of a play. After notice, defendants refused to discontinue the use of the title "Happiness" and advertised it extensively in the press and otherwise under this title and continued performing in motion pictures under said title in various cities mentioned in the affidavits. In addition to this, the plaintiff personally visited and called upon Mr. Rothapfel, manager of the defendant theatre company, and protested against the use of this title.

Dodd, Mead & Co. are the plaintiff's publishers and have acquired from the plaintiff sole right to publish, plaintiff reserving the dramatic rights and the rights of presentation upon the stage in any and every form.

The defense interposed is that on November 12, 1910, a lady named Spiegelberg gave a performance of a tragedy in one act entitled "Happiness," and this was performed in her country residence in Westchester County, New York, and for which a charge of $5 was made for the benefit of a hospital. And further the presentation of a play called "Happiness" by the Chautauqua Association. However, this latter play was produced in 1916, two years after the production by the plaintiff of his play and after his play had been copyrighted. Upon notice and protest by the plaintiff the Chautauqua Association changed the title of the play to "The Quest for Happiness." The defendants having received notice of the

"The House of a Thousand Candles." A month after the release of the plaintiff's picture the defendants offered

claim of the plaintiff proceeded to produce their photoplay under this title, and the capital was thus invested after due and timely notice, and can only be based upon insistence that they were right in the position which they took. Therefore it will not be unfair to grant this injunction as against the defendants unless the strict rule of law forbids the granting of such relief. And in addition thereto it is claimed, and properly so, by the plaintiff that the matter of change of title by the defendants is a simple one if the photoplay is permitted to continue. What is now probably a five and ten cent moving picture performance will undoubtedly take from a valuable asset the trade name of this play, which will be produced under expensive auspices to a theatre-going public.

If the title "Happiness" is infringed, it can be protected on the doctrine of unfair competition. *Corbett* v. *Purdy*, 80 Fed. 901; *Glaser* v. *St. Elmo Co.*, 175 Fed. 276.

The courts have exercised their equitable jurisdiction and enjoined defendants from using as the title of photoplay the plaintiff's title, such as "A Fool There Was," where the plaintiff had been using it as the title of a drama. *Klaw & Erlanger* v. *General Film Co.*, 156 N. Y. Supp. 1128. Valuable titles which have been used as trade names have been protected in the following cases: *Schook* v. *Woods*, 32 Leg. Int. 264; *Outcault* v. *Lamar*, 135 App. Div. 110; *Frohman* v. *Morris*, 68 Misc. 641; *Frohman* v. *Payton*, 34 Misc. 275. A fanciful title such as "The Come Back" was protected by Judge Clark in the state court, 160 N. Y. Supp. 609.

In *Aaronson* v. *Fleckenstein*, 28 Fed. 75, the rule was laid down that the name given a composition by its author, by which it has become known to the public, is a property right which should be protected, and that it is a fraud upon the public and the complainant to permit its use.

The use of the title "Happiness" in a prominent theatre in New York City, staged for performance by one of the foremost actresses of her time, has given to such title a value and asset

for exhibition a motion picture entitled "The House of a Thousand Scandals." At the commencement of the

as to constitute a property right in this plaintiff which should be protected. While it is true that the title of a copyrighted play is not protected by the copyright, the use of that title is none the less to be secured to the owner of the copyrighted matter as a trade mark if the title so first employed by him has acquired a trade significance as an arbitrary designation. If the word "Happiness," even though a word in common use, was adopted by the plaintiff and at the time of its adoption was not employed by another as the designation of the title of a play, it may become a trade name or trade mark. The title may in no sense be descriptive of the drama as such, and indeed, it may be an arbitrary title employed to identify rather than describe the composition itself. If the title is serviceable as a description of the subject portrayed in the play, it was open to adoption by the plaintiff, and if such use gave it a secondary meaning in identification of the plaintiff's dramatic composition, it became so associated with the good will of the drama as to be established in the production of the play and was a trade mark.

I think the circumstances and use of the title by the plaintiff herein justify the conclusion that the plaintiff had secured a trade mark or trade name in said title. After full notice, the defendants having chosen the title and advertised it in a photoplay, did so at their peril. Justification for this use cannot be found in the isolated case of the production of a play of a similar title at Mrs. Spiegelberg's home.

The right to a title vests in the first to apply and use the title. *McLean* v. *Fleming*, 96 U. S. 245. In *G. & C. Merriam Co.* v. *Saalfield*, 198 Fed. 369, it was said: "A trade mark is a trade mark because it is indicative of the origin of the goods. The original right to its exclusive use was not based upon any statute, but upon the principles of equity and the right is acquired not by discovery or invention or registration but by adoption and use."

In Drone on Copyrights (p. 535) it is said: "There can be no copyright in a title; but on general principles of equity an injunction will be granted restraining a person from appropriating the title of a well known publication for a rival work, nor will a person be allowed to use a title which is a mere colorable imitation of another for the purpose of misleading the public into buying one publication in the belief that it is the other."

I think the use of the title for a motion picture play as used by the defendants is an infringement of the plaintiff's sole right to the title as the title of a play in drama on the stage, and that the injunction should be granted. *Kalem* v. *Harper*, 222 U. S. 61."

On appeal, reversed upon the ground that no actual prior user was shown, but the rule involved was expressly recognized—C. C. A., 2d Circuit, November 13, 1917. Ward, J.

See also: *Iliodor Picture Corp.* v. *Michailoff et al.* (1917), N. Y. Law Journal, October 6. Hough, C. J.: "This action is sustainable only as a copyright bill, a finding based on the citizenship and residence of the necessary parties.

"A threatened infringement of copyright is enough to sustain a bill.

"I assume that defendant Export & Import Film Co.'s photoplay deals with entirely different scenes, times and surroundings from those employed by plaintiff. Ivan the Terrible was not a Romanoff, and the sixteenth was different from the twentieth century, even in Russia. This is common knowledge.

"But when a copyrighted play is registered as The Fall of the Romanoffs, and Iliodor is a prominent character therein, defendants' acts in advertising The Tyranny of the Romanoffs with Iliodor are nonsense, unless intended to create the belief that the play so named did or does deal with the same matters naturally suggested by The Fall of the Romanoffs with Iliodor as an actor.

"Where the title of a play is descriptive it may be part of the right or property covered by the copyright. The dividing line between copyright or trade-mark infringement and unfair competition is not easy to draw in many cases.

"Here there is plainly such unfairness, but there is a threat of infringement also by the appropriation of name and actual infringement in the simulation of Iliodor's costume in advertising matter.

"Injunction pendente lite will continue against Blumenthal, The Export & Import Film Company,

action an application was made by the plaintiff for an injunction pendente lite, which was granted.[25] After a trial upon the merits, judgment was found for the defendant and the complaint dismissed, the court holding that there was no such similarity between the titles as would mislead or deceive the public.[26]

Inc., and Chadwick, preventing their use of the title 'The Tyranny of the Romanoffs with Iliodor,' and from using, showing &c., any photograph of Iliodor in a costume shown on that person in plaintiff's copyrighted photoplay.

"I am satisfied that defendants have pirated one of plaintiff's copyrighted photographs of Iliodor, hence this last direction.

"To avoid (if possible) further motions it may be said that I should not consider 'The Tyranny of the Romanoffs' a copying or infringement of 'The Fall of the Romanoffs.' It is the phrase 'with Iliodor' which under the circumstances constitutes the actionable *threat* of infringement, a threat not the less actionable because a story concerning Ivan the Terrible would not and could not make the threat good.

"This of course is entirely apart from the above mentioned appropriation of Iliodor's photograph.

"Plaintiff will give security in $5,000. Settle order on notice. The stay order as against all defendants not above named will be vacated."

[25] *Selig Polyscope Co.* v. *Mutual Film Corp.* (1915), N. Y. Law Journal, September 28.

[26] *Selig Polyscope Co.* v. *Mutual Film Corp.* (1917), N. Y. Law Journal, February 1. Opinion after final hearing. Pendleton, J.: "This is an action brought to enjoin defendants from using as the name or title of a photoplay "The House of a Thousand Scandals." Plaintiff, under permission from the author or his assigns of a novel entitled "The House of a Thousand Candles," produced or made a film for a picture play following the story and incidents set forth in the novel and about August, 1915, commenced exhibiting such moving picture play under the name of "The House of a Thou-

The question in the last mentioned case was further complicated by the fact that the plaintiff based his action

sand Candles." Defendants or their predecessors in interest made a film for a picture play with the title or name of "The House of a Thousand Scandals," the story or plot of which is not taken from or based on the story of the novel, and proposes to exhibit the same under the above name. Both parties have expended considerable sums of money and extensively advertised their productions under the respective names aforesaid. The action is in equity to restrain and prevent unfair competition. Although there is evidence as to copyrights secured, the cause of action does not arise thereunder and such facts are only material as showing the history of the case. The gist of the action is that the public is liable to be misled or deceived. *Ball* v. *Broadway Bazaar*, 194 N. Y. 435; *Klaw* v. *General Film Co.*, 154 N. Y. S. 988. The plays themselves are entirely dissimilar. The words and language of the respective titles are to some extent descriptive of the two plays and the differences in the plots. Plaintiff advertises its play as taken from the novel. There is nothing, either in word or similarity of design in defendants' advertisements of its play outside of and apart from the alleged similarity in the name or title, tending to show or suggest that defendants' play was taken from the novel or is in any way similar to plaintiff's play, and there is no evidence that any one has been misled or any confusion occasioned between the two productions. In fact there is some evidence that there has been no such confusion and that the two plays have been exhibited in the same theatres at different times, a circumstance going to show that they have been regarded and treated as distinct and different exhibitions. Even if it be assumed that the title "The House of a Thousand Candles" is not descriptive, but an arbitrary or fanciful title, the use of which as a trade name will be protected, where the unfair competition is based on alleged similarity the resemblance must be such as to deceive a person making natural and ordinary use of his senses. *Munro* v. *Tousey*, 129 N. Y. 38. While there is some similarity here as idem sonans, the words

upon its rights in the famous novel by Meredith Nicholson as well as upon the rights accruing to it because of the production and exhibition by it of a motion picture under such title.

This brings us to the question whether the owner of a novel who has not as yet made a motion picture reproduction of the same may enjoin a motion picture produced under the same title as that of his novel.

Offhand, they do not seem to be in the same class of goods, and hence not in competition with one another. In *Atlas* v. *Street & Smith*,[27] the leading case in this country in which the question was touched, this position was taken by the court.

A great deal, however, may be said in favor of those who take the position that there is direct competition between the two. Under the copyright law the copyright owner of the novel has the sole and exclusive right to make a dramatization of his novel. A dramatization having been held to include a motion picture reproduction of a work, it is argued that a stranger who puts out a motion picture with the same title anticipates a right which the novelist is given under the copyright; and

"Candles" and "Scandals" have respectively well defined meanings and represent entirely different conceptions. As defendants' title is not in terms misleading and there is no evidence that any one has been misled or that any confusion has been created, it can not be said that it is calculated to deceive or that deception or confusion is probable, and as defendants have not been shown to have done any other acts tending or liable to deceive or mislead a case for an injunction has not been made out. Judgment for defendants."

[27] *Atlas* v. *Street & Smith* (1913), 204 Fed. (C. C. A.) 398.

when the novelist attempts to avail himself of his right to reproduce his work in motion pictures under his copyright, he finds that he cannot use the very title which he has conceived. Should he use the same title he would be unfairly competing with the stranger, who, by prior user, had acquired a superior right to the title with respect to a motion picture. In other words, a potentiality of his novel is the development of the same in the form of a motion picture, and the production of a motion picture under the same title by a stranger cuts off that potential development of his work.

His predicament is extreme, for should he exercise his privilege under his copyright and make a motion picture reproduction of his novel under another title, as he would be compelled to do, he would at once lose all rights conferred upon him by his copyright of the novel, under the rule that the exploitation of the copyrighted work under a title different from that applied to it when securing copyright, amounts to a dedication of the work.[28]

In other words, his copyright gives the novelist certain specified rights. In attempting to exercise those rights he is prevented from so doing by the laws of unfair competition. To escape the consequences of unfair competition, he must change the title of the motion picture reproduction of his novel; and the moment he does that, he loses his copyright entirely. He is placed in the position where he must not exercise the motion picture rights derived from his copyright under penalty either of losing

[28] *Collier* v. *Imp. Films Co.* (1913), 214 Fed. (D. C.) 272; See also Section 142.

his entire copyright or of competing unfairly with his neighbor.

To realize the practical effect of this rule, we may take the case of a famous novel which has enjoyed a circulation of half a million. A stranger comes along, while the fame of the novel is at its height, and puts out a picture entirely unrelated to the novel in story, plot, theme, characterization or situation—but with the identical title. If it is the law that there is no competition between them, the novelist is barred from producing a motion picture of his novel under any title, and the motion picture producer may with impunity palm off his mediocre work as the product of the novelist, and thereby reap the benefit of the latter's genius.

On the other hand, it may be said that the whole theory of unfair competition is founded on the protection of the trader in the conduct of his business. Would the production of a picture bearing the same title as a novel, decrease the sales of such novel? Would there in any event be actual competition? Would the picture influence the public not to purchase the novel? It may also be asked whether a novel published under the same title as that of a prior motion picture would result in a decreased attendance at the exhibition of the picture. The argument advanced is that the effect of one upon the other is too problematical and remote to permit the aggrieved party to invoke the law of unfair competition for his protection.

It has generally been assumed that *Atlas* v. *Street & Smith* has settled the law in this country to the effect that there is no competition between a novel and a motion picture. While in the prevailing opinion that statement is made, it is pure obiter dictum. The question involved in that case was not between a novel and a picture, but between a series of publications and a picture. There a series of works, each under a different title, had been published from time to time, the entire series being known under the name "Nick Carter." The court was right in its conclusion, for the exhibition of a picture under the same title could not very well affect the trade in the series; the situation is analogous to that of a motion picture published under the same title as that of a periodical. How can it be said that a person contemplating attendance at the exhibition of a motion picture may be under the impression that he will see reproduced a periodical!

The question has not yet come squarely before the courts.[29]

[29] See: *Harper* v. *Ranous* (1895), 67 Fed. (C. C.) 904. This case was brought under the Copyright Act for an infringement. The defendant performed a dramatic composition bearing the same title as the plaintiff's novel. The plot, scenes and dialogue of the novel, not having been imitated or adapted, the court held that an action did not lie, as the copyright law did not protect a title alone, but only in so far as it was a part of the copyrighted work.

This case has sometimes been cited in support of the proposition that there is no unfair competition between a novel and a dramatic composition but it will be noted that unfair competition was not at all involved in the case.

See: *Astor* v. *W. 82nd St. Realty Co.* (1915), 167 A. D. (N. Y.) 273; 152 N. Y. Supp. 631. An hotel and an apartment hotel bore the same title, "Apthorp." *Held*, that since one desiring rooms by the day or longer in a hotel would not be apt to lease an apartment in an apartment hotel, there was no direct competition between them, and no injunction would lie.

Section 122.—Use of title after copyright in work expires.

After the literary work falls into the public domain, the title of such work becomes public property as well. It has been noted before that a title is protected only in conjunction with a work with which it has become associated.[30] Hence, if the work becomes public property, the title also becomes public property. Anyone may thereafter appropriate the title for use in connection with any literary work.[31] The courts will not perpetuate the rights in a literary work under the copyright law upon any theory of unfair competition.[32]

See also: *Simplex Automobile* v. *Kahnweiler* (1914), 162 A. D. (N. Y.) 480; 147 N. Y. Supp. 617. Plaintiff affixed the title "*Simplex*" to an automobile. Defendant affixed the same title to a fire extinguisher. *Held*, that there could be no recovery.

A discussion of the law of unfair competition including trade names and trade marks is contained in 20 C. C. A. at page 165. See also: 30 C. C. A. 376; 50 C. C. A. 323.

Where the title of a play was used as the title of a musical composition and the composition was published in such a manner as to lead the public to believe that the musical composition was a part of the play, when not so in fact, held that the owners of the play were entitled to an injunction and damages. See: *Elkin & Co.* v. *Francis Day & Hunter* (Eng.) (1910), Times, Oct. 27.

[30] *Black* v. *Ehrich* (1891), 44 Fed. (C. C.) 793; *Aronson* v. *Fleckenstein* (1886), 28 Fed. (C. C.) 75.

[31] *Merriam Co.* v. *Strauss* (1904), 136 Fed. (C. C.) 477; *Merriam Co.* v. *Halloway Pub. Co.* (1890), 43 Fed. (C. C.) 450; *Merriam Co.* v. *Texas Siftings Co.* (1892), 49 Fed. (C. C.) 944; *Merriam Co.* v. *Famous S. & C. Co.* (1891), 47 Fed. (C. C.) 411; *Merriam* v. *Saulfield* (1912), 198 Fed. (C. C. A.) 369.

[32] *Ogilvie* v. *Merriam Co.* (1907), 149 Fed. (C. C.) 858; *G. & C. Merriam* v. *Ogilvie* (1908), 159 Fed. (C. C. A.) 638.

This rule, however, is limited to the extent that the title must not be used in such a manner as to lead the public to believe that the later work to which the title is applied is the identical literary production of the former work. The courts have always required the subsequent user of such title to affix thereto some phrase or expression which will distinguish to the public the old and the new work.[33]

[33] *Atlas Mfg. Co.* v. *Street & Smith* (1913), 204 Fed. (C. C. A.) 398. Van Valkenburgh, J.: "So the copyright of a book does not prevent others from taking the same title for another book, though the copyright has not expired; and on the expiration of the copyright of a novel any person may use the plot for a play, copy or publish it or make any other use of it as he may see fit. . . . The right to use a copyrighted name upon the expiration of the copyright becomes public property, subject to the limitation that the right be so exercised as not to deceive members of the public or lead them to believe that they are buying the particular thing which was produced under the copyright."

Glaser v. *St. Elmo* (1909), 175 Fed. (C. C.) 276. "The rule is well settled that, on the expiration of a patent for an article which has become identified by some particular name, as the name of the inventor, although it is open to the public to manufacture the patented article and to call it by the name by which it is commonly known, it is unfair competition to do so unless the person making the article affixes to it a plain notice that it is not made by the owner of the original patent, but by some one else. *Singer Mfg. Co.* v. *June Mfg. Co.*, 163 U. S. 169; 16 Sup. Ct. 1002; *Merriam* v. *Famous Shoe etc. Co.*, 47 Fed. (C. C.) 411. The same rule has been applied to copyrights. *Merriam Co.* v. *Ogilvie*, 159 Fed. (C. C. A.) 638."

Estes v. *Williams* (1884), 21 Fed. (C. C.) 189; *Estes* v. *Leslie* (1886), 27 Fed. (C. C.) 22; *Estes* v. *Worthington* (1887), 21 Fed. (C. C.) 154.

Section 123.—Infringement of titles—Titles held to infringe.

Defendants, who had obtained the services of one Heney to revise an old work, and had entitled it, *Heney's New and Revised Edition of Jousse's Royal Standard Pianoforte Tutor* and had printed the word "Heney" in large letters, both on the title page and cover, were held to infringe the plaintiff's work *Heney's Royal Modern Tutor for the Pianoforte.*[34]

So, too, were the titles *Canadian Bookseller and Literary Journal* and *Canada Bookseller and Stationer* held to infringe.[35]

The plaintiffs and one Beatty had carried on the business of publishing and selling copybooks under the title of *Beatty's Head Line Copy-Book.* Subsequently Beatty withdrew from the firm, received twenty thousand dollars for his interest therein, and registered his name in connection with copybooks. He then contracted with the defendant to prepare copybooks, and these were to be sold under the title *Beatty's New and Improved Head-Line Copy Books.* It was held that he could not do so.[36]

[34] *Metzler* v. *Wood* (Eng.) (1876), 8 Ch. D. 606. "But when the defendant came to print the cover, fair trading required that the exterior of the work should bear the name of *Jousse* as the prominent word, and that the name of *Henrey* as editor should be made subordinate. The question is whether the cover of the book is not calculated to deceive. The cases rest in a simple proposition enunciated by Lord Longdale in *Croft* v. *Day*, 7 Beav. 84, which is 'that no man has a right to sell his own goods as the goods of another.' That is the principle on which I decide this case."

[35] *Rose* v. *McLean* (Can.) (1896), 24 Ont. App. 240.

[36] *Canada Publ. Co.* v. *Beatty*

Plaintiff published a magazine under the title of *Suburban Life*. Defendant attempted the publication of a periodical, *Philadelphia Suburban Life*. He was enjoined.[37] The title *J. Gruber's Hagerstown Town and County Almanack* was held to infringe upon the title *T. G. Robertson's Hagerstown Almanack*.[38]

The title *Sherlock Holmes, Detective*, has been held to infringe *Sherlock Holmes*.[39]

A book or pamphlet published by the plaintiff under the title of *Payson, Drunton & Scribner's National System of Penmanship*, was held infringed by defendant's book, *Independent National System of Penmanship*.[40]

(Can.) (1885), 11 Can. Sup. Ct. 306. "In my opinion the plaintiff had the exclusive right to use the name 'Beatty' in connection with, and as denoting copy books of his manufacture, and no one has the right to the word for the purpose of passing off his books as those of the plaintiff, or even when innocent of that purpose, to use it in any way calculated to deceive, or aid in deceiving the public, to the detriment of the plaintiff . . . ."

[37] *Suburban Press* v. *Phila. Co.* (1910), 227 Pa. 148; 75 Atl. 1037. "There are two classes of cases involving judicial interference with the use of names; first, where the intent is to get an unfair and fraudulent share of another's business, and second, where the effect of defendant's action, *irrespective of his intent*, is to produce confusion in the public mind and consequent loss to the plaintiff."

Citing *American Clay Mfg. Co.* v. *American Clay Mfg. Co.* (1901), 198 Pa. 189; 47 Atl. 936.

[38] *Robertson* v. *Berry* (1878), 50 Md. 591.

[39] *Hopkins Amusement Co.* v. *Frohman* (1903), 202 Ill. 541; 67 N. E. 391.

[40] *Potter* v. *McPherson* (1880), 21 Hun, 559. "Where such a simulated resemblance is found in the title made use of by one person to that previously used by another long engaged in the same business, the inference is just and natural that the motive for doing so is to acquire improp-

The title *Dr. Eliot's Five-Foot Shelf of the World's Best Books* and the title *Dr. Eliot's Five-Foot Shelf of the World's Greatest Books* were both held to compete unfairly with the expression *Dr. Eliot's Five-Foot Shelf of Books.*[41]

The title *Chatterbox* on a series of publications has been held to infringe a prior series under that title.[42]

Comfort and *Home Comfort* have been declared in competition, the latter infringing on the former.[43]

Plaintiffs had for many years printed the well-known *Oxford Bible.* The defendant published a bible specified in the title page as an *Oxford Bible, The S. S. Teacher's Edition* and on the back as a *Holy Bible; Oxford, S. S. Teacher's Edition.* Held that was an infringement, and should be restrained.[44]

The use of the title *Webster's Dictionary,* unless there was an explanation published in such manner as to indicate clearly that plaintiffs were not its publishers, was held to be unfair competition.[45]

The complainant published a trade journal under the title *The United States Investor.* The defendant issued a similar publication entitled *The Investor* and inserted at

erly the patronage and trade of the other, and no reason exists for excluding this case from the control of that presumption."

[41] *Collier* v. *Jones* (1910), 66 Misc. (N. Y.) 97; 120 N. Y. Supp. 991; modified 140 A. D. (N. Y.) 911; 125 N. Y. Supp. 1116.

[42] *Estes* v. *Leslie* (1886), 27 (C. C.) 22; *Estes* v. *Worthington* (1887), 31 Fed. (C. C.) 154.

[43] *Gannert* v. *Rupert* (1904), 127 Fed. (C. C. A.) 962.

[44] *Chancellor Oxford Univ.* v. *Wilmore Andrews* (1900), 101 Fed. (C. C.) 443.

[45] *Ogilvie* v. *Merriam Co.* (1907), 149 Fed. (C. C.) 858; *Merriam Co.* v. *Ogilvie* (1908), 159 Fed. (C. C. A.) 638.

the head of its editorial page the following: *Published by the Investor Publishing Company*. It was held that the bill of complaint stated a cause of action for unfair competition.[46] A newspaper called *United States Police Gazette* was held to infringe upon one called *The National Police Gazette*.[47] A periodical entitled *Bon Ton* was protected against unfair competition by another periodical which was issued under the title *Gazette du Bon Ton*.[48]

The word *Chanticlair* as the title of a play was held to infringe the title *Chantecler*.[49]

The title *Buster Brown* in connection with a play was held capable of being protected upon the theory of unfair competition;[50] so also the title *Erminie*[51] as well as *L'Aiglon*.[52] And the title *Mercedes* as that of a vaudeville sketch was likewise protected.[53]

It was held that there was unfair competition between a dramatic composition and a motion picture both bearing the same title, to wit: *The Miracle*;[54] so also in respect

[46] *Investor Publishing Co. of Mass.* v. *Dobinson* (1896), 72 Fed. (C. C.) 603.

[47] *Matsell* v. *Flanagan* (1867), 2 Abb. Pr. R. (N. S.) 459. The defendant was not the publisher but the vendor of the infringing publication; still, he was held liable as a joint tort feasor.

[48] *Taylor* v. *Nast* (1915), 154 N. Y. Supp. 982.

[49] *Frohman* v. *Morris* (1910), 68 Misc. (N. Y.) 461; 123 N. Y. Supp. 1090.

[50] *Outcault* v. *Lamar* (1910), 135 A. D. (N. Y.) 110; 119 N. Y. Supp. 930.

[51] *Aronson* v. *Fleckenstein* (1886), 28 Fed. (C. C.) 75.

[52] *Frohman* v. *Payton* (1901), 34 Misc. (N. Y.) 275; 68 N. Y. Supp. 849.

[53] *Howard* v. *Lovett*, Michigan Circuit Ct., Wayne County, Feb. 24, 1916; Trade Mark Reporter, Vol. 6, p. 229.

[54] *Miracle Co.* v. *Danziger* (1913), N. Y. Law Journal, March 8.

of the title *A Fool There Was*; [55] and also where the title was *The Come Back*,[56] and where it was *Happiness*.[57]

In the case of the titles *The House of a Thousand Candles* and *The House of a Thousand Scandals* as the names of two motion pictures, they were held to unfairly compete with each other upon the hearing for an injunction pendente lite; [58] but upon final hearing they were held *not* to infringe each other.[59]

In the case of the title *The Rosary* the contrary was the situation. The Justice presiding at the time the application for an injunction pendente lite was made, held there was no infringement of title where two motion pictures bore that name.[60] Upon final hearing the contrary conclusion was reached, the Justice then presiding holding that the motion picture bearing that title and released subsequently in point of time was unfairly competing with the other.[61]

The title *Follies of 1917* as the name of a theatrical

[55] *Marc Klaw* v. *General Film Co.* (1915), 154 N. Y. Supp. 988; aff'd 171 A. D. (N. Y.) 945; 156 N. Y. Supp. 1128.

[56] *Dickey* v. *Mutual Film Corp.* (1915), 160 N. Y. Supp. 609; *Dickey* v. *Metro Pictures Corporation* (1917), N. Y. Law Journal, April 28.

[57] *Manners* v. *Triangle* (1917), U. S. District Court, Southern District of New York, N. Y. Law Journal, June 21.

[58] *Selig Polyscope Co.* v. *Mutual Film Corp.* (1915), N. Y. Law Journal, September 28.

[59] *Selig Polyscope Co.* v. *Mutual Film Corporation* (1917), N. Y. Law Journal, February 1.

[60] *Selig Polyscope Co,* v. *Unicorn Film Service Corp.* (1916), N. Y. Law Journal, September 16.

[61] *Selig Polyscope Co.* v. *Unicorn Film Service Corp.* (1917), 163 N. Y. Supp. 62.

production was held infringed by the title *Gus Hill's Follies of 1917*.[62]

In England, defendant was restrained from using the title *Current Quotations* as the title of its catalogue unless it affixed thereto distinguishing words.[63] And where plaintiff's work was entitled *The Birthday Scripture Text Book* and that of defendant *The Children's Birthday Text Book*, they were held to compete unfairly.[64]

So also the publisher of a magazine entitled *The Monthly Odd Volume* was enjoined from selling his periodical upon the ground that such title competed unfairly with the plaintiff's annual publication entitled *The Odd Volume*.[65]

The defendant was enjoined from exhibiting a motion picture under the title *Sealed Orders* upon the ground that a film under such title would unfairly compete with plaintiff's dramatic composition bearing the same title.[66]

In Australia, the title of a play *The Wrong Mr. Wright*, was held to be infringed by that of another play called *The Wrong Mrs. Wright*.[67]

Section 124.—Infringement of titles—Titles held not to infringe.

The Spice of Life and *The Good Things of Life* as the

[62] *Ziegfield Follies Inc.* v. *Gus Hill* (1916), N. Y. Law Journal, December 5.

[63] *Ewen's Colonial Stamp Market Ltd.* v. *Federal Stamp Co.* (Eng.) (1907), Times, February 23.

[64] *Mack* v. *Petter* (Eng.), L. R. 14 Eq. 431.

[65] *Alden* v. *Arnsky-Wilson* (Eng.) (1911), Times, May 13.

[66] *Raleigh* v. *Kinematograph Trading Company* (Eng.) (1914), Times, March 12.

[67] *Broadhurst* v. *Nichols* (Australian) (1903), N. S. W. 3 S. R. 147.

titles of two books were held not to infringe;[68] so also where the titles were *Social Register* and *Newport Social Index.*[69]

In the case of newspapers where the titles *New Era* and *Republican New Era* were used, they were held not to compete unfairly.[70] The same was held with respect to the titles *The Commercial Advertiser* and *New York Commercial.*[71] The title *The New Northwest* and *The Northwest News* were held not to compete;[72] so also where the titles were *The National Advocate* and *The New York National Advocate.*[73]

Where the titles of monthly magazines for the young were *Our Young Folks* and *Our Folks' Illustrated Paper,* they were held not to infringe,[74] so too, where the titles were *Motor Boat* and *Motor Boating Magazine.*[75]

Plaintiff published a book entitled *Farthest North Nansen.* Defendant's book was entitled *The Fram Expedition. Nansen in the Frozen World. Including Earlier Arctic Explorations.* It was held not to infringe.[76]

[68] *Stokes* v. *Allen & White* (1890), 56 Hun (N. Y.), 526; 9 N. Y. Supp. 846.

[69] *Social Register Assoc'n* v. *Murphy* (1904), 128 Fed. (C. C.) 116.

[70] *Bell* v. *Locke* (1840), 8 Paige (N. Y.), 74; see also: *Grocers Journal Co.* v. *Midland Publishing Co.* (1907), 127 Mo. App. 356.

[71] *Commercial Advertising Ass'n* v. *Hoques* (1898), 26 A. D. (N. Y.) 279; 49 N. Y. Supp. 938.

[72] *Duniway Publ. Co.* v. *The Northwest Printing & Publ. Co.* (1884), 11 Oregon, 322; 8 Pac. 283.

[73] *Snowden* v. *Noah,* Hopkins Ch. R. 347; Cox 1.

[74] *Osgood* v. *Allen* (1872), Fed. Cas. 10603.

[75] *Motorboat Pub. Co.* v. *Motor Boating Co.* (1907), 57 Misc. (N. Y.) 108; 107 N. Y. Supp. 468.

[76] *Harper & Bros.* v. *Lare et al.* (1900), 103 Fed. (C. C. A.) 203.

Charley's Uncle was held not to infringe the title of plaintiff's play *Charley's Aunt.*[77]

Defendants were permitted to use the title *St. Elmo* as the name of their play notwithstanding the fact that prior to defendant's use plaintiffs had produced a play under the same title.[78]

So also with respect to the title, *Charity* [79] and to the title *The Shadow.*[80]

The title *Nick Carter* as that of a motion picture was held not to unfairly compete with the same title as the name of a weekly periodical.[81]

Plaintiff, the publisher of a series of pamphlet works of fiction entitled the *Old Sleuth Library*, sought to restrain defendant who published a similar series of pamphlets under the title *New York Detective Library*, from publishing any book or pamphlet containing in its title, or in any part of it, the word *Sleuth*. The complaint was dismissed.[82]

Defendant produced a motion picture under the title *The Girl Who Did Not Care*. Plaintiff had produced a motion picture before defendant's entitled *The Girl Who Doesn't Know*. Injunction was denied.[83]

It was held in Canada that there was no unfair com-

[77] *Frohman* v. *Miller* (1894), 8 Misc. (N. Y.) 379; 29 N. Y. Supp. 1109.

[78] *Glaser* v. *St. Elmo Co.* (1909), 175 Fed. (C. C.) 276.

[79] *Isaacs* v. *Daly* (1874), 7 Jones & Spencer (N. Y.), 511.

[80] *Stringer* v. *Frohman* (1915), 152 N. Y. Supp. 935.

[81] *Atlas Manufacturing Co.* v. *Street & Smith* (1913), 204 Fed. (C. C. A.) 398.

[82] *Munro* v. *Tousey* (1891), 129 N. Y. 38; 29 N. E. 9.

[83] *B. S. Moss Motion Picture Corp.* v. *Ivan Film Prod. Inc.* (1917), N. Y. Law Journal, Jan. 23.

petition in the case of two books entitled *The New Canadian Bird Book* and *The Canadian Bird Book* respectively.[84]

In England the title *The Evening Post* was held not to infringe the title *The Morning Post;* [85] so also when the titles were *The North Express* and *The Daily Express;* [86] the *Mail* and *Morning Mail.*[87]

Where the titles of two magazines were *The Field* and *The Field and Kennel,*[88] there was no unfair competition. No injunction was granted where the titles of the magazine were *Everybody's Magazine* and *Everybody's Weekly.*[89] The court also refused an injunction where the titles of the plaintiff's magazines were *The Plumber and Decorator* and *The Decorators' and Painters' Magazine,* and that of defendant's publication *The Decorator.*[90] Plaintiffs issued a periodical entitled *M. A. P.*, the title being an abbreviation for *Mainly About People.* The defendant's publication was entitled *P. T. O.*, being an abbreviation for *People Talked Of.* No injunction was allowed.[91] And a publication entitled *Punch & Judy* could not enjoin a publication under the title of either *Punch* or *Judy.*[92]

[84] *McIndoo* v. *Musson Book Co.* (Can.) (1913), 35 O. L. R. 42.

[85] *Borthwick* v. *The Evening Post* (Eng.) (1888), 37 Ch. Div. 449.

See also: *Kelly* v. *Byles* (Eng.) (1880), 13 Ch. Div. 682.

[86] *Dillon* v. *Pearson* (Eng.) (1901), Times, December 23.

[87] *Walter* v. *Emmott* (Eng.) (1885), 54 L. J. Ch. 1059; 53 L. T. 437.

[88] *Cox* v. *Sports Publishing Co.* (Eng.) (1902), Times, June 14.

[89] *Ridgway Co.* v. *Amalgamated Press* (Eng.) (1911), 28 T. L. R. 149.

[90] *Dale Reynolds* v. *Trade Papers Publ. Co.* (Eng.) (1902), Times, December 9.

[91] *C. Arthur Pearson Ltd.* v. *T. P. O'Connor* (Eng.) (1906), Times, May 12.

[92] *Bradbury* v. *Beeton* (Eng.) (1869), 18 W. R. 33.

Plaintiff and defendant both published books under the title *Cottage Homes of England.* The books were of an entirely different character. No injunction was allowed;[93] so also in the case of the title *Our Sailor King,* the court holding that the books appealed to different classes of customers, hence no competition, even though the text was quite similar.[94]

It was held that plaintiff, the owner of a play entitled *Where there's a Will, there's a Way,* was not entitled to enjoin the production of defendant's play entitled *Where there's a Will.*[95]

Section 125.—Acquiescence and abandonment.

Mere non-user of a title for a length of time is not in itself an abandonment of the right to its exclusive use.[96] There must be something more tangible, some express act to evince such an intent to abandon, or a series of acts from which such intent may be clearly implied. "To establish the defense of abandonment it is necessary to show not only acts indicating a practical abandonment, but an actual intent to abandon. Acts which unexplained would be sufficient to establish abandonment, may be answered by showing that there never was an intention to give up and relinquish the right claimed." [97]

[93] *Crotch* v. *Arnold* (Eng.) (1909), 54 S. J. 49.

[94] *John F. Shaw & Co.* v. *Collins* (Eng.) (1911), Times, June 2.

[95] *Broemel* v. *Meyer* (Eng.) (1912), 29 T. L. R. 148.

[96] *Janney* v. *Pan-Coast Ventilator Mfg. Co.* (1904), 128 Fed. (C. C.) 121. The failure to put out the article for a short period so that it is not in the market at the time of the commencement of suit, does not constitute abandonment.

[97] *Saxlehner* v. *Eisner et al.* (1900), 179 U. S. 19; 21 Sup.

The mere fact that third parties have made use of the plaintiff's title is not of itself conclusive or presumptive evidence of an abandonment.[98] The burden always remains upon the defendant to establish the abandonment.[99] Having established such abandonment, however, the courts will refuse to enjoin the defendant from using the title; it will follow then as a matter of course that the plaintiff will receive neither an accounting of profits nor damages.[100]

Ct. 7. Quoted with approval in *Baglin* v. *Cusenier Co.* (1911), 221 U. S. 580; 31 Sup. Ct. 669, where it was said: "There must be found an intent to abandon or the property is not lost."

[98] *Cuervo* v. *Henkell* (1892), 50 Fed. (C. C.) 471. . . . "And as to other imitations of his own trade-mark, there is not a particle of evidence to show that these were made or sold with his consent or acquiescence. This defense has been so frequently and forcibly condemned by authority that further discussion is profitless. (Citing cases)."

International Cheese Co. v. *Phoenix Cheese Co.* (1907), 118 A. D. (N. Y.) 499; 103 N. Y. Supp. 362. "And the fact that hotels and restaurants were selling other brands of cheese as Philadelphia cream cheese does not show an intent by defendant to abandon its trade-name or to make it public property."

[99] *Julian* v. *Hoosier Drill Co.* (1881), 78 Ind. 408; *Indian Rubber Co.* v. *Rubber Comb Co.* (1879), 45 Super. Ct. (N. Y.) 258; *Saxlehner* v. *Eisner* (1900), 179 U. S. 19; 21 Sup. Ct. 7.

Actiengesellschaft v. *Arnberg* (1901), 109 Fed. (C. C. A.) 151. "It is no answer to his complaint against any particular person who has so used it to say that such trespasser is not the only one who has done so, for a trespasser cannot justify upon the ground that others have committed like trespasses. . . ."

[100] *Blackwell* v. *Dibrell* (1878), Fed. Cas. (C. C.) 1475; *Royal Baking Powder* v. *Raymond* (1895), 70 Fed. (C. C.) 376; *Menendez* v. *Holt* (1888), 128 U. S. 514; 9 Sup. Ct. 143.

Acquiescence may consist in either permitting a third party to use the title for a time without making any protest, or in allowing the defendant to use it for a long time before commencing the action to enjoin.

To constitute acquiescence there must be full *scienter* on the part of the plaintiff. Unless he knows of the infringing acts, he cannot be said to acquiesce in them.

It is no defense to an accounting and claim for damages to establish user of the title by third parties, unless in addition thereto the defendant shows acquiescence in such user.[101]

Where the plaintiff has knowingly permitted the defendant or others to use his title for a long time and has made no attempt to assert his rights as against them, he will not be permitted to pick out the defendant as a special infringer, pursue him alone, and recover an account of profits.

The English rule penalizes a plaintiff by refusing all relief including injunction. The American courts, how-

[101] *Selig Polyscope Co.* v. *Unicorn Film Service Corp.* (1917), 163 N. Y. Supp. 62. "Justification for this use of the plaintiff's trade-mark cannot be found in the fact that the catalogues in evidence disclose the designation of other motion picture films by the use of the word 'Rosary.' So far as these catalogues have any value as proof, they indicate no more than that other persons in three instances have so named their films at dates long after the plaintiffs Rowland and Clifford acquired their trade-mark by original adoption. Whether the films referred to were actually exhibited under the conditions which the plaintiffs might or might not have *found* to be injurious to their rights is a matter of speculation, but the defendant's case is not aided by pointing to a possible invasion of these rights by others."

ever, will ordinarily grant injunction when the right thereto is made out, even though there be acquiescence, but will in such cases deny an account of profits and an award of damages.[102] Nor will they in such cases grant a temporary injunction.[103]

The reason for the American rule is that where the plaintiff has stood by without protest and permitted the defendant to infringe upon his rights, and has allowed him to expend moneys in marketing and advertising his product, he is not equitably entitled to the fruits of the defendant's enterprise, or to make any claim for damages sustained by him. But not having divested himself of his property right, equity will protect him against any future infringement thereof.[104]

[102] *McLean* v. *Fleming* (1877), 96 U. S. 245. "Cases frequently arise where a court of equity will refuse the prayer of the plaintiff for an account of gains and profits on the ground of delay in asserting his rights, even when the facts proved render it proper to grant an injunction to prevent further infringements."

Allen v. *Walker* (1916), 235 Fed. (D. C.) 230. Where defendant had been infringing for two years, and had not been notified to desist it was held such laches as to preclude an accounting.

Strauss v. *Notaseme Co.* (1915), 240 U. S. 179; 36 Sup. Ct. 288; *Menendez* v. *Holt* (1888), 128 U. S. 514; 9 Sup. Ct. 143; *Amoskeag* v. *Spear* (1849), 2 Sandf. S. C. 599.

See in this connection: *Sawyer* v. *Kellogg* (1881), 9 Fed. (C. C.) 601.

[103] *Burns* v. *Burns* (1902), 118 Fed. (C. C.) 944; *Virginia Hot Springs* v. *Hegeman* (1905), 138 Fed. (C. C.) 855.

[104] *Menendez* v. *Holt* (1888), 128 U. S. 514; 9 Sup. Ct. 143; *Fairbanks* v. *Luckel* (1902), 116 Fed. (C. C. A.) 332; *Sawyer* v. *Kellogg* (1881), 9 Fed. (C. C.) 601; *McLean* v. *Fleming* (1877), 96 U. S. 245.

Where the defendant had originally manufactured and sold "Royal" baking powder and had become bankrupt, he could not after a lapse of twenty-three years, resume the use of that trade name, the plaintiff having in the meantime built up a large business under the same trade name.[105]

Some writers have sought to draw a distinction between "laches" and "acquiescence" although the terms have been used interchangeably by the courts. We cannot see any real distinction between the two. Both involve knowledge on the part of the plaintiff of the defendant's invasion of his rights. Both contemplate a standing by and a tacit permission to the defendant to continue his infringement.

Section 126.—Relief.

In actions of this kind the plaintiff is entitled to an injunction, an accounting of defendant's profits, and damages sustained by him. It does not necessarily follow that in every case the plaintiff is entitled to all these modes of relief. He is ordinarily entitled to an injunction where he has not abandoned the title.[106]

Whether he is entitled to an accounting or damages is a question to be determined from the facts of each particular case. The cases thus far have not laid down uniform rules. For instance, in several cases the use of the identical title was held sufficient to entitle the plaintiff

[105] *Royal Baking Co.* v. *Raymond* (1895), 70 Fed. (C. C.) 376.

[106] *Le Page Co.* v. *Russian Cement Co.* (1892), 51 Fed. (C. C. A.) 941; *Noebius* v. *De Jonge & Co.* (1914), 215 Fed. (D. C.) 443; *United Drug Co.* v. *Rectanus Co.* (1913), 206 Fed. (D. C.) 570.

to an accounting and damages, even though nothing else was proven.[107] Then again, to entitle the plaintiff to an

[107] *Miracle* v. *Danziger* (1913), N. Y. Law Journal, March 8; *Klaw* v. *General Film Co.* (1915), 154 N. Y. Supp. 988; aff'd 171 A. D. (N. Y.) 945; 156 N. Y. Supp. 1128; *Selig Polyscope* v. *Unicorn Film* (1917), N. Y. Law Journal; 163 N. Y. Supp. 62.

Ziegfeld Follies v. *Gus Hill* (1916), N. Y. Law Journal, December 5. "Plaintiff does not claim on this motion any exclusive right to the use of the word "Follies" as a name applied to theatrical attractions. It merely asks to be protected against the appropriation by the defendant of the name or title "Follies of 1917" or "Follies of" any particular year and his using it as the title of a theatrical production, on the very sufficient ground that it or its predecessors in interest created and applied that title to a successful theatrical production nearly ten years ago, and have used it ever since as the name of a distinctive and very popular theatrical production, which by the expenditure of a very large sum of money the plaintiff and its predecessors in interest have popularized and identified with their ownership, management and control. The defendant disclaims any intention of misappropriating plaintiff's property rights or trading on plaintiff's name and points to the fact that the title he uses is "Gus Hill's Follies of 1917," claiming that the important part of the name, so far as drawing power is concerned, is in his own name "Gus Hill," which is widely known throughout the country and identified with a certain class of productions. It is doubtless true that the defendant's name is widely known and serves to identify in the minds of the public the kind of production to be expected under his management or direction. But if, as the defendant claims, it is his name that attracts, rather than the fanciful name of the production, whatever it might be, it is difficult to see why he deliberately adopts the particular name that plaintiff has popularized and has so long used, or why he insists so strongly upon using this particular name. It is a case where, as Judge Coxe observed in *Florence Co.* v. *J. C. Dowd*, 178 Fed. Rep. 73, 76, "if honest he should stop voluntarily, and if dishonest he should be

accounting and an assessment of damages, it was held that he must establish actual losses as well as fraud.[108]

compelled to stop. Motion granted."

Walter v. *Emmott* (Eng.) (1885), 54 L. J. Ch. 1059; 53 L. T. 437. Plaintiff who owned a newspaper called the *Mail* attempted to restrain defendant from publishing a paper called the *Morning Mail*. Lord Justice Bowen said:

"The use of a similar name, for instance, is not, as a matter of law, conclusive to show that there is an intention to deceive, or as a matter of law, that there would be such a deception as would cause an interference with or damage to the business of another, because we can conceive cases where the use of a similar name might be so hedged round by other circumstances as to destroy the natural effect of such an act. But I do think in nine cases out of ten the use of a name would be evidence from which few minds could draw any other inference except that damage would be done by deceiving the customer or public in respect of the two businesses."

Taendsticksfabriks A. Vulcan v. *Meyers* (1893), 139 N. Y. 364; 34 N. E. 904. "It is not necessary to sustain an action of this kind either to establish a guilty knowledge or fraudulent intent on the part of the wrong-doer. It is sufficient that the proprietary right of the party and its actual infringement is shown."

See also: *Howard Co.* v. *Carlton* (1915), 219 Fed. (D. C.) 913; *Oneida Community* v. *Oneida* (1914), 150 N. Y. Supp. 923; modified 168 A. D. (N. Y.) 769; 154 N. Y. Supp. 391; *Salvation Army* v. *Salvation Army* (1909), 135 A. D. (N. Y.) 268; 120 N. Y. Supp. 471; *Clinton Metallic Paint* v. *N. Y. Metallic Paint* (1898), 23 Misc. (N. Y.) 66; (1898), 50 N. Y. Supp. 437.

[108] *Elgin Nat. Watch Co.* v. *Illinois Watch Co.* (1900), 179 U. S. 665; 21 Sup. Ct. 270; *Osgood* v. *Allen* (1872), 1 Holmes (C. C.), 185; Fed. Cas. 10603; *Day* v. *Webster*, 23 A. D. (N. Y.) 601; 49 N. Y. Supp. 314; *Kipling* v. *Putnam* (1903), 120 Fed. (C. C. A.) 641; *Morgan* v. *Walton* (1898), 86 Fed. (C. C. A.) 605; *N. K. Fairbank Co.* v. *Windsor* (1903), 124 Fed. (C. C. A.) 200; *Billiken Co.* v. *Baker & B. Co.* (1909), 174 Fed. (C. C.) 829.

United Drug Co. v. *Rectanus Co.*

Some cases hold that although fraud is not established specifically, and there is no direct proof of actual loss, nevertheless an accounting and damages will be allowed.[109]

Each case must be decided upon its own peculiar facts. Where a play has achieved national or international renown, and is well known to the public, the mere appropriation of the title, no matter whether it be accidental or deliberate, is in itself sufficient to establish a wrongful intent, giving the rights to injunction, accounting and damages.[110] On the other hand, where the plaintiff's

(1913), 206 Fed. (D.C.) 570. ". . . We are clearly of opinion that the facts stated require us, under the express mandate of the authorities cited, to hold that the right of the plaintiff to the exclusive use of the word Rex in connection with medicinal preparations for dyspepsia and kindred diseases of the stomach and digestive organs must be sustained. The following, among many cases, while requiring that judgment, also show that while an injunction against the future use of the word Rex in connection with the character of preparations indicated should be granted, no accounting for profits, nor any assessment of damages for unfair trade, need on the facts found be decreed. *Saxlehner* v. *Eisner and Mendelsohn Co.* (1900), 179 U. S. 19; *Saxlehner* v. *Siegel-Cooper Co.* (1900), 179 U. S. 42; *Menendez* v. *Holt* (1888), 128 U. S. 514; *McLean* v. *Fleming* (1877), 96 U. S. 245."

[109] *Dickey* v. *Mutual* (1916), 160 N. Y. Supp. 609; *N. K. Fairbank Co.* v. *Windsor* (1903), 124 Fed. (C. C. A.) 200.

[110] *Frohman* v. *Payton* (1901), 34 Misc. (N. Y.) 275; 68 N. Y. Supp. 849; *Frohman* v. *Morris* (1910), 68 Misc. (N. Y.) 461; 123 N. Y. Supp. 1090. See in this connection: *Kathreiner* v. *Pastor-Kneipp* (1879), 82 Fed. (C. C. A.) 321.

See also in this connection: *Hier* v. *Abrahams* (1880), 82 N. Y. 519. To maintain an action for unfair competition because of the use of the same trade name, trade-mark, symbol or device it is not necessary to show that there is an intent to defraud.

play is not nationally or universally known, an innocent party will only be enjoined from future infringements. In any case where there is an intentional infringement, or fraud is perpetrated, the plaintiff is entitled to an accounting and damages; so too, where an innocent infringer after notice persists in the use of the title.[111]

Notice may be given by word of mouth or by letter. Registration of a play in the office of the Register of Copyrights is notice in like manner as the recording of a deed.[112] Suit actually commenced and service of a summons therein is the best form of notice.[113]

See also *Dutton* v. *Cupples*, (1907), 117 A. D. (N. Y.) 172; 102 N. Y. Supp. 309.

[111] *Fuller* v. *Huff* (1900), 104 Fed. (C. C. A.) 143. "Although the intent of the defendant's principal when it commenced to use the name 'Health Food,' may have been innocent, the continuance, after it had learned of the complainant's prior use indicates its deliberate intention to use the name without reference to the complainant's possible prior rights. *Orr* v. *Johnson* (Eng.), 13 Ch. Div. 434."

Singer Mfg. Co. v. *Long* (Eng.) (1882), L. R. 8 App. Cas. 15. "It is not honest for them (the infringers) to persevere in their intention, though originally the intention might not have been otherwise than honest."

To the same effect: *Dickey* v. *Metro Pictures Corporation* (1917), N. Y. Law Journal, April 28th.

[112] *National Car Brake Co.* v. *Terre Haute Co.* (1884), 19 Fed. (C. C.) 520. "In reference to this subject of knowledge of the patent, I say to you that everyone is bound to take notice of the existence of a patent and the rights of parties under it, and is held responsible to pay for every infringement that he actually perpetrates, just as if he did know it. *It is like the record of a deed;* the record of patents of Washington is notice to everyone just as your title deeds in the records of the proper county are notice to all the world of your title."

[113] Section 25 (b), Copyright Law of the United States of 1909. "But the foregoing exceptions

In all these cases the relief granted is primarily directed toward the protection of the trader rather than the protection of the public.[114]

Actual deception is not required to be proven. It is sufficient that the use of the title is *calculated* to deceive the public.[115]

shall not deprive the copyright proprietor of any other remedy given him under this law, nor shall the limitation as to the amount of recovery apply to infringements occurring after the actual notice to a defendant, either by service of process in a suit or other written notice served upon him."

[114] *Aunt Jemima Mills Co.* v. *Rignay & Co.* (1916), 234 Fed. (D. C.) 804. "The fundamental basis of the private remedy is however not the protection of the public from imposition, but injury to the complainant. That the public is deceived may be evidence of the fact that the original proprietor's rights are being invaded. If, however, the rights of the original proprietor are in nowise interfered with, the deception of the public is no concern of a court of chancery."

Hanover Milling Co. v. *Metcalf* (1915), 240 U. S. 403; 36 Sup. Ct. 357. "The redress that is accorded in trade-mark cases is based upon the party's right to be protected in the good-will of a trade or business. The primary and proper function of a trade-mark is to identify the origin or ownership of the article to which it is affixed. Where a party has been in the habit of labelling his goods with a distinctive mark, so that purchasers recognize goods thus marked as being of his production, others are debarred from applying the same mark to goods of the same description, because to do so would in effect, represent their goods to be of his production and would tend to deprive him of the profit he might make through the sale of the goods which the purchaser intended to buy. Courts afford redress or relief upon the ground that a party has a valuable interest in the good-will of his trade or business, and in the trade-mark adopted to maintain and extend it."

[115] *Frohman* v. *Miller* (1894),

While some of the text writers have attempted to distinguish between unfair competition and actions based on the unfair use of a trade-mark or trade name, we see no such difference. Actions based on the wrongful use of a trade name are embraced within the greater field of unfair competition.[116]

The plaintiff is not compelled to wait until there is an actual infringement. He may apply for and secure an

8 Misc. (N. Y.) 379; 29 N. Y. Supp. 1109. Quoting from *Shook* v. *Wood*, 32 Leg. Int. 264, the court said, "If it was not the defendant's intention to produce the plaintiff's play *the effect of it was to mislead the public* and thereby injure the plaintiffs in their future business."

Roy Watch Co. v. *Carman Roy Watch Co.* (1899), 28 Misc. (N. Y.) 45; 58 N. Y. Supp. 979; *Fischer* v. *Blanch* (1893), 138 N. Y. 244; 33 N. E. 1040. "The true test is whether the resemblance is such that it is *calculated* to deceive and does in fact deceive under the ordinary conditions which prevail in the conduct of the particular traffic to which the controversy relates."

Oneida Community v. *Oneida G. T. Co.* (1914), 150 N. Y. Supp. 923; modified 168 A. D. (N. Y.) 769; 154 N. Y. Supp. 391. "The word 'calculate' is not used in the consideration of this evidence as planning, organizing, thinking out, or devising on the part of defendant an inscription, word, or name with intention to deceive, *but rather the inherent properties of such name or description are such that in and of themselves to the innocently concerned, they may confuse or deceive.*"

Walter M. Steppacher & Bro. v. *Karr* (1916), 236 Fed. (D. C.) 151. "There is no direct evidence of any confusion of goods . . . It is not necessary for the plaintiff to establish by evidence that any person has actually been deceived by the imitation. The question is whether there is a liability to deception through the defendant's use of the word 'Emerald.' "

[116] *Amoskeag Mfg. Co.* v. *Spear* (1849), 2 Sandf. 599; *Scriven* v. *North* (1904), 134 Fed. (C. C. A.) 366.

injunction against one who threatens to compete unfairly with him.[117]

It has been held that a cause of action for unfair competition may be properly united with one involving the infringement of patent. The courts take the position that the unfair competition is an aggravation of the infringement. It would seem to follow from this, that a cause of action in unfair competition may be united with one involving the infringement of a copyright.[118]

Section 127.—Marks and devices.

As in other trades, the motion picture producers and distributors have adopted distinguishing marks, brand-marks, signs, devices, designs, symbols and emblems to identify to the public more readily their own product. These marks can be protected both under the general principles of equity and by the state or Federal statutes relating to trade-marks.

While the decisions speak with more or less confusion of trade-marks, technical trade-marks and unfair competition, the basic principle underlying all these classes of cases seems to be the protection of the trader from the use of unfair methods.[119] In technical trade-mark cases, the fraud is presumed from the mere use of the same

[117] *Edison Storage Battery* v. *Edison* (1904), 67 N. J. Eq. 44; 55 Atl. 861; *Taendsticksfabriks A. Vulcan* v. *Meyers* (1893), 139 N. Y. 364; 34 N. E. 904.

[118] *Farmers' Handy Wagon Co.* v. *Beaver* (1916), 236 Fed. (C. C. A.) 731; *Adams* v. *Folger* (1903), 120 Fed. (C. C. A.) 260; *Ludwigh* v. *Payson* (1913), 206 Fed. (C. C. A.) 64.

[119] *Amoskeag Manufacturing Co.* v. *Spear* (1849), 2 Sandf. 599.

The similarity between the marks and devices must in general be such as to deceive the ordinary purchaser. For cases where some similarity existed but not enough

symbol or mark,[120] while in the other class of cases, fraud or a fraudulent intent must be actually proven or indicated by the facts.[121]

The tendency at the present time, however, is to eliminate all these fine distinctions, and to view the offender in the broad light of unfair competition generally.[122] As in the law of trade-names, prior user gives the exclusive right.[123] Also the same rules with respect to acquiescence and abandonment apply.

The registration of a trade-mark gives no greater rights to the owner; its practical effect is to create a presumption

to cause such deception see: Hubinger v. *Eddy* (1896), 74 Fed. (C. C.) 551, where a manufacturer of starch used as a trade-mark a flat-iron and the defendant used a trade-mark consisting of a picture of a colored woman holdup in her extended arms a freshly ironed shirt bosom, underneath which was a table upon which a small sized flat-iron appeared.

Liggett and Myers Tobacco Co. v. *Finzer* (1888), 128 U. S. 182; 9 Sup. Ct. 60, where complainant's trade-mark consisted of a star of tin and defendant's of a red star on a round piece of gilded paper with the word "light" underneath and other words referring to the defendant as the manufacturer.

120 *Simmons* v. *Mansfield* (1893), 93 Tenn. 84; 23 S. W. 165; *Lawrence Mfg.* v. *Tennessee Mfg.* (1891), 138 U. S. 537; 11 Sup. Ct. 396; *Tobacco Co.* v. *Hynes* (1884), 20 Fed. (D. C.) 883; *Coffeen* v. *Brunton* (1849), Fed. Cas. (C. C.) 2946; *Millington* v. *Fox* (Eng.) (1838), 3 Mylne & C. 338; *Johnston* v. *Orr-Ewing* (Eng.) (1882), 7 App. Cas. 219; *Edelstein* v. *Edelstein* (Eng.) (1863), 1 De Gex J. & S. 185; *Manufacturing Co.* v. *Wilson*, 3 App. Cas. 376.

121 *Hostetter* v. *Brueggeman* (1891), 46 Fed. (C. C.) 188.

122 *Denison Mfg. Co.* v. *Thomas Mfg. Co.* (1899), 94 Fed. (C. C.) 651; *Church & Dwight* v. *Russ* (1900), 99 Fed. (C. C.) 276; *Reymer & Bros* v. *Huyler's* (1911), 190 Fed. (C. C.) 83.

123 *Hainque* v. *Cyclops Iron Works* (1902), 136 Cal. 351; 68 Pac. 1014.

in favor of the owner as to use and adoption, relieving him from the burden of offering proof of these facts—it is a prima facie evidence of ownership. In addition thereto it awards treble damages as against an infringer under the Federal statute.[124]

So far as notice is concerned, it has been held that registration does not ipso facto constitute either actual or constructive notice.[125]

Motion picture producers and distributors have vied with each other in conceiving original introductions to their pictures upon the screen. Thus they flash as an introduction or interlude to or between pictures distinctive symbols such as moving stars, triangles grouping themselves in designs, and other devices of a similar nature. In the same manner, the picture is brought to a close by some like ingenious method, either an invisible hand spelling out the name of the maker of the picture, or a grouping of figures or letters in some form or combination peculiarly distinctive.

These devices are accorded protection in the same manner and for the same reasons enumerated above.

Each firm adopts a peculiar color scheme or series of designs recurring throughout the exhibition of the motion picture. These may be said to resemble closely the wrappers of packages in which goods are put upon the market; and any simulation of a device, scheme or design of this nature, will be protected upon the general theory of unfair competition.[126]

[124] Sec. 9501, Compiled Statutes of U. S., 1913.

[125] *Restanus Co.* v. *United Drug Co.* (1915), 226 Fed. (C. C. A.) 545.

[126] See in this connection: *Day*

Billing and advertising matter, heralds, clip sheets and material of a similar character are important and significant indicia upon the question of unfair dealing and carry great weight with the court.

The use of letters of the alphabet has been held to designate grade and quality rather than ownership, and will not be protected as a trade-mark.[127]

Section 128.—Transferability.

There is no exclusive right to the title as such, even though it be originated and first used by the possessor. The right to the exclusive use of the title exists solely in conjunction with the work with which it has become identified. It is, therefore, a species of property that

v. *Webster* (1897), 23 A. D. (N. Y.) 601; 49 N. Y. Supp. 314. In an action based upon unfair competition the court said: "It is true that the similarity of the alleged wrongdoer's label may be so great that fraud will be inferred from a mere inspection of the respective labels. Where, however, the similarity is not so great as upon a mere inspection to warrant the conclusion of fraud resort may be and usually is had to evidence *aliunde.*"

[127] *Stevens* v. *William* (1904), 127 Fed. (C. C. A.) 950.

On the question whether geographical names which have acquired a secondary meaning will be protected see: *La Republique Française* v. *Saratoga Spring Co.* (1903), 191 U. S. 427; *Shaver* v. *Heller & Herz* (1901), 108 Fed. (C. C. A.) 821; *American Waltham Watch* v. *U. S. Watch Co.* (1899), 173 Mass. 85; 53 N. E. 141; *American Clay Mfg. Co.* v. *American Clay Mfg. Co.* (1901), 198 Penn. St. 189; 47 Atl. 936; *British-American Tobacco Co.* v. *Brit. Amer. C. S. Co.* (1914), 211 Fed. (C. C. A.) 933; *Hamilton Shoe Co.* v. *Wolf* (1916), 240 U. S. 251; 36 Sup Ct. 269; *Pettes* v. *American Clock Co.* (1903), 89 A. D. (N. Y.) 345; 85 N. Y. Supp. 900; *Elgin Nat. Watch Co.* v. *Illinois Co.* (1900), 179 U. S. 665; 21 Sup. Ct. 270.

may be assigned only when the work to which it attaches is likewise assigned. In the eyes of the law it has no separate existence. The author or proprietor of a literary product may not part with his rights to the work, and still reserve his right to the title thereof to the exclusion of the whole world.

He may, however, part with a portion of his right to the work and still keep his exclusive right to the title. Thus, the owner of a play may assign to a third party his motion picture rights to the play, and he may at the same time under a negative covenant reserve the right that the motion picture be not produced under that title. In that event, his right to the title still remains exclusive. He may also permit the licensee to use the title for the motion picture, and yet retain his right to exploit the play under its old title. In such case both he and his licensee have exclusive right to the title, each for his particular work.

In other words, as long as some right to the original work remains, the title may be reserved. When all rights in the work are sold, the right to the title likewise ceases with respect to the original owner, and passes to the assignee. Indeed, the latter may even enjoin his own assignor from the use of the title.

Where the proprietor of the rights in the work dies, the property in the work passes either by bequest or descent, and the right to the title passes with it as an incident thereto. The title need not be specifically bequeathed; it will pass to the legatee with the work itself.

In like manner the right to the title passes to the trustee in bankruptcy where he succeeds to the rights in the work.

So also, the rights to a trade-mark, consisting of a device, symbol, mark, sign, brand-mark, emblem or other distinguishing feature may be sold or assigned, but only in connection with the business with which it has become identified; [128] they may also pass by bequest or descent; [129]

[128] *Eiseman* v. *Schiffer* (1907), 157 Fed. (C. C.) 473. Since a trade-mark may not be separately asisgned without the good will of the business, one to whom such assignment is made acquires no rights under it; and where, after such assignment the assignor discontinues the use of the trade-mark, that is an abandonment, and neither one can enjoin a third party.

Jacoway v. *Young* (1915), 228 Fed. (C. C. A.) 630. "A trade-mark has no efficacy except in connection with the business in which it is used. It cannot be assigned separately therefrom, and ordinarily passes with a transfer of the business."

". . . It (the trade-mark) was applied for and secured by complainant in connection with his business. Root, the individual, going from complainant to respondent, in the capacity of a mere employe, dealing with goods and a business not his own, could not carry with him a registered trade-mark, nor personal rights destructive thereof. The doctrine of prior use does not apply in such a case, because the exclusive right to the use of a trade-mark rests not on invention, but on such use as makes it point out the origin of the claimant's goods."

Allen v. *Walker* (1916), 235 Fed. (D. C.) 230. "When Allen transferred the business to the corporation, he passed title to the trade-mark, even if he did not lawfully assign it to M. E. Allen."

See also: *Crossman* v. *Griggs* (1904), 186 Mass. 275; 71 N. E. 560; *Kidd* v. *Johnson* (1879), 100 U. S. 617.

[129] *Finney's Orchestra* v. *Finney's Famous Orchestra* (1910), 161 Mich. 289; 126 N. W. 198.

Excerpt from headnote:

"Members of Finney's Orchestra who, after the founder's death, in accordance with his will maintain the name and organization and continue to carry on business as a musical organization, have a right to the exclusive use of the name and will be pro-

and a trustee in bankruptcy succeeds as well to such trade-marks.[130] The assignee may also enjoin his assignor from making any use thereof.[131]

While in the case of a title, the property right thereto exists only with respect to a particular piece of property and passes only as an incident in conjunction therewith, the right to the use of a mark or device is in the nature of the good will and assets generally of a particular business.

In the former case, the concrete work is of the essence of the right. In the latter case, it is the abstract right to the use of the mark or device to a particular class of goods, which is accorded protection.

This distinction is the more readily apparent upon examination of an old English case wherein the title of a magazine alone was put up and sold at auction. There

tected by injunction against former members who organize a corporation under the name of Finney's Famous Orchestra, and represent themselves to be the original association; the attempt being unfair competition and a fraud on the public."

The court cites *Messer* v. *Fadettes* (1897), 168 Mass. 140; 46 N. E. 407, in support of this proposition.

Burton v. *Stratton* (1882), 12 Fed. (C. C.) 696; *Atlantic Milling Co.* v. *Robinson* (1884), 20 Fed. (C. C.) 217; *Morgan* v. *Rogers* (1884), 19 Fed. (C. C.) 596; *Burrow* v. *Marceau* (1908), 124 A. D. (N. Y.) 665; 109 N. Y. Supp. 105.

[130] *Pepper* v. *Labrot* (1881), 8 Fed. (C. C.) 29.

[131] *Russia Cement* v. *Le Page* (1888), 147 Mass. 206; 17 N. E. 304; *Celluloid Mfg. Co.* v. *Cellonite Co.* (1887), 32 Fed. (C. C.) 94; *Hoxey* v. *Chaney* (1887), 143 Mass. 592; 10 N. E. 713; *Jurgens* v. *Woodberry* (1907), 56 Misc. (N. Y.) 404; 106 N. Y. Supp. 571; *Probosco* v. *Bonyon* (1876), 1 Mo. App. 241; *Burton* v. *Stratton* (1882), 12 Fed. (C. C.) 696.

the title was not treated as the title of a literary work since it identified no particular work, but it was held to designate a series of publications issued under that name, and as such was a trade-mark. As the title constituted the sole valuable asset of the business, the sale of the title was equivalent to the sale of the entire good will of the business.[132]

Section 129.—Parties.

It is important to determine who may be held liable for the infringement of the title. We have the producer, the firm that actually manufactures the picture, the distributor, who releases it to the trade, and the exhibitor, who does the actual injury by showing it to the public. All of them are proper parties to the action, and each is liable to account to the successful plaintiff, and to pay him damages.[133]

When the action is in equity, it may be brought against

[132] *Bradbury* v. *Dickens* (Eng.), 27 Beav. 53. Upon a dissolution of co-partnership the title of a magazine, *Household Words* was, by order of the court put up for sale at auction and sold for £3,550. "The court said that property in a literary periodical like this is confined purely to the mere title, and that forms part of the partnership assets and must be sold for the benefit of the partners, if of any value. The decree ordered the sale of the right to use the name of the periodical, and the right to publish, under the same name and title any periodical or other work, whether in continuance of said periodical called *Household Words*, or otherwise as the purchaser might think fit."

Excerpt from opinion in *G. & H. Mfg. Co.* v. *Hall* (1874), 61 N. Y. 226, and the principle therein stated approved and applied by the court.

[133] *Hennessy* v. *Herrmann* (1898), 89 Fed. (C. C.) 669.

all of the infringers at the same time, so that the court may in the one action grant all the relief requisite with respect to each infringer.[134]

But this does not prevent the plaintiff from pursuing any one of the infringers without joining the others.[135] If he does so, however, he cannot subsequently maintain separate actions against the others.

The courts have gone so far as to hold the officers and directors of a corporation personally liable to a plaintiff in a case where the infringement was of a willful nature.[136] All employes and agents are proper parties.[137]

In actions at law the same rule obtains, since the action is founded on a tort, and there is only one suit available to the plaintiff.

Section 130.—Actions at law.

We have been dealing thus far with actions where the relief sought is equitable in its nature. Indeed, this is the common and usual form of action adopted by the trader in securing speedy and permanent relief.

There is, however, a remedy for the trader, in an action at law. Here the trader may recover a sum of money by way of balm to his injuries. An action of this kind

[134] *Jewish Col. Ass'n* v. *Solomon* (1903), 125 Fed. (C. C.) 994.

[135] *Hill* v. *Lockwood* (1887), 32 Fed. (C. C.) 389; *Appollinaris* v. *Scherer* (1886), 27 Fed. (C. C.) 18.

[136] *Saxlehner* v. *Eisner* (1906), 147 Fed. (C. C. A.) 189; *California Fig Syrup Co.* v. *Imp. Co.* (1892), 51 Fed. (C. C.) 296; *Armstrong* v. *Savannah Soap Works* (1892), 53 Fed. (C. C.) 124; *Rogers* v. *International Silver Co.* (1902), 118 Fed. (C. C. A.) 133.

[137] *Sawyer* v. *Kellogg* (1881), 7 Fed. (C. C.) 721; (1881), 9 Fed. (C. C.) 601; *Roberts* v. *Sheldon* (1879), 8 Biss. (C. C.) 398.

is based upon the common-law theory of fraud and deceit.[138]

Since the basis of the action is fraud, it is necessary that a fraudulent intent be actually proved, and that some actual damage be established.

It is hence readily apparent why an injured plaintiff prefers to go into equity for redress rather than into law.

Section 131.—Trade-mark in title of cartoon.

In a recent case the New York Supreme Court held that cartoons were to be treated as commodities of barter and sale and in like manner as tangible goods. It held that the title affixed to such cartoons and with which they had become identified to the public, would be protected against unfair use by third parties, and that such titles were in the eyes of the law trade-marks.

In view of the importance of this case because of the re-

[138] *Hagan & Dodd Co.* v. *Rigbers* (1907), 1 Ga. App. 100; 57 S. E. 970. "We have been unable, however, to find any case holding that jurisdiction of such subject-matters is exclusively with a court of equity; on the contrary, we think the principle clearly deducible from all the authorities is that a party who has been injured and damaged by a fraudulent use of his trade-mark, or by any unfair competition in trade, has an election of remedies. He may waive this purely equitable relief, such as accounting, discovery, injunction, etc., and sue at law for the damages that he has suffered as the result of such unlawful and unfair conduct."

Edelstein v. *Edelstein* (Eng.) (1863), 1 De G. J. & S. 185; *Rodgers* v. *Nowill* (Eng.) (1853), 6 Hare, 325; *Day* v. *Woodworth* (1851), 13 How. 363; *Warner* v. *Roehr* (1884), Fed. Cas. (C. C.) No. 17189A; *Le Page Co.* v. *Russia Cement* (1892), 51 Fed. (C. C. A.) 941; *Southern* v. *How* (Eng.) (1618), 2 Popham, 144; *Thedford Medicine Co.* v. *Curry* (1895), 96 Ga. 89.

cent development in the making of animated cartoons, the opinion in its entirety is given below.[139]

[139] *Star Company* v. *Wheeler Syndicate* (1916), N. Y. Law Journal, August 15, Greenbaum, J:

" The controversy in this action has narrowed itself to the inquiry whether the plaintiff, the Star Company, has acquired a trademark in the words "Mutt and Jeff" as a title to a series of cartoons published in its paper known as the *American.* The controlling facts upon which the rights of the parties depend are practically undisputed. Harry C. Fisher, known by the nom de plume of "Bud Fisher," was concededly the creator of two grotesque figures which he named "Mutt and Jeff," respectively, and which he utilized in a series of cartoons, each publication being in the form of what in newspaper parlance is called a "comic strip." Each strip consisted of four or more pictures in which the chief characters, "Mutt and Jeff," were delineated in various attitudes and situations and were represented as exchanging views on a variety of topics, the words of the dialogue being printed in a balloon-shaped scroll emanating from the lips of the speakers. Mr. Fisher began this series of cartoons on November 15, 1907, in the *San Francisco Chronicle* with the character of "Mutt." Commencing on December 11, 1907, he continued the publication of these cartoons in the *San Francisco Examiner* until April 9, 1909. During this period and as early as March and April, 1908, which was prior to the time he entered in plaintiff's employ, he introduced the figure "Jeff" in his comic strip, and the cartoons became known to the public as "Mutt and Jeff," although these words had not formally appeared in the headings of the pictures. He started on the *Chronicle* with a weekly salary of $15, which he shortly after increased to $27.50. When he entered into the employ of the *Examiner* his salary became $50 a week, subsequently increased to $60, and then to $75. In February, 1909, he made a three-year contract with the *Examiner*, which was owned or controlled by William R. Hearst, the virtual owner of the *New York American* and other newspapers. In May, 1909, he came to New York City and prepared daily

Upon reargument of the case the court went one step further, and held that it would enjoin not only the use of

cartoons for the *American* until August, 1910, when a new contract was made with the plaintiff for a term of five years at a salary of $200 a week for the first year; $250 during the second, third and fourth years, and $300 a week during the fifth year. The contracts of February, 1909, and August, 1910, provided for Fisher's exclusive services at a weekly salary on "publications and newspapér enterprises in which William R. Hearst is or may be interested." One of these enterprises was and is known as the International News Service. During substantially the entire period of these contracts Fisher's cartoons appeared daily in the Hearst publications and in other publications under agreements made with the International News Service. The first time that the words "Mutt and Jeff" were employed in the caption of the cartoons was under date of November 20, 1909, as follows: "Mutt and Jeff do a Little Ticket Scalping at the Big Game—by 'Bud' Fisher." As a matter of fact Fisher himself prepared the titles or headings to the cartoons, and they were uniformly published as prepared by him until December 11, 1914, when the words "Mutt and Jeff" were printed for the first time as the heading of the Fisher comic strip, reading as follows: "Mutt and Jeff—The Little Fellow Also knows some Law and Proves it." This heading was published without the knowledge of Mr. Fisher, who promptly protested against its use, with the result that the succeeding publications contained only headings or titles as prepared by Fisher in accordance with previous practice. It may here be observed that at about this time ineffectual negotiations had been in progress for plaintiff's renewal of the Fisher contract, and in December, 1914, Mr. Fisher had concluded a contract with the Wheeler Syndicate to commence upon the expiration of the term of the subsisting agreement with plaintiff, and it was therein provided that he was to receive a minimum of $1,000 weekly for his "Mutt and Jeff" cartoons. On January 19, 1915, and down to the end of that month the *American* again published the Fisher cartoons with the title "Mutt and

the title with respect to cartoons, but would enjoin as well, the publication of cartoons drawn in imitation of those

Jeff—by 'Bud' Fisher." When these titles appeared Mr. Fisher again protested against their use, and upon the plaintiff's failure to discontinue them he ceased furnishing any further drawings for the plaintiff. It may further be noticed that the plaintiff at times during the term of its contract with Fisher extensively advertised that "Mutt and Jeff will appear in the *New York American* daily." These advertisements were printed in its Sunday editions and also on cards in subway and elevated stations, on billboards, newsstands and upon plaintiff's newspaper delivery wagons. Broadly stated, the contention of the plaintiff is that, being the first one to use the title "Mutt and Jeff" in connection with its comic series, it is entitled to the exclusive right to the use of such title as a trade-mark or trade name. It doubtless is the law that the exclusive right to a trade-mark does not belong to the one who suggested or invented it, but to the party who was the first to appropriate and use it in his business and give it a name and reputation. *Caswell* v. *Hazard*, 121 N. Y. 494; *Columbia Mill Co.* v. *Alcon*, 150 U. S. 460, 463; 28 Am. & Eng. Enc. of Law, pp. 393, 394, 2d ed. The plaintiff insists that the facts of this case bring it within the decision in *Herald Co.* v. *Star Co.*, 146 Fed. Rep. 204, aff'd by Circuit Court of Appeals, 146 Fed. Rep. 1023, and *Outcault* v. *N. Y. Herald*, 146 Fed. 205, popularly known as the "Buster Brown" case. While the facts in the "Buster Brown" case are quite analogous in some features to those here appearing, yet they may be differentiated in material respects. In the "Buster Brown" case the court found as a fact that the *New York Herald* was the first to use the words "Buster Brown" as the "title of a comic section" of its newspaper. In the case at bar the plaintiff had published the cartoons for about five years without the title of "Mutt and Jeff" and the only titles employed were those prepared by Fisher, which varied from day to day, the captions being appropriate to the subject-matter of the given strip. In the "Buster Brown" case it appeared that the *New York Herald* had used the title for a number of years as a heading to a comic section of its paper. In the case at bar no such situation existed. Under all the circumstances here appearing it may not be fairly held that the plaintiff had actually used "Mutt and Jeff" as a title of Fisher's comic strips, even if it be assumed that a strip may be regarded as a comic section of the paper. The fact is that during the entire period of its contract with Mr. Fisher plaintiff published these strips without any title of its own. The mere circumstance that in its advertisements the cartoons were referred to in connection with the words "Mutt and Jeff" is of no special significance, since it is also the fact that since September 22, 1910, Fisher published upwards of 300,000 copies of his books of cartoons selected from those which had appeared in the *American* under the title of "The Mutt and Jeff Cartoons by Bud Fisher." It is thus evident that the plaintiff was not the first user of the words "Mutt and Jeff" as a title or trade-mark, and that these words had not been appropriated by it as a trade-mark or trade name to designate its comic section or a portion thereof, except upon the few occasions during the expiring months of the agreements, after the plaintiff realized that a renewal of the Fisher contract was out of the question. It is clear that this is not a case where the plaintiff had been in the habit of labeling its comic strips with a distinctive mark, or where it may be fairly said that it had acquired by user the words "Mutt and Jeff" as against Fisher. Nor is this a case where it may be held that the plaintiff, being entitled to the exclusive services of Fisher in the drawing of the cartoons in question, became entitled to the use of the title "Mutt and Jeff" since those words originated with Fisher before he entered in the employ of plaintiff and the cartoons had already acquired a reputation as "Mutt and Jeff" cartoons. The facts in this case, too, are different from these appearing in *Jaeger's Co.* v. *Le Boutillier*, 47 Hun, 521, where it was shown that Professor Jaeger had never been engaged in the business of selling goods and therefore had never acquired any proprietary right in a trademark. On the other hand, the facts established in this case are, that Fisher was most actively engaged for some time prior to his employment with plaintiff in producing the cartoons with

"Mutt and Jeff" characters. These cartoons, in effect the products of Fisher's hand and brain, are to be treated as a commodity of barter and sale, the same as tangible goods or merchandise which may be sold under a distinctive mark or name which the vendor may exclusively use as a trade-mark or trade name in the sale of such goods. The mere circumstance that for a period of time Fisher obligated himself to produce his cartoons exclusively for the plaintiff no more deprived him of the exclusive right to use the trade-mark or trade name of his productions than would a manufacturer of goods known by a trade name be deprived of the exclusive right to such trade name, because he had agreed for a definite time to manufacture them exclusively for a given firm. Of course, during the time when Fisher was obliged to furnish his cartoons exclusively to the plaintiff, the latter had the exclusive right to the use of the trade name which went with the exclusive right to all of Fisher's output; but when the contract terminated Fisher was at liberty to sell this output to whomsoever he wished. The law of the case is so well considered in *Hanover Milling Co.* v. *Metcalf*, 240 U. S. 403 et seq. that citation of further authorities would be superfluous. In the opinion of the court the plaintiff is not entitled to the use of the trade name or trade-mark "Mutt and Jeff," the right thereto being now vested in the Wheeler Syndicate under its subsisting contract with Fisher, subject to such rights, if any, reserved therein to Fisher. There must be a decree in favor of defendant.

Fisher v. *Star Co.* For the reasons stated in the opinion filed in *Star Co.* v. *Wheeler Syndicate*, a decree will be entered in favor of plaintiff.

Wheeler Syndicate v. *Star Co.* Upon the opinion filed this day in *Star Co.* v. *Wheeler Syndicate*, a decree will be entered in favor of plaintiff."

See also opinion of Weeks, J., in denying the motion for an injunction pendente made by the Star Company in its action against the Wheeler Syndicate, reported in (1915), 91 Misc. (N. Y.) 640.

See also: *Outcault* v. *New York Herald* (1906), 146 Fed. (C. C.) 205. "The contention of complainant is that it is unfair competition in trade for any one else to draw or offer for sale any other pictures in which, although the

put out by the cartoonist who was the proprietor of the title.[140]

scenes and incidents are different, some of the characters are imitations of those which appeared in the earlier pictures which complainant sold to defendant. In other words, that deponent, although he never copyrighted them and did not acquire any right to the title in connection with newspaper publication, has, nevertheless, some common-law title to individual figures therein displayed, which he can maintain to the exclusion of others, who depict them in other scenes and situations. It is sufficient to say that no authority is cited supporting this proposition, which seems entirely novel and does not commend itself as sound."

See also: *New York Herald* v. *Star Co.* (1906), 146 Fed. (C. C.) 204; aff'd 146 Fed. (C. C. A.) 1023. Temporary injunction was issued enjoining defendant from using title "Buster Brown" in such a manner as to lead the public to believe that it contemplated the publication of a comic section under that title.

See also: *N. Y. Herald* v. *Ottawa Citizen* (Can.), 41 Can. S. C. R. 229. Registration of a title "Buster Brown" for the comic section of a newspaper was held invalid.

[140] *Fisher* v. *Star Company* (1917), N. Y. Law Journal, Jan. 26. "The only question reserved by the court for determination was whether the defendant is to be enjoined from hereafter publishing cartoons drawn in imitation of Mr. Fisher's creations, "Mutt and Jeff." It seems to me that, viewing this question from a standpoint of unfair competition, there should be but one answer thereto, and that is that the publication of such cartoons would be calculated to deceive the public into believing that they were the genuine productions of Mr. Fisher. The cases that recognize these principles as applied to ordinary merchandise are fully stated in such cases as *Hanover Milling Co.* v. *Metcalf*, 240 U. S. 403; *E. P. Dutton & Co.* v. *Cupples*, 117 App. Div. 172, and *Yale & Towne Mfg. Co.* v. *Adler*, 154 Fed. Rep. 37. I can find no difference in principle between that class of cases and the one under review excepting that it is here sought to protect an individual possessed of special skill in the production of cartoons of

his own creation. My attention has been called to the opinion written by the examiner of interferences upon an application of the defendant for cancellation of the trade-mark "Mutt and Jeff" registered by the plaintiff Fisher as a trade-mark for a series of cartoons. The examiner refers to recent works on trade-marks in which the distinction is observed between a personal and impersonal trade-mark. Special reference is made to Paul on Trade-Marks and the English work of Sebastian (4th ed., p. 100), concerning which the examiner states that a "personal trade-mark is discussed at some length with the citation of authorities and is referred to as a mark which benefits the article to which it is attached with the personal skill or supervision of an individual." I can see no reason on principle why such a trade-mark should not be recognized as the property of Fisher in this case. In passing upon the voluminous findings submitted by the defendant I desire to observe that because reference is made to certain copyrights in the plaintiff's findings there is no implication that this court is disposing of this case upon the theory that a copyright is involved. The facts with reference to the copyright are merely incidental in the determination of the ultimate questions presented."

CHAPTER XI

UNFAIR COMPETITION (CONTINUED)

Miscellaneous Matters

SEC. 132. Right to use or assign one's own name.
133. Limitations on use—price fixing.
134. Restraint of trade.

Section 132.—The right to use or assign one's own name.

It is well settled that every individual has a right to use his own name in connection with his business. He may not, however, use the name in a manner so as to lead the public to believe that his goods are those of some person bearing the same name.[1]

While many forms of business enterprises are con-

[1] *Cream Co.* v. *Keller* (1898), 85 Fed. (C. C.) 643; *Chapman* v. *Waterman* (1917), N. Y. App. Div., N. Y. Law Journal, Apr. 4; *Rogers* v. *Rogers* (1895), 70 Fed. (C. C. A.) 1017; *Devlin* v. *Devlin* (1877), 69 N. Y. 212; *Frazer* v. *Frazer* (1887), 121 Ill. 147; 13 N. E. 639; *Landreth* v. *Landreth* (1884), 22 Fed. (C. C.) 41.

Howard v. *Lovett*, Michigan Circuit Ct., Wayne County, Feb. 24, 1916. Trade-Mark Reporter, Vol. 6, p. 229. Plaintiff was granted an injunction restraining the use of the word "Mercedes" as the title of a vaudeville act upon the ground that plaintiff had first used that title with respect to a vaudeville act. The injunction was granted notwithstanding that one of the defendant's middle name was Mercedes and that the act was named after such defendant.

stantly changing hands under their original names, it is well to bear in mind that there are limitations upon this right which are peculiarly applicable to the motion picture industry.

Some of the foremost companies in the industry have adopted as the corporate title the name of some prominent director or producer whose work is devoted to the productions of that company. Should the company later dispense with the services of that particular individual, or should the original interests attempt to withdraw or sell out, the question arises, how far may this be legally done?

It has been held that where the value of a trade name is dependent upon the personal reputation, skill, experience of and is indissolubly connected or associated with the owner, it cannot be assigned, for that would effect a fraud upon the public.[2] This rule has been applied to

[2] *Messer* v. *The Fadettes* (1897), 168 Mass. 140; 46 N. E. 407. The leader of an orchestra attempted to sell all her right, title and interest in and to a musical organization or orchestra together with the name by which it was designated, the "Fadette Ladies Orchestra." Said the court: "So far as Ethel Atwood (the assignor) had any right or ownership in the trade-name which designated the organization under her management, it was personal to herself, depending upon her personal reputation and skill, *and it was not assignable*. . . . The case is not like those in which there is a sale of fixed property and a local business to which the name belongs and whose principal features remain unchanged after the sale. If the use by the plaintiff of the name 'Fadette Ladies Orchestra' would have any influence beneficial to herself upon the public who wished to procure the services of such an organization, it would be only to mislead and defraud them by implying that she and such musicians as she employed were the same per-

artists, authors, musicians, and lawyers; and they will not be permitted to assign to others the use of their own names.[3] That limitation exists even where a corporation

sons who had formerly gained a good reputation under this name. It is well settled that the courts will not enforce a claim of this kind, which contains a misrepresentation to the public."

Hegeman v. *Hegeman* (1880), 8 Daly (N. Y.), 1, holds certain kinds of names non-assignable. "When, however, the whole pecuniary value of a name . . . is derived solely from the personal qualities of the one to whom the name belongs, such as his skill, special knowledge and experience, or from the fact that the article is produced under his personal supervision, which imparts to it a special value, then the right to the name is not transmissible." *Leather Cloth Co.* v. *Am. Leather Cl. Co.* (Eng.), 11 H. L. Cas. 523; *Kidd* v. *Johnson* (1879), 100 U. S. 617; *Dixon Crucible Co.* v. *Guggenheim*, 2 Brewster, 321.

Hughes v. *Statham* (Eng.) (1825), 4 Barnewell & Cresswell, 187. An agreement between two attorneys which provided for the transfer of the business besides the use of the name was held invalid in so far as the name was concerned. See also: *Dean* v. *Emerson* (1869), 102 Mass. 480; *Hoxie* v. *Chaney* (1887), 143 Mass. 592; 10 N. E. 713. *In re Swezey* (1881), 62 Howard's Pr. (N. Y.) 215; *Skinner* v. *Oakes* (1881), 10 Mo. App. 45.

[3] *Blakely* v. *Sousa* (1900), 197 Pa. 305; 47 Atl. 286. Plaintiff's intestate had contracted with defendant, the leader of a band, whereby he was to act in the general capacity of a business manager. Four years later plaintiff died.

Held that there was the relation of employer and employe, which terminated at death. That each party relied to a great extent upon the purely personal qualifications of the other, and for that reason the contract was not assignable, even though the plaintiff's intestate had been given the right to assign the contract to a corporation.

Held also that one could not assign to another the use of his *own* name, as that was contrary to public policy, in the case of an artist, an author, musician or lawyer, as the value of such a

has been formed to take over the use of the name, for even in that case assignability is not permitted.[4]

In New York, a defendant who, as executor, had acquired the right to the use of a surname which was the same as his own, conveyed the business together with the trade name to another. He, thereafter in his individual capacity, attempted to grant to a third party the right to the use of his own name in connection with a similar business. The court enjoined him.[5]

name was entirely dependent upon the personal reputation, skill, experience and indissolubly connected or associated with the owner.

But this rule was not followed in the older New York cases.

See: *Christy* v. *Murphy* (1856), 12 How. Pr. (N. Y.) 77.

See also: *Booth* v. *Jarrett* (1876), 52 How. 169. Lessor's name was on theatre ("Booth's Theatre"); lessee was held entitled to use name on theatre since the name was identified with the goods sold—the theatre.

[4] *Blakely* v. *Sousa* (1900), 197 Pa. 305; 47 Atl. 286.

Skinner v. *Oakes* (1881), 10 Mo. App. 45. "We think the answer to this question depends upon the effect which the use of the name in each particular instance is shown to have upon the minds of the public. If it leads the public to believe the particular goods are in fact made by the person whose name is thus stamped upon them, or in whose name they are advertised, whereas they are in fact made by another person, then such a use of the name will not be protected by the courts, for to do so would be to protect the perpetration of a fraud upon the people. See also: *Oakes* v. *Tonsmierre* (1883), 49 Fed. (C. C.) 447.

[5] *Burrow* v. *Marceau* (1908), 124 A. D. (N. Y.) 665; 109 N. Y. Supp. 105. "Each case must depend upon its own facts, but where it is clearly established that an attempt is being made by one person to get the business of another by any means that involves fraud or deceit, a court of equity will protect the honest trader and restrain a dishonest one from carrying out his scheme."

Section 133.—Limitations on use—price fixing.

The fundamental distinction between the rights derived under the copyright and patent laws is that in the former there is granted the exclusive right to print, publish and vend,[6] while in the latter the exclusive right is given to make, *use* or vend the patented article. In other words, the right granted under the patent law which is not given to the copyright proprietor is the sole right to use.[7]

This means, in effect, that the owner of a patent may attach any and all conditions with respect to the use of his patented article, and those conditions are binding upon all persons into whose possession the patented article may come. This is a right irrespective of any contract, and attaches to the patented commodity in a manner which may best be described as a "covenant running with the land." [8]

In copyright, on the other hand, the sole right to use is not granted to the proprietor of the work. Hence, any limitation in the use of the work, must be sought for in some contract, and only parties privy to the contract are bound by such limitations.

The "vending" rights in both patent and copyright

Kurtzmann v. *Kurtzmann* (1914), 84 Misc. (N. Y.) 478; 147 N. Y. Supp. 673. The use of one's own name may in certain cases be restrained.

See also: *Romeike* v. *Romeike*, Trade-Mark Rep. (1917), Vol. 7, p. 360.

[6] Section one of the Copyright Act of 1909.

[7] Section 9428 of the Compiled Statutes 1916, p. 10031.

[8] *Bloomer* v. *McQuewan* (1852), 14 How. 549; *Mitchell* v. *Hawley* (1872), 16 Wallace, 544; *Adams* v. *Burke* (1873), 17 Wallace, 453.

are identical. In neither case may the proprietor restrict the selling price of the article of one who is not a party to a contract with him.

This distinction is emphasized clearly in the "Sanatogen" case.[9] The restriction placed upon each package was in the form of a notice reading as follows:

"Notice to the Retailer

"This size package of Sanatogen is licensed by us for sale and use at a price not less than One dollar ($1.00). Any sale in violation of this condition, or use when so sold, will constitute an infringement of our patent No. 601,995, under which Sanatogen is manufactured, and all persons so selling or using packages or contents will be liable to injunction and damages."

"A purchase is an acceptance of this condition. All rights revert to the undersigned in the event of violation.

"THE BAUER CHEMICAL CO."

The court held that this limitation placed upon the patented article was not with respect to its use, but related to its sale merely, and, as such, was unenforcible in the absence of any special contract between the parties to the action.

The court aptly states its position: "The real question is whether in the exclusive right secured by statute to 'vend' a patented article, there is included the right, by notice, to dictate the price at which subsequent sales of the article may be made. The patentee relies solely upon the notice quoted to control future prices in the

[9] *Bauer* v. *O'Donnell* (1913), 229 U. S. 1; 33 Sup. Ct. 616.

resale by a purchaser of an article said to be of great utility and highly desirable for general use. The appellee and the jobbers from whom he purchased were neither the agents nor the licensees of the patentee. They had the title to, and the right to sell, the article purchased without accounting for the proceeds to the patentee, and without making any further payment than had already been made in the purchase from the agent of the patentee. Upon such facts as are now presented we think the right to *vend* secured in the patent statute is not distinguishable from the right of *vending* given under the Copyright Act. In both instances it was the intention of Congress to secure an exclusive right to sell, and there is no grant of a privilege to keep up prices, and prevent competition by notices restricting the price at which the article may be resold. The right to vend conferred by the patent law has been exercised, and the added restriction is beyond the protection and purpose of the act."

This rule was even more forcibly reiterated in the recent case of *Straus* v. *Victor*.[10] There the Victor Company

[10] *Straus* v. *Victor*, U. S. Supreme Court, decided April 9, 1917. "It thus becomes clear that this 'License Notice,' is not intended as a security for any further payment upon the machine, for the full price, called a 'royalty,' was paid before the plaintiff parted with the possession of it; that it is not to be used as a basis for tracing and keeping the plaintiff informed as to the condition or use of the machine, for no report of any character is required from the 'ultimate user' after he has paid the stipulated price; that, notwithstanding its apparently studied avoidance of the use of the word 'sale' and its frequent reference to the word 'use,' the most obvious requirements for securing a bona

by means of a complicated license notice attached to its talking machines, ostensibly sought to restrict the use of the machine. One of the conditions attached thereto was that the "royalty" to be paid for the "use" of the machine was not to be less than the amount specified upon the notice.

The court, brushing aside the other conditions imposed by this license notice, found that the sole and real purpose of the notice was to restrict the price at which the machine could be sold after the plaintiff had been paid in full for it, and re-affirmed *Bauer* v. *O'Donnell.*

The courts have even placed limitations upon the extent to which the exclusive right to use the article may be applied by the patentee. Until recently, the rule was that the proprietor of the patent had the right to place any restrictions he deemed proper upon the use of his patent. In the "Mimeograph" case [11] it was held proper for the patentee to control the use of his article by imposing a condition that the machine was to be used only with the supplies made by the patentee.

fide enforcement of the restrictions of the notice as to 'use' are omitted; and that, even by its own terms, the title to the machines ultimately vests in the 'ultimate users,' without further payment or action on their part, except patiently waiting for patents to expire on inventions, which, so far as this notice shows, may or may not be incorporated in the machine. There remains for this 'License Notice' so far as we can discover, the function only, of fixing and maintaining the price of plaintiff's machines to its agents and to the public, and this we cannot doubt is the purpose for which it really was designed."

[11] *Henry* v. *A. B. Dick Co.* (1911), 224 U. S. 1; 32 Sup. Ct. 364.

That decision, however, was overruled in the case of *Motion Picture Patent Co.* v. *Universal Film Mfg. Co.*[12] In this case, the plaintiff, the owner of a patent for a motion picture projecting machine, attempted to impose a restriction upon the use of the machine to the effect that such machine was to be used solely for exhibiting or projecting motion picture films containing the inventions of certain letters patent, such films being controlled by a licensee of the plaintiff.

Subsequently to the expiration of the patents upon the film, the plaintiff sought to restrain one of the defendants from using any film in its projecting machine other than the film of plaintiff's licensee. It contended that the use of such other film constituted an infringement of its patent in the projecting machine.

Mr. Justice Clarke, writing for the court, held that such a restriction was invalid; that it was an attempt without statutory warrant, to continue the patent monopoly in the film of plaintiff's licensee after such patent had expired; that "to enforce it would be to create a monopoly in the manufacture and use of moving picture films wholly outside of the patent in suit and of the patent law."

The court said, "The exclusive right granted in every patent must be limited to the invention described in the claims of the patent, and that it is not competent for the owner of a patent by notice attached to its machine to, in effect, extend the scope of its patent monopoly by restricting the use of it to materials neces-

[12] *Motion Picture Patents Co.* v. *Universal Film*, U. S. Sup. Court, decided April 9, 1917. See also: *Universal Film Co.* v. *Copperman* (1914), 218 Fed. (C. C. A.) 577.

sary in its operation, but which are no part of the patented invention."

The court also held that any provision in the license notice to the effect that the proprietor of the patent shall have the right to impose any new conditions upon the use of the patented article from time to time was invalid.

It is easy to understand why the court has reversed itself, and has taken the position declared in the "*Motion Picture Patents Case*" when we consider the primary purpose of the patent laws. In the words of the court: "Since *Pennock* v. *Dialogue,* 2 Pet. 1, was decided in 1829, this court has consistently held that the primary purpose of our patent laws is not the creation of private fortunes for the owners of patents, but is to promote the progress of science and the useful arts." (Constitution, Art. 1, Sec. 8.)

In the *Bobbs-Merrill* v. *Strauss* case [13] the court clearly

[13] *Bobbs-Merrill Co.* v. *Strauss* (1908), 210 U. S. 339; 28 Sup. Ct. 722; *Scribner* v. *Strauss* (1908), 210 U. S. 352; 28 Sup. Ct. 735.

See: Hammond Publishing Co. v. *Smythe* (1886), 27 Fed. (C. C.) 914; *Harrison* v. *Maynard-Merrill Co.* (1894), 61 Fed. (C. C. A.) 689; *Clemens* v. *Estes* (1885), 22 Fed. (C. C.) 899; *Werckmeister* v. *Am. Lithographic Co.* (1904), 134 Fed. (C. C. A.) 321; *Doan* v. *Am. Book Co.* (1901), 105 Fed. (C. C. A.) 772; *Kipling* v. *G. P. Putnam's Sons* (1903), 120 Fed. (C. C. A.) 631; *Bobbs-Merrill Co.* v. *Snellenburg* (1904), 131 Fed. (C. C.) 530; *Dodd* v. *Smith* (1891), 144 Pa. St. 340; 22 Atl. 710; *Authors' & Newspapers' Assn.* v. *O'Gorman Co.* (1906), 147 Fed. (C. C.) 616.

Harrison v. *Maynard, Merrill & Co.* (1894), 61 Fed. (C. C. A.) 689. ". . . The copy having been absolutely sold to him, the ordinary incidents of ownership in personal property, among which is the right of alienation, attach to it. If he has agreed that he will not sell it for certain purposes

defined its position with respect to the right to limit the price at which a copyrighted work could be re-sold. The court held that unless there was a contract, and the parties to the suit were privy to it, an attempted restriction upon the price of a copyrighted work was unenforcible, and that the sole right to vend under the copyright statute did not permit the holder of a copyright to fasten by notice in a book or upon one of the articles mentioned within the statute, a restriction upon the subsequent alienation of the subject matter of copyright after the owner had parted with the title to one who had acquired full dominion over it, and had given a satisfactory price for it.

The court stated its position in the following language: "In our view the copyright statutes, while protecting the owner of the copyright in his right to multiply and sell his production, do not create the right to impose, by notice, such as is disclosed in this case, a limitation at which the book shall be sold, at retail, by future purchasers, with whom there is no privity of contract."

Section 134.—Restraint of trade.

In the year 1908, the motion picture business had reached a point where it was regarded as one of the leading industries of the country. At that time there were two aggregations of manufacturers, competing with each other. One group controlled the patents pertaining to the various parts of the camera used in the taking of pictures. The other group was in control of divers patents in connection with the machine, whereby the picture was projected upon the screen. At the close of that year, finding competition and litigation between them ruinous, they combined by pooling their patents, and formed the Motion Picture Patents Co., with a subsidiary distributing company, the General Film Company.

"The plan . . . was first to combine the defendants, who were manufacturers and importers of films, in an agreement to act as one man might have acted. Lists of exchanges and of theatres were prepared, and no exchange was permitted to have films, and no theatre to exhibit them, unless with the consent of all the defendants. The names of none appeared upon this list except such as bought all supplies from the defendants, and any who dealt otherwise were dropped. Every theatre was required to pay a royalty for the use of a projecting machine, even when the machine had been owned by the exhibitor before the combination was formed. The films passed into the possession of exchanges and exhibitors under an agreement which enabled the defendants to recall them at will." [14]

or to certain persons and violates his agreement, and sells to an innocent purchaser, he can be punished for a violation of his agreement, but neither is guilty under the copyright statutes of an infringement."

Copyright and patent statutes differ in the extent of protection granted by such statutes. Hence the rights of a patent owner are not necessarily to be applied by analogy to those of a copyright owner.

[14] *United States* v. *Motion Picture Patents Co.* (1915), 225 Fed. (D. C.) 800. *Dickinson, J.*: ". . . It is evident that whoever controls the films referred to controls the motion-picture business, but the point with which we are now concerned is that trade in these films is within the statute. . . ."

The methods of the combination were so thorough and effective that at the time the government tried its

And in arriving at its conclusion, after deciding that films were articles of commerce and as such within the statute, the court said:

"We are constrained, however, to find that there was no such relation, but that the end, directly proposed, was the imposition upon the trade of an undue and unreasonable restraint, in order that as the immediate and direct effect and result of the combination, the defendants might monopolize the trade in all the accessories of the motion picture art so far as they are articles of commerce. A further end proposed, and which has largely been achieved, is the domination of the motion picture business itself, and it requires no prophetic vision to foresee that the ultimate result would be that no play would be written or dramatically enacted, except by authors and artists favored by the defendants."

An earlier case, decided in the United States Supreme Court in which various owners of patents had pooled their patents and had thereby effected a combination in violation of the Sherman Law is the case of *Standard Sanitary Co.* v. *U. S.*, commonly referred to as the "Bathtub" case (1912), 226 U. S. 20; 33 Sup. Ct. 9.

See also: *N. Y. Motion Picture Co.* v. *Universal Film* (1912), 77 Misc. (N. Y.) 581; 137 N. Y. Supp. 278; *Metropolitan Opera Co.* v. *Hammerstein* (1914), 162 A. D. (N. Y.) 691; 147 N. Y. Supp. 532; *People* v. *Klaw* (1907), 55 Misc. (N. Y.) 72; 106 N. Y. Supp. 341; *Matter of Jackson* (1907), 57 Misc. (N. Y.) 1; 107 N. Y. Supp. 799.

For a case where various owners of copyrights pooled their respective copyrights and thereby effectuated a combination which tended to create a monopoly in violation of statute, see *Straus* v. *Am. Pub. Ass'n* (1913), 231 U. S. 222; 34 Sup. Ct. 84. "So, in the present case, it cannot be successfully contended that the monopoly of a copyright is in this respect any more extensive than that secured under the patent law. No more than the patent statute was the Copyright Act intended to authorize agreements in unlawful restraint of trade and tending to monopoly in violation of the specific

suit to dissolve the combination (Oct. 1, 1915) out of one hundred and sixteen independent manufacturers, there was but one solitary survivor.

Fortunately, for the business and for the public as well, the combination was dissolved under the "Sherman Anti-Trust Law." [15]

Although this decision has had an enormous beneficial effect in revivifying and stimulating the industry to a more active and higher-class standard of production, we believe that it has resulted in a great waste of money. Each group of manufacturers has attempted to conduct its business independently of the others, and to that end numerous and vast chains of distributing centres have been formed. These are unnecessary, and might well be eliminated. The inevitable trend of the industry is to recombine as formerly, not, however, for the purpose of restraining trade and destroying competition, but with the object of effecting greater efficiency and economy by doing away with so many exchanges, and distributing through a common source.

terms of the Sherman Law, which is broadly designed to reach all combinations in unlawful restraint of trade and tending because of the agreements or combinations entered into to build up and to perpetuate monopolies." See also: *Mines* v. *Scribner* (1906), 147 Fed. (C. C.) 927.

[15] For a history of the litigation leading up to the formation of the combination, see: *Edison* v. *Am. Mutoscope* (1902), 114 Fed. (C. C. A.) 926; *Edison* v. *Am. Mutoscope* (1907), 151 Fed. (C. C. A.) 767; *Greater N. Y. Film Rental Co.* v. *Biograph*, U. S. Dist. Court, S. D. N. Y., July 12, 1912, reversed 203 Fed. 39.

CHAPTER XII

COPYRIGHT

In General

SEC. 135. Common-law rights.
136. What is secured by copyright.
137. How copyright is secured.
138. Publication.
139. Notice of copyright.
140. Licensee's failure to insert notice.
141. False notice of copyright.
142. Title—Changing title.
143. Who may secure copyright.
144. Belligerent aliens.
145. In what name copyright may be taken out.
146. Subjects of copyright—in general.
147. Immoral and seditious works.
148. Gags, stage business, contrivances, cartoons, advertisements.
149. Burlesques, parodies, inferior copies.
150. Copyrighting revised edition of work.
151. Works in public domain.
152. Component parts.
153. Term of copyright.
154. Renewal of copyright.
155. Assignment of copyright.
156. Difference between assignment and license.

Section 135.—Common-law rights.

The author of a work is not bound to copyright it,

in this country, in order to protect it. He has a common-law right [1] which in many ways resembles copyright, and

[1] *Palmer* v. *De Witt* (1872), 47 N. Y. 532. "An author or proprietor of an unpublished literary work has then a property in such work, recognized and protected both here and in England, and the use and enjoyment of it is secured to him as a right. This property in a manuscript is not distinguishable from any other personal property. It is governed by the same rules of transfer and succession, and is protected by the same process, and has the benefit of all the remedies accorded to other property so far as applicable."

See also the other two leading cases in this country on common-law rights: *Tompkins* v. *Hallock* (1882), 133 Mass. 32; *Carter* v. *Bailey* (1874), 64 Me. 458.

See also: *Aronson* v. *Fleckenstein* (1886), 28 Fed. (C. C.) 75; *Boucicault* v. *Fox* (1862), 5 Blatch. (C. C.) 87; *Banker* v. *Caldwell* (1859), 3 Minn. 46; *Oertel* v. *Wood* (1870), 40 How. Pr. (N. Y.) 10; *Shook* v. *Daly* (1875), 49 How. Pr. (N. Y.) 366; *French* v. *McGuire* (1878), 55 How. Pr. (N. Y.) 471; *Shook* v. *Rankin* (1875), 6 Biss. (C. C.) 477; *Boucicault* v. *Wood* (1867), 2 Biss. (C. C.) 34; *Crowe* v. *Aiken* (1870), 2 Biss. (C. C.) 208; *Boucicault* v. *Hart* (1875), 13 Blatch. (C. C.) 47; Fed. Cas. No. 1692; *Parton* v. *Prang* (1872), 3 Cliff. (C. C.) 537.

For English cases see: *Southey* v. *Sherwood* (Eng.) (1817), 2 Mer. 435; *Tonson* v. *Collins* (Eng.), 1 W. Bl. 301; *Jeffries* v. *Boosey* (Eng.) (1854), 4 H. L. Cas. 815; 3 C. L. R. 625; 24 L. J. Ex. 81; *Prince Albert* v. *Strange* (Eng.) (1849), 1 Mac. & G. 25; 1 H. & T. 1; 18 L. J. Ch. 120; 13 Jur. 109; *Queensberry* v. *Shebbeare* (Eng.) (1758), 2 Eden, 329; *Mansell* v. *Valley Printing Co.* (Eng.) (1908), L. R. 2 Ch. 441; 77 L. J. Ch. 742; 99 L. T. 464; 28 T. L. R. 802.

As to whether copyright is considered personal property see: Latour v. *Bland* (Eng.) (1818), 2 Stark, 382; *Palmer* v. *De Witt* (1872), 47 N. Y. 532.

As to whether common-law rights in an unpublished manuscript may be acquired by adverse possession see: O'Neill v. *General Film Company* (1916), 171 A. D. (N. Y.) 854; 157 N. Y. Supp. 1028; modifying 152 N. Y. Supp.

which he may enforce in the state courts [2] or in the Federal courts, if other jurisdictional elements are present.[3]

These rights are not lost by the sale of the manuscript, but on the contrary pass to the purchaser, who may in turn sell the manuscript and thus convey the rights to the new purchaser. Where the owner of the manuscript dies, the common-law rights in it pass to his next of kin or legatee, and the rights continue indefinitely until they are lost by publication or copyright.[4]

This is well illustrated in *O'Neill* v. *General Film Company*,[5] where the action was brought for an injunction and an accounting by reason of defendants' infringement of plaintiff's unpublished manuscript of a play entitled "Count of Monte Cristo." The court found that one Charles Fechter made a dramatic version of the novel of that title prior to the year 1883; that in that year one John Stetson, the proprietor of a theatre in Boston was the owner of the Fechter version manuscript; that in 1885 the said John Stetson sold the manuscript to the plaintiff

599. See also *Hart* v. *Fox* (1917), N. Y. Law Journal, August 24.

[2] *Palmer* v. *De Witt* (1872), 47 N. Y. 532; *Tompkins* v. *Hallock* (1882), 133 Mass. 32; *Carter* v. *Bailey* (1874), 64 Me. 458.

[3] *Press Publ. Co.* v. *Monroe* (1896), 73 Fed. (C. C. A.) 196.

[4] *White* v. *Geroch* (Eng.) (1819), 22 R. R. 786; 2 B. & Ald. 298; 1 Chit. 24; *Palmer* v. *De Witt* (1872), 47 N. Y. 532.

See also: *Lytton* v. *Devey* (Eng.) (1884), 52 L. T. 121. The personal representatives of a decedent prevented the publication of the decedent's letters. *Macmillan Co.* v. *Dent* (Eng.) (1906), 1 Ch. 101 (Times, Nov. 8); 23 T. L. R. 45; *Philip* v. *Pennell* (Eng.) (1907), L. R. 2 Ch. 577; 76 L. J. Ch. 663; 97 L. T. 386; 23 T. L. R. 718.

[5] *O'Neill* v. *General Film Co.* (1916), 171 A. D. (N. Y.) 85[illegible]; 157 N. Y. Supp. 1028.

in the action who, since that time had been in "continuous uninterrupted open possession of the said play." Indeed the court found it so difficult to prove a chain of title that judgment for plaintiff was really given upon the theory of adverse possession. An injunction was granted enjoining the exhibition of defendants' infringing motion picture.

Common-law rights obtained in England as well as in this country prior to 1911 when they were altogether abrogated in England, and the author was thenceforth bound to look for protection only to the Copyright Statute. In the United States, however, there has been no change in the common-law rule, and common-law rights are still recognized and protected.[6] The present copyright statute expressly provides that nothing in the Act shall be construed to annul or limit the right of an author or proprietor of an unpublished work, at common law or in equity, to prevent infringements thereof.[7]

Under the common law the author has the exclusive right to perform his unpublished dramatic composition; and as long as the work remains unpublished he may enjoin anyone from infringing upon that right.[8] He also has the right to a first publication. But by publication he loses all his common-law rights.

"As author of the work . . . the literary property

[6] *Palmer* v. *DeWitt* (1872), 47 N. Y. 532; *Tompkins* v. *Hallock* (1882), 133 Mass. 32; *Carter* v. *Bailey* (1874), 64 Me. 458; *Press Pub. Co.* v. *Monroe* (1896), 73 Fed. (C. C. A.) 196.

[7] Copyright Act of 1909—Section two.

[8] *Palmer* v. *DeWitt* (1872), 47 N. Y. 532; *Tompkins* v. *Hallock* (1882), 133 Mass. 32; *Carter* v. *Bailey* (1874), 64 Me. 458.

vested in her consisted . . . of the following rights, privileges or powers: *Before publication:* The sole exclusive interest, use and control. The right to its name, to control or prevent publication. The right of private exhibition, for criticism or otherwise, reading, representation and restricted circulation; to copy, and permit others to copy, and to give away a copy; to translate or dramatize the work; to print without publication; to make qualified distribution. The right to make the first publication. The right to sell and assign her interest, either absolutely or conditionally, with or without qualification, limitation or restriction, territorial or otherwise, by oral or written transfer. . . .

"*After publication:* Unrestricted publication without copyright, is a transfer to the public to do most of the things the author might do, in common with her, except all rights of transfer and sale which remain to the author; but without advantage, since the work has become, by the publication, common property." [9]

The exclusive right of multiplying and vending copies of an intellectual work is of purely statutory origin.[10] The moment an author multiplies and vends his work he publishes the same, and his common-law rights are forever gone with publication.[11] Publication, however, with-

[9] *Harper* v. *Donohue* (1905), 144 Fed. (C. C.) 491.

[10] *Donaldson* v. *Becket* (Eng.) (1774), 4 Burr. 2408 (English House of Lords); *Wheaton* v. *Peters* (1834), 8 Pet. 591.

[11] *Wheaton* v. *Peters* (1834), 8 Pet. 591. For a historical and important discussion of common-law rights and statutory rights in literary property. It holds in effect that by publication the author loses all his common-law rights and must thereafter

out the consent of the author does not destroy his common-law rights.[12]

In like manner the common-law rights are lost when copyright of the work is obtained.[13] Common-law rights and copyright in the same work are not co-existent. Where one ends the other begins. It is as if the public said to the author, "Give us the benefit of your work, and we will confer an exclusive monopoly upon you with greater rights. In exchange for that, we are to possess it wholly after a definite term."

look to the statute alone for protection.

See also: *Holmes* v. *Hurst* (1899), 174 U. S. 82; 19 Sup. Ct. 606; *Burrow-Giles Lithog. Co.* v. *Sarony* (1884), 111 U. S. 53; 4 Sup. Ct. 279; *Walker* v. *Globe Newspaper Co.* (1908), 210 U. S. 356; 28 Sup. Ct. 726; *Wheaton* v. *Peters* (1834), 8 Pet. 591; *Jewelers' Mercantile Agency* v. *Jewelers* (1898), 155 N. Y. 241; 49 N. E. 872; *Daly* v. *Walrath* (1899), 40 A. D. (N. Y.) 220; 57 N. Y. Supp. 1125; *Palmer* v. *DeWitt* (1872), 147 N. Y. 532; *Rees* v. *Peltzer* (1874), 75 Ill. 475; *Stevens* v. *Cady* (1852), 14 How. 528; *Millar* v. *Taylor* (Eng.) (1769), 4 Burr. 2331; *Read* v. *Conquest* (Eng.) (1861), 9 C. B. (N. S.) 755; 3 L. T. 888; 9 W. R. 434; *Bobbs Merrill* v. *Strauss* (1906), 147 Fed. (C. C. A.) 15; *Caliga* v. *Inter Ocean Newspaper Co.* (1907), 157 Fed. (C. C. A.) 186.

[12] *Harper* v. *Donohue* (1905), 144 Fed. (C. C.) 491–498. "Publication in a foreign country without the consent of the author is not an abandonment, *Boucicault* v. *Wood*, 2 Biss. 34, or without the consent of the owner of the exclusive right to publish in this country. *Goldmark* v. *Kreling* (1888), 35 Fed. (C. C.) 661."

[13] *Savage* v. *Hoffman* (1908), 159 Fed. (C. C.) 584; *Photo Drama Picture Co., Inc.*, v. *Social Film Co.* (1915), 220 Fed. (C. C. A.) 448; *West Publishing Co.* v. *Thompson* (1909), 169 (C. C.) 833; *Jewelers' Mercantile Agency* v. *Jewelers* (1898), 155 N. Y. 241; 49 N. E. 872.

See also cases cited under footnote 11.

When there is a publication of the work and the statute has not been complied with, the work is forever dedicated to the public.[14]

While performing rights were not within the provisions of 8 Anne which gave to authors the sole liberty of printing their books [15] the author now has the sole right of dramatization in his common-law work. As the performance of a play or motion picture is not a "publication" thereof,[16] he may produce the same upon the stage or screen and still retain his common-law rights therein. Hence a motion picture may be protected before publication under the common law.[17]

It has been held that where on assignment of the publication rights, the performing rights in an unpublished drama have been reserved by an author, the statutory performing rights are vested in him, immediately upon

[14] *Koppel* v. *Downing* (1897), 11 App. Dist. Col. 93. Where copyright in a play had not been perfected by the deposit of copies, the licensee could not at a subsequent date obtain valid copyright therein, even though his contract with the proprietor gave him that right.

See also cases cited under footnotes 11, 12 and 13.

[15] *Coleman* v. *Wathen* (Eng.), 5 T. R. 245.

[16] *Aronson* v. *Fleckenstein* (1886), 28 Fed. (C. C.) 75. "The law is now too well settled to require the citation of authorities that the playing of a dramatic composition is not such a publication as makes the composition public property. . . ."

See also: *Thomas* v. *Lennon* (1883), 14 Fed. (C. C.) 849; *Boucicault* v. *Hart* (1875), 13 Blatch. 47; *Palmer* v. *DeWitt* (1872), 47 N. Y. 532; *Macklin* v. *Richardson* (Eng.), Ambler, 694; *Morris* v. *Kelly* (Eng.), 1 Jac. & W. 481.

[17] *Universal Film* v. *Copperman* (1914), 218 Fed. (C. C. A.) 577.

the publication of the work and the securing of copyright therein.[18]

In actions for infringement of the common-law rights in a play or motion picture, the complainant is entitled to an injunction and an account of profits,[19] and even exemplary damages.[20]

[18] *Fitch* v. *Young* (1911), 230 Fed. (D. C.) 743. Complainant's testator, Clyde Fitch, wrote a play he assigned to Macmillan Company. They took out copyright and published the work. Clyde Fitch reserved the performing rights. Thereafter the Macmillan Company assigned the copyright to Clyde Fitch which contained the following clause: "This assignment shall not affect in any way the right of the Macmillan Company to publish the above-described works. The company shall continue to have the sole and exclusive right to publish said works as though this assignment had not been made." The copyright was secured prior to the present statute, and under Rev. St. 4952 which did not give the exclusive right to novelize a play to the copyright proprietor. Defendants published a story in its magazine which it is alleged infringes upon complainant's play. The court after holding that the assignment conveyed only the performing rights but reserved the copyright in the Macmillan Company said:

Hand, J.: "The right to novelize did not, however, exist before the Copyright Act of 1909, and the only basis for suit against a story as piracy which could arise under this copyright would be by virtue of the exclusive right to 'copy' granted by section 4952 of the Revised Statutes, a right which the Macmillan Company, the owner of the copyright, alone has the right to invoke. Any right to novelize the play in such form as does not result in a

[19] *French* v. *Kreling* (1894), 63 Fed. (C. C.) 621.

See also: *O'Neill* v. *General Film* (1916), 171 A. D. (N. Y.) 854; 157 N. Y. Supp. 1028; modifying 152 N. Y. Supp. 599.

[20] *Press Publishing Co.* v. *Monroe* (1896), 73 Fed. (C. C. A.) 196.

Where the manuscript is converted the plaintiff may ask to go to the jury on the question of damages, even though the work has no fixed or definite value.[21]

Section 136.—What is secured by copyright.

The copyrighting of a photoplay gives to the copyright

'copy' is a right in the public domain, and would inhere in the first novelizer, whether he were Clyde Fitch or another; any right so to change the play that a court would still consider it a 'copy' of the play is within the exclusive control of the Macmillan Company."

[21] *Taft* v. *Smith Gray & Co.* (1912), 76 Misc. (N. Y.) 283; 134 N. Y. Supp. 1011. In an action for the conversion of an unpublished manuscript having only a speculative value, evidence of the nature of the property, whether it can be reproduced, its utility to the owner and his estimate of its value, if not otherwise determinable, is competent upon the question of damages.

When the value of property, the reproduction of which is impossible, cannot be definitely ascertained, the question of its value to the owner is for the jury.

Where the property has no market value, the actual value to the owner is the measure of damages. *Leoncini* v. *Post* (1891), 13 N. Y. Supp. 825; *Frankenstein* v. *Thomas* (1872), 4 Daly (N. Y.), 256; *Watson* v. *Cowdrey* (1880), 23 Hun (N. Y.), 169.

In *Spicer* v. *Waters* (1866), 65 Barb. (N. Y.) 227, it is said: "When the property has no market value, such as paintings, *manuscripts*, etc., the damages are in the discretion of the jury. *Press Publ. Co.* v. *Monroe* (1896), 73 Fed. (C. C. A.) 196; *Wood* v. *Cunard Steamship Co.* (1911), 192 Fed. (C. C. A.) 293.

See in this connection: *Stover* v. *Lathrop* (1888), 33 Fed. (C. C.) 348. Where a book is copyrighted and the action is brought in trover and there is no allegation of copyright the jury may not take into consideration in computing the damages the infringement of the copyright in the book occasioned by the conversion.

proprietor thereof the exclusive right to publish, copy and vend the photoplay; to make any other version of the motion picture, to novelize it, to perform it publicly, and to make a transcription thereof in whole or in part so that it may be performed upon the stage with living actors.[22]

Section 137.—How copyright is secured.

Under the present Copyright Act a motion picture may be copyrighted in one of three ways:

1. Where it is sought to be copyrighted as an unpublished work and the motion picture is a photoplay, copyright is secured by the deposit in the office of the Register of Copyright with claim of copyright of the title and description of such photoplay, together with one print taken from each scene or act.[23]

[22] Section one, Subd. (a) (b) (d), of the Copyright Act of 1909.

[23] Copyright Act of 1909, Section eleven.

MOTION PICTURES

DIRECTIONS FOR SECURING REGISTRATION UNDER THE AMENDATORY COPYRIGHT ACT OF AUGUST 24, 1912.

The amendment of the Copyright Act, approved August 24, 1912, provides for obtaining copyright for two new classes of works, namely:

Class "1," "Motion-picture photo-plays"; and class "m," "Motion pictures other than photo-plays."

In order to secure registration of claims to copyright for such works the following steps should be taken in compliance with the express provisions of the Act cited.

MOTION-PICTURE PHOTO-PLAYS

1. Motion-picture photo-plays not reproduced in copies for sale.

Deposit in the Copyright Office, Washington, D. C.

2. Where the motion picture is other than a photoplay and it is sought to copyright the same as an unpublished

(1) The title of the motion-picture photo-play.

(2) A description of the work, preferably either printed or typewritten.

(3) A photograph taken from each scene of every act.

These deposits should be accompanied by an application for recording the claim to copyright. For this purpose use application form "L 2," which will be furnished by the Copyright Office upon request. Also send with the application a post office or express money order to pay the statutory registration fee of $1.00.

II. Motion-picture photo-plays reproduced in copies for sale.

When the motion-picture photo play has been published (i. e., placed on sale, sold, or publicly distributed) with the required notice of copyright upon each copy, promptly after such publication deposit in the Copyright Office two complete copies of the work, accompanied by an application for recording the claim to copyright in the published work. For this purpose use application form "L 1," which will be furnished by the Copyright Office upon request. Also send with the application a post office or express money order to pay the statutory registration fee of $1.00.

MOTION PICTURES OTHER THAN PHOTO-PLAYS

I. Motion pictures other than photo-plays not reproduced in copies for sale.

Deposit in the Copyright Office, Washington, D. C.

(1) The title of the motion picture.

(2) A description of the work, preferably either printed or typewritten.

(3) Two or more photographs taken from different sections of the complete motion picture.

These deposits should be accompanied by an application for recording the claim to copyright. For this purpose use application form "M 2," which will be furnished by the Copyright Office upon request. Also send with the application a post office or express money order to pay the statutory fee of $1.00.

work, copyright is secured by deposit with claim of copyright of the title and description of such motion picture, together with not less than two prints from different sections of the complete motion picture.[24]

3. Where the motion picture, whether it be a photoplay or a work other than a photoplay is sought to be copyrighted as a published work, copyright is secured by publication of the motion picture with the notice of copyright as provided for by the Act.[25]

It is a condition precedent to the maintenance of an action for infringement of a work, the copyright in which has been secured by publication, to deposit in the Copy-

II. Motion pictures other than photo-plays reproduced in copies for sale.

When the work has been published (i. e., placed on sale, sold, or publicly distributed) with the required notice of copyright upon each copy, promptly after such publication deposit in the Copyright Office two complete copies of the work, accompanied by an application for recording the claim to copyright in the published work. For this purpose use application form "M 1," which will be furnished by the Copyright Office upon request. Also send with the application a post office or express money order to pay the statutory fee of $1.00.

In all cases the money order remitting the registration fee should be made payable to the "Register of Copyrights." Send the title, description, prints, copies, application and fee in one parcel, addressed to the Register of Copyrights, Washington, D. C.

If any motion picture has been registered as a work "not reproduced in copies for sale," it must nevertheless be registered a second time if it has been afterward published.

THORVALD SOLBERG,
Register of Copyrights.

[24] Copyright Act of 1909, Section eleven.

[25] Copyright Act of 1909, Section twelve.

N. Y. Times v. *Star Co.* (1912), 195 Fed. (C. C.) 110.

right Office, or in the mail addressed to the Register of Copyrights, Washington, D. C., promptly after such publication, two complete copies of the best edition of the work, together with claim for copyright registration.

Under Section five of the Act the application for registration must specify to which class therein enumerated, the work for which copyright is claimed, belongs.

When the motion picture is a photoplay the application must be made under group (l) and where it is other than a photoplay, under group (m).

The validity of the copyright, however, is not affected because of improper classification [26] and indeed Section five expressly provides that no error in classification shall invalidate or impair the copyright nor limit the subject matter of copyright.

Section 138.—Publication.

Just what constitutes "Publication" with respect to motion pictures has not been defined by the statute, and has not been clearly stated by the courts. Under the Act [27] and under the rules [28] promulgated by the Register of Copyrights, respecting the registration of claims to copyright as provided by the Act, publication takes place where copies of the first authorized edition are

[26] *Green* v. *Luby* (1909), 177 Fed. (C. C.) 287. "But the fact that the sketch was improperly classified as a dramatic composition in taking out the copyright would not affect its validity."

[27] Copyright Act of 1909, Section sixty-two.

[28] Rules and Regulations of Copyright Office, Rule twenty-five.

placed on sale, sold or publicly distributed by the proprietor of the copyright or under his authority.

Clearly, when the motion picture is offered for sale outright, the date when it is first so offered is the date of publication.[29]

The usual method of procedure, however, is for the producing company to place a number of the positive prints of the film in exchanges, where they are rented to exhibitors at fixed compensation. Title in the prints always remains in the producer or distributor. Any exhibitor, upon payment of the stipulated license fee is at liberty to rent the film.

In our opinion the offer of the prints by the exchanges to the exhibitors constitutes a publication within the meaning of the act.

The date of the first publication is the first day upon which exhibitors may obtain the prints, which is ordinarily called in the trade the release date.

There is good authority to sustain this position. In cases where books containing the ratings of merchants were leased for a stated term to any and all persons who accepted them at the proprietor's terms, and where title

[29] *Gottsberger* v. *Aldine* (1887), 33 Fed. (C. C.) 381. Where plaintiff had sold several copies of his work before obtaining copyright, this was a publication, and he could not restrain defendants from infringing.

Stern v. *Jerome H. Remick* (1910), 175 Fed. (C. C.) 282. The sale of a single copy of the song was held sufficient to constitute a publication.

See also: *Palmer* v. *DeWitt* (1872), 47 N. Y. 532; *Tompkins* v. *Halleck* (1882), 133 Mass. 32; *Carter* v. *Bailey* (1874), 64 Me. 461.

remained as well in the credit agency, it was held that there was a publication.[30]

[30] *Jewelers Mercantile Agency* v. *Jewelers* (1898), 155 N. Y. 241; 49 N. E. 872. If a book be put within reach of the general public so that all may have access to it, no matter what limitations be placed upon the use of it by the individual subscriber or lessee, it is published, and what is known as the common-law copyright or right of first publication is gone.

Ladd v. *Oxnard* (1896), 75 Fed. (C. C.) 703. Where a book is issued to subscribers thereof and where there is no limitation upon the number of persons to whom the book may be issued, there is a "publication" although the books are *not sold* and a number of restrictions are placed upon their use.

Larrowe-Loisette v. *O'Laughlin* (1898), 88 Fed. (C. C.) 896. The issuance of a book to all who subscribe for a course of instruction in connection with the book constitutes a publication thereof.

For cases where the placing of a work in a public office was held to be a publication, see:

Wright v. *Eisle* (1903), 86 A. D. (N. Y.) 356; 83 N. Y. Supp. 887, where the filing of plans and specifications with a public department was held to be publication.

Rees v. *Peltzer* (1874), 75 Ill. 475; where the filing of a manuscript map was held a publication.

Vernon Abstr. Co. v. *Waggoner Title Co.* (1908), 107 S. W. (Tex.) 919; where it was held a publication to furnish abstracts of title to owners of property.

D'Ole v. *Kansas City Star* (1899), 94 Fed. (C. C.) 840. An author leaving copies of a book in a public place or giving them away "publishes."

See also: *Kiernan* v. *Man. Tel. Co.* (1876), 50 How. Pr. (N. Y.) 194.

But see: *Stecher* v. *Dunstan* (1916), 233 Fed. (D. C.) 601; where the sending of samples was held not to constitute publication, and *McDermott* v. *Bd. of Trade* (1906), 146 Fed. (C. C. A.) 961, and *Falk* v. *Gast* (1893), 54 Fed. (C. C. A.) 890.

As to the publication of a painting see: *Pierce* v. *Werckmeister* (1896), 72 Fed. (C. C. A.) 54, rev. (1894), 63 Fed. (C. C.) 445, and *Am. Tobacco Co.* v. *Werckmeister* (1907), 207 U. S. 284; 28 Sup. Ct. 72; *Werckmeister*

It is not necessary that a sale be consummated to constitute publication. Where the work is exposed to the general public [31] "so that all may have access to it, no matter what limitations be put upon the use of it by the individual subscriber or lessee, it is published." [32]

Where an author publishes or consents to the publication of his work without complying with the statute, publication constitutes dedication to the public.[33]

v. *Am. Lith. Co.* (1904), 134 Fed. (C. C. A.) 321; *Turner* v. *Robinson* (Irish) (1860), 10 Ir. Ch. Rep. 121, and *Prince Albert* v. *Strange* (Eng.) (1849), 1 Mac. and G. 23.

See in this connection: *Grossman* v. *Canada Cycle Co.* (Can.) (1902), 5 Ont. L. R. 55. The mailing and even delivery of a large number of copies of an American newspaper in England to subscribers thereof was held *not* to be a publication since the work was not made available to the general public. See also: *Francis Day & Hunter* v. *Feldman & Co.* (Eng.) (1914), 2 Ch. 728; 83 L. J. Ch. 906; 111 L. T. 521.

[31] *Bleistein* v. *Donaldson* (1903), 188 U. S. 239; 23 Sup. Ct. 298; rev. 104 Fed. (C. C. A.) 993. "There was no publication until they were exposed to the general public, so that the public, without discrimination as to persons, might enjoy them." (Argument of counsel.)

[32] *Jewelers Mercantile Agency* v. *Jewelers* (1898), 155 N. Y. 241; 49 N. E. 872.

[33] *Wheaton* v. *Peters* (1834), 8 Pet. 591; *Bartlette* v. *Crittenden* (1847), 4 McLean, 300; *Same* v. *Same* (1849), 5 McLean, 32; *Boucicault* v. *Fox* (1862), 5 Blatch. (C. C.) 87; *Parton* v. *Prang* (1872), 3 Cliff. (C. C.) 537; *Boucicault* v. *Hart* (1875), 13 Blatch. (C. C.) 47; *Clemens* v. *Belford* (1883), 14 Fed. (C. C.) 728; *Potter* v. *McPherson* (1880), 21 Hun (N. Y.), 559; *Oertel* v. *Jacoby* (1872), 44 How. Pr. (N. Y.) 179; *Wagner* v. *Conried* (1903), 125 Fed. (C. C.) 798; *State* v. *State Journal Co.* (1905), 106 N. W. (Nebr.) 434.

Wall v. *Gordon* (1872), 12 Abb. Pr. (N. S.) N. Y. 349. Plaintiff, composer and owner of the copyright in a song "When

In *Universal Film Co.* v. *Copperman*,[34] a motion picture was manufactured in Denmark. Copies of the film were sold to purchasers in different countries of Europe, and the contract of sale provided that the prints sold to the purchaser would not be exported or sold for export to any other country; i. e., the right to represent the photoplay was limited to the country wherein the sale took place.

The film was not copyrighted in any of the countries wherein it was sold. Subsequently to such sales and on November 10, 1912 the photoplay was copyrighted in the United States, but in the preceding September one of the prints had been purchased by one of the defendants in England without any knowledge of the restriction contained in the original contract of sale. This film was exhibited in the United States before copyright registration.

The Band Begins to Play," had the same printed in sheet music form and placed 200 copies in the hands of Wrippert & Co., music dealers in London, for sale, with written instructions not to sell any of them until Sept 11, 1871. He came to the United States and secured copyright on Sept. 9, 1871. Before leaving England he had exposed for sale copies of the song without the music.

Held that there was a publication and a dedication to the public.

Holmes v. *Donohue* (1896), 77 Fed. (C. C.) 179. The publication in a magazine of a story in serial form without first depositing the title as required by the then existing statute was held to be a dedication of the work.

[34] *Universal Film Co.* v. *Copperman* (1914), 212 Fed. (D. C.) 301; aff'd 218 Fed. (C. C. A.) 577.

See in this connection: *Daly* v. *Walrath* (1899), 40 A. D. (N. Y.) 220. Where there had been publication of the work in Germany all common-law rights were destroyed.

The court held that the sale of prints of the films in Europe constituted a publication of the film, and that since no copyright had been secured in the film in Europe, the work fell into the public domain.

Even if copyright had been secured in every country wherein the film had been so sold and exhibited, and all such countries came within Section seven, Subdivision B of the Act (granting protection to foreign authors or proprietors of works), the publication of the film in this country in September, 1912, without securing copyright therein under our statute nevertheless amounted to a dedication of such motion picture.[35]

The court defines publication in the following language: "If there be such a dissemination of the thing under consideration among the public as to justify the belief, that it took place with the intention of rendering the work common property then publication occurred."

In discussing the question whether the sale of films as in this action amounted to a publication the court states: "I do not see what more the Nordisk Company could have done toward disseminating its work than to sell it everywhere in Great Britain and Europe with knowledge that the play would be performed and the films shown over most of the civilized world. I do not think it makes any difference that each purchaser agrees not to use out of his own country or to sell for export; it is proven that

[35] See in this connection: *The Mikado Case* (1885), 25 Fed. (C. C.) 183. It is immaterial in what country publication of the work is made. "Such rights of authors as are saved by statute are not recognized extra-territorially. They can only be enforced in the sovereignty of their origin."

more than a month before registration in the United States there was nothing to prevent anybody in any part of Europe from buying, using and seeing this photoplay. How publication could be plainer I do not perceive. . . . Because there was a publication in Europe before registration in the United States this bill must be dismissed."

In *Ferris* v. *Frohman* [36] a play called "The Fatal Card" was first publicly performed in England. At the time of such performance a statute was in force in England under which the first public presentation of a dramatic composition was declared to be in the construction of the act equivalent to the first publication of a book. Complainants' play was never in fact published, but on the contrary was kept in manuscript form.

The complainant Frohman was granted an exclusive license to perform the play in the United States for a specified period. The play was not copyrighted in this country, although produced on the stage.

Thereafter the defendant made an adaptation of the English play for which he secured American copyright.

This action was brought in the state court to protect complainants' common-law rights in their unpublished manuscript. Defendants contended that the presentation upon the stage of the play in England having been a publication thereof under the English Statute in force at the time, complainants had lost their common-law rights in such play; and since the play had not been copyrighted in this country there was a dedication to the public.

[36] *Ferris* v. *Frohman* (1912), 223 U. S. 424; 32 Sup. Ct. 263; aff'g (1909), 238 Ill. 430; 87 N. E. 327.

The United States Supreme Court held that in order to constitute an abandonment of common-law rights there must be a publication of the work in the sense that publication has been established by the common law, to wit: reproduction of the work in copies for sale. That since the play had not been printed and published no publication had taken place; that the English Parliament could at its pleasure define publication and impose such other restrictions upon the common-law rights of the author as it deemed fit, but that such modifications could have no extraterritorial effect, and that the American courts were not bound to accept such changes in the common law. In other words, that while such representation in England amounted to a publication, it did not amount to publication so far as this country was concerned. In the words of the court:

"When Section 20 of the Act of 5 and 6 Vict. C. 45 provided that the first public performance of a play should be deemed equivalent in the construction of that act, to the first publication of a book, it simply defined its meaning with respect to the rights which the statutes conferred. The deprivation of the common-law right by force of the statute, was plainly limited by the territorial bounds within which the operation of the statute was confined."

Section 139.—Notice of copyright.

The statute does not provide for any notice of copyright in the case of works copyrighted as unpublished works. Hence no notice of copyright is required on motion pictures which are copyrighted as unpublished works.

Where the copyright is secured by publication, the notice of copyright must be inserted on each and every copy of the work in strict compliance with Section eighteen of the Act.[37]

Section eighteen provides that the notice shall consist either of the word "Copyright" or the abbreviation "Copr." accompanied by the name of the copyright proprietor. Where the work is a *printed* literary, musical, or dramatic work, the notice must also include the year in which copyright was secured by publication.

Since a motion picture is not a *printed* work in the literal sense that the word *printed* is used throughout the Act, it would seem that the copyright notice af-

[37] *Banks* v. *Manchester* (1888), 128 U. S. 244; 9 Sup. Ct. 36. "It has prescribed such a method, and that method is to be followed. No authority exists for obtaining a copyright, beyond the extent to which Congress has authorized it. A copyright cannot be sustained as a right existing at common law; but as it exists in the United States, it depends wholly on the Legislation of Congress. . . ."

Mifflin v. *White*, *Mifflin* v. *Dutton* (1902), 190 U. S. 260–265; 23 Sup. Ct. 769–771. The statute with respect to form of copyright notice must be complied with, "in substance at least." See *Thompson* v. *Hubbard* (1889), 131 U. S. 123; 9 Sup. Ct. 710.

Pierce v. *Werckmeister* (1896), 72 Fed. (C. C. A.) 54. "To secure a statutory copyright under the laws of the U. S., all the prescribed requisites of the statute must be complied with. *Wheaton* v. *Peters*, 8 Pet. 591, 664; *Parkinson* v. *Laselle* (1875), 3 Sawy. 330, 332, Fed. Cas. No. 10,762 (C. C.); *Boucicault* v. *Hart* (1875), 13 Blatchf. 47, 50, Fed. Cas. No. 1,692 (C. C.); *Lawrence* v. *Dana* (1869), 4 Cliff. 1, 60, Fed. Cas. No. 8, 136 (C. C.)." See also: *Jackson* v. *Walkie* (1886), 29 Fed. (C. C.) 15; *Blume* v. *Spear* (1887), 30 Fed. (C. C.) 629.

fixed to published motion pictures does not require the inclusion of the year when first publication took place.

The question as to the proper form of notice to be placed on motion pictures, has not yet come before the courts; and in view of the fact that the word *printed* may be construed as applying to positive films it is advisable to add to the copyright notice the year when first publication took place.

Section eighteen also provides that in the case of works specified in subsections (f) to (k) of Section five, the notice may consist of the letter "C," inclosed within a circle, accompanied by the initials, monogram, mark or symbol of the copyright proprietor, providing his name shall appear on some accessible portion of the work. As motion pictures are classified under subsections (l) and (m) of section five, the proprietor of a motion picture may not insert such a form of notice, at any rate, not if his motion picture was copyrighted subsequent to August 24, 1912 when the "Townsend Bill" was approved, providing for the separate copyrighting of motion pictures, and creating two new classes of copyrightable works to wit, "(l) Motion-picture photoplays;" and " (m) Motion-pictures other than photoplays."

Prior to that amendment of the Copyright Act, motion pictures were copyrighted as photographs, and as photographs were copyrighted under subsection (j) such form of notice was proper.

The copyright notice should be inserted immediately after the title of the motion picture and should read as follows:

"Copyright or Copr. 191– (insert proper year) by A. B. (insert proper name)".

The notice need not be placed upon the copies deposited with the Register of Copyrights,[38] but it must appear on all the published copies of the work during the full term of the copyright.

In a case where the assignee of the copyright had omitted to print it, he was held debarred from enjoining his very assignor for infringement.[39] Its purpose is to inform the public.[40] It should above all, be legible,[41] and its legibility is a question for the jury.[42]

[38] *Osgood* v. *A. S. Aloe Instrument Co.* (1897), 83 Fed. (C. C.) 470; *Werckmeister* v. *Am. Lith. Co.* (1905), 142 Fed. (C. C.) 827, has even gone so far as to hold that the notice of copyright need not be placed upon the original where the same is a painting.

[39] *Thompson* v. *Hubbard* (1889), 131 U. S. 123; 9 Sup. Ct. 710. "It is not enough that Thompson while he owned the copyright gave the required notice in the copies of every edition he published, while it was *his* copyright. The inhibition of the statute extended to and operated upon Hubbard while he owned the copyright in respect to the copies of every edition which he published, and for his failure he is debarred from maintaining his action."

[40] *Burrow-Giles Lith. Co.* v. *Sarony* (1884), 111 U. S. 53; 4 Sup. Ct. 279; *Pierce* v. *Werckmeister* (1896), 72 Fed. (C. C. A.) 54.

[41] *Alfred Decker Co.* v. *Etchison* (1915), 225 Fed. (D. C.) 135. The notice printed on the work was so small and blurred that in the language of the court it could only be discovered "with a microscope, by a person skilled in the art." *Held* that an innocent infringer who upon learning that the work was copyrighted immediately ceased his infringe-

[42] *Bolles* v. *Outing Co.* (1897), 77 Fed. (C. C. A.) 966; aff'd (1899), 175 U. S. 262; 20 Sup. Ct. 94.

While the statute calls for strict compliance, the courts have gone very far in formulating the rule of "substantial compliance."

Callaghan v. *Myers*,[43] the leading case in the country, held that a variation of one year, reducing the term of copyright for that period, was immaterial. On the other hand it was held that a variation of one year lengthening the term of copyright to that extent, was material and invalidated the copyright.[44]

ment would not be compelled to pay damages, but that he would be enjoined.

Strauss v. *Pen Printing Co.* (1915), 220 Fed. (D. C.) 977. Plaintiff's photograph contained a copyright notice consisting of "C." The mark was blurred. All that could be seen upon inspection was a small blurred print mark the outline of which was roughly semi-circular in shape, with the arc uppermost. *Held* under section twenty of the act that the copyright was not invalidated, and that complainant could recover for infringement, after actual notice. The court did not award any damages to complainant but allowed complainant, defendant's profits as well as costs.

[43] *Callaghan* v. *Myers* (1888), 128 U. S. 617; 9 Sup. Ct. 177.

A reporter of law books containing the judicial opinions of the judges has no copyright in those *opinions*, although he has such copyright in the matter therein which is the result of his own intellectual labor.

A variance of *one year* in the dates between the deposit and the notice of copyright printed in the book is not a material variation, in this instance, because the statement on the book purported to lessen the life of the copyright by one year, so that the public would not be injured. The title was actually deposited in *1867* and the notice read *1866*.

Held also that when the title was deposited by *E. B. Myers & Chandler* and the notice read *E. B. Myers*, the variation was immaterial.

[44] *Baker* v. *Taylor* (1848), 2 Blatch. (C. C.) 182. Plaintiffs

Motion picture producers have frequently used the word "Copyrighted" instead of "Copyright" as provided by the statute, in the notice. Although the use of the word "Copyrighted" has been held to be substantial compliance with the statute,[45] its use should be avoided.

The full meaning of the notice is that the copyright is owned by the person whose name is inserted in the copyright notice. The notice does not necessarily imply that the person mentioned in the copyright notice is the one who originally secured the copyright. It does not necessarily mean that the work is copyrighted by the person therein mentioned. To sustain this interpreta-

published a book and in the copyright notice inserted the year 1847 as the date of publication instead of the 1846, the correct date.

Held that unless there was a strict compliance with the statute no copyright was secured; that the failure to publish a notice in accordance with the act whether caused through inadvertence or intentionally were fatal.

The court said: ". . . I think the point is placed beyond question that the failure, in the present case, to publish the notice demanded by the act, in the manner directed, creates a fatal defect in the plaintiff's title. Even though the failure to publish the statutory notice arose from mistake, this court would have no power to accept the intention of the party, in place of a performance, any more in respect to the insertion of that notice on the proper page, than in respect to the deposit of the title of the book."

[45] *Falk* v. *Shumacher* (1891), 48 Fed. (C. C.) 222. The following notice was held to be a substantial compliance with the statute. "*1889. Copyrighted by B. J. Falk.*"

See also: *Record & Guide Co.* v. *Bromley* (1910), 175 Fed. (C. C.) 156· where the notice was: "*Copyrighted 1907 by C. W. Sweet.*"

tion of the meaning of the notice, reference may be had to that section of the Act which provides that an assignee of a copyright may insert his name in place and stead of that of his assignor. When such substitution takes place, the notice does not imply that the work was copyrighted by the assignee, but it does convey the meaning that the copyright is owned by such assignee.

An abbreviation of the date is substantial compliance,[46] likewise of the Christian name.[47] Nor do additional words harm the notice [48] in every instance. The exact part of the page upon which the notice appears is immaterial.[49]

[46] *Snow* v. *Mast* (1895), 65 Fed. (C. C.) 995. Where the year in a copyright notice is abbreviated to read as follows: "*'94*" there is a substantial compliance with the statute.

Bolles v. *Outing Co.* (1897), 77 Fed. (C. C. A.) 966; aff'd 175 U. S. 262; 20 Sup. Ct. 94. Where the notice of copyright read as follows: "*Copyright 93, by Bolles, Brooklyn*" it was held sufficient.

[47] *Burrow Giles* v. *Sarony* (1883), 17 Fed. (C. C.) 591; aff'd (1884), 111 U. S. 53; 4 Sup. Ct. 279. Where the notice contains the initial of the Christian name and the full surname there is a compliance with the statute.

[48] *Hills* v. *Austrich* (1903), 120 Fed. (C. C.) 862. A notice reading: "*Copyright 1902, published by Hills & Co., Ltd., London, England,*" was held a sufficient compliance with the statute.

See also: *Hills* v. *Hoover* (1905), 136 Fed. (C. C.) 701.

Hefel v. *White Land Co.* (1893), 54 Fed. (C. C.) 179. Where copyright notice contains all the words required by the statute it is sufficient even though additional words are added. Such additional words are treated merely as surplusage.

The notice here contained the additional words, "*Civil Engineer*" printed immediately after the name of the copyright proprietor.

[49] *Blume* v. *Spear* (1887), 30 Fed. (C. C.) 629. Copyright

The date itself may be in arabic or in Roman numerals, as Judge Learned Hand has recently held.[50]

Copyright is not lost where the notice has been omitted by accident or mistake from some of the copies,[51] or where a change was made therein after the work left the hands of the copyright proprietor.[52]

Section twenty provides that: "where the copyright proprietor has sought to comply with the provisions of

was not lost by placing the proper copyright notice below the first page of music.

[50] *Stern* v. *Remick* (1910), 175 Fed. (C. C.) 282. "Nor do I find any difficulty in deciding that Roman numerals conform to the notice prescribed by the statute. Roman numerals are a part of the language of this country. They are constantly in use upon monumental architecture of all sorts and for serial purposes upon books, and they are a part of the language as taught in the public schools, and understood by all but the most illiterate. Nor can one seriously contend that the notice required by the statute would be fulfilled only by Arabic numerals. If the letters were written out in words, it would certainly be a compliance. I regard the writing of it here in Roman numerals as more nearly a literal compliance with the statute than to write out the year in words."

[51] *Stecher* v. *Dunston* (1916), 233 Fed. (D. C.) 601. The omission by accident or mistake of the notice from particular copies does not invalidate the copyright or prevent a recovery after actual notice of the copyright.

See also: *Merriam Co.* v. *United Dictionary Co.* (1907), 208 U. S. 260; 28 Sup. Ct. 290; aff'g (1906), 146 Fed. (C. C. A.) 354. The omission of the notice in the English edition of an American work which was to be sold only in England did not invalidate the copyright.

[52] *Falk* v. *Gast*, 54 Fed. (C. C. A.) 890; aff'g 48 Fed. 262. "If the proper statutory notice of copyright was upon each copy as it left the control and ownership of the proprietor of the copyright he cannot be responsible for any changes which were afterwards improvidently made upon a particular copy before it came into the hands of the last purchaser."

the Act with respect to notice, the omission by accident or mistake of the prescribed notice from a particular copy or copies shall not invalidate the copyright or prevent recovery for infringement against any person who, after actual notice of the copyright, begins an undertaking to infringe it."

The section further provides that there shall be no recovery of damages against an innocent infringer who has been misled by the omission, and that the court may in its discretion refuse a permanent injunction against an innocent infringer unless the copyright proprietor shall reimburse him for his reasonable outlay innocently incurred.

But a notice reading "Registered 3,693, 1883" was held insufficient and an abandonment [53] as were several other notices which showed great discrepancies in the dates [54] and in the form of notice generally.[55]

[53] *Higgins* v. *Keufel* (1887), 30 Fed. (C. C.) 627; aff'd (1891), 140 U. S. 428; 11 Sup. Ct. 731.

[54] *Record & Guide Co.* v. *Bromley* (1910), 175 Fed. (C. C.) 156. Where at the head of the first column on the first page of reading matter the title of a periodical was inserted, and followed by two lines in the following manner:

"Copyright by the Real Estate Record and Builder's Guide Co.

Vol. LXXV. May 6, 1905. No. 1938,

[55] *Lydiard-Peterson* v. *Woodman* (1913), 204 Fed. (C. C. A.) 921. The notice was "*Copyright 1908, Drawn by J. C. Woodman.*" *Held*, improper.

Record & Guide Co. v. *Bromley* (1910), 175 Fed. (C. C.) 156. Where the notice inserted on the front page above the title and read: "*The entire contents of this paper covered by copyright*" or "*contents covered by copyright.*" *Held* non-compliance with statute.

So also where the notice was inserted at the foot of each page and read: "*The text of these pages are copyrighted. All rights reserved. Notice is hereby given that infringement will lead to prosecution.*" Such notice was invalid.

In *Haas* v. *Feist*, the complainant had used his own name in registering his copyright, but had inscribed upon the work, as part of the notice, a trade-name, the use of which was in violation of the laws of his state. It was held that this invalidated his copyright.[56]

Under Section eighteen of the Act, where copyright subsisted in a work at the time the present act went into effect, the notice may be in the form prescribed by that Act or in that prescribed by the Act of June 18, 1874.

It would seem under Section nine that the notice of copyright is required to be affixed only to those copies of the work "published or offered for sale in the United States." For that reason positive prints made for shipment without the United States do not require the notice to be affixed thereon.[56a]

Section 140.—Licensee's failure to insert notice.

The proprietor of the copyright does not lose his rights thereto or dedicate the work where he gives a license

such notice was held invalid upon the ground that it was the evident intention of the author that the date contained in the second line was not to be considered the date of the copyright.

Jackson v. *Walkie* (1886), 29 Fed. (C. C.) 15. The book in question contained the notice "*Entered according to act of congress, in the year 1878, by H. A. Jackson.*"

Held insufficient, distinguishing it from *Myers* v. *Callaghan* where the year of entry was designated as 1866 when in fact it was entered in 1867, thereby abridging the copyright one year and harming nobody.

[56] *Haas* v. *Feist* (1916), 234 Fed. (D. C.) 105; on rehearing 234 Fed. 109.

[56a] See in this connection: *Haggard* v. *Waverly* (1905), 144 Fed. (C. C.) 490.

to publish the work upon the express condition that a proper copyright notice be affixed to each and every copy of the work, and such condition is subsequently breached by the licensee. The wrongful act of the licensee does not forfeit the licensor's right.

"The copyright of the appellee was property of which it could not legally be deprived without its consent. Title to copyright is no more lost by the theft of the manuscript or piratical publication of it than is one's title to a horse by the stealing of it or by the unlawful sale of it to a stranger." [57]

An innocent party who believes such works to be in the public domain and in good faith makes use of it, consequently does so at his peril.

On the other hand, where the proprietor of the copyright licenses another to use the work, but does not, in his contract, provide that the licensee must insert a proper copyright notice in every published copy of the work, he loses his copyright when the licensee publishes the work without a proper notice.

Section 141.—False notice of copyright.

Section twenty-nine provides that any person who, with fraudulent intent shall insert or impress any notice of copyright or words of the same import upon any uncopyrighted work, or shall remove or alter the notice upon a copyrighted work, shall be guilty of a misdemeanor. This section also provides that any person who shall knowingly import, issue or sell any uncopyrighted work

[57] *Am. Press Ass'n* v. *Daily Story Pub. Co.* (1902), 120 Fed. (C. C. A.) 766; App. Dism. 193 U. S. 675; 24 Sup. Ct. 852.

bearing such notice shall be liable to a fine therein specified. Section thirty prohibits the importation of any work bearing a false notice of copyright.

There must be actual participation in the wrongful act before any liability will accrue.[58] The notice, however, must contain all the necessary elements prescribed by the statute for a valid notice,[59] so that if the notice is defective or insufficient, it may not be said to be a false notice of copyright.

Section 142.—Title—Changing title.

While there is an English case holding that copyright protects the title of a work,[60] the great weight of authority is just the other way, and the law may be regarded

[58] *Rigney* v. *Dutton* (1896), 77 Fed. (C. C.) 176. In an action to recover a penalty under the statute for inserting a false notice of copyright, it was held sufficient to maintain the action to allege that defendants had *prepared* a cut with the copyright notice inscribed thereon and caused prints from said cut to be published as part of an advertising page of a trade paper.

Ross v. *Raphael* (1898), 91 Fed. (C. C. A.) 128. This action was brought under section 4963, Rev. St., U. S., as it existed prior to the amendment of 1897 to recover penalties for inserting a copyright notice upon an uncopyrighted book. *Held* that since defendant did not make the books or insert the notice therein it was not liable notwithstanding the fact that defendant knew at the time of the sale of such books that they contained a false notice of copyright.

See also: *McLaughlin* v. *Raphael* (1903), 191 U. S. 267; 24 Sup. Ct. 105; aff'g 115 Fed. 85; *Taft* v. *Stevens* (1889), 38 Fed. (C. C.) 28; *Rigney* v. *Raphael* (1896), 77 Fed. (C. C.) 173.

[59] *Hoertel* v. *Raphael* (1899), 94 Fed. (C. C.) 844.

[60] *Weldon* v. *Dicks* (Eng.) (1878), 48 L. J. Ch. 201; 10 Ch. D. 247; 39 L. T. 467; 27 W. R. 639.

as settled that the title of a book or motion picture has no copyright protection.[61]

However, there is one purpose for which the copyright law regards the title as an integral part of the work, and that is for the purpose of identification. It does not permit the proprietor to copyright the work under one title and exploit it under another which differs substantially. To do otherwise would defeat the whole purpose of notice.[62]

[61] *Corbett* v. *Purdy* (1897), 80 Fed. (C. C.) 901; *Glaser* v. *St. Elmo* (1909), 175 Fed. (C. C.) 276; *Atlas* v. *Street & Smith* (1913), 204 Fed. (C. C. A.) 398; App. Dism. 231 U. S. 348; 34 Sup. Ct. 73; *Harper* v. *Ranous* (1895), 67 Fed. (C. C.) 904.

See also: Section 121.

Dick v. *Yates* (Eng.) (1881), 18 Ch. D. 76; 50 L. J. Ch. 809; 44 L. T. 660. Plaintiff in 1881 had copyrighted his book under the title of "Splendid Misery." The court held that there could be no copyright in the *title* of a book.

See *Crotch* v. *Arnold* (Eng.) (1909), 54 S. J. 49.

[62] *Collier* v. *Imp.* (1913), 214 Fed. (D. C.) 272. After a dramatic composition was copyrighted under the name *A White Slave's Love*, the work was produced under the title *The Undertow*. Hough, J.:

"I am not satisfied that an author can copyright a play under one title, produce it under another, and hold as an infringer a person who has been misled by his actions. But I am not called upon to determine that question, as it does not arise upon these pleadings. The bill avers that the defendant produced the complainant's work with full knowledge of all the facts. As to such person I think it clear that an author or assignee does not forfeit a copyright by a change of the title of the work."

See also: *Blume* v. *Spear* (1887) 30 Fed. (C. C.) 629: "If, however, the orator published the composition under a title different from that by which he copyrighted it, in substance, he would thereby probably so depart from his copyright that he would leave the composition to the public. Drone, Copyrights, 140, 142."

But an immaterial variation whereby none is apt to be misled will not vitiate the copyright.[63]

See in this connection: *Caliga* v. *Inter Ocean Newspaper Co.* (1907), 157 Fed. (C. C. A.) 186.

[63] *Donnelly* v. *Ivers* (1882), 18 Fed. (D. C.) 592. A book was registered for copyright under the title *Over One Thousand Recipes, The Lake-Side Cook-Book; a complete Manual of Practical, Economical, Palatable and Healthful Cookery, Chicago: Donnelley, Loyd & Co., 1878.* The book was subsequently published under the title *The Lake-Side Cook Book, No. 1; a complete Manual of Practical, Economical and Palatable and Healthful Cookery. By N. A. D.*, with place of publication and name of proprietor and notice of copyright. In an action to restrain defendant from infringing it was held the variance was not material.

Carte v. *Evans* (1886), 27 Fed. (C. C.) 861. The name of the filed title here was: *Piano-forte Arrangement of the Comic Opera, The Mikado, or the Town of Titipu, by W. S. Gilbert and Sir Arthur Sullivan. By George L. Tracy.*

The printed book was *Vocal Score of the Mikado, or The Town of Titipu. Arrangement for Piano-forte by George Lowell Tracy (of Boston, U. S. A.) of the above-named opera by W. S. Gilbert and Arthur Sullivan.*

Subsequently another edition was published in which the words "*Piano-forte Score*" were substituted for the words "*Vocal Score.*"

Held no substantial difference in the titles, as "The published title is sufficient to identify it with substantial certainty with the registered copyright, and no one could possibly be misled by the variations between the two."

Patterson v. *Ogilvie Pub. Co.* (1902), 119 Fed. (C. C.) 451. The title of a work deposited in accordance with the statute read:

The Captain of the Rajah. By Howard Patterson. Illustrated by Warren Sheppard. A thrilling and realistic sea story from a noted sailor's pen, and lavishly illustrated by the pencil of America's greatest marine artist.

The book was published with the following title:

The Captain of the Rajah. A Story of the Sea, by Howard Patterson. Illustrated by Warren Sheppard.

Held that the shortening of title did not invalidate copyright.

Under the old Acts where deposit of the title of the work was the first step to secure copyright, the law permitted a change in the title of the work between such deposit and publication, if we may accept *Black* v. *Allen* as an authority.[64]

Section 143.—Who may secure copyright.

Although the Act does not expressly so provide, citizens of the United States are entitled to secure copyright.

The rights of an alien to enjoy copyright are governed by Section eight of the Act.

That section provides that the copyright secured by the Act shall extend to the work of an author or proprietor who is a citizen or subject of a foreign state or nation only when the alien author or proprietor shall be domiciled within the United States at the time of the first publication of the work; or when such foreign state or nation grants either by treaty, convention, agreement or law to citizens of the United States the benefit of Copyright on substantially the same basis as to its own citizens, or copyright protection substantially equal to the protection secured to such foreign author under the Act or by treaty; or when such foreign state or nation is a party

Daly v. *Webster* (1892), 56 Fed. (C. C. A.) 483. A leading case on this proposition.

[64] *Black* v. *Allen* (1893), 56 Fed. (C. C.) 764. "It is easily seen that an author may find it to his advantage to change the title of his work between the time of his taking his first step toward obtaining a copyright and the actual publication of the book. I do not think that the courts should hold that such change of title renders a copyright invalid, unless compelled to do so, and I do not think they are so compelled."

to an international agreement which provides for reciprocity in the granting of copyright, by the terms of which agreement the United States may at its pleasure, become a party thereto.

The section further provides that the existence of the reciprocal conditions aforesaid shall be determined by the President of the United States, by proclamations made from time to time.[65]

[65] Opinion of U. S. Attorney General, dated May 6, 1911, 29 Opinions of Atty. Gen'l, p. 64.

"1: It is the duty of the President to determine and proclaim what foreign countries grant to the citizens of the United States rights similar to those specified in section 1 (e).

2: A proclamation of the President may be made retroactive in that it may determine that either of the conditions have been complied with since a specified date and thereupon the citizens or subjects of the country referred to in the proclamation will be entitled to avail themselves of our copyright from the specific date mentioned in the proclamation.

Germany having complied with one or more of the conditions of Section 8, on or before July 1, 1909, a German citizen could from that date acquire all the rights of our law (except those in Section 1, e) by publishing with copyright notice and complying with the terms of the law. But he could not secure registration of his copyright until after the proclamation of April 9th, 1910.

If an action were instituted between July 1, 1909, and April 9, 1910, it might be maintained by proof of registration after April 9, 1910.

In an action for an infringement committed between July 1, 1909, and April, 1910, the infringer would not have an equitable defense on the ground that at the time of the infringement he did not have any legitimate notice of the existence of the copyright. The notice of copyright printed on the published copies would be notice that the copyright proprietor claims that one of the conditions of Section 8 have been complied with. Every-

The proclamation is conclusive evidence of the existence of reciprocal conditions, and the courts will not review it. The reciprocal conditions will be presumed to continue to exist until the President by proclamation

one must be aware that the absence of the proclamation is not conclusive evidence that the reciprocal conditions have not been complied with.

3: With reference to Section 1 (e) Germany complied with the condition on September 9, 1910, and the proclamation was issued on December 8, 1910, but it does not recite that the condition was complied with prior to its date. Hence there is not sufficient evidence of the compliance with the condition prior to the date of the proclamation to maintain an action for an infringement committed between the two dates.

4: As to the question whether a German citizen could acquire the right specified in Section 1 (e) prior to September 9, 1910, it is clear that it could not be acquired prior to that date. Prior to the compliance by Germany with the condition of Section I (e), the condition of the German citizen with regard to that right was the same as if the act did not exist.

Fraser v. *Yack* (1902), 116 Fed. (C. C. A.) 285. "At the date of this contract, May 8, 1890, copyright was not authorized in this country in favor of foreign authors (Rev. St., Sec. 4952); nor, as it would seem could a foreign author assign or transfer to a citizen his manuscript or common-law right of property therein, so that the latter could have copyright protection within the United States. *Yuengling* v. *Schile*, 12 Fed. 97, 102–107. The international copyright law granting copyright to foreign authors was passed March 13, 1891, and went into effect July 1, 1891. 26 Stat. 1106–1110, c. 565."

See also: *Boucicault* v. *Delafield* (Eng.) (1863), 1 H. & M. 597. Where the author of a play known as "The Colleen Bawn" filed a bill to restrain a piratical production. It appeared that the play had first been represented in New York, and by reason of that fact —there being no copyright convention with the United States— it was held that, under the statute (S. 19, Act 7 & 8 Vict., c. 12) there was no playright in England.

declares the cessation of the existence of such conditions.[66]

Section 144.—Belligerent aliens.

In time of war the status of the belligerent alien is

[66] *Chappell* v. *Fields* (1914), 210 Fed. (C. C. A.) 864. Section eight of the 1909 act respecting rights of alien authors construed.

"On April 9, 1910, President Taft issued a proclamation stating that citizens of Great Britain were entitled to the benefit of our copyright law, with an exception not material in this case. This proclamation is conclusive evidence of the fact that Great Britain at that date gave our citizens the benefit of her copyright laws on substantially the same basis as to her own citizens and the courts have no right to review it. . . . Congress, in our opinion has confided the whole subject to the Executive exclusively. The president is required, by proclamation, to determine from time to time, as the purposes of the act may require, the existence of these reciprocal conditions. As no proclamation has been made since that of April 9, 1910, we are bound to presume that in the opinion of the Executive these conditions do still exist."

Bong v. *Campbell Art Co.* (1908), 214 U. S. 236; 29 Sup. Ct. 628; aff'g 155 Fed. (C. C. A.) 116; 16 Ann. Cas. 1126. The courts will not take judicial notice that a foreign country is a party to an international agreement which provides for reciprocity in the granting of copyright, by the terms of which agreement this country may at its pleasure become a party. Such condition must be determined by a Presidential proclamation.

See: *Bong* v. *Campbell Art Co.* (1908), 214 U. S. 236; 29 Sup. Ct. 628; aff'g 155 Fed. (C. C. A.) 116; 16 Ann. Cas. 1126. Under Section 4952 of the Revised Statutes as amended by the Act of March 3, 1891, the assignee of an author was not entitled to copyright of the work unless such author himself would have been entitled to take out such copyright.

To the same effect *Yuengling* v. *Schile* (1882), 12 Fed. (C. C.) 97.

changed. His copyright is not lost, although it becomes liable to seizure. "During the war the property of alien enemies is subject to confiscation jure belli, and their civil capacity to sue is suspended."[67] The declaration of war does not in itself work a confiscation of the copyright, for an Act of Congress is necessary to bring about this result.[68] But it suspends the remedies of the copyright owner, so that he may neither sue on his contract, license or royalty agreement, nor maintain an action for infringement.[69] He may, however, be sued in the courts of this country (the essential jurisdictional facts being present) by an American citizen.[70]

[67] Judge Story in *Fairfax* v. *Hunter* (1813), 7 Cranch, 603.

See also: Opinions of Attorney General, Vol. 22, p. 268 (1898).

Held that the copyrights of Spanish subjects during the existence of a state of war between this country and Spain were suspended.

[68] *Brown* v. *United States* (1814), 8 Cranch, 112; *Distington Hematite* v. *Possehl* (Eng.) (1916), 32 T. L. R. 349.

[69] *Watts* v. *Unione* (1915), 224 Fed. (D. C.) 192; aff'd 229 Fed. 136. "Where therefore such a contract has been entered into with an alien enemy before the outbreak of the war, and has been performed on his side, the war merely suspends his remedy; in other words, he cannot sue upon it during the existence of hostilities."

Cohen v. *Mutual Life* (1872), 50 N. Y. 616. "All intercourse, commercial or otherwise, between them is unlawful; and all contracts existing at the commencement of the war suspended, and all made during its existence void. . . ."

Sands v. *N. Y. Life Ins. Co.* (1872), 50 N. Y. 632. "Clearly it is not law, nor do these or any recognized authorities 'intend to hold that a valid debt by note, bond or contract, existing when the war began . . . was nullified by the war. The debt is suspended until peace returns."

[70] *Watts* v. *Unione* (1915), 224 Fed. (D. C.) 192; aff'd 229 Fed.

As between two belligerents suing each other in the courts of this country, it is always discretionary with the United States Courts whether or not they will entertain jurisdiction.[71] That question is eliminated, however, the moment the United States enters the war with one of the belligerents.

If the copyright of the work is technically in the name of a domestic corporation, but all or the great majority of the stockholders and directors are enemy aliens residing in the belligerent country, the courts will undoubtedly follow the doctrine expressed in *Daimler* v. *Continental Tire Rubber Co.*,[72] and hold the company disqualified to sue. The English courts have consistently held to the rule that outward semblances must be disregarded, and that the ultimate disposition of the property remains the chief element for the court's consideration.[73]

136. "It is apparent therefore that to hold that a subject's right of action in his own country against an alien enemy is suspended, would be to defeat the very object of the suspensory rule, and to turn a disability into a relief."

[71] *Richards* v. *Wreschner* (1915), 156 N. Y. Supp. 1054; *Kaiser Wilhelm II* (1916), 230 Fed. (D. C.) 717; *Watts* v. *Unione* (1915), 224 Fed. (D. C.) 192; aff'd 229 Fed. 136.

[72] *Daimler Co.* v. *Continental Tire Rubber Co.* (Eng.) (1916), 114 L. T. 1049; 32 T. L. R. 624. The company was declared under a disability to sue on a trade debt, Baron Reading holding that to permit such suit would be to sanction "trading with the enemy."

[73] *Stephen M. Weld* v. *Fruhling* (1916), 32 T. L. R. 469; *Moss* v. *Donahue* (1916), 32 T. L. R. 343. In this connection the decision of Judge McAvoy of the City Court of the City of New York is of interest, but we are unable to agree with the learned court in its conclusions therein expressed.

Copyright owned by partners, one or more of whom is a resident of the belligerent country, comes within the rule of disability.[74] Such partners do not necessarily have to be belligerents, for even a citizen of this country who resides in the belligerent country during the war is treated on a par with a belligerent alien.[75]

Agency between a belligerent alien residing in his country and an enemy alien residing in this country is not affected by the war;[76] but the declaration of war ipso-facto terminates the agency between such belligerent alien and an American citizen residing in this country, just as it terminates partnerships under the same circumstances.[77] Where the agency survives, an American may pay over royalties to such resident agent,[78] al-

Schulz v. *Raimes*, N. Y. Law Journal, Apr. 19, 1917.

[74] *G. Candilis & Son* v. *Harold Victor & Co.* (Eng.) C. A. (1916), W. N. 424. Two of the partners were residents of Trebizond, Black Sea, which is a part of Turkey, with whom England was waging war.

[75] *Porter* v. *Freudenberg* (Eng.) (1915), 112 L. T. R. 313.

[76] *Porter* v. *Freudenberg* (Eng.) (1915), 112 L. T. R. 313.

[77] *Distington Hematite Co.* v. *Possehl* (Eng.) (1916), 32 T. L. R. 349; *Cohen* v. *Mutual Life* (1872), 50 N. Y. 616. "All existing partnerships between citizens or subjects of the two countries are dissolved. . . ."

[78] *Hubbard* v. *Mathews* (1873), 54 N. Y. 43. "Moneys received by such an agent are lawfully paid and lawfully received, though a remittance by him to his enemy principal would be unlawful."

Buchanan v. *Curry* (1821), 19 Johns. (N. Y.) 137. "The rule is founded in public policy, which forbids during war, that money or other resources shall be transferred, so as to aid or strengthen our enemies. The crime consists in exporting the money or property, or placing it in the power of the enemy; not in delivering it to an alien enemy, or his agent, residing here, under the control of our own government."

though the agent is not permitted to remit them to his principal.[79]

To remit royalties direct to the belligerent alien is treasonable. This prohibition extends not only to American citizens, but as well to all aliens residing here.[80]

The right of a licensee of a belligerent copyright proprietor to sue for infringement here during the war is not easy to define. The question seems to be complicated enough in times of peace,[81] but becomes doubly so on a declaration of war. However, the rule may be adduced that in cases where the licensee is required to join his belligerent proprietor as a party he may not sue; but where his license is so broad that it may be regarded in law as an assignment, he may enforce all his rights in the American courts, irrespective of the belligerent origin of his grant, provided, of course, that he is not himself an enemy alien.

Great Britain passed a statute on August 10, 1916 with respect to copyright, in its nature supplementary

[79] *United States* v. *Greathouse* (1863), 4 Sawyer, 472. "Whereever overt acts are committed, which in their natural consequence, if successful, would encourage and advance the interests of the rebellion, in judgment of law aid and comfort are given."

See Foster's Crown Law, 217.

[80] *Carlisle* v. *United States* (1872), 16 Wall. 147. "An alien, while domiciled in the country owes a local and temporary allegiance, which continues during the period of his residence."

[81] *Tully* v. *Triangle Film Co.* (1916), 229 Fed. (D. C.) 297; *New Fiction Pub. Co.* v. *Star Co.* (1915), 220 Fed. (D. C.) 994; *Aaronson* v. *Fleckenstein* (1886), 28 Fed. (C. C.) 75; *Wooster* v. *Crane* (1906), 147 Fed. (C. C. A.) 515; *Saake* v. *Lederer* (1909), 174 Fed. (C. C. A.) 135.

See also Section 161.

to the Trading with the Enemy Act of 1914, which greatly simplifies these questions. Under the terms of the Act the Public Trustee or Custodian is vested with title in all such copyrights, and holds the same until the end of the war.[82] The act, however, is limited to such works as are first published or made in the enemy country, and makes no mention of works first published in England before the war and owned by enemies. It is the disposition of this class of copyrights which raises the greatest problems.

Section 145.—In what name copyright may be taken out.

The copyright need not necessarily be taken out in the name of an individual. It may be obtained in the co-partnership or firm name of the individual, or even in a trade name or an assumed partnership name.[83] A corporation may likewise be the proprietor of the copyright.[84]

But there is a limitation on this rule. The trade name

[82] Chapter 32, 6 & 7 Geo. 5 (1916). An Act to make provision with respect to Copyright in Works first Published or made in an enemy country During the Present War.

[83] Section 23 of the Copyright Act of 1909; *Scribner* v. *Clark* (1888), 50 Fed. (C. C.) 473; aff'd as *Belford* v. *Scribner* (1891), 144 U. S. 488; 12 Sup. Ct. 734; *Callaghan* v. *Myers* (1888), 128 U. S. 617; 9 Sup. Ct. 177; *Scribner* v. *Allen Co.* (1892), 49 Fed. (C. C.) 854; *Werckmeister* v. *Springer Lith. Co.* (1894), 63 Fed. (C. C.) 808; *Rock* v. *Lazarus* (Eng.), Law Reports, 15 Eq. Cases, 104; *Weldon* v. *Dicks* (Eng.) (1878), Law Reports, 10 Ch. Div. 247; *Fruit Cleaning Co.* v. *Fresno Home Packing Co.* (1899), 94 Fed. (C. C.) 845.

[84] *Nat'l Cloak & Suit* v. *Kaufman* (1911), 189 Fed. (C. C.) 215.

or firm name must be one which the individual has a lawful right to use.

The assumption of a "nom de plume" does not confer any greater rights upon the author than the use of his own name.[85]

Haas v. *Feist* [86] was an action for the infringement of a song. The complainant's assignors had taken out copyright in the name of Deutsch & Cahalin, but they had neglected to file a certificate with the County Clerk giving the names and addresses of the members of the firm, as required by the New York Statute. The court on rehearing, held that inasmuch as this was a violation of the State statute, it went to the essence of the copyright and destroyed it. The complainants could not obtain the protection of the law in the very act of doing something illegal.

This decision may have a far reaching effect. Suppose a motion picture company has been using a trade name which is in unfair competition with another, and while so doing, and before injunction is granted, it takes out copyright in its trade name in numerous pictures. Would that destroy the copyright? We think

[85] *Clemens* v. *Belford* (The "Mark Twain" Case) (1883), 14 Fed. (C. C.) 728. By adopting the nom de plume "Mark Twain," he acquired no greater rights than he would have had in his own name. For exclusive monopoly in his published work the author must look to the copyright statutes, and where the work is dedicated to the public, the defendant was at liberty to publish copies of it with the nom de plume and all, as long as it did not hold out to the public something as having been written which was in fact not written by the plaintiff.

[86] *Haas* v. *Feist* (1916), 234 Fed. (D. C.) 105.

it would. In the *Haas* v. *Feist* case the violation was of a penal statute. In the supposititious case there is, however, only the violation of the civil law. The courts may, and we believe, will follow the rule enunciated by Judge Hand.

Section 146.—Subjects of copyright—In general.

Section four of the Act provides that the works for which copyright may be secured under the Act shall include all the writings of an author.

A literary work need not be of the highest class of literature in order to be copyrightable,[87] nor must it be altogether an original work.

It is the arrangement, combination and development of the theme which call for the exercise of skill and ingenuity on the part of the author that establishes his right to copyright therein.[88] Even if the material with which he works is hackneyed, but he makes a new arrangement of it, he is entitled to copyright the work. The

[87] *Atlas* v. *Street & Smith* (1913), 204 Fed. (C. C. A.) 398; App. Dism. 231 U. S. 348; 34 Sup. Ct. 323.

See also: *Henderson* v. *Tompkins* (1894), 60 Fed. (C. C.) 758.

[88] *Lover* v. *Davidson* (Eng.) (1856), 1 C. B. N. S. 182. Where one takes an old song which is in the public domain and embellishes it with an original arrangement and new accompaniments, the work acquires originality and some labor and skill, sufficient to warrant copyright.

Lawrence v. *Dana* (1869), 4 Cliff. 1, Fed. Cas. No. 8136 (C. C.). *Held* that where the author of a book took the material from sources common to all writers, if he arranged and combined the material in a new way and if he exercised skill and discretion in his independent work he was entitled to protect the work by copyright.

See Section 157 for detailed discussion.

test is not originality of theme, but originality of plan, arrangement, development, treatment and combination.[89]

Section 147.—Immoral and seditious works.

On broad principles of public policy copyright will not protect a work which is immoral or treasonable.[90] This was recently illustrated in a case wherein the proprietor of the copyright in a novel sought to restrain the exhibition of a motion picture. The court held that as the novel was immoral, copyright protection would be denied it, and no injunction would be granted.[91] And the same rule was held to apply where the love affairs of a notorious courtesan had been elaborated on.[92]

The principle is well stated in a leading American case:[93]

[89] *Hoffman* v. *Le Traunik* (1913), 209 Fed. (D. C.) 375. "To be entitled to be copyrighted the composition must be original, meritorious and free from illegality or immorality. 'And a work, in order to be copyrighted, must be original in the sense that the author has created it by his own skill, labor, and judgment, without directly copying or evasively imitating the work of another.' However 'a new and original plan, arrangement or combination of materials, will entitle the author to a copyright therein, whether the materials themselves be new or old.' "

See in this connection: *Baker* v. *Selden* (1879), 101 U. S. 99. See Section 157 for detailed discussion.

Henderson v. *Tompkins* (1894), 60 Fed. (C. C.) 758. See on the question as to amount of originality and literary quality necessary to have copyrightable work.

[90] *Hoffman* v. *Le Traunik* (1913), 209 Fed. (D. C.) 375.

[91] *Glyn* v. *Western Feature Film Co.* (Eng.) (1916), W. N. 5; 140 L. T. Jo. 176, on the novel "Three Weeks."

[92] *Stockdale* v. *Onwhyn* (Eng.) (1826), 5 B. and C. 173; 2 C. and P. 163.

[93] *Martinetti* v. *Maguire* (1861), Fed. Cas. No. 9173 (C. C.).

See also: *Dunlop* v. *United*

"From this it expressly appears that the constitution did not intend that Congress should pass laws to promote immorality or anything except science and the useful arts. . . . So a real dramatic composition if grossly indecent and calculated to corrupt the morals of the people, would not be entitled to a copyright. Such an exhibition neither 'promotes the progress of science or the useful arts' but on the contrary. The Constitution does not authorize the protection of such productions, and Congress cannot be presumed to have intended to have gone beyond their power to give them such protection."

This would seem to apply to motion pictures, quite irrespective of the question of censorship. One scene in a picture, whether immoral or seditious would suffice to destroy copyright therein. But if the objectionable scene or scenes are eliminated, the film may be copyrighted.[94]

Section 148.—Gags, stage business, contrivances, cartoons, advertisements.

It is not always an easy matter to determine what may be a proper subject of copyright. Generally speaking, stage business, gags, gestures, tricks of make-up, dance steps and tones of voice are not copyrightable.[95]

States (1896), 165 U. S. 501; 17 Sup. Ct. 375.

[94] *Broder* v. *Zeno Mauvais Co.* (1898), 88 Fed. (C. C.) 74.

[95] *Chappell* v. *Fields* (1914), 210 Fed. (C. C. A.) 864.

Savage v. *Hoffman* (1908), 159 Fed. (C. C.) 584. Plaintiff was producing an operetta entitled "The Merry Widow." Defendant produced a vaudeville sketch in which two people danced to the same music as in the operetta. *Held* no injunction.

"Obviously the complainant has no literary property in the manner in which Barbanell and Brian dance. They if anyone have the right to complain. The manner and method of every dancer and actor is individual, and utterly unlike the railroad scene which was held the subject of literary property in *Daly* v. *Palmer* (1868), 6 Blatchf. (D. C.) 256."

Barnes v. *Miner* (1903), 122 Fed. (C. C.) 480. Plaintiff and defendant gave impersonations on the stage interspersed with motion pictures showing them changing their costumes. Each had copyrighted the act as a whole. *Held* that there was no cause of action as there was nothing original in the act, and that such act was not a proper subject for copyright.

Bloom v. *Nixon* (1903), 125 Fed. (C. C.) 977. Following the English cases of *Tate* v. *Fullbrook* and *Bishop* v. *Viviana & Co.* The song was merely a vehicle to enable the singer to impersonate another, and the imitation was done in good faith. From the dicta of this decision it would appear that a *parody* would not infringe upon the copyright of the work parodied.

Another rule, however, would apply where the imitation or parody was merely a pretense for singing the song.

Keene v. *Clarke* (1867), 28 N. Y. Super. Ct. 38. It was held that interpolations technically known in the profession as "gags" were not entitled to protection if the original work was dedicated.

Tate v. *Fullbrook* (Eng.) (1908), 1 K. B. 821; *Karno* v. *Pathé Frères* (Eng.) (1908), 99 L. T. 114; 24 T. L. R. 588. Follows *Tate* v. *Fullbrook* and holds a vaudeville sketch made up entirely of stage-business and "gags" with no sustained dialogue is not the subject of protection under the English Copyright Act. Court refused to restrain a motion picture reproduction thereof.

Distinguishing mechanical arrangements from dramatic performances: *Harris* v. *Commonwealth* (1885), 81 Va. 240; *Jacko* v. *State* (1853), 22 Ala. 73; *Carte* v. *Duff* (1885), 23 Blatchf. 347; 25 Fed. (C. C.) 183.

Nor will a description of a dance, no matter how original or unique be protected,[96] and the same holds true with respect to mechanical contrivances.[97]

Cartoons, of course, may be copyrighted as such, but whether a series of cartoons, expressing a connected story, may be copyrighted as a "dramatic composition" is open to question, although there is authority to support the conclusion that they may be so copyrighted.[98]

[96] *Fuller* v. *Bemis* (1892), 50 Fed. (C. C.) 926.

[97] *Serrena* v. *Jefferson* (1888), 33 Fed. (C. C.) 347. "The plaintiffs' contention is founded solely upon the circumstance that in their play the river into which the fall takes place is mimicked by a tank filled with real water, instead of by an apparatus constructed of cloth, canvas or painted paste board. Such a mechanical contrivance, however, is not protected by a copyright of the play in which it is introduced. The decisions which extend the definition of 'dramatic compositions' so as to include situations and 'scenic' effects, do not cover the mere mechanical instrumentalities by which such effects or situations are produced." The court then distinguishes the instant case from *Daly* v. *Palmer*, 6 Blatchf. 264.

Freligh v. *Carroll* (1871), Fed. Cas. 5092*a* (C. C.). Where a mechanical contrivance was used in connection with a copyrighted play, the copyright did not protect the mechanical device.

See in this connection *Sherman* v. *Marinelli* (1916), 232 Fed. (D. C.) 730.

[98] *Empire City Am. Co.* v. *Wilton* (1903), 134 Fed. (C. C.) 132. ". . . I still think that the court cannot here decide upon demurrer that there is no dramatic right, so called, in a series of cartoons. *The Supreme Court has lately shown a tendency to widen, rather than to narrow, the scope of the copyright act. . . .*"

As to whether an exhibition of "living pictures" infringes upon a copyright in cartoons, see: Brad-

Photographs are copyrightable,[99] as well as theatrical posters.[100]

Editorials and special matter in a newspaper may be copyrighted, although there may be no general copy-

bury, *Agnew* v. *Day* (Eng.) (1916), 32 T. L. R. 349; where it was so held and an injunction and damages were awarded to plaintiff.

See in this connection: *Hene* v. *Samstag* (1912), 198 Fed. (D. C.) 359, where one McManus, a cartoonist, devised a character "Napoleon, the Newlywed's Baby," and contracted with his co-plaintiffs to give them a license to reproduce such character in the form of a doll. *Held*, that such agreement could not be exclusive, as he had never obtained a copyright on a doll, and defendants could not be enjoined from putting out any such doll.

[99] See Section five of the Copyright Act of 1909. See also: *Pagano* v. *Beseler* (1916), 234 Fed. (D. C.) 963.

As to who is entitled to copyright of a photograph see: Ellis v. *Ogden* (Eng.) (1884), 11 T. L. R. 50. Where the sitter had not paid for her photograph, the copyright therein vested in the photographer. But where such photographs were paid for, copyright vested in the sitter. See, in support of the latter proposition, *Ellis* v. *Marshall* (Eng.) (1895), 11 T. L. R. 522.

See also: *Gross* v. *Seligman* (1914), 212 Fed. (C. C. A.) 930. Plaintiff owned the copyright of a photograph of a woman. Defendant caused the same model to pose for a photograph. The light, shade, background and pose were practically identical. Defendant was held to infringe.

See in this connection: *Bracken* v. *Rosenthal* (1907), 151 Fed. (C. C.) 136. It is an infringement to make a photograph of a copyrighted piece of sculpture. "This definition is fully sustained by the authorities . . . so that it seems clear that the word 'copy' may be used to designate a picture of a piece of statuary without in any way straining the well-established use of the word."

[100] *Bleistein* v. *Donaldson* (1902), 188 U. S. 239; 23 Sup. Ct. 298; rev. 104 Fed. 993.

right in the same paper.[101] But government publications cannot be protected.[102]

Nor may a motion picture scenario be copyrighted as a "dramatic composition" although it may be copyrighted as a "book." The distinction is artificial and incorrect in law, for a scenario is as much a dramatic composition as the lines of the play in the famous railroad scene in *Daly* v. *Webster*.[103]

There seems to be a conflict of authority among the Circuit Courts as to whether advertisements and catalogues may be the subject of copyright. Some incline

[101] *Tribune Co. of Chicago* v. *Ass'td Press* (1900), 116 Fed. (C. C.) 126. "However the rule may be in reference to original matter published in such form, I am of opinion that there can be no general copyright of a newspaper composed in large part of matter not entitled to protection."

"Under the amendment (authorizing copyright in America on foreign publications) whatever rights may be vested either in the *Times* or the *Tribune* through contract with it, to copyright any editorials or special matter, I am satisfied that it can be exercised only for matter distinctly set apart for the purpose and so distinguished in the publication, and that the publication in this country must be substantially identical with that in the foreign country, to bring it within the intent of the statute."

[102] *Du Puy* v. *Post Telegram Co.* (1914), 210 Fed. (C. C. A.) 883.

[103] *Daly* v. *Webster* (1892), 56 Fed. (C. C. A.) 483. "In plays of this class the series of events is the only composition of any importance. The dialogue is unimportant, and as a work of art trivial. The effort of the composer is directed to arranging for the stage a series of events so realistically presented, and so worked out by the display of feeling or earnestness on the part of the actors, as to produce a corresponding emotion in the audience. . . ."

For detailed discussion, see Section 4.

to the opinion that they are not "writings" within the intent of the framers of the Constitution, and therefore not copyrightable,[104] but others hold that there is enough of originality and skill displayed in getting up such advertisements as to warrant holding them copyrightable.[105]

Section 149.—Burlesques, parodies, inferior copies.

A genuine criticism, burlesque or parody of a copyrighted work is not an infringement.

"A copyrighted work is subject to fair criticism, serious

[104] *Mott Iron Works* v. *Clow* (1897), 82 Fed. (C. C. A.) 316. "So far as the decisions of the Supreme Court have gone, we think they hold to the proposition that mere advertisements, whether by letter press or by pictures, are not within the protection of the copyright laws" referring to pictorial illustrations of artistic plumbing fixtures in a catalogue. See also: *Lamb* v. *Grand Rapids Furniture* (1889), 39 Fed. (C. C.) 474, involving similar illustrations of furniture.

Stone v. *Dugan* (1915), 220 Fed. (C. C. A.) 837; aff'g 210 Fed. 399. A pamphlet made up of advertisements which are extravagant, misleading and untrue, is not copyrightable.

[105] *White* v. *Shapiro* (1915), 227 Fed. (D. C.) 957. *Held* a catalogue of brass goods, which consisted principally of trimmings for electric light fixtures copyrightable.

Court cites in support of its position: *Da Prato Statuary Co.* v. *Giuliani Statuary Co.* (1911), 189 Fed. (C. C.) 90; *Nat'l. Cloak & Suit Co.* v. *Kaufman* (1911), 189 Fed. (C. C.) 215; *Bleistein* v. *Donaldson Lithographing Co.* (1902), 188 U. S. 239; 23 Sup. Ct. 298.

Meccano v. *Wagner* (1916), 234 Fed. (D. C.) 912. A manual explaining the workings of mechanical toys held copyrightable.

See also: *De Jong* v. *Brueker* (1911), 182 Fed. (C. C.) 150; aff'd 191 Fed. 35.

But see in this connection *Nat'l Cloak & Suit Co.* v. *Standard Mail Order Co.* (1911), 191 Fed. (C. C.) 528.

or humorous. So far as is necessary to that end quotations may be made from it, and it may be described by words, representations, pictures or suggestions. It is not always easy to say where the line should be drawn between the use which for such purposes is permitted and that which is forbidden.

One test which when applicable would seem to be ordinarily decisive, is whether or not so much has been reproduced as will materially reduce the demand for the original. If it has, the rights of the owner of the copyright have been injuriously affected.

A word of explanation will here be necessary. The reduction in demand, to be a ground of complaint must result from the partial satisfaction of that demand by the alleged infringing production. A criticism of the original work which lessened its money value by showing that it was not worth seeing or hearing, could not give any right of action for infringement of Copyright." [106]

Nor will the "imitation" of a work ordinarily be considered an infringement.[107]

But where the so-called imitation or impersonation was merely a vehicle for performing the whole of a copyrighted work, defendant's claim that she was simply

[106] *Hill* v. *Whalen* (1914), 220 Fed. (D. C.) 359.

See also: *Glyn* v. *Western Feature Film Co.* (1916) (Eng.), W. N. 5; 140 L. T. Jr. 176; Times, December 22d, 32 T. L. R. 235. It was held that a genuine burlesque in a film of a serious work or novel was not an infringement of the copyright if what had been taken had been subjected to such mental labor and such a revision and alteration as to produce an original result.

[107] *Green* v. *Minzensheimer* (1909), 177 Fed. (C. C.) 286.

mimicking the complainant's song was held untenable.[108]

A vulgar and grossly inferior copy of a work will nevertheless amount to an infringement thereof.[109]

Section 150.—Copyrighting revised edition of work.

Under Section six of the Act, compilations, abridgments, adaptations, arrangements, dramatizations, translations or other versions of works in the public domain, or of copyrighted works, when produced with the consent of the proprietor of the copyright in such works, or works republished with new matter, are regarded as new works, subject to copyright under the provisions of the Act; but the section further provides that the publication of any such new works shall not affect the force or validity of any subsisting copyright upon the matter employed or any part thereof, or be construed to imply an exclusive right to such use of the original works, or to secure or extend copyright in such original works.

Thus a later edition of a copyrighted work may be protected by copyright where substantial new matter has been added,[110] and a later edition of a work in the

[108] *Green* v. *Luby* (1909), 177 Fed. (C. C.) 287.

[109] *Hanfstaengl* v. *Smith* (Eng.) (1905), L. R. 1 Ch. 519; 74 L. J. Ch. 304; 92 L. T. 351; 21 T. L. R. 291.

[110] *West Pub. Co.* v. *Edward Thompson Co.* (1910), 176 Fed. (C. C. A.) 833; modifying 169 Fed. 833. It was held that under the copyright statutes prior to the 1909 Act as well as under that Act a work which had been previously copyrighted, might be copyrighted again as a new work where new matter had been added to the previous edition.

public domain, when copyrighted, protects that part of the work which is new and original.[111]

Where it is desirable to elaborate a one or two reel picture previously copyrighted, into a feature, it is important that care be taken that the new work be copyrighted, otherwise not only will the new work be dedicated but the old work as well.

Section 151.—Works in public domain.

Section seven of the Act provides that no copyright shall subsist in the original text of any work which is in the public domain, or in any work which was published in this country or any foreign country prior to the going into effect of the present copyright act, and which has not been already copyrighted in the United States.

Although portions of a work may be in the public domain or non-copyrightable matter, the work, as a whole, may be the subject of copyright.[112]

Section 152.—Component parts.

A revolutionary section, and one which will greatly

[111] *Kipling* v. *Putnam* (1903), 120 Fed. (C. C. A.) 631.

See also: *Bentley* v. *Tibbals* (1915), 223 Fed. (C. C. A.) 247. Where the complainant after copyrighting a work included the entire copyrighted work in a larger edition, printed the larger edition in England with a copyright notice and sold copies of such edition in the United States it was held that the copyrighted work was dedicated as the public could not know which part of the larger edition was protected by copyright and which was not.

[112] *Lawrence* v. *Bushnell* (India), 35 Ind. L. R. Calc. 463; *Kipling* v. *Putnam* (1903), 120 Fed. (C. C. A.) 631.

enhance the value of copyright, especially with respect to dramatic works and motion pictures, is Section three, which provides in effect that by copyrighting the work all the component parts of it are protected.[113] That section has already shown its utility in several decisions, one in the copyrighting of a catalogue; [114] and in the right to use the words of a copyrighted song in conjunction with mechanical contrivances.[115]

The protection afforded by this section of the Act has reference to the separate chapters, subdivisions, acts, etc., of a work and not to the subdivision of rights, licenses or privileges.[116]

The section also provides that in the case of composite works or periodicals the copyright thereon shall give to

[113] *Mail & Express* v. *Life Pub. Co.* (1912), 192 Fed. (C. C. A.) 899.

[114] *Da Prato* v. *Giuliani* (1911), 189 Fed. (C. C.) 90. "The complainant having copyrighted its entire catalogue was entitled to the protection of the copyright law as to each cut contained therein."

[115] *Witmark* v. *Standard Music Roll* (1914), 213 Fed. (D. C.) 532; aff'd 221 Fed. 376. The copyright of a work as a musical composition prior to 1909 protected the music but not the words. Under the 1909 act, however, copyright of a musical composition was held to protect all the copyrightable component parts thereof.

And see: *Mills* v. *Standard Music Roll Co.* (1915), 223 Fed. (D. C.) 849, aff'd by United States Circuit Court of Appeals—Third Circuit at March, 1917 term. See opinion of the Circuit Court of Appeals, holding that as to musical compositions copyrighted subsequent to 1909 the words, being a component part of the work, were entitled to full protection, even though not separately copyrighted.

[116] *New Fiction Publishing Co.* v. *Star Co.* (1915), 220 Fed. (D. C.) 994.

the proprietor all the rights in respect thereto which he would have received if each part were separately copyrighted.[117]

Section 153.—Term of copyright.

Copyright secured under the Act endures for twenty-eight years from the date of first publication, under Section twenty-three.

A difficulty presents itself when we attempt to fix the duration of copyright secured in unpublished works pursuant to Section eleven. Congress has apparently overlooked the necessity for a provision in that section limiting or defining the period for which copyright is to run.

The Register of Copyrights issues a certificate upon the making of the deposit called for in that section, which provides that copyright in the work shall endure for twenty-eight years from the date of the certificate.

When the question comes before the courts the Register of Copyrights will probably be sustained in his action. Since the constitution provides that the term of copyright must be limited, the courts will no doubt fix the time of protection of the unpublished work for the same period as that granted to the published work.

They will also hold, we believe, that where the unpublished work is thereafter reproduced in copies for sale, the original term will run, not from the date of first publication, but from the date of the deposit of the copy

[117] *Ford* v. *Blaney* (1906), 148 Fed. (C. C.) 642; *Dam* v. *Kirk La Shelle* (1910), 175 Fed. (C. C. A.) 902; *Mifflin* v. *White* (1902), 190 U. S. 260; 23 Sup. Ct. 769; *Holmes* v. *Hurst* (1899), 174 U. S. 82; 19 Sup. Ct. 606.

called for in Section eleven and the issuance of the certificate for such unpublished work by the Register of Copyrights.

If this were not so and one who had obtained copyright in a play as an unpublished work, refrained from publication for a period of twenty-seven years and then first published, the original term would be extended for twenty-eight years and in addition there would be the right of renewal for an additional twenty-eight years.

Section 154.—Renewal of copyright.

The monopoly of copyright is extended by Section twenty-four of the Act for an additional period of twenty-eight years, but only to the author, if still living, or the widow, widower, or children of the author, if the author be not living, or if such author, widow, widower or children be not living, then by the author's executors, or in the absence of a will, to his next of kin, except that as provided in Section twenty-three of the Act in the case of a posthumous work, a composite work upon which the copyright was originally secured by the proprietor thereof, or of any work copyrighted by a corporate body (otherwise than as assignee or licensee of the individual author) or by an employer for whom such work is made for hire, the proprietor of such copyright shall be entitled to a renewal and extension of such copyright for the twenty-eight year period.

The application for renewal must in any event be made to the copyright office and duly registered therein within one year prior to the expiration of the original term of the copyright.

The right of renewal can only be exercised by those mentioned in the Statute.[118]

An assignment of the renewal copyright executed more than one year before the expiration of the original copyright is insufficient to give the assignee the right to apply for the renewal of the copyright in his own name.

The application for the renewal cannot be made except during the year preceding the expiration of the original copyright. During that year the right of renewal accrues to the author, if he is still living, or to his widow or children, if the author is not then living.

During that year the author can assign his right to apply for a renewal and under such an assignment, made during that year, the assignee has a right to apply for the renewal.

The Register of Copyrights will not accept a renewal application unless it is signed by the author or by the

[118] *White-Smith* v. *Goff* (1911), 187 Fed. (C. C. A.) 247; aff'g 180 Fed. 256. The right of renewal can only be exercised by those mentioned in the statute. "It is to be noted that in each statute the grant of the original copyright is to the author or proprietor, while as to the provision for an extension the word 'proprietor' is studiously stricken out. . . ."

See also: *Pierpont* v. *Fowle* (1846), Fed. Cas. 11,152. When an author was employed to compile a book and in consideration of a specified sum sold the copyright to the publisher and the author's name was published on the title page as such author, the author alone was entitled to the renewal.

As to the right of an author who has assigned the copyright to enjoin his assignee, upon securing a renewal thereof see: Paige v. *Banks* (1870), 7 Blatch. 152.

assignee in case the assignment was made during the last year of the original term.

If the author has assigned the renewal right more than a year before the expiration of the original term, and during the last year of the term refuses to sign an application, he could be compelled in an equity action to sign such application. The difficulty of relying on such an action, however, lies in the fact that the action could not be commenced until after the commencement of the last year of the original term, and that it might not be brought to judgment until after the expiration of that year. In that event no application would be made during the last year of the original term and the right of renewal would be entirely lost.

In case the assignment was made more than a year before the expiration of the original term, and the author dies thereafter, the assignment will become worthless, and the renewal copyright will belong absolutely to the persons designated in the statute. If, however, the assignment was made during the last year of the original term, application for the renewal copyright would vest such renewal right in the assignee, and the rights so vested would not be lost in case the author dies after the assignee has acquired the renewal copyright.

After securing the renewal of the copyright, the copyright notice should give the year when the renewal copyright commences and the name of the author in whose name the renewal right was obtained. Where the renewal right has been assigned and the assignment recorded as provided by the Act then the assignee may substitute his name in the notice in place of that of the author.

Section 155.—Assignment of copyright.

Copyright is not a divisible right but the rights under it may be cut up, and a part of the right assigned to one and part of the right retained by the proprietor or assigned to another party. There is no restriction in equity upon the power of the copyright proprietor to assign all or any portion of his right. An assignment of the whole or of an undivided part of the copyright to each of two or more persons makes the holders thereof joint owners.[119]

No formal assignment of the *right* to copyright is necessary; mere consent is sufficient to constitute one the proprietor.[120]

[119] *Black* v. *Allen* (1890), 42 Fed. (C. C.) 618; (1893), 56 Fed. (C. C.) 764. There is no restriction in equity upon the power of a copyright proprietor to assign or transfer an exclusive right to use a copyrighted work. In such case the legal title remains in the proprietor; and a beneficial interest, to the extent which is agreed upon vests in the other party who has acquired an equitable right in the copyright and who may be properly styled an "assignee of an equitable interest."

[120] *Carte* v. *Evans* (1886), 27 Fed. (C. C.) 861; *Schumacher* v. *Schwenke* (1885), 25 Fed. (C. C.) 466; *Little* v. *Gould* (1852), Fed. Cas. 8395 (C. C.); *Laurence* v. *Dana* (1869), Fed. Cas. 8,136 (C. C.); *Sweet* v. *Benning* (1855), 1 K. & J. 169; aff'd 6 De G. M. & G. 223; *Gill* v. *United States* (1896), 160 U. S. 426; 16 Sup. Ct. 322; *Callaghan* v. *Meyers* (1888), 128 U. S. 617; 9 Sup. Ct. 177; *Black* v. *Allen* (1890), 42 Fed. (C. C.) 618; *White-Smith* v. *Apollo* (1905), 139 Fed. (C. C.) 427; aff'd 209 U. S. 17; 28 Sup. Ct. 319; *Marsh* v. *Conquest* (Eng.) (1864), 17 C. B. N. S. 418; 33 L. J. P. C. 319; 10 Jur. N. S. 989; 10 L. T. 717; 12 W. R. 309.

Gould v. *Banks* (1832), 8 Wend. (N. Y.) 562. An assignment or relinquishment in the copyright of a book, or of an interest in such copyright, is void if not in writing, although

To, however, assign a copyright which has already been secured, it is necessary that the assignment shall be in writing under Section forty-two of the Act which expressly provides that copyright secured under the present or previous Acts "may be assigned, granted, or mortgaged by *an instrument in writing*" signed by the proprietor of the copyright, or may be bequeathed by will.

Where the assignment is executed in a foreign country, under section forty-three it must be acknowledged by the assignor before a consular office or secretary of legation of the United States authorized by law to administer oaths or perform notarial acts.

Section forty-four directs that every assignment of copyright shall be recorded in the copyright office within three calendar months after its execution in the United States or within six calendar months after its execution without the limits of the United States, in default of which such assignment shall be void as against any subsequent purchaser or mortgagee for a valuable consideration, without notice, whose assignment has been duly recorded.

Where a copyright is bequeathed, the executor in whom the copyright is vested must legally qualify before he may execute a valid assignment thereof.[121]

The assignment need not be drawn in any special form or arrangement. Any writing which evidences an inten-

an *agreement* to assign or relinquish may be by parol.

[121] *Mackay* v. *Mackay* (Scotch) (1912), 2 Scots Law Times, 445. Trustees appointed under a will, in whom the copyrights belonging to the testator were bequeathed, purported to assign such copyrights before having legally qualified as such trustees. *Held* that assignment was invalid.

tion to grant or convey the copyright will be deemed sufficient.[122] And upon the sale of a business, a general statement that all copyrights belonging to such business are included, suffices to pass such copyrights.[123]

An assignment of all the dramatization rights carries with it the rights to make both a dramatic and motion picture version,[124] but since the copyright in the play and in the film may be separately assigned, assignments of the copyright therein must be recorded to avail the assignee; and failure to record gives a bona fide purchaser of all or some of the rights a clear title.[125]

[122] *Kyle* v. *Jefferys* (Eng.) (1859), 3 Macq. 611. A receipt in payment of the copyright has been held to constitute a valid assignment.

Robinson v. *Illustrated London News* (Eng.) (1907), Times, Apr. 26. Discusses the sufficiency of an instrument which operated to assign the entire copyright in a painting.

See also: *Landeker* v. *Wolff* (Eng.) (1907), 52 Sol. J. 45; *Cumberland* v. *Copeland* (Eng.) (1862), 1 H. and C. 194; 31 L. J. Ex. 353; 9 Jur. (N. S.) 253; 7 L. T. 334; *Leyland* v. *Stewart* (Eng.) (1876), 4 Ch. D. 419; 46 L. J. Ch. 103; 25 W. R. 225.

See also: *Hardacre* v. *Armstrong* (Eng.) (1904), Times, Dec. 20; 21 T. L. R. 189; (1905), Times, Jan. 12–13–17. The copyright may be assigned by a separate writing, and if doubt exist as to which one of several copyrights the assignment refers, it becomes a question for the jury.

[123] *Banks Law Pub. Co.* v. *Lawyers Co-operative* (1909), 169 Fed. (C. C. A.) 386.

[124] See Section 1.

[125] *Brady* v. *Reliance* (1916), 229 Fed. (C. C. A.) 137. Complainant delivered to Munsey Company a manuscript and received therefor a specified sum. The receipt signed by complainant contained the following "Author reserves right of book publication and dramatic rights, if any, after a trial publication is completed." The Munsey Company duly copyrighted the story and assigned the motion picture rights to the defendant Mutual Com-

Failure to record the assignment is not available as a defense by an infringer. The purpose of the statute which requires recording is to protect subsequent purchasers and mortgagees of the copyright, not infringers, and the assignee always has a cause of action against the infringer irrespective of the record.[126]

An action brought to compel an assignment or reassignment of a copyright is not an action under the copyright law, and may be brought in a State court.[127]

pany which employed the defendant Reliance Company to manufacture the picture.

The complainant demanded that the Munsey Company be required to reassign to him all rights in and to the copyright except the right of serial publication and that the other defendants be enjoined from selling or leasing the motion picture.

Held, assuming that complainant could have required the Munsey Company, after serial publication to reassign to him all the other rights, that such assignment would have been void against subsequent purchasers and mortgagees without notice, for a valuable consideration, unless recorded in the office of the Librarian of Congress within sixty days after its execution. "Such persons can surely not be worse off when no actual assignment whatever has been made. Moreover, without reference to any statute, when one clothes another with apparent ownership, though actually as trustee, he cannot defeat the title of those who act in good faith, for a valuable consideration, and without notice deal with the trustee."

See also: *Photo-Drama Motion Picture* v. *Social Uplift* (1915), 220 Fed. (C. C. A.) 448, aff'g 213 Fed. 374.

[126] *New Fiction* v. *Star* (1915), 220 Fed. (D. C.) 994.

[127] *Hoyt* v. *Bates* (1897), 81 Fed. (C. C.) 641.

See also: *Albright* v. *Teas* (1882), 106 U. S. 613; 1 Sup. Ct. 550, a patent case.

An agreement to assign a copyright can be specifically enforced.[128]

The assignee is permitted by Section forty-six of the Act when the assignment has been recorded to substitute his name for that of the assignor in the statutory notice of copyright.

Copyright is distinct from the property in the material object copyrighted. The Act provides in Section forty-one that the sale or conveyance by gift or otherwise of the material object shall not of itself constitute a transfer of the copyright, and in like manner, that the assignment of the copyright shall not constitute a transfer to the material object.[129]

As was said in the leading case of *Stevens* v. *Cady:* [130]

[128] *Thombleson* v. *Black* (Eng.) (1837), 1 Jur. 198.

[129] *Harper* v. *Donohue* (1905), 144 Fed. (C. C.) 491; *Patterson* v. *Ogilvie Pub. Co.* (1902), 119 Fed. (C. C.) 451; *Wilder* v. *Kent* (1883), 15 Fed. (C. C.) 217; *Parton* v. *Prang* (1872), 3 Cliff. (C. C.) 537; *Marshall* v. *Bull* (Eng.) (1901), 85 L. T. 77; *Cooper* v. *Stephens* (Eng.) (1895), 1 Ch. Div. 567.

[130] *Stevens* v. *Cady* (1852), 14 How. 528. "No doubt the property may be reached by a creditor's bill and be applied to the payment of the debts of the author. . . . But in case of such remedy, we suppose, it would be necessary for the court to compel a transfer to the purchaser in conformity with the requirements of the copyright act, in order to vest him with a complete title to the property."

See also: *Stevens* v. *Gladding* (1854), 17 How. 447. "So if he has not acquired the right to print the map, he cannot use his plate for that purpose, because he has not made himself the owner of something as necessary to printing as paper and ink, and as clearly a distinct species of property as either of these articles. He may make any other use of the plate of which it is susceptible. He may keep it

"The copyright is an exclusive right to the multiplication of the copies for the benefit of the author or his assigns disconnected from the plate or any other physical existence. It is an incorporeal right to print and publish the map or as said by Lord Mansfield in *Millar* v. *Taylor*, 4 Burr, 2396, 'a property in notion, and has no corporeal tangible substance.'"

It was held in that case that a sale of plates on an execution against the owner of the copyright did not pass the right to reproduce copies therefrom.

Applying that rule to motion pictures, a sale of a positive film, without the assignment of the copyright therein, will not vest in the purchaser the right to make prints therefrom.[131]

Assignment of the copyright has become one of the methods by which certain of the rights are secured to the author. An author wishes to publish his story in a magazine, but he does not desire to lose his dramatization rights. He assigns his right to copyright to the proprietor of the magazine. As the title now vests in the latter, the story

until the expiration of the limited time, during which the exclusive right exists, and then use it to print maps. . . ."

[131] *Universal Film Mfg. Co.* v. *Copperman* (1914), 218 Fed. (C. C. A.) 577. When positive prints of a film are sold, but the copyright therein is retained by the seller, the purchaser secures merely the right to perform the film; he does not secure the right to reproduce the film in copies.

"When it sold a positive film, which was the only means of performing the play, it conferred the performing right on the purchaser and his assigns. No one, by virtue of that sale, would acquire the right to re-enact the play and take a negative of it, or make, if that could be done, a new negative from the positive film."

is properly copyrighted by the copyrighting of the entire magazine, for under Section three of the Act the copyright upon composite works or periodicals gives to the proprietor thereof all the rights in respect thereto which he would have if each part were individually copyrighted. The proprietor of the magazine then re-assigns all but the publishing rights to the author, who becomes in this way re-possessed of his performing rights.

This roundabout way is necessary, for unless the proprietor of the magazine owns the copyright, beneficially or as trustee, publication of the story in the magazine operates as a dedication, even though the magazine as a whole is copyrighted.[132]

Where the author, in his unpublished and uncopyrighted play, assigns the publishing rights to another and reserves the performing rights to himself, although he loses his common-law rights as soon as the play is published, the publisher nevertheless holds as a trustee for the author the new dramatization rights which are created under

[132] *Mifflin* v. *White* (1903), 190 U. S. 260, 23 Sup. Ct. 769. While the author gave his publishers the right to print, publish and sell his work in a magazine but did not give them the right to obtain copyright either in their name or his, the publication of such work serially in the magazine destroyed the copyright in it.

See also: *Ford* v. *Blaney* (1906), 148 Fed. (C. C.) 642; *Dam* v. *Kirk La Shelle* (1910), 175 Fed. (C. C. A.) 902; *Holmes* v. *Hurst* (1899), 174 U. S. 82, 19 Sup. Ct. 606.

See also: *Press Pub. Co.* v. *Monroe* (1896), 73 Fed. (C. C. A.) 196. Plaintiff sold certain rights to a poem which she had composed. Before the publication of the poem defendant without her consent published the work in its newspaper. *Held* that defendant infringed plaintiff's reserved rights in the manuscript.

the copyright, and may be compelled to assign the same to the author.[133]

It would seem that there is an implied warranty of title where a copyright is assigned.[134]

Section 156.—Difference between assignment and license.

There is a great difference between an assignment of the copyright and a license, arising especially in the question of suit.[135] But for all purposes an exclusive license of a particular right under the copyright for the entire

[133] *Fitch* v. *Young* (1915), 230 Fed. (D. C.) 743.

See also: *Ford* v. *Blaney* (1906), 148 Fed. (C. C.) 842.

[134] *Sims* v. *Marryat* (Eng.) (1851), 17 Q. B. 281.

[135] *As to what constitutes an assignment of the copyright or the mere giving of a license see: Landeker* v. *Wolff* (Eng.) (1907), 52 Sol. J. 45; *Tree* v. *Bowkett* (Eng.) (1896), 74 L. T. 77; *Lucas* v. *Cooke* (Eng.) (1880), 13 Ch. D. 872; *Lacy* v. *Toole* (Eng.) (1867), 15 L. T. 512.

For a careful discussion of the differences in the rights granted see: Heap v. *Hartley* (Eng.) (1889), 42 Ch. D. 461.

Re The Liedertafel Series (Eng.) (1907), L. R. 1 Ch. 651; 96 L. T. 766, 76 L. J. Ch. 542; 23 T. L. R. 461. Giving one "the sole and exclusive right of printing and publishing the series" did not operate as an assignment of the copyright.

In re Clinical Obstetrics (Eng.) (1908), Ch. D. Dec. 4. "The whole and exclusive right in all countries to print and publish the work" was construed to confer an exclusive license and not an assignment of the copyright.

Black v. *Imperial Book Co.* (Can.) (1904), 5 Ont. L. R. 184. An agreement giving the exclusive right to publish and vend a work for a period less than the unexpired term of the copyright is a license and not a partial assignment of the copyright.

term of such copyright operates in law as an assignment of that right.[136]

Instruments purporting to convey certain grants or licenses, especially dramatizations and motion picture rights, are constantly coming up for construction.[137]

Dam v. *Kirk LaShelle* contains a valuable discussion on the reservation of rights and the methods of construing such grants.[138]

[136] *Fitch* v. *Young* (1916), 230 Fed. (D. C.) 743. "The analogy of patents is apt in which the form of an assignment does not count, and in which even a license for the term of the patent to use, make and vend will, if exclusive, operate as an assignment."

See in this connection: *Edwards* v. *Cotton* (Eng.) (1902), 19 T. L. R. 34. Plaintiffs sought injunction to restrain defendant from singing in public a certain song which they had composed and which was taken from an operetta composed by them. Defendant offered to show that one of the plaintiffs had sent her a pencil copy of the song with the words, "Herewith the MS of your song 'Men.'" The court held that this was not a permanent and irrevocable license to sing the song, and granted injunction.

[137] See Section 1 for a detailed discussion of the decisions.

[138] *Dam* v. *Kirk La Shelle* (1908), 166 Fed. (D. C.) 589; aff'd 175 Fed. (C. C. A.) 902.

CHAPTER XIII

COPYRIGHT (CONTINUED)

Infringement

SEC. 157. Tests—What is protected.
158. Primary test.
159. Common sources.
160. Substantial similarity by coincidence.
161. Who may maintain action—Misjoinder of parties—Joinder of causes of action.
162. Where action may be brought.
163. Who is liable—Intent.
164. What must be alleged and proved.
165. Bill of particulars.

It is this branch of the Copyright Law with which most of the litigation concerns itself. Piracy is a broad term, and no statute nor court may with any degree of definitiveness say that this or that degree of similarity is sufficient to constitute piracy. Just as there are infinite works which will be entitled to copyright, so there may be an infinite variety of arrangements of other works which may or may not infringe upon the originals; and to guide them in determining whether or not piracy exists, the courts have laid down certain rules and tests which time has shown to be of great value.

Section 157.—Tests—What is protected.

We must keep in mind the all important rule that

"There is no inherent property right in ideas, sentiments or creations of the imagination expressed by an author, apart either from the manuscript in which they are contained or the concrete form which he has given them, and the language in which he has clothed them." [1]

It is not the intellectual conception, or the thought or the idea which is copyrighted, but the writings of the author, the form of expression and the arrangement of the words.[2]

"The right thus secured by the copyright act is not a right to the use of certain words, because they are the common property of the human race, and are as little susceptible of private appropriation as air or sunlight; nor is it the right to ideas alone, since in the absence of means of communicating them they are of value to no one but the

[1] *Maxwell* v. *Goodwin* (1899), 93 Fed. (C. C.) 665. The court quoting from *Stowe* v. *Thomas* (1853), Fed. Cas. No. 13,514 (C. C.).

See also: *Jeffrys* v. *Boosey* (Eng.) (1854), 4 H. C. L. 867, and *Reade* v. *Conquest* (Eng.) (1862), 11 C. B. (N. S.) 479; MacGillivray on Copyright, and Copinger on Copyright, 5th ed., for the earlier English cases formulating this rule.

See generally for discussion of infringement of dramatic compositions: *Schlotz* v. *Amasis* (Eng.) (1909), Times, May 19.

[2] *Holmes* v. *Hurst* (1899), 174 U. S. 86; 19 Sup. Ct. 606; *White-Smith* v. *Apollo* (1907), 209 U. S. 17, 28 Sup. Ct. 319; *Stowe* v. *Thomas* (1853), 2 Wall. Jr. (C. C.) 547, 23 Fed. Cas. 201; *Baker* v. *Selden* (1879), 101 U. S. 99; *Johnson* v. *Donaldson* (1880), 3 Fed. (C. C.) 22; *Perris* v. *Hexamer* (1878), 99 U. S. 674, 676; *Bobbs-Merrill Co.* v. *Strauss* (1908), 210 U. S. 339, 347; 28 Sup. Ct. 722.

Cartwright v. *Wharton* (Can.) (1912), 25 Ont. L. R. 357. Copyright extends only to the expression, development and sequence of the work, not to the ideas themselves.

author. But the right is to that arrangement of words which the author has selected to express his ideas." [3]

The purpose of affording protection to authors is "to promote the progress of science and useful arts." [4] If an author could secure a monopoly of the ideas and intellectual conceptions contained in his writings, the protection given to authors would impede rather than advance the arts as each author by his appropriation would narrow the field of thought to which authors go for their material.[5]

In the words of Lord Mansfield:

"We must take care to guard against two extremes equally prejudicial—the one, that men of ability, who have employed their time for the service of the community may not be deprived of their just merits and the reward of their ingenuity and labor; the other, that the world may not be deprived of improvements, nor the progress of the arts be retarded. The act that secures copyright to authors guards against the piracy of the words and sentiments, but it does not prohibit writing on the same subject." [6]

Keeping this rule of law constantly before us, we will readily understand the primary test that is applied to determine infringement or piracy of a work.

Section 158.—Primary test.

In the leading English case of *Chatterton* v. *Cave*,[7] cited

[3] *Holmes* v. *Hurst* (1899), 174 U. S. 82; 19 Sup. Ct. 606.

[4] Constitution of the United States, Article one, Section eight.

[5] *Holmes* v. *Hurst* (1899), 174 U. S. 86; 19 Sup. Ct. 606.

[6] *Sayre* v. *Moore* (Eng.), 1 East, 361.

[7] *Chatterton* v. *Cave* (Eng.) (1878), 3 App. Cas. 483; 47 L. J. Q. B. 545; 38 L. T. 397; 26 W. R. 498. For an earlier leading Eng-

time and again with approval in American cases, the rule of piracy was expounded that in order to maintain an action for infringement a "substantial and material part" of the work must be taken.

That rule is now accepted as the primary test of infringement, and was laid down in the early American case of *Emerson* v. *Davies*,[8] where Judge Story, speaking of the infringement of one book by another, said:

"It is not sufficient to show that it may have been suggested by Emerson's, or that some parts and pages of it have resemblances in method and details and illustrations to Emerson's. It must be further shown that the resemblances in those parts and pages are so close, so full, so striking, as fairly to lead to the conclusion that the one is a substantial copy of the other or mainly borrowed from it."

This rule has been reiterated, clothed in different language, in the more important cases of infringement which have come before the American courts.

Judge Blatchford lays it down in *Daly* v. *Palmer*.[9] In that case complainant represented in his play a railroad scene in which the hero was tied to a railroad track to be killed by an oncoming train. Shortly before the arrival

lish case, see *Planche* v. *Braham* (1837), 4 Bing. N. C. 17.

In *Trengrouse* v. "*Sol*" *Syndicate* (Eng.) (1901), Times, Sept. 26, the taking of a single page of a large book was held sufficient to entitle plaintiff to an injunction.

[8] *Emerson* v. *Davies* (1845), 3 Story, 768.

[9] *Daly* v. *Palmer* (1868), 6 Blatch. 256.

See also: *Chappell* v. *Fields* (1914), 210 Fed. (C. C. A.) 864, and *Ricordi* v. *Mason* (1911), 201 Fed. (C. C.) 182; aff'd 210 Fed. 277.

of the train, the hero was released by a woman, and immediately thereafter the train was seen rushing by. This was the climax of the play.

The defendant reproduced a similar scene in his play, the development of the action and the dénouement being practically identical in both scenes.

The court said:

"All that is substantial and material in the plaintiff's railroad scene has been used by Boucicault in the same order and sequence of events, and in a manner to convey the same sensations and impressions to those who see it represented, as in the plaintiff's play. Boucicault has indeed adapted the plaintiff's series of events to the story of his play, and in doing so has evinced skill and art; but the same use is made in both plays of the same series of events to excite by representation the same emotions in the same sequence. . . . As in the case of a musical composition, the air is the invention of the author, and a piracy is committed if that in which the whole meritorious part of the invention consists is incorporated in another work without any material alteration in sequence of bars; so in the case of a dramatic composition designed or suited for representation the series of events directed in writing by the author in any particular scene is his invention, and a piracy is committed if that in which the whole merit of the scene consists is incorporated in another work without any material alteration in the constituent parts of the series of events or in the sequence of the events in the series."

When in another action [10] the question of the infringe-

[10] *Brady* v. *Daly* (1899), 175 U. S. 148, 20 Sup. Ct. 62. See

ment of the same scene reached the Supreme Court, that tribunal restated the rule as follows:

"When anyone, without the owner's permission publicly performs substantially that whole railroad scene, he substantially performs a dramatic composition which is covered by the owner's copyright."

In *Fischel* v. *Lueckel*,[11] involving the infringement of the copyright of a photogravure, the court said:

"The appropriation of part of a work is no less an infringement than the appropriation of the whole, provided the alleged infringing part contains any substantial repetitions of any material parts which are original and distinctive."

Where the infringement of a dramatic composition was involved,[12] Seaman, J., quoting from an earlier case [13] stated:

"As the owner of material possessions may assert his

also: *Farmer* v. *Elstner* (1888), 33 Fed. (C. C.) 494, and Drone on Copyright, p. 408, and cases therein cited.

[11] *Fishel* v. *Lueckel* (1892), 53 Fed. (C. C.) 499.

See also: *Falk* v. *Donaldson* (1893), 57 Fed. (C. C.) 32, where the court said: "But the real question is not one as to admission of fact, but whether the lithograph is an illegal appropriation of the *substantial* parts of the photograph. In such a case the inquiry always is whether the alleged infringer has appropriated the results of the original conception of the artist. It is not a question of quantity but of quality and value; not whether the part appropriated is a literal copy of the original production, but whether it is a *substantial and material part.*"

See also: *Gray* v. *Russell* (1839), 1 Story, 11; *Folsom* v. *Marsh* (1841), 2 Story, 115.

[12] *Maxwell* v. *Goodwin* (1899), 93 Fed. (C. C.) 665.

[13] *Stowe* v. *Thomas* (1853), Fed. Cas. (C. C.) No. 13,514.

rights wherever or in whatever disguise his property is found, so the author of a literary composition may claim it as his own in whatever language or form of words it can be identified as his production. The true test of piracy then is not whether a composition is copied in the same language or in the exact words of the original, but whether in substance it is reproduced, not whether the whole, but a material part is taken. . . . The controlling question is whether the substance of the work is taken without authority."

The court, continuing, in holding that defendant's play did not infringe, said:

"When the two plays are compared, read either as an entire production or in detail in any parts or form I can find no copying in plot, scene, dialogue, sentiment, characters or dramatic situations, and no similarity aside from the general features and subjects . . . indeed there is marked dissimilarity in the portrayal of all the characters and in thought, treatment and expression both in detail and throughout the plays."

In another case [14] it was held that there was no infringement between the two plays:

"Analyzing the details of the situation as presented in these two plays, the points of essential difference so far outnumber the points of similarity that it is difficult to understand how anyone could persuade himself that the one was borrowed from the other."

A published story in a magazine was held infringed by the performance of a dramatic composition in *Dam* v.

[14] *Hubges* v. *Belasco* (1904), 130 Fed. (C. C.) 388.

Kirk LaShelle,[15] one of the leading American cases. There the theme of the story was the change of the disposition and character of "Dan" the central figure, from a man of submissive temperament in his household and towards his wife and mother-in-law, to a man of commanding and asserting mien upon his becoming a father. The court held that the theme of the story was "substantially" imitated in the defendant's play:

"It is true the dialogue of the drama is not in the words of the copyrighted story; but its exact phraseology was not necessary to the adaptation of the plot or subject or the portrayal of the different characters to the play . . . it is enough if the essence of a play is taken from an original literary production. . . . He has cleverly staged the play and by the use of language and characters has given the subject of the story an excellent interpretation. But this is unimportant, if he has taken, as I think he has, the substance of complainant's authorship."

On affirmance[16] the Circuit Court of Appeals held:

"The playwright expanded the plot. He made a successful drama. The story was but a framework. But the theme of the story is the theme of the play, viz.: the change produced in the character of a husband by becoming a father."

A practical method of arriving at the conclusion of

[15] *Dam* v. *Kirk La Shelle* (1908), 166 Fed. (C. C.) 589.

[16] *Dam* v. *Kirk La Shelle* (1910), 175 Fed. (C. C. A.) 902.

See also: for a case where there is an appropriation of a theme: *Eisfeldt* v. *Campbell* (1909), 171 Fed. (C. C.) 594.

infringement or no infringement has been expounded by Judge Mayer in *Vernon* v. *Shubert*.[17] He says:

"The only way to arrive at a conclusion on the merits in a case like this is to endeavor to discover the theory of the play, and, generally speaking, the method of its execution."

Attention may be here called to the extensive litigation which grew out of the infringement of the play "Under the Gaslight." Many interesting copyright questions were at one time or another passed upon by the courts in the course of these controversies. A statement giving the history of the litigation will be found below.[18]

[17] *Vernon* v. *Shubert* (1915), 220 Fed. (D. C.) 694.

See also: *Nethersole* v. *Bell* (Eng.) (1903), Times, July 4, 31, which involved the right of defendant to produce a play "Sapho" written by a M. Espinasse. *Held* that there was a substantial pirating of situation and plot from "Sapho" written by Clyde Fitch, and injunction was granted.

[18] "Under the Gaslight." In the extensive litigation growing out of the infringement of the play "Under the Gaslight" many interesting copyright questions were at one time or another passed upon by the courts. The first case was for infringement of the railroad scene, where the court found in favor of the plaintiff. *Daly* v. *Palmer* (1868), 6 Blatch. (D. C.) 256. This decision was never appealed from.

The second action first came up in the form of an application for injunction pendente lite which was denied, *Daly* v. *Brady* (1889), 39 Fed. (C. C.) 265, upon the ground that there was a material variation in the title as filed and the title as used.

On final hearing the Bill of Complaint was dismissed, the court following the decision on the motion. *Daly* v. *Webster* (1891), 47 Fed. (C. C.) 903.

An appeal was taken, and the Court of Appeals reversed the Circuit Court, and remanded the case with instructions to enter

Section 159.—Common sources.

The usual defense set up in an infringement action is that complainant and defendant have derived their works from a common source, which is in the public domain; or that complainant's theme is a part of the common stock of literary material; and that complainant's copyright does not protect that which is public property.

a decree for an account and injunction [*Daly* v. *Webster* (1892), 56 Fed. (C. C. A.) 483, 1 U. S. App. 573], on the ground that the variation in the titles was immaterial, and there had been an infringement.

After the coming in of the master's report and entry of final decree, an appeal was taken by the defendant, and the decree was affirmed without opinion. *Webster* v. *Daly*, 11 U. S. App. 791.

The appeal was dismissed by the Supreme Court. *Webster* v. *Daly* (1895), 163 U. S. 155, 16 Sup. Ct. 961.

The final decree in that action did not provide for profits. Thereupon a *new* action was commenced to recover statutory damages for the infringement [*Daly* v. *Brady* (1895), 69 Fed. (C. C.) 285], and judgment was entered in favor of the defendant on the ground that insufficient testimony was presented. Thereafter plaintiff moved for a new trial which was granted. The cause came on before the same judge, and judgment was found in plaintiff's favor.

An appeal was taken, and the judgment was affirmed. *Brady* v. *Daly* (1897), 83 Fed. (C. C. A.) 1007, 51 U. S. App. 621.

On writ of error to the U. S. Supreme Court judgment was affirmed. *Brady* v. *Daly* (1899), 175 U. S. 148, 20 Sup. Ct. 62.

"The Octoroon." Another play productive of copyright litigation was that entitled "The Octoroon." The opinions will be found to contain valuable discussions on the law of literary property. *Boucicault* v. *Fox* (1862), 5 Blatch. (D. C.) 87; *Boucicault* v. *Wood* (1867), 2 Biss. (C. C.) 34. And in the play "Shoughraun" reported in *Boucicault* v. *Hart* (1875), 13 Blatch. (D. C.) 47, and *Boucicault* v. *Chatterton* (Eng.) (1876), 5 Ch. Div. 267.

In a case where both the complainant's play and the defendant's motion picture were alleged to have been based upon a foreign work which was in the public domain, the test of infringement in such case was stated by the court as follows:

"Defendants would undoubtedly have the right to make an independent translation of their own, with such modifications as their own ingenuity might suggest. They had no right, however, to transfer into their own adaptation variations from and additions to the French play which were original with Jackson (complainant's assignor) who first translated it and copyrighted it here." [19]

The courts have recognized the fact:

"That the points of similarity in two dramatizations of the same novel must necessarily be much greater than should be possible in any two original dramas, if each were written entirely independent of any knowledge of the other." [20]

Judge Story has held that:

"It has been truly said, that the subject of both of these works is of such a nature that there must be close

[19] *Stevenson* v. *Fox* (1915), 226 Fed. (D. C.) 990.

Goldmark v. *Kreling* (1888), 35 Fed. (C. C.) 661. For a careful analysis of two plays alleged to be derived from a common source showing what suffices to show infringement.

Daly v. *Palmer* (1868), 6 Blatch. 256. "The true test of whether there is piracy or not, is to ascertain whether there is a servile or evasive imitation of the plaintiff's work, or whether there is a bona fide original compilation, made up from common materials, and common sources, with resemblances which are merely accidental, or result from the nature of the subject."

[20] *Nixon* v. *Doran* (1909), 168 Fed. (C. C.) 575.

resemblances between them. But the real question on this point is not whether such resemblances exist, but whether these resemblances are purely accidental and undesigned, and unborrowed because arising from common sources accessible to both the authors, and the use of materials open equally to both; whether, in fact, the defendant Davies used the plaintiff's work as his model, and imitated and copied that, and did not draw from such common sources or common materials.[21]"

Where it is contended that the theme of complainant's work is one which is part of the common stock of ideas, one which has been used by authors and playwrights for many years, the defendant will not be restrained unless he has gone directly or indirectly to the complainant's work and taken that portion of it which is the creation of the complainant,—that is to say, the complainant's embellishment and original treatment will be jealously guarded by the courts.[22] But no author will be permitted to appropriate unto himself a literary theme to the exclusion of others.[23]

[21] *Emerson* v. *Davies* (1845), Fed. Cas. No. 4,436, and see 3 Story, 768.

See also: *Pike* v. *Nicholas* (Eng.) (1869), 5 Ch. App. 251. "When once it was established that there were common sources it would be naturally expected that there would be great similarity in the statements of the facts which were narrated from those common sources. Accordingly there might be traced throughout the work of the defendant a great similarity to the outline and plan of that of the plaintiff."

[22] *Aronson* v. *Fleckenstein* (1886), 28 Fed. (C. C.) 75.

[23] *Nixon* v. *Doran* (1909), 168 Fed. (C. C.) 575. "In the same way a copyright of the dramatization of a novel, if the novel is free to the world by the expiration of the original copyright,

Judge Lacombe has humorously illustrated the rule in the following language:

"There is nothing original in the incident thus represented on the stage. Heroes and heroines, as well as villains of both sexes, have for a time whereof the memory

can protect merely the original portions of the drama, and the original arrangement of scenes and characters in so far as they are not an exact reproduction of the book."

Glaser v. *St. Elmo* (1909), 175 Fed. (C. C.) 276. Holt, D. J.: "By the expiration of the term of the copyright of the novel, however, any person could make any use of the novel which he saw fit. He could copy it or publish or make a play of it. It was no longer protected by the copyright act. But although a person could make a play from the novel, using its plot and incidents in such play, he could not copy the play of 'St. Elmo,' already written and copyrighted, further than to make such a general use of the plot and incidents of the novel as was open to the public generally."

Simms v. *Stanton* (1896), 75 Fed. (C. C.) 6. "The copyright obtained by complainant for his works did not protect him in the use of material which had originated or had been utilized by some previous writer on the same subject."

Robl v. *Palace Theatre* (Eng.) (1911), 28 T. L. R. 69. The representation of a dramatic piece in which the similarities to a piece previously produced are due to mere coincidence—both plays being derived independently from the common stock of dramatic ideas—is not an infringement of the rights given by the Dramatic Copyright Act 1833, to the author of the play first produced.

See in this connection: *Griggs* v. *Perrin* (1892), 49 Fed. (C. C.) 15. "A party may invent a new machine and write a book describing it for which he may obtain a copyright. This does not prevent another author from describing the same machine. He must not copy the copyrighted book, but he may write one of his own. . . . The copyrighted book is sacred, but not the subject of which it treats."

See also: *Burnell* v. *Chown* (1895), 69 Fed. (C. C.) 993.

of the theatre-goer runneth not to the contrary, been precipitated into conventional ponds, lakes, rivers and seas. So frequent a catastrophe may fairly be regarded as the common property of all playwrights." [24]

In *Vernon* v. *Shubert*,[25] the court speaking of themes upon which authors draw for their literary productions said:

"Of course, as so often happens, there are some characters in both plays having a similarity, and there are here and there some instances of similar phraseology. But that is a very old story in playwriting, because, after all, there are not so many themes around which a play may be plotted. Secret marriages, district attorneys, murders, office boys, blackmailing, good people and bad people have walked about behind the footlights for many a day."

And again the same court said:

"It is to be expected that two playwrights writing independently from a common source may develop similarity in their plots and in their lines." [26]

On affirmance the Circuit Court of Appeals held that:

"This does not entitle the person who first presents that suggested situation in a copyrighted play from depriving other persons to whom the same situation naturally presents itself, upon perusal of the narrative which is the common source, from also presenting it in a book or a play, provided that the later one gets the idea from the common source, not from the copyrighted play."[27]

[24] *Serrena* v. *Jefferson* (1888), 33 Fed. (C. C.) 347.

[25] *Vernon* v. *Shubert* (1915), 220 Fed. (D. C.) 694.

[26] *Bachman* v. *Belasco* (1913), 224 Fed. (D. C.) 815.

[27] *Bachman* v. *Belasco* (1913), 224 Fed. (C. C. A.) 817.

Judge Lacombe states the proposition as follows:

"The copyright cannot protect the fundamental plot which was common property long before the story was written; it will protect the embellishment with which the author added elements of literary value to the old plot, but it will not operate to prohibit the presentation by someone else of the same old plot without the particular embellishments." [28]

A practical test commonly used in the case of works based upon a common source is to see whether the alterations, omissions and additions which first appeared in the complainant's version are followed by the defendant.[29]

In connection with the application of this test, absence

On the question whether defendant may make use of complainant's work where the same is based upon common property, see Johnson v. *Donaldson* (1880), 3 Fed. (C. C.) 22; *Glaser* v. *St. Elmo* (1909), 175 Fed. (C. C.) 276; *Stevenson* v. *Fox* (1915), 226 Fed. (D. C.) 990.

[28] *London* v. *Biograph* (1916), 231 Fed. (C. C. A.) 696.

See also on the same question: *Bobbs-Merrill* v. *Equitable* (1916), 232 Fed. (D. C.) 791; *Stevenson* v. *Harris* (1917), 238 Fed. (D. C.) 432; *Eichel & Colligan* v. *Woods* (1917), District Court of the United States Southern District of New York, Manton, J., April 2d.

[29] *Stevenson* v. *Fox* (1915), 226 Fed. (D. C.) 990; *O'Neill* v. *Gen. Film Co.* (1916), 157 N. Y. Supp. 1028.

See: *Rees* v. *Robbins* (1914), London Times, Jan. 29, Feb. 14, and July 4, for a careful examination of two plays by the court where the contention was that the material in both plays was taken from the common stock of ideas.

See also: *Jacobson* v. *De Mille*, District Court of the United States, Southern District of New York, opinion by Sheppard, J., October 1, 1916, where the same defense was interposed in an action for infringement of a play.

of any proof from the person who produced defendant's work to explain the reasons for the same variations from the original work will be construed against the defendant.[30]

Section 160.—Substantial similarity by coincidence.

It was held in an earlier line of cases that where the similarity or identity between two works was caused by mere coincidence, each author working independently of the other, no cause of action existed for infringement of either a statutory copyright [31] or the common-law right in an unpublished work.[32]

An extreme late case [33] where this principle was applied was one where the action was based on the common-law rights in a well-known unpublished play "Peg O' My

[30] *O'Neill* v. *General Film Co.* (1915), 157 N. Y. Supp. 1028; *Stevenson* v. *Fox* (1915), 226 Fed. (D. C.) 990.

See also: *Bleistein* v. *Donaldson* (1903), 188 U. S. 239; 23 Sup. Ct. 298.

[31] *Reed* v. *Carusi* (1845), 20 Fed. Cas. (C. C.) 11,642.

Johnson v. *Donaldson* (1880), 3 Fed. (C. C.) 22. "If each of two persons should compose a poem identically alike, he who first composed it would have no priority of title over the other, nor would he acquire priority by first publishing it. The law of copyright would protect each in his own manuscript, but would not prevent either from using his own.

S. S. White Dental Co. v. *Sibley* (1889), 38 Fed. (C. C.) 751. "If he (defendant) devised the same plan in ignorance of what the plaintiff had done, it is clear, we believe, that he has not infringed. . . ."

See also: *Schwarz* v. *Wylie* (Eng.) (1911), Times, Nov. 17; *Reichart* v. *Sapte* (Eng.) (1893), 2 Q. B. 308.

[32] *Morosco* v. *Fendell*, State of Wisconsin, Circuit Court, Fond du Lac County, opinion of Judge Chester A. Fowler, March 31, 1917.

[33] *Morosco* v. *Fendell*, supra.

Heart." Not only was the theme identical, but a number of the situations and the title as well were similar and the names of the two chief characters were alike. The court, nevertheless, found no infringement, as it was satisfied that the defendant had conceived and written his play without having ever read, seen or heard of the plaintiff's drama..

The law is expressed by the learned court:

"Priority of conception and completion and production altogether do not give the plaintiff the right to enjoin the production of the defendant's play, unless the latter was based or founded upon the former; unless it was copied from or made in imitation of it; unless the former was used in the production of it, so that the latter is a reproduction of the former; unless the latter was 'pirated' from the former. Even substantial similarity, founded upon coincidence, and not the result of piracy, direct or indirect, is insufficient to establish infringement (citing cases). This is stated of copyright matter, but with equal or greater reason it would be true of non-copyrighted matter. It is the taking and appropriation by one person of the literary work of another that is prohibited. If one play is as much the original conception and the result of the original mental labor of the one producing it as another play is of its author, the authors are equally entitled to the fruits of their original labors, notwithstanding the works be similar. This seems to me the common sense view of the matter."

This principle, however, has been modified lately with respect to works protected under the Copyright Act. The federal courts take the position that since sole and exclusive rights are granted by the copyright, any invasion of them, whether made innocently through coincidence or otherwise, subjects the invader to an action by the owner of the rights.

"Defendant contends that in order to infringe a copyright the defendant must have actually copied or pirated the production of the plaintiff, and not merely, while ignorant, have himself produced substantially the same thing. . . .

"The cause now before me involves only the property right of the original composer in his copyright. The act in force when this copyright was issued (citing case) provides that the author of a musical composition, upon complying with the provisions of the Copyright statute, shall have the sole liberty of printing, publishing and vending the same. We are referred to no authority, and know of no reason for holding that the person to whom the right is secured may not maintain it by injunction against another person who threatens to invade it." [34]

The present condition of the law may be said to be that where the complainant relies upon his common-law rights, he must establish piracy. Where, however, the action is based upon a statutory copyright, it is sufficient

[34] *Hein* v. *Harris* (1910), 183 Fed. (C. C. A.) 107; aff'g 175 Fed. 875.

But see: *Corelli* v. *Gray* (Eng.) (1913), Times, May 21, 22, 23, 24, June 5 and Nov. 21. This case takes the opposite view adopted by the Federal court in *Hein* v. *Harris*. Here the court holds that, under the English Copyright Act of 1911, where the similarity in both works is by coincidence there is no remedy under the act for infringement.

To the same effect: *Robl* v. *Palace Theatre* (Eng.) (1911), Times, Nov. 14, 17.

to show an invasion of such statutory right. It is immaterial whether such invasion has been caused by coincidence, accident (where defendant believes plaintiff's work to be in the public domain) or piracy.

It is obvious that the copyrighting of a work confers at least this one advantage which is not secured under common law.

Section 161.—Who may maintain action—Misjoinder of parties—Joinder of causes of action.

Under the Act,[35] the action for infringement may be maintained by the proprietor of the copyright, and it is immaterial whether he is the proprietor of record or an assignee of the copyright whose assignment has not been recorded,[36] since the section respecting the recording of assignments protects subsequent purchasers or mortgagees for value, but has no reference to infringers.

Of course, when the proprietor has not parted with any of the rights secured under the copyright either by way of sale or license, he is the only proper party plaintiff to the action.

A frequent situation, however, that presents itself, is one where the proprietor has either made an assignment or granted a license with respect to some of his rights, and the party who is injured by the infringement is not the copyright proprietor, but on the contrary, is his assignee or licensee.

[35] Section 25, subdivision (b). See also: *Harper & Bros.* v. *Donohue* (1905), 144 Fed. (C. C.) 491.

[36] *New Fiction Co.* v. *Star Co.* (1915), 220 Fed. (D. C.) 994.

Although the law is clear that where an assignee of some of the rights is injured, he is a proper party plaintiff, together with the copyright proprietor, yet, where a licensee has been harmed, the law is not entirely clear as to whether or not such licensee should be joined.

It is well settled that a licensee cannot in any event sue in his own name alone.[37] It would seem, however, that where the rights granted to the licensee are infringed upon by the defendant, then such licensee may sue in his own name providing he joins in his action the legal owner of the entire copyright.

Gaumont v. *Hatch* decided in 1913, seems to support the last mentioned rule.[38] There the Gaumont Co., owner of a

[37] *Wooster* v. *Crane & Co.* (1906), 147 Fed. (C. C. A.) 515. "It is the general rule that a mere licensee cannot in its own name sue strangers who infringe. *Birdsell* v. *Shaliol*, 112 U. S. 485. Here, however, the complainant is not a mere licensee, but has the full equitable title, and Wooster, who has the legal title, is one of the infringers and occupies a position altogether hostile to the complainant."

See also: *New Fiction* v. *Star* (1915), 220 Fed. (D. C.) 994.

Neilson v. *Horniman* (Eng.) (1909), 26 T. L. R. 188, C. A. Copyright owners of play granted plaintiff "the sole license" to produce play for a period of one year except in London and suburbs. Defendants produced the play at Manchester without having secured permission of plaintiffs. *Held*, that as plaintiff did not hold an assignment of acting rights but only a "sole license" he had no title to sue in his own name.

See also: *Mackay* v. *Edwardes* (Eng.) (1906), Times, Jan. 30, April 27.

[38] *Gaumont* v. *Hatch* (1913), 208 Fed. (D. C.) 378. The lessor of a film and his lessees are all proper parties plaintiff in an action brought for infringement of the film.

Young, D. J.: "It appears from the allegations of the bill as amended that the Gaumont Company is the owner of the film and

motion picture film, had leased copies of the film to the other plaintiffs in the action, Schwalm and Rothleder, for a specified period, and for exhibition within a limited territory. The lease provided for a return of the films upon the termination of the lease. The court held that the Gaumont Co. having a present existing beneficial interest in the films, and their lessees, were all proper parties plaintiff to the action, under Equity Rule nineteen, which provides that all persons having an interest in the subject in the action in obtaining the relief demanded, may join as plaintiffs.

the lessor and is entitled to have the film returned at the termination of the lease. It is therefore interested in preventing by injunction the removal of the film, or any copy thereof, beyond the jurisdiction of this court, as such removal into another jurisdiction, would result in the necessity of more and probably of a multiplicity of suits. The lessees, Schwalm and Rothleder, are interested in preventing the exhibition of the film at any other place within the territory secured to them by the lease. They have a vital interest in the relief sought. Both the lessor, the Gaumont Company, and the lessees, Schwalm and Rothleder, are parties in interest, and, under the nineteenth rule in equity (198 Fed. xxviii, 115 C. C. A. xxviii) are proper parties plaintiff. This ground of dismissal must therefore be overruled.

See also: *Worthington* v. *Batty* (1889), 40 Fed. (C. C.) 479. Plaintiff contracted with an authoress for the publication of her book. In violation of her agreement she subsequently allowed a newspaper to print the book, and plaintiff brought suit to restrain the paper. Motion for preliminary injunction was denied because the authoress who had an interest in the copyright should have been made a party to the action.

See also: *Macmillan* v. *Dent* (Eng.) (1906), Times, Nov. 8, 23 T. L. R. 45. The proprietor and his licensee may join as co-plaintiffs in the action.

The same rule in its converse application is illustrated in *New Fiction Co.* v. *Star*,[39] where the licensee of the "serial" rights in a dramatic composition brought the action in his own name against a newspaper which had published the work. The invasion was clearly of the licensee's rights. It was held that a mere licensee could not maintain an action in his own name for infringement of the copyrighted work, since the statute gave the right to maintain actions for infringement to the "copyright proprietor." The court at the foot of its opinion, makes the following significant statement:

"It will be understood that I am not passing on the question which would be presented if Goodman (the copyright proprietor) were a party plaintiff."

Tully v. *Triangle* [40] holds that where the rights of the

[39] *New Fiction* v. *Star* (1915), 220 Fed. (D. C.) 994.

See also the cases referred to in the opinion: *Jude's Liedertafel Case*, L. R. (Eng.) (1907), 1 Ch. 651; *Empire City Am. Co.* v. *Wilbou* (1903), 134 Fed. (C. C.) 132.

[40] *Tully* v. *Triangle* (1916), 229 Fed. (D. C.) 297. Complainant Tully was the author of an original dramatic composition which he duly copyrighted. Complainant Espladian Producing Co. was granted by Tully the exclusive license to produce the play upon the stage with living actors. Defendant produced a film which complainants alleged infringed upon Tully's play. *Held* that Espladian Producing Company, had no interest in the subject of the action, hence an improper party and bill multifarious.

"From the foregoing it will be seen that the Espladian Producing Company is the exclusive licensee to produce the play 'upon the stage by a company of players,' and that all other rights, such as motion picture rights, remain in and were reserved by Tully, the author. When, therefore, the Espladian Producing Company became such licensee, it did so with the knowl-

exclusive licensee are not infringed by the defendant, he is not a proper party to the action.

In some instances the courts have permitted an exclusive licensee of portions of the rights secured by the copyright to maintain an action in his own name and alone against an infringer of the rights granted to him. In *Aronson* v. *Fleckenstein*, the plaintiff, while an exclusive licensee of the American rights for a limited period, was by the terms of his license empowered to bring all necessary suits for the protection of his rights, and copyrighted the work in order to safeguard his rights. It was held that not only was he entitled to maintain suit in his own name, but that he was the only one who could do so.[41]

edge that Tully at any time and at any place could produce a so-called motion picture photoplay, and if Tully could do this, then, of course, any licensee of his could do the same. It seems to me entirely clear that the Espladian Producing Company has no right or interest in respect of the presentation by motion pictures of 'A Bird of Paradise.'"

See in this connection: *Menchen* v. *Denville* (Eng.) (1913), Times, Dec. 3. *Held* that the plaintiff who was a grantee of the copyright proprietor of the motion picture rights was not entitled to enjoin the production upon the stage of a play under the same title although the owner of the copyright might have been entitled to do so.

[41] *Aronson* v. *Fleckenstein* (1886), 28 Fed. (C. C.) 75.

See also: *Roberts* v. *Myers* (1860), 20 Fed. Cas. No. 11,906 (C. C.). "The respondent is a mere wrong-doer who has invaded this copyright. . . . It is quite clear that this copyright being infringed and in danger of further violation by a person who has no color of right, the true owner ought to have a remedy. But it is said that Boucicault (author) ought to be the complainant, or at least join with Roberts. Why so? His interest has not been invaded or endangered, nor can

The equitable owner of a copyright is a proper party to an action for infringement.[42]

Where the complainant has full equitable title to the copyright and the legal title therein is in one who is an infringer, who occupies a position altogether hostile to the complainant, the owner of the equitable title may maintain the action in his own name.[43]

Where a licensee has an exclusive license under the copyright for the entire term of such copyright the courts by analogy with the rule followed in the case of patents will regard the license as an assignment and plaintiff will be permitted to sue in his own name.[44]

the non-joinder of Boucicault in any way affect the defendant . . . to require him then to be joined with Roberts would be an idle and nugatory act. . . ."

In this case it was held that the assignee of the exclusive right of representing a drama for one year in the United States could maintain suit in his own name.

Hill v. *Whalen* (1914), 220 Fed. (D. C.) 359. An exclusive licensee of the dramatic rights of copyrighted cartoons was granted an injunction restraining the production of play wherein two characters impersonated the cartoons and used a number of the phrases placed in the mouths of the cartoons by the original artist.

See also: *Keene* v. *Wheatley* (1861), Fed. Cas. No. 7,644 (C. C.)

For a case where the court permitted the owner of a copyright in the words of a song, and not in the music, to sue for infringement, see: Francis v. *Oliver* (Eng.) (1907), Times, March 20.

[42] *Historical Pub. Co.* v. *Jones* (1916), 231 Fed. (C. C. A.) 638.

[43] *Wooster* v. *Crane* (1906), 147 Fed. (C. C. A.) 515. Citing: *Littlefield* v. *Perry* (1874), 21 Wall. 205; *Waterman* v. *McKenzie* (1890), 138 U. S. 252, 11 Sup. Ct. 334; *Excelsior* v. *Pacific* (1901), 185 U. S. 282; 22 Sup. Ct. 681; *Root* v. *Railway* (1881), 105 U. S. 189; *Little* v. *Gould* (1852), 15 Fed. Cas. 604 (C. C.) No. 8,395; *Ruggles* v. *Eddy* (1872), 20 Fed. Cas. 1,317 (C. C.) No. 12,117.

[44] *Fitch* v. *Young* (1911), 230 Fed. (D. C.) 743.

Where the rights conveyed by the author did not give the right to copyright, the one obtaining such rights may not copyright the work or maintain suit on the copyright for its infringement.[45]

It was held that where the action was brought by the legal holder of the copyright, although the beneficial ownership thereof was in another, the defendant could not take any advantage of the trust relation existing between such legal owner and some third party.[46]

As to unpublished works, not copyrighted, it was held in *Tams* v. *Witmark*,[47] that the "exclusive owners of the right to produce and perform" an operetta in the United States could maintain an action in their own name without joining their assignors, the court following the rule laid down in an earlier case where the same situation was presented.[48] This rule has likewise been followed in the federal courts.[49]

[45] *Saake* v. *Lederer* (1909), 174 Fed. (C. C. A.) 135; Rev. 166 Fed. (C. C.) 810.

[46] *Hanson* v. *Jaccard* (1887), 32 Fed. (C. C.) 202.

[47] *Tams* v. *Witmark* (1900), 30 Misc. (N. Y.) 293; 63 N. Y. Supp. 721, aff'd 48 A. D. (N. Y.) 632; 63 N. Y. Supp. 1117.

[48] *Palmer* v. *DeWitt* (1872), 47 N. Y. 532.

See also: *Tompkins* v. *Halleck* (1882), 133 Mass. 32. Where an unpublished and uncopyrighted play was assigned to plaintiffs with the exclusive right to represent the same in the New England states, plaintiffs were granted an injunction and accounting for damages.

[49] *Goldmark* v. *Kreling* (1888), 35 Fed. (C. C.) 661. Plaintiffs acquired the American rights to the operetta "Nanon." Subsequently the authors published the piano-score in Europe, and defendants making their own orchestration, produced it over here.

"The authors certainly could not have sold and conveyed any right to a third party to perform

From the above it is apparent that the rule as to the joinder of licensee and proprietor is not stringently applied in the state or federal courts with respect to unpublished-uncopyrighted works, while it is strictly adhered to in cases involving statutory copyright infringement. The reason is probably found in the wording of the Copyright Act which gives various remedies to the "copyright proprietor," thereby compelling such proprietor to be brought in. There being no such limitation in common-law works, the courts are disposed to permit greater freedom of action on the part of the licensee and a more liberal construction of the remedies open to him.

Misjoinder must be raised either by way of motion or by way of defense in the answer. Failure by the defendant to do so, will preclude him from raising the question on appeal.[50]

It has been held that an action brought to restrain the infringement of a patent may be joined with one for unfair competition where the jurisdictional facts are present as to the latter cause of action.[51] We see no reason

their operetta in America, so as to cut off the prior exclusive right conveyed to Goldmark and Conreid. If they could not cut them off by subsequent sale, we do not perceive how they could do it by a subsequent dedication to the public by publication."

Crowe v. *Aiken* (1870), 2 Biss. (C. C.) 208. One Tom Taylor of London wrote a play for Miss Bateman, a famous actress. The play was first produced in London. Subsequently Taylor sold the exclusive rights for the United States for 5 years to the plaintiff, Miss Bateman's husband, who brought the play to this country, and sued to enjoin defendant from infringing. *Held*, that plaintiff could maintain the action in his own name.

[50] *Historical Publ. Co.* v. *Jones* (1916), 231 Fed. (C. C. A.) 638.

[51] *Farmers Handy Wagon Co.* v. *Beaver* (1916), 236 Fed. (C. C. A.)

why the same should not hold true when the infringement of a copyright is involved instead of that of a patent.

An instance where such a situation may arise is when not only the body of the work is appropriated, but the title as well. Since the copyright covering the work does not extend to the title, the proprietor is not entitled to enjoin the use of the title in his infringement suit unless he sets forth another cause of action based upon the unfair use of the title.

A complaint containing a count in infringement and another in trespass has been held to be demurrable.[52]

Section 162.—Where action may be brought.

Under Section thirty-four of the Copyright Act, all actions, suits or proceedings arising under the copyright law "shall be originally cognizable by the Circuit Courts of the United States, the District Court of any territory, the Supreme Court of the District of Columbia, the Dis-

731. "The bill seeks to restrain infringement of the patent and also to restrain unfair competition. These are properly joined, independent of the question of citizenship. *Adams* v. *Folger* (1903), 120 Fed. (C. C. A.) 260; *Ludwigs* v. *Payson* (1913), 206 Fed. (C. C. A.) 64.

"Appellant is entitled to have its patent sustained, infringement thereof and unfair competition found and restrained, and an accounting taken."

See also: *McIndoo* v. *Musson Book Co.* (Can.) (1915), 35 O. L. R. 42.

[52] *Ohman* v. *City of New York* (1909), 168 Fed. (C. C.) 953. Defendant was sued for having printed in the City Record mutilated copies of plaintiff's maps. The causes of action sought to unite an action for infringement under the copyright laws with an action for trespass. Demurrer was sustained.

trict Courts of Alaska, Hawaii or Porto Rico and the courts of first instance of the Philippine Islands." And such courts may proceed under Section twenty-six in any action, suit or proceeding instituted for violation of any provision of the act to enter any judgment or decree enforcing the remedies therein provided.

As the Circuit Courts have been abolished since the passage of the 1909 Act, all actions are now originally cognizable by the District Courts.

The federal courts have exclusive jurisdiction over all actions arising under the Copyright Act.

Where the action is brought to enforce the rights of the proprietor of an unpublished and uncopyrighted work, the state courts have concurrent jurisdiction with the federal courts to enforce the rights of such proprietor; that is, the action may in any event be brought in a state Court, and where the jurisdictional facts are present it may be maintained in the federal courts.[53]

All civil actions, suits, or proceedings may under Section thirty-five be instituted in the district of which the defendant or his agent resides, or in which he may be found.[54]

Section 163.—Who is liable—Intent.

Anyone infringing any of the rights granted to the

[53] *Palmer* v. *De Witt* (1872), 47 N. Y. 532; *Tompkins* v. *Halleck* (1882), 133 Mass. 32; *Carter* v. *Bailey* (1874), 64 Me. 458; *Crowe* v. *Aiken* (1870), 2 Biss. (C. C.) 208.

[54] *Lederer* v. *Rankin* (1898), 90 Fed. (C. C.) 449; *Fraser* v. *Barrei* (1900), 105 Fed. (C. C.) 787; *Lederer* v. *Ferris* (1906), 149 Fed. (C. C.) 250; *Wagner* v. *Wilson* (1915), 225 Fed. (D. C.) 912.

copyright proprietor of a motion picture renders himself liable to an action under the Act.

Thus one offering the infringing work for sale for the purpose of exhibition, though not himself exhibiting the same, has been held to be an infringer.[55]

And the lessor of a theatre who lets his theatre to one whose exhibition is an infringement, is liable, where he has knowledge of the infringing performance and does not make any attempt to stop it.[56]

[55] *Kalem* v. *Harper* (1911), 222 U. S. 55; 32 Sup. Ct. 20. The court gives the following cases in support of this proposition: *Rupp & Wittgenfeld* v. *Elliot* (1904), 131 Fed. (C. C. A.) 730, 732; *Harper* v. *Shoppell* (1886), 28 Fed. (C. C.) 613; *Morgan Envelope Co.* v. *Albany Paper Co.* (1894), 152 U. S. 425; 14 Sup. Ct. 627.

Daly v. *Palmer* (1868), 6 Blatch. (D. C.) 256. Where one of the defendants had not produced the infringing play but had merely sold it to another who himself produced it, the defendant was held liable.

Fenning Film Service v. *Wolverhampton and District Cinemas* (Eng.) (1914), Law Times, June 20. *Held* that under Copyright Act of 1911 one who announced by posters and handbills that he would exhibit a motion picture, had authorized a performance and was guilty of infringement although he never in fact exhibited the motion picture.

[56] *Marsh* v. *Conquest* (Eng.) (1864), 17 C. B. (N. S.) 418. Where the company of players and the stage manager was in the proprietor's employ he was held liable.

Wall v. *Taylor* (Eng.) (1883), 11 Q. B. D. 102; 52 L. J. Q. B. 558; 31 W. R. 712. Suit for penalties for infringement of performing rights of a song by defendant who gave the same in his hall where admission was by refreshment ticket, price *8d.* *Held* that plaintiff was entitled to recover.

Monahan v. *Taylor* (Eng.) (1886), 2 T. L. R. 685; *Sarpy* v. *Holland* (Eng.) (1908), L. R. 2 Ch. 198; 77 L. J. Ch. 637; 99 L. T. 317; 24 T. L. R. 600; *Fire Department* v. *Hill* (1891), 14 N. Y. Supp. 158.

The courts have even gone so far as to hold that it is not necessary for the defendant to know that the performance is unlawful, where he has rented his theatre and derivéd profit thereby.[57] This position was taken by Lord Coleridge on the ground that if it were necessary to prove knowledge in the defendant, it would be extremely difficult to protect the copyright.

In the words of Lord Justice Bowen:

"It is not unreasonable to require that the person who lets his premises for a concert should make inquiries as to the copyright of the pieces performed." [58]

Defendants, producers of motion pictures, had invited the public to view the films for the purpose of selling them. It was held that such an exhibition was not a "performance" of the same within the meaning of the English

But see: *Russell* v. *Briant* (Eng.) (1849), 8 C. B. 836. Where the proprietor of the theatre did not authorize the performance, had no management in the production and was not associated in business with the one controlling the performance, he was held not liable for infringement.

And see: *Moul* v. *The Coronet Theatre, Ltd.* (Eng.) (1903), Times, Feb. 4. Action for infringement of performing rights in musical selection against proprietor of theatre. *Held* that defendant was not liable since *actual knowledge* of the infringement on his part had not been established.

[57] *Monahan* v. *Taylor* (Eng.) (1886), 2 T. L. R. 685; *Marsh* v. *Conquest* (Eng.) (1864), 17 C. B. (N. S.) 418; *French* v. *Day* (Eng.) (1893), 9 L. T. R. 548.

[58] *Monahan* v. *Taylor* (Eng.) (1886), 2 T. L. R. 685. In this connection it is interesting to note that where an employer expressly directs his servants not to violate the law he is nevertheless bound by the unlawful acts of the servant, so far as violating the ordinances of the city are concerned. *Matter of Hammerstein* (1907), 52 Misc. (N. Y.) 608; 102 N. Y. Supp. 950.

Act in force at the time, and did not render defendants liable for infringement.[59]

Where, under the English Act, the sole claim was that the infringement was of the exclusive performing rights, the manufacturer was not a joint tort feasor.[60]

In an earlier American case the manufacturer of the electrotype plates from which the infringing copies were made, was held not liable, in the absence of guilty knowledge or intent.[61] This does not seem to be altogether the true rule at the present time.

The attitude of the courts to-day is to hold everyone liable who in any manner has helped to create the in-

[59] *Glenville* v. *Selig Polyscope Co.* (Eng.) (1911), 27 L. T. R. 554. Defendants, who were producers of motion pictures, fitted up a room at their place of business and issued advertisements to the public to see films showing certain scenes of a play which plaintiffs alleged to infringe their rights.

Held, without deciding on the infringement, that such a room was not a place "of dramatic entertainment" within meaning of Section 2 of the Dramatic Copyright Act, 1833, inasmuch as the public were merely invited with the object of getting them to purchase the films.

[60] *Karno* v. *Pathé Frères* (Eng.) (1908), 100 L. T. 260; 53 S. J. 228; 25 T. L. R. 242. Defendants manufactured films which reproduced plaintiff's music hall sketch as "living pictures." *Held*, assuming the plaintiff's sketch to be a "dramatic piece" or entertainment within the meaning of § 1 of the Dramatic Copyright Act of 1833 the defendants did not "cause to be presented" the plaintiff's sketch within the meaning of § 2 of the Act.

[61] *Harper* v. *Shoppell* (1886), 26 Fed. (C. C.) 519 (1886), 28 Fed. (C. C.) 613. "The law will not assume without evidence or simply upon proof that the defendant sold the plate to the proprietors of a newspaper, that he intended to authorize a violation of the plaintiff's rights."

fringing work.[62] Thus, it would seem that the manufacturer of a film, its releasor or distributor and its exhibitor, would all be liable whether they had acted innocently or otherwise, and this liability exists even where the infringing acts were committed by an employe.[63] On the other hand, it has been held that an employe is not liable for an infringing act of his employer, where the act is done without his knowledge and contrary to his express instructions, he being an officer of the defendant.[64]

[62] *Belford* v. *Scribner* (1892), 144 U. S. 488; 12 Sup. Ct. 734; *Gross* v. *Van Dyke* (1916), 230 Fed. (C. C. A.) 412.

See also: *Stevens* v. *Gladding* (1854), 17 How. 447.

[63] *Trow Directory* v. *Boyd* (1899), 97 Fed. (C. C.) 586.

See also: *West Pub. Co.* v. *Lawyers Co-op.* (1897), 79 Fed. (C. C. A.) 756.

Schumacher v. *Schwencke* (1887), 30 Fed. (C. C.) 690; re-affirming, on final hearing, (1885), 25 Fed. (C. C.) 466. "It is clear that the defendants are wrongdoers. They have invaded the complainant's territory. They have copied the painting. It is immaterial how this was accomplished, whether directly or indirectly. . . ."

Gilmore v. *Anderson* (1889), 38 Fed. (C. C.) 846. "Some of the material from Gilmore's book so used by Alger (defendant) had previously been used by others, without right, and was taken by him from their works. . . . These acts of others would not however remove the protection of the copyright, nor furnish any excuse for him."

Although all those who had helped to create the infringing work are liable as infringers the courts will not require those who did not share in the profits to account for the same. They will, however, be enjoined and required to pay complainant's damages. *Gross* v. *Van Dyk Gravure Co.* (1916), 230 Fed. (C. C. A.) 412.

[64] *Stuart* v. *Smith* (1895), 68 Fed. (C. C.) 189.

See also: *French* v. *Gregory* (Eng.) (1893), 9 T. L. R. 548. The manager of the theatre was held not liable, the proprietor

Knowledge is at best a difficult matter to establish in a court of law; it is doubly so in an infringement case. For that reason knowledge or intent has been held to be immaterial.[65] It must be understood that this rule does not apply to the criminal section of the Act, where it is specifically provided that the infringer must have knowingly and wilfully aided in the commission of the Act. Nor did it apply to the penalty sections of former statutes.[66]

alone being responsible for the infringing performance.

See in this connection: *Howell* v. *Miller* (1898), 91 Fed. (C. C. A.) 129. Where officers of a state prepare a work which is the property of the state, and the work infringes upon the copyright of another work, the copyright proprietor of the latter work may maintain an action for infringement.

[65] *Fisher* v. *Lueckel* (1892), 53 Fed. (C. C.) 499. "When the infringement is otherwise established, the intention is immaterial. *Reed* v. *Holliday*, 19 Fed. 325."

"The evidence shows that the defendants bought the pictures from complainants, furnished them to the photogravure company, ordered the copies made, and gave general directions as to how the work should be done. The defendants procured the infringing act to be done. They are therefore liable as joint tort feasors. *Estes* v. *Worthington* (1887), 30 Fed. (C. C.) 465; Rob. Pat., Sec. 910."

Weatherby & Sons v. *Intern'l Horse Agency* (Eng.) (1910), 2 Ch. 297; 79 L. J. Ch. 609; 102 L. T. 856; 26 T. L. R. 527; *Carlton Illustrators* v. *Coleman* (Eng.) (1910), 27 T. L. R. 65; *Smith* v. *Daily News, Ltd.*, (Eng.) (1910), Times, Dec. 2.

Where the manuscript has been submitted to the infringer, that fact may be taken into consideration. *Maxwell* v. *Goodwin* (1899), 93 Fed. (C. C.) 665; *Bird* v. *Thanhauser* (1911), 160 Ill. App. 653; *Fraser* v. *Edwardes* (Eng.) (1905), Times, March 23, 24, 25, 28, 29, 30.

[66] *Taylor, Jr.*, v. *Gilman* (1885), 24 Fed. (C. C.) 632; *McDonald* v. *Hearst* (1899), 95 Fed. (D. C.) 656; *Schreiber* v. *Sharpless* (1881), 6 Fed. (D. C.) 175.

This present trend is illustrated in *Haas* v. *Feist*,[67] where, notwithstanding the innocence of one of the defendants, the court decreed on account of profits and damages as against him, for the Copyright Act "imposes upon everyone the duty to learn the facts conveyed by the notice."

An author may be guilty of infringement of his own work.[68]

When a work, including the copyright therein, is sold, the vendor is liable for any infringement of such work by himself and he will not be permitted in an action for such infringement to maintain the defense that the work is not copyrightable.[69]

[67] *Haas* v. *Feist* (1916), 234 Fed. (D. C.) 105.

[68] *George T. Birel Co.* v. *Welsh* (1904), 131 Fed. (C. C.) 564.

[69] *Lavin* v. *Birch* (Eng.) (1903), Times, Apr. 4; *Hardacre* v. *Armstrong* (Eng.) (1904), Times, Oct. 27.

See generally the line of cases to the effect that a licensee under a patent will not be permitted to question his licensor's title in an action for royalties: Nillson v. *De Haven* (1900), 47 A. D. (N. Y.) 537, 62 N. Y. Supp. 506; *Saltus* v. *Bedford Co.* (1892), 133 N. Y. 499; 33 N. E. 518; *Baylies* v. *Bullock* (1900), 32 Misc. (N. Y.) 218; 66 N. Y. Supp. 253; reversed on other grounds (1901), 59 A. D. (N. Y.) 576; 69 N. Y. Supp. 693; *Marston* v. *Swett* (1876), 66 N. Y. 206; *Sizer* v. *Ray* (1881), 87 N. Y. 220; *Maitland* v. *Company* (1894), 7 Misc. (N. Y.) 408; 27 N. Y. Supp. 965; *Montgomery* v. *Waterbury* (1893), 2 Misc. (N. Y.) 145; 21 N. Y. Supp. 631; aff'd 142 N. Y. 652; 37 N. E. 569; *O'Brien* v. *Jones* (1883), 91 N. Y. 192; *McGiffen* v. *Baird* (1875), 62 N. Y. 329; *Akin* v. *Meeker* (1894), 78 Hun, 387; 29 N. Y. Supp. 132; aff'd 149 N. Y. 610; 44 N. E. 1120.

And as to a play see: *Hart* v. *Fox* (1917), N. Y. Law Journal, August 24; *Outcault* v. *Bonheur* (1907), 120 A. D. (N. Y.) 168; 104 N. Y. Supp. 1099.

A licensee who oversteps the grant of his license is as much an infringer as a stranger.[70] To illustrate, a party who is given the exclusive right to exhibit a film for a limited time within a specified territory, is guilty of infringement if he exhibits the film or causes it to be exhibited in other territory.

Section 164.—What must be alleged and proved.

As the action for infringement is purely statutory, the complaint must allege every fact necessary to show that complainant is entitled to maintain his action under the Act.[71]

[70] *Duck* v. *Mayer* (Eng.) (1892), 8 T. L. R. 339. Where defendant had overstepped the grant of her license in producing a play, held liable for infringement.

See also Section 75.

[71] *Saake* v. *Lederer* (1909), 174 Fed. (C. C. A.) 135; *De Jonge* v. *Brenker & Kessler* (1911), 191 Fed. (C. C. A.) 35; *Lederer* v. *Saake* (1909), 166 Fed. (C. C.) 810; *Freeman* v. *Trade Reg.* (1909), 173 Fed. (C. C.) 419; *Merriam* v. *United Dictionary* (1905), 140 Fed. (C. C.) 768; *Merrill* v. *Tice* (1881), 104 U. S. 557; *Osgood* v. *Aloe Instrument Co.* (1897), 83 Fed. (C. C.) 470; *Jones* v. *Van Zandt* (1846), 5 How. 372; *Pierce* v. *Werckmeister* (1896), 72 Fed. (C. C. A.) 54; *Boucicault* v. *Hart* (1875), 13 Blatch. (C. C.) 47; *Empire City* v. *Wilton* (1903), 134 Fed. (C. C.) 132; *Banks* v. *Manchester* (1888), 128 U. S. 244; 9 Sup. Ct. 36; *Trow City Directory* v. *Curtin* (1888), 36 Fed. (C. C.) 829.

Chicago Mus. Co. v. *Butler* (1884), 19 Fed. (C. C.) 758. In an action for the infringement of a copyright the complaint must set forth the various steps by which complainant acquired that right.

"The plaintiff must show that he has taken the steps required by law."

This rule differs from the rule in patent cases because there is a presumption in patents, from the issuance of the letters patent, the examination before the commissioner and so on. No procedure

The complaint must specifically allege the necessary steps taken to secure copyright, otherwise the bill is demurrable.[72] As the rule has been expressed:

is necessary to be gone through in copyright other than the formal deposit, and under the old Act, the filing of the title.

Bosselman v. *Richardson* (1909), 174 Fed. (C. C. A.) 622. "Such a certificate (a copyright certificate) is wholly unlike letters patent, which are issued under § 4884 after a quasi judicial examination of the applicant's rights, and which grant him, his heirs, or assigns, the exclusive right to make, use and vend the invention patented. A patentee accordingly makes a prima facie case when he puts his letters in evidence and proves infringement. *The owner of a copyright, on the other hand, is bound to prove compliance with all the statutory conditions*, viz.: in this case that his assignor was the author and that neither he nor his assignor had published the painting before copyright. 8 Pet. 593, 669; 104 U. S. 557, 96 Pet. 213. *The certificate of the Librarian of Congress is no proof of compliance with these conditions.*"

See also: *Patterson* v. *Ogilvie Pub. Co.* (1902), 119 Fed. (C. C.) 451. Where the certificate described the author as "of New York" and the author testified that he was a resident of New York and that he mailed the copies of the work from that locality. *Held* sufficient evidence showing that author was a citizen of the United States.

See also: *Webb* v. *Powers* (1847), Fed. Cas. 17323 (C. C.). An allegation of citizen in a bill of complaint, not denied by the answer is sufficient, and no other evidence on that point is necessary.

See generally on demurrer or motion to dismiss bill of complaint: Crown Feature Film v. *Betts* (1913), 206 Fed. (D. C.) 362; *Henderson* v. *Tompkins* (1894,) 60 Fed. (C. C.) 758; *Boucicault* v. *Hart* (1875), Fed. Cas. 1692 (C. C.); *Atwill* v. *Ferrett* (1846), Fed. Cas. 640 (C. C.), *Farmer* v. *Calvert* (1872), Fed. Cas. 4651 (C. C.); *Trow City Directory* v. *Curtin* (1888), 36 Fed. (C. C.) 829.

[72] *Ford* v. *Blaney Amuse. Co.* (1906), 148 Fed. (C. C.) 642; *Huebsch* v. *Christ* (1914), 209

"An author suing for infringement of a copyright has the burden of showing a literal compliance with each and every statutory requirement in the nature of condition precedent to the acquisition of a valid copyright." [73]

And to the same effect:

"The bill must show strict compliance with the requirements of the copyright law, and if a failure so to do appears on the face of the bill, then the bill fails to state a cause of action under the statute." [74]

In numerous actions which were brought for infringement, complainants were non-suited because of their failure to allege or establish compliance with all the provisions of the statute.

Fed. (D. C.) 885. Even where there *is no denial* of plaintiff's copyright he is bound to prove the same.

[73] *Osgood* v. *Aloe Inst. Co.* (1897), 83 Fed. (C. C.) 470.

[74] *Crown Feature Co.* v. *Levy* (1912), 202 Fed. (D. C.) 805. "Complainant states merely that its assignor was 'the sole and exclusive owner and proprietor of certain photographs entitled St. George and the Dragon, Part I, . . . and of all rights and privileges thereunder and therein in and to the United States and the territories thereof.' There is no allegation that Powers was the author or that there was any author or producer in the United States or elsewhere, or how, if Powers was not the author, he became the proprietor. I think under the present act even more strongly than heretofore, complainant must show his title not merely by an allegation that he is the proprietor, but by setting forth facts which show how he became proprietor, and why he has the right to bring the action. While *Bosselman* v. *Richardson*, 174 Fed. 622, and *Ford* v. *Blaney Amusement Co.*, 148 Fed. 642, arose under the previous law, yet they are in principle applicable to the case here under consideration."

See also: *Freeman* v. *The Trade Register* (1909), 173 Fed. (C. C.) 419. Copyright statute must be strictly complied with.

Where the complaint alleged that "two complete copies of said photographs" had been deposited, the allegation was held not to satisfy the requirement of the statute which provides for the deposit of "two complete copies of the best edition thereof then published." [75] In the same case the court expressed the view that the bill was demurrable because as the court said: "There is nothing to show that the photograph is a copyrightable work."

Where the action is brought by the proprietor of a copyright who is not himself the author, it is incumbent upon him to allege the manner in which he acquired title.[76]

It is interesting to note that in an action brought in the state court for infringement of an unpublished operetta, it was held on demurrer that it was sufficient to allege that the plaintiff "duly acquired and became exclusive owners" of the work, and the the court would not treat such an allegation as a conclusion of law.[77]

[75] *Crown Feature Co.* v. *Levy* (1912), 202 Fed. (D. C.) 805.

[76] *Burrow-Giles Lithographic Co.* v. *Sarony* (1884), 111 U. S. 53, 4 Sup. Ct. 279; *Nottage* v. *Jackson* (Eng.) (1883), 11 Q. B. D. 627; *Atwell* v. *Ferrett* (1846), 2 Blatchf. (C. C.) 39; *Bimms* v. *Woodworth,* 4 Wash. C. C. Rep. 48; *Black* v. *Allen Co.* (1890), 42 Fed. (C. C.) 618; S. C. 56, Fed. 764; *Press Publ. Co.* v. *Falk* (1894), 59 Fed. (C. C.) 324; *Pollard* v. *Photograph Co.* (Eng.) (1888), 40 Ch. Div. 345; *Moore* v. *Rugg* (1890), 46 N. W. (Minn.) 141; *Dielman* v. *White* (1900), 102 Fed. (C. C.) 892; *Parton* v. *Prang* (1872), 3 Clifford (C. C.), 537; *Little* v. *Good* (1851), 2 Blatchf. (C. C.) 165; *Hardacre* v. *Armstrong* (Eng.) (1904), Times, Oct. 27.

[77] *Tams* v. *Witmark* (1900), 30 Misc. (N. Y.) 293; 63 N. Y. Supp. 721; aff'd 48 A. D. (N. Y.) 632; 63 N. Y. Supp. 1117.

The complainant is always under the obligation of establishing the authorship of the work.[78]

Under Section twelve of the Act no action or proceeding may be maintained for infringement of copyright unless the provisions of the Act with respect to the deposit of copies and registration of the work have been complied with. Hence, where the complaint does not allege the deposit of copies and registration of the work, the bill is demurrable.[79]

[78] *Bullinger* v. *Mackey* (1879), 15 Blatch. (C. C.) 550; Fed. Cas. 2,127, p. 651. "I next notice the point made, that the plaintiff has not produced proper evidence to show himself the author or proprietor of his works, within the meaning of the copyright laws. The argument here is, that no one but the plaintiff himself can legally establish the fact that the plan, arrangement, and combination of his works originated in his brain. But, there is evidence showing that the plaintiff, by his own labor and that of persons employed by him, and working under his direction, gathered together from various original sources the material of his book; that the manuscript in which the matter was arranged was partly in his handwriting; and that from the manuscript the work was printed for him at his expense. It was not necessary that these acts of the plaintiff should be proved by the testimony of the plaintiff. The testimony of any person who saw them done is primary and direct evidence of their having been done, and, in the absence of any testimony to the contrary, established the fact that the plaintiff gathered together information conveyed by his book, arranged that information as it appears in the book, and caused it to be printed in that form. The acts of the plaintiff thus proved to have been done in preparing his work are those of a compiler. A compiler is an author, within the meaning of the constitution and the copyright laws. . . ."

But see in this connection: *Reed* v. *Carusi* (1845), 20 Fed. Cas. No. 11,642 (C. C.).

[79] *N. Y. Times* v. *Star Co.*

After the obtaining of a temporary restraining order, it appearing that two copies of the work had not been deposited in the copyright office or in the mail addressed to the Register of Copyrights, the court held that it had no jurisdiction to maintain the action.[80]

The Certificate of Copyright Registration is prima facie evidence of the facts stated therein under Section fifty-five of the Act, and has been so held by the courts.[81]

The proper method of proving the exhibition of a

(1912), 195 Fed. (C. C.) 110; *N. Y. Times Co.* v. *Sun Printing & Pub. Ass'n* (1913), 204 Fed. (C. C. A.) 586; *Davies* v. *Bowes* (1914), 219 Fed. (C. C. A.) 178.

Caliga v. *Interocean Newsp. Co.* (1907), 157 Fed. (C. C. A.) 186. But, on the other hand, where complainant had registered her painting twice she lost all copyright therein. It follows that it is just as dangerous to do too much as too little in the registration for copyright.

[80] *N. Y. Times Co.* v. *Star Co.* (1912), 195 Fed. (C. C.) 110. Where complainant had obtained a restraining order on March 8th, but had not mailed two copies of the work to Washington, *held* that the court had no jurisdiction to maintain the action, as such deposit is a condition precedent.

[81] *Chataugua School* v. *Nat'l School* (1914), 211 Fed. (D. C.) 1014; reversed in (1916), 238 Fed. (C. C. A.) 151, on the question that a compilation of methods for giving hypodermic injections did not disclose originality.

Huebsch v. *Christ* (1914), 209 Fed. (D. C.) 885. It would seem that a certificate of the copyright office showing deposit of two copies of the work is competent evidence of such deposit.

See also in this connection: *Merrell* v. *Tice* (1881), 104 U. S. 557; *Saake* v. *Lederer* (1909), 174 Fed. (C. C. A.) 135; *Belford* v. *Scribner* (1891), 144 U. S. 488; 12 Sup. Ct. 734; *Callaghan v. Myers* (1888), 128 U. S. 617; 9 Sup. Ct. 177; *Bosselman* v. *Richardson* (1909), 174 Fed. (C. C. A.) 622; *Lederer* v. *Saake* (1909), 166 Fed. (C. C.) 810.

motion picture is not by the production of the film, but by a witness who has seen it reproduced.[82]

Section 165.—Bill of particulars.

The defendant in an infringement suit is entitled to a bill of particulars setting forth in detail the specific parts of complainant's work, which complainant claims to be infringed.[83]

Equity rule twenty expressly gives this right: "A further and better statement of the nature of the claim or defense or further and better particulars of any matter stated in any pleading may in any case be ordered upon such terms as to costs and otherwise as may be just."

Where the action is based upon a number of copyrights, complainant will be required, upon defendant's motion, to separately state and number his causes of action.[84] And no affidavit will be required on a motion to separately state and number, as that can be determined from the inspection of the pleadings alone.[85]

[82] *Glyn* v. *Western Feature Film Co.* (Eng.) (1916), 114 L. T. 354, 32 T. L. R. 235.

[83] *Liddell* v. *Copp-Clark Co.* (Can.), 19 O. Pr. 332. In an action for copyright infringement defendant was entitled to a bill of particulars showing the date of registration of the plaintiff's copyright, and showing what part of the defendant's work was an infringement.

[84] See for non-copyright actions: *Maxwell Steel Vault Co.* v. *Nat'l Casket Co.* (1913), 205 Fed. (D. C.) 522; *Muser* v. *Robertson* (1883), 17 Fed. (C. C.) 500; *Gause* v. *Knapp* (1880), 1 Fed. (C. C.) 292; Foster's "Federal Practice," 5th ed., §§ 240–241.

[85] *Deubert* v. *City of New York* (1908), 126 A. D. (N. Y.) 359; 110 N. Y. Supp. 403; *Harrington* v. *Stillman* (1907), 120 A. D. (N. Y.) 659; 105 N. Y. Supp. 75.

The defendant's right to ask for a more definite and certain complaint was involved in a patent case where [86] Judge Chatfield, in granting the motion to the extent of directing the plaintiff to make his complaint more definite and certain, stated:

"But, before answering, the defendant is entitled to a definite and certain complaint, and is entitled to know that with which it is charged, so as to determine whether the information upon which its answer is to be drawn is within its own possession. The plaintiff has alleged infringement both before and after the letters patent referred to were granted. The defendant, in its correspondence and affidavits presented upon this motion, alleges the use and sale of no articles except those made under the Almond patent, No. 434,748, granted August 19, 1890, which has already expired, and the Scognamillo patent, No. 785,523, issued March 21, 1905, and upon the papers it would seem that the defendant has the right to operate under these patents, unless they are the object of attack.

"The plaintiff should be required to particularize sufficiently, so that an issue can be raised, and so that the allegations of fact of the complaint can be definitely made out, for the purpose of framing the issue."

[86] *Fischer* v. *Automobile Supply Co.* (1912), 199 Fed. (D. C.) 191.

CHAPTER XIV

COPYRIGHT (CONTINUED)

Remedies

SEC. 166. Actions in equity—In general.
167. Preliminary injunction.
168. Final hearing.
169. Injunction as to part.
170. Writ of seizure.
171. Accounting.
172. Actions at law.
173. Actions purporting to be brought under the Copyright Act.
174. Willful infringements.
175. Statute of limitations.
176. Construction of forfeiture and penalty clauses.
177. Appeal.

Section thirty-six of the Copyright Act expressly provides that the courts which have jurisdiction over copyright actions or the judges thereof shall have the power upon bill in equity filed by any party aggrieved to grant injunctions to prevent and restrain the violation of any right secured by the copyright laws according to the course and principles of the courts of equity, on such terms as said court or judge may deem reasonable.

This section further provides that any injunction which may be granted restraining and enjoining the doing of anything forbidden by the Act, may be served on the parties against whom such injunction may be granted anywhere in the United States, and shall be operative throughout the United States and be enforceable by proceedings in contempt or otherwise by any other court or judge possessing jurisdiction of the defendants.

The copyright proprietor, however, is not confined to a bill in equity for his relief. He may maintain an action at law triable before a court and jury, as will be more fully discussed hereafter.

Section 166.—Actions in equity—In general.

Rule one of the Supreme Court Rules for the practice and procedure to be followed in actions under Section twenty-five of the Act provides that the existing rules of equity practice so far as they may be applicable, shall be enforced in all proceedings instituted under that section of the Act.

Section 167.—Preliminary injunction.

An aggrieved party is not required to wait until there is a final determination before equitable relief will be granted to him. Nor is he required to wait until the infringement has actually taken place, before filing his bill. A threatened invasion of his rights is sufficient to entitle complainant to injunctive relief.[1]

The rule respecting the granting of injunctions pendente lite has been enforced more liberally in favor of the plaintiff in actions involving the infringement of literary prop-

[1] *Historical Pub. Co.* v. *Jones* (1916), 231 Fed. (C. C. A.) 638.

erty than in actions of another nature, since the delay involved in waiting for a final decree would generally amount to a denial of justice.[2]

Notwithstanding this broad rule, however, the courts will require that complainant before obtaining a temporary injunction, establish a clear case.[3] And he must show affirmatively "beyond any doubt that he has complied with the copyright law"; in other words, if there is any doubt as to the validity of complainant's copyright, no injunction pendente lite will issue.[4]

Indeed, where complainant's copyright is attacked the court is disposed rather to restrict its interference by injunction, and in such case it will give great weight to the consideration of the questions, first, as to which side is more likely to suffer by an erroneous or hasty judgment, and secondly, as to the prejudicial effect the injunction may have upon the trial of the action.[5]

The true rule may be said to be that where the complainant's copyright is not seriously contested and the court is satisfied that there is an infringement, an injunction will be granted regardless of the consequences of the same to the defendant. If, however, the complainant's copyright is seriously contested and some doubt is raised

[2] *Chappell* v. *Fields* (1914), 210 Fed. (C. C. A.) 864; *Nixon* v. *Doran* (1909), 168 Fed. (C. C.) 575.

[3] *Harper* v. *Holman* (1897), 84 Fed. (C. C.) 224; *Hoffman* v. *LeTraunik* (1913), 209 Fed. (D. C.) 375; *American Malting Co.* v. *Keitel* (1913), 209 Fed. (C. C. A.) 351; *Nixon* v. *Doran* (1909), 168 Fed. (C. C.) 575; *Benton* v. *Van Dyke* (1909), 170 Fed. (C. C.) 203.

[4] *American Trotting Reg.* v. *Gocher* (1895), 70 Fed. (C. C.) 237.

[5] *McNeill* v. *Williams* (Eng.) (1847), 11 Jur. 344.

as to its validity, then the court will consider before issuing its mandate whether the defendant will suffer great loss. For if it should then turn out upon final hearing that complainant's copyright is invalid, defendant's loss may be of such a character as to be impossible of computation, and a recovery on the undertaking given on injunction would not return the defendant to his former position.

The wisdom of this rule is readily apparent in a case where a motion picture has been released for exhibition, and, shortly after its release, and before it has run its course, an injunction issues. It may be, and usually is, several months before a final hearing can be had. If complainant's copyright is held to be invalid upon final hearing, defendant's injury cannot be compensated by recovery under the undertaking, for the life of a picture is ephemeral. After vacating the injunction the picture has in all likelihood grown stale, and defendant has lost not only his investment but his profit as well. He may, under the undertaking, recover the cost of his film, but since future profits in works of this character are to a great extent speculative, he must suffer this loss without redress.

A motion for a temporary injunction will not be allowed to operate as a means of obtaining a premature expression, where unnecessary, of the opinion by the court upon the merits of the controversy.[6]

Where the defendant denies that the work annexed to the bill of complaint and alleged to be the work infringed is such in fact, the complainant must affirmatively show

[6] *Pott* v. *Altemus* (1894), 60 Fed. (C. C.) 339.

that the copy which he annexes is indeed a true copy of the work.[7]

And where defendant claimed that he had an oral license to produce complainant's work by reason of the fact that the complainant was aware of the preparations which the defendant was making for his production, complainant's motion for a temporary injunction was denied.[8]

In all cases where an injunction pendente lite is granted, the injunction will not become effective except upon the complainant giving security in such sum as the court or judge may deem proper conditioned upon the payment of such costs and damages as may be incurred or suffered by the party who may be found to have been wrongfully enjoined or restrained thereby.[9]

In some instances it becomes necessary to secure a temporary restraining order to enjoin the alleged infringers until the hearing and determination of a motion for injunction pendente lite. The courts will only issue such an extraordinary order where it clearly appears by affidavit or by verified bill of complaint that immediate

[7] *Humphries* v. *Armstrong* (1887), 30 Fed. (C. C.) 66. On motion for preliminary injunction the plaintiff must show that the copy of his book is a copy of the book which was copyrighted, where the defendant denies this to be the fact.

Tully v. *Triangle* (1916), 229 Fed. (D. C.) 297. The court holds that rule two of the Supreme Court rules requiring that a copy of the infringed and infringing works shall accompany the complaint should be followed whenever possible.

[8] *G. Ricordi* v. *Hammerstein* (1907), 150 Fed. (C. C.) 450.

[9] Act Oct 15th, 1914, Chapter 323, § 18, U. S. Compiled Statutes 1916, § 1243b, p. 1963.

or irreparable injury, loss or damage will result to the complainant before notice can be served and a hearing had thereon.[10] Here as well, complainant must give security in a sum fixed by the court or judge granting the order.[11]

The injunction pendente lite and the temporary restraining order are binding upon the parties to the suit, their officers, agents, servants, employes and attorneys or those in active concert or participating with them, and who shall by personal service *or otherwise* have received actual notice of the same.[12]

The statute prescribes the requisites of the order for the injunction or restraining order, and care should be taken that the statute be literally complied with.[13]

Where an injunction will work very serious injury to the defendant, and the damages of complainant, if he should sustain his cause of action, may be computed with some degree of certainty, the court may in its discretion grant an injunction pendente lite, but suspend the operation of the same upon the defendant filing an undertaking in a specified sum. The court may also attach further conditions precedent to the suspension of the injunction. It occasionally requires the defendant in such cases to file statements at specified periods showing gross sales

[10] Act Oct. 15th, 1914, Chapter 323, § 17, U. S. Compiled Statutes, 1916, § 1243a, p. 1962.

[11] Act Oct. 15th, 1914, Chapter 323, § 18, U. S. Complied Statutes, 1916, § 1243b, p. 1963.

[12] Act Oct. 15th, 1914, Chapter 323, § 19, U. S. Compiled Statutes, 1916, § 1243c, p. 1963.

[13] Act Oct. 15th, 1914, Chapter 323, § 19, U. S. Compiled Statutes, 1916, § 1243c, p. 1963.

or receipts derived from the exploitation of the alleged infringing work.[14]

It has been said that the real basis for the granting of injunctions pendente lite is to maintain the status quo.[15]

Laches of the complainant will bar his right to a temporary injunction. But laches must not be confused with mere lapse of time. It is the element of time in conjunction with the element of knowledge which goes

[14] *Boosey* v. *Empire* (1915), 224 Fed. (D. C.) 646. A motion for a temporary injunction was granted in the case of an infringement of a musical composition, but the injunction was suspended upon the defendant filing a bond in a specified sum, and also statements semimonthly showing gross sales and receipts therefrom.

See also: *Hubbard* v. *Thompson* (1882), 14 Fed. (C. C.) 689.

[15] *Ladd* v. *Oxnard* (1896), 75 Fed. (C. C.) 703.

Colgate v. *White* (1909), 169 Fed. (C. C.) 887.

"While there is much doubt about the questions discussed in the briefs, I am inclined to the opinion that the complainant presents a case calling for the preservation, so far as practicable, of the status quo of the parties pending the litigation. If an injunction is not issued the complainant may suffer the very injury of which he complains, before the cause can be heard. If it is issued the defendant will suffer no special harm, and for any possible injury should be protected by a bond.

"Upon filing a proper and sufficient bond, therefore, an injunction may be issued restraining the defendants pendente lite from publishing the complainant's portrait, or his biography so far as the same may be based upon information obtained from him, and from enforcing the subscription contract."

On the question whether an injunction will be granted restraining a newspaper from publishing an outline of the plot of a play prior to its première see: Gilbert v. *The Star* (Eng.) (1894), 11 T. L. R. 4; which holds in the affirmative.

to make up laches. "The cases in which laches has been considered a bar to equitable relief proceed on the assumption that the party to whom it is imputed has knowledge of his rights." [16]

Section 168.—Final hearing.

Upon final hearing in an action in equity complainant is entitled to a permanent injunction, to damages, to an accounting of profits and to full costs which may in the discretion of the court include a reasonable counsel fee. He is not necessarily entitled to all these forms of relief.

He is ordinarily entitled to an injunction where an infringement is made out,[17] even though there is no proof of any damage to complainant.[18] There are, however,

[16] *Encyclopædia Britannica* v. *American Newspaper Ass'n* (1904), 130 Fed. (C. C.) 460, aff'd 134 Fed. (C. C. A.) 831.

For summary of the cases where laches was set up as a defense to infringement of copyright see notes to Taylor v. *Sawyer Spindle Co.*, 22 C. C. A. 211; *Richardson* v. *D. M. Osborn & Co.*, 36 C. C. A. 613.

See also: *Halstead* v. *Grinnan* (1894), 152 U. S. 412; 14 Sup. Ct. 641; *Ritchie* v. *Sayres* (1900), 100 Fed. (C. C.) 520; *Galliher* v. *Cadwell* (1892), 145 U. S. 368; 12 Sup. Ct. 873; *Old Colony Trust Co.* v. *Dubuque Co.* (1898), 89 Fed. (C. C.) 794.

As to whether the bill of complaint must be verified where a temporary injunction is prayed for see: Rule twenty-five, subdivision fifth of the Equity Rules; *Fichtel* v. *Barthel* (1909), 173 Fed. (C. C.) 489; *Black* v. *Henry G. Allen Co.* (1890), 42 Fed. (C. C.) 618; which hold in the affirmative.

[17] *Reed* v. *Holliday* (1884), 19 Fed. (C. C.) 325.

[18] *McMillan* v. *King* (1914), 223 Fed. (D. C.) 862. "Proof of actual damage is not necessary for the issuance of an injunction, if infringement appears and damage may probably follow from its continuance. *Reed* v. *Holliday* (1884), 19 Fed. (C. C.)

two exceptions to his right to an injunction. Where, during the pendency of the litigation, the term of complainant's copyright expires, he will not be granted an injunction, although he may be given damages and an account of profits.[19] And where the complainant is guilty of gross laches, equity will not grant an injunction.[20]

325, 327; *Sampson, etc., Co.* v. *Seaver, etc., Co.* (1905), 134 Fed. (C. C.) 890; Id., 140 Fed. (C. C. A.) 539."

See in this connection: *D'Ole* v. *Kansas City Star* (1899), 94 Fed. (C. C.) 840.

[19] *Hartford Print. Co.* v. *Hartford Directory* (1906), 146 Fed. (C. C.) 332.

See also: *Blank* v. *Mfg. Co.* (1856), Fed. Cas. (C. C.) No. 1532.

Root v. *Railway Co.* (1881), 105 U. S. 193. Plaintiff brought action after the expiration of his patent for an accounting of profits and damages for infringement within the term of the patent. Demurrer to bill was sustained, the court holding that plaintiff had an adequate remedy at law for his damages.

[20] *West Publ. Co.* v. *Edward Thompson Co.* (1908), 157 Fed. (C. C. A.) 1003, (1909), 169 Fed. (C. C.) 833, mod. 176 Fed. 833. "The complainant knew at least as early as 1893 that its syllabi were being paraphrased or copied by the defendant's writers, or some of them. Its conduct shows that it must have considered this to have been a fair use of its publications because it did not begin this action until the defendant *after 18 years* of labor and immense outlay of money, had published almost its entire work. The laches of the complainant and the hardship upon the defendant are such that we think the trial judge, 'according to the course and principles of courts of equity,' was right in refusing an injunction and accounting of profits. But we also think that the court can give damages in this case by way of compensation. . . . *This court, having obtained jurisdiction of the cause and having the power to grant an injunction, has the right to do justice between the parties and to dispose of it finally, even if this involves withholding injunctive relief and awarding damages.*"

See also: *Lawrence* v. *Dana*

It may be stated as a general rule that the right to an account of profits is incident to the right to injunction.[21]

Indeed, Section twenty-five, subdivision (b) of the Act expressly provides that any person who shall infringe a copyright shall pay to the copyright proprietor such damages as he may have suffered, due to the infringement, as well as all the profits which the defendant has made by such infringement.

Complainant is entitled, not only to an account of profits, but his actual damages as well. And this right is expressly given by the above-mentioned section of the Act.

The copyright proprietor may secure in lieu of actual damages and profits such damages as to the court shall appear to be just, and in assessing such damages the court may in its discretion award the sums fixed by Section twenty-five, subdivision (b) as follows: Where the motion picture is a photoplay, (its exhibition being a dramatic performance [22]) the court may award one hun-

(1869), Fed. Cas. No. 8136 (C.C.); and *Werner* v. *Encyclopedia* (1905), 134 Fed. (C. C. A.) 831.

See: *Masson's Appeal* (1871), 70 Pa. St. 26; *Valentine* v. *Richardt* (1891), 126 N. Y. 272; 27 N. E. 255; *Waite* v. *O'Neil* (1896), 76 Fed. (C. C. A.) 408; *Andrus* v. *Berkshire Co.* (1906), 147 Fed. (C. C. A.) 76; *New York City* v. *Pine* (1902), 185 U. S. 93, 22 Sup. Ct. 592.

[21] *Stevens* v. *Gladding* (1854), 17 How. 447; *Fischel* v. *Leuckel* (1892), 53 Fed. (C. C.) 499; *Sanborn* v. *Dakin* (1889), 39 Fed. (C. C.) 266; *Belford* v. *Scribner* (1892), 144 U. S. 488; 12 Sup. Ct. 734; *Gast* v. *Falk* (1893), 54 Fed. (C. C. A.) 890; *Stevens* v. *Cady* (1854), Fed. Cas. No. 13,395 (C. C.).

[22] *Kalem* v. *Harper* (1911), 222 U. S. 55; 32 Sup. Ct. 20.

dred dollars for the first, and fifty dollars for every subsequent infringing performance under subsection four of subdivision (b).

Where the motion picture, however, is other than a photoplay, the interesting question presents itself as to whether the court may assess damages pursuant to subsection four. The question has not at this writing come up for decision. Equity would seem to demand that the owner of a copyright in such a motion picture, which is frequently as valuable as a motion picture photoplay, should be entitled to receive the same rate of damages as in the case of motion pictures which are photoplays.

Such damages when fixed by the court in lieu of actual damages and profits must not be less than two hundred and fifty dollars nor be more than five thousand dollars. But such limitation does not apply to infringements occurring after actual notice to the defendant either by service of process in the suit or other written notice served upon him. In that event the recovery is unlimited.

There is dictum, however, and a decision of the District Court to the effect that Section twenty-five leaves the question of the arbitrary award of damages in lieu of actual damages and profits within the sound discretion of the court to allow or refuse the same entirely.[23] In a later case decided by the Circuit Court of Appeals, it was held that Section twenty-five prohibited the award of merely nominal damages. It held that where there was an in-

[23] *Decker* v. *Etchison* (1915), 225 Fed. (D. C.) 135; *Woodman* v. *Lydiard-Peterson Co.* (1912), 192 Fed. (C. C.) 67.

fringement the court was bound to assess at least the minimum amount as damage.[24]

We believe that the rule laid down by the Circuit Court of Appeals is the correct one.

The very purpose of Congress in fixing a minimum was to enable an injured party to obtain some substantial compensation for the injury done to him even where he was unable to show actual damage. Even if the complainant has not been actually damaged, he has by reason of the infringement, been put to the trouble and expense of commencing and maintaining a lawsuit to defend his property rights, and the infringing party should in equity be compelled to reimburse the complainant for his outlay.

When we consider that there is also a maximum we can readily see the justice of the statute. The maximum protects the innocent infringer, and in the same manner the minimum protects the aggrieved complainant.

But where motion pictures infringe upon an undramatized or non-dramatic work, and the infringer shows that he was not aware that he was infringing, and that such infringement could not have been reasonably foreseen, such damages under Section twenty-five may not exceed the sum of one hundred dollars.

And in the case of an infringement of a copyrighted dramatic or dramatico-musical work by a maker of motion pictures and his agencies for distribution thereof to exhibitors, where such infringer shows that he was not aware that he was infringing a copyrighted work, and that such infringement could not reasonably have been foreseen, the entire sum of such damages recoverable by the copy-

[24] *Westermann* v. *Dispatch* (1916), 233 Fed. (C. C. A.) 609.

right proprietor from such infringing maker and his agencies for the distribution to exhibitors of such infringing motion picture may not exceed the sum of five thousand dollars nor be less than two hundred and fifty dollars.

But the foregoing exceptions do not deprive the copyright proprietor of any other remedy given him under the Act and, here as well, the limitation as to the amount of recovery does not apply to infringements occurring after actual notice.

Plaintiff is entitled to damages down to the date of the trial.[25]

The rule as to profits under the present Act is strictly enforced.[26] One who infringes does so at his peril, and stands in danger of being compelled to turn over all his profits to the complainant. And this is so no matter how great the disparity in the nature of the respective works,

[25] *Hardacre* v. *Armstrong* (Eng.) (1904), Times, Oct. 27.

[26] *Haas* v. *Feist* (1916), 234 Fed. (D. C.) 105. "The plaintiff's right to damages against the defendant Feist, regardless of its innocence, is unquestionable. *Gross* v. *Van Dyk Gravure Co.*, 230 Fed. 412. And in spite of some language in that opinion looking to a different rule for profits I think the same should apply to them as to damages. When, as in copyright, the law provides a form of notice, it imposes upon everyone at his peril the duty to learn the facts conveyed by the notice. Without some such rule it could not be a tort innocently to copy a copyrighted work, because it could not be said that among the reasonable results of the defendant's acts was comprised an infringement. It becomes a tort, only when the statute imposes a duty on everyone to advise himself of the copyright. I cannot see why there should be any difference between damages and profits in this respect."

See also: *Huebsch* v. *Christ* (1914), 209 Fed. (D. C.) 885.

no matter how big a production defendant has made, nor how small and insignificant the complainant's copyrighted work.[27]

It does not matter that only a portion of the defendant's work infringes. He must pay over all his profits in the entire work, especially so in the case of dramatic compositions, where only a small portion of the work infringes.[28] The courts will not attempt to discover what portion of the profits is derived from that part of complainant's work which was made use of by defendant.[29]

Although the copyright proprietor is prima facie entitled to an account of profits and damages, situations may arise, however, where, because of some act of omission or commission equity will not give the complainant such relief.

Where a copyright proprietor stands by and permits an infringer to expend large sums of money in exploiting the infringing work, with a view to later appropriating such profits, he will not be permitted to recover any of the profits derived by the infringer after the time of his discovery of the infringement.[30] And where he is guilty of laches, he will not be awarded an account of profits or damages, although he will receive his injunction.[31]

[27] *Dam* v. *Kirk La Shelle* (1910), 175 Fed. (C. C. A.) 902.

See also: *Callaghan* v. *Meyers* (1888), 128 U. S. 617; 9 Sup. Ct. 177.

[28] *Brady* v. *Daly* (1899), 175 U. S. 148; 20 Sup. Ct. 62.

[29] *Dam* v. *Kirk La Shelle* (1910), 175 Fed. (C. C. A.) 902; *Callaghan* v. *Meyers* (1888), 128 U. S. 617; 9 Sup. Ct. 177; *Belford* v. *Scribner* (1892), 144 U. S. 488; 12 Sup. Ct. 734.

[30] *Haas* v. *Feist* (1916), 234 Fed. (D. C.) 105.

[31] *Wooster* v. *Crane & Co.* (1906), 147 Fed. (C. C. A.) 515.

The maxim that equity will not aid a complainant who comes into court with unclean hands applies as well in an action brought for infringement of copyright.[32]

[32] *Harms* v. *Stern* (1916), 231 Fed. (C. C. A.) 645. Vacating former order of the Circuit Court of Appeals reported in 229 Fed. 42 and affirming order of District Court reported in 222 Fed. 581.

A contract was made between defendants Harms and one Romberg whereby Romberg agreed to assign to Harms all musical compositions which he would write for a specified number of years. Romberg sold one of his musical compositions, written during the period of the contract, to the complainant Stern, who copyrighted the song. Defendants Harms published the song and this action was brought for infringement of Stern's copyright. Relief was denied to Stern upon the ground that they as assignees of Romberg stood in his shoes and that he, having been guilty of iniquitous conduct would not be aided by a court of equity; that the fact that an injunction was asked for to protect a copyright did not take the case out of the general principle that a complainant was required to come into equity with clean hands.

"In our opinion the plaintiffs did not come into court with clean hands. Their misconduct relates to the matter now in litigation. Their right is the right of Romberg and the latter's misconduct is for the purposes of this suit theirs. Having agreed by a binding contract to assign this song to these defendants, he has not done as he agreed, but has repudiated the legal and moral obligations which the agreement imposed upon him. In doing so he has committed iniquity as respects this copyrighted song and the relation of these defendants thereto. And with his hands thus unclean he has no standing in a court of equity in asking an injunction to restrain these defendants from exercising a right which he bound himself to give exclusively to them. As the plaintiffs stand in his shoes we must decline to grant them what we could not grant to Romberg."

See Kerr on Injunction (5th Ed.), 413.

Slingsby v. *Bradford Truck Co.* (Eng.) (1905), W. N. 122.

This need not be pleaded as a defense in order to be available; the court may of its own motion refuse relief to a complainant where the record discloses the unconscionable act.[33] But it must be remembered that the maxim applies only where the misconduct is in connection with the matter in litigation.[34]

And where the court refuses upon final hearing to give relief to complainant because of the immorality of complainant's work it may nevertheless refuse to award damages to defendant upon an undertaking given by complainant upon the issuance of a temporary restraining order, where defendant has in fact infringed complainant's work.[35]

Under Section forty of the Act the prevailing party is entitled as a matter of right to full costs except in actions

A catalogue which, in violation of the law, misrepresents articles as having been patented, will not be protected.

Davies v. *Bowes* (1913), 209 Fed. (D. C.) 53, aff'd 219 Fed. 178. Where an article, which is fiction and comes from the imagination of the reporter is held out as a news item in a newspaper, a copyright of the newspaper does not include the alleged news item above referred to. Anyone of the public may thereafter make use of the statements made in the news item, for the purpose of literary development.

See also: *Wright* v. *Tullis* (Eng.) (1845), 1 C. B. 873, where a publisher pretended that a copyrighted work was a translation from a well known foreign writer, when in fact it was the original work of a native. It was held that such pretense vitiated the copyright; and see: *Tribune Co.* v. *Associated Press* (1900), 116 Fed. (C. C.) 126.

[33] *Bentley* v. *Tibbals* (1915), 223 Fed. (C. C. A.) 247.

[34] *Bentley* v. *Tibbals* (1915), 223 Fed. (C. C. A.) 247.

[35] *Broder* v. *Zeno Mauvais Music Co.* (1898), 88 Fed. (C. C.) 74.

brought by or against the United States or any officer thereof, and the court may award a reasonable attorney's fee as part of the costs.[36]

[36] *Strauss* v. *Penn Printing & Publishing Co.* (1915), 220 Fed. (D. C.) 977. "Under the circumstances in this case the complainant is entitled to reasonable attorney's fee as part of the costs under the provisions of section 40 of the Act. If in the answer the defendant had admitted that the complainant was entitled to the relief granted herein, as was conceded at the trial, it is questionable whether an attorney's fee would have been allowed. *The answer, however, compelled the complainant to sustain by proof its right to any relief whatever.* Under these circumstances, taking into consideration on the other hand, that the issues involved are clearly defined and settled and raise no intricate questions of law, an attorney's fee of seventy-five ($75.00) dollars is awarded as part of the costs."

Hendricks v. *Thomas Publishing Co.*, N. Y. Law Journal (1917), April 18 (United States Circuit Court of Appeals—Second Circuit), Judge Hough in allowing twenty-five hundred ($2,500.00) dollars counsel fee said:

"It has often been held that allowance of counsel fees is a matter peculiarly within the discretion of the court awarding the same, because that court can (and always does) proceed upon its own knowledge of the value and extent of the professional services rendered. We have lately approved this rule in *Central Trust Co.* v. *United States, &c., Co.*, 233 Fed. Rep. 420. Discretionary matters are reviewable only when abuse of discretion is shown. Certainly no abuse is here demonstrated, and having ourselves examined this record, whereof the printed testimony is far less important than the enormous and ill-digested mass of exhibits requiring much labor to prove an infringement now admitted, we are the less inclined to disagree. There is nothing in *Universal Film, &c., Co.* v. *Copperman*, 218 Fed. Rep. 577, especially applicable to this case. *In both cases the trial judge inquired as to the value in a particular litigation of the professional services rendered, and fixed them by his own knowledge of the facts and professional custom.* We

The court upon final hearing will not consider itself bound by any order made in an application for an injunction pendente lite,[37] as the purpose of temporary injunctions is to hold matters in status quo and not to adjudicate.[38]

An author who assigned his copyright was not thereafter permitted upon securing a renewal thereof to enjoin his assignee.[39]

If the primary and controlling purpose of a suit is to enforce a right secured by the copyright laws, the Federal courts have jurisdiction of the action, although it incidentally involves questions respecting the validity, interpretation and effect of a contract through which complainant derives title.[40]

The usual procedure in an action for injunction where the court finds that there has been an infringement of the complainant's copyright is to enter an interlocutory decree providing for an injunction and sending the cause to a master to take proof of damages or profits or both.[41]

decline to disturb the award of counsel fees."

Gross v. *Van Dyke Gravure* (1916), 230 Fed. (C. C. A.) 412. A counsel fee of $350 was awarded.

Mills v. *Standard Music Roll Co.* (2 cases), 223 Fed. (D. C.) 849. A counsel fee of $75 was allowed in each case.

Gross v. *Van Dyke* (1916), 230 Fed. (C. C. A.) 412. The court may award a counsel fee and relieve one of the defendants who is an innocent infringer from paying it.

[37] *Millar* v. *Taylor* (Eng.) (1769), 4 Burr. 2380.

[38] *Ladd* v. *Oxnard* (1896), 75 Fed. (C. C.) 703.

[39] *Paige* v. *Banks* (1870), 7 Blatchf. (C. C.) 152.

[40] *Wooster* v. *Crane & Co.* (1906), 147 Fed. (C. C. A.) 515; *Ferris* v. *Frohman* (1912), 223 U. S. 424; 32 Sup. Ct. 263.

[41] *Huebsch* v. *Christ* (1914), 209 Fed. (D. C.) 885; *Patterson* v.

Upon the return of the master's report a final decree is entered awarding complainant damages or profits or both, together with costs, and in the discretion of the court a reasonable counsel fee as part of the costs.[42]

The court may, instead of referring the cause to a master, itself fix the damages as well as the profits.[43]

Where in an action for infringement defendant claims title to the copyright upon which the complainant is suing, the court has jurisdiction to adjudicate the question of title.[44]

Where the copyright was secured under an Act prior to 1909 but the infringement occurred subsequent to the going into effect of the 1909 Act, the complainant may pursue the remedies given under the 1909 Act.[45]

Under Section twenty-seven of the Act the proceedings for injunction, damages and profits and those for the seizure of infringing copies and plates, may be united in one action.

Section 169.—Injunction as to part.

The court has the right, infringement being established,

Ogilvie Pub. Co. (1902), 119 Fed. (C. C.) 451.

[42] *Patterson* v. *Ogilvie Pub. Co.* (1902), 119 Fed. (C. C.) 451. The decision in this case provided that complainant might take a final decree for injunction and six cents damages, or an interlocutory decree for an injunction, with reference to a master.

See also: § 40 of the Copyright Act of 1909. *Heubsch* v. *Crist* (1914), 209 Fed. (D. C.) 885.

[43] *Patterson* v. *Ogilvie Pub. Co.* (1902), 119 Fed. (C. C.) 451; *Mills* v. *Standard Music Roll*, 223 Fed. (D. C.) 849; aff'd March, 1917; *Gross* v. *Van Dyke Gravure Co.* (1916), 230 Fed. (C. C. A.) 412.

[44] *Binns* v. *Woodruff* (1821), Fed. Cas. (C. C.) No. 1424.

[45] *Huebsch* v. *Christ* (1914), 209 Fed. (D. C.) 885.

to enjoin the further performance of the defendant's entire work. It may, however, in its sound discretion, issue its injunction only as against that portion of the work which infringes where the defendant may readily expurgate such part of the infringing work.[46]

The court will ordinarily issue such an injunction when the infringement has not been wilfully caused or where both works are based upon a common source, and the defendant has taken only a small portion of his work from the complainant.[47]

This is especially true, where the damage done to the defendant by an injunction would be out of all proportion to complainant's damage.[48]

But this will not be done where the part which infringes and that which does not cannot be readily separated.[49]

"If an individual chooses in any work to mix my literary matter with his own, he must be restrained from publishing the literary matter which belongs to me; and if the other parts of the work cannot be separated, and if by that means the injunction which restrains the publication

[46] *Historical Pub. Co.* v. *Jones* (1916), 231 Fed. (C. C. A.) 638.

See also: *Farmer* v. *Elstner* (1888), 33 Fed. (C. C.) 494; *Samson* v. *Seaver* (1905), 140 Fed. (C. C. A.) 539.

[47] *Stevenson* v. *Fox* (1915), 226 Fed. (D. C.) 990.

[48] *Farmer* v. *Elstner* (1888), 33 Fed. (C. C.) 494.

[49] *Park & Pollard Co.* v. *Kellerstrass* (1910), 181 Fed. (C. C.) 431. "Yet, as what is permissible and what is improper are so interwoven and combined in one and the same book that the defendant without elimination cannot use or employ what is his own without employing and using that which is not, he ought not at this juncture exact of the court the task of such separation so as to relieve him therefrom."

of my matter prevents also the publication of his own literary matter, he has only himself to blame." [50]

Secton 170.—Writ of seizure.

The aggrieved party need not wait until final adjudication before he secures the seizure of the infringing copies of his motion picture.

Section twenty-five of the Act, subdivisions (c) and (d), provide that the infringer shall be liable to deliver upon oath to be impounded during the pendency of the action upon such terms and conditions as the court may prescribe all articles alleged to infringe a copyright, and that the infringer shall also be liable after final hearing to deliver up, on oath, for destruction all the infringing copies or devices as well as all plates, moulds, matrices or other means for making such infringing copies as the court may order.

The Supreme Court of the United States in pursuance of the authority vested in it under this section of the Act has adopted rules for the practice and procedure to be followed in the impounding and destruction of the infringing devices, plates, etc., and these rules are contained in Rules three to thirteen inclusive, thereof.

The rules in substance provide that upon the institution of the suit or at any time before final judgment, the complainant or his agent may file an affidavit giving the number and location to the best of his knowledge of the alleged infringing copies, plates, etc., and the value

[50] Lord Eldon in *Mawman* v. *Tegg* (Eng.) (1826), 2 Russ. 385. See also: *Webb* v. *Powers* (Eng.), 2 Woodb. & M. 497; *Greene* v. *Bishop* (1858), 1 Cliff, (C. C.) 186.

of the same, together with a bond in twice the reasonable value of such infringing copies and plates. The clerk is thereupon required to issue a writ directed to the Marshal directing him to seize and hold the same subject to the order of the court. The rules are given in full in the appendix herein.

It has been held that a motion for an order to show cause why films seized by the Marshal pursuant to Section twenty-five, subdivision (c) of the Act should not be returned, will not be entertained by the court unless it is shown pursuant to the Supreme Court rules that the articles seized are not infringing copies.[51]

Where the defendant has been successful in the action, he may recover his damages under the complainant's bond. *Universal Film Mfg. Co.* v. *Copperman,*[52] has a detailed discussion of the mode of fixing the damages in a situation of this kind. The court there fixes defendant's loss as the moneys which he would have received from exhibitions of the film during the period of detention of the film.

The court follows the line of reasoning suggested in *Schlesinger* v. *Bedford,*[53] where a recovery was permitted for the prevention of dramatic performances, and holds in effect that the modern trend of thought in awarding damages is to compensate the aggrieved party for all of his loss; for one who prevents another from pursuing his business has in mind the nature and incidents of such

[51] *Crown Feature Film* v. *Betts* (1913), 206 Fed. (D. C.) 362.

[52] *Universal Film* v. *Copperman* (1914), 218 Fed. (D. C.) 580.

[53] *Schlesinger* v. *Bedford* (1893), 28 Weekly Notes, 57.

business, and should be liable for the losses sustained by reason of his acts, whether the loss be in the nature of future profits or investment or both.

Actions brought under the Copyright Act are statutory actions, as distinguished from common-law actions; hence, attachments and replevins, not being specifically provided for in the Act, may not be maintained.[54]

And the rules of the state courts wherein the writ is issued pertaining to attachment and replevin have no reference thereto.[55]

Section 171.—Accounting.

Section twenty-five, subdivision (b) provides that in proving profits the plaintiff shall be required to prove sales only, and the defendant shall be required to prove every element of costs which he claims. While this rule primarily applies to works which are reproduced in copies

[54] *Dixon* v. *Corinne* (1914), 214 Fed. (D. C.) 418. On attachment.

Hillis & Co. v. *Hoover* (1906), 142 Fed. (C. C.) 904. On replevin.

Gustin v. *Record Pub. Co.* (1904), 127 Fed. (C. C.) 603. On replevin.

But see: *Morrison* v. *Pettibone* (1897), 87 Fed. (C. C.) 330.

[55] *Richardson* v. *Bosselman* (1907), 164 Fed. (C. C.) 781; *Hills* v. *Hoover* (1906), 142 Fed. (C. C.) 904; *Gustin* v. *Record Pub. Co.* (1904), 127 Fed. (C. C.) 603; *Reinhardt* v. *Smith* (1903), 121 Fed. (C. C.) 148; *Falk* v. *Curtis* (1900), 102 Fed. (C. C.) 967.

But see in this connection: *Am. Tobacco Co.* v. *Werckmeister* (1907), 207 U. S. 284; 28 Sup. Ct. 72. This was the ordinary action for replevin under the New York Code based on 4965, Rev. St. of U. S. *Held* that as the question of the propriety of bringing such a form of action was not raised until on a motion for a new trial, it could not be heard on appeal.

for sale, it may be stated that where the infringement is of a dramatic work, and the complainant wishes to secure defendant's profits, he must only show the gross receipts, and the defendant is obligated to show the actual cost of production and the disbursements necessarily incurred by him in the exploitation of the work.

As a matter of practice, the procedure which is ordinarily followed is the one outlined in the old Chancery Practice Rule one hundred and seven.[56]

[56] Chancery Rule one hundred and seven: "All parties accounting before a master shall bring in their accounts in the form of debtor and creditor, and any one of the other parties who shall not be satisfied with the accounts so brought in shall be at liberty to examine the accounting party upon interrogatories, as the master may direct. On any reference to take or state an account, the master shall be at liberty to allow interest as shall be just and equitable, without any special directions for that purpose, unless a contrary direction is contained in the order of reference, and every change, discharge or state of facts, brought in before the master shall be verified by oath as true, either positively or upon information and belief."

New York Bank Note Co. v. *Hamilton Eng. Co.* (1900), 56 A. D. (N. Y.) 488; 67 N. Y. Supp. 827. "*When the account is presented, the plaintiff is at liberty to surcharge the same with any sums which he can prove ought to be added thereto, and he may examine the party presenting the account for that purpose. The defendant may also show matters, within the scope of the accounting, which tend to relieve him from the apparent amount which would otherwise be charged against him.*"

The question was again considered in *Kliger* v. *Rosenfeld* (1907), 120 A. D. (N. Y.) 396, 105 N. Y. Supp. 214. "The proper practice where a party is adjudged to account either before the court or a referee appointed by it, is that prescribed by the 107th Chancery Rule, and the party so directed should prepare and file and verify an account of the matter as he

After the parties appear before the Master, the defendant is directed to file his account. The defendant charges himself with the gross receipts and credits himself with his disbursements. The account is verified. If the complainant is dissatisfied with any portion of the account he files exceptions thereto, stating specifically the nature of his objections, and if it is with respect to any particular item of the account, by pointing out the same.

Hearings are then had before the Master on the items to which objections have been taken.

It would seem under the rule laid down by Section twenty-five, that if the objection is taken to any part of the receipts, the burden is on the complainant. He may subpœna the books of account [57] as well as the defendant himself, or its officers, if a corporation, as well as other witnesses.

If, on the other hand, the objection is taken with respect to the disbursements of the defendant, then the defendant must prove by competent evidence the correctness of the items to which the objections have been taken, otherwise those items are stricken from the account, and the defendant is surcharged with them.[58]

claims the facts to be. *New York Bank Note Co.* v. *Hamilton Engraving Co.* (1900), 56 A. D. (N. Y.) 488, 67 N. Y. Supp. 827. *If such account is satisfactory to the opposing party, that is an end of the matter. If it is not, the other party should file his objections and specify what is wrong and what surcharges he claims should be made. In this manner issues for litigation are made concerning specific items and the mass of uncontested items are eliminated from proof and further consideration until the making up of the findings and report.*"

[57] *Callaghan* v. *Meyers* (1888), 128 U. S. 617; 9 Sup. Ct. 177.

[58] *Ginn* v. *Appollo* (1915), 228

In this respect the old Chancery Rule above mentioned has been modified by the Act.[59]

Section 172.—Actions at law.

A copyright proprietor may bring his action on the law side of the court and ask for damages by reason of the infringement. He acquires thereby the absolute right to a trial by jury. The question of infringement, which is a question of fact, then becomes one for the jury.[60]

Fed. (D. C.) 214. "In patent cases, the profits are found by contrasting the amount of proceeds of sales made with the total cost of production. In copyright cases, under the Act of 1912 (Act Aug. 24, 1912) the plaintiff may show only the receipts, or debit side of the account, and put upon the defendant the burden of proving the cost of production, or the plaintiff may exact the penalty. A successful plaintiff is thus given something in the nature of certain options. He may take damages and profits or the penalty imposed. If he takes profits, he may avail himself of the method of proving profits given by the Act of 1912. This method, however, is not exclusive. Whatever method he adopts he may apply it by calling upon the defendant to account, or by proving either sales or profits through and by evidence introduced or witnesses called by him."

[59] In the following cases miscellaneous questions arising upon an accounting, such as "proper elements of cost," "items properly included in gross receipts" etc., etc., are discussed. *Callaghan* v. *Meyers* (1888), 128 U. S. 617; 9 Sup. Ct. 177; *Stevens* v. *Gladding* (1856), Fed. Cas. No. 13,397 (C. C.) *Hartford Co. v. Hartford D. Co.* (1906), 148 Fed. (C. C.) 470, and *Dam* v. *Kirk La Shelle* (1911), 189 Fed. (C. C.) 842, particularly, which involves the accounting on an infringement of a dramatic composition.

See also: *Chils* v. *Gronland* (1890), 41 Fed. (C. C.) 145.

[60] *Maxwell* v. *Goodwin* (1899),

Section twenty-five, subdivision (b) providing for the payment of damages as well as profits, applies to an action at law as well as to one in equity. The difference is that in one the jury, instead of the master, assesses the damages; and the use of the word "court" in the statute does not require the judge acting by himself to assess the damages, but on the contrary, he is permitted to direct the jury to assess the damages within the prescribed limits.[61]

It has been held no error to instruct the jury that it may award exemplary damages in the case of a wanton or malicious disregard of complainant's rights in his work.[62]

Where the action is tried at law, the judge must submit the issues of infringement to the jury, but where the verdict of the jury is clearly against the weight of evidence, the trial justice may set it aside.[63]

It would seem that a complainant may bring his action for damages for infringement in the law branch of the court, and during the pendency of that action may institute a new action for an injunction, upon the theory that the action at law is designed to secure indemnity for the past, and the injunction protection for the future.[64]

93 Fed. (C. C.) 665. "Applying the rule held in patent causes at law, that issues of infringement and identity must be passed upon by the jury," it is proper to submit the issue of infringement or piracy to a jury in a copyright action.

Dam v. *Kirk La Shelle* (1910), 175 Fed. (C. C. A.) 902.

[61] *Mail & Express* v. *Life Pub. Co.* (1912), 192 Fed. (C. C. A.) 899.

[62] *Press Pub. Co.* v. *Monroe* (1896), 73 Fed. (C. C. A.) 196.

[63] *Maxwell* v. *Goodwin* (1899), 93 Fed. (C. C.) 665.

[64] *Schumacher* v. *Schwencke* (1885), 25 Fed. (C. C.) 466. "The copyright law seems to contem-

Section 173.—Actions purporting to be brought under the Copyright Act.

Complainants occasionally mistake their remedies. Actions are brought under the Copyright Act where the questions involved have reference solely to contractual relations between the parties. The Federal courts will not entertain such actions, unless the other jurisdictional facts are present.[65]

plate both remedies; and no reason is suggested why a party who seeks the first should be deprived of the second."

[65] Editorial in N. Y. Law Journal, September 19, 1917.

Suits in State Courts affecting Patentable and Literary Rights.

The decision of the Supreme Judicial Court of Massachusetts in *Aronson* v. *Orlov* (July, 1917, 116 N. E. 951) is of more than usual interest because of Chief Justice Rugg's treatment of a defense that is very frequently raised when patentable or copyrightable rights are incidentally, though not directly, brought in issue in State courts. It appeared that two of the defendants, former employees of the plaintiffs, associated themselves with a third person in the manufacture of petticoats in accordance with an idea to secure elasticity in connection with the seams originated by one of the plaintiffs and secretly communicated to the defendants in the course of their employment. The plaintiff originator had applied for a patent embodying such idea, but his application had been disallowed. The defendants had applied for a patent involving the same idea and their application had been neither allowed nor disallowed but was still pending. In such condition of the facts an injunction with damages is granted prohibiting the defendants from disclosing and using the plaintiff's idea for an elastic seam on the ground that it is a protectable trade secret.

While there is considerable novelty in this branch of the case, the principal general interest lies in the determination, after discussion, that the subject-matter of the suit is not within the cognizance of the Federal courts,

For instance, where the legal title in copyrighted books was not in the copyright proprietor, his remedy for breach

but that the State court has jurisdiction. The entire opinion will amply repay perusal. After showing by the citation of many authorities that prior to the issuance of a patent no case can arise under the patent laws respecting the relative rights of parties to or under a patent, the learned Chief Justice said in part as follows:

"The case at bar, in our opinion, does not arise 'under the patent laws' of the United States. The plaintiffs do not rest upon any right secured by the patent laws, and they do not assail any monopoly conferred upon the defendants by such laws. Every reference to the application for a patent and to the patent laws might be stricken from the bill, and every fact respecting that subject might be eliminated from the master's report, without affecting or impairing the fundamental rights upon which the plaintiffs' case rests. On the other hand, giving full effect to every allegation in the bill touching patents and to every fact found by the master relative to that subject, involves no right arising under the patent laws. Even when a patent has been granted, business transactions entered upon and executed before the patent was granted are not ordinarily affected. Concededly, no patent was granted to anybody for anything respecting this subject until long after this suit was instituted. The question which the plaintiffs are seeking to have settled in this cause is not their right to a patent, but their right to be protected from unlawful trade interference. The circumstance that priority of conception of an idea, which may or may not involve a patentable invention, was incidentally involved in one respect of that unlawful interference, renders the subject of the Patent Laws of the United States, if a patent ever should be granted, collateral and incidental to a cause over which the state courts have jurisdiction.

"This suit is not brought to determine the priority of an invention, and hence the right to a patent. It is brought to prevent the unlawful use of information, which may relate in part to an invention about the patentability of which there is contention,

of a contract respecting the sale of the books was held to be one for breach of contract, and not one cognizable

which has been obtained under such confidential circumstances that it ought not to be used to their harm. See *Agawan Co.* v. *Jordan*, 7 Wall. 583, 602, 19 L. Ed. 177. Therefore the statement of the Circuit Court judge in *Standard Scale & Foundry Co.* v. *McDonald*, 127 Fed. 709, 710, that 'it was never in the mind of Congress that the inventor, without complying with the statutory scheme of submitting his claim to the Patent Office for its action thereon, could go into a United States court in the first instance, to have determined the question of his right to a patent,' has no application to the facts here disclosed.

"The plaintiffs' cause of action seems far more remote from the patent laws of the United States than actions on notes given for patents where the voidness of the patent (*Dickinson* v. *Hall*, 14 Pick. 217, 25 Am. Dec. 390), its invalidity because of fraudulent procurement (*Bliss* v. *Negus*, 8 Mass., 46), its want of utility (*Bierce* v. *Stocking*, 11 Gray, 174), and its utter worthlessness (*Lester* v. *Palmer*, 4 Allen, 145), have been considered as defenses and directly adjudicated by this court. All of these cases were cited with approval in *Pratt* v. *Paris Gaslight & Coke Co.*, 168 U. S. 255, 260, 261, 18 Sup. Ct. 62, 41 L. Ed. 458), together with an amplitude of other authorities showing the wide scope of jurisdiction rightly taken by state courts of questions involving incidentally the validity of patents when the action was not brought directly and chiefly for infringement or to test the validity of a patent."

As to actions in state courts affecting property that might be the subject of copyright it should be kept in mind that the American Copyright Act now in force expressly provides that nothing therein contained "shall be construed to annul or limit the right of the author or proprietor of an unpublished work, at common law or in equity, to prevent the copying, publication or use of such unpublished work without his consent, and to obtain damages therefor." (U. S. Comp. Stat., 1913, § 9518. The American Act differs from the English Copyright Act of 1911 in that the latter "confers copyright in unpublished as well as published works, and abolishes the quasi-copyright at common law previously enjoyed by the former, preserving, however, the common-law right to have a period of trust or confidence restrained." The Law of Copyright, by George Stuart Roberts, 1912, Preface.

In the United States common-law rights in literary property must be sued on in a state court unless the matter in dispute is sufficiently large and an alien is a party, or the suit is between citizens of different states, so as to confer jurisdiction upon a federal court. In like manner as in suits incidentally concerning patentable rights, the contention is not infrequently made in actions in state courts affecting literary or artistic property rights that the Federal courts have exclusive jurisdiction. On Monday last we referred to the decision of Mr. Justice Greenbaum in *Fisher* v. *Star Company* (N. Y. Law Journal, January 26, 1917, p. 1497), which turned upon a question of trade-mark or trade name. It appeared, among other things, that a cartoonist, whose rights to the trade-mark in "Mutt and Jeff" were upheld, had not only registered those words as a trade-mark in his name, but further, that he had published and copyrighted in his name books containing some of his drawings and published under the title "The Mutt and Jeff cartoons, by 'Bud' Fisher." Mr. Justice Greenbaum felt constrained to remark in reply to points made by counsel that "in passing upon the voluminous findings submitted by the defendant I desire to observe that because reference is made to certain copyrights in the plaintiff's findings there is no implication that this court is disposing of this case upon the theory that a copyright is involved. The facts with reference to the copyright are merely incidental in the determination of the ultimate questions presented."

The test of jurisdiction is similar to that applied in the Massachusetts case as to patentable property, that is whether the suit is really to uphold or recover damages for infringement of "any right protected under this (the Copyright) act." And a state court or a Federal court, if for special reasons it has jurisdiction, may, in upholding merely common-law rights in literary property, grant remedies that are similar to those under the Copyright Act.[66] And where the suit was to enforce a contract between a publisher and an author, it was held not to be an action arising under the Copyright Act.[67] A covenant in a contract between a proprietor of a

prescribed by the Copyright Act for infringement of literary works that have actually been copyrighted. *French* v. *Kreling*, 63 Fed. 621.

[66] *Harrison* v. *Maynard* (1894), 61 Fed. (C. C. A.) 689.

[67] *Silver* v. *Holt* (1895), 84 Fed. (C. C.) 809.

Baldwin v. *Baird* (1885), 25 Fed. (C. C.) 293. Two parties had contracted for the sale of a book each one to have a certain territory. Subsequently the successors of one party brought out a new edition of the work and invaded the other's territory. *Held* that this was not a question of copyright but of contract, and injunction was granted restraining.

Pulte v. *Derby* (1852), 5 McLean, 328. The author of a book sought to restrain the publishers, who had copyrighted the book in their own names, from publishing a third edition. The parties had, before the book was copyrighted, entered into an agreement whereby the right was granted to the defendants to publish a first edition and as many copies of the second edition as they could sell. The defendants in a cross bill claimed that as the copyright was in them, the complainant had no right to publish a revised edition and prayed that he be enjoined. The court held that the rights of the parties depended upon the construction of the contract alone and that there was no question in the case which could be said to arise under the Copyright Act.

See also: *Albright* v. *Teas* (1882), 106 U. S. 613; 1 Sup. Ct. 550. *Held* that a suit involving contract rights granted in a patented invention did not involve patent rights as such, and could not be brought in the United States courts.

"The controversy between them as stated by the appellants themselves is whether certain goods manufactured by them embody the invention covered by the appellee's patents. This does not necessarily involve a construction of the patents. Both parties may agree as to

copyright and a licensee, whereby the licensee binds himself not to infringe, is enforceable in a state court in the same manner as the contractual rights and obligations arising out of any other negative covenant in the contract.[68]

what the patented invention is and yet disagree on the question whether the invention is employed in the manufacture of certain specified goods. The controversy between the parties in this case is clearly of the latter kind."

See also: *Herzog* v. *Heyman* (1897), 151 N. Y. 587; 45 N. E. 1127; *Waterman* v. *Shipman* (1891), 130 N. Y. 301; 29 N. E. 111.

[68] *Comerma Co.* v. *Comerma and Tile Arch Const. Co.*, N. Y. Law Journal (1917), June 1st. "The evidence establishes that the plaintiff was a licensee under the patents mentioned in the agreement between the parties, and it is admitted that the plaintiff's license was not an exclusive one even within a limited territory. It may be presumed that the plaintiff has the mere naked right of user of the patented article for a consideration paid or to be paid. Under the agreement between the parties to this action, defendant Comerma stipulated not to infringe the two patents in question and not to question their validity. Inasmuch as plaintiff's claim does not arise under the Patent Laws, but under a contract, it is evident that the plaintiff could not enforce its rights against defendants in the Federal courts, which have exclusive power to adjudicate rights under the Patent Laws of the United States, but have no jurisdiction to adjudicate rights, which depend entirely upon contractual obligations in relation to patents. If the plaintiff may not assert its rights under the Patent Laws, it seems clear that he never could assert them unless the state courts had jurisdiction to enforce them. We are thus required to construe the contract and determine what the parties meant when Comerma agreed not to "infringe" the patents. If the word "infringe" were construed to refer to the making, selling or using without right of a patented article, which is the sense

Section 174.—Willful infringements.

Section twenty-eight of the Act provides that any person who willfully and for profit shall infringe any copyright secured by the Act or who shall knowingly and willfully aid or abet such infringement shall be deemed guilty of a misdemeanor, and upon conviction thereof, shall be punished by imprisonment for not exceeding one year or by a fine of not less than one hundred dollars nor more than one thousand dollars or both in the discretion of the court.

The interesting question that arises under this section of the Act is as to the respective criminal liabilities of the various parties who participate in the "duping" of a film.

The making of a negative "dupe" from a positive print of a motion picture, when made for the purpose of profit in any form, comes within this section. The intent to

in which the word is ordinarily employed (*Goodyear Shoe Mfg. Co.* v. *Jackson*, 112 Fed. 146, 148), then no effect could be given to the word "infringe" in the contract. But reading that portion of the contract, under which the defendant agreed not to "infringe," in conjunction with the other portions thereof and the circumstances disclosed upon the trial, it is evident that what the parties meant was that the defendant Comerma would not make the articles specified in these patents within the territory prescribed. In other words, the question of a violation of the covenant not to infringe the patented article is cognizable in the state court in the same manner as that court may construe the contractual rights and obligations arising out of any negative covenant in a contract. The word "infringe" would thus be construed to mean as between the parties that Comerma would not make or be interested in any such article as is described in the patents."

derive profit need not be expressly shown, but may be inferred from the circumstances of the case, as where the defendant is engaged in the motion picture business and is caught making a negative "dupe." Here, clearly, the court will hold that the defendant's intent as expressed by his outward acts, was to derive a profit.

The Act makes a distinction between the person who infringes and him who aids or abets such infringement. In the former it must be established that the act was done willfully and for profit. In the latter it is sufficient to show that the defendants knowingly and willfully aided or abetted. In the second case profit is entirely eliminated.

Every one who participates in the "duping" process and in the sale or other disposition of the "duped" negatives and positives is equally liable under the Act. Thus the photographer, the developer, the printer, distributor and exhibitor may all be liable.

The criminal and civil remedies under the Act are not exclusive. They may be pursued concurrently if desired, so that the complainant may at one and the same time move for his injunction pendente lite, secure a writ of seizure for the "duped" films, and obtain his warrant for the arrest of the infringer.[69]

[69] *R.* v. *Baldoli* (Eng.) (1913), Times, Nov. 27. See for conviction under English Copyright Act for knowingly having a positive print of a film in the possession of defendant with intent to make infringing copies therefrom: *Rex* v. *Willetts* (Eng.) (1906), Times, Jan. 20. The defendants had conspired to pirate the plaintiff's music, and the conviction was had on the theory of conspiracy.

Some of the states have enacted laws making it a crime to publicly perform unpublished works. See

Section 175.—Statute of limitations.

Section thirty-nine of the Act provides that no criminal proceeding shall be maintained under the provisions of the Act, unless the same is commenced within three years after the cause of action has arisen.

The present statute does not contain any statute of limitation with respect to civil remedies. Under the statute in force prior to the present Act there was a provision limiting the commencement of actions for a forfeiture or penalty within two years after the cause of action had arisen.[70]

Section 176.—Construction of forfeiture and penalty clauses.

Under the earlier statutes, all the copies of the infringer's work, found in his possession, were forfeited, and in addition thereto, he was liable to a penalty, half of the proceeds going to the plaintiff and half to the United States Government. An action brought under these statutes was not in equity, for equity does not enforce penalties and forfeitures,[71] but was in the nature of a *qui*

Penal Laws of New York, § 441, which makes it a misdemeanor to perform an undedicated work in that state.

[70] Revised Statute, 4968. See also: *Wheeler* v. *Cobbey* (1895), 70 Fed. (C. C.) 487.

[71] *Stevens* v. *Gladding* (1854), 17 How. 447. For a full discussion as to the power of a court by equity to enforce the forfeiture provisions of the Copyright Act. It would seem that in the absence of express jurisdiction conferred by Congress such courts will not enforce penalties or forfeitures (p. 455).

Chapman v. *Ferry* (1882), 12 Fed. (C. C.) 693; *U. S.* v. *White* (1883), 17 Fed. (C. C.) 561; *Fletcher* v. *New Orleans* (1884), 20 Fed. (C. C.) 345; *Trow City*

tam action which abated with the death of the defendant.[72] It was civil in its nature,[73] although the statute, being highly penal [74] called for a strict construction.[75]

So that when the alleged wrongful acts were committed by defendant's agent without his knowledge or consent, he was not liable,[76] nor where he had parted with possession of the infringing copies.[77]

On the other hand, the complainant was not required to allege a demand and refusal,[78] nor was it material whether or not he was damaged by the infringement.[79]

Under the 1909 Act most of these fine distinctions seem to have been done away with. From the language of the statute the penalties are expressly declared to be given in lieu of damages and not to be regarded as penal-

Directory v. *Curtin* (1888), 36 Fed. (C. C.) 829; *Lillard* v. *Sun Printing Co.* (1898), 87 Fed. (C. C.) 213.

[72] *Schreiber* v. *Sharpless* (1883), 17 Fed. (D. C.) 589.

[73] *Journal Pub. Co.* v. *Drake* (1912), 199 Fed. (C. C. A.) 572. "The action is founded upon that implied contract which every person enters into with the state to observe its laws. *Stearns* v. *U. S.*, 2 Paine, 300; Fed. Cas. No. 13,341. . . . Actions for penalties are civil actions both in form and in substance, according to Blackstone."

[74] *McDonald* v. *Hearst* (1900), 95 Fed. (C. C.) 656.

[75] *Falk* v. *Curtis* (1900), 98 Fed. (C. C.) 989; 100 Fed. 77; *Snow* v. *Laird* (1900), 98 Fed. (C. C. A.) 813; *Bennett* v. *Carr* (1899), 96 Fed. (C. C. A.) 213; *Boston Traveler Co.* v. *Purdy* (1905), 137 Fed. (C. C. A.) 717; *Caliga* v. *Interocean Newspaper Co.* (1907), 157 Fed. (C. C. A.) 186; aff'd 215 U. S. 182; 30 Sup. Ct. 38.

[76] *Taylor* v. *Gilman* (1885), 24 Fed. (C. C.) 632.

[77] *Sarony* v. *Ehrich* (1886), 28 Fed. (C. C.) 79.

[78] *Hegeman* v. *Springer* (1901), 110 Fed. (C. C. A.) 374; aff'd 189 U. S. 505; 23 Sup. Ct. 849.

[79] *Springer* v. *Falk* (1894), 59 Fed. (C. C. A.) 707.

ties.[80] And this construction has been placed upon the statute in *Westermann* v. *Despatch.*[81]

This reçent construction of the statute is of interest, for if the action is not construed as being one for a penalty, but rather one for liquidated damages, then the Statute of Limitations for penalties in the former Copyright Act even if it is held that the repealing clause of the present Act has not repealed this provision, does not apply.[82]

Section 177.—Appeal.

Section thirty-eight provides that the orders, judgments or decrees of any court having jurisdiction of the actions, suits or proceedings brought under the Act may be reviewed on appeal or writ of error, in the manner and to the extent provided by law for the review of cases determined in said courts respectively.

[80] Section 25, Copyright Act of 1909. See also: *Brady* v. *Daly* (1899), 175 U. S. 148; 20 Sup. Ct. 62.

[81] *Westermann* v. *Despatch* (1916), 233 Fed. (C. C. A.) 609. Construing § 25 of the 1909 Act, *Held* that the "in lieu of" clause providing that the court might in its discretion allow a specified sum for every infringing copy or performance of a work was not to be regarded as imposing a penalty.

"It would seem that the words 'shall not be regarded as a penalty' were added out of abundant caution, for under such a situation as usually exists on this subject the awarding of a round sum in damages is no more a penalty when the damages are liquidated by a court than when they are liquidated by a contract."

[82] For cases under the former statute see: *Patterson* v. *Ogilvie Pub. Co.* (1902), 119 Fed. (C. C.) 451; *Wheeler* v. *Cobbey* (1895), 70 Fed. (C. C.) 487; see also generally: *Brady* v. *Daly* (1899), 175 U. S. 148; 20 Sup. Ct. 148.

CHAPTER XV

COPYRIGHT (CONTINUED)

Miscellaneous Matters

SEC. 178. Return of copies deposited.
179. Prohibition of importation of piratical copies.
180. Ad interim protection.
181. Bankruptcy—Title in trustee.
182. Selling secondhand copies.
183. Taxability.
184. Music in theatres.
185. Co-authorship.
186. Employer and employe.
187. Restraint of trade—Price fixing—Monopoly.

Section 178.—Return of copies deposited.

Section sixty of the Act provides that any works deposited pursuant to the Act and not disposed of in accordance therewith may in the discretion of the Librarian of Congress and Register of Copyrights be destroyed after an opportunity has been given to the author, copyright proprietor or other lawful claimant to claim and remove the same.

The Register of Copyrights has also permitted the withdrawal of one copy of published works deposited with him, where the claimant gives some valid reason why it is necessary for him to have such copy removed.

Section 179.—Prohibition of importation of piratical copies.

Section thirty of the Act expressly prohibits the importation into the United States of any piratical copies of a work in which there is subsisting a United States copyright.

Where a film has been "duped" and an attempt is made to bring into this country "duped" copies of the film, the copyright proprietor may prevent the entry of such films under Sections thirty-two and thirty-three of the Act.

Where, however, the motion picture for which entry is sought is merely an infringement of the copyright in a work, which itself is not a motion picture, the copyright proprietor may not avail himself of the benefit of this section.[1]

[1] *Ruling of the Treasury Department dated December 21, 1912, on the importation of the motion picture "The Miracle."* "The Department is in receipt of your letter of the 18th instant in relation to the importation at New York on the 9th idem of a moving picture film which is claimed to be a reproduction of a drama entitled 'The Miracle.'

" It is represented that Messrs. Ed. Bote and G. Bock of Berlin, Germany, are the proprietors of the copyright of the dramatic composition entitled 'The Miracle'; that Bote and Bock by virtue of paragraph D of § 1 of the Copyright Act have the exclusive right to make all moving pictures representing this dramatic composition; that the Miracle Company by certain contracts have acquired the sole rights in the said dramatic composition and also the moving picture right therein for the United States, and that the film belonging to the Miracle Company was advertised on the 8th of this month to be exhibited in London, England, on the 21st instant.

" I inclose herewith for your

Section 180.—Ad interim protection.

Sections twenty-one and twenty-two providing for ad interim protection of works published abroad in the

information a copy of the Department's letter of the 18th instant to the collector of customs at New York authorizing the release of the film in question. As it is not shown either in the collector's letter or in your communication that the film imported is a piratical copy, the Department knows of no provision of law which would authorize the exclusion of the same from entry as § 30 of the Copyright Act prohibits the importation only of articles bearing a false notice of copyright when there is no existing copyright thereon in the United States or of piratical copies of any work copyrighted in the United States.

"Therefore the question of whether the imported film is an infringement of the dramatic composition or of the moving picture film advertised to be exhibited in London on the 21st instant is one for the determination of the courts after the film is released from customs custody.

"Respectfully,

"J. F. Curtis,

"Assistant Secretary."

Letter referred to in the above ruling:—

"December 18, 1917.

"The Collector of Customs,

"New York, N. Y.

"Sir:

"The Department is in receipt of your letter of the 18th instant, reporting in relation to an importation of a moving picture film made at your port on the 9th instant, entry No. 332691, and which is claimed to be a reproduction of a drama entitled 'The Miracle,' of which Mr. A. H. Woods of New York City is the American copyright proprietor.

"It appears that the film was duly entered and released, but that the same has been returned to you by the New York Film Company, pending the determination of the matter by the Department, and that Mr. Woods claims the film was imported in violation of paragraph D of section 1 of the Act of March 4, 1909, as being a reproduction of the drama entitled 'The Miracle' as exhibited in London.

"Paragraph D of section 1 of

English language before publication in this country have no application to motion pictures, but refer solely to books.

the Copyright Act merely defines the exclusive rights given to the copyright proprietor in dramatic works.

"Under section 30 of the same Act the importation into the United States of any article bearing a false notice of copyright, when there is no existing copyright thereon in the United States or of any piratical copies of any work copyrighted in the United States, is prohibited, and as it is not shown or claimed that the film in question is a prohibited importation under this provision of law, the Department is of the opinion that the same should be released to the importer. You will be governed accordingly.

"Respectfully,

"(signed) F. M. Halstead,

"Chief, Division of Customs."

See the following treasury ruling as to what constitutes piratical copies of a film: (T. D. 33258.)

Copyright—Films—Moving pictures—Piratical copies

Regulations governing the importation of moving-picture films under the copyright act of March 4, 1909.—T. D. 31754 of July 17, 1911, modified.

Treasury Department,
March 10, 1913.

To collectors and other officers of the customs:

Attention is invited to section 30 of the copyright act of March 4, 1909, as follows:

That the importation into the United States of any article bearing a false notice of copyright when there is no existing copyright thereon in the United States, or of any piratical copies of any work copyrighted in the United States, is prohibited.

The following regulations governing the importation of moving picture films are hereby promulgated for the guidance of officers of the customs:

1. A "piratical copy" of a film is defined as a film which constitutes either an actual copy or a substantial reproduction of a legally copyrighted film produced and imported in contravention of the rights of the copyright proprietor.

2. Collectors will admit to entry imported films concerning which either (*a*) adverse copy-

Section 181.—Bankruptcy—Title in trustee.

The trustee in bankruptcy acquires title to the copyrights owned by the bankrupt proprietor, and he may

rights are claimed by parties interested, or (*b*) an infringement only is claimed by a copyright proprietor other than the importer. In such cases the copyright claimants will be remitted to their rights at law or in equity.

3. Collectors will not permit entry of imported films concerning which either (*a*) representations are made that they are piratical copies and such representations are not denied by the importers, or (*b*) if the collector is satisfied they do, in fact, constitute piratical copies as above defined.

4. Collectors will detain films covered by the preceding regulation and report the facts to the department for instructions.

5. If the collector is not satisfied that an imported film is a piratical copy, and the importer files an affidavit denying that it is in fact such a piratical copy, and alleging that the detention of the film will result in a material depreciation of its value or loss or damage to him, the film will be admitted to entry, unless a written demand for its exclusion is filed by the copyright proprietor or other party in interest, setting forth that the imported film is a piratical copy of a film legally copyrighted in the United States, and unless there is also filed with the collector a good and sufficient bond conditioned to hold the importer or owner of such film harmless from any loss or damage resulting from its detention in the event that the same is held by the department not to be prohibited from importation under section 30.

6. Upon the filing of such demand and bond the collector will cause the film to be detained, and will fix a time at which the parties in interest may submit evidence to substantiate their respective claims, which evidence shall be reduced to writing at the expense of the parties in interest and transmitted by the collector to the department, with such report and recommendation as he may deem proper.

7. No film will be presumed to be prohibited from entry as a piratical copy under said act, and the burden of proof that any

exercise dominion thereto either by way of a sale or otherwise. But whether or not he is vested with title in the common-law rights of an unpublished work, is open to question.[2]

A sheriff, levying upon the copyrighted property and thereafter selling the same, does not sell the copyright, as that still remains in the judgment debtor, and he has not been divested therefrom.[3] All that the Sheriff sells

film is in fact a piratical copy will be upon the party making such claim.

8. If the film is held by the department to be a piratical copy, its seizure and forfeiture will be directed in accordance with section 32 of the copyright act, and the bond will be returned to the copyright proprietor, but if not so held, the collector will be directed to release the film and transmit the bond to the importer.

9. Regulations contained in T. D. 31754 of July 17, 1911, so far as they relate to moving picture films, are hereby modified accordingly.

James F. Curtis, *Assistant Secretary*.

[2] See: *In re McDonnell* (1900), 101 Fed. (D. C.) 239; *Gillett* v. *Bate* (1881), 86 N. Y. 87; *In re Dann* (1904), 129 Fed. (D. C.) 495.

[3] *Patterson* v. *Ogilvie Pub. Co.* (1902), 119 Fed. (C. C.) 451. Plaintiff, the author of a book, became financially embarrassed; a judgment was secured against him, and upon execution the sheets and plates of the book were levied on and sold by the sheriff. Defendant purchased the plates from some one to whom they had passed from the purchaser at the sheriff's sale. The court said:—

"The copyright was not sold, and complainant has not lost his right to enforce it because he failed to prevent the sale of the plates. They were mere pieces of metal, which became the property of the purchaser, but gave him no right to publish the copyrighted work which could be printed from them. Complainant did not abandon his copyright by failing to buy them in, and is not estopped thereby from enforcing his statutory rights."

in such case is the physical work itself, not the intangible and incorporeal copyright, and the original proprietor may in his own name enjoin subsequent infringers.[4]

The trustee in bankruptcy does not acquire title to a license agreement for the use of a copyrighted work, as that kind of an agreement is strictly personal in its nature, and is ipso facto abrogated by the adjudication of bankruptcy, unless a contrary intention is therein expressly stipulated.

In a case where a publishing firm had become bankrupt and the trustee attempted to sell its rights, the learned Referee, awarding the rights to the author, said:

" . . . I am of the opinion that the claimant is entitled to the copyrights in question, because I must find on the facts and law that the contract was a personal engagement between author and publisher, involving trust and confidence which cannot be assigned or delegated to another without the author's consent." [5]

[4] *Wilder* v. *Kent* (1883), 15 Fed. (C. C.) 217. Where a copyrighted map or its copper plate are seized by the sheriff on execution, the purchaser of the same acquires no right to make copies thereof.

See also: *Stevens* v. *Gladding* (1854), 17 How. 447; *Stevens* v. *Cady* (1852), 14 How. 528; *Patterson* v. *Ogilvie Pub. Co.* (1902), 119 Fed. (C. C.) 451.

[5] *In re D. H. McBride & Co.* (1904), 132 Fed. (D. C.) 285. The contract involved was one between an author and publisher. On the bankruptcy of the publisher the author attempted to obtain a re-assignment of the copyright. The Special Commission held that he could do so:

"It is true that the author reserved her own right to assign her royalties, but she also expressly reserved to herself the right to object to an assignment on the part of the corporation."

See also: *Arkansas Smelting Co.* v. *Belden* (1888), 127 U. S. 379, 8 Sup. Ct. 1308; *Bancroft* v.

But where there was no mere license but an assignment, or a license which amounted in law to an assignment, the trustee became legally vested with title on the bankruptcy of such assignee or licensee, and could not be compelled to turn over the copyright to the assignor or licensor.[6]

Section 182.—Selling secondhand copies.

In view of the practice of buying up old motion pictures and again distributing them, it is of interest to note that these second-hand copies even though copyrighted, may lawfully be touched up and restored as closely as possible to their original condition. The purchaser may also exhibit or cause the same to be exhibited. He may not, however, make copies of the film, as that would violate the rights of the copyright proprietor of such film.

While there is no reported decision on this proposition directly involving motion pictures, the case of *Doan* v.

Scribner (1896), 72 Fed. (C. C. A.) 988.

So that a license under a patent right is held personal to the licensee and does not pass to a receiver or administrator by operation of law. *Oliver* v. *Rumford Chem. Works* (1883), 109 U. S. 75; 3 Sup. Ct. 61; *Waterman* v. *Shipman* (1893), 55 Fed. (C. C. A.) 982.

Also *Griffith* v. *Tower Pub. Co.* (Eng.) (1897), 1 Chancery, 21, where the identical question was passed on, and the same conclusion arrived at. *Stevens* v. *Benning* (Eng.) (1854), 1 Kay & Johnson, 168; aff'd 6 De G. M. & G. 223; *Hole* v. *Bradbury* (Eng.) (1879), 12 Chan. Div. 886; *Reade* v. *Bentley* (Eng.) (1858), 4 Kay & Johnson, 656.

[6] *In re Howley Dresser Co.* (1904), 132 Fed. (D. C.) 1002. The copyright was held to go to the trustee in bankruptcy.

"The question always is in such cases whether the agreement is merely an arrangement to publish under the copyright

American Book Co.,[7] which concerned itself with the defendant's right to rebind old books in imitation of the originals, is so closely analogous that it may be said to apply.

This would indicate that the buyer of a film could restore the original title, both in text and design, and use the original advertisements in so far as no attempt was made to mislead the public into believing such motion pictures to be a first issue, or to be exhibited by the copyright proprietor.[8]

or an actual transfer of the copyright."

In re Grant Richards (Eng.) (1907), 2 K. B. 33. Where the publisher held the copyright and agreed to pay royalties it was held that the copyright passed to the trustee in bankruptcy.

[7] *Doan* v. *Am. Book Co.* (1901), 105 Fed. (C. C. A.) 772. Defendant bought up second-hand copies of plaintiff's copyrighted books, and rebound them, making up new covers for that purpose in exact imitation of the originals. *Held* that this was not a violation of the copyright. "The sale of them by the appellee (plaintiff) carried with it the ordinary incidents of ownership in personal property, including the right of alienation (*Harrison* v. *Maynard*, 61 Fed. 689) and the appellants purchasing them had the right to resell them. . . . We think the right of repair with respect to a copyrighted book sold to the extent to which that right is here claimed, may not properly be denied. . . . What was done was merely the restoration of the books to their original condition when sold by the appellee or so nearly so as could be done . . . a right of ownership in the book carries with it and includes the right to maintain the book as nearly as possible in its original condition, so far, at least, as the cover and binding of the book is concerned."

See also: *Dodd* v. *Smith* (1891), 144 Pa. St. 340; 22 Atl. 710; *Harrison* v. *Maynard Merrill & Co.* (1894), 61 Fed. (C. C. A.) 689; *Henry Bill Publ. Co.* v. *Smythe* (1886), 27 Fed. (C. C.) 914.

[8] *Where old books were passed*

Where a secondhand motion picture projecting machine was sold, no false representations as to its origin being made, it was held that such sale was lawful under the original name of the machine.[9]

Section 183.—Taxability.

Copyright may not be taxed. It is a species of intangible property which is exempt from taxation; for to tax it would be to impose a check upon that which is avowedly sought to be encouraged.[10]

off as new, it was held to be unfair competition in: Doan v. *American Book Co.* (1901), 105 Fed. (C. C. A.) 772; *Bureau of Nat'l Literature* v. *Sells* (1914), 211 Fed. (D. C.) 379; *Ginn* v. *Apollo* (1914), 215 Fed. (D. C.) 772; *Kipling* v. *Putnam* (1903), 120 Fed. (C. C. A.) 631.

[9] *Vitascope Co.* v. *U. S. Phonograph Co.* (1897), 83 Fed. (C. C.) 30. Where plaintiff had contracted with Edison for the manufacture by the latter of certain motion picture machines and after his failure to pay for some of them, Edison sold them to a third party under the name which had been given them "Edison Vitascopes," plaintiff could not enjoin the third party from offering them for sale under that name, as that was their name, and no false representation was made to the public.

It is to be noted that no right to the use of the name had been shown to vest exclusively in the plaintiff.

[10] *People ex rel. Johnson* v. *Roberts* (1899), 159 N. Y. 701; 53 N. E. 685. The same rule with respect to patent rights is laid down in *People ex rel. Edison* v. *Assessors* (1898), 156 N. Y. 417; 51 N. E. 269.

People ex rel. United States Aluminum Co. v. *Knight* (1903), 174 N. Y. 475; 67 N. E. 65. A corporation may be taxed by the state even though its property consists of exempt letters patent, bonds or copyrights.

". . . . But they involve the principle that while a tax cannot be assessed upon property that is exempt by Act of Congress, it may be imposed upon the franchise of a corporation to which such exempt property belongs

Section 184.—Music in theatres.

The owner or lessee of a theatre is undoubtedly liable for unauthorized and unlicensed performances of musical compositions given in his theatre. This follows logically from the decisions in *Herbert* v. *Shanley* and *Church* v. *Hilliard* [11] decided in 1917 by the United States Supreme Court.

In each of these cases the plaintiff had brought an action for an injunction and damages on the ground that his music had been unlawfully performed "for profit," in the one case at a popular restaurant, in the other case at a hotel. The performance in each case had been of the kind known as a "cabaret."

and may be measured by the value thereof. The principle applies with the same force to patent rights as to United States bonds, both of which are exempt from taxation. There is no distinction in this respect between United States bonds, patent rights and copyrights."

Harper v. *Donohue* (1905), 144 Fed. (C. C.) 491. "Such literary property is not subject either to execution or taxation, because this might include a forced sale, the very thing the owner has a right to prevent."

[11] *Herbert* v. *Shanley Co.* (1917), 242 U. S. 591; 37 Sup. Ct. 232; *Church* v. *Hilliard* (1917), 242 U. S. 591; 37 Sup. Ct. 232.

For an English case taking the same position as the Supreme Court see *Sarpy* v. *Holland* (Eng.) (1908), L. R. 2 Ch. 198; 77 L. J. Ch. 637; 99 L. T. 317; 24 T. L. R. 600.

See the following English cases where the owner of a theatre was required to obtain a music license in addition to his theatrical license if the music was more than a subsidiary part of the entertainment. *Gregory* v. *Tavernor* (1833), 6 C. & P. 280; *Hall* v. *Green* (1853), 9 Exch. 247; *Quaglieni* v. *Matthews* (1865), 6 B. & S. 474; *Syers* v. *Conquest* (1873), 37 J. P. 342; *Fay* v. *Brignell* (1883), Cab. & El. 112.

Defendants claimed that the performance was not "for profit" within the meaning of Section one, subdivision (e) of the Copyright Act, as no admission was charged at the door, the only revenue exacted being for the refreshments served. It was held that this plea was untenable, for, as Mr. Justice Holmes pointed out: "If the rights under the copyright are infringed only by a performance where money is taken at the door, they are very imperfectly protected. Performances not different in kind from those of the defendants could be given that might compete with and even destroy the success of the monopoly that the law intends the plaintiffs to have. It is enough that there is no need to construe the statute so narrowly. The defendant's performances are not eleemosynary. They are part of a total for which the public pays, and the fact that the price of the whole is attributed to a particular item which those present are expected to order is not important. It is true that the music is not the sole object, but neither is the food, which probably could be got cheaper elsewhere. The object is a repast in surroundings that to people having limited powers of conversation or disliking the rival noise, give a luxurious pleasure not to be had from eating a silent meal. If music did not pay it would be given up. If it pays, it pays out of the public's pocket. Whether it pays or not, the purpose of employing it is profit and that is enough."

In the case of a motion picture theatre where admission is charged at the door, there can be no defense on that score, for admittedly the entire performance is for profit and gain, a profit which is obtained by direct methods.

The music which is played to accompany the exhibition of the pictures is as much a part of the entertainment as the pictures themselves.

Indeed the tendency has been to elaborate the musical program, and in many instances special music has been composed for feature pictures. Under these circumstances it is difficult to see how the theatre proprietor can escape liability when he performs music without a license from the copyright owners.

In *Hubbell* v. *Royal Pastime Amusement Co.* plaintiffs, owners of the Copyright, sought to restrain defendant from further performances of their music in its theatre. On motion to dismiss the bill of complaint the point was made that inasmuch as the bill failed to allege that the musical compositions involved were written for the purpose of public performance for profit, defendant was at liberty to perform the same. In denying the motion the court held that when the composer took the proper steps to secure copyright in his work, it might fairly be inferred that copyright was secured to obtain all the rights granted by the statute to the copyright proprietor, including the exclusive right to perform the work for profit.[12]

[12] *Hubbell* v. *Royal Pastime Amusement Co.* (1917), May 26th, District Court U. S., S. D. New York.

Mayer, J: "This is a motion to dismiss the bill on the ground that the facts stated therein are insufficient to constitute a cause of action under the Copyright Act of March 4th, 1909, as amended. The sole point urged is that the bill is defective because it fails to allege that the musical compositions involved were written for the purpose of public performance for profit.

"As a mere matter of pleading I am inclined to think that when the composer composes his composition with an unlimited copy-

This rule as to public performance for profit applies with equal force to performances rendered by mechanical reproduction; for the language in Section one, subdivision (e) governing the compulsory licensing of musical compositions for mechanical purposes, explicitly excepts from its provisions public performance for profit. The language of the last paragraph of Section one permits the use of coin-operated machines, but again prohibits such use where an admission fee is charged to the place where the machines are operated.

It is plainly the intent of Congress to prohibit the performance of a musical composition for profit without the consent of the owner of the copyright.

The rule of liability for unlicensed public performance for profit of copyrighted music is the same as that for the infringement of any other copyrighted work.[13]

right notice it may fairly be inferred that he had written the work for the purpose of securing all the rights attainable under the Copyright Act including the exclusive right publicly to perform it for profit.

"But the controversy goes deeper than a mere matter of pleading, for I am entirely satisfied that a semi-colon should precede the words 'and for the purpose of a public performance for profit.' This is borne out by a reading of the committee reports and the reading of the statute. See *Tyrrell* v. *The Mayor* (1899), 159 N. Y. 239; 53 N. E. 1111, as to the rules of construction where punctuation is involved. If the semi-colon is not inserted at the place above indicated, subdivision e of section 1 does not seem to make sense.

"Eliminating the semi-colon the most, however, that the section amounts to is a protection in favor of those persons who do not perform publicly for profit the musical composition—

[13] See Section 163.

Section 185.—Co-authorship.

This subject has been treated in detail in Sections 9 and 10, to which the reader is referred.

Section 186.—Employer and employe.

For a discussion of the rights of the above parties the reader is referred to Section 8.

Section 187.—Restraint of trade—Price fixing—Monopoly.

The reader is referred to Sections 133 and 134 for a detailed discussion of the law on this subject.

as in the case of street parades, school, educational or similar public occasions and exhibitions.

"Putting the matter another way, the contention of the defendant is that the person who becomes entitled to the copyright by complying with the act must state what was in his mind at the time that he obtained his copyright. I am unable to see any justification for this view because the purpose or mental attitude of the composer is immaterial. The procedure is that he complies with the act and as a result of that compliance certain benefits follow by virtue of the statute.

"The subject could be further and somewhat elaborately developed, but I see no occasion so to do upon this motion, as the point which defendant makes will be preserved should a trial be had. Motion denied."

CHAPTER XVI

COPYRIGHT (CONTINUED)

British, Colonial and International Copyright

SEC. 188. Copyright in United Kingdom and Protectorates.
189. Copyright in Newfoundland.
190. Copyright in Commonwealth of Australia.
191. Copyright in Dominion of New Zealand.
192. Copyright in Union of South Africa.
193. Copyright in Dominion of Canada.
194. International Copyright.

Section 188.—Copyright in United Kingdom and Protectorates.

Under the English Copyright Act of 1911, copyright will subsist, in a published work, where such work was first published in any part of the British Dominions to which the Act extends. For the purposes of this Act "a work shall be deemed to be first published within the parts of His Majesty's Dominions to which this Act extends, notwithstanding that it has been published simultaneously in some other place . . . and a work shall be deemed to be published simultaneously in two places if the time between the publication in one such place and the publication in the other place does not exceed fourteen days, or such longer period as may, for the time being, be fixed by Order in Council."

An American citizen may secure copyright in a motion picture produced in this country by publishing the same simultaneously (that is, within fourteen days) in this country and in any part of the British dominions to which the 1911 Act extends.

At the time of the going into effect of the 1911 Act, the Act extended to all of the British dominions with the exception of the self-governing dominions, to wit: Dominion of Canada, Commonwealth of Australia, Dominion of New Zealand, Union of South Africa, and Newfoundland.

Since then, Newfoundland has adopted the Act in its entirety without any qualifications.

Australia and the Union of South Africa have adopted the Act with certain modifications and additions.

New Zealand has passed a Copyright Act which is based upon the 1911 Act, and which grants to British subjects rights substantially identical with those given under the 1911 Act.

Canada, however, has not as yet seen fit to take any action with respect to such Act, and the provisions of the Act do not extend to that dominion.

Under an Order in Council, which was expressly authorized by the Act, Cyprus and the British protectorates were included within its provisions; the protectorates specified in that Order in Council are Cyprus, Bechuanaland Protectorate, East Africa Protectorate, Northern Nigeria Protectorate, Northern Territories of the Gold Coast, Nyassaland Protectorate, Northern Rhodesia, Southern Rhodesia, Siera Leone Protectorate, Somaliland Protectorate, Southern Nigeria Protectorate, Solomon

Island Protectorate, Swaziland, Uganda Protectorate and Weihaiwei.

Deposit of Books in British Museum

The provision of the 1911 Act with respect to deposit in the British Museum and other libraries has reference only to books. This section of the Act may be disregarded so far as motion pictures are concerned.

Publication

Under Section three of the Act of 1911 "publication in relation to any work means the issue of copies of the work to the public." There must be a bona fide issue of copies, for under Section thirty-five of Subdivision three "a colourable publication, and one 'not intended to satisfy the reasonable requirements of the public,' will not be in conformity with the statute." *Francis Day* and *Hunter* v. *B. Feldman & Co.* (1914), L. R., 2 Ch. 728.

Unpublished Works

Great Britain issued an Order in Council on February 3, 1915, under Section twenty-nine of the 1911 Act containing the following provision: "The Copyright Act of 1911 including the provisions as to existing works, shall, subject to the provisions of the said Act and of this Order, apply: (a) To literary, dramatic, musical and artistic works, the authors whereof were at the time of the making of the works, citizens of the United States of

America, in like manner as if the authors had been British subjects; (b) In respect of residence in the United States of America, in like manner as if such residence had been residence in the parts of His Majesty's Dominions to which the said Act extends."

The Order further provides that the enjoyment of the rights given by the Order shall be subject to the accomplishment of the conditions and formalities prescribed by the law of the United States, and that the term of copyright shall not exceed that conferred by the American law.

Under this Order in Council a citizen of or resident in the United States is entitled to the benefits of the English Copyright Law of all his unpublished works composed by him while he was such citizen or resident, provided he has complied with the conditions and formalities prescribed by the United States Copyright Laws.

As soon as that formality has been complied with by the author of any American work he becomes vested with the rights secured by the English Copyright Law in unpublished works.

It is not necessary for him to take any steps or comply with any formalities whatever in Great Britain.

It is to be remembered, however, that the right thus secured will continue in effect only as long as the work remains unpublished.

As soon as the work is published in the United States, the benefits of the English Copyright Law will be lost unless the work is simultaneously published in the United Kingdom of Great Britain and Ireland, or in such other parts of the British Dominions to which the 1911 Act extends, or published in such Dominions within fourteen days after publication in the United States.

The Order, however, provides that it shall not extend to the self-governing dominions. Until each self-governing dominion approves of the provisions of the Order, it does not extend to such dominions.

Section 189.—Copyright in Newfoundland.

Newfoundland adopted the British Copyright Act of 1911 in full by an enactment of its Legislature in 1912, except those clauses which are expressly restricted to the United Kingdom. She has in addition become a party to the revised Berne convention of Berlin of 1908.

Since Newfoundland has become a part of the British Dominions to which the Act of 1911 extends, first or simultaneous publication of an American film in Newfoundland secures copyright under the 1911 Act throughout the British dominions to which the Act extends; and in like manner first or simultaneous publication in any part of the British dominions to which the Act extends secures copyright thereunder enforceable in Newfoundland.

Section 190.—Copyright in Commonwealth of Australia.

In 1912, Australia passed a Copyright Act which declared the Act of 1911 to be in force in its territory subject, however, to certain modifications. The modifications have reference chiefly to summary remedies granted under the Australian Act which are broader than those granted under the 1911 Act.

Provision is also made for registration of copyright and deposit of copies; such registration and deposit, however, being optional and not mandatory. The chief advantage of registration and deposit is that the registered owner is given the right to pursue certain summary remedies which may not otherwise be invoked.

The Australian Act has not affected the Act of 1911 with respect to the persons who may secure copyright. Anyone entitled to secure copyright under the 1911 Act is accorded protection in Australia.

As Australia by its acceptance of the 1911 Act has come within its provisions, publication in Australia is for the purposes of the 1911 Act publication within the British dominions to which the Act extends. First or simultaneous publication in England or any other part of the British dominions to which the Act extends gives British copyright which is enforceable in Australia.

Section 191.—Copyright in Dominion of New Zealand.

New Zealand passed a Copyright Act in 1913, which went into effect on April 1st, 1914, based upon the 1911 Act. There were modifications as to summary remedies and provisions for optional registration and deposit similar to the Australian Act.

The Act provides that copyright shall subsist in a published work if first publication takes place in New Zealand, and that in the case of an unpublished work, copyright shall subsist therein only if at the date of the making of the work the author is a British subject or resident in New Zealand. The Act further provides that copyright shall be extended to no other works except such as may be given protection by an Order in Council of the Governor. An Order in Council has been made by the Governor of New Zealand extending the Act to Great Britain, so that first publication in Great Britain is equivalent to a first publication in New Zealand, and will afford protection under the New Zealand Act.

In addition thereto an Order in Council has been made by the Governor extending the provisions of the Act to countries belonging to the Copyright Union as of April 1st, 1914, from which date New Zealand may be regarded as a party to the Revised Berne Convention of Berlin of 1908.

Section 192.—Copyright in Union of South Africa.

Like Australia the Union of South Africa passed an Act in 1916 adopting the 1911 Act in accordance with Section twenty-five thereof, and declared the same to be in force in the Union subject to certain modifications and additions, consisting chiefly of a system of registration and deposit, and the imposition of severer penalties for infringements.

Section 193.—Copyright in Dominion of Canada.

Method No. 1

Canada has not yet taken any step toward accepting in whole or in part the 1911 Act, nor has she passed any legislation repealing or modifying any of the Acts of Parliament in so far as they affected her at the time of the taking effect of the 1911 Act, although this right was expressly conferred upon her by Section twenty-six of that Act.

All those Acts of Parliament, therefore, which were in force in Canada on July 1st, 1912, are still valid and subsisting in Canada. Those Acts, so far as they may affect copyright in motion pictures, are the Literary Copyright Act of 1842 and the International Copyright Act of 1886.[1]

When the 1842 Act was passed the art of motion pictures was unknown, and there is no specific provision in that Act conferring copyright in motion pictures. Section II, however, in defining the meaning of the words "dramatic piece," (protected under that Act) as that phrase is used in the Act, provides that such phrase "shall be construed to mean and include every tragedy, comedy, play, opera, farce, or other *scenic*, musical, or dramatic entertainment." While we know of no decision which holds that motion pictures are included within that definition, we believe that the provision is broad enough to include a motion picture, especially in view of the use of the words "scenic . . . entertainment" and "dramatic entertainment."

The 1842 Act, while containing no express provision where publication was first to take place, was held to have intended first publication in the United Kingdom alone.[2]

The Act provides in Section XXIV that the copyrighted work shall be registered in the Book of Registry of the Stationers Company.

[1] See *Black* v. *Imperial Book Co.* (Can.) (1904), 8 Ont. L. R. 9; aff'd 35 Can. Sup. Ct. 488.

[2] Copinger, Law of Copyrights, 4th Ed., p. 89; *Chappell* v. *Purday* (Eng.) (1845), 4 W. & C. 485; *Routledge* v. *Low* (Eng.) (1865), L. R. 3 H. L. 100.

Failure to comply with registration does not affect the validity of the copyright, but prevents the maintenance of an action for infringement.

Not only may a British subject secure copyright under this Act, but any alien, as well, who resided at the time of first publication, in the British Dominions.[3]

We now come to the interesting question whether under this Act a non-resident alien, first publishing in the United Kingdom, may secure copyright thereunder. In *Routledge* v. *Low*, an American authoress, who had taken up a nominal residence in Canada for the sole purpose of being in the British dominions at the moment of first publication of the work in England, was held to have acquired a valid British copyright. Although it was not necessary for the court to pass upon the question of a non-resident alien acquiring British copyright under this Act, the court nevertheless discussed this proposition at length. Lord Cairns said: "Protection is given to every author who publishes in the United Kingdom, wheresoever that author may be resident, or of whatever state he may be the subject. The intention of the Act is to obtain a benefit for the people of this country by the publication to them of works of learning, of utility, of amusement. The benefit is obtained, in the opinion of the legislature, by offering a certain amount of protection to the author, thereby inducing him to publish his work here.

[3] *Routledge* v. *Low* (Eng.) (1868), L. R. 3 H. L. 100, 37 L. J. (C. H.) 454, 18 L. T. 874; *Jeffreys* v. *Boosey* (Eng.) (1854), 4 H. L. C. 815; *Buxton* v. *James* (Eng.) (1851), 5 De G. & Sm. 80, 16 Jur. 15; *Ollendorf* v. *Black* (Eng.) (1850), 4 De G. & Sm. 209; 20 L. J. (C. H.) 165.

This is or may be, a benefit to the author, but it is a benefit given, not for the sake of the author of the work, but for the sake of those to whom the work is communicated. . . . I am glad to be able to entertain no doubt that a construction of the Act so consistent with a wise and liberal policy is the proper construction to be placed upon it."

In addition to the weight to be given to the above dicta, we have the assurance, given by Lord Salisbury to the United States government, at the time of the passage of the Chace Act of 1891, in a despatch dated June 16th, 1891, to the President of the United States, that residence in the British Dominions was not essential in order to obtain the protection of the British Copyright Laws.

The International Copyright Act of 1886 extended the 1842 Act by making it possible to secure British copyright by first publishing the work in *any* British possession, provided, however, that where such first publication took place in any such possession, the enactments contained in the Act of 1842 respecting the registry of the copyright in such work should not apply, if the law of such possession provided for the registration of such copyright, and the local statute in force in the possession where first publication took place had to be complied with.

The 1886 Act contains the significant provision that nothing in that Act or in the 1842 Act "shall prevent the passing in a British possession of any Act or ordinance respecting the copyright within the limits of such possession, of works first produced in that possession." [4]

[4] Section eight, subsection four.

The significance of this section lies in the fact that under the local Canadian statute now in force, copyright may be acquired thereunder only by those who are "domiciled in Canada or in any part of the British possessions or any citizen of any country which has an international copyright treaty with the United Kingdom." [5]

Canada has consistently refused to recognize any relation existing between the United States and Great Britain which would bring the former within these provisions. Since the American may not apply for Canadian copyright under the local statute, then he may not, under the International Act of 1886, secure British copyright by first publishing in Canada.

To secure protection, therefore, in Canada, under the English Acts of 1842 and 1886, he must publish in those parts of the British dominions which permit him to secure copyright under the local statute, in which event he must comply with the local statute with respect to registration, where the statute makes provision for the same. And if there is no such provision in the local statute he must register in Stationers' Hall and make the deposit when so required.

To avoid any complications, the safest course to pursue is to first publish in the United Kingdom and register in Stationers' Hall.

The rights of an American citizen, non-resident in the British dominions, who first published in the United Kingdom, were not affected by this Act of 1886, and these

[5] Canadian Copyright Act 1886, § 4 (now Part I, chapter 70, of the Revised Statutes of Canada of 1906, as amended by the Laws of 1908). See Appendix.

rights were expressly recognized by the British government in 1891 by Lord Salisbury.

In short, under the 1842 and 1886 English Acts, still in force in Canada, an American citizen, resident in the United States, by first publishing his motion picture in the United Kingdom, secures copyright in his film; and by registration in Stationers' Hall, is entitled to enforce his copyright in Canada.

First publication has been held to take place under the Act of 1842 where there is simultaneous publication in this country and in the United Kingdom.[6] And simultaneous publication will be deemed to be equivalent to first publication under the Act of 1886 in view of the official assurance given to the United States.[7]

It must be borne in mind that the simultaneous publication here spoken of is not made pursuant to the 1911 Act, and the fourteen days' grace provided for in the 1911 Act has no application whatsoever. Simultaneous publication as here used, means publication made on the same day in both countries.

Although it has been held that registration in Stationers' Hall is no longer possible because of the 1911 Act,[8] yet, as a matter of fact, as late as July 20th, 1917, a com-

[6] *Grossman* v. *Canada Cycle Co.* (Can.) (1902), 5 O. L. R. 55; *Cocks* v. *Purday* (Eng.) (1846), 2 Car. & Kirw. 269; *Routledge* v. *Low* (Eng.) (1868), L. R., 3 H. L. 100. Publications in England and abroad simultaneously will not prevent copyright in England. See also: Copinger, Law of Copyright, 4th Ed., p. 89.

[7] Lord Salisbury: Official British Dispatch addressed to the President of the United States dated June 16th, 1891.

[8] *Evans* v. *Morris* (Eng.) (1913), W. N. 58.

munication emanating from an official of the Stationers' Company stated that works were still offered and accepted for registration under the Act of 1842.[9]

Objection has been made to the regularity of this procedure, upon the ground that the Act of 1911 has repealed the Act of 1842, in the United Kingdom, and that the steps of publication and registration may not be taken in that territory under a repealed Act having no force therein.

If that were the correct view, the provision under the 1911 Act holding the Acts of 1842 and 1886 valid with respect to the self-governing dominions, would be nugatory.

For example, if this were so, a subject and resident of the United Kingdom desirous of protecting his copyright in Canada would be unable to protect his work by registration, his 1911 Act would not extend into Canadian territory, and he would be compelled to comply with the local Canadian statute, which would necessitate republication by him in Canada and full compliance with the Canadian statute.

A Canadian, on the other hand, by first publishing in Canada and complying with the Canadian statute with

[9] "Stationers' Hall
" London, E. C.
" July 20th, 1917.

"Books published in Canada are still registered here by the registering officer under the Act of 1842, but registration of works first published in Great Britain or any British possession which has adopted the Act of 1911 seems wholly unnecessary and useless expense. The fee is 5*s*. per entry, not 2*s*."

The above information and letter were secured from "The Publishers' Circular" Westrand, London, issue of September 1st, 1917.

respect to registration, would secure a valid copyright in Canada as well as throughout the British dominions, including the United Kingdom.

We would have the anomalous situation of a Canadian having greater rights than those accorded a subject and resident of the United Kingdom.

We do not believe that this was the intention of Parliament. The 1911 Act rather intended to maintain the status quo with respect to England and her self-governing dominions which existed prior to its taking effect, until such time as each dominion saw fit to modify its law with respect to copyright.

Method No. 2

Instead of relying upon the protection given in Canada by complying with the English Acts of 1842 and 1886 as above outlined, many Americans have sought to obtain copyright in Canada under the local statute by first securing copyright in their work in the United Kingdom under the present English statute, and thereafter claiming copyright under the local Canadian statute by virtue of Section 6 thereof.

That section (Section 6 of the Canadian Act of 1886) provides: "Every work of which the copyright has been granted, and copyright of which is not secured or subsisting in Canada, under any act of the Parliament of Canada . . . shall, when printed and published, or reprinted and republished in Canada be entitled to copyright under this Act."

The American, having secured British copyright in his work, would seem to be entitled to apply for local

Canadian copyright by re-printing and re-publishing his work in Canada.

Although the precise question has not yet come before the Canadian courts, the Canadian Department of Agriculture has expressly recognized the right of a citizen of the United States who has a subsisting British Copyright in his work, to secure copyright therein under the Canadian statute by complying with the requirements of the Canadian Act with respect to printing, publication, notice and deposit. The bulletin of the Department (Circular No. 4a) is given in full below.[10] The Canadian Act is given in full in the appendix.

It should be remembered that where copyright protection is secured under the local Canadian statute, such protection does not give the exclusive right to perform the copyrighted work, since the Canadian statute confers no performing rights.

This defect in the statute practically destroyed the

[10] Circular No. 4a

DEPARTMENT OF AGRICULTURE,

Copyright and Trade Mark Branch,
Ottawa, Canada,

SIR,

I beg herewith to enclose Circular containing The Copyright Act with Rules and Forms under the same.

I would direct your attention to Sections 4, 6, 8, 11, 14 and 24 of the Act, to Rule IV, page 17, and to Forms A and A1, pages 19 and 20 of the Circular.

Canadian Copyright of a work will be registered in favor of a citizen of the United States upon the applicant shewing that he has subsisting British copyright of such work and otherwise complying with the requirements of the Act, Rules and Forms.

I have the honor to be,
Sir,
Your obedient servant,
P. E. RITCHIE,
Registrar of Copyright, &c.

value of dramatic works which depended for their copyright upon the local statute. To remedy this condition, an act was passed in 1915 making it a crime to perform without the written consent of the copyright proprietor, "in public and for private profit the whole or any part of any dramatic or operatic work or musical composition in which copyright subsists." [11]

Method No. 3

It has been contended, and with much logic, that an American, resident in the United States, and first pub-

[11] An Act to Amend the Criminal Code

5 George 5, Chap. 12 (April 15, 1915)

Section 508A. "Any person who, without the written consent of the owner of the copyright or of his legal representative, knowingly performs or causes to be performed in public and for private profit the whole or any part, constituting an infringement, of any dramatic or operatic work or musical composition in which copyright subsists in Canada, shall be guilty of an offence, and shall be liable on summary conviction to a fine not exceeding two hundred and fifty dollars, or, in the case of a second or subsequent offence, either to such fine or to imprisonment for a time not exceeding two months, or to both."

Section 508B. "Any person who makes or causes to be made any change in or suppression of the title, or the name of the author, of any dramatic or operatic work or musical composition in which copyright subsists in Canada, or who makes or causes to be made any change in such work or composition itself without the written consent of the author or of his legal representative, in order that the same may be performed in whole or in part in public for private profit, shall be guilty of an offence, and shall be liable on summary conviction to a fine not exceeding five hundred dollars, or, in the case of a second or subsequent offence, either to such fine or to imprisonment for a term not exceeding four months, or to both."

lishing in Canada, is entitled by reason of the Berne Convention to the full protection accorded to resident Canadians under the Canadian statute.

Canada is by proxy a member of the Berne Convention, and of the additional Act of Paris of 1896 modifying the Berne Convention.[12] Article three of the Berne Convention, as modified by the additional Act of Paris, reads as follows: "Authors not belonging to one of the countries of the Union, who shall have published or caused to be published for the first time their literary or artistic works in a country which is a party to the Union, shall enjoy, in respect of such works, the protection accorded by the Berne Convention and by the present additional act."

The Berne Convention and the additional Act of Paris are at the present time in full force and effect so far as Canada is concerned. The Berlin Convention of 1908, indeed, expressly provides in Article 27, that the Berne Convention and the additional Act "shall remain in force in regard to relations with states which do not ratify the present convention."

Canada, not having taken any action with respect to the Berlin Convention is therefore bound by the Berne Convention and the additional Act of Paris. An American then under Article 3 would seemingly have the right

[12] Berne Convention was signed by Great Britain September 5, 1887, and on November 28, 1887, an Order in Council was made by Great Britain giving full effect to the convention throughout the British Dominions.

Great Britain, by Order in Council, adopted the additional act of Paris on March 7, 1898.

See *Mary* v. *Hubert* (Can.) (1906), 15 Que. K. B. 381.

to first publish in Canada and thereby secure copyright in Canada; and any provision in the Canadian statutes which attempts to deprive him of that right, is in derogation of a solemn international compact.[13]

The fact remains, however, that Canada refuses to consider herself bound by the Convention with respect to American authors.[14]

[13] See in this connection: Copinger, Fifth Ed., p. 342, citing *Smiles* v. *Belford* (Can.) (1877), 1 Ont. App. R. 436; *Morang* v. *Publishers' Syndicate* (Can). (1900), 32 O. R. 393; *Black* v. *Imperial Book Co.* (Can.) (1903), 5 Ont. L. R. 184, (1905), 21 T. L. R. 540; *Hawkes* v. *Whaley, Royce & Co.*, "The Author" for 1913, p. 202.

See also: Briggs on International Copyright (Stevens & Haynes, London, 1906), p. 625: "Even as it is, it may be pointed out that the Canadian law now in force, which renders printing and publishing, or reprinting and republishing in Canada, though without any limit of time, a condition of copyright, cannot operate to prevent the author of a British work from gaining protection in Canada without publishing in that country. He gets this right under Imperial legislation, which no Canadian statute can override."

[14] *History of Canadian Copyright legislation:*

While Imperial copyright has been greatly simplified by the Act of 1911, and this especially so with reference to motion pictures, Canadian copyright has been thrown into confusion.

The following is a brief review of the history of Canadian copyright legislation which is essential to a proper understanding of the subject.

The English Literary Act of 1842 extended to every part of the British dominions, including of course Canada. Under that Act a British subject publishing in England obtained copyright in Canada as well, and was thereby enabled to prevent the importation of cheap reprints or editions of his work into the colonies.

This state of affairs gave rise to dissatisfaction in Canada, as it made the colony dependent upon the mother country for her

Section 194.—International Copyright.

The revised Berne Convention of 1908, more popularly known as the Berlin Convention, provides in Article 6:

books, and compelled her to purchase the expensive English editions. English publishers, on the other hand, feared to publish cheap editions for the colonies because such books were apt to find their way back to England.

To relieve this condition the Foreign Reprints Act of 1847 was passed in England. Under this Act, British reprints were allowed to be imported into Canada under certain conditions, but the Act proved wholly unsatisfactory to Canada, and failed to remedy the conditions of which that dominion complained. The position as to reprints was greatly modified by the 1875 Act hereinafter discussed under which the British subject, by publishing and printing a Canadian edition, could exclude foreign reprints, although not himself permitted to import his British edition, and under which, if he did not publish and print in Canada, he was permitted to import his British edition and suppress multiplication of copies in Canada, but could not, under the terms of the 1847 Act, prevent the importation of foreign reprints.

The Foreign Reprints Act concerns itself only with books.

In 1862 The Fine Arts Act was passed in England giving protection to drawings, paintings and photographs. This Act was held, however, not to extend to Canada. *Graves* v. *Garrie* (Can.) (1903), A. C. 496; *Tuck & Sons* v. *Priester* (Can.) (1887), 19 Q. B. D. 629. It will thus be seen that in 1862 photographs were copyrightable in England, but were not protected in Canada, while literary works first published in England enjoyed copyright protection in Canada. While one first publishing a literary work in the United Kingdom secured copyright enforceable in Canada, a Canadian, first publishing in Canada secured no such reciprocal rights in England until the International Copyright Act of 1886.

Although she had passed a copyright statute in 1832, Canada passed her first important local copyright law in 1875. This act was repealed by the Act

"Authors not being subjects or citizens of one of the countries of the Union, who first publish their works in

of 1886 which is the fundamental copyright statute now in force.

This statute grants protections for twenty-eight years to persons domiciled in Canada or the British dominions, and subjects of countries having treaties with Great Britain. The Act also provides that all works given the protection of copyright are required to be first published in Canada, a deposit of copies made and a notice of copyright printed.

The effect of this act and its amendatory acts of 1889 (never approved by the Crown) and 1900 have been much discussed in their relation to the Imperial Acts, and the weight of authority now seems to be that the local acts of the Colony may not in any way abrogate the Imperial Statutes. In other words, Canada may not, unless expressly authorized by England, pass any act which will affect any subsisting British Copyright. She could and she did pass acts which conferred local copyright, but in so far as these acts attempt to curtail or destroy any rights granted under the British Acts or treaties they must be deemed ineffective.

As a colony, however, Canada always felt that she was empowered to legislate for herself with respect to copyright, and this position was considerably strengthened by the British North American Act of 1867 which provided for the consolidation of Canada, Nova Scotia and New Brunswick, and for a Parliament which was expressly empowered to legislate exclusively, among other subjects, on copyright. The abortive Act of 1889 illustrates the length to which the Canadian Parliament went to enact copyright legislation which was not only openly hostile to the United States but to England as well. The Act was never approved by the Crown, but owing to the feeling on Canada's part that she was the subject of discrimination on the part of the United States, a concession was made to her by the mother country and another Act passed by the Canadian Parliament in 1900 was approved, by which Canada was enabled in certain instances to prevent the importations of books copyrighted in the United Kingdom but printed elsewhere.

Canada's chief grievance

one of those countries shall enjoy in that country the same rights as native authors, and in the other countries of the Union the rights granted by the present Convention."

This provision in effect gives international copyright to an American author who merely first publishes in any country of the Union (e. g., in the United Kingdom).

Since the Convention provides that the enjoyment and exercise of the rights granted thereunder shall not be subject to the performance of any formality, the mere first publication confers protection.

This convention has been modified by the additional Protocol of 1914 to the extent that where any country outside of the Union fails to give adequate protection to the works of authors who are subjects or citizens of one of the Union countries, nothing in the provisions of the convention shall be deemed to prejudice in any manner whatsoever the right of the contracting states to impose restrictions upon the protection accorded to works the authors of which are, at the time when such works are first published, subjects or citizens of any such country outside the Union, and not actually domiciled in one of the Union countries.

against the United States is that the American statute makes it obligatory for foreign English books (which include Canadian books) to be set up in type and printed within the United States, while American works in which British copyright is subsisting, may be imported into Canada without such restriction. Her chief effort has been to pass retaliatory legislation, but in that respect England has balked her, a policy to which England feels herself committed by reason of her membership in the international copyright convention.

It is important to bear in mind that no protection is accorded by the convention to the unpublished works of citizens of a non-union country.

The countries who are members of the Berlin Convention are, the United Kingdom of Great Britain and Ireland, India, Germany, Belgium, Denmark, Spain, France, Italy, Japan, Republic of Liberia, Luxemburg, Monaco, Norway, Sweden, Switzerland, and Tunis.

APPENDIX

UNITED STATES COPYRIGHT ACT OF 1909, AS AMENDED BY THE ACTS OF 1912, 1913 AND 1914

An Act to Amend and Consolidate the Acts Respecting Copyright

---

Be it enacted by the Senate and House of Representatives of the United States of America in Congress assembled, That any person entitled thereto, upon complying with the provisions of this Act, shall have the exclusive right:

(*a*) To print, reprint, publish, copy, and vend the copyrighted work;

(*b*) To translate the copyrighted work into other languages or dialects, or make any other version thereof, if it be a literary work; to dramatize it if it be a nondramatic work; to convert it into a novel or other nondramatic work if it be a drama; to arrange or adapt it if it be a musical work; to complete, execute, and finish it if it be a model or design for a work of art;

(*c*) To deliver or authorize the delivery of the copyrighted work in public for profit if it be a lecture, sermon, address, or similar production;

(*d*) To perform or represent the copyrighted work publicly if it be a drama or, if it be a dramatic work and not reproduced in copies for sale, to vend any manuscript or any record whatsoever thereof; to make or to procure the making of any transcription or record thereof by or from which, in whole or in part, it may in any manner or by any method be exhibited, performed, represented, produced, or reproduced; and to exhibit, perform, represent, produce, or reproduce it in any manner or by any method whatsoever;

(*e*) To perform the copyrighted work publicly for profit if it be a musical composition and for the purpose of public performance for profit; and for the purposes set forth in subsection (a) hereof, to make any arrangement or setting of it or of the melody of it in any system of notation or any form of record in which the thought of an author may be recorded and from which it may be read or reproduced: *Provided*, That the provisions of this Act, so far as they secure copyright controlling the parts of instruments serving to reproduce mechanically the musical work, shall include only compositions published and copyrighted after this Act goes into effect, and shall not include the works of a foreign author or composer unless the foreign state or nation of which such author or composer is a citizen or subject grants, either by treaty, convention, agreement, or law, to citizens of the United States similar rights: *And provided further, and as a condition of extending the copyright control to such mechanical reproductions*, That whenever the owner of a musical copyright has used or permitted or knowingly acquiesced in the use of the copyrighted work upon the parts of instruments serving to reproduce mechanically the musical work, any other person may make similar use of the copyrighted work upon the payment to the copyright proprietor of a royalty of two cents on each such part manufactured, to be paid by the manufacturer thereof; and the copyright proprietor may require, and if so the manufacturer shall furnish, a report under oath on the twentieth day of each month on the number of parts of instruments manufactured during the previous month serving to reproduce mechanically said musical work, and royalties shall be due on the parts manufactured during any month upon the twentieth of the next succeeding month. The payment of the royalty provided for by this section shall free the articles or devices for which such royalty has been paid from further contribution to the copyright except in case of public performance for profit: *And provided further*, That it shall be the duty of the copyright owner, if he uses the musical composition himself for the manufacture of parts of instruments serving to reproduce mechanically the musical work, or licenses others to do so, to file notice thereof, accompanied by a recording fee, in the copyright office, and any failure to file such notice shall be a complete defense to any suit, action, or proceeding for any infringement of such copyright.

In case of the failure of such manufacturer to pay to the copyright proprietor within thirty days after demand in writing the full sum of royalties due at said rate at the date of such demand the court may award taxable costs to the plaintiff and a reasonable counsel fee, and the court may, in its discretion, enter judgment therein for any sum in addition over the amount found to be due as royalty in accordance with the terms of this Act, not exceeding three times such amount.

The reproduction or rendition of a musical composition by or upon coin-operated machines shall not be deemed a public performance for profit unless a fee is charged for admission to the place where such reproduction or rendition occurs.

SEC. 2. That nothing in this Act shall be construed to annul or limit the right of the author or proprietor of an unpublished work, at common law or in equity, to prevent the copying, publication, or use of such unpublished work without his consent, and to obtain damages therefor.

SEC. 3. That the copyright provided by this Act shall protect all the copyrightable component parts of the work copyrighted, and all matter therein in which copyright is already subsisting, but without extending the duration or scope of such copyright. The copyright upon composite works or periodicals shall give to the proprietor thereof all the rights in respect thereto which he would have if each part were individually copyrighted under this Act.

SEC. 4. That the works for which copyright may be secured under this Act shall include all the writings of an author.

SEC. 5. That the application for registration shall specify to which of the following classes the work in which copyright is claimed belongs:

(*a*) Books, including composite and cyclopædic works, directories, gazetteers, and other compilations;

(*b*) Periodicals, including newspapers;

(*c*) Lectures, sermons, addresses (prepared for oral delivery);

(*d*) Dramatic or dramatico-musical compositions;

(*e*) Musical compositions;

(*f*) Maps;

(*g*) Works of art; models or designs for works of art;

(*h*) Reproductions of a work of art;

(*i*) Drawings or plastic works of a scientific or technical character;

(*j*) Photographs;

(*k*) Prints and pictorial illustrations;

(*l*) *Motion-picture photoplays;*

(*m*) *Motion pictures other than photoplays.*[1]

Provided, nevertheless, That the above specifications shall not be held to limit the subject-matter of copyright as defined in section four of this Act, nor shall any error in classification invalidate or impair the copyright protection secured under this Act.

SEC. 6. That compilations or abridgments, adaptations, arrangements, dramatizations, translations, or other versions of works in the public domain, or of copyrighted works when produced with the consent of the proprietor of the copyright in such works, or works republished with new matter, shall be regarded as new works subject to copyright under the provisions of this Act; but the publication of any such new works shall not affect the force or validity of any subsisting copyright upon the matter employed or any part thereof, or be construed to imply an exclusive right to such use of the original works, or to secure or extend copyright in such original works.

SEC. 7. That no copyright shall subsist in the original

[1] The changes marked, and the addition of the words printed in italics are authorized by the amendatory Act of August 24, 1912.

text of any work which is in the public domain, or in any work which was published in this country or any foreign country prior to the going into effect of this Act and has not been already copyrighted in the United States, or in any publication of the United States Government, or any reprint, in whole or in part, thereof: *Provided, however,* That the publication or republication by the Government, either separately or in a public document, of any material in which copyright is subsisting shall not be taken to cause any abridgment or annulment of the copyright or to authorize any use or appropriation of such copyright material without the consent of the copyright proprietor.

SEC. 8. That the author or proprietor of any work made the subject of copyright by this Act, or his executors, administrators, or assigns, shall have copyright for such work under the conditions and for the terms specified in this Act: *Provided, however,* That the copyright secured by this Act shall extend to the work of an author or proprietor who is a citizen or subject of a foreign state or nation, only:

(*a*) When an alien author or proprietor shall be domiciled within the United States at the time of the first publication of his work; or

(*b*) When the foreign state or nation of which such author or proprietor is a citizen or subject grants, either by treaty, convention, agreement, or law, to citizens of the United States the benefit of copyright on substantially the same basis as to its own citizens, or copyright protection substantially equal to the protection secured to such foreign author under this Act or by treaty; or when such foreign state or nation is a party to an international agreement which provides for reciprocity in the granting of copyright, by the terms of which agreement the United States may, at its pleasure, become a party thereto.

The existence of the reciprocal conditions aforesaid shall be determined by the President of the United States, by proclamation made from time to time, as the purposes of this Act may require.

SEC. 9. That any person entitled thereto by this Act may secure copyright for his work by publication thereof with the notice of copyright required by this Act; and such notice shall be affixed to each copy thereof published or offered for sale in the United States by authority of the copyright proprietor, except in the case of books seeking ad interim protection under section twenty-one of this Act.

SEC. 10. That such person may obtain registration of his claim to copyright by complying with the provisions of this Act, including the deposit of copies, and upon such compliance the register of copyrights shall issue to him the certificate provided for in section fifty-five of this Act.

SEC. 11. That copyright may also be had of the works of an author of which copies are not reproduced for sale, by the deposit, with claim of copyright, of one complete copy of such work if it be a lecture or similar production or a dramatic, musical, or *dramatico-musical* composition; *of a title and description, with one print taken from each scene or act, if the work be a motion-picture photoplay;* of a photographic print if the work be a photograph; *of a title and description, with not less than two prints taken from different sections of a complete motion picture, if the work be a motion picture other than a photoplay;* [1] or of a photograph or other identifying reproduction thereof, if it be a work of art or a plastic work or drawing. But the privilege of registration of copyright secured hereunder shall not exempt the copyright proprietor from the deposit of copies, under sections twelve and thirteen of this Act, where the work is later reproduced in copies for sale.

SEC. 12. That after copyright has been secured by publication of the work with the notice of copyright as provided in section nine of this Act, there shall be promptly deposited in the copyright office or in the mail addressed to the register of copyrights, Washington, District of Columbia, two complete copies of the best edition thereof then published, *or if the work is by an author who is a citizen or subject of a foreign state or nation and has been published in a foreign country, one complete copy of the best edition then published in such foreign country,* which copies *or copy,* [2] if the work be a book or periodical, shall have been produced in accordance with the manufacturing provisions specified in section fifteen of this Act; or if such work be a contribution to a periodical, for which contribution special registration is requested, one copy of the issue or issues containing such contribution; or if the work is not reproduced in copies for sale, there shall be deposited the copy, print, photograph, or other identify-

[1] The words printed in italics indicate the amendments authorized by the amendatory Act of August 24, 1912.

[2] The words printed in italics in sec. 12 are inserted by the amendatory Act of Mar. 28, 1914, which also provides "That all Acts or parts of Acts in conflict with the provisions of this Act are hereby repealed."

ing reproduction provided by section eleven of this Act, such copies or copy, print, photograph, or other reproduction to be accompanied in each case by a claim of copyright. No action or proceeding shall be maintained for infringement of copyright in any work until the provisions of this Act with respect to the deposit of copies and registration of such work shall have been complied with.

SEC. 13. That should the copies called for by section twelve of this Act not be promptly deposited as herein provided, the register of copyrights may at any time after the publication of the work, upon actual notice, require the proprietor of the copyright to deposit them, and after the said demand shall have been made, in default of the deposit of copies of the work within three months from any part of the United States, except an outlying territorial possession of the United States, or within six months from any outlying territorial possession of the United States, or from any foreign country, the proprietor of the copyright shall be liable to a fine of one hundred dollars and to pay to the Library of Congress twice the amount of the retail price of the best edition of the work, and the copyright shall become void.

SEC. 14. That the postmaster to whom are delivered the articles deposited as provided in sections eleven and twelve of this act shall, if requested, give a receipt therefor and shall mail them to their destination without cost to the copyright claimant.

SEC. 15. That of the printed book or periodical specified in section five, subsections (a) and (b) of this act, except the original text of a book of foreign origin in a language or languages other than English, the text of all copies accorded protection under this act, except as below provided, shall be printed from type set within the limits of the United States, either by hand or by the aid of any kind of typesetting machine, or from plates made within the limits of the United States from type set therein, or, if the text be produced by lithographic process, or photo-engraving process, then by a process wholly performed within the limits of the United States, and the printing of the text and binding of the said book shall be performed within the limits of the United States; which requirements shall extend also to the illustrations within a book consisting of printed text and illustrations produced by lithographic process, or photo-engraving process, and also to separate lithographs or photo-engravings, except where in either case the subjects represented are located in a foreign country and illustrate a scientific work or reproduce a work of art; but they shall not apply to works in raised characters for the use of the blind, or to books of foreign origin in a language or languages other than English, or to books published abroad in the English language seeking ad interim protection under this act.

SEC. 16. That in the case of the book the copies so deposited shall be accompanied by an affidavit, under the official seal of any officer authorized to administer oaths within the United States, duly made by the person claiming copyright or by his duly authorized agent or representative residing in the United States, or by the printer who has printed the book, setting forth that the copies deposited have been printed from type set within the limits of the United States or from plates made within the limits of the United States from type set therein; or, if the text be produced by lithographic process, or photo-engraving process, that such process was wholly performed within the limits of the United States, and that the printing of the text and binding of the said book have also been performed within the limits of the United States. Such affidavit shall state also the place where and the establishment or establishments in which such type was set or plates were made or lithographic process, or photo-engraving process or printing and binding were performed and the date of the completion of the printing of the book or the date of publication.

SEC. 17. That any person who, for the purpose of obtaining registration of a claim to copyright, shall knowingly make a false affidavit as to his having complied with the above conditions shall be deemed guilty of a misdemeanor, and upon conviction thereof shall be punished by a fine of not more than one thousand dollars, and all of his rights and privileges under said copyright shall thereafter be forfeited.

SEC. 18. That the notice of copyright required by section nine of this act shall consist either of the word "Copyright" or the abbreviation "Copr.," accompanied by the name of the copyright proprietor, and if the work be a printed literary, musical, or dramatic work, the notice shall include also the year in which the copyright was secured by publication. In the case, however, of copies of works specified in subsections (f) to (k), inclusive, of section five of this act, the notice may consist of the letter C inclosed within a circle, thus: ©, accompanied by the initials, monogram, mark, or symbol of the copyright proprietor: *Provided,* That on some accessible portion of such copies or of the margin, back, permanent base, or pedestal, or of the substance on which such copies shall be mounted, his name shall appear. But in the case of works in which copyright is subsisting when this act shall go into effect, the notice of copyright may be either in one of the forms prescribed herein or in one of those prescribed by the Act of June eighteenth, eighteen hundred and seventy-four.

SEC. 19. That the notice of copyright shall be applied, in the case of a book or other printed publication, upon its title-page or the page immediately following, or if a periodical either upon the title-page or upon the first page of text of each separate number or under the title heading, or if a musical work either upon its title-page or the first page of music: *Provided*, That one notice of copyright in each volume or in each number of a newspaper or periodical published shall suffice.

SEC. 20. That where the copyright proprietor has sought to comply with the provisions of this Act with respect to notice, the omission by accident or mistake of the prescribed notice from a particular copy or copies shall not invalidate the copyright or prevent recovery for infringement against any person who, after actual notice of the copyright, begins an undertaking to infringe it, but shall prevent the recovery of damages against an innocent infringer who has been misled by the omission of the notice; and in a suit for infringement no permanent injunction shall be had unless the copyright proprietor shall reimburse to the innocent infringer his reasonable outlay innocently incurred if the court, in its discretion, shall so direct.

SEC. 21. That in the case of a book published abroad in the English language before publication in this country, the deposit in the copyright office, not later than thirty days after its publication abroad, of one complete copy of the foreign edition, with a request for the reservation of the copyright and a statement of the name and nationality of the author and of the copyright proprietor and of the date of publication of the said book, shall secure to the author or proprietor an ad interim copyright, which shall have all the force and effect given to copyright by this Act, and shall endure until the expiration of thirty days after such deposit in the copyright office.

SEC. 22. That whenever within the period of such ad interim protection an authorized edition of such book shall be published within the United States, in accordance with the manufacturing provisions specified in section fifteen of this Act, and whenever the provisions of this Act as to deposit of copies, registration, filing of affidavit, and the printing of the copyright notice shall have been duly complied with, the copyright shall be extended to endure in such book for the full term elsewhere provided in this Act.

SEC. 23. That the copyright secured by this Act shall endure for twenty-eight years from the date of first publication, whether the copyrighted work bears the author's true name or is published anonymously or under an assumed name: *Provided,* That in the case of any posthumous work or of any periodical, cyclopædic, or other composite work upon which the copyright was originally secured by the proprietor thereof, or of any work copyrighted by a corporate body (otherwise than as assignee or licensee of the individual author) or by an employer for whom such work is made for hire, the proprietor of such copyright shall be entitled to a renewal and extension of the copyright in such work for the further term of twenty-eight years when application for such renewal and extension shall have been made to the copyright office and duly registered therein within one year prior to the expiration of the original term of copyright: *And provided further,* That in the case of any other copyrighted work, including a contribution by an individual author to a periodical or to a cyclopædic or other composite work when such contribution has been separately registered, the author of such work, if still living, or the widow, widower, or children of the author, if the author be not living, or if such author, widow, widower, or children be not living, then the author's executors, or in the absence of a will, his next of kin shall be entitled to a renewal and extension of the copyright in such work for a further term of twenty-eight years when application for such renewal and extension shall have been made to the copyright office and duly registered therein within one year prior to the expiration of the original term of copyright: *And provided further,* That in default of the registration of such application for renewal and extension, the copyright in any work shall determine at the expiration of twenty-eight years from first publication.

SEC. 24. That the copyright subsisting in any work at the time when this Act goes into effect may, at the expiration of the term provided for under existing law, be renewed and extended by the author of such work if still living, or the widow, widower, or children of the author, if the author be not living, or if such author, widow, widower, or children be not living, then by the author's executors, or in the absence of a will, his next of kin, for a further period such that the entire term shall be equal to that secured by this Act, including the renewal period: *Provided, however,* That if the work be a composite work upon which copyright was originally secured by the proprietor thereof, then such proprietor shall be entitled to the privilege of renewal and extension granted under this section: *Provided,* That application for such renewal and extension shall be made to the copyright office and duly registered therein within one year prior to the expiration of the existing term.

SEC. 25. That if any person shall infringe the copyright in any work protected under the copyright laws of the United States such person shall be liable:

(*a*) To an injunction restraining such infringement;

(*b*) To pay to the copyright proprietor such damages as the copyright proprietor may have suffered due to the infringement, as well as all the profits which the infringer shall have made from such infringement, and in proving profits the plaintiff shall be required to prove sales only and the defendant shall be required to prove every element of cost which he claims, or in lieu of actual damages and profits such damages as to the court shall appear to be just, and in assessing such damages the court may, in its discretion, allow the amounts as hereinafter stated, but in [1] case of a newspaper reproduction of a copy-

[1] The word "the" before the words "case of a newspaper reproduction," etc., was struck out by the amendatory Act of August 24, 1912.

righted photograph such damages shall not exceed the sum of two hundred dollars nor be less than the sum of fifty dollars, *and in the case of the infringement of an undramatized or nondramatic work by means of motion pictures, where the infringer shall show that he was not aware that he was infringing, and that such infringement could not have been reasonably foreseen, such damages shall not exceed the sum of one hundred dollars; and in the case of an infringement of a copyrighted dramatic or dramatico-musical work by a maker of motion pictures and his agencies for distribution thereof to exhibitors, where such infringer shows that he was not aware that he was infringing a copyrighted work, and that such infringements could not reasonably have been foreseen, the entire sum of such damages recoverable by the copyright proprietor from such infringing maker and his agencies for the distribution to exhibitors of such infringing motion picture shall not exceed the sum of five thousand dollars nor be less than two hundred and fifty dollars,* and such damages shall in no other case exceed the sum of five thousand dollars nor be less than the sum of two hundred and fifty dollars, and shall not be regarded as a penalty. *But the foregoing exceptions shall not deprive the copyright proprietor of any other remedy given him under this law, nor shall the limitation as to the amount of recovery apply to infringements occurring after the actual notice to a defendant, either by service of process in a suit or other written notice served upon him.*[1]

First. In the case of a painting, statue, or sculpture, ten dollars for every infringing copy made or

[1] The words printed in italics indicate the amendments authorized by the amendatory Act of August 24, 1912.

sold by or found in the possession of the infringer or his agents or employees;

Second. In the case of any work enumerated in section five of this Act, except a painting, statue, or sculpture, one dollar for every infringing copy made or sold by or found in the possession of the infringer or his agents or employees;

Third. In the case of a lecture, sermon, or address, fifty dollars for every infringing delivery;

Fourth. In the case of a dramatic or dramatico-musical or a choral or orchestral composition, one hundred dollars for the first and fifty dollars for every subsequent infringing performance; in the case of other musical compositions, ten dollars for every infringing performance;

(*c*) To deliver up on oath, to be impounded during the pendency of the action, upon such terms and conditions as the court may prescribe, all articles alleged to infringe a copyright;

(*d*) To deliver up on oath for destruction all the infringing copies or devices, as well as all plates, molds, matrices, or other means for making such infringing copies as the court may order;

(*e*) Whenever the owner of a musical copyright has used or permitted the use of the copyrighted work upon the parts of musical instruments serving to reproduce mechanically the musical work, then in case of infringement of such copyright by the unauthorized manufacture, use, or sale of interchangeable parts, such as disks, rolls, bands, or cylinders for use in mechanical music-producing machines adapted to reproduce the copyrighted music, no criminal action shall be brought, but in a civil action an injunction may be granted upon such terms as the court may impose, and the plaintiff shall be entitled to recover in lieu of profits and damages a royalty as provided in section one, subsection (e), of this Act: *Provided also,* That whenever any person, in the absence of a license agreement, intends to use a copyrighted musical composition upon the parts of instruments serving to reproduce mechanically the musical work, relying upon the compulsory license provision of this Act, he shall serve notice of such intention, by registered mail, upon the copyright proprietor at his last address disclosed by the records of the copyright office, sending to the copyright office a duplicate of such notice; and in case of his failure so to do the court may, in its discretion, in addition to sums hereinabove mentioned, award the complainant a further sum, not to exceed three times the amount provided by section one, subsection (e), by way of damages, and not as a penalty, and also a temporary injunction until the full award is paid.

Rules and regulations for practice and procedure under this section shall be prescribed by the Supreme Court of the United States.

SEC. 26. That any court given jurisdiction under section thirty-four of this Act may proceed in any action, suit, or proceeding instituted for violation of any provision hereof to enter a judgment or decree enforcing the remedies herein provided.

SEC. 27. That the proceedings for an injunction, damages, and profits, and those for the seizure of infringing copies, plates, molds, matrices, and so forth, aforementioned, may be united in one action.

SEC. 28. That any person who willfully and for profit shall infringe any copyright secured by this Act, or who shall knowingly and willfully aid or abet such infringement, shall be deemed guilty of a misdemeanor, and upon conviction thereof shall be punished by imprisonment for not exceeding one year or by a fine of not less than one hundred dollars nor more than one thousand dollars, or both, in the discretion of the court: *Provided, however,* That nothing in this Act shall be so construed as to prevent the performance of religious or secular works, such as oratorios, cantatas, masses, or octavo choruses by public schools, church choirs, or vocal societies, rented, borrowed, or obtained from some public library, public school, church choir, school choir, or vocal society, provided the performance is given for charitable or educational purposes and not for profit.

SEC. 29. That any person who, with fraudulent intent, shall insert or impress any notice of copyright required by this Act, or words of the same purport, in or upon any uncopyrighted article, or with fraudulent intent shall remove or alter the copyright notice upon any article duly copyrighted shall be guilty of a misdemeanor, punishable by a fine of not less than one hundred dollars and not more than one thousand dollars. Any person who shall knowingly issue or sell any article bearing a notice of United States copyright which has not been copyrighted in this country, or who shall knowingly import any article bearing such notice or words of the same purport, which has not been copyrighted in this country, shall be liable to a fine of one hundred dollars.

SEC. 30. That the importation into the United States

of any article bearing a false notice of copyright when there is no existing copyright thereon in the United States, or of any piratical copies of any work copyrighted in the United States, is prohibited.

SEC. 31. That during the existence of the American copyright in any book the importation into the United States of any piratical copies thereof or of any copies thereof (although authorized by the author or proprietor) which have not been produced in accordance with the manufacturing provisions specified in section fifteen of this Act, or any plates of the same not made from type set within the limits of the United States, or any copies thereof produced by lithographic or photo-engraving process not performed within the limits of the United States, in accordance with the provisions of section fifteen of this Act, shall be, and is hereby, prohibited: *Provided, however,* That, except as regards piratical copies, such prohibition shall not apply:

(*a*) To works in raised characters for the use of the blind;

(*b*) To a foreign newspaper or magazine, although containing matter copyrighted in the United States printed or reprinted by authority of the copyright proprietor, unless such newspaper or magazine contains also copyright matter printed or reprinted without such authorization:

(*c*) To the authorized edition of a book in a foreign language or languages of which only a translation into English has been copyrighted in this country;

(*d*) To any book published abroad with the authorization of the author or copyright proprietor when imported under the circumstances stated in one of the four subdivisions following, that is to say:

First. When imported, not more than one copy at one time, for individual use and not for sale; but such privilege of importation shall not extend to a foreign reprint of a book by an American author copyrighted in the United States;

Second. When imported by the authority or for the use of the United States;

Third. When imported, for use and not for sale, not more than one copy of any such book in any one invoice, in good faith, by or for any society or institution incorporated for educational, literary, philosophical, scientific, or religious purposes, or for the encouragement of the fine arts, or for any college, academy, school, or seminary of learning, or for any State, school, college, university, or free public library in the United States;

Fourth. When such books form parts of libraries or collections purchased en bloc for the use of societies, institutions, or libraries designated in the foregoing paragraph, or form parts of the libraries or personal baggage belonging to persons or families arriving from foreign countries and are not intended for sale:

Provided, That copies imported as above may not lawfully be used in any way to violate the rights of the proprietor of the American copyright or annul or limit the copyright protection secured by this Act, and such unlawful use shall be deemed an infringement of copyright.

Sec. 32. That any and all articles prohibited importation by this Act which are brought into the United States from any foreign country (except in the mails) shall be seized and forfeited by like proceedings as those provided by law for the seizure and condemnation of property imported into the United States in violation of the customs revenue laws. Such articles when forfeited shall be destroyed in such manner as the Secretary of the Treasury or the court, as the case may be, shall direct: *Provided, however*, That all copies of authorized editions of copyright books imported in the mails or otherwise in violation of the provisions of this Act may be exported and returned to the country of export whenever it is shown to the satisfaction of the Secretary of the Treasury, in a written application, that such importation does not involve willful negligence or fraud.

Sec. 33. That the Secretary of the Treasury and the Postmaster-General are hereby empowered and required to make and enforce such joint rules and regulations as shall prevent the importation into the United States in the mails of articles prohibited importation by this Act, and may require notice to be given to the Treasury Department or Post-Office Department, as the case may be, by copyright proprietors or injured parties, of the actual or contemplated importation of articles prohibited importation by this Act, and which infringe the rights of such copyright proprietors or injured parties.

Sec. 34. That all actions, suits, or proceedings arising under the copyright laws of the United States shall be originally cognizable by the circuit courts of the United States, the district court of any Territory, the supreme court of the District of Columbia, the district courts of Alaska, Hawaii, and Porto Rico, and the courts of first instance of the Philippine Islands.

SEC. 35. That civil actions, suits, or proceedings arising under this Act may be instituted in the district of which the defendant or his agent is an inhabitant, or in which he may be found.

SEC. 36. That any such court or judge thereof shall have power, upon bill in equity filed by any party aggrieved, to grant injunctions to prevent and restrain the violation of any right secured by said laws, according to the course and principles of courts of equity, on such terms as said court or judge may deem reasonable. Any injunction that may be granted restraining and enjoining the doing of anything forbidden by this Act may be served on the parties against whom such injunction may be granted anywhere in the United States, and shall be operative throughout the United States and be enforceable by proceedings in contempt or otherwise by any other court or judge possessing jurisdiction of the defendants.

SEC. 37. That the clerk of the court, or judge granting the injunction, shall, when required so to do by the court hearing the application to enforce said injunction, transmit without delay to said court a certified copy of all the papers in said cause that are on file in his office.

SEC. 38. That the orders, judgments, or decrees of any court mentioned in section thirty-four of this Act arising under the copyright laws of the United States may be reviewed on appeal or writ of error in the manner and to the extent now provided by law for the review of cases determined in said courts, respectively.

Sec. 39. That no criminal proceeding shall be maintained under the provisions of this Act unless the same is commenced within three years after the cause of action arose.

Sec. 40. That in all actions, suits, or proceedings under this Act, except when brought by or against the United States or any officer thereof, full costs shall be allowed, and the court may award to the prevailing party a reasonable attorney's fee as part of the costs.

Sec. 41. That the copyright is distinct from the property in the material object copyrighted, and the sale or conveyance, by gift or otherwise, of the material object shall not of itself constitute a transfer of the copyright, nor shall the assignment of the copyright constitute a transfer of the title to the material object; but nothing in this Act shall be deemed to forbid, prevent, or restrict the transfer of any copy of a copyrighted work the possession of which has been lawfully obtained.

Sec. 42. That copyright secured under this or previous Acts of the United States may be assigned, granted, or mortgaged by an instrument in writing signed by the proprietor of the copyright, or may be bequeathed by will.

Sec. 43. That every assignment of copyright executed in a foreign country shall be acknowledged by the assignor before a consular officer or secretary of legation of the United States authorized by law to administer oaths or perform notarial acts. The certificate of such acknowledgment under the hand and official seal of such consular officer or secretary of legation shall be prima facie evidence of the execution of the instrument.

SEC. 44. That every assignment of copyright shall be recorded in the copyright office within three calendar months after its execution in the United States or within six calendar months after its execution without the limits of the United States, in default of which it shall be void as against any subsequent purchaser or mortgagee for a valuable consideration, without notice, whose assignment has been duly recorded.

SEC. 45. That the register of copyrights shall, upon payment of the prescribed fee, record such assignment, and shall return it to the sender with a certificate of record attached under seal of the copyright office, and upon the payment of the fee prescribed by this Act he shall furnish to any person requesting the same a certified copy thereof under the said seal.

SEC. 46. That when an assignment of the copyright in a specified book or other work has been recorded the assignee may substitute his name for that of the assignor in the statutory notice of copyright prescribed by this Act.

SEC. 47. That all records and other things relating to copyrights required by law to be preserved shall be kept and preserved in the copyright office, Library of Congress, District of Columbia, and shall be under the control of the register of copyrights, who shall, under the direction and supervision of the Librarian of Congress, perform all the duties relating to the registration of copyrights.

SEC. 48. That there shall be appointed by the Librarian of Congress a register of copyrights, at a salary of four thousand dollars per annum, and one assistant register of copyrights, at a salary of three thousand dollars per annum, who shall have authority during the absence of the register of copyrights to attach the copyright office seal to all papers issued from the said office and to sign such certificates and other papers as may be necessary. There shall also be appointed by the Librarian such subordinate assistants to the register as may from time to time be authorized by law.

SEC. 49. That the register of copyrights shall make daily deposits in some bank in the District of Columbia, designated for this purpose by the Secretary of the Treasury as a national depository, of all moneys received to be applied as copyright fees, and shall make weekly deposits with the Secretary of the Treasury in such manner as the latter shall direct, of all copyright fees actually applied under the provisions of this Act, and annual deposits of sums received which it has not been possible to apply as copyright fees or to return to the remitters, and shall also make monthly reports to the Secretary of the Treasury and to the Librarian of Congress of the applied copyright fees for each calendar month, together with a statement of all remittances received, trust funds on hand, moneys refunded, and unpaid balances.

SEC. 50. That the register of copyrights shall give bond to the United States in the sum of twenty thousand dollars, in form to be approved by the Solicitor of the Treasury and with sureties satisfactory to the Secretary of the Treasury, for the faithful discharge of his duties.

SEC. 51. That the register of copyrights shall make an annual report to the Librarian of Congress, to be printed in the annual report on the Library of Congress, of all copyright business for the previous fiscal year, including the number and kind of works which have been deposited in the copyright office during the fiscal year, under the provisions of this Act.

Sec. 52. That the seal provided under the Act of July eighth, eighteen hundred and seventy, and at present used in the copyright office, shall continue to be the seal thereof, and by it all papers issued from the copyright office requiring authentication shall be authenticated.

Sec. 53. That, subject to the approval of the Librarian of Congress, the register of copyrights shall be authorized to make rules and regulations for the registration of claims to copyright as provided by this Act.

Sec. 54. That the register of copyrights shall provide and keep such record books in the copyright office as are required to carry out the provisions of this Act, and whenever deposit has been made in the copyright office of a copy of any work under the provisions of this Act he shall make entry thereof.

Sec. 55. That in the case of each entry the person recorded as the claimant of the copyright shall be entitled to a certificate of registration under seal of the copyright office, to contain the name and address of said claimant, *the name of the country of which the author of the work is a citizen or subject, and when an alien author domiciled in the United States at the time of said registration, then a statement of that fact, including his place of domicile, the name of the author (when the records of the copyright office shall show the same)*, the title of the work *which is registered* for which copyright is claimed, the date of the deposit of the copies of such work, *the date of publication if the work has been reproduced in copies for sale, or publicly distributed,* and such marks as to class designation and entry number as shall fully identify the entry. In the case of a book the certificate shall also state the receipt of the affidavit, as provided by section sixteen of this Act, and the date of the completion of the printing, or the date of the publication of the book, as stated in the said affidavit. The register of copyrights shall prepare a printed form for the said certificate, to be filled out in each case as above provided for *in the case of all registrations made after this Act goes into effect, and in the case of all previous registrations so far as the copyright office record books shall show such facts,*[1] which certificate, sealed with the seal of the copyright office, shall, upon payment of the prescribed fee, be given to any person making application for the same. Said certificate shall be admitted in any court as prima facie evidence of the facts stated therein. In addition to such certificate the register of copyrights shall furnish, upon request, without additional fee, a receipt for the copies of the work deposited to complete the registration.

SEC. 56. That the register of copyrights shall fully index all copyright registrations and assignments and shall print at periodic intervals a catalogue of the titles of articles deposited and registered for copyright, together with suitable indexes, and at stated intervals shall print complete and indexed catalogues for each class of copyright entries, and may thereupon, if expedient, destroy

[1] The words printed in italics indicate the amendments authorized by the amendatory Act of March 2, 1913.

the original manuscript catalogue cards containing the titles included in such printed volumes and representing the entries made during such intervals. The current catalogues of copyright entries and the index volumes herein provided for shall be admitted in any court as prima facie evidence of the facts stated therein as regards any copyright registration.

SEC. 57. That the said printed current catalogues as they are issued shall be promptly distributed by the copyright office to the collectors of customs of the United States and to the postmasters of all exchange offices of receipt of foreign mails, in accordance with revised lists of such collectors of customs and postmasters prepared by the Secretary of the Treasury and the Postmaster-General, and they shall also be furnished to all parties desiring them at a price to be determined by the register of copyrights, not exceeding five dollars per annum for the complete catalogue of copyright entries and not exceeding one dollar per annum for the catalogues issued during the year for any one class of subjects. The consolidated catalogues and indexes shall also be supplied to all persons ordering them at such prices as may be determined to be reasonable, and all subscriptions for the catalogues shall be received by the Superintendent of Public Documents, who shall forward the said publications; and the moneys thus received shall be paid into the Treasury of the United States and accounted for under such laws and Treasury regulations as shall be in force at the time.

SEC. 58. That the record books of the copyright office, together with the indexes to such record books, and all works deposited and retained in the copyright office, shall be open to public inspection; and copies may be taken of the copyright entries actually made in such record books, subject to such safeguards and regulations as shall be prescribed by the register of copyrights and approved by the Librarian of Congress.

SEC. 59. That of the articles deposited in the copyright office under the provisions of the copyright laws of the United States or of this Act, the Librarian of Congress shall determine what books and other articles shall be transferred to the permanent collections of the Library of Congress, including the law library, and what other books or articles shall be placed in the reserve collections of the Library of Congress for sale or exchange, or be transferred to other governmental libraries in the District of Columbia for use therein.

SEC. 60. That of any articles undisposed of as above provided, together with all titles and correspondence relating thereto, the Librarian of Congress and the register of copyrights jointly shall, at suitable intervals, determine what of these received during any period of years it is desirable or useful to preserve in the permanent files of the copyright office, and, after due notice as hereinafter provided, may within their discretion cause the remaining articles and other things to be destroyed: *Provided*, That there shall be printed in the Catalogue of Copyright Entries from February to November, inclusive, a statement of the years of receipt of such articles and a notice to permit any author, copyright proprietor, or other lawful claimant to claim and remove before the expiration of the month of December of that year anything found which relates to any of his productions deposited or registered for copyright within the period of years stated, not reserved or disposed of as provided for in this Act: *And provided further,* That no manuscript of an unpublished work shall be destroyed during its term of copyright without specific notice to the copyright proprietor of record, permitting him to claim and remove it.

SEC. 61. That the register of copyrights shall receive, and the persons to whom the services designated are rendered shall pay, the following fees: For the registration of any work subject to copyright, deposited under the provisions of this Act, one dollar, which sum is to include a certificate of registration under seal: *Provided,* That in the case of photographs the fee shall be fifty cents where a certificate is not demanded. For every additional certificate of registration made, fifty cents. For recording and certifying any instrument of writing for the assignment of copyright, or any such license specified in section one, subsection (e), or for any copy of such assignment or license, duly certified, if not over three hundred words in length, one dollar; if more than three hundred and less than one thousand words in length, two dollars; if more than one thousand words in length, one dollar additional for each one thousand words or fraction thereof over three hundred words. For recording the notice of user or acquiescence specified in section one, subsection (e), twenty-five cents for each notice if not over fifty words, and an additional twenty-five cents for each additional one hundred words. For comparing any copy of an assignment with the record of such document in the copyright office and certifying the same under seal, one dollar. For recording the extension or renewal of copyright provided for in sections twenty-three and twenty-four of this Act, fifty cents. For recording the transfer of the proprietorship of copyrighted articles, ten cents for each title of a book or other article, in addition to the fee prescribed for recording the instrument of assignment. For any requested search of copyright office records, indexes, or deposits, fifty cents for each full hour of time consumed in making such search: *Provided,* That only one registration at one fee shall be required in the case of several volumes of the same book deposited at the same time.

SEC. 62. That in the interpretation and construction of this Act "the date of publication" shall in the case of a work of which copies are reproduced for sale or distribution be held to be the earliest date when copies of the first authorized edition were placed on sale, sold, or publicly distributed by the proprietor of the copyright or under his authority, and the word "author" shall include an employer in the case of works made for hire.

SEC. 63. That all laws or parts of laws in conflict with the provisions of this Act are hereby repealed, but nothing in this Act shall affect causes of action for infringement of copyright heretofore committed now pending in courts of the United States, or which may hereafter be instituted; but such causes shall be prosecuted to a conclusion in the manner heretofore provided by law.

SEC. 64. That this Act shall go into effect on the first day of July, nineteen hundred and nine.

Approved, March 4, 1909.

NOTE TO SECTION 18, PROVISO

The Act of June 18, 1874, provides that the notice of copyright to be inscribed on each copy of a copyrighted work shall consist of the following words:

"Entered according to Act of Congress, in the year ——, by A. B., in the office of the Librarian of Congress, at Washington"; or, . . . the word "Copyright," together with the year the copyright was entered, and the name of the party by whom it was taken out, thus: "Copyright, 18—, by A. B."

PRESIDENTIAL PROCLAMATIONS

[See Sec. 8]

The following proclamations have been issued by the President, by which copyright protection is granted in the United States to works of authors who are citizens or subjects of the countries named. It is to be noted that this protection does not include "copyright controlling the parts of instruments serving to reproduce mechanically the musical work" provided in Sec. 1 (e) of the Act of March 4, 1909, except in the case of the countries named in the second part of this list, viz: Belgium, Cuba, Germany, Great Britain, Hungary, Italy, Luxemburg, and Norway.

July 1, 1891—Belgium, France, Great Britain and the British possessions, and Switzerland. (Stat. L., vol. 27, pp. 981–982.)

April 15, 1892—Germany. (Stat. L., vol. 27, pp. 1021–1022.)

October 31, 1892—Italy. (Stat. L., vol. 27, p. 1043.)

May 8, 1893—Denmark. (Stat. L., vol. 28, p. 1219.)

July 20, 1893—Portugal. (Stat. L., vol. 28, p. 1222.)

July 10, 1895—Spain. (Stat. L., vol. 29, p. 871.)

February 27, 1896—Mexico. (Stat. L., vol. 29, p. 877.)

May 25, 1896—Chile. (Stat. L., vol. 29, p. 880.)

October 19, 1899—Costa Rica. (Stat. L., vol. 31, pp. 1955–1956.)

November 20, 1899—Netherlands and possessions. (Stat. L., vol. 31, p. 1961.)

November 17, 1903—Cuba. (Stat. L., vol. 33, pt. 2, p. 2324.)

January 13, 1904—China. (Treaty of October 8, 1903, Article XI.) (Stat. L., vol. 33, pt. 2, pp. 2208, 2213–2214.)

July 1, 1905—Norway. (Stat. L., vol. 34, pt. 3, pp. 3111–3112.)

May 17, 1906—Japan. (Treaty of November 10, 1905.) (Stat. L., vol. 34, pt. 3, pp. 2890–2891.)

September 20, 1907—Austria. (Stat. L., vol. 35, pt. 2, p. 2155.)

April 9, 1908—Convention between the United States and other powers on literary and artistic copyrights, signed at the City of Mexico, January 27, 1902. (This treaty is effective from July 1, 1908, as between the United States and the following countries: Guatemala, Salvador, Costa Rica, Honduras, and Nicaragua.) (Stat. L., vol. 35, pt. 2, pp. 1934–1946. English, French, and Spanish texts.)

August 11, 1908—Japan. (Treaty of May 19, 1908, for protection in China.) (Stat. L., vol. 35, pt. 2, pp. 2044–2046.)

August 11, 1908—Japan. (Treaty of May 19, 1908, for protection in Korea.) (Stat. L., vol. 35, pt. 2, pp. 2041–2043.)

April 9, 1910—Austria, Belgium, Chile, Costa Rica, Cuba, Denmark, France, Germany, Great Britain and her possessions, Italy, Mexico, the Netherlands and possessions, Norway, Portugal, Spain, and Switzerland. (Stat. L., vol. 36, pt. 2, pp. 2685–2686.)

June 29, 1910—Luxemburg. (Stat. L., vol. 36, pt. 2, p. 2716.)

May 26, 1911—Sweden. (Effective June 1, 1911.) (Stat. L., vol. 37, pt. 2, pp. 1682–1683.)

October 4, 1912—Tunis. (Stat. L., vol. 37, pt. 2, p. 1765.)

October 15, 1912—Hungary. [Copyright convention between the United States and Hungary, effective October 16, 1912, including protection under Sec. 1 (e).] (Stat. L., vol. 37, pt. 2, pp. 1631–1633.)

July 13, 1914—Copyright convention between the United States and other American Republics, signed at Buenos Aires, August 11, 1910. (Effective from July 13, 1914, as between the United States and the following countries: Dominican Republic, Guatemala, Honduras, Panama, Nicaragua, and Ecuador. The Governments of Bolivia, Brazil, Costa Rica, and Salvador have announced through diplomatic channels the adhesion of those countries to this convention.) (Stat. L., vol. 38, pt. 2, pp. 1785–1798. Spanish, English, Portuguese, and French texts.)

PRESIDENTIAL PROCLAMATIONS UNDER SECTION 1 (e)

December 8, 1910—Germany. (Stat. L., vol. 36, pt. 2, pp. 2761–2762.)

June 14, 1911—Belgium, Luxemburg, and Norway. (Stat. L., vol. 37, pt. 2, pp. 1687–1690.)

November 27, 1911—Cuba. (Stat. L., vol. 37, pt. 2, pp. 1721–1722.)

October 15, 1912—Hungary. (See above.)

January 1, 1915—Great Britain. (British order in council issued February 3, 1915, effective January 1, 1915.) (Stat. L., vol. 38, pt. 2, pp. 2044–2045.)

May 1, 1915—Italy.

RULES ADOPTED BY THE SUPREME COURT OF THE UNITED STATES FOR PRACTICE AND PROCEDURE UNDER SECTION 25 OF AN ACT TO AMEND AND CONSOLIDATE THE ACTS RESPECTING COPYRIGHT, APPROVED MARCH 4, 1909. TO GO INTO EFFECT JULY 1, 1909

1

The existing rules of equity practice, so far as they may be applicable, shall be enforced in proceedings instituted under section twenty-five (25) of the act of March fourth, nineteen hundred and nine, entitled "An act to amend and consolidate the acts respecting copyright."

2

A copy of the alleged infringement of copyright, if actually made, and a copy of the work alleged to be infringed, should accompany the petition, or its absence be explained; except in cases of alleged infringement by the public performance of dramatic and dramatico-musical compositions, the delivery of lectures, sermons, addresses, and so forth, the infringement of copyright upon sculptures and other similar works and in any case where it is not feasible.

3

Upon the institution of any action, suit, or proceeding, or at any time thereafter, and before the entry of final judgment or decree therein, the plaintiff or complainant, or his authorized agent or attorney, may file with the clerk of any court given jurisdiction under section 34 of the act of March 4, 1909, an affidavit stating, upon the best of his knowledge, information, and belief, the number and location, as near as may be, of the alleged infringing copies, records, plates, molds, matrices, etc., or other means for making the copies alleged to infringe the copyright, and the value of the same, and with such affidavit shall file with the clerk a bond executed by at least two sureties and approved by the court or a commissioner thereof.

4

Such bond shall bind the sureties in a specified sum, to be fixed by the court, but not less than twice the reasonable value of such infringing copies, plates, records, molds, matrices, or other means for making such infringing copies, and be conditioned for the prompt prosecution of the action, suit or proceeding; for the return of said articles to the defendant, if they or any of them are adjudged not to be infringements, or if the action abates, or is discontinued before they are returned to the defendant; and for the payment to the defendant of any damages which the court may award to him against the plaintiff or complainant. Upon the filing of said affidavit and bond, and the approval of said bond, the clerk shall issue a writ directed to the marshal of the district where the said infringing copies, plates, records, molds, matrices, etc., or other means of making such infringing copies shall be stated in said affidavit to be located, and generally to any marshal of the United States, directing the said marshal to forthwith seize and hold the same subject to the order of the court issuing said writ, or of the court of the district in which the seizure shall be made.

5

The marshal shall thereupon seize said articles or any smaller or larger part thereof he may then or thereafter find, using such force as may be reasonably necessary in the premises, and serve on the defendant a copy of the affidavit, writ, and bond by delivering the same to him personally, if he can be found within the district or if he can not be found, to his agent, if any, or to the person from whose possession the articles are taken, or if the owner, agent, or such person can not be found within the district by leaving said copy at the usual place of abode of such owner or agent, with a person of suitable age and discretion, or at the place where said articles are found, and shall make immediate return of such seizure, or attempted seizure, to the court. He shall also attach to said articles a tag or label stating the fact of such seizure and warning all persons from in any manner interfering therewith.

6

A marshal who has seized alleged infringing articles, shall retain them in his possession, keeping them in a secure place, subject to the order of the court.

7

Within three days after the articles are seized, and a copy of the affidavit, writ and bond are served as hereinbefore provided, the defendant shall serve upon the clerk a notice that he excepts to the amount of the penalty of the bond, or to the sureties of the plaintiff or complainant, or both, otherwise he shall be deemed to have waived all objection to the amount of the penalty of the bond and the sufficiency of the sureties thereon. If the court sustain the exceptions it may order a new bond to be executed by the plaintiff or complainant, or in default thereof within a time to be named by the court, the property to be returned to the defendant.

8

Within ten days after service of such notice, the attorney of the plaintiff or complainant shall serve upon the defendant or his attorney a notice of the justification of the sureties, and said sureties shall justify before the court or a judge thereof at the time therein stated.

9

The defendant, if he does not except to the amount of the penalty of the bond or the sufficiency of the sureties of the plaintiff or complainant, may make application to the court for the return to him of the articles seized, upon filing an affidavit stating all material facts and circumstances tending to show that the articles seized are not infringing copies, records, plates, molds, matrices, or means for making the copies alleged to infringe the copyright.

10

Thereupon the court in its discretion, and after such hearing as it may direct, may order such return upon the filing by the defendant of a bond executed by at least two sureties, binding them in a specified sum to be fixed in the discretion of the court, and conditioned for the delivery of said specified articles to abide the order of the court. The plaintiff or complainant may require such sureties to justify within ten days of the filing of such bond.

11

Upon the granting of such application and the justification of the sureties on the bond, the marshal shall immediately deliver the articles seized to the defendant.

12

Any service required to be performed by any marshal may be performed by any deputy of such marshal.

13

For services in cases arising under this section, the marshal shall be entitled to the same fees as are allowed for similar services in other cases.

COPYRIGHT

By the President of the United States of America

A PROCLAMATION

Whereas it is provided by the act of Congress of March 4, 1909, entitled "An act to amend and consolidate the acts respecting copyright," that the benefits of said act, excepting the benefits under section 1 (*e*) thereof, as to which special conditions are imposed, shall extend to the work of an author or proprietor who is a citizen or subject of a foreign State or nation, only upon certain conditions set forth in section 8 of said act, to wit:

(*a*) When an alien author or proprietor shall be domiciled within the United States at the time of the first publication of his work; or

(*b*) When the foreign State or nation of which such author or proprietor is a citizen or subject grants, either by treaty, convention, agreement, or law, to citizens of the United States the benefit of copyright on substantially the same basis as to its own citizens, or copyright protection substantially equal to the protection secured to such foreign author under this act or by treaty; or when such foreign State or nation is a party to an international agreement which provides for reciprocity in the granting of copyright, by the terms of which agreement the United States may, at its pleasure, become a party thereto:

And whereas it is also provided by said section that "The existence of the reciprocal conditions aforesaid shall be determined by the President of the United States, by proclamation made from time to time as the purposes of this act may require":

And whereas satisfactory evidence has been received that in Austria, Belgium, Chile, Costa Rica, Cuba, Denmark, France, Germany, Great Britain and her possessions, Italy, Mexico, the Netherlands and possessions, Norway, Portugal, Spain, and Switzerland the law permits and since July 1, 1909, has permitted to citizens of the United States the benefit of copyright on substantially the same basis as to citizens of those countries:

Now, therefore, I, William Howard Taft, President of the United States of America, do declare and proclaim that one of the alternative conditions specified in section 8, of the act of March 4, 1909, is now fulfilled, and since July 1, 1909, has continuously been fulfilled, in respect to the citizens or subjects of Austria, Belgium, Chile, Costa Rica, Cuba, Denmark, France, Germany, Great Britain and her possessions, Italy, Mexico, the Netherlands and possessions, Norway, Portugal, Spain, and Switzerland, and that the citizens or subjects of the aforementioned countries are and since July 1, 1909, have been entitled to all of the benefits of the said act other than the benefits under section 1 (*e*) thereof, as to which the inquiry is still pending.

In testimony whereof, I have hereunto set my hand and caused the seal of the United States to be affixed.

Done at the city of Washington this ninth day of April, in the year of our Lord one [SEAL] thousand nine hundred and ten, and of the Independence of the United States of America the one hundred and thirty-fourth.

WM. H. TAFT.

By the President:

P. C. KNOX,

Secretary of State.

In "The Statutes at Large of the United States of America, from March, 1909, to March, 1911." Vol. 36, part 2. 8vo. Washington, 1911, pp. 2685–2686.

COPYRIGHT CONVENTION

UNITED STATES AND HUNGARY

IN FORCE OCTOBER 16, 1912

The President of the United States of America and His Majesty the Emperor of Austria, King of Bohemia, etc., and Apostolic King of Hungary, desiring to provide, between the United States of America and Hungary, for a reciprocal legal protection in regard to copyright of the citizens and subjects of the two countries, have, to this end, decided to conclude a convention, and have appointed as their plenipotentiaries:

The President of the United States of America—

Richard C. Kerens, Ambassador Extraordinary and Plenipotentiary of the United States of America to His Imperial and Royal Apostolic Majesty; and

His Majesty the Emperor of Austria, King of Bohemia, etc., and Apostolic King of Hungary—

Count Paul Esterházy, Baron of Galántha, Viscount of Fraknó, Privy Councillor and Chamberlain, Chief of Section in the Ministry of the Imperial and Royal House and of Foreign Affairs, and

Dr. Gustavus de Töry, Secretary of State in the Royal Hungarian Ministry of Justice;

Who, having communicated to each other their full powers, found to be in good and due form, have agreed as follows:

Article 1

Authors who are citizens or subjects of one of the two countries or their assigns shall enjoy in the other country, for their literary, artistic, dramatic, musical, and photographic works (whether unpublished or published in one of the two countries) the same rights which the respective laws do now or may hereafter grant to natives.

The above provision includes the copyright control of mechanical musical reproductions.

Article 2

The enjoyment and the exercise of the rights secured by the present Convention are subject to the performance of the conditions and formalities prescribed by the laws and regulations of the country where protection is claimed under the present Convention; such enjoyment and such exercise are independent of the existence of protection in the country of origin of the work.

Article 3

The term of copyright protection granted by the present Convention shall be regulated by the law of the country where protection is claimed.

Article 4

The present Convention shall be ratified and the ratifications shall be exchanged at Washington as soon as possible.

Article 5

The present Convention shall be put in force one month after the exchange of ratifications, and shall remain in force until the termination of a year from the day on which it may have been denounced.

In faith whereof the Plenipotentiaries have signed the present Convention in two copies, each in English and Hungarian languages, and have affixed thereto their seals.

Done at Budapest, the 30th day of January, 1912.

(SEAL) RICHARD C. KERENS.
(SEAL) ESTERHÁZY PÁL.
(SEAL) TÖRY GUSTÁV.

NOTE.—Ratification was advised by the Senate, July 23, 1912; ratifications were exchanged, September 16, 1912; proclaimed by the President, October 15, 1912. The Convention went into force October 16, 1912.

In "The Statutes at Large of the United States of America, from March, 1911, to March, 1913." Vol. 37, part 2. 8vo. Washington, 1913, pp. 1631–1633.

COPYRIGHT CONVENTION BETWEEN THE UNITED STATES AND OTHER AMERICAN REPUBLICS

Signed at Buenos Aires, August 11, 1910; ratification advised by the Senate, February 15, 1911; ratified by the President, March 12, 1911; ratification of the United States deposited with the Government of the Argentine Republic, May 1, 1911; proclaimed July 13, 1914

By the President of the United States of America

A PROCLAMATION

Whereas, a Convention on Literary and Artistic Copyright between the United States of America and the Argentine Republic, Brazil, Chile, Colombia, Costa Rica, Cuba, Dominican Republic, Ecuador, Guatemala, Haiti, Honduras, Mexico, Nicaragua, Panama, Paraguay, Peru, Salvador, Uruguay, and Venezuela was concluded and signed by their respective Plenipotentiaries at Buenos Aires on the eleventh day of August, one thousand nine hundred and ten, the original of which Convention, being in the Spanish, English, Portuguese and French languages, is word for word as follows:

Fourth International American Convention

LITERARY AND ARTISTIC COPYRIGHT

Their Excellencies the Presidents of the United States of America, the Argentine Republic, Brazil, Chili, Colombia, Costa Rica, Cuba, Dominican Republic, Ecuador, Guatemala, Haiti, Honduras, Mexico, Nicaragua, Panama, Paraguay, Peru, Salvador, Uruguay and Venezuela;

Being desirous that their respective countries may be represented at the Fourth International American Conference, have sent thereto the following Delegates duly authorized to approve the recommendations, resolutions, conventions and treaties which they might deem advantageous to the interests of America:

[Here follow the names of the respective delegates, omitted.]

Who, after having presented their credentials and the same having been found in due and proper form, have agreed upon the following Convention on Literary and Artistic Copyright.

ARTICLE 1. The signatory States acknowledge and protect the rights of Literary and Artistic Property in conformity with the stipulations of the present Convention.

ARTICLE 2. In the expression "Literary and Artistic works" are included books, writings, pamphlets of all kinds, whatever may be the subject of which they treat, and whatever the number of their pages; dramatic or dramatico-musical works; choreographic and musical compositions, with or without words; drawings, paintings, sculpture, engravings; photographic works; astronomical or geographical globes; plans, sketches or plastic works relating to geography, geology or topography, architecture or any other science; and, finally, all productions that can be published by any means of impression or reproduction.

ARTICLE 3. The acknowledgment of a copyright obtained in one State, in conformity with its laws, shall produce its effects of full right, in all the other States, without the necessity of complying with any other formality, provided always there shall appear in the work a statement that indicates the reservation of the property right.

ARTICLE 4. The copyright of a literary or artistic work, includes for its author or assigns the exclusive power of disposing of the same, of publishing, assigning, translating, or authorizing its translation and reproducing it in any form whether wholly or in part.

ARTICLE 5. The author of a protected work, except in case of proof to the contrary, shall be considered the person whose name or well known nom de plume is indicated therein; consequently suit brought by such author or his representative against counterfeiters or violators, shall be admitted by the Courts of the Signatory States.

ARTICLE 6. The authors or their assigns, citizens or domiciled foreigners, shall enjoy in the signatory countries the rights that the respective laws accord, without those rights being allowed to exceed the term of protection granted in the country of origin.

For works comprising several volumes that are not published simultaneously, as well as for bulletins, or parts, or periodical publications, the term of the copyright will commence to run, with respect to each volume, bulletin, part, or periodical publication, from the respective date of its publication.

ARTICLE 7. The country of origin of a work will be deemed that of its first publication in America, and if it shall have appeared simultaneously in several of the signatory countries, that which fixes the shortest period of protection.

ARTICLE 8. A work which was not originally copyrighted shall not be entitled to copyright in subsequent editions.

ARTICLE 9. Authorized translations shall be protected in the same manner as original works.

Translators of works concerning which no right of guaranteed property exists, or the guaranteed copyright of which may have been extinguished, may obtain for their translations the rights of property set forth in Article 3rd but they shall not prevent the publication of other translations of the same work.

ARTICLE 10. Addresses or discourses delivered or read before deliberative assemblies, Courts of Justice, or at public meeting, may be printed in the daily press without the necessity of any authorization, with due regard, however, to the provisions of the domestic legislation of each nation.

ARTICLE 11. Literary, scientific or artistic writings, whatever may be their subjects, published in newspapers or magazines, in any one of the countries of the Union, shall not be reproduced in the other countries without the consent of the authors. With the exception of the works mentioned, any article in a newspaper may be reprinted by others, if it has not been expressly prohibited, but in every case, the source from which it is taken must be cited.

News and miscellaneous items published merely for general information, do not enjoy protection under this convention.

ARTICLE 12. The reproduction of extracts from literary

or artistic publications for the purpose of instruction or chrestomathy, does not confer any right of property, and may, therefore, be freely made in all the signatory countries.

ARTICLE 13. The indirect appropriation of unauthorized parts of a literary or artistic work, having no original character, shall be deemed an illicit reproduction, in so far as effects civil liability.

The reproduction in any form of an entire work, or of the greater part thereof, accompanied by notes or commentaries under the pretext of literary criticism or amplification, or supplement to the original work, shall also be considered illicit.

ARTICLE 14. Every publication infringing a copyright may be confiscated in the signatory countries in which the original work had the right to be legally protected, without prejudice to the indemnities or penalties which the counterfeiters may have incurred according to the laws of the country in which the fraud may have been committed.

ARTICLE 15. Each of the Governments of the signatory countries, shall retain the right to permit, inspect, or prohibit the circulation, representation or exhibition of works or productions, concerning which the proper authority may have to exercise that right.

ARTICLE 16. The present Convention shall become operative between the Signatory States which ratify it, three months after they shall have communicated their ratification to the Argentine Government, and it shall remain in force among them until a year after the date when it may be denounced. This denunciation shall be addressed to the Argentine Government and shall be without force except with respect to the country making it.

In witness whereof, the Plenipotentiaries have signed the present treaty and affixed thereto the Seal of the Fourth International American Conference.

Made and signed in the City of Buenos Aires on the eleventh day of August in the year one thousand nine hundred and ten, in Spanish, English, Portuguese and French, and deposited in the Ministry of Foreign Affairs of the Argentine Republic, in order that certified copies be made for transmission to each one of the signatory nations through the appropriate diplomatic channels.

[Here follow the signatures (omitted) of the delegates of the United States of America and the other nineteen contracting states: Argentine Republic, Brazil, Chili, Colombia, Costa Rica, Cuba, Dominican Republic, Ecuador, Guatemala, Haiti, Honduras, Mexico, Nicaragua, Panama, Paraguay, Peru, Salvador, Uruguay, Venezuela.]

And whereas, the said Convention has been ratified by the Government of the United States, by and with the advice and consent of the Senate thereof, and by the Governments of the Dominican Republic, Guatemala, Honduras, Panama, Nicaragua, and Ecuador,[1] and the ratifications of the said Governments were, by the provisions of Article 16 of the said Convention, deposited by their respective Plenipotentiaries with the Government of the Argentine Republic;

[1] The Governments of Bolivia, Brazil, Costa Rica, and Salvador have announced through diplomatic channels the adhesion of those countries to this copyright convention.

Now, therefore, be it known that I, Woodrow Wilson, President of the United States of America, have caused the said Convention to be made public, to the end that the same and every article and clause thereof may be observed and fulfilled with good faith by the United States and the citizens thereof.

In testimony whereof, I have hereunto set my hand and caused the seal of the United States to be affixed.

Done at the City of Washington this thirteenth day of July in the year of our Lord one thousand nine [SEAL] hundred and fourteen, and of the Independence of the United States of America the one hundred and thirty-ninth.

WOODROW WILSON.

By the President:
W. J. BRYAN,
Secretary of State.

In "The Statutes at Large of the United States of America, from March, 1913, to March, 1915." Vol. 38, part 2. 8vo. Washington, 1915, pages 1785–1798. (Spanish, English, Portuguese, and French texts.)

GREAT BRITAIN

Order in Council under the Copyright Act, 1911 (1 & 2 Geo. 5, c. 46), regulating Copyright Relations with the United States of America.

At the Court at Buckingham Palace, the 3d day of February, 1915.

Present, THE KING'S MOST EXCELLENT MAJESTY, LORD PRESIDENT, VISCOUNT KNOLLYS, LORD CHAMBERLAIN, MR. SECRETARY HARCOURT, MR. ARTHUR HENDERSON, SIR WILLIAM MACGREGOR, LORD JUSTICE BANKES.

Whereas by a Proclamation of the President of the United States of America, dated the 9th April, 1910, the benefits of the United States Act of 1909, entitled "An Act to Amend and Consolidate the Acts respecting Copyright," were extended to the subjects of Great Britain and her possessions, but no provision was made therein for the protection of the musical works of British subjects against reproduction by means of mechanical contrivances:

And whereas His Majesty is advised that the Government of the United States of America has undertaken, upon the issue of this Order, to grant such protection to the musical works of British subjects:

And whereas by reason of these premises His Majesty is satisfied that the Government of the United States of America has made, or has undertaken to make, such provision as it is expedient to require for the protection of works entitled to copyright under the provisions of Part I of the Copyright Act, 1911:

And whereas by the Copyright Act, 1911, authority is conferred upon His Majesty to extend, by Order in Council, the protection of the said Act to certain classes of foreign works within any part of His Majesty's Dominions, other than self-governing dominions, to which the said Act extends:

And whereas it is desirable to provide protection within the said dominions for the unpublished works of citizens of the United States of America:

Now, therefore, His Majesty, by and with the advice of His Privy Council, and by virtue of the authority conferred upon him by the Copyright Act, 1911, is pleased to order, and it is hereby ordered, as follows:—

1. The Copyright Act, 1911, including the provisions as to existing works, shall, subject to the provisions of the said Act and of this Order, apply—

(*a*) to literary, dramatic, musical and artistic works the authors whereof were at the time of the making of the works Citizens of the United States of America, in like manner as if the authors had been British Subjects:

(*b*) in respect of residence in the United States of America, in like manner as if such residence had been residence in the parts of His Majesty's dominions to which the said Act extends.

Provided that—

(i) The term of copyright within the parts of His Majesty's dominions to which this Order applies shall not exceed that conferred by the law of the United States of America:

(ii) the enjoyment of the rights conferred by this Order shall be subject to the accomplishment of the conditions and formalities prescribed by the law of the United States of America:

(iii) in the application to existing works of the provisions of Section 24 of the Copyright Act, 1911, the commencement of this Order shall be substituted for the 26th July, 1910, in subsection 1 (*b*).

2. This Order shall apply to all His Majesty's Dominions, Colonies and Possessions, with the exception of those hereinafter named, that is to say:

The Dominion of Canada.
The Commonwealth of Australia.
The Dominion of New Zealand.
The Union of South Africa.
Newfoundland.

3. This Order shall come into operation on the 1st day of January, 1915, which day is in this Order referred to as the commencement of this Order.

And the Lords Commissioners of His Majesty's Treasury are to give the necessary Orders accordingly.

ALMERIC FITZROY.

COPYRIGHT—GREAT BRITAIN

BY THE PRESIDENT OF THE UNITED STATES OF AMERICA

A PROCLAMATION

Whereas it is provided by the Act of Congress of March 4, 1909, entitled "An Act to Amend and Consolidate the Acts Respecting Copyright," that the provisions of said Act, "so far as they secure copyright controlling the parts of instruments serving to reproduce mechanically the musical work, shall include only compositions published and copyrighted after this Act goes into effect, and shall not include the works of a foreign author or composer unless the foreign state or nation of which such author or composer is a citizen or subject grants, either by treaty, convention, agreement, or law, to citizens of the United States similar rights":

And whereas it is further provided that the copyright secured by the Act shall extend to the work of an author or proprietor who is a citizen or subject of a foreign state or nation, only upon certain conditions set forth in section 8 of said Act, to wit:

(*a*) When an alien author or proprietor shall be domiciled within the United States at the time of the first publication of his work; or

(*b*) When the foreign state or nation of which such author or proprietor is a citizen or subject grants, either by treaty, convention, agreement, or law, to citizens of the United States the benefit of copyright on substantially the same basis as to its own citizens, or copyright protection substantially equal to the protection secured to such foreign author under this Act or by treaty; or when such foreign state or nation is a party to an international agreement which provides for reciprocity in the granting of copyright, by the terms of which agreement the United States may, at its pleasure, become a party thereto:

And whereas it is also provided by said section that "The existence of the reciprocal conditions aforesaid shall be determined by the President of the United States, by proclamation made from time to time as the purposes of this Act may require":

And whereas satisfactory official assurance has been given that, by virtue of the authority conferred by the British Copyright Act, 1911, a British Order in Council has been issued of even date with this Proclamation directing:—

1. That "the Copyright Act, 1911, including the provisions as to existing works, shall, subject to the provisions of the said Act and of this Order, apply—

"(*a*) to literary, dramatic, musical and artistic works the authors whereof were at the time of the making of the works citizens of the United States of America, in like manner as if the authors had been British subjects:

"(*b*) in respect of residence in the United States of America, in like manner as if such residence had been residence in the parts of His Majesty's dominions to which the said Act extends.

"Provided that—

"(i) the term of copyright within the parts of His Majesty's dominions to which this Order applies shall not exceed that conferred by the law of the United States of America:

"(ii) the enjoyment of the rights conferred by this Order shall be subject to the accomplishment of the conditions and formalities prescribed by the law of the United States of America:

"(iii) in the application to existing works of the provisions of Section 24 of the Copyright Act, 1911, the commencement of this Order shall be substituted for the 26th July, 1910, in subsection 1 (*b*)."

2. That "this Order shall apply to all His Majesty's dominions, colonies and possessions with the exception of those hereinafter named, that is to say:—The Dominion of Canada, The Commonwealth of Australia, The Dominion of New Zealand, The Union of South Africa, Newfoundland."

3. That "this Order shall come into operation on the first day of January, 1915, which day is in this Order referred to as the commencement of this Order.

"And the Lords Commissioners of His Majesty's Treasury are to give the necessary Orders accordingly."

Now, therefore, I, Woodrow Wilson, President of the United States of America, do declare and proclaim that one of the alternative conditions specified in section 8 (*b*) of the Act of March 4, 1909, now exists and is fulfilled in respect to the subjects of Great Britain and the British dominions, colonies and possessions, with the exception of Canada, Australia, New Zealand, South Africa, and

Newfoundland, and that such subjects shall be entitled to all the benefits of section 1 (*e*) of the said Act, on and after January 1, 1915.

In testimony whereof, I have hereunto set my hand and caused the seal of the United States to be affixed.

Done at the City of Washington this first day of January, in the year of our Lord one thousand nine [SEAL] hundred and fifteen, and of the Independence of the United States of America the one hundred and thirty-ninth.

WOODROW WILSON.

By THE PRESIDENT:
W. J. BRYAN,
Secretary of State.

In "The Statutes at Large of the United States of America, from March, 1913, to March, 1915." Vol. 38, part 2. 8vo. Washington, 1915, pp. 2044–2045.

COPYRIGHT OF LABELS AND PRINTS DESIGNED TO BE USED FOR ARTICLES OF MANUFACTURE

The new copyright law approved March 4, 1909, going into effect on July 1, 1909, did not repeal the copyright act of June 18, 1874, according to the opinion of the Attorney-General, of December 22, 1909. Labels or prints designed to be used for articles of manufacture should therefore be registered in the Patent Office.

Section 3 of the act of June 18, 1874, reads as follows:

SEC. 3. That in the construction of this act the words "engraving, cut, and print" shall be applied only to pictorial illustrations or works connected with the fine arts, and no prints or labels designed to be used for any other articles of manufacture shall be entered under the copyright law, but may be registered in the Patent Office. And the Commissioner of Patents is hereby charged with the supervision and control of the entry or registry of such prints or labels, in conformity with the regulations provided by law as to copyright of prints, except that there shall be paid for recording the title of any print or label, not a trade-mark, six dollars, which shall cover the expense of furnishing a copy of the record, under the seal of the Commissioner of Patents, to the party entering the same.

RULES AND REGULATIONS FOR THE REGISTRATION OF CLAIMS TO COPYRIGHT

(As revised and issued in November, 1917)

1. Copyright under the act of Congress entitled: "An act to amend and consolidate the acts respecting copyright," approved March 4, 1909,[1] is ordinarily secured by printing and publishing a copyrightable work with a notice of claim in the form prescribed by the statute. Registration can be made *after* such publication, but the statute expressly provides, in certain cases, for registration of manuscript works.

WHO MAY SECURE COPYRIGHT

2. The persons entitled by the act to copyright protection for their works are:

(1) The *author* of the work, if he is:

(*a*) A citizen of the United States, or

(*b*) An alien author domiciled in the United States at the time of the first publication of his work, or

(*c*) A citizen or subject of any country which grants either by treaty, convention, agreement, or law, to

[1] Amendatory acts were approved August 24, 1912 (providing for the registration of motion pictures), March 2, 1913 (amending sec. 55, with regard to the certificate of registration), and March 28, 1914 (amending sec. 12, to provide for deposit of only one copy in case of works of foreign authors published abroad in foreign languages).

citizens of the United States the benefit of copyright on substantially the same basis as to its own citizens. The existence of reciprocal copyright conditions is determined by presidential proclamation.[1]

[1] Presidential copyright proclamations have been issued securing copyright privileges in the United States to the citizens or subjects of the following countries: Austria, Belgium, Chile, China, Costa Rica, Cuba, Denmark, Dominican Republic, Ecuador, France, Germany, Great Britain and the British possessions, Guatemala, Honduras, Hungary, Italy, Japan, Luxemburg, Mexico, Netherlands (Holland) and possessions, Nicaragua, Norway, Panama, Portugal, Salvador, Spain, Sweden, Switzerland, and Tunis.

The commercial treaty with China of October 8, 1903, proclaimed by the President on January 13, 1904, contains Article XI relating to copyright. A copyright convention with Japan was signed at Tokyo November 10, 1905, and proclaimed in the United States on May 17, 1906. Two additional treaties with Japan, which were signed at Washington May 19, 1908, and proclaimed August 11, 1908, deal with the protection of patents, trade-marks, and copyrights in China and Korea, respectively. The copyright convention with Hungary was signed at Budapest on January 30, 1912, and was proclaimed by the President on October 15, 1912.

The convention to protect literary and artistic property signed at Mexico on January 27, 1902, was proclaimed by the President on April 9, 1908, who announced the ratification of this treaty also by Costa Rica, Guatemala, Honduras, Nicaragua, and Salvador. The Pan American Copyright Convention signed at Buenos Aires on August 11, 1910, was proclaimed on July 13, 1914, announcing its ratification also by the Dominican Republic, Ecuador, Guatemala, Honduras, Nicaragua, and Panama. Since that date announcement has been made of the adhesion to this convention of Bolivia, Brazil, Costa Rica, Paraguay, and Salvador.

Copyright proclamations under section 1 (e), "to secure copyright controlling the parts of instruments serving to reproduce mechanically

(2) The *proprietor* of a work. The word "proprietor" is here used to indicate a person who derives his title to the work from the author. If the author of the work should be a person who could not himself claim the benefit of the copyright act, the proprietor can not claim it.

(3) The *executors, administrators,* or *assigns* of the above-mentioned author or proprietor.

REGISTRATION

3. After the publication of any work entitled to copyright, the claimant of copyright should register his claim in the Copyright Office. An action for infringement of copyright can not be maintained in court until the provisions with respect to the deposit of copies and registration of such work shall have been complied with.

A certificate of registration is issued to the claimant and duplicates thereof may be obtained on payment of the statutory fee of 50 cents.

SUBJECT-MATTER OF COPYRIGHT

4. The act provides that no copyright shall subsist in the original text of any work published prior to July 1, 1909, which has not been already copyrighted in the United States "or in any publication of the United States

musical works" have been issued in behalf of Belgium (June 14, 1911), Cuba (November 27, 1911), Germany (December 8, 1910), Great Britain (January 1, 1915), Italy (May 1, 1915), Luxemburg (June 14, 1911), New Zealand (December 1, 1916), and Norway (June 14, 1911). Protection under this section is also included in the copyright convention with Hungary, proclaimed on October 15, 1912.

government or any reprint in whole or in part thereof" (sec. 7).

Section 5 of the act names the thirteen classes of works for which copyright may be secured, as follows:

(*a*) *Books.*—This term includes "composite and cyclopædic works, directories, gazetteers and other compilations" and generally all printed literary works (except dramatic compositions) whether published in the ordinary shape of a book or pamphlet, or printed as a leaflet, card, or single page. The term "book" as used in the law includes tabulated forms of information, frequently called charts; tables of figures showing the results of mathematical computations, such as logarithmic tables, interest, cost, and wage tables, etc., single poems, and the words of a song when printed and published without music; descriptions of motion pictures or spectacles; catalogues; circulars or folders containing information in the form of reading matter and literary contributions to periodicals or newspapers.

5. The term "book" can not be applied to—

Blank books for use in business or in carrying out any system of transacting affairs, such as record books, account books, memorandum books, blank diaries or journals, bank deposit and check books; forms of contracts or leases which do not contain original copyrightable matter; coupons; forms for use in commercial, legal, or financial transactions, which are wholly or partly blank and whose value lies in their usefulness.

6. (*b*) *Periodicals.*—This term includes newspapers, magazines, reviews, and serial publications appearing oftener than once a year; bulletins or proceedings of

societies, etc., which appear regularly at intervals of less than a year; and, generally, periodical publications which would be registered as second-class matter at the post office. Serial publications which are not clearly "periodicals" should be registered as *books* and the application for registration should be accompanied by the required affidavit.

7. (*c*) *Lectures, sermons, addresses,* or similar productions, prepared for oral delivery.

8. (*d*) *Dramatic and dramatico-musical compositions,* such as dramas, comedies, operas, operettas, and similar works.

The designation "dramatic composition" does not include the following: Dances, motion-picture shows; stage settings or mechanical devices by which dramatic effects are produced, or "stage business"; animal shows, sleight-of-hand performances, acrobatic or circus tricks of any kind; scenarios for, or descriptions of motion pictures or of settings for the production of motion pictures. (These, however, when printed and published, are registrable as "books.")

9. *Dramatico-musical compositions* include principally operas, operettas, and musical comedies, or similar productions which are to be acted as well as sung.

10. (*e*) *Musical compositions,* including other vocal and instrumental compositions, with or without words and separately published songs from operas and operettas, when not intended to be acted.

The words of a song printed alone should be registered as a "book," not as a "musical composition."

"Adaptations" and "arrangements" may be registered

as "new works" under the provisions of section 6. Mere transpositions into different keys are not provided for in the copyright act.

11. (*f*) *Maps.*—This term includes all cartographical works, such as terrestrial maps, plats, marine charts, star maps, but not diagrams, astrological charts, or landscapes.

12. (*g*) *Works of art and models or designs for works of art.*—This term includes all works belonging fairly to the so-called fine arts. (Paintings, drawings, and sculpture.)

The protection of productions of the industrial arts utilitarian in purpose and character even if artistically made or ornamented depends upon action under the patent law; but registration in the Copyright Office has been made to protect artistic drawings notwithstanding they may afterwards be utilized for articles of manufacture.

Toys, games, dolls, advertising novelties, instruments or tools of any kind, glassware, embroideries, garments, laces, woven fabrics, or similar articles, are examples. The exclusive right to make and sell such articles should not be sought by copyright registration.

13. (*h*) *Reproductions of works of art.*—This term refers to such reproductions (engravings, woodcuts, etchings, casts, etc.) as contain in themselves an artistic element distinct from that of the original work of art which has been reproduced.

14. (*i*) *Drawings or plastic works of a scientific or technical character.*—This term includes diagrams or models illustrating scientific or technical works, architects' plans, designs for engineering work, relief maps, etc.

15. (*j*) *Photographs.*—This term covers all photo-

graphic prints, but not half tones or other photo-engravings.

16. (*k*) *Prints and pictorial illustrations.*—This term comprises printed pictures, such as lithographs, photo-engravings, etc.

17. (*l*) *Motion-picture photoplays.*

18. (*m*) *Motion pictures other than photoplays.*

Postal cards can not be copyrighted as such. The pictures thereon may be registered as "prints or pictorial illustrations" or as "photographs." Text matter on a postal card may be of such a character that it may be registered as a "book."

Trade-marks can not be registered in the Copyright Office. Application should be made to the Commissioner of Patents.

Labels and prints for articles of manufacture are required by the Act of June 18, 1874, to be registered for copyright in the Patent Office. The Copyright Office will register a claim of copyright in a pictorial drawing to protect such drawing; but if it is used for a label or print, the label or print should be registered at the Patent Office.

HOW TO SECURE REGISTRATION

19. Copyright registration may be secured for:
(1) Unpublished works.
(2) Published works.

UNPUBLISHED WORKS

Unpublished works are such as have not at the time of registration been printed or reproduced in copies for sale or been publicly distributed. They include only the works enumerated in Section 11: Lectures, sermons, addresses, or similar productions for oral delivery; dramatic musical and dramatico-musical compositions; photographs; works of art (paintings, drawings and sculptures); plastic works; motion-picture photoplays; and motion pictures other than photoplays.

In order to secure copyright in such unpublished works, the following steps are necessary:

20. (1) In the case of lectures, sermons, addresses, and dramatic musical and dramatico-musical compositions, deposit one complete copy of the work.

This copy (which may be written or typewritten) should be in convenient form, clean and legible, the leaves securely fastened together, and should bear the title of the work corresponding to that given in the application.

The entire work in each case should be deposited. It is not sufficient to deposit a mere outline or epitome, or, in the case of a play, a mere scenario, or a scenario with the synopsis of the dialogue.

21. (2) In the case of unpublished photographs, deposit one copy of the work. (Photo-engravings or photogravures are not photographs within the meaning of this provision.)

22. (3) In the case of works of art, models or designs for works of art, or drawings or plastic works of a scientific or technical character, deposit a photograph or other identifying reproduction.

(4) In the case of motion-picture photoplays, deposit a title and description, with one print taken from each scene or act.

(5) In the case of motion pictures other than photoplays, deposit a title and description, with not less than two prints taken from different sections of the complete motion picture.

In each case the deposited article must be accompanied by a claim of copyright, an application for registration, and a money order for the amount of the statutory fee.

23. Any work which has been registered under section 11, if published, *i. e.*, reproduced in copies for sale or distribution, must be deposited a second time (accompanied by an application for registration and the statutory fee) in the same manner as is required in the case of works published in the first place.

PUBLISHED WORKS

Deposit of Copies

24. Promptly after first publication of the work with the copyright notice inscribed, two *complete* copies of the best edition of the work then published must be sent to the Copyright Office, with a proper application for registration correctly filled out and a money order for the amount of the legal fee.

The statute requires that the deposit of the copyright work shall be made "promptly," which has been defined as "without unnecessary delay." It is not essential, however, that the deposit be made on the very day of publication.

25. Published works are such as are printed or otherwise produced and "placed on sale, sold, or publicly distributed." Works intended for sale or general dis-

tribution should first be printed with the statutory form of copyright notice inscribed on every copy published or offered for sale in the United States.

The following works cannot be registered until after they have been published: Books, periodicals, maps, prints and pictorial illustrations.

NOTICE OF COPYRIGHT

26. The ordinary form of copyright notice for books, periodicals, dramatic and musical compositions is "Copyright, 19— (the year of publication), by A. B. (the name of the claimant)." The name of the claimant printed in the notice should be the real name of a living person, or his trade name if he always uses one (but not a pseudonym or pen name), or the name of the firm or corporation claiming to own the copyright.

27. In the case of maps, photographs, reproductions of works of art, prints or pictorial illustrations, works of art, models or designs for works of art, and plastic works of a scientific or technical character, the notice may consist of the letter C, inclosed within a circle, thus ©, accompanied by the initials, monogram, mark, or symbol of the copyright proprietor. But in such cases the name itself of the copyright proprietor must appear on some accessible portion of the work, or on the mount of the picture or map, or on the margin, back, or permanent base or pedestal of the work.

28. The prescribed notice must be affixed to each copy of the work published or offered for sale in the United States. But no notice is required in the case of foreign books printed abroad seeking *ad interim* protection in

the United States, as provided in section 21 of the copyright act.

AMERICAN MANUFACTURE OF COPYRIGHT BOOKS

29. The following works must be manufactured in the United States in order to secure copyright:

(*a*) All "books" in the English language and books in any language by a citizen or domiciled resident of the United States must be printed from type set within the limits of the United States, either by hand or by the aid of any kind of typesetting machine, or from plates made within the limits of the United States from type set therein, or, if the text of such books be produced by lithographic process or photo-engraving process, then by a process wholly performed within the limits of the United States; and the printing of the text and binding of the book must be performed within the limits of the United States.

(*b*) All *illustrations* within a book produced by lithographic process or photo-engraving process and all *separate lithographs* or *photo-engravings* must be produced by lithographic or photo-engraving process wholly performed within the limits of the United States, except when the subjects represented in such illustrations in a book or such separate lithographs or photo-engravings "are located in a foreign country and illustrate a scientific work or reproduce a work of art."

30. Books by foreign authors in any language other than English are not required to be printed in the United States.

In the case of books printed abroad in the English

language an *ad interim* term of copyright of thirty days from registration made in the Copyright Office within thirty days after publication abroad may be secured; but in order to extend the copyright to the full term of protection, an edition of the work must be published in the United States within the thirty days *ad interim* term, printed or produced within the limits of the United States as required in section 15 of the copyright act.

APPLICATION FOR REGISTRATION

31. The application for copyright registration required to be sent with each work must state the following facts:

(1) The *name*, nationality and exact address of the claimant of copyright.

(2) The name of the country of which the author of the work is a citizen or subject.

(3) The *title* of the work.

(4) The name and address of person to whom certificate is to be sent.

(5) In the case of works reproduced in copies for sale or publicly distributed, the actual date (year, month, and day) when the work was published.

32. In addition, it is desirable that the application should state for record the name of the author. If, however, the work is published anonymously or under a pseudonym and it is not desired to place on record the real name of the author, this may be omitted. By the nationality of the author is meant citizenship, not race; a person naturalized in the United States should be described as a citizen. An author, a citizen of a foreign country having no copyright relations with the United

States, may only secure copyright in this country, if at the time of publication of his work he is domiciled in the United States. The fact of such domicile in the United States should be expressly stated in the application, including a statement of this place of domicile. Care should be taken that the title of the work, the name of the author, and the name of the copyright claimant should be correctly stated in the application, and that they should agree exactly with the same statements made in the work itself.

APPLICATION FORMS

33. The Copyright Office has issued the following application forms, which will be furnished on request, and should be used when applying for copyright registration:

A1. New book printed and published for the first time in the United States; also United States edition of English book.

A2. Book reprinted in the United States with new copyright matter.

A3. Book by foreign author in foreign language.

A4. Ad interim for 30 days for book published abroad in the English language.

A5. Contribution to a newspaper or periodical.

B1. Periodical. For registration of single issue.

B2. Periodical. For use with trust fund.

C. Lecture, sermon, or address.

D1. Published dramatic composition.

D2. Dramatic composition not reproduced for sale.

D3. Published dramatico-musical composition.

D4. Unpublished dramatico-musical composition.

E. New musical composition published for the first time.

E1. Musical composition republished with new copyright matter.

E2. Musical composition not reproduced for sale.

F. Published map.

G. Work of art (painting, drawing, or sculpture); or model or design for a work of art.

I1. Published drawing or plastic work of a scientific or technical character.

I2. Unpublished drawing or plastic work of a scientific or technical character.

J1. Photograph published for sale.

J2. Photograph not reproduced for sale.

K. Print or pictorial illustration.

L1. Motion-picture photoplay reproduced for sale.

L2. Motion-picture photoplay not reproduced for sale.

M1. Motion picture, not a photoplay, reproduced for sale.

M2. Motion picture, not a photoplay, not reproduced for sale.

R1. Renewal of a copyright for 28 years.

R2. Extension of a renewal copyright for 14 years.

U. Notice of use of music on mechanical instruments.

AFFIDAVIT OF MANUFACTURE

34. In the case of books by American authors and all books in the English language the application must be accompanied by an affidavit, showing the following facts:

(1) That the copies deposited have been printed from type set within the limits of the United States; or from

plates made within the limits of the United States from type set therein; or if the text be produced by lithographic process or photo-engraving process, that such process was wholly performed within the limits of the United States, stating, in either case, the place and the establishment where such work was done.

(2) That the printing of the text has been performed within the limits of the United States, showing the place and the name of the establishment doing the work.

(3) That the binding of such book (if bound) has been performed within the limits of the United States, showing the place and the name of the establishment where the work was done.

(4) That the completion of the printing of said book was on a stated day, or that the book was published on a given date.

Section 62 of the copyright act defines the date of publication (in the case of a work of which copies are reproduced for sale or distribution) as "the earliest date when copies of the first authorized edition *were placed on sale, sold, or publicly distributed* by the proprietor of the copyright or under his authority."

35. The affidavit may be made before any officer authorized to administer oaths within the United States who can affix his official seal to the instrument.

The affiant and the officer administering the oath for such affidavit are specially requested to make sure that the instrument is properly executed, so as to avoid the delay of having it returned for amendment. Experience shows that among the common errors made by applicants are the following:

Failure to write in the "venue"—that is, the name of the county and State—and to make sure that the notary's statement agrees.

Reciting a corporation or partnership as affiant. Oaths can be taken only by individuals.

Failure to state in what capacity the affiant makes the oath, whether as claimant, agent of the claimant, or printer. Where a corporation or firm is the claimant, the affiant should swear as agent.

Failure to state the *exact date* of publication or completion of printing. The month alone is insufficient.

Failure to sign the affidavit. The signature should correspond exactly with the name of the affiant stated at the beginning. Corporation or firm names must not appear in this place.

Failure to obtain signature of the notary after swearing to the contents.

Failure to obtain the seal of the notary.

Swearing before an officer not authorized to act in the place stated in the venue, or an officer who has no official seal.

Variance between names and dates as stated in the affidavit and the application.

The affidavit must never be made *before* publication has taken place.

36. The affidavit may be made by: (1) The person claiming the copyright; or (2) his duly authorized agent or representative residing in the United States; or (3) the printer who has printed the book.

The person making the affidavit should state in which of the above-mentioned capacities he does so.

37. In the case of a foreign author applying for a book in a language other than English, no affidavit is required, as such books are not subject to the manufacturing clause.

In the case of a foreign author applying for a book in the English language, the same affidavit must be made as in that of an American author, except where a book is deposited for *ad interim* protection under section 21. In such cases the affidavit must be filed when the *ad interim* copyright is sought to be extended to the full term by the publication of an edition printed in the United States.

The affidavit is only required for BOOKS.

PERIODICALS (FORM B)

38. Application should be made in the same manner as for books, depositing two copies, but no affidavit is required.

Separate registration is necessary for each number of the periodical published with a notice of copyright, and can only be made after publication. It is not possible to register the title of the periodical in advance of publication.

CONTRIBUTIONS TO PERIODICALS (FORM A5)

39. If special registration is requested for any contribution to a periodical, *one* copy of the number of the periodical in which the contribution appears should be deposited promptly after publication.

The entire copy should be sent; sending a mere clipping or page containing the contribution does not comply with the statute.

The date of publication of a periodical is not necessarily the date stated on the title-page. The application should state the day on which the issue is "first placed on sale, sold, or publicly distributed," which may be earlier or later than the date printed on the title-page.

AD INTERIM APPLICATIONS (FORM A4)

40. Where a book in the English language has been printed abroad, an *ad interim* copyright may be secured by depositing in the Copyright Office one complete copy of the foreign edition, with an application containing a request for the reservation and a money order for $1. Such applications should state: (1) Name and nationality of the author; (2) Name, nationality, and address of the copyright claimant; (3) Exact date of original publication abroad.

The deposit must be made not later than thirty days after its publication abroad. Whenever, within the thirty days' period of *ad interim* protection, an authorized edition manufactured in the United States has been published and two copies have thereafter been promptly deposited, the copyright claim therein may be registered the same as any other book (Form A1).

MAILING APPLICATIONS AND COPIES

41. All deposits and other material intended for the Copyright Office should be addressed to the "Register of Copyrights, Library of Congress, Washington, D. C." Letters dealing with copyright matters should not be addressed to clerks or individuals in the Copyright Office.

The copies of works sent to be registered for copyright may be mailed to the Copyright Office free (under sec. 14 of the copyright law) if directly delivered for that purpose to the postmaster, who will attach his frank label to the parcel. The Copyright Office can not furnish franking labels.

The money order (or other remittance) to pay the statutory registration fee is not entitled to free postal transmission according to the ruling of the Post Office Department. This with the application should therefore be forwarded in an envelope, to which letter postage has been affixed, addressed to the Register of Copyrights.

FEES

42. The fee required to be paid for copyright registration is $1, except that in case of photographs it is only 50 cents when no certificate of registration is desired.

All remittances to the Copyright Office should be sent by money order or bank draft. Postage stamps should not be sent for fees or postage. Checks can not be accepted unless certified. Coin or currency inclosed in letter or packages if sent will be at the remitter's risk.

Publishers may for their own convenience deposit in the Copyright Office a sum of money in advance against which each registration will be charged.

ASSIGNMENTS OF COPYRIGHT

43. When a copyright has been assigned the instrument in writing signed by the proprietor of the copyright may be filed in this office for record within six calendar months after its execution without the limits of the

United States or three calendar months within the United States.

After having been recorded the original assignment will be returned to the sender with a sealed certificate of record attached. The assignment will be returned by registered mail, if the post-office registration fee (10 cents) is sent for that purpose.

44. The fee for recording and certifying an assignment is $1 up to 300 words; $2 from 300 to 1,000 words; and another dollar for each additional thousand words or fraction thereof over 300 words.

45. After the assignment has been duly recorded, the assignee may substitute his name for that of the assignor in the copyright notice on the work assigned. Such substitution or transfer of ownership will be indexed in this office upon request, at a cost of 10 cents for each work assigned.

NOTICE OF USER OF MUSICAL COMPOSITIONS

46. Whenever the owner of the copyright in a musical composition uses such music upon the parts of instruments serving to reproduce it mechanically himself or permits anyone else to do so, he must send a notice of such use by him or by any other person to the Copyright Office to be recorded.[1]

47. Whenever any person in the absence of a license intends to use a copyrighted musical composition upon

[1] Presidential proclamations have been issued under section 1 (*e*), securing "copyright controlling the parts of instruments serving to reproduce mechanically the musical work" in behalf of Belgium, Cuba, Germany, Great Britain, Hungary, Italy, Luxemburg, New Zealand and Norway.

the parts of instruments serving to reproduce the same mechanically, the act requires that he shall serve notice of such intention upon the copyright proprietor and must also send a duplicate of such notice to the Copyright Office.

APPLICATION FOR THE RENEWAL OR EXTENSION OF SUBSISTING COPYRIGHTS

48. Application for the renewal or extension of a subsisting copyright may be filed within one year prior to the expiration of the existing term by:

(1) The author of the work if still living;

(2) The widow, widower, or children of the author if the author is not living;

(3) The author's executor, if such author, widow, widower, or children be not living;

(4) If the author, widow, widower, and children are all dead, and the author left no will, then the next of kin.

49. If the work be a composite work upon which copyright was originally secured by the proprietor thereof, then such proprietor is entitled to the privilege of renewal and extension.

50. The fee for the recording of the renewal claim is 50 cents. Application for the renewal or extension of copyright can not be recorded in the name of an assignee nor in that of any person not expressly mentioned in section 24 of the act.

SEARCHES

51. Upon application to the Register of Copyrights search of the records, indexes, or deposits will be made

for such information as they may contain relative to copyright claims. Persons desiring searches to be made should state clearly the nature of the work, its title, the name of the claimant of copyright and probable date of entry; in the case of an assignment, the name of the assignor or assignee or both, and the name of the copyright claimant and the title of the music referred to in case of notice of user.[1]

The statutory fee for searches is 50 cents for each full hour of time consumed in making such search.

[1] NOTE.—The law provides as follows: "That the record books of the copyright office, together with the indexes to such record books, and all works deposited and retained in the copyright office, shall be open to public inspection; and copies may be taken of the copyright entries actually made in such record books, subject to such safeguards and regulations as shall be prescribed by the register of copyrights and approved by the Librarian of Congress." (Sec. 58, act of Mar. 4, 1909.)

BRITISH COPYRIGHT ACT OF 1911

(1 & 2 Geo. 5. Ch. 46)

CHAPTER 46

AN ACT to amend and consolidate the Law relating to Copyright. [16th December, 1911.]

Be it enacted by the King's most Excellent Majesty, by and with the advice and consent of the Lords Spiritual and Temporal, and Commons, in this present Parliament assembled, and by the authority of the same, as follows:

Part I

IMPERIAL COPYRIGHT

RIGHTS

1. (1) Subject to the provisions of this Act, copyright shall subsist throughout the parts of His Majesty's dominions to which this Act extends for the term hereinafter mentioned in every original literary, dramatic, musical and artistic work, if—

(*a*) in the case of a published work, the work was first published within such parts of His Majesty's dominions as aforesaid; and

(*b*) in the case of an unpublished work, the author was at the date of the making of the work a British subject or resident within such parts of His Majesty's dominions as aforesaid;

but in no other works, except so far as the protection conferred by this Act is extended by Orders in Council thereunder relating to self-governing dominions to which this Act does not extend and to foreign countries.

(2) For the purposes of this Act, "copyright" means the sole right to produce or reproduce the work or any substantial part thereof in any material form whatsoever, to perform, or in the case of a lecture to deliver, the work or any substantial part thereof in public; if the work is unpublished, to publish the work or any substantial part thereof; and shall include the sole right,—

(*a*) to produce, reproduce, perform, or publish any translation of the work;

(*b*) in the case of a dramatic work, to convert it into a novel or other non-dramatic work;

(*c*) in the case of a novel or other non-dramatic work, or of an artistic work, to convert it into a dramatic work, by way of performance in public or otherwise;

(*d*) in the case of a literary, dramatic, or musical work, to make any record, perforated roll, cinematograph film, or other contrivance by means of which the work may be mechanically performed or delivered,

and to authorize any such acts as aforesaid.

(3) For the purposes of this Act, publication, in relation to any work, means the issue of copies of the work to the public, and does not include the performance in public of a dramatic or musical work, the delivery in public of a lecture, the exhibition in public of an artistic work, or the construction of an architectural work of art,

but, for the purposes of this provision, the issue of photographs and engravings of works of sculpture and architectural works of art shall not be deemed to be publication of such works.

2. (1) Copyright in a work shall be deemed to be infringed by any person who, without the consent of the owner of the copyright, does anything the sole right to do which is by this Act conferred on the owner of the copyright: Provided that the following acts shall not constitute an infringement of copyright:

(i) Any fair dealing with any work for the purposes of private study, research, criticism, review, or newspaper summary:

(ii) Where the author of an artistic work is not the owner of the copyright therein, the use by the author of any mould, cast, sketch, plan, model, or study made by him for the purpose of the work, provided that he does not thereby repeat or imitate the main design of that work:

(iii) The making or publishing of paintings, drawings, engravings, or photographs of a work of sculpture or artistic craftsmanship, if permanently situate in a public place or building, or the making or publishing of paintings, drawings, engravings, or photographs (which are not in the nature of architectural drawings or plans) of any architectural work of art:

(iv) The publication in a collection, mainly composed of non-copyright matter, bonâ fide intended for the use of schools, and so described in the title and in any advertisements issued by the publisher, of short passages from published literary works not themselves published for the use of schools in which copyright subsists: Provided that not more than two of such passages from works by the same author are published by the same publisher within five years, and that the source from which such passages are taken is acknowledged:

(v) The publication in a newspaper of a report of a lecture delivered in public, unless the report is prohibited by conspicuous written or printed notice affixed before and maintained during the lecture at or about the main entrance of the building in which the lecture is given, and, except whilst the building is being used for public worship, in a position near the lecturer; but nothing in this paragraph shall affect the provisions in paragraph (i) as to newspaper summaries:

(vi) The reading or recitation in public by one person of any reasonable extract from any published work.

(2) Copyright in a work shall also be deemed to be infringed by any person who—

(*a*) sells or lets for hire, or by way of trade exposes or offers for sale or hire; or

(*b*) distributes either for the purposes of trade or to such an extent as to affect prejudicially the owner of the copyright; or

(*c*) by way of trade exhibits in public; or

(*d*) imports for sale or hire into any part of His Majesty's dominions to which this Act extends, any work which to his knowledge infringes copyright or would infringe copyright if it had been made within the part of His Majesty's dominions in or into which the sale or hiring, exposure, offering for sale or hire, distribution, exhibition, or importation took place.

(3) Copyright in a work shall also be deemed to be infringed by any person who for his private profit permits a theatre or other place of entertainment to be used for the performance in public of the work without the consent of the owner of the copyright, unless he was not aware, and had no reasonable ground for suspecting, that the performance would be an infringement of copyright.

3. The term for which copyright shall subsist shall, except as otherwise expressly provided by this Act, be the life of the author and a period of fifty years after his death:

Provided that at any time after the expiration of twenty-five years, or in the case of a work in which copyright subsists at the passing of this Act thirty years, from the death of the author of a published work, copyright in the work shall not be deemed to be infringed by the reproduction of the work for sale if the person reproducing the work proves that he has given the prescribed notice in writing of his intention to reproduce the work, and that he has paid in the prescribed manner to, or for the benefit of, the owner of the copyright royalties in respect of all copies of the work sold by him calculated at the rate of ten per cent. on the price at which he publishes the work; and, for the purposes of this proviso, the Board of Trade may make regulations prescribing the mode in which notices are to be given, and the particulars to be given in such notices, and the mode, time, and frequency of the payment of royalties, including (if they think fit) regulations requiring payment in advance or otherwise securing the payment of royalties.

4. If at any time after the death of the author of a literary, dramatic, or musical work which has been published or performed in public a complaint is made to the Judicial Committee of the Privy Council that the owner of the copyright in the work has refused to republish or to allow the republication of the work or has refused to allow the performance in public of the work, and that by reason of such refusal the work is withheld from the public, the owner of the copyright may be ordered to grant a license to reproduce the work or perform the work in public, as the case may be, on such terms and subject to such conditions as the Judicial Committee may think fit.

5. (1) Subject to the provisions of this Act, the author of a work shall be the first owner of the copyright therein: Provided that—

(*a*) where, in the case of an engraving, photograph, or portrait, the plate or other original was ordered by some other person and was made for valuable consideration in pursuance of that order, then, in the absence of any agreement to the contrary, the person by whom such plate or other original was ordered shall be the first owner of the copyright; and

(*b*) where the author was in the employment of some other person under a contract of service or apprenticeship and the work was made in the course of his employment by that person, the person by whom the author was employed shall, in the absence of any agreement to the contrary, be the first owner of the copyright, but where the work is an article or other contribution to a newspaper, magazine, or similar periodical, there shall, in the absence of any agreement to the contrary, be deemed to be reserved to the author a right to restrain the publication of the work, otherwise than as part of a newspaper, magazine, or similar periodical.

(2) The owner of the copyright in any work may assign the right, either wholly or partially, and either generally or subject to limitations to the United Kingdom or any self-governing dominion or other part of His Majesty's dominions to which this Act extends, and either for the whole term of the copyright or for any part thereof, and may grant any interest in the right by license, but no such assignment or grant shall be valid unless it is in writing signed by the owner of the right in respect of which the assignment or grant is made, or by his duly authorized agent:

Provided that, where the author of a work is the first owner of the copyright therein, no assignment of the copyright, and no grant of any interest therein, made by him (otherwise than by will) after the passing of this Act, shall be operative to vest in the assignee or grantee any rights with respect to the copyright in the work beyond the expiration of twenty-five years from the death of the author, and the reversionary interest in the copyright expectant on the termination of that period shall, on the death of the author, notwithstanding any agreement to the contrary, devolve on his legal personal representatives as part of his estate, and any agreement entered into by him as to the disposition of such reversionary interest shall be null and void, but nothing in this proviso shall be construed as applying to the assignment of the copyright in a collective work or a license to publish a work or part of a work as part of a collective work.

(3) Where, under any partial assignment of copyright, the assignee becomes entitled to any right comprised in copyright, the assignee as respects the right so assigned, and the assignor as respects the rights not assigned, shall be treated for the purposes of this Act as the owner of the copyright, and the provisions of this Act shall have effect accordingly.

CIVIL REMEDIES

6. (1) Where copyright in any work has been infringed, the owner of the copyright shall, except as otherwise provided by this Act, be entitled to all such remedies by way of injunction or interdict, damages, accounts, and otherwise, as are or may be conferred by law for the infringement of a right.

(2) The costs of all parties in any proceedings in respect of the infringement of copyright shall be in the absolute discretion of the Court.

(3) In any action for infringement of copyright in any work, the work shall be presumed to be a work in which copyright subsists and the plaintiff shall be presumed to be the owner of the copyright, unless the defendant puts in issue the existence of the copyright, or, as the case may

be, the title of the plaintiff, and where any such question is in issue, then—

(*a*) if a name purporting to be that of the author of the work is printed or otherwise indicated thereon in the usual manner, the person whose name is so printed or indicated shall, unless the contrary is proved, be presumed to be the author of the work;

(*b*) if no name is so printed or indicated, or if the name so printed or indicated is not the author's true name or the name by which he is commonly known, and a name purporting to be that of the publisher or proprietor of the work is printed or otherwise indicated thereon in the usual manner, the person whose name is so printed or indicated shall, unless the contrary is proved, be presumed to be the owner of the copyright in the work for the purposes of proceedings in respect of the infringement of copyright therein.

7. All infringing copies of any work in which copyright subsists, or of any substantial part thereof, and all plates used or intended to be used for the production of such infringing copies, shall be deemed to be the property of the owner of the copyright, who accordingly may take proceedings for the recovery of the possession thereof or in respect of the conversion thereof.

8. Where proceedings are taken in respect of the infringement of the copyright in any work and the defendant in his defence alleges that he was not aware of the existence of the copyright in the work, the plaintiff shall not be entitled to any remedy other than an injunction or

interdict in respect of the infringement if the defendant proves that at the date of the infringement he was not aware and had no reasonable ground for suspecting that copyright subsisted in the work.

9. (1) Where the construction of a building or other structure which infringes or which, if completed, would infringe the copyright in some other work has been commenced, the owner of the copyright shall not be entitled to obtain an injunction or interdict to restrain the construction of such building or structure or to order its demolition.

(2) Such of the other provisions of this Act as provide that an infringing copy of a work shall be deemed to be the property of the owner of the copyright, or as impose summary penalties, shall not apply in any case to which this section applies.

10. An action in respect of infringement of copyright shall not be commenced after the expiration of three years next after the infringement.

SUMMARY REMEDIES

11. (1) If any person knowingly—

(*a*) makes for sale or hire any infringing copy of a work in which copyright subsists; or

(*b*) sell or lets for hire, or by way of trade exposes or offers for sale or hire any infringing copy of any such work; or

(*c*) distributes infringing copies of any such work either for the purposes of trade or to such an extent as to affect prejudicially the owner of the copyright; or (*d*) by way of trade exhibits in public any infringing copy of any such work; or

(*e*) imports for sale or hire into the United Kingdom any infringing copy of any such work:

he shall be guilty of an offence under this Act and be liable on summary conviction to a fine not exceeding forty shillings for every copy dealt with in contravention of this section, but not exceeding fifty pounds in respect of the same transaction; or, in the case of a second or subsequent offence, either to such fine or to imprisonment with or without hard labor for a term not exceeding two months.

(2) If any person knowingly makes or has in his possession any plate for the purpose of making infringing copies of any work in which copyright subsists, or knowingly and for his private profit causes any such work to be performed in public without the consent of the owner of the copyright, he shall be guilty of an offence under this Act, and be liable on summary conviction to a fine not exceeding fifty pounds, or, in the case of a second or subsequent offence, either to such fine or to imprisonment with or without hard labor for a term not exceeding two months.

(3) The court before which any such proceedings are taken may, whether the alleged offender is convicted or not, order that all copies of the work or all plates in the possession of the alleged offender, which appear to it to be infringing copies or plates for the purpose of making infringing copies, be destroyed or delivered up to the owner of the copyright or otherwise dealt with as the court may think fit.

(4) Nothing in this section shall, as respects musical works, affect the provisions of the Musical (Summary Proceedings) Copyright Act, 1902, or the Musical Copyright Act, 1906.

12. Any person aggrieved by a summary conviction of an offence under the foregoing provisions of this Act may in England and Ireland appeal to a court of quarter sessions and in Scotland under and in terms of the Summary Jurisdiction (Scotland) Acts.

13. The provisions of this Act with respect to summary remedies shall extend only to the United Kingdom.

IMPORTATION OF COPIES

14. (1) Copies made out of the United Kingdom of any work in which copyright subsists which if made in the United Kingdom would infringe copyright, and as to which the owner of the copyright gives notice in writing by himself or his agent to the Commissioners of Customs and Excise, that he is desirous that such copies should not be imported into the United Kingdom, shall not be so imported, and shall, subject to the provisions of this section, be deemed to be included in the table of prohibitions and restrictions contained in section forty-two of the Customs Consolidation Act, 1876, and that section shall apply accordingly.

(2) Before detaining any such copies or taking any further proceedings with a view to the forfeiture thereof under the law relating to the Customs, the Commissioners of Customs and Excise may require the regulations under this section, whether as to information, conditions, or

other matters, to be complied with, and may satisfy themselves in accordance with those regulations that the copies are such as are prohibited by this section to be imported.

(3) The Commissioners of Customs and Excise may make regulations, either general or special, respecting the detention and forfeiture of copies the importation of which is prohibited by this section, and the conditions, if any, to be fulfilled before such detention and forfeiture, and may, by such regulations, determine the information, notices, and security to be given, and the evidence requisite for any of the purposes of this section, and the mode of verification of such evidence.

(4) The regulations may apply to copies of all works the importation of copies of which is prohibited by this section, or different regulations may be made respecting different classes of such works.

(5) The regulations may provide for the informant reimbursing the Commissioners of Customs and Excise all expenses and damages incurred in respect of any detention made on his information, and of any proceedings consequent on such detention; and may provide for notices under any enactment repealed by this Act being treated as notices given under this section.

(6) The foregoing provisions of this section shall have effect as if they were part of the Customs Consolidation Act, 1876: Provided that, notwithstanding anything in that Act, the Isle of Man shall not be treated as part of the United Kingdom for the purposes of this section.

(7) This section shall, with the necessary modifications, apply to the importation into a British possession to

which this Act extends of copies of works made out of that possession.

DELIVERY OF BOOKS TO LIBRARIES

15. (1) The publisher of every book published in the United Kingdom shall, within one month after the publication, deliver, at his own expense, a copy of the book to the trustees of the British Museum, who shall give a written receipt for it.

(2) He shall also, if written demand is made before the expiration of twelve months after publication, deliver within one month after receipt of that written demand or, if the demand was made before publication, within one month after publication, to some depôt in London named in the demand a copy of the book for, or in accordance with the directions of, the authority having the control of each of the following libraries, namely: the Bodleian Library, Oxford, the University Library, Cambridge, the Library of the Faculty of Advocates at Edinburgh, and the Library of Trinity College, Dublin, and subject to the provisions of this section the National Library of Wales. In the case of an encyclopædia, newspaper, review, magazine, or work published in a series of numbers or parts, the written demand may include all numbers or parts of the work which may be subsequently published.

(3) The copy delivered to the trustees of the British Museum shall be a copy of the whole book with all maps and illustrations belonging thereto, finished and colored in the same manner as the best copies of the book are

published, and shall be bound, sewed, or stitched together, and on the best paper on which the book is printed.

(4) The copy delivered for the other authorities mentioned in this section shall be on the paper on which the largest number of copies of the book is printed for sale, and shall be in the like condition as the books prepared for sale.

(5) The books of which copies are to be delivered to the National Library of Wales shall not include books of such classes as may be specified in regulations to be made by the Board of Trade.

(6) If a publisher fails to comply with this section, he shall be liable on summary conviction to a fine not exceeding five pounds and the value of the book, and the fine shall be paid to the trustees or authority to whom the book ought to have been delivered.

(7) For the purposes of this section, the expression "book" includes every part or division of a book, pamphlet, sheet of letter-press, sheet of music, map, plan, chart or table separately published, but shall not include any second or subsequent edition of a book unless such edition contains additions or alterations either in the letter-press or in the maps, prints, or other engravings belonging thereto.

SPECIAL PROVISIONS AS TO CERTAIN WORKS

16. (1) In the case of a work of joint authorship, copyright shall subsist during the life of the author who first dies and for a term of fifty years after his death, or during the life of the author who dies last, whichever period is the longer, and references in this Act to the

period after the expiration of any specified number of years from the death of the author shall be construed as references to the period after the expiration of the like number of years from the death of the author who dies first or after the death of the author who dies last, whichever period may be the shorter, and in the provisions of this Act with respect to the grant of compulsory licenses a reference to the date of the death of the author who dies last shall be substituted for the reference to the date of the death of the author.

(2) Where, in the case of a work of joint authorship, some one or more of the joint authors do not satisfy the conditions conferring copyright laid down by this Act, the work shall be treated for the purposes of this Act as if the other author or authors had been the sole author or authors thereof:

Provided that the term of the copyright shall be the same as it would have been if all the authors had satisfied such conditions as aforesaid.

(3) For the purposes of this Act, "a work of joint authorship" means a work produced by the collaboration of two or more authors in which the contribution of one author is not distinct from the contribution of the other author or authors.

(4) Where a married woman and her husband are joint authors of a work the interest of such married woman therein shall be her separate property.

17. (1) In the case of a literary dramatic or musical work, or an engraving, in which copyright subsists at the date of the death of the author or, in the case of a work of joint authorship, at or immediately before the date of the

death of the author who dies last, but which has not been published, nor, in the case of a dramatic or musical work, been performed in public, nor, in the case of a lecture, been delivered in public, before that date, copyright shall subsist till publication, or performance or delivery in public, whichever may first happen, and for a term of fifty years thereafter, and the proviso to section three of this Act shall, in the case of such a work, apply as if the author had died at the date of such publication or performance or delivery in public as aforesaid.

(2) The ownership of an author's manuscript after his death, where such ownership has been acquired under a testamentary disposition made by the author and the manuscript is of a work which has not been published nor performed in public nor delivered in public, shall be prima facie proof of the copyright being with the owner of the manuscript.

18. Without prejudice to any rights or privileges of the Crown, where any work has, whether before or after the commencement of this Act, been prepared or published by or under the direction or control of His Majesty or any Government department, the copyright in the work shall, subject to any agreement with the author, belong to His Majesty, and in such case shall continue for a period of fifty years from the date of the first publication of the work.

19. (1) Copyright shall subsist in records, perforated rolls, and other contrivances by means of which sounds may be mechanically reproduced, in like manner as if such contrivances were musical works, but the term of copyright shall be fifty years from the making of the

original plate from which the contrivance was directly or indirectly derived, and the person who was the owner of such original plate at the time when such plate was made shall be deemed to be the author of the work, and, where such owner is a body corporate, the body corporate shall be deemed for the purposes of this Act to reside within the parts of His Majesty's dominions to which this Act extends if it has established a place of business within such parts.

(2) It shall not be deemed to be an infringement of copyright in any musical work for any person to make within the parts of His Majesty's dominions to which this Act extends records, perforated rolls, or other contrivances by means of which the work may be mechanically performed, if such person proves—

(*a*) that such contrivances have previously been made by, or with the consent or acquiescence of, the owner of the copyright in the work; and

(*b*) that he has given the prescribed notice of his intention to make the contrivances, and has paid in the prescribed manner to, or for the benefit of, the owner of the copyright in the work royalties in respect of all such contrivances sold by him, calculated at the rate hereinafter mentioned:

Provided that—

(i) nothing in this provision shall authorize any alterations in, or omissions from, the work reproduced, unless contrivances reproducing the work subject to similar alterations and omissions have been previously made by, or with the consent or acquiescence of, the owner of the copyright, or unless such alterations or omissions are reasonably necessary for the adaptation of the work to the contrivances in question; and

(ii) for the purposes of this provision, a musical work shall be deemed to include any words so closely associated therewith as to form part of the same work, but shall not be deemed to include a contrivance by means of which sounds may be mechanically reproduced.

(3) The rate at which such royalties as aforesaid are to be calculated shall—

(*a*) in the case of contrivances sold within two years after the commencement of this Act by the person making the same, be two and one-half per cent.; and

(*b*) in the case of contrivances sold as aforesaid after the expiration of that period, five per cent.

on the ordinary retail selling price of the contrivance calculated in the prescribed manner, so however that the royalty payable in respect of a contrivance shall, in no case, be less than a half-penny for each separate musical work in which copyright subsists reproduced thereon, and, where the royalty calculated as aforesaid includes a fraction of a farthing, such fraction shall be reckoned as a farthing:

Provided that, if, at any time after the expiration of seven years from the commencement of this Act, it appears to the Board of Trade that such rate as aforesaid is no longer equitable, the Board of Trade may, after holding a public inquiry, make an order either decreasing or increasing that rate to such extent as under the circumstances may seem just, but any order so made shall be provisional only and shall not have any effect unless and until confirmed by Parliament; but, where an order revising the rate has been so made and confirmed, no further revision shall be made before the expiration of fourteen years from the date of the last revision.

(4) If any such contrivance is made reproducing two or more different works in which copyright subsists and the owners of the copyright therein are different persons, the sums payable by way of royalties under this section shall be apportioned amongst the several owners of the copyright in such proportions as, failing agreement, may be determined by arbitration.

(5) When any such contrivances by means of which a musical work may be mechanically performed have been made, then, for the purposes of this section, the owner of the copyright in the work shall, in relation to any person who makes the prescribed inquiries, be deemed to have given his consent to the making of such contrivances if he fails to reply to such inquiries within the prescribed time.

(6) For the purposes of this section, the Board of Trade may make regulations prescribing anything which under this section is to be prescribed, and prescribing the mode in which notices are to be given and the particulars to be given in such notices, and the mode, time, and frequency of the payment of royalties, and any such regulations may, if the Board think fit, include regulations requiring payment in advance or otherwise securing the payment of royalties.

(7) In the case of musical works published before the commencement of this Act, the foregoing provisions shall have effect, subject to the following modifications and additions:

(*a*) The conditions as to the previous making by, or with the consent or acquiescence of, the owner of the copyright in the work, and the restrictions as to alterations in or omissions from the work, shall not apply:

(*b*) The rate of two and one-half per cent. shall be substituted for the rate of five per cent. as the rate at which royalties are to be calculated, but no royalties shall be payable in respect of contrivances sold before the first day of July, nineteen hundred and thirteen, if contrivances reproducing the same work had been lawfully made, or placed on sale, within the parts of His Majesty's dominions to which this Act extends before the first day of July, nineteen hundred and ten:

(*c*) Notwithstanding any assignment made before the passing of this Act of the copyright in a musical work, any rights conferred by this Act in respect of the making, or authorizing the making, of contrivances by means of which the work may be mechanically performed shall belong to the author or his legal personal representatives and not to the assignee, and the royalties aforesaid shall be payable to, and for the benefit of, the author of the work or his legal personal representatives:

(*d*) The saving contained in this Act of the rights and interests arising from, or in connexion with, action taken before the commencement of this Act shall not be construed as authorizing any person who has made contrivances by means of which the work may be mechanically performed to sell any such contrivances, whether made before or after the passing of this Act, except on the terms and subject to the conditions laid down in this section:

(*e*) Where the work is a work on which copyright is conferred by an Order in Council relating to a foreign country, the copyright so conferred shall not, except to such extent as may be provided by the Order, include any rights with respect to the making of records, perforated rolls, or other contrivances by means of which the work may be mechanically performed.

(8) Notwithstanding anything in this Act, where a record, perforated roll, or other contrivance by means of which sounds may be mechanically reproduced has been made before the commencement of this Act, copyright shall, as from the commencement of this Act, subsist therein in like manner and for the like term as if this Act had been in force at the date of the making of the original plate from which the contrivance was directly or indirectly derived:

Provided that—

(i) the person who, at the commencement of this Act, is the owner of such original plate shall be the first owner of such copyright; and

(ii) nothing in this provision shall be construed as conferring copyright in any such contrivance if the making thereof would have infringed copyright in some other contrivance, if this provision had been in force at the time of the making of the first-mentioned contrivance.

20. Notwithstanding anything in this Act, it shall not be an infringement of copyright in an address of a political nature delivered at a public meeting to publish a report thereof in a newspaper.

21. The term for which copyright shall subsist in photographs shall be fifty years from the making of the original negative from which the photograph was directly or indirectly derived, and the person who was owner of such negative at the time when such negative was made shall be deemed to be the author of the work, and, where such owner is a body corporate, the body corporate shall be deemed for the purposes of this Act to reside within the parts of His Majesty's dominions to which this Act extends if it has established a place of business within such parts.

22. (1) This Act shall not apply to designs capable of being registered under the Patents and Designs Act, 1907, except designs which, though capable of being so registered, are not used or intended to be used as models or patterns to be multiplied by any industrial process.

(2) General rules under section eighty-six of the Patents and Designs Act, 1907, may be made for determining the conditions under which a design shall be deemed to be used for such purposes as aforesaid.

23. If it appears to His Majesty that a foreign country

does not give, or has not undertaken to give, adequate protection to the works of British authors, it shall be lawful for His Majesty by Order in Council to direct that such of the provisions of this Act as confer copyright on works first published within the parts of His Majesty's dominions to which this Act extends, shall not apply to works published after the date specified in the Order, the authors whereof are subjects or citizens of such foreign country, and are not resident in His Majesty's dominions, and thereupon those provisions shall not apply to such works.

24. (1) Where any person is immediately before the commencement of this Act entitled to any such right in any work as is specified in the first column of the First Schedule to this Act, or to any interest in such a right, he shall, as from that date, be entitled to the substituted right set forth in the second column of that schedule, or to the same interest in such a substituted right, and to no other right or interest, and such substituted right shall subsist for the term for which it would have subsisted if this Act had been in force at the date when the work was made and the work had been one entitled to copyright thereunder:

Provided that—

(*a*) if the author of any work in which any such right as is specified in the first column of the First Schedule to this Act subsists at the commencement of this Act has, before that date, assigned the right or granted any interest therein for the whole term of the right, then at the date when, but for the passing of this Act, the right would have expired the substituted right conferred by this section shall, in the absence of express agreement, pass to the author of the work, and any interest therein created before the commencement of this Act and then subsisting shall determine; but the person who immediately before the date at which the right would so have expired was the owner of the right or interest shall be entitled at his option either—

(i) on giving such notice as hereinafter mentioned, to an assignment of the right or the grant of a similar interest therein for the remainder of the term of the right for such consideration as, failing agreement, may be determined by arbitration; or

(ii) without any such assignment or grant, to continue to reproduce or perform the work in like manner as theretofore subject to the payment, if demanded by the author within three years after the date at which the right would have so expired, of such royalties to the author as, failing agreement, may be determined by arbitration, or, where the work is incorporated in a collective work and the owner of the right or interest is the proprietor of that collective work, without any such payment;

The notice above referred to must be given not more than one year nor less than six months before the date at which the right would have so expired, and must be sent by registered post to the author, or, if he cannot with reasonable diligence be found, advertised in the London Gazette and in two London newspapers:

(b) where any person has, before the twenty-sixth day of July, nineteen hundred and ten, taken any action whereby he has incurred any expenditure or liability in connexion with the reproduction or performance of any work in a manner which at the time was lawful, or for the purpose of or with a view to the reproduction or performance of a work at a time when such reproduction or performance would, but for the passing of this Act, have been lawful, nothing in this section shall diminish or prejudice any rights or interest arising from or in connexion with such action which are subsisting and valuable at the said date, unless the person who by virtue of this section becomes entitled to restrain such reproduction or performance agrees to pay such compensation as, failing agreement, may be determined by arbitration.

(2) For the purposes of this section, the expression "author" includes the legal personal representatives of a deceased author.

(3) Subject to the provisions of section nineteen subsections (7) and (8) and of section thirty-three of this Act, copyright shall not subsist in any work made before the commencement of this Act, otherwise than under, and in accordance with, the provisions of this section.

APPLICATION TO BRITISH POSSESSIONS

25. (1) This Act, except such of the provisions thereof as are expressly restricted to the United Kingdom, shall extend throughout His Majesty's dominions: Provided that it shall not extend to a self-governing dominion, unless declared by the Legislature of that dominion to be in force therein either without any modifications or additions, or with such modifications and additions relating exclusively to procedure and remedies, or necessary to adapt this Act to the circumstances of the dominion, as may be enacted by such Legislature.

(2) If the Secretary of State certifies by notice published in the London Gazette that any self-governing dominion has passed legislation under which works, the authors whereof were at the date of the making of the works British subjects resident elsewhere than in the dominion or (not being British subjects) were resident in the parts of His Majesty's dominions to which this Act extends, enjoy within the dominion rights substantially identical with those conferred by this Act, then, whilst such legislation continues in force, the dominion shall, for the purposes of the rights conferred by this Act, be treated as if it were a dominion to which this Act extends; and it shall be lawful for the Secretary of State to give such a certificate as aforesaid, notwithstanding that the remedies for enforcing the rights, or the restrictions on the importation of copies of works, manufactured in a foreign country, under the law of the dominion, differ from those under this Act.

26. (1) The Legislature of any self-governing dominion

may, at any time, repeal all or any of the enactments relating to copyright passed by Parliament (including this Act) so far as they are operative within that dominion: Provided that no such repeal shall prejudicially affect any legal rights existing at the time of the repeal, and that, on this Act or any part thereof being so repealed by the Legislature of a self-governing dominion, that dominion shall cease to be a dominion to which this act extends.

(2) In any self-governing dominion to which this Act does not extend, the enactments repealed by this Act shall, so far as they are operative in that dominion, continue in force until repealed by the Legislature of that dominion.

(3) Where his Majesty in Council is satisfied that the law of a self-governing dominion to which this Act does not extend provides adequate protection within the dominion for the works (whether published or unpublished) of authors who at the time of the making of the work were British subjects resident elsewhere than in that dominion, His Majesty in Council may, for the purpose of giving reciprocal protection, direct that this Act, except such parts (if any) thereof as may be specified in the Order, and subject to any conditions contained therein, shall, within the parts of His Majesty's dominions to which this Act extends, apply to works the authors whereof were, at the time of the making of the work, resident within the first-mentioned dominion, and to works first published in that dominion; but, save as provided by such an Order, works the authors whereof were resident in a dominion to which this Act does not extend shall not, whether they are British subjects or

not, be entitled to any protection under this Act except such protection as is by this Act conferred on works first published within the parts of His Majesty's dominions to which this Act extends:

Provided that no such Order shall confer any rights within a self-governing dominion, but the Governor in Council of any self-governing dominion to which this Act extends, may, by Order, confer within that dominion the like rights as His Majesty in Council is, under the foregoing provisions of this subsection, authorized to confer within other parts of His Majesty's dominions.

For the purposes of this subsection, the expression "a dominion to which this Act extends" includes a dominion which is for the purposes of this Act to be treated as if it were a dominion to which this Act extends.

27. The Legislature of any British possession to which this Act extends may modify or add to any of the provisions of this Act in its application to the possession, but, except so far as such modifications and additions relate to procedure and remedies, they shall apply only to works the authors whereof were, at the time of the making of the work, resident in the possession, and to works first published in the possession.

28. His Majesty may, by Order in Council, extend this Act to any territories under his protection and to Cyprus, and, on the making of any such Order, this Act shall, subject to the provisions of the Order, have effect as if the territories to which it applies or Cyprus were part of His Majesty's dominions to which this Act extends.

PART II

INTERNATIONAL COPYRIGHT

29. (1) His Majesty may, by Order in Council, direct that this Act (except such parts, if any, thereof as may be specified in the Order) shall apply—

(*a*) to works first published in a foreign country to which the Order relates, in like manner as if they were first published within the parts of His Majesty's dominions to which this Act extends;

(*b*) to literary, dramatic, musical, and artistic works, or any class thereof, the authors whereof were at the time of the making of the work subjects or citizens of a foreign country to which the order relates, in like manner as if the authors were British subjects;

(*c*) in respect of residence in a foreign country to which the Order relates, in like manner as if such residence were residence in the part of His Majesty's dominions to which this Act extends;

and thereupon, subject to the provisions of this Part of this Act and of the Order, this Act shall apply accordingly:

Provided that—

(i) before making an Order in Council under this section in respect of any foreign country (other than a country with which His Majesty has entered into a convention relating to copyright), His Majesty shall be satisfied that that foreign country has made, or has undertaken to make, such provisions, if any, as it appears to His Majesty expedient to require for the protection of works entitled to copyright under the provisions of Part I. of this Act;

(ii) the Order in Council may provide that the term of copyright within such parts of His Majesty's dominions as aforesaid shall not exceed that conferred by the law of the country to which the Order relates;

(iii) the provisions of this Act as to the delivery of copies of books shall not apply to works first published in such country, except so far as is provided by the Order;

(iv) the Order in Council may provide that the enjoyment of the rights conferred by this Act shall be subject to the accomplishment of such conditions and formalities (if any) as may be prescribed by the Order;

(v) in applying the provision of this Act as to ownership of copyright, the Order in Council may make such modifications as appear necessary having regard to the law of the foreign country;

(vi) in applying the provisions of this Act as to existing works, the Order in Council may make such modifications as appear necessary, and may provide that nothing in those provisions as so applied shall be construed as reviving any right of preventing the production or importation of any translation in any case where the right has ceased by virtue of section five of the International Copyright Act, 1886.

(2) An Order in Council under this section may extend to all the several countries named or described therein.

30. (1) An Order in Council under this Part of this Act shall apply to all His Majesty's dominions to which this Act extends except self-governing dominions and any other possession specified in the order with respect to which it appears to His Majesty expedient that the Order should not apply.

(2) The Governor in Council of any self-governing dominion to which this Act extends may, as respects that dominion, make the like orders as under this Part of this Act His Majesty in Council is authorized to make with respect to His Majesty's dominions other than self-governing dominions, and the provisions of this Part of this Act shall, with the necessary modifications, apply accordingly.

(3) Where it appears to His Majesty expedient to except from the provisions of any order any part of his dominions not being a self-governing dominion, it shall be lawful for His Majesty by the same or any other Order in Council to declare that such order and this Part of this Act shall not, and the same shall not, apply to such part, except so far as is necessary for preventing any prejudice to any rights acquired previously to the date of such Order.

PART III

SUPPLEMENTAL PROVISIONS

31. No person shall be entitled to copyright or any similar right in any literary, dramatic, musical, or artistic work, whether published or unpublished, otherwise than under and in accordance with the provisions of this Act,

or of any other statutory enactment for the time being in force, but nothing in this section shall be construed as abrogating any right or jurisdiction to restrain a breach of trust or confidence.

32. (1) His Majesty in Council may make Orders for altering, revoking, or varying any Order in Council made under this Act, or under any enactments repealed by this Act, but any Order made under this section shall not affect prejudicially any rights or interests acquired or accrued at the date when the Order comes into operation, and shall provide for the protection of such rights and interests.

(2) Every Order in Council made under this Act shall be published in the London Gazette and shall be laid before both Houses of Parliament as soon as may be after it is made, and shall have effect as if enacted in this Act.

33. Nothing in this act shall deprive any of the universities and colleges mentioned in the Copyright Act, 1775, of any copyright they already possess under that Act, but the remedies and penalties for infringement of any such copyright shall be under this Act and not under that Act.

34. There shall continue to be charged on, and paid out of, the Consolidated Fund of the United Kingdom such annual compensation as was immediately before the commencement of this Act payable in pursuance of any Act as compensation to a library for the loss of the right to receive gratuitous copies of books:

Provided that this compensation shall not be paid to a library in any year, unless the Treasury are satisfied that the compensation for the previous year has been applied in the purchase of books for the use of and to be preserved in the library.

35. (1) In this Act, unless the context otherwise requires—

"Literary work" includes maps, charts, plans, tables, and compilations;

"Dramatic work" includes any piece for recitation, choreographic work or entertainment in dumb show, the scenic arrangement or acting form of which is fixed in writing or otherwise, and any cinematograph production where the arrangement or acting form or the combination of incidents represented give the work an original character;

"Artistic work" includes works of painting, drawing, sculpture and artistic craftsmanship, and architectural works of art and engravings and photographs;

"Work of sculpture" includes casts and models;

"Architectural work of art" means any building or structure having an artistic character or design, in respect of such character or design, or any model for such building or structure, provided that the protection afforded by this Act shall be confined to the artistic character and design, and shall not extend to processes or methods of construction;

"Engravings" include etchings, lithographs, woodcuts, prints, and other similar works, not being photographs;

"Photograph" includes photo-lithograph and any

work produced by any process analogous to photography;

"Cinematograph" includes any work produced by any process analogous to cinematography;

"Collective work" means—

(*a*) an encyclopædia, dictionary, year book, or similar work;

(*b*) a newspaper, review, magazine, or similar periodical; and

(*c*) any work written in distinct parts by different authors, or in which works or parts of works of different authors are incorporated;

"Infringing," when applied to a copy of a work in which copyright subsists, means any copy, including any colorable imitation, made, or imported in contravention of the provisions of this Act;

"Performance" means any acoustic representation of a work and any visual representation of any dramatic action in a work, including such a representation made by means of any mechanical instrument;

"Delivery," in relation to a lecture, includes delivery by means of any mechanical instrument;

"Plate" includes any stereotype or other plate, stone, block, mould, matrix, transfer, or negative used or intended to be used for printing or reproducing copies of any work, and any matrix or other appliance by which records, perforated rolls or other contrivances for the acoustic representation of the work are or are intended to be made;

"Lecture" includes address, speech, and sermon;

"Self-governing dominion" means the Dominion of Canada, the Commonwealth of Australia, the Dominion of New Zealand, the Union of South Africa, and Newfoundland.

(2) For the purposes of this Act (other than those relating to infringements of copyright), a work shall not be deemed to be published or performed in public, and a lecture shall not be deemed to be delivered in public, if published, performed in public, or delivered in public, without the consent or acquiescence of the author, his executors, administrators or assigns.

(3) For the purposes of this Act, a work shall be deemed to be first published within the parts of His Majesty's dominions to which this Act extends, notwithstanding that it has been published simultaneously in some other place, unless the publication in such parts of His Majesty's dominions as aforesaid is colorable only and is not intended to satisfy the reasonable requirements of the public, and a work shall be deemed to be published simultaneously in two places if the time between the publication in one such place and the publication in the other place does not exceed fourteen days, or such longer period as may, for the time being, be fixed by Order in Council.

(4) Where, in the case of an unpublished work, the making of a work has extended over a considerable period, the conditions of this Act conferring copyright shall be deemed to have been complied with, if the author was, during any substantial part of that period, a British subject or a resident within the parts of His Majesty's dominions to which this Act extends.

(5) For the purposes of the provisions of this Act as to residence, an author of a work shall be deemed to be a resident in the parts of His Majesty's dominions to which this Act extends if he is domiciled within any such part.

36. Subject to the provisions of this Act, the enactments mentioned in the Second Schedule to this Act are hereby repealed to the extent specified in the third column of that schedule:

Provided that this repeal shall not take effect in any part of His Majesty's dominions until this Act comes into operation in that part.

37. (1) This Act may be cited as the Copyright Act, 1911.

(2) This Act shall come into operation—

(*a*) in the United Kingdom, on the first day of July nineteen hundred and twelve or such earlier date as may be fixed by Order in Council;

(*b*) in a self-governing dominion to which this Act extends, at such date as may be fixed by the Legislature of that dominion;

(*c*) in the Channel Islands, at such date as may be fixed by the States of those islands respectively;

(*d*) in any other British possession to which this Act extends, on the proclamation thereof within the possession by the Governor.

SCHEDULES

First Schedule

EXISTING RIGHTS

Existing Right	Substituted Right
	(a) *In the case of Works other than Dramatic and Musical Works*
Copyright.	Copyright as defined by this Act.[1]
	(b) *In the case of Musical and Dramatic Works*
Both copyright and performing right.	Copyright as defined by this Act.[1]
Copyright, but not performing right.	Copyright as defined by this Act, except the sole right to perform the work or any substantial part thereof in public.
Performing right but not copyright.	The sole right to perform the work in public, but none of the other rights comprised in copyright as defined by this Act.

For the purposes of this Schedule the following expressions, where used in the first column thereof, have the following meanings:

"Copyright," in the case of a work which according to the law in force immediately before the commencement of this Act has not been published before that date and statutory copyright wherein depends on publication, includes the right at common law (if any) to restrain publication or other dealing with the work;

"Performing right," in the case of a work which has not been performed in public before the commencement of this Act, includes the right at common law

[1] In the case of an essay, article, or portion forming part of and first published in a review, magazine, or other periodical or work of a like nature, the right shall be subject to any right of publishing the essay, article, or portion in a separate form to which the author is entitled at the commencement of this Act, or would, if this Act had not been passed, have become entitled under section eighteen of the Copyright Act, 1842.

(if any) to restrain the performance thereof in public.

SECOND SCHEDULE

ENACTMENTS REPEALED

Session and Chapter	Short Title	Extent of Repeal
8 Geo 2. c. 13.......	The Engraving Copyright Act, 1734...	The whole Act.
7 Geo. 3. c. 38.......	The Engraving Copyright Act, 1767...	The whole Act.
15 Geo. 3. c. 53......	The Copyright Act, 1775...........	The whole Act.
17 Geo. 3. c. 57......	The Prints Copyright Act, 1777......	The whole Act.
54 Geo. 3. c. 56......	The Sculpture Copyright Act, 1814....	The whole Act.
3 & 4 Will. 4. c. 15...	The Dramatic Copyright Act, 1833....	The whole Act.
5 & 6 Will. 4. c. 65...	The Lectures Copyright Act, 1835....	The whole Act.
6 & 7 Will. 4. c. 59...	The Prints and Engravings Copyright (Ireland) Act, 1836.	The whole Act.
6 & 7 Will. 4. c. 110..	The Copyright Act, 1836............	The whole Act.
5 & 6 Vict. c. 45.....	The Copyright Act, 1842............	The whole Act.
7 & 8 Vict. c. 12.....	The International Copyright Act, 1844	The whole Act.
10 & 11 Vict. c. 95...	The Colonial Copyright Act, 1847.....	The whole Act.
15 & 16 Vict. c. 12...	The International Copyright Act, 1852	The whole Act.
25 & 26 Vict. c. 68...	The Fine Arts Copyright Act, 1862....	Sections one to six. In section eight the words "and pursuant to any Act for the protection of copyright engravings," and "and in any such Act as aforesaid." Sections nine to twelve.
38 & 39 Vict. c. 12...	The International Copyright Act, 1875	The whole Act.
39 & 40 Vict. c. 36...	The Customs Consolidation Act, 1876 .	Section forty-two, from "Books wherein" to "such copyright will expire." Sections forty-four, forty-five and one hundred and fifty-two.
45 & 46 Vict. c. 40...	The Copyright (Musical Compositions) Act, 1882.	The whole Act.
49 & 50 Vict. c. 33...	The International Copyright Act, 1886	The whole Act.
51 & 52 Vict. c. 17...	The Copyright (Musical Compositions) Act, 1888.	The whole Act.
52 & 53 Vict. c. 42...	The Revenue Act, 1889.............	Section one, from "Books first published" to "as provided in that section."
6 Edw. 7. c. 36......	The Musical Copyright Act, 1906.....	In section three the words "and which has been registered in accordance with the provisions of the Copyright Act, 1842, or of the International Copyright Act, 1844, which registration may be effected notwithstanding anything in the International Copyright Act, 1886."

[From the official edition of the Act printed by Eyre and Spottiswoode for Rowland Bailey, the King's Printer, London. ii, 29 pp. sm. 4°.]

ADDENDA

PREVIOUS COPYRIGHT ACTS NOT REPEALED

[Repealed matter indicated by italics and brackets]

THE FINE ARTS COPYRIGHT ACT, 1862

25 AND 26 VICTORIA, CHAPTER 68

AN ACT for amending the Law relating to Copyright in Works of the Fine Arts, and for repressing the Commission of Fraud in the Production and Sale of such Works. [29th July, 1862.]

Whereas by Law, as now established, the Authors of Paintings, Drawings, and Photographs have no Copyright in such their Works, and it is expedient that the Law should in that respect be amended; Be it therefore enacted by the Queen's most Excellent Majesty, by and with the Advice and Consent of the Lords Spiritual and Temporal, and Commons, in this present Parliament assembled, and by the Authority of the same, as follows:

[*Sections 1–6 are repealed by the Copyright Act, 1911.*]

7. No Person shall do or cause to be done any or either of the following Acts; that is to say,

First, no Person shall fraudulently sign or otherwise affix, or fraudulently cause to be signed or otherwise affixed, to or upon any Painting, Drawing, or Photograph, or the Negative thereof, any Name, Initials, or Monogram:

Secondly, no Person shall fraudulently sell, publish, exhibit, or dispose of, or offer for Sale, Exhibition, or Distribution, any Painting, Drawing, or Photograph, or Negative of a Photograph, having thereon the Name, Initials, or Monogram of a Person who did not execute or make such Work:

Thirdly, no Person shall fraudulently utter, dispose of, or put off, or cause to be uttered or disposed of, any Copy or colorable Imitation of any Painting, Drawing, or Photograph, or Negative of a Photograph, whether there shall be subsisting Copyright therein or not, as having been made or executed by the Author or Maker of the original Work from which such Copy or Imitation shall have been taken:

Fourthly, where the Author or Maker of any Painting, Drawing, or Photograph, or Negative of a Photograph, made either before or after the passing of this Act, shall have sold or otherwise parted with the Possession of such Work, if any Alteration shall afterwards be made therein by any other Person, by Addition or otherwise, no Person shall be at liberty during the life of the Author or Maker of such Work, without his Consent, to make or knowingly to sell or publish, or offer for Sale, such Work or any Copies of such Work so altered as aforesaid, or of any Part thereof, as or for the unaltered Work of such Author or Maker:

Every Offender under this Section shall, upon Conviction, forfeit to the Person aggrieved a Sum not exceeding Ten Pounds, or not exceeding double the full Price, if any, at which all such Copies, Engravings, Imitations, or altered Works shall have been sold or offered for Sale; and all such Copies, Engravings, Imitations, or altered Works shall be forfeited to the Person, or the Assigns or legal Representatives of the Person, whose Name, Initials, or Monogram shall be so fraudulently signed or affixed thereto, or to whom such spurious or altered Work shall be so fraudulently or falsely ascribed as aforesaid: Provided always, that the Penalties imposed by this Section shall not be incurred unless the Person whose Name, Initials, or Monogram shall be so fraudulently signed or affixed, or to whom such spurious or altered Work shall be so fraudulently or falsely ascribed as aforesaid, shall have been living at or within Twenty Years next before the Time when the Offence may have been committed.

8. All pecuniary Penalties which shall be incurred, and all such unlawful Copies, Imitations, and all other Effects and Things as shall have been forfeited by Offenders, pursuant to this Act [*and pursuant to any Act for the Protection of Copyright Engravings*], may be recovered by the Person herein-before [*and in any such Act as aforesaid*] empowered to recover the same respectively, and herein-after called the Complainant or the Complainer, as follows:

In England and Ireland, either by Action against the Party offending, or by summary Proceeding before any two Justices having Jurisdiction where the Party offending resides:

In Scotland by Action before the Court of Session in ordinary Form, or by summary Action before the Sheriff of the County where the Offence may be committed or the Offender resides, * * * and any Judgment so to be pronounced by the Sheriff in such summary Application shall be final and conclusive, and not subject to Review by [*Advocation*], Suspension, Reduction, or otherwise.

[*Secs. 9–12 repealed by the Copyright Act, 1911.*]

[From "The Statutes of the United Kingdom of Great Britain and Ireland." Vol. 25, 4°. By G: Kettilby Rickards. London, G: E: Eyre and W: Spottiswoode, 1862, pp. 750–752.]

THE CUSTOMS CONSOLIDATION ACT, 1876

39 and 40 VICTORIA, CHAPTER 36

AN ACT to consolidate the Customs Laws. [24th July, 1876.]

* * * * *

AS TO THE IMPORTATION, PROHIBITION, ENTRY, EXAMINATION, LANDING, AND WAREHOUSING OF GOODS

* * * * *

42. The goods enumerated and described in the following table of prohibitions and restrictions inwards are hereby prohibited to be imported or brought into the United Kingdom, save as thereby excepted, and if any goods so enumerated and described shall be imported or brought into the United Kingdom contrary to the prohibitions or restrictions contained therein, such goods shall be forfeited, and may be destroyed or otherwise disposed of as the Commissioners of Customs may direct.

A TABLE OF PROHIBITIONS AND RESTRICTIONS INWARDS

Goods prohibited to be imported

[*Books wherein the copyright shall be first subsisting, first composed, or written or printed, in the United King-*

dom, and printed or reprinted in any other country, as to which the proprietor of such copyright or his agent shall have given to the Commissioners of Customs a notice in writing, duly declared, that such copyright subsists, such notice also stating when such copyright will expire.]

* * * * *

Indecent or obscene prints, paintings, photographs, books, cards, lithographic or other engravings, or any other indecent or obscene articles.

[*Secs. 44 and 45 are repealed by the Copyright Act, 1911.*]

* * * * *

151. The Customs Acts shall extend to and be of full force and effect in the several British possessions abroad, except where otherwise expressly provided for by the said Acts, or limited by express reference to the United Kingdom or the Channel Islands, and except also as to any such possession as shall by local Act or ordinance have provided, or may hereafter, with the sanction and approbation of Her Majesty and her successors, make entire provision for the management and regulation of the Customs of any such possession, or make in like manner express provisions in lieu or variation of any of the clauses of the said Act for the purposes of such possession.

[*Sec. 152 repealed by the Copyright Act, 1911.*]

[From "The Law Reports. The Public General Statutes, 1876." Vol. 11, 8°. London, William Clowes and Sons, 1876, pp. 171, 181-182, 210.]

The Musical (Summary Proceedings) Copyright Act, 1902

2 Edward VII., Chapter 15

AN ACT to amend the Law relating to Musical Copyright. [22nd July, 1902.]

Be it enacted by the King's most Excellent Majesty, by and with the advice and consent of the Lords Spiritual and Temporal, and Commons, in this present Parliament assembled, and by the authority of the same, as follows:

1. A court of summary jurisdiction, upon the application of the owner of the copyright in any musical work, may act as follows: If satisfied by evidence that there is reasonable ground for believing that pirated copies of such musical work are being hawked, carried about, sold or offered for sale, may, by order, authorize a constable to seize such copies without warrant and to bring them before the court, and the court, on proof that the copies are pirated, may order them to be destroyed, or to be delivered up to the owner of the copyright if he makes application for that delivery.

2. If any person shall hawk, carry about, sell or offer for sale any pirated copy of any musical work, every such pirated copy may be seized by any constable without warrant, on the request in writing of the apparent owner of the copyright in such work, or of his agent thereto authorized in writing, and at the risk of such owner.

On seizure of any such copies, they shall be conveyed by such constable before a court of summary jurisdiction, and, on proof that they are infringements of copyright, shall be forfeited or destroyed, or otherwise dealt with, as the court may think fit.

3. "Musical copyright" means the exclusive right of the owner of such copyright, under the Copyright Acts in force for the time being, to do, or to authorize another person to do, all or any of the following things in respect of a musical work:—

(1) To make copies by writing or otherwise of such musical work.

(2) To abridge such musical work.

(3) To make any new adaptation, arrangement or setting of such musical work, or of the melody thereof, in any notation or system.

"Musical work" means any combination of melody and harmony, or either of them, printed, reduced to writing, or otherwise graphically produced or reproduced.

"Pirated musical work" means any musical work written, printed or otherwise reproduced, without the consent lawfully given by the owner of the copyright in such musical work.

4. This Act may be cited as The Musical (Summary Proceedings) Copyright Act, 1902, and shall come into operation on the first day of October one thousand nine hundred and two, and shall apply only to the United Kingdom.

[From "The Law Reports. The Public General Statutes, 1902." Vol. 40, 8°. London, William Clowes & Sons, Ltd., 1903, p. 18.]

The Musical Copyright Act, 1906

6 Edward VII., Chapter 36

AN ACT to amend the law relating to Musical Copyright. [4th August, 1906.]

Be it enacted by the King's most Excellent Majesty, by and with the advice and consent of the Lords Spiritual and Temporal, and Commons, in this present Parliament assembled, and by the authority of the same, as follows:

1. (1) Every person who prints, reproduces, or sells, or exposes, offers, or has in his possession for sale, any pirated copies of any musical work, or has in his possession any plates for the purpose of printing or reproducing pirated copies of any musical work, shall (unless he proves that he acted innocently) be guilty of an offence punishable on summary conviction, and shall be liable to a fine not exceeding five pounds, and on a second or subsequent conviction to imprisonment with or without hard labor for a term not exceeding two months or to a fine not exceeding ten pounds: Provided that a person convicted of an offence under this Act who has not previously been convicted of such an offence, and who proves that the copies of the musical work in respect of which the offence was committed had printed on the title page thereof a name and address purporting to be that of the printer or publisher, shall not be liable to any penalty under this Act unless it is proved that the copies were to his knowledge pirated copies.

(2) Any constable may take into custody without war-

rant any person who in any street or public place sells or exposes, offers, or has in his possession for sale any pirated copies of any such musical work as may be specified in any general written authority addressed to the chief officer of police, and signed by the apparent owner of the copyright in such work or his agent thereto authorized in writing, requesting the arrest, at the risk of such owner, of all persons found committing offences under this section in respect to such work, or who offers for sale any pirated copies of any such specified musical work by personal canvass or by personally delivering advertisements or circulars.

(3) A copy of every written authority addressed to a chief officer of police under this section shall be open to inspection at all reasonable hours by any person without payment of any fee, and any person may take copies of or make extracts from any such authority.

(4) Any person aggrieved by a summary conviction under this section may in England or Ireland appeal to a court of quarter sessions, and in Scotland under and in terms of the Summary Prosecutions Appeals (Scotland) Act, 1875.

2. (1) If a court of summary jurisdiction is satisfied by information on oath that there is reasonable ground for suspecting that an offence against this Act is being committed on any premises, the court may grant a search warrant authorizing the constable named therein to enter the premises between the hours of six of the clock in the morning and nine of the clock in the evening, and, if necessary, to use force for making such entry, whether by breaking open doors or otherwise, and to seize any copies

of any musical work or any plates in respect of which he has reasonable ground for suspecting that an offence against this Act is being committed.

(2) All copies of any musical work and plates seized under this section shall be brought before a court of summary jurisdiction, and if proved to be pirated copies or plates intended to be used for the printing or reproduction of pirated copies shall be forfeited and destroyed or otherwise dealt with as the court think fit.

3. In this Act—

The expression "pirated copies" means any copies of any musical work written, printed, or otherwise reproduced without the consent lawfully given by the owner of the copyright in such musical work:

The expression "musical work" means a musical work in which there is a subsisting copyright, [*and which has been registered in accordance with the provisions of the Copyright Act, 1842, or of the International Copyright Act, 1844, which registration may be effected notwithstanding anything in the International Copyright Act, 1886*]:

The expression "plates" includes any stereotype or other plates, stones, matrices, transfers, or negatives used or intended to be used for printing or reproducing copies of any musical work: Provided that the expressions "pirated copies" and "plates" shall not, for the purposes of this Act, be deemed to include perforated music rolls used for playing mechanical instruments, or records used for the reproduction of sound waves, or the matrices or other appliances by which such rolls or records respectively are made:

The expression "chief officer of police"—

(*a*) with respect to the City of London, means the Commissioner of City Police;

(*b*) elsewhere in England has the same meaning as in the Police Act, 1890;

(*c*) in Scotland has the same meaning as in the Police (Scotland) Act, 1890;

(*d*) in the police district of Dublin metropolis means either of the Commissioners of Police for the said district;

(*e*) elsewhere in Ireland means the District Inspector of the Royal Irish Constabulary:

The expression "court of summary jurisdiction" in Scotland means the sheriff or any magistrate of any royal, parliamentary, or police burgh officiating under the provisions of any local or general police Act.

4. This Act may be cited as the Musical Copyright Act, 1906.

[From "The Law Reports. The Public General Statutes, 1906." Vol. 44, 8°. London, Rowland Bailey, 1906, pp. 98–100.]

CANADIAN COPYRIGHT ACT

CHAPTER 70

AN ACT respecting Copyright

SHORT TITLE

1. This Act may be cited as the Copyright Act. R. S., c. 62, s. 1.

INTERPRETATION

2. In this Act, unless the context otherwise requires,—

(*a*) "Minister" means the Minister of Agriculture;

(*b*) "Department" means the Department of Agriculture;

(*c*) "legal representatives" includes heirs, executors, administrators and assigns, or other legal representatives. R. S., c. 62, s. 2.

PART I

REGISTERS OF COPYRIGHTS

3. The Minister shall cause to be kept, at the Department, books to be called the Registers of Copyrights, in which proprietors of literary, scientific and artistic works or compositions, may have the same registered in accordance with the provisions of this Act. R. S., c. 62, s. 3.

SUBJECTS AND CONDITIONS OF COPYRIGHT

4. Any person domiciled in Canada or in any part of the British possessions, or any citizen of any country which has an international copyright treaty with the United Kingdom, who is the author of any book, map, chart or musical composition, or of any original painting, drawing, statue, sculpture or photograph, or who invents, designs, etches, engraves or causes to be engraved, etched or made from his own design, any print, cut, or engraving, and the legal representatives of such person or citizen, shall for the term of twenty-eight years, from the time of recording the copyright thereof in the manner hereinafter directed, have the sole and exclusive right and liberty of printing, reprinting, publishing, reproducing and vending such literary, scientific or artistic work or composition, in whole or in part, and of allowing translations of such work from one language into other languages to be printed or reprinted and sold. R. S., c. 62, s. 4.

5. In no case shall the said sole and exclusive right and liberty in Canada continue to exist after it has expired elsewhere. R. S., c. 62, s. 5.

6. The condition for obtaining such copyright shall be that the said literary, scientific or artistic works shall be printed and published or reprinted and republished in Canada, or in the case of works of art that they shall be produced or reproduced in Canada, whether they are so published or produced for the first time, or contemporaneously with or subsequently to publication or production elsewhere. R. S., c. 62, s. 5.

7. No literary, scientific or artistic work which is im-

moral, licentious, irreligious, or treasonable or seditious, shall be the legitimate subject of such registration or copyright. R. S., c. 62, s. 5.

8. Every work of which the copyright has been granted and is subsisting in the United Kingdom, and copyright of which is not secured or subsisting in Canada, under any Act of the Parliament of Canada, or of the Legislature of the late province of Canada, or of the legislature of any of the provinces forming part of Canada, shall, when printed and published, or reprinted and republished in Canada, be entitled to copyright under this Act; but nothing in this Act shall, except as hereinafter provided, be held to prohibit the importation from the United Kingdom of copies of any such work lawfully printed there.

2. If any such copyright work is reprinted subsequently to its publication in the United Kingdom, any person who has, previously to the date of entry of such work upon the Registers of Copyright, imported any foreign reprints, may dispose of such reprints by sale or otherwise; but the burden of proof of establishing the extent and regularity of the transaction shall in such case be upon such person. R. S., c. 62, s. 6; 63–64 V., c. 25, s. 1.

9. Any literary work intended to be published in pamphlet or book form, but which is first published in separate articles in a newspaper or periodical, may be registered under this Act while it is so preliminarily published, if the title of the manuscript and a short analysis of the work are deposited at the Department, and if every separate article so published is preceded by the words, *Registered in accordance with the Copyright Act:* Provided

that the work, when published in book or pamphlet form, shall be subject, also, to the other requirements of this Act. R. S., c. 62, s. 7.

10. If a book is published anonymously, it shall be sufficient to enter it in the name of the first publisher thereof, either on behalf of the un-named author or on behalf of such first publisher, as the case may be. R. S., c. 62, s. 8.

11. No person shall be entitled to the benefit of this Act unless he has deposited at the Department three copies of the book, map, chart, musical composition, photograph, print, cut, or engraving, and in the case of paintings, drawings, statuary and sculpture, unless he has furnished a written description of such works of art; and the Minister shall cause the copyright of the same to be recorded forthwith in a book to be kept for that purpose, in the manner adopted by him, or prescribed by the rules and forms made, from time to time, as herein provided. R. S., c. 62, s. 9; 58-59 V., c. 37, s. 1.

12. The Minister shall cause one of such three copies of such book, map, chart, musical composition, photograph, print, cut, or engraving, to be deposited in the Library of the Parliament of Canada and one in the British Museum. R. S., c. 62, s. 10; 58-59 V., c. 37, s. 2.

13. It shall not be requisite to deliver any printed copy of the second or of any subsequent edition of any book unless the same contains very important alterations or additions. R. S., c. 62, s. 11.

14. No person shall be entitled to the benefit of this Act unless he gives information of the copyright being secured,—

(*a*) if the work is a book, by causing to be inserted in the several copies of every edition published during the term secured, on the title page, or on the page immediately following; or,

(*b*) if the work is a map, chart, musical composition, print, cut, engraving or photograph, by causing to be impressed on the face thereof; or,

(*c*) if the work is a volume of maps, charts, music, engravings or photographs, by causing to be impressed upon the title page or frontispiece thereof;

the words,—"Copyright, Canada, 190 , by A. B." 7-8 Ed. VII., c. 17, s. 1.

2. As regards paintings, drawings, statuary and sculptures, the signature of the artist shall be deemed a sufficient notice of such proprietorship. R. S., c. 62, s. 12.

15. The author of any literary, scientific or artistic work or his legal representatives, may, pending the publication or republication thereof in Canada, obtain an interim copyright therefor by depositing at the Department a copy of the title or a designation of such work, intended for publication or republication in Canada.

2. Such title or designation shall be registered in an interim copyright register at the Department to secure to such author aforesaid or his legal representatives, the exclusive rights recognized by this Act, previous to publication or republication in Canada.

3. Such interim registration shall not endure for more than one month from the date of the original publication elsewhere, within which period the work shall be printed or reprinted and published in Canada.

4. In every case of interim registration under this Act

the author or his legal representatives shall cause notice of such registration to be inserted once in the *Canada Gazette*. R. S., c. 62, s. 13.

16. The application for the registration of a copyright, or of a temporary or of an interim copyright may be made in the name of the author or of his legal representatives, by any person purporting to be agent of such author or legal representatives.

2. Any damage caused by a fraudulent or an erroneous assumption of such authority shall be recoverable in any court of competent jurisdiction. R. S., c. 62, s. 14.

ASSIGNMENTS AND RENEWALS

17. The right of an author of a literary, scientific or artistic work to obtain a copyright, and the copyright when obtained, shall be assignable in law, either as to the whole interest or any part thereof, by an instrument in writing, made in duplicate, and which shall be registered at the Department on production of both duplicates and payment of the fee hereinafter mentioned.

2. One of the duplicates shall be retained at the Department, and the other shall be returned, with a certificate of registration, to the person depositing it. R. S., c. 62, s. 15.

18. Whenever the author of a literary, scientific or artistic work or composition which may be the subject of copyright has executed the same for another person, or has sold the same to another person for due consideration, such author shall not be entitled to obtain or to retain the proprietorship of such copyright, which is, by the said transaction, virtually transferred to the purchaser,

and such purchaser may avail himself of such privilege, unless a reserve of the privilege is specially made by the author or artist in a deed duly executed. R. S., c. 62, s. 16.

19. If, at the expiration of the said term of twenty-eight years, the author, or any of the authors when the work has been originally composed and made by more than one person, is still living, or if such author is dead and has left a widow or a child, or children living, the same sole and exclusive right and liberty shall be continued to such author, or to such authors still living, or, if dead, then to such widow and child or children, as the case may be, for the further term of fourteen years; but in such case, within one year after the expiration of such term of twenty-eight years, the title of the work secured shall be a second time registered, and all other regulations herein required to be observed in regard to original copyrights shall be complied with in respect to such renewed copyright. R. S., c. 62, s. 17.

20. In all cases of renewal of copyright under this Act the author or proprietor shall, within two months from the date of such renewal, cause notice of the registration thereof to be published once in the *Canada Gazette*. R. S., c. 62, s. 18.

CONFLICTING CLAIMS TO COPYRIGHT

21. In case of any person making application to register as his own, the copyright of a literary, scientific or artistic work already registered in the name of another person, or in case of simultaneous conflicting applications, or of an application made by any person other than the person entered as proprietor of a registered copyright, to cancel

the said copyright, the person so applying shall be notified by the Minister that the question is one for the decision of a court of competent jurisdiction, and no further proceedings shall be had or taken by the Minister concerning the application until a judgment is produced maintaining, cancelling or otherwise deciding the matter.

2. Such registration, cancellation or adjustment of the said right shall then be made by the Minister in accordance with such decision.

3. The Exchequer Court of Canada shall be a competent court within the meaning of this Act, and shall have jurisdiction to adjudicate upon any question arising under this section, upon information in the name of the Attorney General of Canada, or at the suit of any person interested. R. S., c. 62, s. 19, 53 V., c. 12, s. 1; 54–55 V., c. 34, s. 1.

UNAUTHORIZED PUBLICATION OF MANUSCRIPT

22. Every person who, without the consent of the author or lawful proprietor thereof first obtained, prints or publishes or causes to be printed or published, any manuscript not previously printed in Canada or elsewhere, shall be liable to the author or proprietor for all damages occasioned by such publication, and the same shall be recoverable in any court of competent jurisdiction. R. S., c. 62, s. 20.

LICENSES TO RE-PUBLISH

23. If a work copyrighted in Canada becomes out of print, a complaint may be lodged by any person with the Minister, who, on the fact being ascertained to his satis-

faction, shall notify the owner of the copyright of the complaint and of the fact; and if, within a reasonable time, no remedy is applied by such owner, the Minister may grant a license to any person to publish a new edition or to import the work, specifying the number of copies and the royalty to be paid on each to the owner of the copyright. R. S., c. 62, s. 21.

FEES

24. The following fees shall be paid to the Minister before an application for any of the following purposes is received, that is to say:—

Registering a copyright	$1.00
Registering an interim copyright	0.50
Registering a temporary copyright	0.50
Registering an assignment	1.00
Certified copy of registration	0.50
Registering any decision of a court of justice, for every folio	0.50

For office copies of documents not above mentioned, the following charges shall be made:—

Every single or first folio of one hundred words, certified copy	$0.50
Every such subsequent folio (fractions of or under one-half not being counted, and of one-half or more being counted)	0.25

2. The said fees shall be in full of all services performed under this Act by the Minister or by any person employed by him.

3. All fees received under this Act shall be paid over to the Minister of Finance and shall form part of the Consolidated Revenue Fund of Canada.

4. No person shall be exempt from the payment of any fee or charge payable in respect of any services performed under this Act for such person, and no fee paid shall be returned to the person who paid it. R. S., c. 62, s. 22.

RIGHT TO REPRESENT SCENE OR OBJECT

25. Nothing herein contained shall prejudice the right of any person to represent any scene or object, notwithstanding that there may be copyright in some other representation of such scene or object. R. S., c. 62, s. 23.

FOREIGN NEWSPAPERS AND MAGAZINES

26. Newspapers and magazines published in foreign countries, and which contain, together with foreign original matter, portions of British copyright works republished with the consent of the author or his legal representatives, or under the law of the country where such copyright exists, may be imported into Canada. R. S., c. 62, s. 24.

CLERICAL ERRORS NOT TO INVALIDATE

27. Clerical errors which occur in the framing or copying of any instrument drawn by any officer or employee in or of the Department shall not be construed as invalidating such instrument, but when discovered they may be corrected under the authority of the Minister. R. S., c. 62, s. 25.

IMPORTATION

28. If a book as to which there is subsisting copyright under this Act has been first lawfully published in any part of His Majesty's dominions, other than Canada, and if it is proved to the satisfaction of the Minister that the owner of the copyright so subsisting and of the copyright acquired by such publication has lawfully granted a license to reproduce in Canada, from movable or other types, or from stereotype plates, or from electroplates, or from lithograph stones, or by any process for facsimile reproduction, an edition or editions of such book designed for sale only in Canada, the Minister may, notwithstanding anything in this Act, by order under his hand, prohibit the importation into Canada, except with the written consent of the licensee, of any copies of such book printed elsewhere: Provided that two such copies may be specially imported for the *bona fide* use of any public free library or any university or college library, or for the library of any duly incorporated institution or society for the use of the members of such institution or society. 63–64 V., c. 25, s. 1.

29. The Minister may at any time in like manner, by order under his hand, suspend or revoke such prohibition upon importation if it is proved to his satisfaction that,—

(*a*) the license to reproduce in Canada has terminated or expired; or,

(*b*) the reasonable demand for the book in Canada is not sufficiently met without importation; or,

(*c*) the book is not, having regard to the demand therefor in Canada, being suitably printed or published; or, (*d*) any other state of things exists on account of which it is not in the public interest to further prohibit importation. 63–64 V., c. 25, s. 2.

30. At any time after the importation of a book has been so prohibited, any person resident or being in Canada may apply, either directly or through a book-seller or other agent, to the person so licensed to reproduce such book, for a copy of any edition of such book then on sale and reasonably obtainable in the United Kingdom or any other part of His Majesty's dominions, and it shall thereupon be the duty of the person so licensed, as soon as reasonably may be, to import and sell such copy to the person so applying therefor, at the ordinary selling price of such copy in the United Kingdom, or such other part of His Majesty's dominions, with the duty and reasonable forwarding charges added.

2. The failure or neglect, without lawful excuse, of the person so licensed to supply such copy within a reasonable time shall be a reason for which the Minister may, if he sees fit, suspend or revoke the prohibition upon importation. 63–64 V., c. 25, s. 3.

31. The Minister shall forthwith inform the Department of Customs of any order made by him under this Act. 63–64 V., c. 25, s. 4.

EVIDENCE

32. All copies or extracts certified from the Department shall be received in evidence without further proof and without production of the originals. R. S., c. 62, s. 26.

33. All documents, executed and accepted by the

Minister shall be held valid, so far as relates to official proceedings under this Act. R. S., c. 62, s. 27.

RULES AND REGULATIONS

34. The Minister may, from time to time, subject to the approval of the Governor in Council, make such rules and regulations, and prescribe such forms as appear to him necessary and expedient for the purposes of this Act; and such regulations and forms, circulated in print for the use of the public, shall be deemed to be correct for the purposes of this Act. R. S., c. 62, s. 27.

OFFENCES AND PENALTIES

35. Every person who wilfully makes or causes to be made any false entry in any of the registry books, hereinbefore mentioned, or who wilfully produces or causes to be tendered in evidence, any paper which falsely purports to be a copy of an entry in any of the said books, is guilty of an indictable offence, and shall be punished accordingly. R. S., c. 62, s. 28.

36. Every person who fraudulently assumes authority to act as agent of the author, or of his legal representative, for the registration of a copyright, or of a temporary or of an interim copyright, is guilty of an indictable offence and shall be punished accordingly. R. S., c. 62, s. 29.

37. Every person who,—

(*a*) after the interim registration of the title of any book according to this Act, and within the term herein limited, or after the copyright is secured and during the term or terms of its duration, prints, publishes, or reprints or republishes, or imports, or causes to be so printed, published or imported, any copy or any translation of such book without having first obtained the right so to do by assignment from the person lawfully entitled to the copyright thereof; or,

(*b*) knowing the same to be so printed or imported, publishes, sells or exposes for sale, or causes to be published, sold or exposed for sale, any copy of such book without such consent;

shall forfeit every copy of such book to the person then lawfully entitled to the copyright thereof; and shall forfeit and pay for every such copy which is found in his possession, either printed or being printed, published, imported or exposed for sale, contrary to the provisions of this Act, such sum, not exceeding one dollar, and not less than ten cents, as the court determines, which forfeiture shall be enforceable or recoverable in any court of competent jurisdiction.

2. A moiety of such sum shall belong to His Majesty for the public uses of Canada, and the other moiety shall belong to the lawful owner of such copyright. R. S., c. 62, s. 30.

38. Every person who, after the registering of any painting, drawing, statue or other work of art, and within the term or terms limited by this Act, reproduces in any manner, or causes to be reproduced, made or sold, in whole or in part, any copy of any such work of art, without the consent of the proprietor shall forfeit the plate or plates on which such reproduction has been made, and every sheet thereof so reproduced, to the proprietor of the copyright thereof; and shall also forfeit for every

sheet of such reproduction published or exposed for sale, contrary to this Act, such sum, not exceeding one dollar and not less than ten cents, as the court determines, which forfeiture shall be enforceable or recoverable in any court of competent jurisdiction.

2. A moiety of such sum shall belong to His Majesty for the public uses of Canada, and the other moiety shall belong to the lawful owner of such copyright. R. S., c. 62, s. 31.

39. Every person who, without the consent of the proprietor of the copyright first obtained,—

(*a*) after the registering of any print, cut or engraving, map, chart, musical composition or photograph, according to the provisions of this Act, and within the term or terms limited by this Act, engraves, etches or works, sells or copies, or causes to be engraved, etched or copied, made or sold any such print, cut or engraving, map, chart, musical composition or photograph, or any part thereof, either as a whole or by varying, adding to or diminishing the main design with intent to evade the law; or,

(*b*) prints or reprints or imports for sale, or causes to be so printed or reprinted or imported for sale, any such map, chart, musical composition, print, cut or engraving, or any part thereof; or,

(*c*) knowing the same to be so reprinted, printed or imported without such consent, publishes, sells or exposes for sale, or in any manner disposes of any such map, chart, musical composition, engraving, cut, photograph, or print;

shall forfeit the plate or plates on which such map, chart,

musical composition, engraving, cut, photograph or print has been copied, and also every sheet thereof, so copied or printed as aforesaid, to the proprietor of the copyright thereof; and shall also forfeit, for every sheet of such map, musical composition, print, cut or engraving found in his possession, printed or published or exposed for sale, contrary to this Act, such sum, not exceeding one dollar and not less than ten cents, as the court determines, which forfeiture shall be enforceable or recoverable in any court of competent jurisdiction.

2. A moiety of such sum shall belong to His Majesty for the public uses of Canada, and the other moiety shall belong to the lawful owner of such copyright. R. S., c. 62, s. 32.

40. Every person who has not lawfully acquired the copyright of a literary, scientific or artistic work, and who inserts in any copy thereof printed, produced, reproduced or imported, or who impresses on any such copy, that the same has been entered according to this Act, or words purporting to assert the existence of a Canadian copyright in relation thereto, shall incur a penalty not exceeding three hundred dollars. R. S., c. 62, s. 33.

41. Every person who causes any work to be registered in the register of interim copyright and fails to print and publish, or reprint and republish the same within the time prescribed, shall incur a penalty not exceeding one hundred dollars. R. S., c. 62, s. 33.

42. Every penalty incurred under either of the last two preceding sections shall be recoverable in any court of competent jurisdiction.

2. A moiety of any such penalty shall belong to His

Majesty for the public uses of Canada, and the other moiety shall belong to the person who sues for the same. R. S., c. 62, s. 33.

43. All books imported in contravention of any order, prohibiting such importation, made under the hand of the Minister; by the authority of this Act, may be seized by any officer of Customs, and shall be forfeited to the Crown and destroyed; and any person importing, or causing or permitting the importation of any book in contravention of such order shall, for each offence, be liable, upon summary conviction, to a penalty not exceeding one hundred dollars. 63–64 V., c. 25, s. 5.

44. No action or prosecution for the recovery of any penalty under this Act, shall be commenced more than two years after the cause of action arises. R. S., c. 62, s. 34.

PART II

APPLICATION

45. This Part shall come into force on a day to be named by proclamation of the Governor General. 52 V., c. 29, s. 7.

46. Nothing in this Part contained shall be deemed to,—

(*a*) prohibit the importation from the United Kingdom of copies of works of which the copyright is there existing and which are lawfully printed and published there; or,

(*b*) except as in this Part otherwise expressly provided, apply to any work for which, before the coming into force of this Part, copyright had been obtained in the United Kingdom, or in any country which has an international copyright treaty with the United Kingdom, in which Canada is included.

2. The law in force at the time of the coming into effect of this Part shall be deemed to continue in force as respects such works. 52 V., c. 29, s. 6.

REPEAL

47. Sections four, five, six and eight of Part I. of this Act are repealed. 52 V., c. 29, ss. 1 and 2.

SUBJECTS AND CONDITIONS OF COPYRIGHT

48. Any person domiciled in Canada or in any part of the British possessions, or any citizen of any country which has an international copyright treaty with the United Kingdom, in which Canada is included, who is the author of any book, map, chart or musical or literary composition, or of any original painting, drawing, statue, sculpture or photograph, or who invents, designs, etches, engraves or causes to be engraved, etched or made from his own design, any print or engraving, and the legal representatives of such person or citizen, shall, for the term of twenty-eight years from the time of recording the copyright thereof, have the sole and exclusive right and liberty of printing, reprinting, publishing, reproducing and vending such literary, scientific, musical or artistic work or composition, in whole or in part, and of allowing translations of such literary work, from one language into other languages, to be printed or reprinted and sold in the manner and on the conditions, and subject to the restrictions hereinafter set forth. 52 V., c. 29, s. 1.

49. The conditions for obtaining such copyright shall be that the said literary, scientific, musical or artistic work shall, before publication or production elsewhere, or simultaneously with the first publication or production thereof elsewhere, be registered in the office of the Minister, by the author or his legal representative, and further that such work shall be printed and published or produced in Canada, or reprinted and republished or reproduced in Canada, within one month after publication or production elsewhere. 52 V., c. 29, s. 1.

50. In no case shall the sole and exclusive right and privilege in Canada continue to exist after it has expired in the country of origin. 52 V., c. 29, s 1.

LICENSES

51. If any person entitled to copyright of a work under this Act,—

(*a*) neglects or fails to take advantage of its provisions; or,

(*b*) having obtained copyright thereunder, at any time after the first publication in Canada of the work for which copyright has been so obtained, fails to print and publish the work in Canada in sufficient numbers and in such manner as to meet the demand in Canada for such work;

the Minister may grant a license or licenses to any person or persons domiciled in Canada to print and publish or to reproduce such work in Canada, but no such license shall convey any exclusive right to print and publish or reproduce any work.

2. A license shall be granted to any applicant agreeing

to pay the author or his legal representatives a royalty of ten per centum on the retail price of each copy or reproduction issued of the work which is the subject of the license, and giving security for such payment to the satisfaction of the Minister. 52 V., c. 29, s. 3; 58–59 V., c. 37, s. 3.

52. As to any work for which copyright has been obtained in Canada, the Governor in Council may, upon its being established to his satisfaction that the holder of such copyright is prepared and *bona fide* intends, during the remaining period of his term of copyright, to print and publish such work in Canada in sufficient numbers and in such manner as to supply the demand for such work in Canada, revoke all licenses for the printing and publication of such work then in force.

2. Such revocation shall not render unlawful the subsequent sale and disposal in Canada of all or any of the copies of such work then printed under the authority of the license so revoked. 58–59 V., c. 37, s. 5.

53. The royalty in this Part provided for shall be collected by the officers of the Department of Inland Revenue, and paid over to the persons entitled thereto, under regulations approved by the Governor in Council; but the Government shall not be liable to account for any such royalty not actually collected. 52 V., c. 29, s. 4.

54. Whenever, under the foregoing provisions of this Part, a license has been issued permitting the printing and publishing or the producing of any work, and evidence has been adduced to the satisfaction of the Governor in Council that such work is in course of being printed and published or produced in such manner as to meet the

demand therefor in Canada, the Governor General may, by proclamation published in the *Canada Gazette*, prohibit the importation, while the author's copyright or that of his assigns is in force, or would have been in force had copyright for the work been obtained in Canada under the foregoing provisions of this Part, of any copies or reproductions of the work to which such license relates.

2. If, at any time thereafter, it is made to appear to the Governor in Council that such work is not, under such license, printed and published or produced in such manner as to meet such demand, the Governor General may, by proclamation published as aforesaid, revoke such prohibition. 52 V., c. 29, s. 5; 58–59 V., c. 37, s. 4.

RULES OF THE

CANADIAN DEPARTMENT OF AGRICULTURE

UNDER

THE COPYRIGHT ACT

Approved by the Governor in Council, on the 3rd day of December, 1907

RULES

I

There is no necessity for any personal appearance at the Department of Agriculture, unless specially called for by order of the Minister or the Deputy, every transaction being carried on by writing.

II

In every case the applicant or depositor of any paper is responsible for the merits of his allegations and for the validity of the instruments furnished by him or his agent.

III

The correspondence is carried on with the applicant or his agent, but with one person only, and will be conveyed through the Canadian mails free of charge.

IV

All papers are to be clearly and neatly written on foolscap paper, and every word of them is to be distinctly legible.

All copies of books deposited shall be bound in boards, and all copies of maps and photographs shall be mounted.

V

An application for registration shall be signed by the applicant or by an agent duly authorized.

A partner may sign for a firm. A director or secretary or other principal officer of a company may sign for the company.

VI

All communications to be addressed in the following words:—To the Minister of Agriculture, (Trade-Mark and Copyright Branch), Ottawa.

VII

As regards proceedings not specially provided for in the following forms, any form being conformable to the letter and spirit of the law will be accepted, and if not so conformable will be returned for correction.

VIII

A copy of the Act and the Rules with a particular section marked, sent to any person making an inquiry, is intended as a respectful answer by the office.

IX

Information as to subsisting registrations will not be furnished by the office, the registers and indexes being open for inspection free of charge.

CONVENTION CREATING THE INTERNATIONAL COPYRIGHT UNION. REVISED TEXT, 1908

PRELIMINARY REMARKS

The Berne Convention creating the International Copyright Union for the protection of works of literature and art was signed on September 9, 1886, and went into force on December 5, 1887. The Additional Agreement formulated at the first conference of revision, which met in Paris, was signed on May 4, 1896, and went into effect on December 9, 1897. This modified Articles 2, 3, 5, 7, 12, and 20 of the Convention, and Numbers 1 and 4 of the "Protocole de Clôture." A declaration interpreting certain provisions of the Berne Convention of 1886 and the Additional Agreement of Paris of 1896 was also signed on May 4, 1896, to go into effect on September 9, 1897.

A second conference of revision was held in Berlin from October 14 to November 14, 1908, and a new text to take the place of the three documents cited above was formulated by the representatives of the following fifteen countries: Belgium, Denmark, France, Germany, Great Britain, Italy, Japan, Liberia, Luxembourg, Monaco, Norway, Spain, Sweden, Switzerland, and Tunis.

Representatives from the following non-Union countries were also present at the conference: Argentina, Chile, China, Colombia, Ecuador, Greece, Guatemala, Mexico, the Netherlands (Holland), Nicaragua, Peru, Persia,

Portugal, Rumania, Russia, Siam, the United States, Uruguay, and Venezuela.

The representative from the United States was present only to "observe and report," with no power to take part in the discussions, and, beyond making a statement to that effect, took no part in the proceedings of the Conference. Mr. Arthur Orr, Third Secretary of the United States Embassy at Berlin, was also present at the sittings of the Conference but took no part in the proceedings.

The Convention was signed on November 13th and the Conference closed on November 14th. To give publicity to the proposed treaty the official text was, by resolution of the Conference, published in the organ of the International Copyright Bureau at Berne, "Le Droit d'Auteur," for November 15th. This is the French text of the treaty printed below.

The English translation here printed is made from the text as published in "Le Droit d'Auteur." Where doubt has been felt as to the best English equivalent, the words of the French text have been added, and the full official text in French follows the English text.

Article 28 of the Convention provides that it shall be ratified, and the ratifications exchanged at Berlin, not later than the first of July, 1910.

THORVALD SOLBERG,
Register of Copyrights.

Statement by Thorvald Solberg, Register of Copyrights, Delegate of the United States to the Berlin Conference to Revise the Berne International Copyright Convention, October 15, 1908.

In 1885 and 1886, at the conferences convened to draft the convention to create the International Union for the protection of literary and artistic property, the United States was represented. At that time, however, it was not deemed possible to send a plenipotentiary delegate, nor could such a representative be sent to attend the first Conference of revision, which met in Paris in 1896.

When the present Conference was arranged for—early in this year—the German Ambassador at Washington wrote to the Secretary of State of the United States a letter explaining the purpose and scope of this Congress, inviting the Government of the United States to send delegates. The Ambassador's letter explained that, in addition to delegates representing Governments in the Union, there would be present representatives from a considerable number of non-Union nations. It was further stated that the attendance of such delegates from non-Union countries would be greeted with special pleasure. This because of the conviction that whatever might be the final position taken by the non-Union countries, or their laws, in relation to copyright, the participation in the proceedings of this Conference by such delegates from non-Union countries would at all events contribute to arouse and increase interest in the Berne Union and its beneficial work.

The German Ambassador's letter further explained that the delegates from non-Union countries attending the Conference would have full freedom of action; that they might confine themselves to following the discussions without taking any stand with regard to them, and that it would be left to the discretion of the non-Union Governments as to whether they would empower their delegates to join the Berne Union.

The Government of the United States again finds it impracticable to send a delegate authorized to commit the United States to actual adhesion at this time to the Berne Convention. Nevertheless, it has been felt that the representation of the United States, even within the limitations indicated, might be beneficial: first, to indicate the sympathy of our Government with the general purposes of the International Copyright Union: second, to secure such information regarding the proceedings of the Conference as might prove valuable; and third, to place (by means of such representation) at the disposal of the Conference, authoritative knowledge as to the facts of copyright legislation and procedure within the United States—information which it is hoped may be of use to the members of the Conference in their deliberations.

The Secretary of State of the United States has done me the honor to designate me to attend this Conference as a delegate on the part of the United States.

It is with the sincere desire that my attendance here may contribute in some degree to the attainment of each of these three objects, that I have crossed the ocean to be present. I trust, also, that this long journey taken for the purpose of being present here may be held to testify to my personal most sincere interest in, and admiration for, the objects of the Berne Union—that admirable association of many nations to secure adequate protection for literary and artistic productions.

It will be for me a great pleasure if my attendance here can be of service to the Conference, or to any of its members.

Some of the questions to be discussed here are now pending before the Congress of the United States in the Copyright Bill now under discussion. I should wish to avoid, therefore, taking any position in regard to the special matters in question—any position which might tend to commit the United States in advance to any line of policy which might embarrass the legislative branch of the Government of the United States in taking such action regarding these matters as it may finally deem advisable. But within that limitation—with the most hearty and cordial expression of my sympathy for the ends and purposes of the Berne Union—I beg to place myself at the service of the Conference.

CONVENTION CREATING AN INTERNATIONAL UNION FOR THE PROTECTION OF LITERARY AND ARTISTIC WORKS, SIGNED AT BERLIN, NOVEMBER 13, 1908

Article 1

Union to protect literary and artistic works.

The contracting countries are constituted into a Union for the protection of the rights of authors in their literary and artistic works.

Article 2

Definition of "literary and artistic works."

The expression "literary and artistic works" includes all productions in the literary, scientific or artistic domain, whatever the mode or form of reproduction, such as: books, pamphlets and other writings; dramatic or dramatico-musical works; choreographic works and pantomimes, the stage directions ("*mise en scène*") of which are fixed in writing or otherwise; musical compositions with or without words; drawings, paintings; works of architecture and sculpture; engravings and lithographs; illustrations; geographical charts; plans, sketches and plastic works relating to geography, topography, architecture, or the sciences.

Translations, adaptations, arrangements of

music and other reproductions transformed from a literary or artistic work, as well as compilations from different works, are protected as original works without prejudice to the rights of the author of the original work.

Translations, arrangements, and adaptations protected.

The contracting countries are pledged to secure protection in the case of the works mentioned above.

Works of art applied to industry are protected so far as the domestic legislation of each country allows.

Works of art applied to industry.

Article 3

The present Convention applies to photographic works and to works obtained by any process analogous to photography. The contracting countries are pledged to guarantee protection to such works.

Photographic works to be protected.

Article 4

Authors within the jurisdiction of one of the countries of the Union enjoy for their works, whether unpublished or published for the first time in one of the countries of the Union, such rights, in the countries other than the country of origin of the work, as the respective laws now accord or shall hereafter accord to natives, as well as the rights specially accorded by the present Convention.

Authors to enjoy in countries of the Union the rights granted to natives.

No formalities required. The enjoyment and the exercise of such rights are not subject to any formality; such enjoyment and such exercise are independent of the existence of protection in the country of origin of the work. Consequently, apart from the stipulations of the present Convention, the extent of the protection, as well as the means of redress guaranteed to the author to safeguard his rights, are regulated exclusively according to the legislation of the country where the protection is claimed.

Definition of country of origin. The following is considered as the country of origin of the work: for unpublished works, the country to which the author belongs; for published works, the country of first publication, and for works published simultaneously in several countries of the Union, the country among them whose legislation grants the shortest term of protection. For works published simultaneously in a country outside of the Union and in a country within the Union, it is the latter country which is exclusively considered as the country of origin.

Published works. By published works ("*œuvres publiées*") must be understood, according to the present Convention, works which have been issued ("*œuvres éditées*"). The representation of a dramatic or dramatico-musical work, the performance of a musical work, the exhibition of a work of art and the construction of a work of architecture do not constitute publication.

ARTICLE 5

Authors within the jurisdiction of one of the countries of the Union who publish their works for the first time in another country of the Union, have in this latter country the same rights as national authors.

Authors of countries of the Union have same rights as natives of other countries.

ARTICLE 6

Authors not within the jurisdiction of any one of the countries of the Union, who publish for the first time their works in one of these countries, enjoy in that country the same rights as national authors, and in the other countries of the Union the rights accorded by the present Convention.

Authors not belonging to countries of the Union also protected if they first publish in a Union country.

ARTICLE 7

The term of protection granted by the present Convention comprises the life of the author and fifty years after his death.

Term of protection: Life and 50 years.

In case this term, however, should not be adopted uniformly by all the countries of the Union, the duration of the protection shall be regulated by the law of the country where protection is claimed, and can not exceed the term granted in the country of origin of the work. The contracting countries will consequently be required to apply

If not adopted; Laws of country to govern term.

the provision of the preceding paragraph only to the extent to which it agrees with their domestic law.

Term for photographic, posthumous, anonymous or pseudonymous works.

For photographic works and works obtained by a process analogous to photography, for posthumous works, for anonymous or pseudonymous works, the term of protection is regulated by the law of the country where protection is claimed, but this term may not exceed the term fixed in the country of origin of the work.

Article 8

Exclusive right of translation for entire term.

Authors of unpublished works within the jurisdiction of one of the countries of the Union, and authors of works published for the first time in one of these countries, enjoy in the other countries of the Union during the whole term of the right in the original work the exclusive right to make or to authorize the translation of their works.

Article 9

Serial novels protected when published in newspapers or periodicals.

Serial stories ("*romans-feuilletons*"), novels and all other works, whether literary, scientific or artistic, whatever may be their subject, published in newspapers or periodicals of one of the countries of the Union, may not be reproduced in the other countries without the consent of the authors.

With the exception of serial stories and of novels ("*romans-feuilletons et des nouvelles*") any newspaper article may be reproduced by another newspaper if reproduction has not been expressly forbidden. The source, however, must be indicated. The confirmation of this obligation shall be determined by the legislation of the country where protection is claimed.

Reproduction of newspaper articles.

The protection of the present Convention does not apply to news of the day or to miscellaneous news having the character merely of press information.

News items not protected.

Article 10

As concerns the right of borrowing lawfully from literary or artistic works for use in publications intended for instruction or having a scientific character, or for chrestomathies, the provisions of the legislation of the countries of the Union and of the special treaties existing or to be concluded between them shall govern.

Extracts from literary or artistic works for educational publications.

Article 11

The stipulations of the present Convention apply to the public representation of dramatic or dramatico-musical works and to the public performance of musical works, whether these works are published or not.

Representation of dramatic or dramatico-musical works.

Representation of translations of dramatic works.

Authors of dramatic or dramatico-musical works are protected, during the term of their copyright in the original work, against the unauthorized public representation of a translation of their works.

Notice of reservation of performance not required.

In order to enjoy the protection of this article, authors, in publishing their works, are not obliged to prohibit the public representation or public performance of them.

Article 12

Adaptations, etc., considered as infringements.

Among the unlawful reproductions to which the present Convention applies are specially included indirect, unauthorized appropriations of a literary or artistic work, such as adaptations, arrangements of music, transformations of a romance or novel or of a poem into a theatrical piece and vice-versâ, etc., when they are only the reproduction of such work in the same form or in another form with non-essential changes, additions or abridgments and without presenting the character of a new, original work.

Article 13

Adaptation of musical works to mechanical instruments.

Authors of musical works have the exclusive right to authorize: (1) the adaptation of these works to instruments serving to reproduce them mechanically; (2) the public performance of the same works by means of these instruments.

The limitations and conditions relative to the application of this article shall be determined by the domestic legislation of each country in its own case; but all limitations and conditions of this nature shall have an effect strictly limited to the country which shall have adopted them.

Each country to regulate for itself the manner in which Convention shall apply.

The provisions of paragraph 1 have no retroactive effect, and therefore are not applicable in a country of the Union to works which, in that country, shall have been lawfully adapted to mechanical instruments before the going into force of the present Convention.

Not retroactive.

The adaptations made by virtue of paragraphs 2 and 3 of this article and imported without the authorization of the parties interested into a country where they are not lawful, may be seized there.

Importation of mechanical appliances prohibited.

ARTICLE 14

Authors of literary, scientific or artistic works have the exclusive right to authorize the reproduction and the public representation of their works by means of the cinematograph.

Reproduction by cinematograph.

Cinematographic productions are protected as literary or artistic works when by the

Cinematographic productions protected.

arrangement of the stage effects or by the combination of incidents represented, the author shall have given to the work a personal and original character.

Cinematographs copyrightable.

Without prejudice to the rights of the author in the original work, the reproduction by the cinematograph of a literary, scientific or artistic work is protected as an original work.

Also any analogous production.

The preceding provisions apply to the reproduction or production obtained by any other process analogous to that of the cinematograph.

Article 15

Author's name indicated on work sufficient proof of authorship.

In order that the authors of the works protected by the present Convention may be considered as such, until proof to the contrary, and admitted in consequence before the courts of the various countries of the Union to proceed against infringers, it is sufficient that the author's name be indicated upon the work in the usual manner.

Publisher of anonymous or pseudonymous works considered as representative of author.

For anonymous or pseudonymous works, the publisher whose name is indicated upon the work is entitled to protect the rights of the author. He is without other proofs considered the legal representative of the anonymous or pseudonymous author.

ARTICLE 16

All infringing works may be seized by the competent authorities of the countries of the Union where the original work has a right to legal protection.

Seizure of pirated copies.

Seizure may also be made in these countries of reproductions which come from a country where the copyright in the work has terminated, or where the work has not been protected.

The seizure takes place in conformity with the domestic legislation of each country.

Seizure to be made according to the laws of each country.

ARTICLE 17

The provisions of the present Convention may not prejudice in any way the right which belongs to the Government of each of the countries of the Union to permit, to supervise, or to forbid, by means of legislation or of domestic police, the circulation, the representation or the exhibition of every work or production in regard to which competent authority may have to exercise this right.

Each government to exercise supervision as to circulation, representation or exhibition of works.

ARTICLE 18

The present Convention applies to all works which, at the time it goes into effect, have not fallen into the public domain of their country of origin because of the expiration of the term of protection.

Convention to apply to all works not in public domain at the time of its going into force.

But if a work by reason of the expiration of the term of protection which was previously secured for it has fallen into the public domain of the country where protection is claimed, such work will not be protected anew.

Special Conventions and domestic legislation may govern.

This principle will be applied in accordance with the stipulations to that effect contained in the special Conventions either existing or to be concluded between countries of the Union, and in default of such stipulations, its application will be regulated by each country in its own case.

Provisions of Convention to apply to new accessions.

The preceding provisions apply equally in the case of new accessions to the Union and where the term of protection would be extended by the application of Article 7.

Article 19

More extensive rights may be granted by domestic legislation.

The provisions of the present Convention do not prevent a claim for the application of more favorable provisions which may be enacted by the legislation of a country of the Union in favor of foreigners in general.

Article 20

More extensive right may be secured by special treaties.

The governments of the countries of the Union reserve the right to make between themselves special treaties, when these treaties would confer upon authors more extended rights than those accorded by the Union, or when they contain other stipulations not conflicting with the present Convention. The provisions of existing treaties which answer the aforesaid conditions remain in force.

ARTICLE 21

Bureau of the International Union.

The international office instituted under the name of "Bureau of the International Union for the Protection of Literary and Artistic Works" ("Bureau de l'Union internationale pour la protection des œuvres littéraires et artistiques") is maintained.

Under control of Switzerland.

This Bureau is placed under the high authority of the Government of the Swiss Confederation, which controls its organization and supervises its working.

Language of Bureau to be French.

The official language of the Bureau is the French language.

ARTICLE 22

Duties of International Bureau.

The International Bureau brings together, arranges and publishes information of every kind relating to the protection of the rights of authors in their literary and artistic works. It studies questions of mutual utility interesting to the Union, and edits, with the aid of documents placed at its disposal by the various administrations, a periodical in the French language, treating questions concerning the purpose of the Union. The governments of the countries of the Union reserve the right to authorize the Bureau by common accord to publish an edition in one or more other languages, in case experience demonstrates the need.

Will furnish information as to copyright. The International Bureau must hold itself at all times at the disposal of members of the Union to furnish them, in relation to questions concerning the protection of literary and artistic works, the special information of which they have need.

Annual report of Director of International Bureau. The Director of the International Bureau makes an annual report on his administration, which is communicated to all the members of the Union.

Article 23

Expenses of the International Bureau to be shared by contracting states. The expenses of the Bureau of the International Union are shared in common by the contracting countries. Until a new decision, they may not exceed sixty thousand francs per year. This sum may be increased when needful by the simple decision of one of the Conferences provided for in Article 24.

Method of sharing expenses. To determine the part of this sum total of expenses to be paid by each of the countries, the contracting countries and those which later adhere to the Union are divided into six classes each contributing in proportion to a certain number of units, to wit:

1st class................25 units
2d class................20 units
3d class................15 units
4th class................10 units
5th class................ 5 units
6th class................ 3 units

These coefficients are multiplied by the number of countries of each class, and the sum of the products thus obtained furnishes the number of units by which the total expense is to be divided. The quotient gives the amount of the unit of expense.

Each country shall declare, at the time of its accession, in which of the above-mentioned classes it desires to be placed.

Swiss Administration to prepare the budget of the International Bureau, etc.

The Swiss Administration prepares the budget of the Bureau and superintends its expenditures, makes necessary advances and draws up the annual account, which shall be communicated to all the other administrations.

ARTICLE 24

Revisions of Convention.

The present Convention may be subjected to revision with a view to the introduction of amendments calculated to perfect the system of the Union.

To take place successively in the countries of the Union.

Questions of this nature, as well as those which from other points of view pertain to the development of the Union, are considered in the Conferences which will take place successively in the countries of the

Union between the delegates of the said countries. The administration of the country where a Conference is to be held will, with the co-operation of the International Bureau, prepare the business of the same. The Director of the Bureau will attend the meetings of the Conferences and take part in the discussions without a deliberative voice.

Changes require unanimous consent. No change in the present Convention is valid for the Union except on condition of the unanimous consent of the countries which compose it.

Article 25

Accession of other countries. The States outside of the Union which assure legal protection of the rights which are the object of the present Convention, may accede to it upon their request.

To be made known by Switzerland. This accession shall be made known in writing to the Government of the Swiss Confederation and by the latter to all the others.

May substitute provisions of previous conventions. Such accession shall imply full adhesion to all the clauses and admission to all the advantages stipulated in the present Convention. It may, however, indicate such provisions of the Convention of September 9, 1886, or of the Additional Act of May 4, 1896, as it may be judged necessary to substitute provisionally, at least, for the corresponding provisions of the present Convention.

Article 26

The contracting countries have the right to accede at any time to the present Convention for their colonies or foreign possessions. Accession for colonies of foreign possessions.

They may, for that purpose, either make a general declaration by which all their colonies or possessions are included in the accession, or name expressly those which are included therein, or confine themselves to indicating those which are excluded from it.

This declaration shall be made known in writing to the Government of the Swiss Confederation, and by the latter to all the others.

Article 27

The present Convention shall replace, in the relations between the contracting States, the Convention of Berne of September 9, 1886, including the Additional Article and the Final Protocol of the same day, as well as the Additional Act and the Interpretative Declaration of May 4, 1896. The conventional acts above-mentioned shall remain in force in the relations with the States which do not ratify the present Convention. Present Convention to replace Berne Convention and Additional Articles. But Berne Convention remains in force between countries not signatory to present Convention.

The States signatory to the present Convention may, at the time of the exchange of

Signatory States may declare themselves bound by former Conventions upon certain points.

ratifications, declare that they intend, upon such or such point, still to remain bound by the provisions of the Conventions to which they have previously subscribed.

Article 28

Convention to be ratified not later than July 1, 1910.

The present Convention shall be ratified, and the ratifications shall be exchanged at Berlin, not later than the first of July, 1910.

Instrument to be filed with Swiss Government.

Each contracting party shall send, for the exchange of ratifications, a single instrument, which shall be deposited, with those of the other countries, in the archives of the Government of the Swiss Confederation. Each party shall receive in return a copy of the *procès-verbal* of the exchange of ratifications, signed by the Plenipotentiaries who shall have taken part therein.

Article 29

Convention to take effect three months after exchange of ratifications.

The present Convention shall be put into execution three months after the exchange of the ratifications and shall remain in force for an indefinite time, until the expiration of one year from the day when denunciation of it shall have been made.

Withdrawal from the Convention.

This denunciation shall be addressed to the Government of the Swiss Confederation. It shall be effective only as regards the country which shall have made it, the Convention remaining in force for the other countries of the Union.

Article 30

The States which introduce into their legislation the term of protection of fifty years * provided for by Article 7, paragraph 1, of the present Convention, shall make it known to the Government of the Swiss Confederation by a written notification which shall be communicated at once by that Government to all the other countries of the Union.

Adoption of term of life and 50 years to be notified.

It shall be the same for such States as shall renounce any reservations made by them in virtue of Articles 25, 26, and 27.

Notice shall be given of renouncement of any reservations.

In testimony of which, the respective Plenipotentiaries have signed the present Convention and have attached thereto their seals.

Signatures.

Done at Berlin, the thirteenth of November, one thousand nine hundred eight, in a single copy, which shall be deposited in the archives of the Government of the Swiss Confederation, and of which copies, properly certified, shall be sent through diplomatic channels to the contracting countries.

Date of signing, November 13, 1908.

* Article 7 provides for a general term of protection for life and fifty years.

CONVENTION DE BERNE REVISÉE POUR LA PROTECTION DES ŒUVRES LITTÉRAIRES ET ARTISTIQUES DU 13 NOVEMBRE 1908.

ARTICLE 1. Les Pays contractants sont constitués à l'état d'Union pour la protection des droits des auteurs sur leurs œuvres littéraires et artistiques.

ART. 2. L'expression "œuvres littéraires et artistiques" comprend toute production du domaine littéraire, scientifique ou artistique, quel qu'en soit le mode ou la forme de reproduction, telle que: les livres, brochures, et autres écrits; les œuvres dramatiques ou dramatico-musicales, les œuvres chorégraphiques et les pantomimes, dont la mise en scène est fixée par écrit ou autrement; les compositions musicales avec ou sans paroles; les œuvres de dessin, de peinture, d'architecture, de sculpture, de gravure et de lithographie; les illustrations, les cartes géographiques; les plans, croquis et ouvrages plastiques, relatifs à la géographie, à la topographie, à l'architecture ou aux sciences.

Sont protégés comme des ouvrages originaux, sans préjudice des droits de l'auteur de l'œuvre originale, les traductions, adaptations, arrangements de musique et autres reproductions transformées d'une œuvre littéraire ou artistique, ainsi que les recueils de différentes œuvres.

Les Pays contractants sont tenus d'assurer la protection des œuvres mentionnées ci-dessus.

Les œuvres d'art appliqué à l'industrie sont protégées

autant que permet de le faire la législation intérieure de chaque pays.

Art. 3. La présente Convention s'applique aux œuvres photographiques et aux œuvres obtenues par un procédé analogue à la photographie. Les Pays contractants sont tenus d'en assurer la protection.

Art. 4. Les auteurs ressortissant à l'un des pays de l'Union jouissent, dans les pays autres que le pays d'origine de l'œuvre, pour leurs œuvres, soit non publiées, soit publiées pour la première fois dans un pays de l'Union, des droits que les lois respectives accordent actuellement ou accorderont par la suite aux nationaux, ainsi que des droits spécialement accordés par la présente Convention.

La jouissance et l'exercice de ces droits ne sont subordonnés à aucune formalité; cette jouissance et cet exercice sont indépendants de l'existence de la protection dans le pays d'origine de l'œuvre. Par suite, en dehors des stipulations de la présente Convention, l'étendue de la protection ainsi que les moyens de recours garantis à l'auteur pour sauvegarder ses droits se règlent exclusivement d'après la législation du pays où la protection est réclamée.

Est considéré comme pays d'origine de l'œuvre: pour les œuvres non publiées, celui auquel appartient l'auteur; pour les œuvres publiées, celui de la première publication, et pour les œuvres publiées simultanément dans plusieurs pays de l'Union, celui d'entre eux dont la législation accorde la durée de protection la plus courte. Pour les œuvres publiées simultanément dans un pays étranger à l'Union et dans un pays de l'Union, c'est ce dernier pays qui est exclusivement considéré comme pays d'origine.

Par œuvres publiees, il faut, dans le sens de la présente Convention, entendre les œuvres éditées. La représentation d'une œuvre dramatique ou dramatico-musicale, l'exécution d'une œuvre musicale, l'exposition d'une œuvre d'art et la construction d'une œuvre d'architecture ne constituent pas une publication.

ART. 5. Les ressortissants de l'un des pays de l'Union, qui publient pour la première fois leurs œuvres dans un autre pays de l'Union, ont, dans ce dernier pays, les mêmes droits que les auteurs nationaux.

ART. 6. Les auteurs ne ressortissant pas à l'un des pays de l'Union, qui publient pour la première fois leurs œuvres dans l'un de ces pays, jouissent, dans ce pays, des mêmes droits que les auteurs nationaux, et dans les autres pays de l'Union, des droits accordés par la présente Convention.

ART. 7. La durée de la protection accordée par la présente Convention comprend la vie de l'auteur et cinquante ans après sa mort.

Toutefois, dans le cas où cette durée ne serait pas uniformément adoptée par tous les pays de l'Union, la durée sera réglée par la loi du pays où la protection sera réclamée et elle ne pourra excéder la durée fixée dans le pays d'origine de l'œuvre. Les Pays contractants ne seront, en conséquence, tenus d'appliquer la disposition de l'alinéa précédent que dans la mesure où elle se concilie avec leur droit interne.

Pour les œuvres photographiques et les œuvres obtenues par un procédé analogue à la photographie, pour les œuvres posthumes, pour les œuvres anonymes ou pseudonymes, la durée de la protection est réglée par la loi du pays où la protection est réclamée, sans que cette durée puisse excéder la durée fixée dans le pays d'origine de l'œuvre.

ART. 8. Les auteurs d'œuvres non publiées, ressortissant à l'un des pays de l'Union, et les auteurs d'œuvres publiées pour la première fois dans un de ces pays jouissent, dans les autres pays de l'Union, pendant toute la durée du droit sur l'œuvre originale, du droit exclusif de faire ou d'autoriser la traduction de leurs œuvres.

ART. 9. Les romans-feuilletons, les nouvelles et toutes autres œuvres, soit littéraires, soit scientifiques, soit artistiques, quel qu'en soit l'objet, publiés dans les journaux ou recueils périodiques d'un des pays de l'Union, ne peuvent être reproduits dans les autres pays sans le consentment des auteurs.

A l'exclusion des romans-feuilletons et des nouvelles, tout article de journal peut être reproduit par un autre journal, si la reproduction n'en est pas expressément interdite. Toutefois, la source doit être indiquée; la sanction de cette obligation est déterminée par la législation du pays où la protection est réclamée.

La protection de la présente Convention ne s'applique pas aux nouvelles du jour ou aux faits divers qui ont le caractère de simples informations de presse.

ART. 10. En ce qui concerne la faculté de faire licitement des emprunts à des œuvres littéraires ou artistiques pour des publications destinées à l'enseignement ou ayant un caractère scientifique, ou pour des chrestomathies, est réservé l'effet de la législation des pays de l'Union et des arrangements particuliers existants ou à conclure entre eux.

ART. 11. Les stipulations de la présente Convention

s'appliquent à la représentation publique des œuvres dramatiques ou dramatico-musicales, et à l'exécution publique des œuvres musicales, que ces œuvres soient publiées ou non.

Les auteurs d'œuvres dramatiques ou dramatico-musicales sont, pendant la durée de leur droit sur l'œuvre originale, protégés contre la représentation publique non autorisée de la traduction de leurs ouvrages.

Pour jouir de la protection du présent article, les auteurs, en publiant leurs œuvres, ne sont pas tenus d'en interdire la représentation ou l'exécution publique.

Art. 12. Sont spécialement comprises parmi les reproductions illicites auxquelles s'applique la présente Convention, les appropriations indirectes non autorisées d'un ouvrage littéraire ou artistique, telles que adaptations, arrangements de musique, transformations d'un roman, d'une nouvelle ou d'une poésie en pièce de théâtre et réciproquement, etc., lorsqu'elles ne sont que la reproduction de cet ouvrage, dans la même forme ou sous une autre forme, avec des changements, additions ou retranchements, non essentiels, et sans présenter le caractère d'une nouvelle œuvre originale.

Art. 13. Les auteurs d'œuvres musicales ont le droit exclusif d'autoriser: 1° l'adaptation de ces œuvres à des instruments servant à les reproduire mécaniquement; 2° l'exécution publique des mêmes œuvres au moyen de ces instruments.

Des réserves et conditions relatives à l'application de cet article pourront être déterminées par la législation intérieure de chaque pays, en ce qui le concerne; mais toutes réserves et conditions de cette nature n'auront qu'un effet strictement limité au pays qui les aurait établies.

La disposition de l'alinéa 1er n'a pas d'effet rétroactif et, par suite, n'est pas applicable, dans un pays de l'Union, aux œuvres qui, dans ce pays, auront été adaptées licitement aux instruments mécaniques avant la mise en vigueur de la présente Convention.

Les adaptations faites en vertu des alinéas 2 et 3 du présent article et importées, sans autorisation des parties intéressées, dans un pays où elles ne seraient pas licites, pourront y être saisies.

Art. 14. Les auteurs d'œuvres littéraires, scientifiques ou artistiques ont le droit exclusif d'autoriser la reproduction et la représentation publique de leurs œuvres par la cinématographie.

Sont protégées comme œuvres littéraires ou artistiques les productions cinématographiques lorsque, par les dispositifs de la mise en scène ou les combinaisons des incidents représentés, l'auteur aura donné à l'œuvre un caractère personnel et original.

Sans préjudice des droits de l'auteur de l'œuvre originale, la reproduction par la cinématographie d'une œuvre littéraire, scientifique ou artistique est protégée comme une œuvre originale.

Les dispositions qui précèdent s'appliquent à la reproduction ou production obtenue par tout autre procédé analogue à la cinématographie.

Art. 15. Pour que les auteurs des ouvrages protégés par la présente Convention soient, jusqu'à preuve contraire, considérés comme tels et admis, en conséquence, devant les tribunaux des divers pays de l'Union, à exercer des poursuites contre les contrefacteurs, il suffit que leur nom soit indiqué sur l'ouvrage en la manière usitée.

Pour les œuvres anonymes ou pseudonymes, l'éditeur dont le nom est indiqué sur l'ouvrage est fondé à sauvegarder les droits appartenant à l'auteur. Il est, sans auteurs preuves, réputé ayant cause de l'auteur anonyme ou pseudonyme.

Art. 16. Toute œuvre contrefaite peut être saisie par les autorités compétentes des pays de l'Union où l'œuvre originale a droit à la protection légale.

Dans ces pays, la saisies peut aussi s'appliquer aux reproductions provenant d'un pays où l'œuvre n'est pas protégée ou a cessé de l'être.

La saisie a lieu conformément à la législation intérieure de chaque pays.

Art. 17. Les dispositions de la présente Convention ne peuvent porter préjudice, en quoi que ce soit, au droit qui appartient au Gouvernement de chacun des pays de l'Union de permettre, de surveiller, d'interdire, par des mesures de législation ou de police intérieure, la circulation, la représentation, l'exposition de tout ouvrage ou production à l'égard desquels l'autorité compétente aurait à exercer ce droit.

Art. 18. La présente Convention s'applique à toutes les œuvres qui, au moment de son entrée en vigueur, ne sont pas encore tombées dans le domaine public de leur pays d'origine par l'expiration de la durée de la protection.

Cependant, si une œuvre, par l'expiration de la durée de protection qui lui était antérieurement reconnue, est tombée dans le domaine public du pays où la protection est réclamée, cette œuvre n'y sera pas protégée à nouveau.

L'application de ce principe aura lieu suivant les stipulations contenues dans les conventions spéciales existantes ou à conclure à cet effet entre pays de l'Union. A défaut de semblables stipulations, les pays respectifs régleront, chacun pour ce qui le concerne, les modalités relatives à cette application.

Les dispositions qui précèdent s'appliquent également en cas de nouvelles accessions à l'Union et dans le cas où la durée de la protection serait étendue par application de l'article 7.

ART. 19. Les dispositions de la présente Convention n'empêchent pas de revendiquer l'application de dispositions plus larges qui seraient édictées par la législation d'un pays de l'Union en faveur des étrangers en général.

ART. 20. Les Gouvernements des pays de l'Union se réservent le droit de prendre entre eux des arrangements particuliers, en tant que ces arrangements confèreraient aux auteurs des droits plus étendus que ceux accordés par l'Union, ou qu'ils renfermeraient d'autres stipulations non contraires à la présente Convention. Les dispositions des arrangements existants qui répondent aux conditions précitées restent applicables.

ART. 21. Est maintenu l'office international institué sous le nom de "Bureau de l'Union internationale pour la protection des œuvres littéraires et artistiques."

Ce Bureau est placé sous la haute autorité du Gouvernement de la Confédération Suisse, qui en règle l'organisation et en surveille le fonctionnement.

La langue officielle du Bureau est la langue française.

Art. 22. Le Bureau international centralise les renseignements de toute nature relatifs à la protection des droits des auteurs sur leurs œuvres littéraires et artistiques. Il les coordonne et les publie. Il procède aux études d'utilité commune intéressant l'Union et rédige, à l'aide des documents qui sont mis à sa disposition par les diverses Administrations, une feuille périodique, en langue française, sur les questions concernant l'objet de l'Union. Les Gouvernements des pays de l'Union se réservent d'autoriser, d'un commun accord, le Bureau à publier une édition dans une ou plusieurs autres langues, pour le cas où l'expérience en aurait démontré le besoin.

Le Bureau international doit se tenir en tout temps à la disposition des membres de l'Union pour leur fournir, sur les questions relatives à la protection des œuvres littéraires et artistiques, les renseignements spéciaux dont ils pourraient avoir besoin.

Le Directeur du Bureau international fait sur sa gestion un rapport annuel qui est communiqué à tous les membres de l'Union.

Art. 23. Les dépenses du Bureau de l'Union internationale sont supportées en commun par les Pays contractants. Jusqu'à nouvelle décision, elles ne pourront pas dépasser la somme de soixante mille francs par année. Cette somme pourra être augmentée au besoin par simple décision d'une des Conférences prévues à l'article 24.

Pour déterminer la part contributive de chacun des pays dans cette somme totale des frais, les Pays contractants et ceux qui adhéreront ultérieurement à l'Union sont divisés en six classes contribuant chacune dans la proportion d'un certain nombre d'unités, savoir:

1re classe	25 unités
2me classe	20 unités
3me classe	15 unités
4me classe	10 unités
5me classe	5 unités
6me classe	3 unités

Ces coefficients sont multipliés par le nombre des pays de chaque classe, et la somme des produits ainsi obtenus fournit le nombre d'unités par lequel la dépense totale doit être divisée. Le quotient donne le montant de l'unité de dépense.

Chaque pays déclarera, au moment de son accession, dans laquelle des susdites classes il demande à être rangé.

L'Administration suisse prépare le budget du Bureau et en surveille les dépenses, fait les avances nécessaires et établit le compte annuel qui sera communiqué à toutes les autres Administrations.

Art. 24. La présente Convention peut être soumise à des revisions en vue d'y introduire les améliorations de nature à perfectionner le système de l'Union.

Les questions de cette nature, ainsi que celles qui intéressant à d'autres points de vue le développement de l'-Union, sont traitées dans des Conférences qui auront lieu successivement dans les pays de l'Union entre les délégués desdits pays. L'Administration du pays où doit siéger une Conférence prépare, avec le concours du Bureau international, les travaux de celle-ci. Le Directeur du Bureau assiste aux séances des Conférences et prend part aux discussions sans voix délibérative.

Aucun changement à la présente Convention n'est

valable pour l'Union que moyennant l'assentiment unanime des pays qui la composent.

Art. 25. Les États étrangers à l'Union et qui assurent la protection légale des droits faisant l'objet de la présente Convention, peuvent y accéder sur leur demande.

Cette accession sera notifiée par écrit au Gouvernement de la Confédération Suisse, et par celui-ci à tous les autres.

Elle emportera, de plein droit, adhésion à toutes les clauses et admission à tous les avantages stipulés dans la présente Convention. Toutefois, elle pourra contenir l'indication des dispositions de la Convention du 9 septembre 1886 ou de l'Acte additionnel du 4 mai 1896 qu'ils jugeraient nécessaire de substituer, provisoirement au moins, aux dispositions correspondantes de la présente Convention.

Art. 26. Les Pays contractants ont le droit d'accéder en tout temps à la présente Convention pour leurs colonies ou possessions étrangères.

Ils peuvent, à cet effet, soit faire une déclaration générale par laquelle toutes leurs colonies ou possessions sont comprises dans l'accession, soit nommer expressément celles qui y sont comprises, soit se borner à indiquer celles qui en sont exclues.

Cette déclaration sera notifiée par écrit au Gouvernement de la Confédération Suisse, et par celui-ci à tous les autres.

Art. 27. La présente Convention remplacera, dans les rapports entre les États contractants, la Convention de Berne du 9 septembre 1886, y compris l'Article additionnel et le Protocole de clôture du même jour, ainsi que l'Acte additionnel et la Déclaration interprétative du 4 mai 1896.

Les actes conventionnels précités resteront en vigueur dans les rapports avec les États qui ne ratifieraient pas la présente Convention.

Les États signataires de la présente Convention pourront, lors de l'échange des ratifications, déclarer qu'ils entendent, sur tel ou tel point, rester encore liés par les dispositions des Conventions auxquelles ils ont souscrit antérieurement.

ART. 28. La présente Convention sera ratifiée, et les ratifications en seront échangées à Berlin au plus tard le 1er juillet 1910.

Chaque Partie contractante remettra, pour l'échange des ratifications, un seul instrument, qui sera déposé, avec ceux des autres pays, aux archives du Gouvernement de la Confédération Suisse. Chaque Partie recevra en retour un exemplaire du procès-verbal d'échange des ratifications, signé par les Plénipotentiaires qui y auront pris part.

ART. 29. La présente Convention sera mise à exécution trois mois après l'échange des ratifications et demeurera en vigueur pendant un temps indéterminé, jusqu'à l'expiration d'une année à partir du jour où la dénonciation en aura été faite.

Cette dénonciation sera adressée au Gouvernement de la Confédération Suisse. Elle ne produira son effet qu'à l'égard du pays qui l'aura faite, la Convention restant exécutoire pour les autres pays de l'Union.

ART. 30. Les États qui introduiront dans leur législation la durée de protection de cinquante ans prévue par l'article 7, alinéa 1er, de la présente Convention, le feront connaître au Gouvernement de la Confédération Suisse par une notification écrite qui sera communiquée aussitôt par ce Gouvernement à tous les autres États de l'Union.

Il en sera de même pour les États qui renonceront aux réserves faites par eux en vertu des articles 25, 26 et 27.

En foi de quoi, les Plénipotentiaires respectifs ont signé la présente Convention et y ont apposé leurs cachets.

Fait à Berlin, le 13 novembre mil neuf cent huit, en un seul exemplaire, qui sera déposé dans les archives du Gouvernement de la Confédération Suisse et dont des copies, certifiées conformes, seront remises par la voie diplomatique aux Pays contractants.

(*Suivent les signatures.*)

INDEX

A

Abandonment PAGE
in use of title 449

Abbreviations
in notice of copyright 516

Accident
film destroyed by 226
in theatre, see "Theatre."
miscellaneous, in theatre 323

Accounting
defenses to, in copyright action 614
in copyright action, method of procedure 623
in unfair competition 453
infringement of common-law rights 498
not given where acquiescence shown 452
of profits in copyright action 608, 613
ordered even where no knowledge 592

Acquiescence
in use of title 449
right to injunction though not to accounting 452
scienter 451

Action
allegations and proof required in copyright 593
cause of, for malicious discharge of actor 146
cause of, in copyright and unfair competition joined 584
copyright, in equity 602
joinder of causes of 577
misjoinder of parties to 577
on copyright, where brought 585

Action—*Continued*

PAGE

on unpublished work, where brought . . . 586
proceedings for injunction, damages, profits and those for seizure of infringing copies and plates may be united in one . . . 619
proprietor must show how he acquired copyright . . . 596
purporting to be brought under Copyright Act . . . 628
who may maintain, for infringement . . . 577

Action at Law

in copyright actions . . . 626
may be pursued in copyright actions concurrently with one in equity . . . 627

Actor

a wage-earner under Bankruptcy Act . . . 263
actor's breach of contract—damages . . . 166
anticipatory breach by producer . . . 135
booking agencies . . . 178
changing motion picture . . . 169
contract for transportation—damages . . . 193
contract for work on Sunday . . . 125
contract labor and exclusion laws . . . 191
contract with infants . . . 173
control of exhibition of motion picture . . . 173
costumes . . . 197
death terminates contract . . . 164
enticement of . . . 198
escrow agents . . . 186
exclusive contract not in restraint of trade . . . 96
exposure to obscenity, ridicule, degradation, etc . . . 136
failure to rehearse . . . 156
form of notice of discharge to be given to . . . 164
garnishment of salary . . . 184
grounds for discharge . . . 156
how many causes of action for breach . . . 145
illness of . . . 157
immorality of . . . 162
inability of producer—when studio closed by authorities . . . 176
incapacity to perform . . . 157
incompetency . . . 158

Actor—*Continued* PAGE
"incompetency" not equivalent "unsatisfactory" 159
injunction for breach of contract where services are special, unique and extraordinary 95
injunction pendente lite 108
injuries by, to patrons 319
insolence of 162
insubordination of 162
intoxication of 163
law governing validity of contract 190
length of engagement 117
liability of manager for negligence of 319
libel of 202
liquidated damage clause for breach 152
measure of damages in event of breach of contract 147
modification of contract 142
not required to play inferior part 139
performance in unlicensed theatre 192
power of company's officer to contract—agency 195
producer's offer of reëmployment after breach 154
profits as a basis for damage 149
proprietor liable for insulting language of 322
questions of travel 177
remedy for breach of contract 146
remedy for malicious discharge 146
remedy where mutilation of motion picture occurs 171
renewal of contract 142
right to perform part of contract 105
royalties in addition to salary 190
services "actually performed" 131
substantial performance 133
tender of services after breach 147
two weeks' notice and other customs 119
unfaithfulness of 162
warranty of requisite skill and ability 159
when contract between actor and producer a joint venture 187
where contract with producer not one of joint venture 168
where he poses in serial story 185
where services are to be "satisfactory" 112
Workmen Compensation Acts 180

Act

PAGE

of play a component part thereof 545
word " Act " a descriptive title 410

Ad Interim Protection

of foreign works 641

Admission Fee

for Sunday performances 392

Advertisements

billboard 228
contract with lithographer for posters 228
copyright in 536, 539, 540
curtain displays 228, 229
curtain displays in first-class theatres 230
immoral 377
important in unfair competition 463
insertion of infringing, makes one liable . . . . . 587, note
misleading not copyrightable 541

Agency

between belligerent alien and citizen 530
payment of royalties to agent 531
power of company's officer to contract for services of actor 195

Aisle

chairs and fixed seats in 366
patron injured in 306
space in rear of orchestra 366
standing in 365

Alien

belligerent, status of, for copyright 527
right to secure copyright 524
see " War."
see " Belligerent Aliens."

Allegations

necessary in copyright action 593

American Citizen PAGE
how to secure copyright in United Kingdom and Protectorates.. 654
how to secure copyright in Newfoundland.................... 658
how to secure copyright in Australia.......................... 658
how to secure copyright in New Zealand... 659
how to secure copyright in Union of South Africa............. 660
how to secure copyright in Canada.......................... 660

Animals
see "Wild animals."

Anonymous Name
may be maintained by author.............................. 60

Appeal
in copyright actions.................................... 638

Application
for copyright registration of motion picture.................. 500
for renewal of copyright when made......................... 547

Aquarium
when theatre license required for........................... 340

Arrangement
copyright in, of words.................................. 560
new, of work... 534
of theme, confers copyright............................. 534

Assault
liability of theatre proprietor for........................... 326

Assignability
of contracts between co-authors........................... 51
of contracts between co-authors and publishers............... 51
of contracts for literary works............................ 67
of marks and devices.................................... 465
of name by executor.................................... 480
of one's own name...................................... 477
of title... 463
of trade-mark and trade name............................ 465

Assignee PAGE
name of, on notice after renewal ... 549
of copyright may sue ... 577
when not entitled to renewal of copyright ... 548

Assignment
exclusive license of entire term an ... 582
right to make, under common law ... 495

Assignment of Copyright
action to compel, may be brought in state court ... 553
and license distinguished ... 557
agreement for, specifically enforced ... 554
by author to magazine proprietor ... 555
exclusive license is ... 558
failure to record, will not avail infringer ... 553
implied warranty of title on ... 557
in film and in play ... 552
in general ... 550
made in foreign country ... 551
must be in writing ... 551
must be recorded ... 551, 552
no formal assignment of right to copyright ... 550
no restriction on ... 550
sale of a number of copyrights is an ... 552
sale of work is not an ... 554
to two people makes them joint-owners ... 550

Assumed Name
copyright may be taken out in ... 532
copyrights do not confer greater rights ... 533

Australia
copyright in Commonwealth of ... 655, 658

Author
akin to actor ... 54
compensation guaranteed ... 79
contract of, with producer personal ... 67
contract of, containing negative covenant enforceable ... 71

Author—*Continued* PAGE
contract to write specifically enforced .92
death of, as affecting right to renewal of copyright 549
death of, title of work passes 464
entitled to royalties, whether work produced or not 82
forfeiture for non-payment of royalties 84
grants sole license 73
grants license with limitations 74
his common-law rights 491
ideas of, not copyrightable 560
injunctions pendente lite more readily granted 92
manuscript lost after submission 87
may be guilty of infringement of his own work 592
may maintain action against third parties 92
may not part with work and retain title 464
may part with portion of work and retain title 464
may reserve dramatic rights in contribution to magazine 16, 17
may copyright magazine article in his own name 18
may not recover for libelous, immoral or seditious work 73
mutilation of his work 53
name of deceased 61
name falsely imputed to work 61
nature of contract of co-authorship 45
of magazine article reserving dramatization rights 555
of work must be established in copyright action 597
paid stipulated amount 80
proprietor of copyright must show how he acquired same from 596
purchaser required to produce work 89
receives percentage of profits 77
refund of advance payments 90
renewal of copyright to 547
rights where motion picture based upon dramatic composition 1
rights where motion picture based upon novel 11
rights where motion picture based upon historical work 11
rights where motion picture based upon short story 15
rights where motion picture based upon sketch 15
rights where motion picture based upon poem 15
rights where motion picture based upon lecture 15
rights where motion picture based upon sermon 15
rights where motion picture based upon original scenario 19

Author—*Continued*

PAGE

rights where motion picture based upon news item.............. 23
rights where motion picture based upon work in public domain.. 24
rights where motion picture produced in serial form........... 25
rights as between employer and employe..................... 26
rights of co-author...35, 45
rights of, where music composed for picture.................. 51
rights of, where changes have been made in the text of his work. 53
rights of, where his work is criticised....................... 63
stipulated damages for breach.............................. 83
when contribution to magazine falls into public domain........ 18
when he may rescind.. 90
when producer may rescind.................................. 90
when work to be done to satisfaction........................ 73
work of libelous, immoral or seditious nature................. 73
work secured by prize contest................................ 88
work to be produced at definite time......................... 75

B

Balcony
falling over, see "Theatre."
patron falling over... 303

Ballet-Dancing
not immoral...357, 379

Bankruptcy
actor is a wage-earner...................................... 263
distributor not a "trader" under the Act.................... 261
effect on contracts for literary or dramatic productions........68, 69
exhibitor's contract does not pass to trustee................. 227
license does not pass to trustee in.......................... 263
motion picture "trade" or "profession"....................... 263
right to title of work passes to trustee....................... 464
right to trade mark and trade name.......................... 465
right to mark and device.................................... 465
with respect to copyright.................................... 643

Barring Clause
in actor's contract... 107

Belligerent Aliens PAGE
agency and partnership 530
copyright owned by partners 530
copyright suspended 528
may be sued 528
ownership of copyright in 529
right of licensee to sue 531
right of, to sue on their copyright 528

Benefit Performances
breach by theatre owner 259, 260
proceeds devoted to charity 259
when license required 260

Berlin Convention
of 1906—Text in English 836
of 1906—Text in French 858

Bill
see "Complaint" "Action."

Bill of Particulars
in copyright action 599
of several causes of action 599

Bill-Poster
immoral 377
may be copyrighted 539

Book
scenario copyrighted as a 540
title of, not protected by copyright 403
various titles of 440

Booking Agency
power to bind producer when booking actor 196
with respect to actors 178

Booking Agreements
circuit agent for theatre owner 256
not interstate commerce 258

Booking Agreements—*Continued* PAGE
specific performance of 257
theatre owner sued by manager 256
when interstate commerce 261

Book Rights
defined 26

Booth
regulations with respect to 367, 368
when a theatre license required for 340

Bowling-Alley
when a theatre license required for 340

Breach
anticipatory, by producer 135
of actor's contract to expose to obscenity, ridicule, degradation, etc. 136
of contract by actor—damages 166
of contract of actor—number of causes of action 145
producer's offer of re-employment after 154
remedy of actor for 146

Burlesques
copyright 541
whether infringement on copyright 537

C

Cabaret
theatre license not required 341, 348

Canada
copyright in Dominion of 655, 660

Cartoonist
tardiness ground for discharge of . . . . . 158, note

Cartoons
animated 469, 470
copyright in 536
"dramatic compositions" 538

Cartoons—*Continued* PAGE
how protected 469
in conflict with play 405
infringement of dramatic rights in 582

Catalogues
copyright in 540

Censorship
boards of 383
extent of discretion in boards of 390
Federal Board 388
in general 383

Certificate
of copyright, as evidence 598

Chancery Rule
number one hundred and seven followed in accountings in copyright actions 624

Chandelier
dropping of, liability for 311
inspection of, no defense 311

Changes
in text of work see "Literary Works" and "Author"

Chapters
of a work, component parts 545

Charitable
performance violating Sunday statute 401

Charitable Entertainments
not relieved from obtaining licenses 347
see "Benefit Performances."

Church
distance from theatre 364, 371
license refused theatre for proximity to 358

Circulation

PAGE

right of restricted, under common law........................ 495

Circus

a private enterprise.. 385
when a theatre license required for......................... 340

Citizen

may secure copyright.. 524
see "American Citizen."

Civil Rights

English doctrine.. 272
exclusion from theatres..................................... 295
exclusion from theatres for race, creed or color............ 296
Federal doctrine.. 272
New York statute prohibiting use of name or picture......... 271
use of name or picture of individual prohibited............. 271

Civil Rights Law of N. Y.

applies to "Weekly News Pictures"........................... 285
cause of action personal.................................... 278
consent—to be in writing.................................... 275
history of.. 271
infant may maintain action.................................. 278
name used without consent enjoined.......................... 275
not intended to prevent dissemination of news............... 281
picture enjoined where plaintiff had not posed.............. 274
remedy at law or in equity.................................. 271
right not possessed by persons of prominence................ 278
right not possessed by criminals............................ 279
statute strictly construed.................................. 279
use of name or picture libelous............................. 282
use must be for trade or advertising........................ 271
when estopped from invoking statute......................... 281
when picture libelous....................................... 272
who has abandoned the right................................. 278
who liable for violation.................................... 278
wholly prospective.. 271

Co-authors PAGE

are tenants in common.... 37
composer of music and scenario writer.... 53
contract of co-authorship not assignable.... 51
contract of co-authorship entire.... 51
contracts between themselves.... 45
contracts between themselves and publishers.... 45
contracts between themselves and publishers are for personal services.... 46
effect of death of one.... 47
elements of skill and confidence.... 48
in action by one, all to be joined.... 44
in action by one, against licensee, others need not be joined.... 45
in general....35–45
may grant rights without consent of co-author.... 37
may not however grant exclusive rights....38, 39
may not destroy rights of co-author.... 40
may not be compelled to account.... 41
may sue each other for infringement of the common work.... 45
not co-partners....42, 46
not joint-venturers.... 46
partnership by special contract dissolved by death of one.... 47
test as to what constitutes.... 35

Classification

validity of copyright not affected by.... 503

Collaborators

in general....35–45

Combination

of theme confers copyright.... 534

Combinations

see "Restraint of Trade."

Comedy

is a descriptive title....408, note

Competition

see "Unfair Competition."

Common Errors PAGE
as a test of infringement . . . 573

Common-law Rights
adverse possession . . . 494
coincidence as a defense . . . 576
conversion of manuscript—damages . . . 499
death of owner of manuscript . . . 493
enforceable in state courts . . . 493
in England . . . 494
in United States . . . 494
infringement . . . 498
in general . . . 491
not co-existent with copyright . . . 496
pass to purchaser of manuscript . . . 493
publication . . . 495
publication in England not necessarily publication here . . . 510
reserving performing rights . . . 497
what is publication . . . 503
what rights are secured to author under . . . 494
what rights are secured to author before publication . . . 495
what rights are secured to author after publication . . . 495

Common Sources
defense . . . 568

Compensation
of actor an element in granting equitable relief . . . 104

Complaint
demurrer to, on copyright . . . 594
how "deposit of copies" pleaded . . . 596
motion to make more definite in copyright action . . . 599
must show authorship . . . 597
must show deposit . . . 596
must show registration . . . 596
must show steps taken to secure copyright . . . 594

Compliance
of copyright statute as to notice . . . 514

Component Parts PAGE
copyright in 544

Composite Work
renewal of copyright 547
reserving rights to contribution to 556

Concert
license does not permit stage plays 344
when a theatre license required for 339, 343

Condition
license granted on, that theatre remain closed on Sunday 360
license for theatre granted upon 358

Coincidence
similarity by 574

Constitutionality
of censorship statutes 384
of statutes regulating "ticket-scalping" 381
of statutes requiring theatre licenses 345
of Sunday statutes 399

Contract
anticipatory breach by producer 135
breach by actor where services are special, unique and extraordinary 95
breach of, to expose actor to obscenity, ridicule, degradation, etc. 136
breach of executory, to play at theatre 149
breach by actor—damages 166
court not bound by provision as to liquidated damages 167
court not ousted of jurisdiction by provisions in 190
for advertising 228
for assignment of copyright specifically enforced 554
for rental of film for Sunday 129
for transportation of actor—damage 193
grounds for discharge of actor 156
law governing validity of actor's 190
liability of producer to actor where studio closed by authorities . . 176
liquidated damages where breach by actor 166

Contract—*Continued* PAGE
made in one state for theatrical production in another 261
of actor, how many causes of action for breach 145
of actor—modification 142
of actor, personal in its nature 157
of actor providing for "no play, no pay" 132
of actor providing for royalties in addition to salary 190
of actor providing for sharing of profits does not constitute joint venture 168
of actor—renewal 142
producer's offer of re-employment after breach of 154
providing for performances in unlicensed theatre 192
recovery by actor where substantial performance 133
recovery on a quantum meruit where actor ill or dead 133
remedy of actor for breach 146
set-off by producer or distributor 218
set-off of moneys received by distributor 218
services of actor to be "satisfactory" to employer 112
stipulation that services of actor are unique, not binding 108
tender of actor's services after breach 147
theatre leases 237
to assign copyright may be by parol 551
where contract between actor and producer a joint venture 187
with actor for work on Sunday 125
with actor must be mutual to be enforceable in equity 102
with actor providing for payment only when "actually performing" 131
with infant actors 173

Contract Labor and Exclusion Laws
with respect to actor 191

Control
right to, publication 495
sole exclusive, in work before publication 495

Co-Partnership
copyright may be taken out in name of 532

Contrivances
copyright in 536, 538

Conversion PAGE

predicated on wrongful use of film 225

Copy

copyright in inferior 541
inferior, may be infringement 543
right to, under common law 495
right to, under copyright 500
right to permit others to, under common law 495
right to give away a, under common law 495

Copyright

action on, where brought 585
ad interim protection 641
advertisements 536
and patent rights distinguished 481
assignee may sue 577
assignment of 550
assignment and license distinguished 557
bankruptcy—title in trustee 643
belligerent aliens 527
bill of particulars 599
bill-posters 539
British, Colonial and International 654
burlesques 541
cartoons 536
catalogues 540
certificate of, as evidence 598
changing title of work 521
common-law rights 491
common sources 568
component parts 544
contrivances 536, 538
criticism 541
distinct from right in material work 554
does not prevent sale of physical property 644
duration of 546
editorials 539
facts to be alleged and proved 593
failure of licensee to insert notice 519

Copyright—*Continued*

PAGE

false notice of 520
gags 536
government publications 540
how secured 500
immoral and seditious works 536
implied warranty of title where, is assigned 557
improper name on notice 519
inferior copies 541
infringement, test of 559
intent to infringe 586, 591
in Commonwealth of Australia 655, 658
in Dominion of Canada 655, 660
in Dominion of New Zealand 655, 659
in Newfoundland 655, 658
in Union of South Africa 655, 660
in United Kingdom and Protectorates 654
international 672
in what name it may be taken out 532
joinder of action in, with action in Unfair Competition 584
joinder of causes of action 577
knowledge and intent not necessary to infringe 588, 591
knowledge and intent, early American rule 589
may unite cause of action for, with Unfair Competition 460
method of obtaining, for motion picture 500
misjoinder of parties 577
music in theatres 649
new matter 543
newspaper 539
not always lost by omission of notice 517
not co-existent with common-law right 496
notice of 510
object of granting 561
of labels and prints 739
one advantage of 577
parodies 541
performance of play not a publication 497
performing rights 497
photographs subjects of 539
pooling 489

Copyright—*Continued* PAGE
presidential proclamations 525
primary test of infringement 561
prohibition of importation of piratical copies 640
proprietor must sue 577
publication generally 494
public domain 544
Remedies
accounting 623
actions at law 626
actions in equity—in general 602
actions purporting to be brought under Copyright Act 628
appeal 638
construction of forfeiture and penalty clauses 636
final hearing 608
injunction as to part 619
preliminary injunction 602
statute of limitations 636
willful infringements 634
writ of seizure 621
renewal of 547
restrictions in re-sale of work 487
return of copies deposited 639
revised edition 543
right to, when not conveyed 583
right secured by 499
scenario 540
selling second-hand copies 646
similarity by coincidence 574
stage-business 536
strict compliance with statute necessary 593
subjects of 534
taken out in wrongful trade name 534
taxability 648
term of 546
test of what is subject of 535
title not protected by 403
unpublished works 546
use of title after expiration of 438
validity of, not affected by classification 503

Copyright—*Continued* PAGE
what complaint must show 594
what is publication 503
when work secured by prize contest 88
who is liable for infringement 586
who may maintain action 577
who may secure 524

Copyright Act
British, of 1911—text 762
Canadian, of 1906—text 812
United States, of 1909, as amended by Acts of 1912, 1913, 1914—text 677

Copyright Conventions
of United States and Hungary—text 722
of United States and other American Republics—text 725

Copyright Office
rules and regulations of United States—text 740
rules and regulations of Canadian—text 833

Corporation
copyright may be taken out in name of 532
renewal of work copyrighted by 547

Costs
in copyright action 608, 616, 617

Costumes
of actor 197

Courts
not bound by stipulation that services of actor are unique 108

Criminal
knowledge necessary in, proceedings 591

Critic
may exclude, from theatre 295

Criticism PAGE
not infringement of copyright 541
of play, when a libel 266
private exhibition for, under common law 495
work of the author 63

Crowds
theatre proprietor must provide for safety of 318, 319

Customs
definition of 122
how pleaded 125
in theatrical profession 119
miscellaneous, in theatrical profession 123
two weeks' custom 119
what are 119

D

Damages
actor bound to mitigate 147
breach of contract by actor 166
contracts for transportation of actor 193
conversion of manuscript 499
evidence of experts on receipts of theatre 247
in copyright action 608, 610
in unfair competition 455
liquidated, breach by actor 166
liquidated damage clause 152
measure of, breach of actor's contract 147
measure of, failure to produce film 220
measure of, for breach of contract to produce 216
method of ascertaining, on producer's default 220
ordered even where no knowledge 592
plaintiff entitled to recover actual losses as a part of 151
profits as a basis for 149
prospective profits a measure of 149
punitive, awarded for assault of patron of theatre 331
where actor's contract subject to two weeks' notice 121
where irreparable, injunction will issue against actor 95
where stipulated between author and producer 83

Dance Steps PAGE.
copyright in.......... 536

Dance-halls
regulation of..........346, note

Dancing
distinguished from skating.......... 341
no license required for..........342, 343

Date
in copyright notice may be in roman numerals.......... 517

Death
of actor terminates contract.......... 164
of author, as affecting right to renewal of copyright.......... 549
of owner of common-law rights to manuscript.......... 493
of performer of troupe cancels contract.......... 161

Deception
need only be calculation for.......... 458

Decree
final, in copyright action.......... 618
interlocutory decree ordinarily entered after finding of infringement.......... 618

Dedicated
when work dedicated.......... 497
when publication of story in magazine is a dedication.......... 556
work published without compliance with statute is.......... 506

Defense
by producer of actor's earnings after discharge.......... 148
in copyright action, laches..........608, note
of coincidence.......... 576
of common sources.......... 568
offer of re-employment to actor after breach.......... 156
two weeks' custom—how pleaded.......... 125

Degradation PAGE
exposure of actor to 136

Deposit
of copies after temporary injunction 598
of copies, how pleaded 596
of copies necessary to maintain action 503
of title and description 500
return of copies deposited in copyright office 639
to be made promptly after publication 503

Description
deposit of, as unpublished work 500

Descriptive
title, not protected 407

Development
of theme confers copyright 534

Devices
see "Marks and Devices."

Director
his rights in general 209

Discharge
actor must seek other employment after 147
damages recoverable by actor for, when fixed beforehand 165
grounds for, of actor 156
of actor for insolence 162
of actor for insubordination 162
of actor for drunkenness 163
of actor for non-adherence to union 164
of actor for his failure to secure proper license required by law 164
of actor for violation of provisions of contract 156
of actor for failure to appear at rehearsals 156
of actor for illness 157
of actor for incompetency 158
of actor for "unsatisfactory" services 112, 159

Discharge—*Continued* PAGE
of actor for immorality . . . 162
of actor for incapacity to perform . . . 157
of actor equivalent to notice where contract subject to two weeks' notice . . . 121
see "Actor."

Discretionary Power
to grant theatre licenses . . . 349, 351, 352

Distances
of theatre from church or school . . . 364, 371
regulation of theatre with respect to . . . 362

Distribution
right to make qualified, under common law . . . 495

Distributor
bankruptcy . . . 261
exhibitor and, licensee and licensor . . . 225
franchise and booking agreements . . . 256
in general . . . 214
interstate commerce . . . 260
liable with producer and exhibitor . . . 467
libel . . . 264
may enjoin infringement of state rights . . . 222
may not injure high standard . . . 221
may restrain producer from granting other "state-rights" . . . 223
must release regularly . . . 222
must release under producer's name . . . 222
not a "trader" under Bankruptcy Act . . . 261
not entitled to mutilate film . . . 221
of film liable for infringement . . . 590
replevin of film and machine . . . 235
to bear loss for destroyed film . . . 226
when entitled to exploit "state-right" films . . . 222

Drama
is a descriptive title . . . 410
see "Play."

Dramatic Composition PAGE
cartoons, whether copyrightable as 538
common sources 568
infringements of 562–565
is a descriptive title . . . . . 408, note
rights of author, where motion picture based upon 1
scenario not copyrighted as 19–21, 540

Dramatic Entertainment
a motion picture exhibition is a 338
motion picture held, in Sunday statute 397
when license required for 338–343

Dramatization Rights
assignment of, carries picture rights 552
author of magazine article reserving 555
construing "presentation on the stage" 7
construing "dramatic version" 8
construing "all dramatization rights" 5–9
grant of "all dramatization rights" 5
grant of, does not necessarily divest author of picture rights 5
in cartoons infringed 582
in unpublished works 556
licensor may reserve stage rights 10
stage rights given subsequently to picture rights 9
time of grant important as showing intent 8–9
when in unfair competition with picture rights 5
when motion picture rights not in contemplation 2
when picture rights suspended 5
when suspension perpetual 7
when they include motion picture rights 2

Dramatize
right to, under common law 495

Dressing-room
actress hurt in 310

Drunkenness
of actor 163

Duping

PAGE

of films 634
"state-rights" owner not to "dupe" 224

Duration

of copyright 546

E

Edition

revised, copyright in 543

Editorials

copyright in 539

Employe

rights of author when relationship that of 26
when author, no formal assignment of work necessary 27
when author engaged in writing only incidentally 29, 34
when not liable for infringement 590
who is paid salary to write has no rights in work 32
who receives profits as well as salary has no rights in work 32
who is paid space rates has no rights in work 33

Employer

author's works vest in, as soon as created 33
rights of author when relationship that of employe 26
right to renewal of copyright 547
when deemed proprietor of author's work 27

Engagement of Actor

length 117

English

common-law rights 494
copyright 654
war copyright statute 532

Enticement

of actor 198

Equitable

owner of copyright may be party 582

Equity PAGE
copyright actions in........ 602
copyright action in, may be pursued concurrently with one at law 627
copyright action in, procedure after finding of infringement...... 618
final hearing in, in copyright action........ 608

Escrow Agents
provision in actor's contract with respect to........ 186

Exchanges
in general........ 214

Exclusion
from theatre, see "Theatre."

Exemplary Damages
for infringement of common-law rights........ 498

Exhibitor
advertising matter........ 228
bankruptcy........ 261
benefit performances........ 258
bill-posters........ 228
distributor and, licensor and licensee........ 225
exhibition of motion picture, how proved........ 598
fixtures........ 232
franchise and booking agreements........ 256
in general........ 214–225
interstate commerce........ 260
liable with producer and distributor........ 467
libel........ 264
libelous film, tort feasor........ 226
may enjoin licensor for violation of exclusive grant........ 227
must pay for film though theatre closed........ 226
of film liable for infringement........ 590
private exhibitions........ 258
programs........ 228
replevin of film and machine........ 235
theatre, when a nuisance........ 251
theatre leases........ 237
when not entitled to specific performance of exclusive grant..... 228

Exit

PAGE

may open on an alley 367
patron injured at, of theatre 306
rear exit, no right to leave by 310
regulations as to 369

Expression

copyright in form of 560

Extraordinary

injunction against actor where services are 95
where services of infant are 173

Extra-territorial

effect of publication 510

F

Facts

which must be alleged and proved in copyright action 593

Farce

is a descriptive title .... 408, note

Feature

elaborating two-reel into 544

Film

all who handle, liable for infringement 590
considered inflammable .... 367, note
exhibition of, how proved 598
importation of, may be censored 389
lessor of, proper party to action 578–579
lessee of, proper party to action 578–579
restrictions on use of 485
sale of, does not convey copyright 555

Final Hearing

in copyright action 608

Fire

film destroyed by 226

Fire—*Continued* PAGE
inspection of theatre . . . 368
regulations with respect to theatres . . . 363

Fire-escapes
of theatre . . . 369

Fire-extinguishers
regulations for theatres . . . 369
theatre proprietor must provide . . . 319

Fireman
may inspect theatre . . . 368
who pays, for supervision of theatre . . . 368

Firm
copyright may be taken out in name of . . . 532

First-class Theatres
curtain displays . . . 230
distributor may not lease to cheaper house . . . 221
is motion picture house a . . . 238–239
picture to be produced in . . . 74
with respect to leases . . . 237

Fixtures
actions to enforce mechanic's lien on . . . 233
balustrades . . . 235
borders . . . 235
carpets . . . 235
carousel . . . 235
chairs . . . 232
clock . . . 235
combination closet . . . 235
curtains . . . 235
dance floors (portable) . . . 235
drop curtain . . . 234, 235
gas appliances . . . 233
lighting appliances . . . 233, 234
oilfitter . . . 235

Fixtures—*Continued* PAGE
piano 235
scenery 234
settees 235
special scenery 234
stage-fittings 234, 235
switchboard 234
ticket-booths 235
wings 235
wires (electric) 234
with reference to theatre buildings 232
wrenches 235

Foreign Work
plays based on, in public domain 569

Forfeiture and Penalty Clause
in copyright statutes 636
non-payment of royalties 84
of license, for failure to pay royalties 84
of license, for insufficient performances 87
of license, for non-production 87

Forgery
to print theatre-ticket wrongfully 383

Franchise Agreements
see "Booking Agreements."

Fraud
in Unfair Competition 455
justifying rescission by author 90
justifying rescission by producer 90
must be proved in actions at law for Unfair Competition 469

G

Gags
copyright in 536

Garnishment
of salary of actor 184

Gestures PAGE
copyright in 536

Government Publications
copyright in 540

Great Britain
copyright in 654
see "English."

Guarantee
of royalties 79–80

H

Hats
regulations as to removal of .... 367, note

Historical Work
rights of author where motion picture based upon 11
when protected as original work 14–15

Horse-race
exhibition license required for 340

Hungary
copyright convention with United States—text 722

I

Ideas
no copyright in 560

Illness
of actor 157

Imitation
not infringement 542
whether infringement on copyright 537

Immoral
advertising matter in general and posters where suggestive 377

Immoral—*Continued* PAGE
ballet dancing not. 357, 379
copyright will not be secured in work which is. 535
exhibitor need not pay for film which is. 226
immorality of actor. 162
need not be exposure of person. 373
preventing exhibition of picture which is. 353
prize-fight. 379
prohibition of pictures which are. 372
race prejudice aroused. 357, 379
seditious works will have no copyright. 535
see "Literary Works."
title suggestive. 377
war pictures suppressed. 357

Impersonation
infringement. 542

Implied Covenant
of warranty of title in copyright. 557

Importation
of films subject to censorship. 388–389
prohibition of, of piratical copies. 640

Incompetency
immortality of actor. 158
of actor not equivalent to dissatisfaction. 113, 159

Independent Contractor
when author is. 27–29
when author retains rights. 27

Individual
copyright may be taken out in name of. 532

Infants
admission of, to theatre. 370
contracts with infant actors. 173
"guardian" might refer to neighbor or friend. . . . . .370, note

Infants—*Continued* PAGE
inability to enforce negative covenant against 173
may sue for violation of civil rights 278
misdemeanor in New York to employ infant actors 175
no injunction for breach of contract 106

Inferior Part
actor not required to play 139

Infringement
criticism 541
defense of common sources 573
for licensee to overstep his grant 593
in cartoons 582
intent 586
joinder of causes of action for 577
knowledge and intent, early American rule 589
may be, of one's own work 592
misjoinder of parties in action for 577
must be of "substantial and material part" 562
of common-law rights 498
of copyright, generally 559
of copyright, when film used at wrong time and place 225
of plays 562–565
plaintiff need not wait until actual 459
primary test 561
private exhibition not an 588
quotations 541
submission of manuscripts considered on 591
test of 542, 559, 561
titles held not to infringe in unfair competition 445
titles held to infringe in unfair competition 440
who is liable for, of copyright 586
who may maintain action for 577
willful 634

Infringer
failure to record assignment will not avail 553

Inflammable
films considered as . . . . . 367, note

Injunction PAGE
against infant actor 173
as between licensee of author and of publisher 13
as to part in copyright action 619
by producer against actor where services are special, unique and extraordinary 95
cannot maintain for violation of Sunday laws 399
deposit of copies after temporary 598
for infringement of common-law rights 498
in unfair competition 453
laches, a defense to, in copyright action 608, 609
not granted against infant actor 106
pendente lite against actor where services are special, unique and extraordinary 108
pendente lite, more readily granted 92
permanent, in copyright action 658
preliminary, more liberally granted in copyright actions 602
preliminary, in copyright action 602
procedure where order is disobeyed 112
producer may enjoin use of other name 222
threatened invasion of copyright sufficient to entitle to preliminary 602
without accounting in unfair competition 452

Injunction Pendente Lite
discretionary with court in case of actor's contract 109
see " Preliminary Injunction."

Insolence
of actor 162

Insubordination
of actor 162

Intellectual Conceptions
no copyright in 560

Intent
early American rule for, as to infringement of copyright 589
in unfair competition 456

Interest PAGE
right to sell or assign, at common law........................ 495
sole exclusive, in work before publication..................... 495

International
copyright.. 672
copyright—text of Berne Convention of 1908—in English...... 836
copyright—text of Berne Convention of 1908—in French...... 858

Interstate Commerce
contracts made in one state for production in another.......... 261
in certain films prohibited.................................. 388
shipment of films.. 261
whether theatricals come within............................. 260

Intoxication
of actor.. 163

J

Joinder
cause of action in copyright with one in unfair competition...... 584
of licensee as co-plaintiff.................................578–580

Joint Venture
contract between actor and producer for sharing of profits not a 168
requirement of good faith in acts of parties to.................. 189
when contract between actor and producer.................. 187

Jurisdiction
of courts not ousted by provisions in actor's contract.......... 190

L

Laches
a bar to preliminary injunction in copyright action............ 607
defense in copyright action...........................608, note
in unfair competition...................................... 449
not equivalent to mere delay in time in copyright action....... 607

Law
actions at, in unfair competition............................ 468
contract labor and exclusion.............................. 191

Lease PAGE
theatre leases in general, see "Theatre Leases."
when distributor's contract a 221

Lecture
rights of author where motion picture based upon 15

Legal Title
defendant estopped from attacking 583
in infringer 582

Legibility
of notice of copyright 513

Lessee
of film proper party to action 578–579

Lessor
of film proper party to action 578–579
of theatre liable for infringing performance 587

Letters
of alphabet not protected as trade-marks 463

Liability
for copyright infringement 586
of lessor of theatre for infringing performance 587
of those who handle film for copyright infringement 590
state officers 591

Libel
criticism of work of author 63
film containing, makes exhibitor tort feasor 226
limits in criticism of play 266
of actor 202
of actor where improper form of billing or type used 203
of actor where mutilation of motion picture 171
to accuse manager of fraud, insolvency and embezzlement 264–265
to allege production to be immoral 264–265
use of name in a "white slave" film 282

Libel—*Continued* PAGE
use of portrait with advertisement........................... 283
works of a libelous nature.................................. 73

License
and assignment of copyright distinguished.................. 557
construction of, one of law for court...................... 7
corporation charter does not remove necessity for obtaining..... 347
distinction between assignment and......................... 71
does not pass to trustee in bankruptcy...................... 263
exclusive, an assignment.................................. 582
exclusive, is assignment of copyright...................... 558
exclusive grant required to restrain invasions............. 6
exclusiveness not presumed................................ 6–7
exclusive, for dramatic production of play................. 2
exhibition, required for horse-racing....................... 340
extent of discretionary power to..........................351–352
fees excessive.. 352
forfeiture of, for failure to pay royalties................. 84
granted on condition that theatre remain closed Sunday........ 360
may not be withheld after building erected................. 363
municipality estopped from suing for fees.................347, note
no custom that license is necessarily an exclusive one.......... 124
necessity for... 345
necessity for license of motion picture exhibitions..........337–343
of stage rights bars picture rights......................... 3–5
of theatre, in general.................................... 337
penalties imposed for failure to procure theatre............... 346
performance of actor in unlicensed theatre.................. 192
power to, discretionary................................... 349
power to, may be delegated................................ 350
refused for proximity to church or school................... 358
right of author to make motion picture after granting exclusive.. 2
right to, on condition.................................... 358
statutes requiring, constitutional.......................... 345
terminated for failure to give required number of performances.. 87
terminated for failure to produce work in time............... 87
theatre, not required for cabaret........................... 341
theatre, not required for skating-rink...................... 341
theatre, required for circus............................... 340

License—*Continued* PAGE
theatre, required for concert.......... 339, 343
theatre, required for opera.......... 340
theatre, required for pantomime.......... 339
theatre, required for aquarium.......... 340
theatre, required for booth.......... 340
theatre, required for bowling-alley.......... 340
theatre, required for singing.......... 339, 342
to operate theatre may be oral.......... 347
theatre, required for museum.......... 340
theatre, and liquor license.......... 361
theatre ticket a revocable.......... 292
theatre ticket not revocable, under English rule.......... 297
time of grant of dramatic rights important as showing intent.... 8–9
to exhibit, purely personal.......... 227
unless exclusive, may be given to others.......... 73
validity of, not to be questioned by licensee.......... 592
when violation of, entitles owner to replevin.......... 235–236
where author grants sole and exclusive.......... 73
where author grants, with limitations.......... 74

License Fees
exhibitor must pay, though theatre closed.......... 226

Licensor
copyright of, not to be questioned by his licensee.......... 592
distributor usually, of exhibitor.......... 225
express covenant not to produce play.......... 10
his picture rights suspended by sale of dramatic rights.......... 7
implied covenant not to produce picture.......... 4
may maintain replevin.......... 237
may reserve stage rights.......... 10
may sue third parties.......... 92
unless exclusive, may grant to others.......... 73
when estopped from granting picture rights.......... 2

Licensee
exclusive, may enjoin others.......... 74
exclusive, may enjoin his licensor.......... 74
exclusive, of part of rights may sue.......... 581
exhibitor usually, of distributor.......... 225

Licensee—*Continued* PAGE
failure of, to insert notice of copyright........................ 519
joined as co-plaintiff....................................578–580
joining proprietor in unpublished work........................ 584
may be enjoined from mutilating work........................ 59
may not question his licensor's copyright.................... 592
may not withhold royalties, when third party infringes......... 82
may restrain invasions only when exclusive.................. 6
need account only to one co-author......................... 42
need not be joined in action between them.................. 43
of "all dramatization rights" secures picture rights........... 5
of belligerent alien, right to sue.......................... 531
of copyright must join proprietor.........................578–580
of copyright proprietor, right to sue........................ 577
of one co-author cannot be sued by other co-author........... 44
of publisher may enjoin licensee of author.................. 14
where rights of exclusive, not infringed..................... 580
who oversteps his grant an infringer........................ 593

Liquidated Damages
courts not bound by provision as to........................ 167
in author's contract.. 83
in theatre lease... 242
where breach by actor...................................... 166

Liquor License
consent required for....................................... 361
theatre proprietor may be required to obtain................. 360

Literary Works
abandonment of contract to write........................... 77
authors may infringe their own............................. 592
author must refund for failure to deliver work on time......... 76
author liable in damages for failure to deliver manuscript....... 76
cannot part with, and retain title.......................... 464
changes in text.. 53
changes in text by outright purchaser....................... 54
changes in text by licensee................................ 54
common-law rights in....................................... 491
contract for several, breach with respect to one, breach of entire contract.. 77
contract for, whether specifically enforced.................. 92

Literary Works—*Continued*

PAGE

copyright in component parts.... 544
criticism.... 63
criticism of, when a libel.... 63
criticism may embody ridicule.... 63
criticism of, limits.... 64
fixing values of.... 78
identity to be preserved.... 57
immoral and seditious have no copyright.... 535
in public domain.... 544
is published when "exposed" to public.... 506–508
libelous, immoral or seditious.... 73
licensee may be enjoined for mutilation.... 56
limitations on use of.... 74, 481
need not be produced unless so contracted.... 89
no right to make changes in serial works.... 57
not produced at time specified.... 75
of any degree of inferiority copyrightable.... 534
outright purchaser may be sued in libel for mutilation.... 54
outright purchaser may be enjoined in certain cases.... 56
performing rights.... 497
producer entitled to maintain high standard of.... 221
producer may waive performance.... 76
protected like other species of property.... 405
publication of, rights prior and subsequent thereto.... 494
restrictions on sale of.... 487
revised editions.... 543
rights of author in.... 1
rights secured under copyright.... 499, 500
sale of, not assignment of copyright.... 554
sole and exclusive licenses in.... 73
specific performance for writing of.... 92
title of, how protected.... 404
to be produced at definite time.... 75
when to be written to satisfaction.... 73
whether work must be produced.... 89

"Living-Pictures"

infringes upon cartoons.... 538
infringement of.... 589

M

PAGE

Magazine
assignment of copyright to proprietor of.................... 555
various titles of.. 441
when proprietor holds as trustee for contributor.............16, 17
when title of, held a trade-mark............................ 467

Magazine Rights
defined.. 26

Make-Up
copyright in... 536

Manufacturer
of film liable for infringement............................. 590

Manuscript
author may recover for conversion........................... 88
author may enjoin wrongful possessor........................ 88
author need not tender, on producer's default................ 76
converted, damages for..................................... 499
damages for failure of author to deliver balance.............. 76
of author lost after submission.............................. 87
submission of, may be considered on infringement..........591, note

Marks and Devices
adopted by producers and distributors........................ 460
assignability.. 465
in unfair competition....................................... 460
right to, and to title distinguished.......................... 466

Master
reference to a master in copyright action after finding of infringement... 618

Master and Servant
no formal assignment from author necessary................... 27
when employer deemed proprietor of author's work...........27–32

Material PAGE
part of work must be taken 562

Misjoinder
of parties, how raised 584

Motion Picture Rights
see "Dramatic Rights."

Multiply
exclusive right to, copies of work 495

Municipality
power to erect theatre 364

Museum
when a theatre license required for 340

Music
abandonment of dramatic rights by sale of libretto, ... 52
composer and scenario-writer co-authors 53
essence in libretto rather than in orchestral accompaniment 52
incidental to picture not dramatic composition 52
in theatres with respect to copyright 649
when owner of words may sue 582
where specially composed for picture 51

Mutilation
of motion picture 171

Mutuality
of contract with actor necessary to secure injunction 102

N

Name
copyright proprietor must have lawful right to use 533
in what, copyright may be taken out 532
no common-law right to prevent use of 270
of author 60
of author a property right 61

Name—*Continued* PAGE

of play, picture or book protected as trade name....407, note
one's own, when not assignable.... 477
right to, under common law.... 495
when executor may not assign.... 480

Negative Covenant

in actor's contract.... 96
to write, enforced.... 71
to write, unique, special and extraordinary.... 72

Negative Print

outright sale.... 215
shipment of, interstate commerce.... 261

Negro

excluding from theatre....298, 328

Newfoundland

copyright in....655, 658

New Matter

entitled to copyright.... 543
of work in public domain.... 544

News Item

rights of author, where motion picture based upon.... 23
when held out as facts, in public domain....23, 24
when held out as fiction, may not be appropriated.... 24

Newspaper

action against, on serial rights.... 580
copyright in.... 539
do not come within Civil Rights Statute.... 281
injunction against, from printing plot of play before premiere... 607
not a private enterprise.... 386
rights of author, where motion picture based upon item in.... 23
"Syndicate Rights" defined.... 26
various titles of.... 440
"Weekly News Pictures" not classified as.... 285
when proprietor holds as trustee for contributor....16, 17

New Zealand

PAGE

copyright in Dominion of 655, 659

Nom de Plume

copyright taken out in 533
when its use may be enjoined 60, 61
when a crime to suppress name 61

Notice

abbreviations 516
date may be in Roman numerals 517
false, of copyright 520
false, must contain elements of valid 521
form of 511–513
legibility 513
meaning of 513–515
need not be on copies deposited 513
no, required on unpublished works 510
of copyright, in general 510
of discharge necessary to be given actor 164
omission of, by accident or mistake 517
on motion picture need not include year 512
on prints for foreign shipment 519
on published works, required 511
on work, after renewal of copyright 549
purpose of 513–515
registered trade-mark no 462
rule of "substantial compliance" 514
superfluous words 516
to infringer in unfair competition 457
where placed 512

Novel

author may prosecute publisher for breach of trust 13
owner of copyright alone may dramatize 12
purchase of picture rights from publisher 12
rights of author where motion picture based upon 11
title of, when in conflict with title of play 434

Novelize

right to, under copyright 500

O

PAGE

Obscene
see "Immoral."

Obscenity
exposure of actor to 136

Opera
when a theatre license required for 340

Operator
regulations with respect to 367–368

Orchestra
space in rear of is "aisle" 366

Order in Council
of Great Britain,—Text, of February 3, 1915 732

Original
work need not be altogether, to be copyrighted 534

Owner
equitable owner of copyright 582

P

Panic
liability of theatre proprietor 312, 317

Pantomime
immoral exhibition . . . . 357, note, 373, note
when a theatre license required for 339

Parodies
copyright 541
no infringement of copyright 537

Part
"substantial and material," must be taken to be infringement . . . 562

Parties PAGE

action in unfair competition against one bar as to other........ 468
misjoinder of................................ 577
to action in unfair competition.............................. 467
when officers, directors and employes liable.................. 468

Patent

copyright and rights under, distinguished.................. 481
history of control and dissolution of motion picture combination 487
pooling.. 488
purpose of patent laws.................................. 486
restrictions after expiration of............................ 485

Penalties

for infraction of fire-regulations.......................369, note
knowledge and intent necessary to recover.................. 591
liability for Sunday performance.......................... 400
see "Liquidated Damages."
seller liable in unfair competition.......................443, note
who liable for.. 379
who liable for, in copyright infringement.................. 586

Pendente Lite

injunction against actor.................................. 108
see "Injunctions," "Preliminary Injunction."

Performance

of actor prevented by illness or death...................... 133
of contract to write within specified time.................. 75
of play not a publication.................................. 497
of unpublished works a crime.........................635, note
private exhibition not a.................................. 588
substantial, by actor.................................... 133

Performer

see "Actor."

Performing Rights

in unpublished work vest statutory.......................... 497
not given under early statutes............................ 497

Performing Rights—*Continued* PAGE
reserved by author . . . 497
right of, under copyright . . . 500

Periodical
reserving dramatization rights in contribution to . . . 555
when proprietor holds as trustee for contributor . . . 16–17

Photographs
infringement to make, of sculpture . . . 539
may be copyrighted . . . 539
no common-law right to prevent use of . . . 269
on post cards . . . 270, note, 277

Piratical Copies
prohibition of importation of . . . 640

Play
copyrighting motion picture which is not a photo . . . 501
grant of producing rights in . . . 1
in conflict with cartoons . . . 405
infringements of . . . 562–565
is a descriptive title . . . 408, note
performance of, not a publication . . . 497
title of, not protected by copyright . . . 403
title of, and title of book . . . 434
to be written to "satisfaction" of manager . . . 115
unfair competition between titles of . . . 443
value of, how estimated . . . 78–79

Playwright
right to retain identity of his work . . . 172
see "author."

Plot
infringement by expanding . . . 566

Poem
rights of author where motion picture based upon . . . 15

Policeman
may inspect theatre . . . 368

Police Power PAGE
Sunday closing 399
see "License," "Regulation."

Positive Prints
in general 215
shipment of, interstate commerce 261

Preliminary Injunction
in copyright action 602
laches a bar in copyright action 607
may be suspended upon certain conditions in copyright action . . 606
newspaper prevented from publishing plot of play before premiere 607
not binding on trial court in copyright action 618
on whom binding in copyright action 606
when temporary restraining order granted in copyright action . . 605
will not become effective in copyright action until security given 605

Presidential Proclamations
see "Proclamations."

Prevent
right to, publication 495

Price-Fixing
in general 481

Print
right to, under common law 495

Privacy
see "Right of Privacy."

Private Enterprise
circus is a 385
motion picture business a 385
newspaper not 386
theatre a 385

Private Exhibitions PAGE
breach by theatre owner.......... 259
for criticism, under common law.......... 495
not infringements.......... 588
proceeds devoted to charity..........259–260
right of, under common law.......... 495
when license required.......... 260
when license not required.......... 260

Private Reading
right of, under common law.......... 495

Prize Contest
when work secured by means of.......... 88

Prize-Fight
interstate shipment prohibited.......... 388
picture of, not permitted.......... 379

Procedure
after finding of infringement in copyright action.......... 618
proceedings for injunction, damages, profits and those for seizure of infringing copies and plates may be united in one action... 619

Proclamations
of President to determine reciprocal rights.......... 525
presidential, itemized.......... 710
presidential—text of April 9, 1910.......... 719
presidential—text of July 13, 1914.......... 725
presidential—text of January 1, 1915.......... 735

Producer
author's work to be done to satisfaction of.......... 73
entitled to have films released regularly.......... 222
his employes other than actor.......... 205
liable with distributor and exhibitor.......... 467
may be enjoined from granting other "state-rights".......... 223
may enjoin licensor.......... 92
may insist on proper advertising.......... 222
may insist on use of his name.......... 222

Producer—*Continued* PAGE
may replevy film for unpaid "state-rights" royalties........... 224
negligence in handling manuscript........................... 88
negligence not predicated in certain cases.................... 88
not required to produce work unless so contracted............ 89
with relation to actor—see "Actor."
with respect to director and other employes.................. 209
with respect to scenario writer.............................. 205
work to be done to his satisfaction......................... 73

Professional Scenario Writer
see "Scenario Writer."

Profits
accounting of, in copyright action........................... 608
as a basis for damages....................................... 149
percentage of, to author..................................... 77
prospective, as a measure of damages......................... 149
to star.. 215
when speculative..79, 216

Prohibition
not included in regulation................................... 371

Proof
required in copyright action................................. 593

Property
lost in theatre.. 335

Proprietor
joined with licensee... 578
joining licensee of unpublished work......................... 584
of theatre, when liable to patron............................ 331
of theatre, when liable for acts of stage-hand............... 334
of theatre, when liable for acts of other employes........... 335
of theatre, liability for act of manager...................197, note

Public, The
duty of theatre proprietor to................................ 291
injuries sustained by patrons of theatre..................... 299

Public, The—*Continued* PAGE
license of theatre in general ... 337
privacy ... 267
regulation of theatres ... 362
right to exclude patrons from theatre ... 291
right of privacy ... 267

Publication
date of first sale is date of ... 504
deposit of copies to be made promptly after ... 503
exclusive right of, under copyright ... 500
in England may not constitute, in United States ... 510
in Europe ... 507, 508
of work secures copyright ... 502
performance of play not a ... 497
rentals or leases constitute ... 504
rights in work before ... 495
rights in work after ... 495
right to first ... 495
simultaneous, in United States and British Dominions ... 654
term of copyright from ... 546
what is ... 503
when title of, held a trade-mark ... 467

Public Domain
and copyright ... 544
foreign work in ... 569
new matter protected, of work in ... 544
title falls into, with work ... 438
title of work in, protected ... 407
translations of works in ... 25
use of title in work falling into ... 438
when work falls into ... 497
where motion picture based upon work in ... 24
works derived from common source ... 568
work may receive original treatment and acquire new protection. 24–25
work published without compliance with statute falls into ... 506

Published Works
all copies of, must bear copyright notice ... 513

Published Works—*Continued* PAGE
copyrighting motion pictures as........................... 502
notice of copyright on, required............................ 511

Publisher
may sell picture rights in novel............................ 12
where nothing on record to show he holds copyright as trustee... 12

Q

Quotations
not infringement.. 542

R

Race-Feeling
aroused by picture.. 379

Receipts
see "Profits."

Refund
advance royalties... 90

Registration
bill must allege.. 597

Regulation
admission of children to theatre............................ 370
aisles, standing in... 365
as to closing theatre....................................... 367
as to removal of hats.................................367, note
censorship.. 383
fireman stationed in.. 368
immoral pictures.. 372
of theatres... 362
operator and booth...................................367, 368
ordinance passed after building erected..................... 363
prohibition not included in power of........................ 371
Sunday performance.. 391
who liable for penalty...................................... 379

Register of Copyrights PAGE
permits withdrawal of one copy of deposited work . . . 639

Rehearsals
failure of actor to attend . . . 156

Release
date of, date of publication . . . 504

Releasor
see "Distributor."

Relief
for infringement of common-law rights . . . 498
injunction against actor whose services are unique . . . 95
injunction pendente lite against actor whose services are unique . 108

Remedies in General
injunction against actor whose services are unique . . . 95
injunction pendente lite against actor whose services are unique . 108
of actor where mutilation occurs . . . 171

Remedies in Copyright Actions
accounting . . . 608, 610, 613, 623
appeal . . . 638
actions at law . . . 626
actions in equity—in general . . . 602
actions purporting to be brought under the Copyright Act . . . 628
bill of particulars . . . 599
civil and criminal may be pursued concurrently . . . 635
construction of forfeiture and penalty clauses . . . 636
costs . . . 608, 616, 617
damages . . . 608, 610
final hearing . . . 608
injunction as to part . . . 619
permanent injunction . . . 608
preliminary injunction . . . 602
procedure after finding of infringement . . . 618
statute of limitations . . . 636

Remedies in Copyright Actions—*Continued* PAGE
willful infringements.. 634
writ of seizure 621

Renewal
by assignee of copyright 548
death of author 549
notice to be placed on work after 549
of copyright 547
when application for, to be made 547

Replevin
for violation of license 235
of films for failure to pay royalties 224
when film taken out of state 236

Rescission
when author entitled to 90
when producer entitled to 90

Restraining Order
on whom binding in copyright action 606
temporary, in copyright action 605

Restraint of Trade
exclusive contract with actor not in 96
in general 487

Revocation
of theatre license 349–351
of theatre license because of unsafe building 351
of theatre license because of immoral picture 354

Ridicule
exposure of actor to 136

Right of Privacy
Civil Rights Law of New York 271
in general 267
libelous use of name or picture 282
no common-law right 269

Right of Privacy—*Continued* PAGE
personal and property rights discussed........................ 267
Weekly News motion pictures.............................. 284
when liable under statute................................. 274
when not liable under statute............................. 278

Rights
motion-picture rights see, "Dramatic Rights."

Royalties
author entitled to, whether work produced or not............. 82
forfeiture for non-payment................................. 84
guarantee of...79, 80
in action for, licensor's copyright not to be questioned......... 592
licensee may not withhold, where third party infringes......... 82
payment to agent.. 531
refund of advance... 90
"state-rights," failure to pay.............................. 224
stipulated, for period or performance........................ 80
to actor in addition to salary.............................. 190
when producer entitled to refund of......................... 90
where stipulated.. 80

Rules
of United States Supreme Court for procedure to secure writ of seizure in copyright action.............................. 621
of United States Supreme Court for practice and procedure under section 25 of the Copyright Act of 1909—text............... 714

Rules and Regulations
of United States Copyright office—text....................... 740
of Canadian Copyright Office—text........................... 833

Rulings
of treasury department on importation of piratical copies...... 640

S

Sale
of dramatic rights perpetually suspends picture rights.......... 7
of scenario vests all rights..............................22, 23

Sale—*Continued*

PAGE

of scenario to several producers.......... 23
of "serial rights" construed.......... 26
one offering infringing work for, liable.......... 587

Satisfaction

author's work to, of producer.......... 73
incompetency not equivalent to dissatisfaction.......... 159
scenario or play to be written to satisfaction of producer.......... 117
services of actor to be to satisfaction of employer.......... 112

Scenario

copyrighted as a book.......... 540
may be developed into short story or novel.......... 21
not copyrightable as a dramatic composition..........19, 540
outright sale divests author of all rights.......... 22
rights of author, where motion picture based upon original.......... 19
sale of, to several producers.......... 23
sale of, "in full payment for story" carried no reservations.......... 22
sale of "to let you have my drama" assigned all rights.......... 23
submitted in prize contest.......... 88
to be written to "satisfaction" of producer.......... 115

Scenario Writer

his rights with respect to producer.......... 205
professional.......... 205
rights in completed motion picture.......... 206
rights in scenario.......... 205

Scenes

are component parts.......... 545

School

distance from theatre.......... 364
license refused theatre for proximity to.......... 358

Sculpture

infringement to photograph.......... 539

Season PAGE
construed 119
when jury may determine length of 231

Seats
inspection of 306
patron injured 305

Second Hand Copies
selling, of copyrighted works 646

Seditious
see "Immoral."
see "Literary Works."

Sell
right to, under common law 495

Serial Rights
belong to owner of rights in drama or novel 24
considered as one publication 26
considered in its secondary meaning 26
licensee of, may maintain action 580
rights of author in serial picture 25
sale of, construed 26

Serial Stories
rights of actor who poses in 185

Sermon
rights of author when motion picture based upon 15

Services
of actor "actually performed" 131
tender of, by actor after breach 147

Set-Off
see "Contract."

Short Story
rights of author where motion picture based upon 15

Singing
PAGE
when a theatre license required for........................339, 342

Skating-Rink
theatre license not required............................341, note
whether skating is dancing...............................341, note

Sketch
is a descriptive title.. 410
rights of author where motion picture based upon............. 15

South Africa
copyright in Union of...................................655, 660

Special
injunction against actor where services are unique, extraordinary and.. 95
where services of infant are.................................. 173

Specific Performance
agreement to assign copyright................................ 554
of contract to write... 92
of contract with actor... 96

Stage-Business
copyright in.. 536

Stage-Hand
when proprietor liable for acts of........................... 334

Standard
producer entitled to maintain................................ 221

State Court
action to compel assignment of copyright may be brought in.... 553

State Rights
breach of condition to pay royalties......................... 224
in general.. 222
purchaser in good faith...................................... 224
third partics infringing, when restrained.................... 222

Statute of Limitations PAGE
in copyright actions.... 636

Statutes—Text
British Copyright Act of 1911.... 762
Canadian Copyright Act of 1906.... 812
United States Copyright Act of 1909, as amended by the Acts of 1912, 1913, 1914.... 677

Steps
patron injured on, of theatre.... 306

Story
infringed by play.... 565

Stranger
acts of, must have been foreseen by theatre proprietor.... 325-327
liability of theatre proprietor for acts of.... 312

Subjects
of copyright.... 534

Substantial
part of work must be taken.... 562

Sunday
charitable performance given on.... 401
civil and criminal liability for violation of.... 399
construction of statutes.... 394-399
contract with actor for work on.... 125
early statutes.... 391
equity will not enjoin violation of.... 399
equity will not enjoin police officials.... 400
is not a dies non.... 391
"labor" to manage a theatre.... 398
legislature the sole judge.... 395
license granted on condition that theatre remain closed on.... 360
motion picture a "theatrical performance".... 397
motion-picture a "place of public amusement".... 397
motion picture a "worldly employment or business".... 397, note

Sunday—*Continued*

PAGE

motion picture an "interlude" . . . 397, note
motion picture a "play" . . . 397, note
motion picture not an "outdoor amusement" . . . 393, 394
motion picture not an "other place of amusement" . . . 396
motion picture not an amusement disturbing the peace . . . 396
New York Laws . . . 393
performance, in general . . . 391
who liable for penalty for performance on . . . 400
"Works of Necessity" . . . 391

Superfluous

words in notice of copyright . . . 516

T

Taxability

of copyrights . . . 648

Tenants in Common

co-authors are . . . 37

Tenants in Common of Literary Property

contracts between themselves . . . 45
contracts between themselves and publishers . . . 45
contracts between themselves and publishers are for personal services . . . 46
contract between them not assignable . . . 51
contract between them entire . . . 51
effect of death of one . . . 47
elements of skill and confidence . . . 48
in action by one, all to be joined . . . 44
in action by one against licensee, others need not be joined . . . 45
may sue each other for infringement of the common work . . . 45
may grant rights without consent of co-tenant . . . 37
may not however grant exclusive rights . . . 38, 39
may not destroy rights of co-tenant . . . 40
may not be compelled to account . . . 41
not co-partners . . . 42, 46
not joint-venturers . . . 46
partnership by special contract dissolved by death of one . . . 47

Tender PAGE
author need not, manuscript where producer defaults 76

Tent
when classified as "building" 363, 364

Term
of copyright 546

Test
of copyright 535
of infringement of copyright 542

Text
changes made in work of author 53

Theatre
a private enterprise .... 293, note, 294
aisles, standing in 365
angle of balcony and guard rail 304
censorship 383
critic may be excluded 295
crowds gathering in front of 252
duty of patron 330
excluding negro from 298
falling over balcony 303
federal censorship board 388
floor giving way 306
immoral exhibitions 372
infants, admission to 370
inspection by proprietor as a defense to action for negligence .. 306–311
inspection of, for fire hazards 368
lessor, liable for infringing performance 587
lessor liable for structure 302
liability of proprietor for manager's refusal to permit officer to enter to serve process on actor .... 197, note
liability to trespasser .... 323, note
license revoked because of unsafe 351
manager not liable for infringing performance .... 590, note
may be a tent 363, 364
measure of proprietor's duty 299

Theatre—*Continued*

PAGE

notice of defects must be shown 303
not a bawdy house 344
not a dwelling house 345
not a nuisance 344
not a nuisance per se ..... 400, note
panic of crowd 312, 317
patron assaulted 326
patron injured by articles dropping 311
patron injured by wild animals 313
patron injured by crowds 318
patron injured by performer 319
patron injured by other accident 322
patron injured by act of stranger 325
patron injured in darkened 306
patron injured in aisles 306
patron injured on steps 306
patron injured at exits 306
patron injured on seat and floor 305
patron injured falling over balcony 303
patrons boisterous 252
patrons trespassing 255
performers noisy 252, 254
power of municipality to erect 364
proximity to church 255
prohibition of giving of performances not regulation 371
property lost in 335
proprietor may refuse to sell ticket 293
proprietor may sell ticket on condition 293
proprietor of, liable for infringing performance 587
proprietor not insurer of safety of patrons 299
property lost in 335
queue 252
regulation of 362
regulation of building 362
regulation as to closing of 367
regulations as to operator and booth 367–368
regulation as to removal of hats ..... 367, note
right to exclude patrons from 291
seats—injuries in—inspection of 306

Theatre—*Continued* PAGE
see "Exhibitor."
Sunday performance 391
ticket of admission a revocable license 292
ticket taker not liable for penalties 379
tripping in 306
what is 337
when a nuisance 251
who liable for injuries to patron 331
who liable for penalties 379

Theatre Leases
adjoining property owners 244
assignments 242
building contracts 242
counterclaim for delay in construction 242
covenant by lessee not to engage in business 246
declarations of patrons part of "res gestæ" 247
deposit as security 250
effect of subsequent ordinances 241
fixed rental as well as profits 245
in action for failure to pay profits, what testimony inadmissible . . 247
in general 237
lessee may sue before date of entry 251
liability of agent contracting 237
liability of owner for repairs . . . . . 245, note
right of municipality to enter into 248
right of way for exit 245
structural defects . . . . . 243–244, note
tenant may not enjoin other tenant for same period 246
theatre shut down by authorities 240
theatre shut down by fire 241
when action to recover deposit maintainable 251
when deposit regarded as penalty 250
when joint venture 245–246
when rent suspended 240–241

Theatre Ticket
a revocable license 292
not revocable, under English rule 297

Theatre Ticket—*Continued*

PAGE

proprietor may refuse to sell 293
proprietor may sell on condition 293
refund of money for . . . . . 393, note
re-sold by speculator 293
"scalping" 381
statutes against "scalping" 381
to print wrongfully is a forgery 383

Theatrical Performance
what is 337

Theme
arrangement of, confers copyright 534

Thought
no copyright in 560

Ticket-Taker
not liable for admission of infants 381

Time
damages for failure to deliver work on 75
producer entitled to refund where work not produced on 76
producer may waive performance on 76
producer must give notice to complete 76
producer must produce within reasonable time 78
use of film at, not agreed upon 225

Title
acquiescence and abandonment 449
after copyright in work expires 438
cannot part with work and retain 464
can part with portion of work and retain title 464
change in, invalidates copyright 522
copyright does not extend to 403
deposit of, as unpublished work 500
descriptive, may not be protected 407
first user obtains exclusive right 410
held not to infringe 445

Title—*Continued* PAGE
held to infringe 413
how protected 404
no copyright in 521
of cartoons protected like trade-marks 469
of novel and play in conflict 434
of work passes on death of author 464
play and motion picture 413
proprietor of copyright must show how he acquired 596
protection in, and in work distinguished 406
right to, and to trade-mark distinguished 466
right to exclusive use of, with work only 463
right to, passes to trustee in bankruptcy 464
similar or same, used 402
those held to infringe 440
transferability of 463
user of, necessary to accord protection 410
using same or similar titles 402
what constitutes prior user 411
where, of magazine held a trade-mark 467
work in public domain protected in 407

Titles of Works
"A Bird of Paradise" 581
"A Fool there Was" 410, 416, 444
"Beatty's Head Line Copy-Book" 440
"Beatty's New and Improved Head-Line Copy Books" 440
"Ben Hur" 3, 413
"Birth Control" 356, 373
"Bon Ton" 443
"Booth's Theatre" 480
"Brewster's Millions" 223
"Buster Brown" 405, 443, 475
"Canadian Bookseller and Literary Journal" 440
"Canada Bookseller and Stationer" 440
"Captain Jinks of the Horse Marines" 2, 413
"Chantecler" 443
"Chanticlair" 443
"Charity" 408, 447
"Charley's Aunt" 447

Titles of Works—*Continued*

PAGE

"Charley's Uncle" . . . 447
"Chatterbox" . . . 442
"Comfort" . . . 442
"Cottage Homes of England" . . . 449
"Count of Monte Cristo" . . . 25
"Current Quotations" . . . 445
"Divorce" . . . 80
"Dr. Eliot's Five-Foot Shelf of the World's Best Books" . . . 442
"Dr. Eliot's Five-Foot Shelf of the World's Greatest Books" . . . 442
"Dr. Eliot's Five-Foot Shelf of Books" . . . 442
"Erminie" . . . 406, 443
"Everybody's Magazine" . . . 409, 448
"Everybody's Weekly" . . . 409, 448
"Fadette Ladies Orchestra" . . . 478
"Farthest North Nansen" . . . 446
"Follies of 1917" . . . 444
"Gazette du Bon Ton" . . . 443
"Gentleman Joe" . . . 60
"Gus Hill's Follies of 1917" . . . 445
"Happiness" . . . 427, 444
"Heney's New and Revised Edition of Jousse's Royal Standard Pianoforte Tutor" . . . 440
"Heney's Royal Modern Tutor for the Pianoforte" . . . 440
"Home Comfort" . . . 410, 442
"Independent National System of Penmanship" . . . 441
"In the Hands of Imposters" . . . 220
"Is Any Girl Safe?" . . . 373
"James Boys and Night Riders" . . . 356
"J. Gruber's Hagerstown Town and County Almanack" . . . 441
"Lady in Red" . . . 51
"L'Aiglon" . . . 443
"La Tosca" . . . 6
"Life" . . . 410
"Mail" . . . 448
"M. A. P. (Mainly About People)" . . . 448
"Mercedes" . . . 443, 477
"Morning Mail" . . . 448
"Motor Boat" . . . 446
"Motor Boating Magazine" . . . 446

Titles of Works—*Continued* PAGE

"Mutt & Jeff" 470
"Napoleon, the Newlywed's Baby" 539
"New Era" 446
"Newport Social Index" 446
"New York Commercial" 446
"New York Detective Library" 447
"Nick Carter" 447
"Old Dutch" 39
"Old Sleuth Library" 405, 447
"Orange Blossoms" 357, 373
"Our Folk's Illustrated Paper" 446
"Our Sailor King" 449
"Our Young Folks" 446
"Oxford Bible" 442
"Payson, Drunton & Scribner's National System of Penmanship" 441
"Peg O' My Heart" 574
"Philadelphia Suburban Life" 441
"Pique" 80
"P. T. O. (People Talked Of)" 448
"Punch & Judy" 448
"Republican New Era" 446
"Sapho" 567
"Sealed Orders" 445
"Sherlock Holmes" 441
"Sherlock Holmes, Detective" 441
"Shoughraun" 568
"Social Register" 408, 446
"St. Elmo" 447, 571
"Suburban Life" 441
"The Awakening of Spring" 356, 376
"The Battles of a Nation" 425
"The Birthday Scripture Text Book" 445
"The Birth of a Nation" 357, 379
"The Black Crook" 247
"The Canadian Bird Book" 412, 448
"The Children's Birthday Text Book" 445
"The Come-Back" 418, 421, 444
"The Commercial Advertiser" 446

Titles of Works—*Continued*

PAGE

"The Daily Express" 448
"The Decorator" 448
"The Decorators' and Painters' Magazine" 448
"The Evening Post" 448
"The Fall of the Romanoffs" 431
"The Fatal Card" 509
"The Field" 448
"The Field and Kennel" 448
"The Fram Expedition. Nansen in the Frozen World" 446
"The Frank Case" 357, 379
"The Girl from Rectors" 357
"The Girl Who did not Care" 426, 447
"The Girl Who Doesn't Know" 426, 447
"The Good Things of Life" 445
"The Hand That Rocks the Cradle" 356, 373
"The House of a Thousand Candles" 428, 432, 444
"The House of a Thousand Scandals" 430, 432, 444
"The House of Bondage" 5
"The Inside of the White Slave Traffic" 356, 372
"The Investor" 442
"The Maid of Plymouth" 80
"The Merry Widow" 536
"The Miracle" 413, 443
"The Monthly Odd Volume" 445
"The Morning Post" 448
"The National Advocate" 446
"The National Police Gazette" 443
"The Ne'er Do Well" 8
"The New Canadian Bird Book" 412, 448
"The New York National Advocate" 446
"The North Express" 448
"The New Northwest" 446
"The Northwest News" 446
"The Octoroon" 29, 568
"The Odd Volume" 445
"The Ordeal" 375
"The Plumber and Decorator" 448
"The Rosary 410, 422, 444
"The Sex Lure" 356, 377

Titles of Works—*Continued* PAGE
"The Shadow" 447
"The Spice of Life" 445
"The Tyranny of the Romanoffs" 431, 432
"The United States Investor" 442
"The Wrong Mr. Wright" 410, 445
"The Wrong Mrs. Wright" 410, 445
"T. G. Robertson's Hagerstown Almanack" 441
"Under the Gaslight" 567
"United States Police Gazette" 443
"Webster's Dictionary" 442
"Where There's a Will" 449
"Where There's a Will, There's a Way" 449
"Willard-Johnson" fight 379

Tort Feasor
When manufacturer not a joint 589

Trade
restraint of 487

Trade-Mark
advantages of registered 461
assignability 465
embraced in unfair competition 459
no protection as, for letters of alphabet 463
registered, no notice 462
right to, and to title distinguished 466
when title of magazine, held a 467

Trade Name
assignability 465
copyright may be taken out in 532
copyright taken out in wrongful 533
embraced in unfair competition 459
right to, and to title distinguished 466
title of work protected on theory of . . . . 407, note

Tragedy
word, is a descriptive title . . . . 408, note

Transcription PAGE
right of, under copyright 500

Translate
right to, under common law 495

Travel
actor entitled to recover for time spent in 134
questions of, of actor 177

Treason
to pay royalties to belligerent alien 531

Trespasser
liability of theatre proprietor to .... 323, note

U

Undertaking
must be given in copyright action to entitle to preliminary injunction 605
must be given in copyright action to entitle to temporary restraining order 605

Unfair Competition
accounting, right to 452, 453
acquiescence and abandonment 449
actions at law 468
action against one, bar as to others 468
acts of third parties 450
between novel and play 434
between stage and picture rights 10
cartoons protected 469
damages 455
deception need not be proven 458
distinction between patent and copyright 481
first user bars others 10
fraud 455
generally 402
importance of advertising matter 463
intent 456

Unfair Competition—*Continued* PAGE
in titles of plays........ 443
in titles of plays and motion pictures........ 443
joinder of action in, with action in copyright........ 584
laches........ 449
marks and devices........ 460
may unite cause of action for, with copyright........ 460
need not wait until actual infringement........ 459
notice to infringer........ 457
parties to the action........ 467
protection primarily of trader........ 458
protects titles as trade names........ 407, note
price-fixing........ 481
relief, generally........ 453
restraint of trade........ 487
right to assign one's name........ 477
seller liable........ 443, note
titles, see "Titles."
titles held to infringe........ 440
titles held not to infringe........ 445
trade names and trade-marks embraced in........ 459
transferability of title........ 463
use of title after copyright in work expires........ 438
work in public domain protected in title........ 407

Unfaithfulness
of actor........ 162

Unique
injunction against actor where services are........ 95
stipulation that services are, not binding on actor........ 108
where services of infant are........ 173

United Kingdom and Protectorates
copyright in........ 654

Unpublished Work
action on, where brought........ 586
coincidence........ 576
duration of protection in........ 540
exclusive license in, protected........ 583

Unpublished Work—*Continued* PAGE
- how copyrighted . . . 500
- may reserve dramatization rights in . . . 556
- performance of, a crime . . . 635, note
- right secured to . . . 495
- rule as to joinder of proprietor and licensee . . . 584
- securing copyright in . . . 501

Use
- exclusive, in work before publication . . . 495
- of film at place not agreed upon . . . 225
- of title necessary where protection sought . . . 410
- period of, intervening . . . 412
- prior user of title . . . 410
- right to "use" in patent may be limited . . . 482
- sole right to, given in patent only . . . 481

V

Validity
- of copyright not affected by classification . . . 503

Value
- of literary work, how estimated . . . 78–79

Vend
- right to, under copyright . . . 500
- right to, a patented article . . . 482

Version
- other, under copyright . . . 500

Voice, Tones of
- copyright in . . . 536

W

War
- license refused to aliens . . . 358
- picture of, when permitted . . . 375
- pictures suppressed . . . 357
- see "Belligerent Aliens."

PAGE

Warranty
of actor of requisite skill and ability........................ 159

Wear and Tear
implied warranty of outline and fitness..................... 227
of film..225–226

Weekly News Pictures
not classified as newspapers............................. 285
see "Right of Privacy."

Wild Animals
negligence to be shown................................. 315
old rule of absolute liability.............................. 313

Words
copyright not a right to use of certain...................... 560

Workmen's Compensation Acts
with respect to actors.................................. 180

Writings
copyright in author's.................................. 560

Writ of Seizure
in copyright action, in general........................... 621
proceedings for, may be united in one action with those for injunction, etc.................................... 619

Y

Year
in notice of copyright after renewal........................ 549
of publication, in notice................................ 511
of publication not required on motion picture................ 512
variation of, in notice of copyright........................ 514

www.ingramcontent.com/pod-product-compliance
Lightning Source LLC
LaVergne TN
LVHW101449200926
848483LV00001B/97